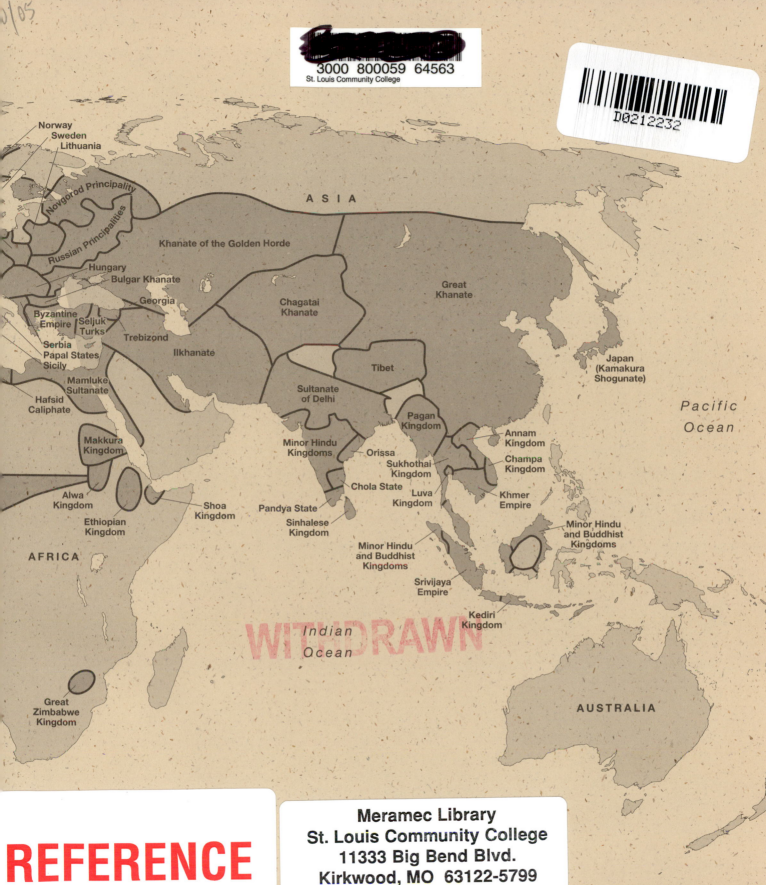

WORLD

MONARCHIES

AND DYNASTIES

VOLUME 2

FR–M

CONSULTING EDITOR

JOHN MIDDLETON

SHARPE REFERENCE

an imprint of M.E. Sharpe, Inc.

Developed, Designed, and Produced by Book Builders LLC

SHARPE REFERENCE

Sharpe Reference is an imprint of M.E. Sharpe, Inc.

M.E. Sharpe, Inc.
80 Business Park Drive
Armonk, NY 10504

Library of Congress Cataloging-in-Publication Data

World monarchies and dynasties / John Middleton, editor.
  p. cm.
Includes bibliographical references and index.
ISBN 0-7656-8050-5 (set : alk. paper)
1. World history.　2. Monarchy—History—Dictionaries.　3. Kings and rulers—History—Dictionaries.　I. Middleton, John.

D21 .W929 2004
903—dc22　　　　　　　　　　　　　　　　　　　　　　　2003023236

Printed and bound in the United States of America

The paper used in this publication meets the minimum requirements of American National Standard for Information Sciences—Permanence of Paper for Printed Library Materials, ANSI Z 39.48.1984.

BM (c) 10 9 8 7 6 5 4 3 2 1

Endpaper Maps: inside front cover: World Monarchies, 1279 c.e.; inside back cover: World Monarchies, Present Day
(IMA for Book Builders LLC)

CONTENTS

LIST OF FEATURES

Royal Rituals

Maps

FRANCIS I (1494–1547 C.E.)

King of France (r. 1515–1547) from the House of Valois, whose rivalry with Charles V (r. 1519–1558), the Holy Roman emperor, led to a series of wars. Francis ruled as an absolute monarch.

Francis was the son of Charles of Orléans, count of Angoulême, and Louise of Savoy. In 1514, he married Claude of Brittany, the daughter of his cousin, Louis XII (r. 1498–1515). After the death of Francis's first wife, he married Eleanor of Austria, sister of Emperor Charles V (r. 1519–1558). Francis was succeeded on the French throne by his son, Henry II (r. 1547–1559).

The year after Francis's marriage to Claude, Louis XII died without a male heir, and Francis succeeded to the throne as next of kin. Before his death, Louis XII had planned an invasion of the duchy of Milan. Francis carried out this plan, resulting in a victory over the Italian forces at Marignano in September 1515.

When the Holy Roman emperor Maximilian I died in 1519, Charles of Habsburg succeeded him as Charles V. Francis also had a claim to that throne, and a fierce rivalry between Francis and Charles led to a series of wars. The first war (1521–1526), resulted in the capture of Francis at Pavia in Italy in 1525. Francis regained his freedom with the Treaty of Madrid (1526), but the cost was the loss of the duchy of Burgundy, the region of Flanders, and Artois. In the next war with Charles (1526–1529), Francis formed the League of Cognac, an alliance with the Italians, including Pope Clement VII. The war ended with the Peace of Cambrai, in which Francis recovered the duchy of Burgundy.

In 1536, Francis took the opportunity, upon the death of the duke of Milan, to make another attempt at taking Milan, which once again led to war with Charles V. Pope Paul III helped to secure the Treaty of Aigues-Mortes, which declared a ten-year truce. In the final war between Francis and Charles, which lasted from 1542 to 1544, Francis tried a final time to obtain Milan, this time forming an alliance with Suleyman I (r. 1520–1566), the sultan of the Ottoman Empire. Charles, meanwhile, formed an alliance with Henry VIII (r. 1509–1547) of England. In the Treaty of Crepy (1544) Francis lost Naples, Flanders, and Artois. In the Treaty of Ardres (1546) with England, he lost Boulogne.

When not at war, Francis I fostered Renaissance culture in France. A patron of artists, writers, and thinkers, he founded the College of France and the Imprimerie Royal. He also commissioned the construction of several palaces and chateaus, including the Louvre, Fontainebleau, and Chambord.

Early in the sixteenth century, Europeans were hoping to find a sea route through North America to the riches of Asia. Hoping to gain a wealthy empire, Francis I sponsored the explorations of Jacques Cartier. Although Cartier failed to find an easy Northwest Passage to Asia, his explorations led to France's land claims in North America.

See also: CHARLES V; FRENCH MONARCHIES; MILAN, DUCHY OF; NAPLES, KINGDOM OF; OTTOMAN EMPIRE; SULEYMAN I, THE MAGNIFICENT; VALOIS DYNASTY.

FRANCONIAN DYNASTY

German dynasty that produced a series of German kings and Holy Roman emperors. These rulers, who descended from the dukes of Franconia, a region in southern Germany, extended their power and territories in Germany and also claimed sovereignty over Italy. Their belief that the emperor was God's representative on earth led to conflict with the papacy.

FOUNDING AND EARLY RULE

Otto of Worms (r. 978–985, 1000–1002), of the Salian House, was the first Salian duke of Franconia. When Henry II, the last emperor of the House of Saxony, died in 1024, Otto's grandson Conrad was chosen to succeed Henry as king of the Germans. The succession of Conrad to the throne as Conrad II (r. 1024–1039) marked the founding of the Franconian line of German kings and Holy Roman emperors. The Franconians are sometimes also known as the Salian dynasty.

In 1026, Conrad II went to Italy and was crowned king of the Lombards in Milan by Archbishop Aribert. However, many of the Lombard margraves, or border lords, and the city of Ravenna revolted against Conrad. After defeating them, Conrad was crowned Holy Roman emperor by the pope in 1027. Conrad expanded his control by forcing the dukes of Bohemia and Poland to acknowledge him as their lord. He took over lands in possession of the Bavarian counts that he claimed had been alienated from the Crown.

In 1036, the lesser Milanese nobles rose up against the rule of the bishop of Milan. Conrad supported these nobles and granted them new rights, such as inheritance rights in their fiefs (lands held from a superior lord). Conrad's action was an early indication of how the Franconian rulers would act in religious matters.

RELATIONS WITH THE CHURCH AND NOBLES

Conrad's son, Henry III (r. 1039–1056), succeeded his father as king of Germany and head of the Franconian dynasty in 1039. While preparing for his imperial coronation by Pope Gregory VI, he learned that Gregory had purchased the papacy—an offense called simony, which was forbidden by the Church. Henry called a synod, which elected a German pope, Clement II, to replace Gregory. Clement crowned Henry emperor in 1046. Thereafter, Henry worked to stamp out abuses in the church, and he played an instrumental role in the election of the next three popes, all of whom were German.

Instead of relying on hereditary succession to fill positions within the empire, Henry III appointed lordship positions, keeping the powers of the duchies of Bavaria, Carinthia, and Swabia in his own hands. The nobility of these areas resented Henry's autocratic rule and plotted an uprising against him, but he died in 1056 before they could act.

INVESTITURE AND STRUGGLE WITH THE PAPACY

Under Henry IV, a struggle began between pope and emperor that became known as the Investiture Controversy. Henry appointed bishops in Italy and claimed to be able to invest them with their lands and regalia, such as the ring and staff that symbolized their earthly power.

After being reprimanded by Pope Gregory VII for making these investitures, Henry convoked a council in the German city of Worms in 1076, which ordered the pope to abdicate. In response, the pope excommunicated Henry and released his subjects from allegiance to him. Henry gained readmission to the Church by dressing as a penitent and standing barefoot in the snow for three days outside the castle of Canossa in Italy, where Pope Gregory was staying. This did not solve Henry's problems, however. Many nobles in Germany opposed his treatment of the

pope, and in 1077 they elected Rudolf of Rheinfelden as a rival king.

In 1080, the pope, influenced by Rudolf, again excommunicated Henry. After defeating Rudolf in battle, Henry invaded Rome with his army in 1084 and was crowned emperor there by his own papal candidate, Clement III. That same year, an army led by Norman nobleman Robert Guiscard came to the pope's aid and drove Henry from Rome, but Gregory died in 1085.

In 1104, the emperor's son Henry, later Emperor Henry V (r. 1106–1125), was concerned that the continued opposition to his father in Germany would damage his own ability to rule, deposed his father and took him prisoner. Henry IV died in 1106.

INVASION OF ITALY AND END OF THE DYNASTY

In 1110, Henry V set out for Rome for his imperial coronation. But because of the continuing investiture controversy, Pope Paschal II refused to crown Henry, who then took the pope prisoner.

To gain his freedom, the pope allowed Henry the power of investiture and crowned him emperor, but in 1112 he retracted his concessions. In 1116, Henry invaded Italy, drove the pope from Rome, and had his empress crowned in 1117 by the antipope (rival pope) Gregory VIII. In 1122, the Concordat of Worms established a compromise on investiture between the pope and the emperor, providing for the free election of bishops and abbots, and allowing the emperor to invest these officials with secular rights and obligations but not spiritual ones.

Henry V died in 1125, ending the rule of the Franconian dynasty as kings and emperors. The Franconians had not succeeded in completely asserting their power in Germany or Italy or in solving their conflict the papacy. This struggle was continued by the Hohenstaufen dynasty.

See also: CONRAD II; CONRAD III; HOHENSTAUFEN DYNASTY; HOLY ROMAN EMPIRE; SALIAN DYNASTY.

FRANKISH KINGDOM (300s–700s C.E.)

Kingdom in northern France and Belgium established by the Franks, a German people who began migrating into Western Europe in the second century.

The Franks, who eventually gave their name to France and the region of Franconia in Germany, were settled along the lower and middle Rhine River, in what is modern-day Belgium; by the third century, there were two main groups of Franks. The Ripuarian Franks lived in the southern region of Gaul. They captured the settlement of Cologne in 463, and made it the capital of their territory, which covered Aachen to Metz in the Rhine Valley.

The Salian (or Salic) Franks lived to the north. By 356, they held territory bounded by the Meuse and Somme rivers and the Atlantic Ocean. The Salian Franks were allies of the Roman Empire and were sometimes invited by the Romans to colonize empty lands. By the fifth century, the Franks had moved into the Roman province of Gaul (present-day France).

In 481, a Frankish leader, Clovis I (r. 481–511), became leader of the Salian Franks after the death of his father, Childeric I (r. 457–481). As ruler, Clovis succeeded in uniting both the Salians and Ripuarians, and he then launched an expansion of Frankish territory that laid the foundation for modern France. Clovis overthrew a Roman army in 486 and established the Merovingian dynasty, which took its name from his grandfather, Merovech (Merovaeus).

Armed conquest was an integral part of Clovis's policy, but shrewd political action was crucial in the rise of the Frankish kingdom. Gaul was occupied by three main barbarian groups in this period—the Burgundians, Visigoths, and Franks—as well as a large group of Gallo-Romans. While the Burgundians and Visigoths adhered to Arian Christianity, a system of beliefs held by the Byzantine Empire, the Gallo-Romans followed the faith practiced by the Church of Rome. Initially, the Franks kept their pagan beliefs, but in 493, Clovis married Clothilde, a Christian princess of Burgundy. In 496, Clovis and 3,000 of his warriors were baptized as Christians by Remi, the bishop of Rheims.

Clovis allowed the Gauls to retain much of the land he conquered. Moreover, many Frankish chieftains intermarried with the remnants of the Gallo-Roman senatorial class of Gaul, thus creating a new aristocracy for the Frankish kingdom.

Beginning in the sixth century and continuing through the ninth century, the Franks conquered most of modern France, as well as present-day Netherlands, west Germany, Austria, Switzerland, and north and central Italy. Around the early sixth century, the Franks created a formal body of laws, called the Salic Law, which would be passed down for centuries. One of the most notable sections of the law stipulated that no woman should inherit the titles or offices of her family. This law was cited when King Edward III of England (r. 1327–1377) tried to claim the throne of France through his mother Isabelle, the daughter of King Philip IV of France (r. 1285–1314). The ensuing dispute over the succession sparked the Hundred Years' War (1337–1453).

Although Clovis I secured his place as king of the Franks, his kingdom was divided upon his death among his four sons. This arrangement severely weakened the power of the Merovingians, who were eventually rulers in name only. In the meantime, the Carolingian "mayors of the palace," the real powers behind the Merovingian throne, increased their power, and, in 751, they supplanted the Merovingian dynasty. Charlemagne (r. 768–814), the second king of the Carolingian dynasty, was the greatest Frankish ruler and one of the most powerful leaders of early medieval Europe.

See also: BURGUNDY KINGDOM; CAROLINGIAN DYNASTY; CHARLEMAGNE; CLOVIS I; FRENCH MONARCHIES; MEROVINGIAN DYNASTY; MEROVINGIAN-FRANKISH KINGDOM.

FURTHER READING

Koenigsberger, H.G. *Medieval Europe 400–1500.* New York: Longman, 1987.

Sauvigny, G. de Bertier de, and David H. Pinkney. *History of France.* Arlington Heights, IL: Forum Press, 1983.

Tierney, Brian, and Sidney Painter. *Western Europe in the Middle Ages, 300–1475.* 6th ed. New York: McGraw-Hill College, 1999.

FRANZ JOSEF (1830–1916 C.E.)

Long-reigning emperor of Austria (r. 1848–1916) and ruler of the Austro-Hungarian Empire. Plagued by personal tragedy throughout his reign, Franz Josef presided over an empire—once one of the most powerful in Europe—that was slowly disintegrating and met complete destruction in World War I. Ruling during a time of increasing nationalist sentiment throughout Europe, Franz Josef was unable to balance effectively the diverse needs and desires of his subjects with the obligations of the monarchy and, ultimately, was unable to prevent the unraveling of Austro-Hungary and the end of the Habsburg dynasty.

EARLY YEARS

Born in a turbulent time in Austria's history, Franz Josef was the son of Austrian Archduke Francis Charles and his wife Sophia, a princess of Bavaria. His uncle, Austrian emperor Ferdinand I (r. 1835–1848), was battling insanity as well as growing discontent among his people. This public discontent came to a head during the European revolutions of 1848, which threw much of the continent into disarray as people rose up against many of the European ruling houses in an effort to achieve more liberal and democratic forms of government. Realizing that Austria would need a strong leader to face the mounting insurrection, the court and Ferdinand's

A member of the Habsburg Dynasty, Franz Josef presided over the waning years of the Austro-Hungarian empire. Though a capable ruler, he was unable to stem the nationalist movements that tore apart his nation and led to the outbreak of World War I.

family convinced him to abdicate the throne in 1848, leaving Franz Josef as emperor at the young age of eighteen.

Franz Josef immediately went to work, first putting down a revolution in the Habsburg kingdom of Hungary in 1849. Following this initial success, Franz Josef won a decisive battle that same year against King Victor Emmanuel II of Sardinia (r. 1849–1861), the emerging favorite as the ruler of a unified Italy. These quick victories helped Franz Josef restore a sense of stability to the Austrians. This semblance of order was enhanced by Franz Josef's marriage to his cousin Elizabeth in 1854 and the birth, in 1858, of Rudolf, the pair's only son and heir to the Austrian throne.

TROUBLE AT HOME AND ABROAD

Subsequent events darkened Franz Josef's reign, however, when Austria suffered defeat in two wars, the Italian War in 1859 and the Austro-Prussian War in 1866. The latter conflict was particularly damaging, for it marked the full ascendancy and military superiority of Prussia and the beginnings of a unified Germany. In addition to such foreign concerns, the internal problems of Franz Josef's empire were beginning to pose a serious challenge.

Although Franz Josef had helped Austria establish one of the most respected civil service systems in Europe, he was not able to successfully manage his large country's ethnic and nationalist problems. After years of agitation for independence, the Hungarians were finally granted some autonomy by the decision in 1867 to create a dual monarchy, known as the Austro-Hungarian monarchy. Essentially, this decision gave Hungarians full control over their internal affairs in return for a pledge to honor Franz Josef as sovereign and to follow Austrian guidance in foreign affairs. In accordance with this agreement, Franz Josef was crowned king of Hungary in 1867.

Though it had some strengths, particularly in matters of trade and commerce, the dual monarchy was beset by serious problems. Ethnic discrimination, particularly against the Slavic Serbians and Czechs, began to create a nationalist backlash among those groups. A separatist movement known as Pan-Slavism began to emerge, with intense support from Russia, which had been engaged in a dispute with Austria over control of the Balkan region. By 1882, Italy, Germany, and Austria-Hungary had formed a secret alliance, known as the Triple Alliance, partly in response to pro-independence movements. Reacting to the formation of this alliance, England, France, and Russia formed a loose alliance of their own known as the Triple Entente. The friction between these two powerful groups set the stage for World War I.

While facing growing foreign and domestic problems, Franz Josef endured a series of personal catastrophes, beginning with the execution of his brother, Emperor Maximilian of Mexico (r. 1864–1867), at the hands of insurgents in 1867. In another act of political violence, Empress Elizabeth fell victim to an assassin in 1898. Most ominously for the future of Europe, however, was the death of Franz Josef's son and heir, the archduke Rudolf, in 1889. Ruled a suicide, the mysterious death of Rudolf left Franz Josef's nephew, Franz Ferdinand, the heir to the Austrian throne. The assassination of Franz Ferdinand by a Serbian nationalist in 1914 was the spark that ignited World War I.

WAR AND DECLINE

Although Franz Ferdinand's assassination was the spark that led to war, the ground for the conflict had already been prepared in Serbia. After having occupied Bosnia and Herzegovina since 1878, Austria fully annexed these two Serbian provinces in 1908. The 1908 crisis did not lead to war, but tensions grew as the Austro-Hungarian monarchy began to face serious threats from internal ethnic nationalist factions clamoring for independence. International pressure from the Triple Entente began to mount as well, and Germany and Austria-Hungary became increasingly poised in opposition to the rest of Europe.

The assassination of Franz Ferdinand in 1914 led Austria to issue a series of punitive declarations to the Serbs, who refused to accept them. Indignant at this refusal, Austria declared war on Serbia, thereby launching all of Europe into World War I. Franz Josef did not live to see the unfortunate end for Austria-Hungary. He died during the war, in 1916, and the Crown passed to his grand-nephew, Charles I (r. 1916–1918), who was the last of the Austrian emperors.

See also: ABDICATION, ROYAL; AUSTRO-HUNGARIAN EMPIRE; HABSBURG DYNASTY; MAXIMILIAN; NATIONALISM; VICTOR EMMANUEL II.

FURTHER READING

Bled, Jean-Paul. *Franz Joseph.* Trans. Teresa Bridgeman. Cambridge, MA: Blackwell, 1992.

FREDERICK I, BARBAROSSA

(1123–1190 C.E.)

Duke of Swabia (r. 1147–1152), king of Germany (r. 1152–1190), and Holy Roman emperor (r. 1155–1190), who united much of Central Europe and died at the beginning of the Third Crusade. A man of enormous energy, Frederick played the games of politics and war with perseverance and focus rather than with the ferocity that his Italian nickname, Barbarossa (Red Beard), might imply. As Holy Roman emperor, he united Central Europe to a greater degree than anyone since Charlemagne (r. 768–814).

EARLY RULE AND THE EMPIRE

Frederick I was the son of Frederick of Hohenstaufen, the duke of Swabia, and the nephew of German King Conrad III (r. 1138–1152). His mother was Judith, a member of the powerful German Welf (or Guelf) dynasty. From an early age, Frederick acted as a mediator between his uncle, King Conrad III, and his mother's family, who were rivals for the imperial throne. Frederick's ministrations and skill impressed Conrad sufficiently to name him his successor, and Frederick was duly and ritually elected the German king in 1152.

The duchy of Swabia and the throne of Germany were hardly adequate for Frederick's ambition, however. He always sought to extend his power, to unify, and to maintain order. He also cheerfully embraced the responsibilities and entanglements that came with every augmentation of his power.

Upon the death of Conrad III in 1152, Frederick was elected king, but his coronation in Rome was delayed for three years. In return for his coronation as Holy Roman emperor, which took place in 1155, Frederick promised Pope Hadrian IV assistance against two papal foes: revolutionaries in Rome led by Arnold of Brescia and the Norman kingdom of Sicily.

CONFLICT IN ITALY

One of the titles accompanying the imperial crown was king of Lombardy—an honor that Frederick's predecessors had ignored since Emperor Henry IV (r. 1084–1105). Frederick saw no reason to let this richest of all Italian provinces remain free of his influence, or perhaps more importantly, free of his tax-gatherers. He thus seized Milan in Lombardy in 1158 and claimed his imperial rights over the province.

Given Frederick's support of the pope's causes in Sicily and Rome, he might have counted on the Church's tacit approval of his enforcement of his overlordship in Lombardy. But Frederick, eager to strengthen the power and hold of his role as monarch, pressed the case for supreme imperial rights and ownership in all temporal issues. He claimed that the emperor owned everything in his empire and could dispose of it as he wished. This included the appointment and dispensation of Church positions and property. This thorny issue, which later became known as the investiture controversy, lasted well beyond Frederick's reign.

Because of his positions on these issues, Frederick had no assistance from the Church in Lombardy. In 1167, various Italian city-states—including Milan, Verona, Vicenza, Padua, Bologna, Modena, Mantua, Treviso, Brescia, Bergamo, Cremona, Piacenza, and Parma—joined together to form the Lombard League in opposition to Frederick. After almost two decades of struggle, they forced Frederick into signing the Treaty of Constance in 1183, in which he affirmed those city-states' rights of self-governance.

RULE IN THE NORTH

Other than in Italy, Frederick was highly successful in extending and consolidating his empire. In 1156, he divorced his first wife, Adelaide of Vohburg, and married Beatrix, the daughter of Count Rainald of Burgundy (r. 1127–1148). Through this marriage, he gained a political foothold in the powerful county of Burgundy.

In succeeding years, Frederick reasserted German control over Bohemia, Poland, and Hungary. One of Frederick's most notable episodes in the north of Europe culminated in 1180, when he deposed the powerful Henry the Lion, duke of Saxony (r. 1142–1180) and Bavaria (r. 1156–1180), after a council of German princes—all of whom had suffered under Henry's rule—recommended that he be deposed. Frederick had raised Henry, who was his cousin, to the dukedom, but Henry had refused to assist Frederick in the emperor's battles against the Lombard League in 1176. Some contemporaries and historians cite this as a factor in Frederick's decision to depose Henry.

LATER YEARS

In 1187, news came to Frederick's court of the reconquest of Jerusalem by the Muslim leader Saladin (r. 1175–1193) and of the pope's call for the Third Crusade. Frederick, now sixty-five years old, responded vigorously to this challenge. He raised an impressive army of 100,000 men and proceeded overland toward Palestine.

Frederick's age and impetuosity, combined with the climate of Palestine, proved stronger than his tremendous will. In 1190, as he bathed in a cool stream in Anatolia (present-day Turkey) after eating a large meal, Frederick suffered what was probably a stroke or cardiac arrest and died. His body was preserved in vinegar and carried before the remnants of his army, already severely depleted by the combined factors of Turkish skirmishes, heat, and disease. Frederick was finally carried to Antioch in southwestern Anatolia and buried there in holy ground. He was succeeded as German king by his sons, Henry VI (r. 1190–1197) and Philip of Swabia (r. 1198–1208).

After his death, Frederick became a symbol of German imperial pride. Stories arose about his accomplishments, and prophecies were told of his inevitable return. Although not an Alexander the Great (r. 336–323 B.C.E.), or even a Charlemagne (r. 768–814), Frederick played a major role in strengthening monarchical rule in Central Europe. He also brought a degree of order and peace to most of Germany, Italy, Hungary, Austria, Bohemia, and Poland that those strife-torn lands had seldom seen.

See also: CHRISTIANITY AND KINGSHIP; CONRAD II; CONRAD III; CRUSADER KINGDOMS; FREDERICK II; HOHENSTAUFEN DYNASTY; HOLY ROMAN EMPIRE; LOMBARD KINGDOM; PAPAL STATES.

FURTHER READING

Barraclough, Geoffrey. *Origins of Modern Germany.* New York: W.W. Norton, 1984

FREDERICK II (1194–1250 C.E.)

King of Sicily (r. 1197–1250), king of Germany (r. 1212–1250), and Holy Roman emperor (r. 1220–1250), who fought with the papacy over control of territories in Italy, and organized and led the Sixth Crusade to the Holy Land in 1228.

EARLY LIFE

A member of the German Hohenstaufen dynasty, Frederick was the son of Henry VI, German king (r.

1190–1197), Holy Roman emperor (r. 1191–1197), and ruler of the Two Sicilies (r. 1194–1197). His mother was Constance, the heiress of Sicily; his paternal grandfather was the great Frederick I, Barbarossa (r. 1155–1190).

After the death of Henry VI in 1197, Frederick's mother Constance placed her young son under the care of Pope Innocent III (r. 1198–1216), the most powerful man in Italy. Soon after, Constance died, leaving the young Frederick orphaned as well as king of Sicily. Innocent III served as the boy's regent in Sicily, leaving Frederick to grow up with little supervision.

The young Frederick was allowed to wander through the streets and *souks*, or marketplaces, of the Sicilian city of Palermo, where Arabic and other languages were as likely to be heard as Italian. Thus began Frederick's informal education, which led eventually to proficiency in nine different languages.

In 1206, at age twelve, Frederick dismissed his rarely seen papal watchdog and began to exert his own will in Sicily. Three years later, in 1209, he married Constance of Aragón, who brought with her to Sicily a small military force with which Frederick began to bring order to a country that had fallen into near-barbarism under the neglect of the papal regency.

SECURING THE THRONE OF THE EMPIRE

In 1212, Pope Innocent III shifted his support from Holy Roman Emperor Otto IV (r. 1198–1218) to Frederick (as the rightful heir of Henry VI), on condition that Frederick pledge to go on Crusade and keep his kingdoms of Germany and Sicily separate. Innocent was concerned that the Papal States would be encircled by German-controlled kingdoms. In 1214, Otto's forces were easily defeated by Frederick's ally, King Philip II Augustus of France (r. 1180–1223), and the following year Frederick was crowned Holy Roman emperor at the city of Aachen.

Frederick loved his southern kingdom, his "haven amidst the floods, a pleasure garden amidst a wilderness of thorns," and soon returned to Sicily after being crowned emperor. Despite his promise to the pope to separate his German realm from Sicily, he left his infant son, Henry VII, on the German throne, with a regency to govern the kingdom. Frederick had thus turned half of his promise to the pope topsy-turvy.

The new pope, Honorius III (r. 1216–1227), urged Frederick's participation in the "Egyptian" Crusade, but revolts swelled in Sicily and Frederick declined to participate. The pope also suggested to the widowed Frederick a new marriage to Isabella, whose father had been the king of Jerusalem. Frederick agreed, and thus a tacit connection with the Holy Land was made.

Recalling the illustrious attempts of his grandfather, Frederick I, Barbarossa, to pacify the independent-minded city-states of northern Italy, Frederick began diplomatic maneuvers in Lombardy, hoping to assert imperial claims. His actions alarmed the papacy and the Italian city-states, which formed an alliance known as the Lombard League in 1224.

THE SIXTH CRUSADE

In 1227, Frederick yielded to the insistent demands of the new pope, Gregory IX (r. 1227–1241), and agreed to honor his pledge to organize a Crusade. Soon after Frederick assembled a large army and prepared to sail for the Holy Land, an epidemic broke out, killing a third of his men, the accompanying king of Thuringia, and infecting Frederick himself. Upon returning to the mainland for a cure, Frederick sent ambassadors to Pope Gregory to explain the delay, but Gregory would not hear them and excommunicated Frederick for his impiety. Unfazed by the pope's action, Frederick dismissed most of his army and, in the summer of 1228, proceeded on to Palestine with a small honor guard.

When he arrived in the Holy Land, Frederick impressed the emissary of the sultan with his extensive knowledge of the Arabic language and culture, and soon he was corresponding intimately with Sultan Al-Kamil Muhammad II (r. 1218–1238). Within a short time, the two rulers signed a remarkable treaty in which the Christians were given the cities of Acre, Sidon, Jaffa, Bethlehem, and Nazareth, as well as all of Jerusalem except the Dome of the Rock, which was sacred to Muslims. The treaty also included a general amnesty and release of all prisoners, along with a ten-year peace.

This astounding achievement was met with scorn and disdain by the ruling aristocrats and warlords on both the Christian and Muslim sides. The infuriated pope refused to verify the treaty. Nevertheless, Frederick crowned himself king of Jerusalem in 1229 (he could not be crowned by clergy because they had been forbidden to interact with the excommunicate). Soon afterward, however, he realized that his peace was hollow and would not be enforceable unless he had enough military force to subdue the greedy aspirations of his own countrymen, who sought greater riches and power in Palestine.

In the meantime, Pope Gregory had fomented revolt against Frederick in Sicily. Frederick returned to Sicily from the Holy Land in 1229 and reconquered his Sicilian estates. However, he refrained from invading the Papal States and was rewarded for this restraint by having his excommunication lifted in 1230.

As Frederick dealt with the situation in Sicily, his relations with his son, the German king Henry VII, were deteriorating. Henry had made many concessions to the German princes, and in 1228, he signed an alliance with Frederick's old foes, the Lombard League. Frederick responded to these challenges with a successful military campaign against Germany, at the end of which, in 1235, he deposed and imprisoned his son.

FINAL STRUGGLES

With Germany resubjugated, Frederick continued his military campaigns against the unrepentant Lombard League. In 1238, however, he was forced to end the siege of Brescia (one of the League's cities) and regroup his forces back to his holdings in southern Italy and Sicily.

Frederick's relationship with the papacy also worsened dramatically at this time. Fearing that Frederick was attempting to encircle the Papal States, Pope Gregory IX once again excommunicated the emperor on Palm Sunday in 1239. Frederick began marshalling his forces against the papacy, but he withdrew them upon the death of Pope Gregory in 1241. Four years later, King Louis IX of France (r. 1226–1270) intervened on Frederick's behalf with the papacy. The fighting ended, and Frederick's excommunication was lifted in 1244. This situation did not last long, however, because Frederick was still intent on subjugating the Lombard League.

By 1250, the struggle against the Italian states had turned in Frederick's favor. But while Louis IX of France was trying to arrange another treaty or armistice with the desperate pope, Frederick succumbed suddenly to dysentery and died in December 1250.

LEGACY

Frederick's legacy, though not obvious, is profound. Ironically, for such a successful general, Frederick's many military victories became meaningless within less than a generation after his death. Even his impressive diplomatic efforts were brief and transitory. However, as founder of the first state-funded nonreligiously affiliated university in Europe (Naples, 1224), as the champion of experimental science and medicine (practiced and encouraged at his court in Sicily), and as the free-thinking precursor of an Italian Renaissance, his influence was enormous and far-reaching.

See also: CRUSADER KINGDOMS; HOHENSTAUFEN DYNASTY; HOLY ROMAN EMPIRE; LOMBARD KINGDOM; LOUIS IX (ST. LOUIS); MILITARY ROLES, ROYAL; PAPAL STATES; SICILY, KINGDOM OF.

FREDERICK II, THE GREAT

(1712–1786 C.E.)

King of Prussia (r. 1740–1786), whose strong leadership, intelligence, and progressive reforms transformed Prussia from a fledgling kingdom into one of the major powers of Europe. Though openly averse to authority as a young man, Frederick II (also known as "Frederick the Great") became perhaps the most successful of Prussian monarchs, leaving a legacy of enlightened governance that greatly influenced the future of the German states.

The oldest son of Prussian king Frederick William I (r. 1713–1740) and Sophia of Hanover, Frederick was trained from a very young age in the arts of war and leadership, with the expectation that he would inherit his father's crown. Frederick rejected this form of schooling, however, and showed a deep and passionate interest in philosophy and the arts. This led very early on to a sharp division between father and son, such that Frederick William openly avowed dislike of Frederick and subjected him to all sorts of cruel punishments, frequently in public. His father was so hard on him that Frederick attempted to flee Prussia for England in 1730 in the company of his good friend Hans Hermann von Katte. The pair were caught, however, and the king made Frederick witness the execution of Katte, who was charged for his role in trying to help the prince flee the country.

Frederick the Great of Prussia was a strong, enlightened leader, who transformed his kingdom into one of the most powerful in Europe. Friends with leading thinkers of the sixteenth century, Frederick II is shown visiting with Voltaire.

Miraculously, Frederick later achieved some reconciliation with his father, largely owing to his acquiescence to an arranged marriage with Elizabeth of Brunswick, a union that Frederick William had encouraged for some time. Frederick and Elizabeth had no children together and lived apart for nearly their entire lives. Most historians now agree that Frederick was homosexual.

Frederick became king upon his father's death in 1740. Known as "the philosopher king," he was a deeply contemplative man, greatly admired, and even befriended by many of the major German and French thinkers of his time, including Goethe and Voltaire, who helped shape his ideas. He was also a cold, calculating, quiet man, and many of his actions seemed rash and foolish at first. In time, however, it became clear that they were the product of careful consideration and prudent analysis.

Almost immediately after taking the throne in 1740, Frederick began to display the qualities of leadership that marked his reign. One of his first actions was to launch a quick and decisive attack, without provocation, against Maria Theresa of Austria (r. 1740–1780), from whom he secured several portions of land for Prussia. Territorial expansion continued throughout Frederick's reign.

Frederick was perhaps most notable as a military tactician, and the techniques he devised for the battlefield changed warfare dramatically and were later adopted by Napoleon I (r. 1804–1814), Adolf Hitler, and others. By the end of the Seven Years' War in 1763, which was fueled by renewed tensions between Prussia and Austria, Prussia was the dominant military power on the European continent, rivaled only by France and Russia.

After securing his borders, Frederick turned inward, embarking on an ambitious program of rebuilding and development that further strengthened the Prussian kingdom. Through intelligent and careful financial planning, Frederick also was able to keep Prussia from falling into debt, even in the aftermath of the destruction of the Seven Years' War. Frederick promoted the development of industry, protected commercial ventures, and provided services and land for sustainable agriculture. In doing so, he improved significantly on initiatives his father had put in place years before. Especially notable for the hands-on approach he took to reform, Frederick personally oversaw many of the changes taking place during his reign, especially in regard to the development of skilled civil servants. Leading by example, Frederick was also a great patron of the arts and was able to generate impressive private support for them.

Frederick's progressive policies carried over into the legal system, where his changes put Prussia on the road to a modern system of jurisprudence. Repealing many of his father's legal guidelines, Frederick abolished corporal punishment and severely curtailed the use of the death penalty. He also promoted freedom of speech, and, most famously, freedom of religion, making one of the first declarations of the separation of church and state. Unfortunately, serfdom in Prussia was too deeply implanted to be abolished.

Although Frederick was a very progressive ruler, he did nothing to further the movement toward democratic government in Prussia. When he died in 1786, Frederick handed down the same system of social stratification and selective citizenship that he inherited from his father. Since Frederick left no direct descendants, upon his death the Crown passed to his nephew, Frederick William II (r. 1786–1797).

See also: COMMERCE AND KINGSHIP; EDUCATION OF KINGS; FREDERICK WILLIAM, THE GREAT ELECTOR; HOMOSEXUALITY AND KINGSHIP; MARIA THERESA; MILITARY ROLES, ROYAL.

FURTHER READING
Fraser, David. *Frederick the Great: King of Prussia.* New York: Fromm, 2001.

FREDERICK WILLIAM, THE GREAT ELECTOR (1620–1688 C.E.)

Elector of Brandenburg (r. 1640–1688), who consolidated the lands of the Hohenzollern dynasty into what later became Prussia, the most powerful state in Germany.

A capable administrator and respected military leader, Frederick William was one of the most successful rulers of the Hohenzollern dynasty. During his reign, Prussia grew from a struggling confederation of local states decimated by foreign armies into a strong and unified nation-state with a commanding voice in European politics.

The son of George William (r. 1620–1640), elector of Brandenburg and duke of Prussia, Frederick William was born in 1620, just after the outbreak of the Thirty Years' War (1618–1648). That conflict dominated the reign of his father, who had attempted to stay neutral and consequently found his lands overrun and occupied until his death in 1640.

Upon inheriting his father's titles, Frederick William immediately set about repairing his damaged homeland, organizing his army into a strong fighting force, driving out an occupying Swedish army, and greatly adding to his family's territory. The Peace of Westphalia in 1648 and a 1657 Polish treaty secured Hohenzollern domain over Prussia and the eastern portions of Pomerania (a region that included parts of Poland), thereby allowing Frederick William to initiate an extensive series of domestic reforms.

Frederick William set the precedent for future governance in Prussia by establishing a strong administrative base that overrode the authority of local leaders for the benefit of the country as a whole. He also initiated a great many public works projects, including a canal on the Oder River that is still in use today. These accomplishments helped fuel the Prussian economy, which quickly bounced back from the ravages of the Thirty Years' War and became the most powerful economy in Germany by the time of Frederick William's death. Frederick William also pursued a policy of widespread religious tolerance, which stifled any religious disputes that might have caused internal discord within Prussia.

Upon Frederick William's death in 1688, he was succeeded by his son, Frederick III (r. 1688–1713). Under Frederick III, who was not nearly as successful a leader as his father, Prussia achieved international recognition in 1701 as a kingdom rather than a duchy. As a result, Frederick's title changed from Frederick III, elector of Brandenburg, to King Frederick I of Prussia (r. 1701–1713), the first Prussian ruler of the Hohenzollern dynasty.

See also: HOHENZOLLERN DYNASTY.

FRENCH MONARCHIES

(ca. 987–1848 C.E.)

Rulers of France from the tenth to the nineteenth century, who were one of the most powerful royal dynasties in Europe during that time.

The French monarchy emerged in the early Middle Ages along with a number of other European dynasties and kingdoms. For the next thousand years, France played a major role in European politics and culture. Its rivalry with England in the Middle Ages and with the Habsburg dynasty of Austria and Spain in the sixteenth through nineteenth centuries shaped the European world. Only three royal families ruled France throughout this long period: the Capetians, the Valois, and the Bourbons.

THE CAPETIAN DYNASTY

The Capetian dynasty did not begin as a powerful family of kings. Instead, they survived, at least in part, because they posed no obvious threat to the more powerful kingdoms around them, such as Flanders and Aquitaine. The Capetians did, however, succeed in founding one of the longest lasting and most powerful monarchies in European history.

The Foundations of French Monarchy

In 987, a Frankish noble named Hugh Capet (r. 987–996) took power in France after the death of Louis V (r. 986–987), the last ruler of the Carolingian dynasty. The Carolingians were the family of the great Charlemagne (r. 768–814), and France was still considered an empire, the Empire of the West, descended from that of Charlemagne. The Capet family origi-

The magnificent Château de Versailles was originally a hunting lodge built by King Louis XIII. Home to the French monarchy for over a century, the palace underwent a vast expansion from 1665 to 1683 under Louis XIV. The Marble Courtyard, shown here, was part of architect Louis Le Vau's sumptuous redesign.

nally ruled only part of that empire (West Francia), and not the largest or most powerful part.

From the accession of Hugh Capet until 1328, the Capetians ruled as kings. Over the nearly three hundred fifty years that the Capetians controlled the French monarchy, one of their most important successes was the creation of a new way of referring to the region. The area became an ideological and historical entity—France—rather than part of a larger territory. The Capetians did this by connecting their rule with the Roman Catholic Church, by carefully parceling out land to loyal nobles, and by enforcing the rule of law.

Feudalism and the Weakness of Central Authority

One of the principal limitations of royal authority during the early Middle Ages was the nature of po-

litical power itself. In the modern world, legitimate political authority emanates from a theoretical consent of the people. However, medieval political power was privately held. In other words, authority, such as the exercise of justice or the collection of taxes, was in the hands of the feudal king. Under the feudal system, a monarch's authority rested on his personal ties with other lords to whom he could distribute authority as property and for whom he often served as arbiter in disputes.

The political world of the early Capetians was often a web of contradictory associations rather than an efficient hierarchy. France, and Europe as a whole, were extremely decentralized, and political action and authority was intensely localized. The monarch's ability to exercise control over his own territory was limited by the loyalty and awe of his high-born allies.

Capetian Dynasty

HUGH CAPET*	987–996
ROBERT II	996–1031
HENRY I	1031–1060
PHILIP I	1060–1108
LOUIS VI	1108–1137
LOUIS VII*	1137–1180
PHILIP II (AUGUSTUS)*	1180–1223
LOUIS VIII	1223–1226
LOUIS IX (ST. LOUIS)*	1226–1270
PHILIP III	1270–1285
PHILIP IV*	1285–1314
LOUIS X	1314–1316
PHILIP V	1316–1322
CHARLES IV	1322–1328

Valois Dynasty

PHILIP VI	1328–1350
JOHN	1350–1364
CHARLES V	1364–1380
CHARLES VI	1380–1422
CHARLES VII*	1422–1461
LOUIS XI*	1461–1483
CHARLES VIII	1483–1498

LOUIS XII	1498–1515
FRANCIS I*	1515–1547
HENRY II	1547–1559
FRANCIS II	1559–1560
CHARLES IX	1560–1574
HENRY III	1574–1589

Bourbon Dynasty

HENRY IV*	1589–1610
LOUIS XIII	1610–1643
LOUIS XIV*	1643–1715
LOUIS XV*	1715–1774
LOUIS XVI*	1774–1792

Restoration Monarchy after the Revolution

NAPOLEON (AS FIRST CONSUL AND EMPEROR)	1799–1814
LOUIS XVIII (BOURBON)	1814–1824
CHARLES X (BOURBON)	1824–1830
LOUIS-PHILIPPE (ORLEANS-BOURBON)*	1830–1848

*Indicates a separate alphabetical entry.

Keys to Success: God and Marriage

Despite their title as kings, the Capetians were weaker than many of the dukes and counts who were their allies. To strengthen their position, the Capetian kings emphasized their special nature as not only political leaders, but also religiously anointed monarchs. Claiming continuity from their Merovingian and Carolingian forebears, the Capetians and their allies in the Church used their sacral status to claim power, making them more like biblical kings than Germanic lords. During the twelfth century, for example, the French monarchy took the fleur-de-lis as a symbol, borrowing it directly from King Solomon of Israel (r. 970–931 B.C.E.). Enthusiastic churchmen, such as Robert the Monk, worked on behalf of the Capetian monarchs, giving their rule a divine purpose, defining the French people as the chosen people of God, and helping establish a consciousness as a nation.

After 1100 C.E., Capetian monarchs gradually increased their power. In 1124, King Louis VI (r. 1108–1137) obtained the right to demand forty days' service from any vassal when the regime was threatened by Germany or England. Allies who refused to serve the king had their lands confiscated, further increasing the Capetian domains. Marriage also consolidated Capetian lands and brought once rival territories together. In 1137, for example, King Louis VII (r. 1137–1180) married Eleanor of Aquitaine; and in 1180, Philip II Augustus (r. 1180–1223) married Isabelle of Hainaut, the daughter of the count of Flanders.

By 1300, the Capetians had built a large and powerful kingdom. They had been smart and fortunate in their rise, taking advantage of the weaknesses of others. But they had also made enemies. In 1152, Louis VII disavowed Eleanor of Aquitaine as his wife, who then married Henry Platagenet, count of Anjou and duke of Normandy, who became King Henry II of England (r. 1154–1189). Henry was a major rival of the Capetians, and the Capetian-Norman rivalry would smolder as a source of conflict for the next several centuries, occasionally breaking out in open warfare (a period known as the First Hundred Years' War, 1159–1299).

THE VALOIS DYNASTY

After eleven consecutive generations of male offspring, the Capetian dynasty finally ended in 1328 when King Charles IV (r. 1322–1328) died without a male heir. His successor was a cousin, Philip of Valois, who became King Philip VI (r. 1328–1350). The Valois dynasty ruled France through a profound transition. While the dynasty began in the late Middle Ages, most of its tenure occurred during the Renaissance, and Valois rule straddled the divide between the medieval and modern periods.

Philip of Valois

The ascension of Philip of Valois to the French throne highlights the changing political and legal values of the time. Under feudal law, inheritance might pass through a female heir (although not technically belonging to that female). By this standard, after the death of Charles IV, there existed a more direct heir to the French throne than Philip. That heir was King Edward III of England (r. 1327–1377), a descendant of the Plantagenet dukes of Normandy.

Edward's accession would have unified France and England into one kingdom. But the growing hatred between the French and English made such a union of crowns impossible. Philip's French supporters thus invoked the ancient Frankish Salic Law, which pre-

ROYAL RITUALS

REIMS CATHEDRAL AND THE FRENCH CORONATION CEREMONY

The cathedral at Reims in northeast France is one of three religious sites directly connected to the French monarchy. Along with Notre-Dame Cathedral and the Abbey of Saint-Denis, the cathedral at Reims served an important role as the traditional site of French royal coronations. According to legend, the Frankish king Clovis was crowned in Reims. The Capetian monarchs, who claimed descent from Clovis, used this legend to establish a divine claim to the French throne. Using holy oil (reputedly delivered by a dove in the ninth century), the archbishop of Reims anointed every king in a solemn ceremony to mark his ascension to the throne. The divinity granted to kings in the ceremony gave them the ability to cure illness through the "royal touch." The last king to be crowned at Reims was also the last to be descended from the original Capetians. In 1825, during the Restoration monarchy, Charles X was crowned at Reims.

ROYAL RELATIVES

PHILIPPE D'ORLEANS

The second son of Louis XIII and Anne of Austria, Philippe spent his entire life in the shadow of his brother, the Sun-King, Louis XIV. Being eclipsed by his brother had several consequences for Philippe. During Philippe's childhood, his mother, who had wanted a daughter, dressed him as a girl. Some historians claim that this reinforced Philippe's sense of inferiority and fostered a sense of frustration with life that became a hallmark of his adulthood. Historians also associate his mother's actions with Philippe's well-known homosexual exploits.

When he became an adult, an obvious source of frustration for Philippe was his father's refusal to allow him any political power. Philippe strove throughout his life to prove himself as capable as his sibling and not a useless dilettante. He won important battles in several of the early wars of his brother's reign, including the defeat of William of Orange at the battle of Cassel in 1677. Such success cost him, however, as Louis refused to allow Philippe further commands after the Dutch War.

Philippe married twice. His first wife Henrietta, daughter of Charles II of England, died in 1670. Philippe was remarried the next year to Elizabeth Charlotte, daughter of the Elector Palatine. He died in 1701 at his palace in Saint-Cloud.

vented kingship from being transmitted to or through a female.

The Hundred Years' War

As a result of the long-standing feud between the Plantagenets (now kings of England) and the kings of France, the new conflict over inheritance sparked renewed warfare and marked the beginning of the so-called Hundred Years' War (1337–1453).

In one of the odd byproducts of feudal ties, Edward III, a king in his own right, owed feudal loyalty to Philip VI (Philip of Valois). Edward was also the duke of Aquitaine, a wealthy province in southwestern France that had become an English territory with the marriage of Henry II of England and Eleanor of Aquitaine. When Philip tried to confiscate land belonging to Edward, claiming that he had not fulfilled his duties as a loyal ally, Edward declared Philip a usurper and claimed the title of king of France. By 1340 France and England were at war.

At first, the war went badly for the French, who lost a series of battles in the north and west. France saw a brief recovery under Charles V (r. 1364–1380)

but fell back once again when his son, Charles VI (r. 1380–1422), went insane, creating disorder among the French leadership. A low point in the conflict was reached after the invasion of France by Henry V (r. 1413–1422) of England and the French defeat at the battle of Agincourt in 1415. Charles VI was forced to disinherit his own son and accept the marriage of his daughter to Henry, making Henry V the heir to the French throne.

France's fortunes turned only with the appearance of Joan of Arc, whose symbolic leadership renewed French confidence and vigor, resulting in a series of decisive victories over England in the 1420s. In the end, however, Charles VII of France (r. 1422–1461) betrayed Joan, as he mistrusted her popularity and her desire for war. The English were finally driven from French soil in 1453.

Religious Wars and the End of a Dynasty

The Hundred Years' War was not the only test of the Valois kings. In the sixteenth century, they faced an even more challenging crisis. After Martin Luther launched the Protestant Reformation in 1517, a flood of new religious ideas spread across Europe. In France, the ideas of Protestant theologian John Calvin spread quickly, creating a community of Protestants in France known as Huguenots.

The Valois monarchs who ruled France after the end of the Hundred Years' War succeeded in strengthening the authority of the Crown. Louis XII (r. 1498–1515), Francis I (r. 1515–1547), and Henry II (r. 1547–1559) all also expanded French territory and, after 1517, coped well with rising religious tensions in France.

In 1559, Henry II died in a jousting accident, leaving his son, Francis II (r. 1559–1560), to rule. A sickly child, Francis died only a year later. Henry's two younger sons, Charles IX (r. 1560–1574) and Henry III (r. 1574–1589), then each succeeded to the throne, but they were dominated by their strong-willed mother, Catherine de Medici. During their reigns, the fragile religious peace between French Catholics and Huguenots disappeared into violent confrontations, including the St. Bartholomew's Day Massacre of Huguenots in Paris in 1572, which was ordered by Charles IX under the instigation of his mother.

None of the later Valois proved up to the challenges of the sixteenth century. Charles IX was poisoned and died a painful death; his brother, Henry III, was assassinated by a Dominican monk, Jacques Clement, in 1589. Neither Charles nor Henry left an heir. Their closest male relative was Henry of Navarre, the leader of the Protestant forces.

THE BOURBONS

Henry of Navarre was the son of Antoine de Bourbon, the duke of Vendome, and Jeanne D'Albret, the staunchly Protestant queen of Navarre (r. 1555–1572). Henry's accession to the French throne in 1589 as Henry IV (r. 1589–1610) inaugurated the third and last royal dynasty in French history: the House of Bourbon.

"The Crown Is Worth a Mass"

To be crowned French king, Henry IV had to give up his Protestant faith and convert to Catholicism. The traditional rite of coronation was too intertwined with Catholic ritual for a Protestant to be king. When confronted with a choice between his religion and the Crown, Henry allegedly remarked, "The crown is worth a mass," and converted to Catholicism.

Henry IV did not turn his back on his former co-religionists, however. As part of the peace settlement of the religious wars that had wracked France, Henry

issued the Edict of Nantes (1598), which gave French Protestants the right to worship, although they could not spread their faith or worship outside established areas. But the peace did not have long to settle in under Henry. He was assassinated in 1610, and his eldest son, Louis XIII (r. 1610–1643), came to the throne while still only a child.

The Sun-King: Absolutism at Its Height

The shape of French and European monarchy took a decisive turn beginning under King Louis XIII (r. 1610–1643). With the aid of his minister of state, Cardinal Richelieu, Louis began to draw upon the sacral nature of monarchy established by the Capetians and claim ancient precedent.

Louis and other French monarchs in the seventeenth century adopted a new vision of monarchical authority called absolutism. This theory of monarchical rule sought to establish unchallenged royal authority by undercutting traditional authority, primarily that of the French nobility or aristocracy. By the second half of the seventeenth century, this political philosophy had evolved into a more mature form—the idea of divine right.

Best articulated by French bishop Jacques Benigne Bossuet, the philosophy of divine right argued that royal authority was sacred and that God had established the monarchy to rule over the French nation. The political and cultural consequences of this idea were reflected most clearly in the magnificent palace at Versailles, built by Louis XIV (r. 1643–1715), who was known as the "Sun-King."

The End of the Monarchy

The power and opulence of the Bourbon monarchs came to an end at the close of the eighteenth century. While the decisiveness and efficiency of absolutism characterized the seventeenth century, the eighteenth century witnessed a revolutionary shift in popular values.

The eighteenth-century movement known as the Enlightenment stressed individual rights and universal justice, values contrary to the often arbitrary absolutist exercise of power. By the reign of King Louis XVI (r. 1774–1792), these values had eroded the prestige of the French monarchy. This degradation combined with a severe economic slowdown and a deepening governmental financial crisis to set the stage for the French Revolution that began in 1789.

Almost three years after the French Revolution began, King Louis XVI and his wife Marie-Antoinette attempted to flee the country. They were caught and eventually executed by the guillotine in 1793. Although several Bourbon relatives returned after Napoleon (1804–1814), the Revolution effectively ended the monarchy in France.

FRENCH MONARCHS AFTER THE REVOLUTION

France was a republic until 1804, when Napoleon declared himself emperor. After Napoleon, two Bourbon relatives, Louis XVIII (r. 1814–1824) and Charles X (r. 1824–1830), ruled in the period known as the Restoration Monarchy.

Charles X, the last Bourbon ruler of France, was deposed in 1830, and Louis Phillipe (r. 1830–1848), duke of Orleans, took power as a constitutional monarch. He abdicated in 1848 and a republic was established in France. Napoleon III (r. 1852–1870) dissolved this republic and named himself emperor, but he was deposed after a disastrous war with Germany. Neither Louis Phillipe nor Napoleon III claimed royal legitimacy.

See also: BOURBON DYNASTY; CAPETIAN DYNASTY; VALOIS DYNASTY.

FURTHER READING

Duby, Georges, and Robert Mandrou. *A History of French Civilization: From the Year 1000 to the Present.* Trans. James Blakely Atkinson. New York: Random House, 1964.

Goubert, Pierre. *The Ancien Régime: French Society, 1600–1750.* New York: Harper and Row, 1973.

Howarth, Thomas E.B. *Citizen-King: The Life of Louis-Philippe, King of the French.* New York: White Lion Publishers, 1975.

Price, Roger. *A Concise History of France.* New York: Cambridge University Press, 1993.

———. *The French Second Empire: An Anatomy of Political Power.* New York: Cambridge University Press, 2001.

FUAD (1868–1936 C.E.)

Sultan and first king of modern Egypt (r. 1917–1936) who ruled during a tumultuous period when Egypt was under the control of Great Britain.

Ahmed Fuad, also known as Fuad I, was the son of Ishmail Pasha, the Egyptian *khedive*, or viceroy. As a member of a prominent Egyptian family, Fuad was sent to Italy for his education. After he returned to Egypt in 1880, he served as a general in the Egyptian army for about ten years. Fuad also made his mark in Egyptian cultural society by helping to found and subsequently administer a university in Giza, now called the University of Cairo, in 1908.

In 1914, Egypt officially was declared a protectorate of Great Britain, and Fuad's eldest brother, Hussein Kamil, was named sultan. Upon Kamil's death in 1917, Fuad succeeded Kamil in that office. At around this time, a new nationalist party, called the Wafd, was formed by Egyptians adamant about regaining Egypt's independence from the British.

As it became clear that the British were not going to honor their promise to give Egypt self-rule, revolts led by the Wafd took place throughout the country. Britain finally relented in 1922, declared Egypt an independent country, and named Fuad king. Nevertheless, Britain remained a presence in Egypt and interceded regularly in its affairs.

A new constitution, adopted in 1924, granted Fuad considerable powers, including the power to dissolve or adjourn parliament, to veto acts of parliament, and to appoint and dismiss prime ministers. He was also named commander-in-chief of the armed forces.

Fuad used his powers often, creating a constant turnover in the country's administration as well as two periods in which Parliament was completely dissolved. For the rest of Fuad's life, Egypt remained in turmoil, with a three-way power struggle between the king, the nationalists, and the British. Upon his death in 1936, Fuad was succeeded by his son, Farouk (r. 1936–1952).

See also: EGYPTIAN KINGDOM, MODERN; FAROUK.

FURTHER READING

Fisher, Sydney Nettleton, and William Ochsenwald. *The Middle East: A History.* 6th ed. Boston: McGraw-Hill, 2004.

FUJIWARA DYNASTY (660s–1185 C.E.)

The civil dictators of Japan from the mid-seventh century to the late twelfth century. The ascendancy of the Fujiwara dynasty coincided with the golden age of the Heian period (794–1185). The Fujiwara family maintained influence at the imperial court in Kyoto by providing generations of daughters as imperial consorts and empresses.

The practice in which great families of Japan manipulated the emperor to their own ends was not new. The Fujiwara replaced the Soga family, who dominated the imperial court from the mid-fifth to the mid-seventh centuries. However, by institutionalizing their role in government as regents and advisors, and by demonstrating competence in their roles, the Fujiwara perpetuated their dynasty and solidified the persistent political dualism in Japanese life—however powerful the leader, he must derive his legitimacy from the puppet imperial court.

THE WISTERIA

The Fujiwara dynasty was founded in the 660s by Fujiwara Kamatara, who was born Nakatomi Kamatori in 614. For Kamatori's support of the imperial house in its struggle against the Soga dynasty, the Emperor Tenji (r. 661–672) awarded him the surname *Fujiwara* (wisteria arbor), which referred to the scene of the victory against the Soga.

Kamatori's son, Fuhito, was grandfather to the Emperor Shomu (r. 724–749) through a daughter who was an imperial consort. He was also father-in-law to the emperor through another daughter, who in 792 became the first empress who was not a princess of royal blood. The marriage between this daughter and Shomu established the tradition by which the Fujiwara married into the imperial house. It became common for emperors to retire early (to enjoy the considerable pleasures of life) and place child emperors born of Fujiwara mothers on the throne under the control of Fujiwara regents.

Fujiwara Yoshifusa (804–872) was the first regent to the Japanese emperor who was not of royal blood. Already a great minister of state, Yoshifusa arranged in 858 for his seven-year-old grandson to be named emperor and declared himself the child's *sessho* or regent, thus institutionalizing the role. Following Yoshifusa as head of the family was Mototsune (836–891), who became regent in 876 to the newest child emperor, Yozei (r. 876–884). As the child grew older, Motosune continued as adviser and created the new role of *kampaku*, or counselor and regent to adult emperors.

Fujiwara Michinaga (966–1028) was the quintes-

sential Fujiwara regent. An obviously capable ruler, he dominated the court at the height of the Heian (Kyoto) imperial splendor. Although he held numerous imperial offices, he never took the kampaku title, however. Four of his daughters married four different emperors, and he was uncle to two emperors and grandfather to three.

Michinaga lived in opulence, with resplendent palaces, many consorts, and extravagant pastimes. He is supposedly one of the models for Prince Genji, hero of *The Tale of Genji*, written around 1004 by imperial lady-in-waiting Murasaki Shikibu and generally considered to be the world's first novel. Michinaga appears many times in *Pillow Book* (ca. 1000), the famous contemporary accounts of imperial court life by Sei Shonagon, a lady of the court.

THE HEIAN PERIOD

During the Heian period, absentee ownership was common, since aristocratic landowners preferred to be in the capital city near the brilliant imperial court. Provincial families, including the Fujiwara, amassed great power and wealth as local managers of the *shoen*, or large fiefdoms, and as designated tax collectors for the landed families.

The continued expansion of private estates in Japan during the Heian period undermined central authority and increasingly encouraged territorial clashes. Despite the brillance of this so-called golden age, growing unrest spread from the countryside to the capital, and Michinaga at times paid warriors of the Minamoto and Taira clans to quell disorder.

Michinaga's son, Fujiwara Yorimichi (992–1074), served more than fifty years as regent for three emperors and dominated court life from 1016 to 1068. During this half century, the control of the central government continued to dissipate. Brigands plundered the imperial palaces, and the provincial lords refused to send taxes.

By the twelfth century, there was constant conflict among the powerful families of Japan. Civil warfare was aggravated by the growing involvement of the *bushi*, or *samurai* retainers. Control belonged to whoever could muster the greatest number of armed men.

INSEI GOVERNANCE

After 1068, Fujiwara power was greatly limited by the *insei* system, the early tradition of cloistered rule that was resurrected by the imperial court. The emperor would abdicate, name a child successor, and retire to a monastery, freeing himself to rule as regent away from the formal and oppressive requirements of court life.

In 1086, Emperor Go-Sanjo (r. 1068–1073), the first emperor without a Fujiwara mother in over a hundred years, retired in favor of his son, Go-Shirakawa (r. 1073–1087). As retired *insei*, or cloistered" emperors, both Go-Sanjo and his son successfully supplanted Fujiwara advisers with their loyal clique of retainers.

Faced with dwindling tax revenues and violent clashes between powerful clans and families, the imperial court and the Fujiwara clan were eventually overtaken by the warrior class. An alliance of Fujiwara and Minamoto warriors lost to the imperial-Taira forces in open conflicts in 1156 and 1159. By 1185, Yoritomo Minamoto, a warrior of the Minamoto clan had concentrated power in his own hands, establishing the Kamakura shogunate. The power and influence of the Fujiwara dynasty was at an end.

See also: KAMAKURA SHOGUNATE; MINAMOTO RULERS; YORITOMO.

FURTHER READING

Bowring, Richard, and Peter Kornicki, eds. *The Cambridge Encyclopedia of Japan.* New York: Cambridge University Press, 1993.

Collcutt, Martin, Marius Jansen, and Isai Jumakura. *Cultural Atlas of Japan.* New York: Facts on File, 1988.

Hall, John W., et al., eds. *The Cambridge History of Japan.* New York: Cambridge University Press, 1988.

FUNAN KINGDOM

(ca. first century–500s C.E.)

Hindu kingdom established in the first century that was one of the first states to emerge in Southeast Asia out of the expanding Indian civilization to the north. Cambodians generally consider the Funan kingdom to be the first Khmer kingdom in the region. Although the exact boundaries of the kingdom are not known, it is generally believed to have occupied an area within present-day Myanmar (Burma), Thailand, Cambodia, and southern Vietnam.

According to Cambodian legends, the Funan kingdom was founded by an Indian leader named Kaundinuya, who came to the region in the first century. Located in the Mekong River Delta, the kingdom flourished as a stopover point for Chinese and Indian trading ships. Such interaction with Chinese and Indian sea traders not only brought goods to the Funan kingdom, but it also encouraged economic reform and development. The Funan people were the first in Southeast Asia to conduct trade with silver coins. The records of a third-century Chinese ambassador described Funan as having walled cities, libraries, a judicial system, and a taxation system.

The Funan civilization derived many of its cultural, religious, and political traditions from India, and then spread them throughout the region. Although Funan never adopted the caste system that was used in India, the Funan people organized themselves into highly sophisticated and centralized states. They are said to have relied on an advanced system of canals and dikes to harness the Mekong River floodwaters and irrigate their inland rice fields.

Among the kings of Funan, Kaundinya Jayavarman (r. ca. 478–514) was known for a mission he sent to China led by a Buddhist monk. King Rudravarman (r. ca. 514–539) encouraged the spread of Buddhism in the kingdom by claiming that a relic of the Buddha was housed in one of the kingdom's temples. By the early sixth century, Theravada Buddhism had begun to flourish in Funan. By that same century, however, the Funan kingdom was in decline. Overrun by Khmer peoples from the Chenla kingdom in the mid-500s, it was eventually replaced by the Chenla Empire.

See also: ANGKOR KINGDOM; CAMBODIAN KINGDOMS; CHAMPA KINGDOM; CHENLA EMPIRE; SOUTHEAST ASIAN KINGDOMS; VIETNAMESE KINGDOMS.

FUNERALS AND MORTUARY RITUALS

The funeral and mortuary practices of royals throughout history have largely reflected their central social role. Although these practices have changed over time and vary depending on the beliefs of the culture and the status of the deceased, several key cross-cultural features have remained consistent.

FUNÉRAILLES DE LA REINE VICTORIA
Au mausolée de Frogmore

The funerals of monarchs are often large ceremonial affairs, marking not only the passing of a ruler but also a change in government. Queen Victoria of Great Britain, who died on January 22, 1901, was honored by a lavish state funeral at St. George's Chapel in London and buried at the Frogmore Mausoleum near Windsor Castle.

The burial of royals tends to celebrate their lives, to preserve their wealth and power beyond death, and to solidify their memory and status in the public for generations to come.

ANCIENT BURIAL CUSTOMS

The first peoples to perfect and perpetuate the mortuary ritual were the Egyptians. The funerary practices of the Egyptians were complex, and the secret of their mummification practices were closely guarded. Much of what we know of this process comes from the early historian Herodotus (484–425 B.C.E.). Embalming is thought to have originated with the Egyptians around 4000 B.C.E. "Embalm" means literally to place in balsam (a fragrant tree), while "mummifica-

tion" refers to the methods used to preserve the body, including the removal of organs, embalming, and wrapping. Upon the death of a pharaoh, his body was given over to the official embalmers who removed the organs and prepared the body for the afterlife; this was likely done in the *ibu* ("place of purification"). The organs were removed and soaked in natron, a natural salt occurring in the Nile River to dry them out and prevent decomposition. The heart was not removed because it was believed to be the center of intelligence.

On the day of the burial, the corpse was the center of elaborate ceremonies symbolizing the life of the god king Osiris, who had been killed and through various processes had been restored to life. It was believed that those who worshiped Osiris and were mummified as he had been could also be brought back to life. The mummy was then lowered into a Great Pyramid, down to the tomb chamber and laid on its left side. The Great Pyramids, future tombs for the pharaohs, were built on such a grand scale that they required more than 2.3 million huge, polished stones and required hundreds of thousands of laborers working continuously for twenty years to complete. Food, drink, and toiletries were left beside the sarcophagus (decorated stone coffin) along with amulets for protection. The chamber leading to the mummy was then filled with sand and gravel to conceal its existence.

Victorian England

It was in England during the reign of Queen Victoria (r. 1837–1901) that the mortuary ritual, funerals, and mourning practices became almost a national obsession. Upon the death of a royal, the country and English court would enter a period of national mourning. In the 1880s, the ascribed length of national mourning for a monarch was twelve weeks, six weeks for the death of the child of the king or queen; mourning lengths were specified down to ten days for a first cousin of the royal family.

Elaborate funerals became common even for minor figures of the royal family. Entire warehouses were devoted to the selling of black fabric and garments to be worn in accordance with the mourning rituals. A mourner would don only black or very dark purple, depending on the relationship of the deceased. This would continue for months or even years. Mourning jewelry was also popular for women

ROYAL RITUALS

ROYAL MAUSOLEA

Mausolea are free-standing structures for housing the dead, larger in size and grander in scale than a tomb. Their origin can be traced to 353 B.C.E. when King Mausolus, ruler of the small Mediterranean kingdom of Caria for twenty-four years, died. His grief-stricken wife Artemisia built the most elaborate tomb in the world to honor him. This tomb would become the standard model used for centuries to come in the burial of royal dead. The original mausoleum was an ornate white marble structure, 140 feet high. It stood for nearly seventeen centuries until damaged by earthquakes.

In early seventeenth-century India in the city of Arga, Utter Pradesh, Shah Jehan (Prince Khurram), the fifth Mughal emperor, built the Taj Mahal to honor Mumtaz Mahal, his deceased wife. Located on the banks of the Yamuna River, the multichambered Taj Mahal, was constructed of a similar white marble and became perhaps the most famous mausoleum in the world.

to wear. The stone or jewel most associated with Victorian mourning was jet, which was made of fossilized driftwood of the monkey-puzzle tree. Queen Victoria wore jet after the death of her husband, Prince Albert, in 1861 until her own in 1901.

See also: VICTORIA.

FURTHER READING

Metcalf, Peter. *Celebrations of Death: The Anthropology of Mortuary Ritual.* New York: Cambridge University Press, 1992

Pearson, Mike Parker. *The Archaeology of Death and Burial.* College Station: Texas A&M University Press, 2001.

Taylor, Lou. *Mourning Dress: A Costume and Social History.* London: Allen & Irwin, 1983

FUR KINGDOM (ca. 1640–1916 C.E.)

Kingdom located in western Sudan, whose wealth and power were derived from its monopoly of the trans-Saharan slave trade through taxes and tariffs.

The sultanate of Dar Fur, also known as the Fur kingdom, was founded in the seventeenth century by Sulayman Solong (r. ca. 1640–1670), who decreed that the state religion would be Islam. However, Sulayman seems not to have made direct efforts to force his subjects to convert, and he made use of traditional Fur ritual practices. The sultanate's rise to importance in the region was due to the deft way in which Sulayman gained monopoly over the wealth that passed through his territory on the trade route between Africa's savanna states and Egypt, a trade in which slaves and ivory were perhaps the most important components.

Sulayman established the Keira dynasty, from which all future sultans would come. He did not, however, establish a permanent capital in which to base his administration. This seems not to have caused insuperable difficulties, however, either for his reign or for the sultans who followed him.

The relatively laissez-faire relationship between Islam and traditional practice in Dar Fur came to an end with the sultanate of Ahmed Bakr (r. 1682–1722), who was not content to see the practice of Islam confined to his court circle. Bakr imported Islamic teachers from Egypt and elsewhere, and embarked upon a program of mosque-building. He also decreed that all his subjects must become Muslims. This decision had important political and economic consequences, for the adoption of Islamic practices included the creation of a form of landholding and labor practices that intimately connected the produce of the land and the land-holding classes to the interests of the state and the sultan himself.

In the latter half of the eighteenth century, the predictability of life centered on control of trade arriving from the West was altered in Dar Fur. This change occurred during the rule of Sultan Muhammad II Tayrab (r. 1756–1787), who sought to expand his kingdom. Tayrab coveted the region of Kordofan, which lay to the west but was, at the time, already claimed as a province of a neighboring kingdom, the Funj sultanate. In the final year of his reign, Tayrab succeeded in winning that territory, which he accomplished while maintaining control over the trade that passed through Dar Fur on its way to Egypt.

Dar Fur faced the first significant challenge to its autonomy in 1821, when Egypt decided to take the province of Kordofan and attempted to gain control over the slave traffic that long enriched the Fur sultanate. Egyptian-sponsored traders established heavily militarized slave camps south of Dar Fur, essentially hijacking the lucrative traffic and giving rise to a rival sultanate, Dar al-Kuti. To strengthen its claim upon the territory, Egypt backed an ambitious trader named Rahma al-Zubayr in his attempt to invade Dar Fur. Zubayr succeeded in defeating the sultan, making the formerly independent sultanate a tributary possession of Egypt. This situation remained unchanged (but not unchallenged) until the rule of Ali Dinar Zakariyya (r. 1898–1916), who restored the Fur sultanate to its former independent status.

The restoration of Dar Fur's independence was not long-lived, however, for Europeans were entering the territory in increasing numbers. Both Britain and France wanted to establish colonial interests in the region, as did Italy, which had already achieved a toe-hold in Libya and wished to expand its authority southward. When World War I broke out in 1914, the ruling Fur sultan, Ali Dinar Zakariyya, made the strategic error of aligning himself with the Islamic Ottoman Empire rather than with the Christian nations of the West, causing the British to declare war on the Fur sultanate. In 1916, after invading the territory of Dar Fur, British troops captured and executed Ali Dinar, bringing the Keira dynasty and the Fur sultanate to an end.

See also: AFRICAN KINGDOMS; SULTANATES.

GAEKWAR DYNASTY. *See* BARODA KINGDOM

GAHADVALAS DYNASTY

(ca. 1080–1192 c.e.)

Last Hindu rulers of the ancient kingdom of Kanauj in northern India.

The Gahadvalas dynasty was founded at Kanauj in the late eleventh century by Chandradeva (r. 1080–1100), a Hindu leader whose ancestry has been claimed by both the Rashtrakuta and Rathor clans. At that time, the Pratihara Empire, which included the Ganges Valley and territory as far east as north Bengal, was disintegrating due to Arab attacks from the west and internal rebellion.

Chandradeva brought political and military order to the troubled region. During his rule, he defeated the armies of the Chandella dynasty and checked the aggression of Vijayasena (r. ca. 1095–1159), a ruler of Bengal. In one ancient inscription, Chandradeva was described as the protector of the holy places of Kasi, Kusika, and Uttarakosala, in the respective cities of Varanasi, Kanauj, and Ayadhya, and of the city of Indrasthana (ancient Delhi.) Based on this source, it is surmised that Chandradeva commanded the whole of what now is the modern state of Uttar Pradesh.

Following Chandradeva's death in 1100, his son, Madanpala (r. 1100–1114), reigned for only a few years. Madanpala was succeeded by his son, Govindachandra (r. 1114–1154), who formed an alliance with King Jayasimha (r. 1128–1149) of Kashmir and Siddharaja Jayasimha (r. 1095–1143), ruler of the kingdom of Gujarat, to defeat a Muslim expedition led by Masud III (r. 1099–1115) of the kingdom of Ghazna. Govindachandra later annexed some of the region of Magadha, which had been under the control of the Pala dynasty of Bengal. Laksmidbara, a learned minister of Govindachandra, wrote the Gahadvalla book of law known as the *Kritya-Kalpataru*.

In 1154, Govindachandra's son, Vijaychandra (r. 1154–1070), succeeded his father on the throne. Early in his reign, Vijaychandra captured Lahore, the capital city of the Punjab kingdom. Vijaychandra ruled as far east as South Bihar, but in the west he lost Delhi around 1160 to Vigraharaja Visaladeva (r. 1153–1164), a king of the Chauhan dynasty.

By the time that Vijaychandra's son, Jayachandra (r. 1070–1093), took the throne, the region around Kanauj was under the control of the Chandella and Chauhan dynasties. In 1192, the kingdom of Ghur launched an invasion against Jayachandra. At the battle of Chandawer in the following year, Jayachandra, the last Hindu ruler of Kanauj, was defeated and killed. The Ghuris then plundered Kanauj and put the entire region under Muslim control.

See also: CHANDELLA DYNASTY; GHUR DYNASTY; INDIAN KINGDOMS; PALA DYNASTY; RASTRAKUTA DYNASTY.

GALAWDEWOS (ca. 1522–1559 C.E.)

Emperor of Ethiopia (r. 1540–1559) who was a descendant of the Salomonic dynasty that ruled Ethiopia from 1268 to the late twentieth century.

The son of Emperor Lebna Dengel (r. 1508–1540), Galawdewos assumed the throne of Ethiopia upon his father's death in 1540. When he became emperor, Galawdewos faced grave challenges to the autonomy of his realm, which was greatly reduced in size. During the previous several years, the territories of the empire had been largely overrun by forces of the Somali Muslim leader Ahmad ibn Ibrahim al-Ghazi, who had declared a *jihad*, or holy war, against Dengel's rule.

Upon taking the throne, Galawdewos had little chance of reclaiming the lost territory on his own. Just one year previously, however, hope had arrived in the form of an expeditionary force sent by Portugal to explore the region. Galawdewos enlisted the aid of these European newcomers, led by Cristovao da Gama, who saw advantages in gaining the gratitude of the Ethiopian emperor. After three years of fighting, during which da Gama was killed by al-Ghazi's forces, Galawdewos ultimately succeeded in routing the invaders. Al-Ghazi himself was killed in battle in 1543.

Upon reclaiming rule of his country, Galawdewos had no intention of relinquishing autonomy to any foreign claimants, including the Portuguese who had helped him regain power. Equally disturbing to Galawdewos were the missionizing activities that accompanied Portuguese trade and exploration. Portugal was allied with the Roman Catholic Church, whereas Ethiopia had, for centuries, been allied with the Coptic Church and its head, the Patriarch of Alexandria.

Having admitted the Portuguese into his kingdom as allies against al-Ghazi, Galawdewos could not easily get rid of them. He was thus forced to deal with the intensifying efforts of Jesuit missionaries to acquire converts for Rome. This ultimately led to his composition, in 1555, of an extraordinary work, *Confession of Faith*, in which he set forth his understanding of the theological and practical value of the Ethiopian Coptic Church. This remarkable document earned Galawdewos the respect of the Jesuits, who allowed him to preserve Coptic tradition within his realm.

Although Galawdewos had defeated al-Ghazi, his reign did not remain untroubled for long. Toward the end of his reign, Ethiopia once again was targeted by a *jihad*, this time launched by al-Ghazi's successor, Amir Nur. Forced to mount another war in defense of his realm, Galawdewos was killed in 1559 while leading his troops against a Muslim attack.

See also: MENELIK II; SUSENYOS; TEWODROS II; ZARA YA'IQOB.

GANDA KINGDOM

(1400s–1966 C.E.; 1993–Present)

Also called Buganda (the Bu- is a prefix in the Bantu language that denotes territory), one of the four traditional kingdoms, along with Nyoro, Toro, and Ankole, that were established in Uganda in central Africa.

The kingdom of Ganda shares with the Nyoro kingdom a creation myth that features Kintu, the supposed first man and founder. Also like the Nyoro, the rulers of Ganda are drawn from the Babito clan. Today, the Ganda constitute the largest ethnic group in the nation of Uganda, and they have held the majority of power within the region since the colonial era.

Buganda began as a subordinate territory under the control of the Bunyoro Kingdom (which was founded around 1200). It became a separate kingdom early in the fifteenth century, and its first king, or *kabaka,* appears to have been a member of the Bunyoro royal family. The name of this ruler was Kimera, who was a descendant of the Babito clan. Oral tradition holds that there were a total of thirty-four Ganda kings from the time of Kimera's rule until the mid-1960s, when the Ugandan national government ordered the abolition of all kingdoms within its borders.

The Ganda kingdom asserted its independence from its Nyoro rulers beginning around 1650. King Mawanda (r. 1674–1704) instituted a policy of expansion, and under his reign the Ganda kingdom achieved preeminent power and influence in the region. His successors built upon his policies, so that by the time British colonizers arrived in 1860, it was with the Buganda king, Mutesa I (r. 1856–1884), that the colonial officers had to negotiate. The British declared Buganda a protectorate in 1891, during the reign of Mutesa's son and successor, Mwanga (r. 1884–1897). In 1896, the British expanded the protectorate to include the lands of the Nyoro, Toro, and Ankole kingdoms as well.

King Mwanga took the Buganda throne at a time of great civil unrest, due largely to the competing efforts of European Protestant and Catholic missionaries. Mwanga sought to quell the unrest by discouraging his people from converting to either group, but this put him at odds with the British colonial office, which supported the Protestants. Mwanga was ultimately ousted from power, exiled to the Seychelles Islands, and replaced on the throne by his son, Daudi Chwa (r. 1897–1942).

Chwa was only four years old when he took the throne, and the British used his youth and inexperience to turn him into a puppet ruler. His son, Mutesa II (r. 1942–1966), proved far less cooperative. During his reign, the British exiled Mutesa for two periods in an effort to render him more willing to cooperate with colonial policies. However, Mutesa II came to power at a time when the popu-

lace throughout Africa had begun calling for an end to colonial rule, and the king became actively involved in political independence movements. Mutesa became the first president of the newly independent nation of Uganda in 1962, but he was was forced out of office in 1966 by his prime minister, Apolo Milton Obote. That same year, Obote dissolved all the kingdoms within Uganda. Mutesa went to live in exile in England, where he died in 1969.

Although Mutesa II was never allowed to return to the Ganda throne, the kingdoms of Uganda were eventually reinstated. In 1993, Mutesa's son, Mutebi II (r. 1993–present), returned to Uganda to assume the Ganda throne.

See also: AFRICAN KINGDOMS; ANKOLE KINGDOM; NYORO KINGDOM; TORO KINGDOM.

FURTHER READING

Shillington, Kevin. *History of Africa.* Rev. ed. New York: St. Martin's Press, 1995.

GAO TI. *See* LIU PANG

GAOZONG. *See* KAO TSUNG

GAUDA KINGDOM (early 600s C.E.)

Short-lived kingdom in the northeastern Bengal region of India, dating from the seventh century, that emerged in the wake of the disintegration of the Gupta Empire.

The Gauda kingdom originated in the early 600s with the overthrow of the Gupta Empire. As the Gupta Empire disintegrated, the various provinces of northern India that had been part of the empire became independent kingdoms. As the borders of these kingdoms shifted, and kings sought to solidify and expand their territories, the Gauda king, Sasanka (r. ca. 606–619), began to extend his political sphere of influence from the region around his capital, Karnasuvarna, into northern Bengal.

Sasanka expanded the Gauda kingdom at the expense of the Guptas. Little is known about this early Gauda king. Much of what is known is inferred from ancient inscriptions and coins from the period. Some evidence suggests that the Gaudas, and specifically Sasanka, descended from the Gupta royal family. Other sources seem to make Sasanka synonymous with another Gauda king, Jayanaga. Still other sources speculate that Jayanaga and his son may have been either predecessors or successors to Sasanka.

The most likely interpretation seems to be that Jayanaga was Sasanka's predecessor. If that is true, then it was during Jayanaga's reign (r. dates unknown) that the Gauda kingdom was pushed out of Bengal by competitor states, namely the Maukari, and relocated further east to the coast of the Bay of Bengal. Nonetheless, by the reign of Sasanka, Gauda was a seaside kingdom in decline. However, this decline was halted by Sasanka, who occupied a number of territories, including Pundavardhana to the north, regions as far west as the city of Benares, and land south to Kongoda, just south of Orissa.

This expansion early in the seventh century, combined with Sasanka's apparent invasion of Kamarupa, prompted King Bhaskaravarman of Kamarupa (r. dates unknown) to ally himself with King Harsha of Vardhana. Having established this alliance, Harsha invaded the Gauda kingdom around 619 (although some sources date it as early as 606).

When King Prabhakara of Thaneswar (r. dates unknown) died, his kingdom came under Harsha's control. This transfer of power to Harsha sparked a rebellion by the Malava, who were tributaries of the Thaneswar. The Malava were also allies of Gaudas, and this alliance was a factor in the Malava rebellion.

The alliance between Malava and the Gauda kingdom made it easier, because of political maneuvering, for Sasanka to personally defeat and kill Harsha's brother, Rajya. Rajya's death served to fuel the hatred that existed between the Gaudas and the Vardhana. This hatred was escalated further by the belief that Rajya was actually unarmed when he met with Sasanka and was murdered.

The killing of his brother provided Harsha with a new motive to invade the Gauda kingdom. This invasion prevented the Gaudas from taking control of the Thaneswar throne and expanding their territory. The loss of Rajya at Sasanka's hand also prompted Harsha to demand that all surrounding kings support Vardhana or run the risk of being invaded.

This led the Vardhana to develop further alliances against the Gaudas, such as gaining the assistance of the king of Kamarupa. Once Sasanka realized that Harsha's armies were advancing on Kanauj, where Sasanka had his men stationed and where Rajya was killed, the Gauda king began to retreat back into his original territories.

Harsha's campaigns against Gauda caused the kingdom to fall into decline, and it was eventually subjugated by the Vardhana. The final victory of Harsha over Gauda probably occurred after Sasanka died. Sasanka's death made Gauda much more vulnerable to its neighbors. After Harsha conquered Gauda, he gave control of its capital, Karnasuvarna, to his ally, the king of Kamarupa. This marked the official end of the Gauda kingdom, which had lasted less than twenty years.

See also: GUPTA EMPIRE; INDIAN KINGDOMS.

FURTHER READING

Basak, Radhagovinda. *The History of North-Eastern India Extending from the Foundation of the Gupta Empire to the Rise of the Pala Dynasty of Bengal (c. 320–760 A.D.).* London: K. Paul Trench, Trubner & Co., 1934.

Duff, Mabel. *The Chronology of Indian History: From the Earliest Times to the 16th Century.* Delhi: Cosmo Publications, 1972.

Smith, Vincent A. *The Oxford History of India.* Ed. Percival Spear. 4th ed. New York: Oxford University Press, 1981.

GENDER AND KINGSHIP

Both male and female monarchs have related in complex ways to gender. Monarchy itself, in most societies, has been strongly or exclusively the domain of males.

The manliness expected of male rulers has many different facets. The idea of the king as a father has been strongest in Christian Europe, where a political theory designated *patriarchalism* emerged in the early modern period. The theory, classically put forward in a work by Englishman Sir Robert Filmer called *Patriarcha*, suggests that the power of monarchs, male or female, is explicitly derived from the power of Adam as father of the human race.

MALE GENDER AND KINGSHIP

An alternative masculine view of kingship is that of the king as husband of the land. Yet another classically male role that kings have been expected to fill has been that of war leader. Many monarchical positions have originated as positions of military command, such as the Roman emperorship, the Mongol khanate, the Japanese shogunate, or the sultanate in Muslim regimes like that of the Mamluks of Egypt. Military monarchical positions have usually been restricted to males.

Positions of religious headship, such as the papacy, caliphate, and Dalai Lamaship, are also male-only. Although Henry VIII of England (r. 1509–1547) called himself Supreme Head of the Church of England, his daughter Elizabeth I (r. 1558–1603) restricted herself to the title of Supreme Governor (the title held by English monarchs ever since.)

FEMALE GENDER AND KINGSHIP

In many monarchical systems, female gender is an absolute disqualification for possession of the throne in one's own right. Despite its emphasis on the emperor's ritual and political rather than military functions, the Chinese empire barred female rulers after Empress Wu Zeitan (r. 690–705) of the T'ang dynasty. Subsequent Confucianists, whose ideology endorsed male dominance, blackened her memory, despite evidence that Empress Wu was a ruler of considerable ability. Before it experienced the full impact of Chinese culture, Japan had several early female rulers, but after 770 it had only two. Women were formally barred from the Japanese imperial succession in the 1800s (under European rather than Chinese influence).

The Islamic world has also usually rejected female rulership. The Muslim historian Siraj described the short reign of one of the rare exceptions: Sultana Raziyya of Delhi (r. 1236–1240), who succeeded her father Iltutmish (r. 1211–1236) in and until her violent death in 1240. In the words of Siraj: "Sultana Raziyya was a great monarch. She was wise, just and generous, a benefactor to her kingdom, a dispenser of justice, the protector of her subjects, and the leader of her armies. She was endowed with all the qualities befitting a king, but she was not born of the right sex, and so, in the estimation of men, all these virtues were worthless."

Christian Europe has had a patchwork of policies regarding gender and kingship. The fundamental distinction is between those countries following the Salic Law first put forth in medieval France and those countries not following it. The Salic Law, so called because of its origins in the ancient customs of the Salian Franks, barred not only women, but also royal descendants in the female line, from succeeding to the throne. It was upheld not only in France, but in many of the principalities of the Holy Roman Empire. The promulgation of the Salic law originated in the desire of French elites to prevent Edward III of

ROYAL RITUALS

AN ANNIVERSARY AS A TIME FOR CRITICISM

On March 10, 1888, England's prince of Wales (the future Edward VII) and his wife, Alexandra of Denmark, celebrated their silver wedding anniversary. London's leading newspaper, the *Times*, took the occasion to publish two editorials that focused on the behavior of the couple. In praising or temperately criticizing some of Edward's and Alexandra's behavior, the *Times* relied on nineteenth-century concepts of gender. Edward was criticized for his patronage of prize-fighters and American cowboys—masculine behavior that was considered excessive and unrefined. Alexandra was praised for acting in a classic wifely role of moderating her husband's aggressiveness. The *Times* credited her with weaning Edward, a keen sportsman, from the cruel practice of pigeon shooting. Such criticism of Edward's behavior suggests that the idea of masculine gender had undergone significant change from the time of his predecessors, who would have been praised for such manly pursuits and interests.

England (r. 1327–1377) from succeeding to the throne. But it also raised the prestige of the French monarchy by making it purely masculine, like the papacy or the emperorship of the Holy Roman Empire. Realms in Southern and Northern Europe generally have been more open to female rulers, although women succeeded to the throne only in default of male heirs—a young son would succeed in preference to his older daughter, but a daughter would succeed if there were no legitimate sons.

Even in societies that have accepted female rulers, it has often been necessary for female monarchs to present themselves as male or androgynous. The most famous example is Queen Hatshepsut (r. 1503–1483 B.C.E.) of ancient Egypt, whose representations depict her with a beard. Queen Elizabeth I of England referred to herself as having the heart and stomach of a king. Both Sultana Raziyya of Delhi and Queen Christina of Sweden (r. 1632–1654), along with many others, have worn male dress. Such use of male dress has been particularly common if a woman exercises military leadership or command. Women rulers with consorts have often had a difficult time balancing between their society's expectation of a wife's submissiveness and a ruler's authority. Many female monarchs, like Christina and Elizabeth I, have avoided this problem by not marrying.

Even where female rulers have been barred from thrones in their own right, however, many have managed to manipulate conventions of female gender roles to exercise considerable formal or informal power. One of the most common ways has been through maternal power. Women have commonly exercised power as regents for their minor children, a role that has sometimes persisted well into the children's majority. Blanche of Castile, the mother of Louis IX (r. 1226–1270) of France, was the effective ruler of the kingdom for many years during her son's reign.

Reigning female monarchs also have projected themselves as mother figures. The mother of the king of Swaziland bears the title *Indlovukazi* ("great she-elephant") and is considered the co-head of state with her son. Consorts have also exercised power as regents for absent husbands, fulfilling a traditional wifely role as steward of the husband's property in the husband's absence.

GENDER CONFUSION AND KINGSHIP

Although some societies have allowed female rule, eunuchs are universally barred from formal monar-

chical power. In the Byzantine Empire, a society in which the imperial throne was never definitively and permanently settled on a particular line or family, this disqualification was particularly useful because it ensured that successful eunuch administrators and generals could not try to take the throne themselves.

Although female rulers sometimes benefited from presenting themselves as male, cross-gendered or gender-inappropriate behavior could harm a male monarch's reputation, particularly if the monarch faced political opposition for other reasons. Roman emperors like Caligula (r. 37–41) and Nero (r. 54–68) were frequently portrayed as cross-dressing or taking a passive role in homosexual intercourse, and this contributed to their reputation as bad emperors. Henry III (r. 1574–1589) of France attracted similar criticism.

Part of the demystification of monarchy that occurred before and during the French Revolution resulted from the feeling that monarchs were not properly fulfilling their gender roles. Louis XVI (r. 1774–1792) was charged with being impotent, and his wife Marie Antoinette was accused of being a bad, quasi-incestuous mother, an adulterous wife, and a lesbian. Many nineteenth- and twentieth-century monarchs have responded to this damaging association between monarchy and gender-deviant behavior by projecting an image of ideal domesticity, an image that is often at variance with reality.

See also: BEHAVIOR, CONVENTIONS OF ROYAL; EUNUCHS, ROYAL; HOMOSEXUALITY AND KINGSHIP; LEGITIMACY; MILITARY ROLES, ROYAL; PRIMOGENITURE; REGENCIES; ROYAL FAMILIES.

FURTHER READING

Filmer, Sir Robert. *Patriarcha and Other Writings.* Ed. Johann P. Somerville. New York: Cambridge University Press, 1991.

Finer, S. E. *The History of Government.* New York: Oxford University Press, 1997.

GENEALOGY, ROYAL

Line of descent or ancestry of a ruler; lineage of a royal family.

Genealogies, originally passed down through oral tradition, have existed for centuries, particularly for noble families. With the advent of writing, family lineages began to be recorded. The Japanese began imperial archives sometime during the third century C.E., and the eighth-century work, *Kojiki,* the oldest surviving text written in Japan, claims to be a history of the royal line since mythological times. Today, the Japanese imperial monarchy proudly traces its ancestry in an unbroken line back to 660 B.C.E., making it the oldest dynasty in the world.

During the Middle Ages, when inheritance of feudal property and titles depended on family lines, genealogies flourished. Even when a new monarch wrested power from a current ruler on the battlefield or through treachery, once the new ruler was established, a blood relative was most likely to be the next on the throne. For example, when William the Conqueror (r. 1066–1087) conquered England, a long line of Norman kings followed the Saxon kings.

CLAIMING KINSHIP

Kings and queens have frequently insisted upon their descent from God or gods, emphasizing that it is their bloodlines that have determined their right to the throne. Royal blood contained the power of the gods, the divine right to rule. For instance, Egyptian pharaohs were considered gods and often wed their brothers or sisters to ensure the royal blood would remain pure.

Even if sovereigns did not claim descent from gods, they wanted to establish the royalty of their lineage. The warrior Conn Cetchathach is reputed to have been the forty-fifth Irish king in a line of descent from Milesius, the legendary Spanish king whose sons conquered Ireland and whose ancestry could be traced back to Adam. Christian monks in other European kingdoms drew similar genealogies for royal families.

The legend of King Arthur expanded after 1066, as the Norman kings endeavored to trace their lineage to the Celtic hero and gain acceptance of their leadership. Another English king, Henry VII (r. 1485–1509), whose right to power might have been weakened by questions of illegitimacy among his ancestors, married Elizabeth of York whose royal bloodline was unquestioned.

INHERITANCE RIGHTS

For much of history, the right to inherit a throne was determined by patrilineal descent (through the father's line). In fourteenth-century France, Salic Law required that inherited titles would go to males and excluded female inheritance. Other monarchies, such as that of England, give preference to the male descendents, but a female may inherit if there are no male heirs. Matrilineal descent (through the mother's line) has been the rule in only a few cultures, such as that of the Lovedu people of South Africa.

The death of a monarch who either had no children or whose children were too young to assume the throne has sometimes brought drastic changes to a nation. Elizabeth I of England (r. 1558–1603) was childless, so upon her death, the Crown went to her Scottish cousin, James I (r. 1603–1625), and the countries of England and Scotland were then united under one rule. At the death of Queen Anne of England (r. 1702–1714), the last of the Stuart line, the nearest relative was a German cousin, George I (r. 1714–1727). Mary, Queen of Scots (r. 1543–1587) inherited the throne when she was only a few days old, so regents ruled Scotland until she was an adult.

In an effort to keep bloodlines pure, royalty generally looked for marriage partners within other royal families. Most European royals shared at least some ancestors and often married—and sometimes murdered—relatives. For example, Margaret Tudor, the daughter of King Henry VII, married the Scottish king and gave birth to a daughter (Mary, Queen of Scots), but she was later beheaded by one of Henry's granddaughters, Elizabeth I of England. Queen Victoria I of England (r. 1837–1901) married her German cousin Prince Albert. Not only did their son, Edward VII (r. 1901–1910), rule England, but their daughter Victoria married the German emperor, and their granddaughters Alexandra, Marie, and Ena were married, respectively, to the tsar of Russia, the king of Romania, and the king of Spain.

Genealogical records, which began primarily as a way for sovereign rulers to establish their right to power and to record their own triumphs for posterity, now allow ordinary people to trace their ancestors and sometimes to establish a connection to kings.

See also: ACCESSION AND CROWNING OF KINGS; DESCENT, ROYAL; DYNASTY; INHERITANCE, ROYAL; PRIMOGENITURE; SUCCESSION, ROYAL.

FURTHER READING
Tuchman, Barbara. *Bible and Sword: England and Palestine from the Bronze Age to Balfour.* New York: Funk and Wagnalls, 1968.

GENGHIS KHAN (ca. 1165–1227 c.e.)

Mongol ruler (r. 1206–1227) who conquered Central Asia, China, and Iran in the early 1200s and created one of the world's great empires, which lasted for a century after his death.

EARLY LIFE AND RISE TO POWER

Named Temuchin at his birth, Genghis Khan (or Jinghiz Khan) was the son of Yisugei, a leader of the Kiyat-Borjigid branch of the Mongol tribe of Central Asia. In 1175, Yisugei was murdered by rival leaders, and Temuchin, his mother, and brothers were deserted by their tribe. Temuchin became a vassal to his father's friend Toghrul, the powerful leader of the Kerait tribe. Through his charisma, Temuchin attracted many followers and gradually rose in power.

Despite a growing group of followers, Temuchin's closest childhood friend, a shepherd named Jamuka, deserted him, possibly because of hostility between Jamuka and some of Temuchin's aristocratic followers. Temuchin had to fight against the alliance that Jamuka formed among the other tribes in the area. Temuchin also quarreled with Toghrul, who plotted to kill him by inviting him to a betrothal feast between his grandson and one of Temuchin's daughters. But Temuchin was warned of the plot and escaped. He later defeated both Toghrul and his old friend Jamuka.

By the early 1200s, Temuchin had gained a great deal of power among the Mongols and was poised to become their ruler. In the spring of 1206, he was enthroned as Mongol leader at the source of the Onon River in present-day Mongolia. He became known as Genghis Khan ("universal ruler" or "universal lord").

RULE AND PERSONAL LIFE

Genghis Khan was then the leader of all the tribes of Central Asia, including those of Turkic and Tungusic origin, who began to call themselves Mongols. Genghis Khan consolidated his power by destroying earlier tribal alliances to form a Mongol nation.

Though illiterate, Genghis Khan understood the importance of the written word. Since the Mongols had no system of writing, he adopted the alphabet of the Uighurs, a Turkic tribe, and saw to the development of a written law code, or *Yasa*, which strictly punished theft and adultery, crimes that had led to frequent feuds among the Mongol tribes.

Genghis Khan often ignored the claims of Mongol aristocrats and put ordinary men into important positions of power. He was kind and generous to loyal friends, and admired loyalty even in his enemies. But he could also be cruel and ruthless.

Genghis Khan's senior wife was named Börte, but he often took new wives from among conquered peoples. He practiced the religion of the Central Asian tribes, which relied on shamans to communicate with spirits, but he was tolerant of other religions, including Christianity, Buddhism, and Islam.

CONQUESTS

After consolidating his power over the Mongols, Genghis Khan set his sights on China. In 1209, he attacked Xixia, the weakest of the three Chinese kingdoms, and then turned to the territory ruled by the non-Chinese Jin (Jurchen) dynasty. Not accustomed to attacking cities and fortifications, the Mongols had a difficult time in China at first. Gradually, however, they took the major cities in the north, and in 1215 they conquered and sacked the city of Pei-Ching (Beijing), the Jin capital.

The Mongol ruler Genghis Khan, shown in this watercolor-and-ink portrait on silk, was the founder of the Yuan Dynasty of China. A great conqueror, he ruled from 1206 to 1227 over an empire that stretched across Central Asia.

In 1219, Genghis Khan led his troops against Sultan Muhammad II (r. 1200–1220) of Khwarizm, whose empire covered much of Central Asia and Afghanistan and the whole of Iran (Persia). The sultan's kingdom was already divided because of tensions between nomadic Turks and settled Iranians, and the sultan's own despotic rule had alienated religious leaders. Genghis Khan cleverly exploited these divisions and conquered the area in 1220. He won many of the sultan's troops as his followers, as he had done with the Jin troops in China.

Genghis Khan's last campaign was against the rebellious Chinese kingdom of Xixia in 1225; by this time he was already ill. There are a number of conflicting stories about his death; some say that he was hurt in a riding accident, while others say he fell victim to illness. He died on August 18, 1227.

LEGACY

The Mongols practiced ultimogeniture, or inheritance by the youngest son of the principal wife. According to this law, Genghis Khan's heir was Tolui, but he preferred his son Ögödei. After Genghis Khan's death, his empire was divided into four parts, one for each of his sons: Jochi (the oldest), Ögödei, Chagatai, and Tolui. Tolui and Ögödei continued the conquest of northern China and gained control of the region in 1234. In 1261, Genghis Khan's grandson, Kublai Khan (r. 1260–1294), moved the capital of his empire to Pei-Ching, and proclaimed the beginning of the Yuan (or Mongol) dynasty in 1271.

Under Genghis Khan's descendants, the Mongols sacked Baghdad; conquered parts of Russia, where they established the Golden Horde Khanate; and invaded Hungary and Poland. However, the empire did not hold together because the rival claimants to the khanate ended up dividing the territory into personal realms without centralized control. The empire also failed to remain united because Genghis Khan did not develop any way for future Mongol rulers to administer the realm.

See also: GOLDEN HORDE KHANATE; IL-KHAN DYNASTY; KHWARAZM-SHAH DYNASTY; KUBLAI KHAN; MONGOL EMPIRE.

FURTHER READING

Ratchnevsky, Paul. *Genghis Khan: His Life and Legacy.* Trans. and ed. Thomas Nivison Haining. Oxford: Basil Blackwell, 1992.

GEORGE I (1660–1727 C.E.)

King of Great Britain and Ireland (r. 1714–1727), and first ruler of the House of Hanover.

The succession of George I, a member of the German house of Hanover, to the English throne was a direct result of the struggle between Catholics and Protestants over what would be the official religion of England. Though ostensibly religious, the succession was chiefly political in both ideology and consequences.

As the Protestant Queen Anne (r. 1702–1714) neared the end of her reign with no surviving children, the English Parliament wanted to avoid the accession of the Catholic, James Edward Stuart, known as the Old Pretender. Parliament had passed the Act of Settlement of 1701, which decreed that the line of English succession would pass only to the Protestant descendants of James I. It was in this way that George Louis of Hanover, the elector of Hanover and great-grandson of James I, became King George I of England.

George I was unpopular with his English subjects. Not only did he have German manners and customs, but he never learned to speak English and resided in Hanover in Germany for much of his reign. Between these cultural issues, and his ceding of much of his power to his prime minister, Robert Walpole, he was thought to be indifferent to English affairs.

George I was also unpopular with the Scots and the English Catholics. Since the Stuarts had a more direct claim to the throne, when they were passed over because they were Catholic, rioting erupted in Scotland and in many towns in England. This culminated in the Jacobite uprising of 1715–1716, which Protestant forces defeated at a battle at Preston. The Jacobite efforts to return the Stuarts to the throne were afterward fairly quiescent until the reign of George's son and successor, George II (r. 1727–1760).

The Protestant and reformist Whig party in England supported George's kingship, and his key advisers were from that group. George depended heavily on these men throughout his reign. Queen Anne's government had been drawn primarily from the opposition Tory party, but the Tories, being suspected supporters of the Stuart ascendancy, were removed from office.

One of George's chief ministers, Robert Walpole,

was a wealthy Norfolk Whig, the leading member in the House of Commons, and a skilled administrator. In 1720, Walpole initiated a plan to take advantage of high interest rates, which had been caused by government military spending. He transformed the South Sea Company, a trading company formed in 1711, into a funds management company by selling company stock in exchange for bonds. Walpole promised that this would get rid of the national debt and create private wealth. The price of stock rose rapidly, but then crashed within the year. The result was that a few individuals became very wealthy, while the public debt was transferred to many unlucky individuals.

Walpole managed to avoid blame for the ensuing crisis, and his clever management gained him power and prestige. He became the first lord of the Treasury, or prime minister, a position from which he controlled George I and ruled the country. When George I died in 1727, he was succeeded by his son, George II. But Walpole's powerful position continued until 1742, well into George II's reign.

See also: ANNE; ENGLISH MONARCHIES; GEORGE II; HANOVER, HOUSE OF; JAMES I OF ENGLAND (JAMES VI OF SCOTLAND); STUART DYNASTY.

FURTHER READING
Black, Jeremy. *A New History of England.* Stroud, Gloucestershire: Sutton, 2000.

GEORGE II (1683–1760 C.E.)

King of Great Britain (r. 1727–1760), a member of the House of Hanover, who ruled during the time of the Jacobite rebellion and its decisive defeat at the battle of Culloden in Scotland in 1746. George II was a noted patron of the arts, especially of music, and retained his father's court musician, Georg Frederic Händel.

The eldest son of George I (r. 1714–1727), George II succeeded his father as king of England while also retaining his title as elector of Hanover, a state in Germany. Although George remained devoted to Hanover, he played a much more active role in ruling England than his father had done. George II also inherited his key adviser, Robert Walpole, from his father.

Walpole had been first lord of the Treasury and the most powerful person in the government of George I—in effect, England's first prime minister. His policies generally secured prosperity and stability, helping preserve the status quo at home, abroad, and within the Church of England. Walpole began to lose his power beginning around 1739, when he was blamed for military losses to Spain. Walpole's lasting legacy was the foundation of a constitutional monarchy in England.

The most significant military event in the reign of George II was the Jacobite Rebellion, an attempt by supporters of the exiled house of Stuart to reclaim the throne for that dynasty. At one point, the Jacobite army advanced as far as Derby in central England, but it was decisively defeated by English forces in 1746 at the battle of Culloden in the Scottish Highlands.

George's reign also saw war in Germany and military engagements with France over colonial expansion in North America, Africa, and India. He was the last English monarch to lead armies in person; he led troops in 1743 at the battle of Dettingen during the War of the Austrian Succession (1740–1748).

George married Caroline of Anspach in 1705, and the couple had three sons and five daughters. The eldest son, Frederick, prince of Wales, predeceased his father in 1751. The second son, George William, died in infancy. The third son, William Augustus, duke of Cumberland, was known as "Bloody Cumberland" for the slaying of both soldiers and civilians after his victory over the Jacobites at the battle of Culloden. When George II died in 1760, he was succeeded by his grandson George (the son of Frederick), who ruled as King George III (r. 1760–1820).

See also: ENGLISH MONARCHIES; GEORGE I; HANOVER, HOUSE OF.

GEORGE III (1738–1820 C.E.)

Long-ruling monarch of Great Britain and Ireland (r. 1760–1820), historically known for both his failure to maintain the British colonies in North America and the insanity that plagued him throughout his reign. George III oversaw a tumultuous but prosperous time in Britain's evolution, an era that began with the nation locked in a power struggle with France and that ended with Great Britain firmly in place as the dominant military power in Europe, if not the world.

A member of the royal House of Hanover, George was born in January 1738, the eldest son of Frederick, prince of Wales, and Princess Augusta of Saxe-Gotha. After George's father died in 1851, he was educated for his future role as king by his domineering mother. The first Hanoverian to speak English as his native tongue, George became king at the age of twenty-two, following the death of his grandfather, King George II (r. 1727–1760). A year later, in 1761, he married Charlotte of Mecklenburg-Strelitz, a marriage that produced fifteen children, including seven sons whose dissolute lives were a continual torment to their father.

The throne George inherited had been weakened considerably by earlier conflicts between the Crown and Parliament, and he ignited a blaze of controversy upon his accession with what many took to be an attempt to recapture royal authority. By staffing government offices with easily influenced and untalented lackeys, and by bribing many of his opponents, George exerted more control over British politics than almost any other monarch of the parliamentary era. The scandals of George's adult sons, who were notorious for their public debauchery, also tarnished George's reputation but did little to affect his political power.

George's influence was most keenly felt in the way Britain dealt with its upstart colonies in North America. The heavy taxes imposed on them by Great Britain led many American colonists to see George as a tyrannical ruler bent on exploitation, and fed the revolutionary fire sweeping the colonies during the 1760s and 1770s. George, who defended the colonial taxes, insisted on dragging out a losing war with the colonists (the American Revolution), which ended with the 1783 surrender to the newly formed United States.

From the 1780s onward, George suffered bouts of insanity, most likely caused by a blood disease known as porphyria. His illness worsened to the extent that in 1811, power was turned over to his profligate son George (later George IV, r. 1820–1830)), who became prince regent. The defeat of Napoleon at Waterloo in 1815 secured British supremacy in Europe for the prince regent. George III died at Windsor Castle in 1820. Despite his struggles with mental illness, he left a legacy of intelligent and informed rule that greatly influenced future British monarchs.

See also: COLONIALISM AND KINGSHIP; ENGLISH MONARCHIES; GEORGE II; HANOVER, HOUSE OF; SAXE-COBURG-GOTHA DYNASTY; TAXATION.

FURTHER READING

Hibbert, Christopher. *George III: A Personal History.* New York: Penguin, 1999.

GEORGE TUPOU I (d. 1893 C.E.)

Ruler (r. 1845–1893) of the Polynesian kingdom of Tonga who unified the various Tongan islands nation and gave the nation a constitution. His successor, George Tupou II (r. 1893–1918), signed a treaty with Great Britain in 1900, making the kingdom a British protectorate.

George Tupou I was descended from the sacred royal line of the Tu'I Tonga, who had ruled the island archipelago since the tenth century. First known as Taufa'ahau Tupou IV when he became king in 1845, he took the name George Tupou I in 1875 when, under his guidance, the kingdom adopted a new code of laws and written constitution and established an administration system.

After uniting the warring communities of Tonga, Tupou guided his kingdom in its transition to a modern country. He converted to Christianity at a time when the traditional Tongan religion was in decline, and he abolished the form of serfdom that existed in the islands. In addition to establishing a new legal code and constitution, Tupou also oversaw the founding of Tonga'a first educational institute. By 1888, he had ensured that Germany, Great Britain, and the United States had each recognized Tonga as a sovereign and independent state.

In 1893, after almost fifty years of rule, George Tupou I died. His great-grandson succeeded to the throne, taking the name of George Tupou II.

See also: SOUTH SEA ISLAND KINGDOMS; TONGA, KINGDOM OF.

GHANA KINGDOM, ANCIENT

(ca. 400–1300 C.E.)

First of the powerful kingdoms of West Africa to arise in response to the growth of the trans-Saharan trade.

The kingdom of Ghana was founded during West Africa's early Iron Age. At its greatest extent, it occupied territory in what is now the southern portion

The ancient kingdom of Ghana was one of the most powerful in West Africa, largely due to its trans-Saharan trade in gold. Ghana's valued exports included both gold nuggets and precious objects, such as this gold ring, fashioned by skilled metalworkers.

of Mauritania and southeastern Mali. The people of this region were predominantly Soninke, who were farmers and iron workers. Local communities, initially simple autonomous villages, grew as their economies prospered and eventually developed into larger multivillage chieftaincies.

Soninke ironworking provided more efficient tools for use in agriculture as well as weaponry that was superior to any available to the Soninke's non-ironworking neighbors. With these advantages, the Soninke were able to conquer greater amounts of territory and, ultimately, to assert their control over a wide region. By the fifth century, the Soninke had established an empire.

Trade was what drove the Soninke to conquer their neighbors. The Soninke were among the first of the people of West Africa to come into contact with

Saharan salt traders who came south looking for new outlets for their goods. On their own, the Soninke could only offer grain in return for salt. But they soon realized that, through conquest, they could control the flow of other trade goods as well. In particular, they knew that gold was highly prized by the trans-Saharan traders and that it was produced in abundance in the forests of Ghana. They conquered that region, establishing themselves along the upper Senegal River, which was the principal route by which gold was transported.

As the gold trade grew in volume over succeeding centuries, the prosperity and power of the kingdom of Ghana grew as well. The trans-Saharan trade expanded, bringing to Ghana goods and visitors from beyond the Red Sea. By the eleventh century, the kingdom of Ghana had reached its peak. Its capital was at the twin cities of Kumbi and Saleh. Kumbi was occupied exclusively by the houses and palace of the king, and the homes of his royal attendants; Saleh was strongly associated with commerce.

According to a description provided by an eleventh-century Arab visitor, al-Bakri, the king of Ghana, was succeeded on the throne by the son of his sister rather than by one of his own offspring. The king's role was primarily to resolve disputes as they arose among the people, to set taxes (payable in gold and slaves) on his subject communities, and to administer justice. The king wore unique clothing and ornaments of gold, and during his public appearances he was accompanied by a retinue of ministers. His audiences with the people were signaled by the sounding of a ritual drum.

The gold trade, which provided the kingdom of Ghana with its wealth and power, probably contributed to its decline as well. Ghana did not mine gold itself, but rather monopolized the entry of this precious metal into trade by controlling the territory through which it had to pass to get from its producers to the Saharan traders. This led to a fierce rivalry between Ghana and the northern traders, which often resulted in raids and violence.

For a time, Ghana appeared to have the upper hand, and around 1050 it successfully expanded its territory to include the important Berber trading town of Awdaghust. Soon, however, Ghana's power began to wane, as traders found ways to elude the king's agents and as new gold fields opened up outside of the king's area of control. With the decline in trade, Ghana began to weaken, and by the early twelfth century, the royal house was beset by rebellions among its subjects. Moreover, much of the territory belonging to the kingdom was lost to the powerful Sosso, who invaded Ghana from the south.

By the early thirteenth century, the kingdom of Ghana had ceased to exist. Those of its subjects who eluded capture or death at the hands of the Sosso drifted away to the south and the west, bringing with them Soninke traditions and their skills in farming and trade. With the fall of the kingdom of Ghana, the stage was set for the rise of new kingdoms in the region, particularly those known collectively as the Akan States.

See also: AFRICAN KINGDOMS; AKAN KINGDOMS; ASANTE KINGDOM; FON KINGDOM; MALI, ANCIENT KINGDOM OF; SONGHAI KINGDOM; SONINKE KINGDOM.

FURTHER READING

Shillington, Kevin. *History of Africa.* Rev. ed. New York: St. Martin's Press, 1995.

GHAZNAVID DYNASTY (977–1186 C.E.)

Turkish dynasty that controlled a large part of the area that is now Afghanistan from the late tenth to the late twelfth centuries, and whose rule marked the beginning of the Islamic era.

The Ghaznavid dynasty was founded in the tenth century by Sebuktigin, a former Turkish slave who married the daughter of the governor of Ghazna (modern Ghazni) when that state was ruled by the Iranian Samanid dynasty. Sebuktigin (r. 977–997) himself became governor of Ghazna in 977 and subsequently took control from the Samanids. Through conquest and diplomacy, he proceeded to extend his realm all the way to the Indian border, ruling his domain until 997.

By Sebuktigin's own request, one of his younger sons, Ismail (r. 997–998), succeeded him as ruler. But his eldest son, Mahmud, who was preferred by many nobles, overwhelmed Ismail in battle, imprisoned him for life, and assumed the throne in 998. Mahmud (r. 998–1030) carried on his father's expansionist strategy, and by 1005, the former Samanid Empire was split into two successor states on either side of the Oxus River. The one in the west was ruled by the Ghaznavids, and the one in the east by the Qarakhanids.

Ghaznavid control reached its peak under Mahmud, who ruled until 1030. He led seventeen military expeditions into India between 1001 and 1026, gaining extensive territories. The empire not only grew substantially in size, but it also became officially Islamic and promoted the Islamic faith wherever it expanded. Mahmud used the wealth he gained from his military conquests to make his capital, Ghazna, one of the most important cities in Central Asia. Mahmud supported scholars and artists, founded colleges, created magnificent gardens, and constructed great mosques, palaces, and other buildings.

Mahmud was succeeded by his son Masud I (r. 1030–1040), who was a much less successful ruler than his father. In 1040, the Seljuk Turks in Khurusan and Khwarezm challenged Ghaznavid dominance, and the Seljuks won all the Ghaznavid regions in Central Asia and Iran at the battle of Dandanqan that year. That left the Ghanavids in control of eastern Afghanistan and northern India, where they ruled until the Ghurids, an Afghan dynasty from Ghur, sacked Ghazna and took over the Ghaznavid state in 1186.

See also: KHWARAZM-SHAH DYNASTY; MAHMUD OF GHAZNA; SAMANID DYNASTY; SELJUQ DYNASTY.

GHUR DYNASTY (1151–1206 C.E.)

Dynasty from Afghanistan that briefly conquered northern India during the twelfth century.

The Ghur region, located in present-day Afghanistan, was originally a feudal territory of the sultan of Ghazna, an Afghan sultanate. As the Ghaznavid dynasty weakened in the twelfth century, the leaders of Ghur increasingly asserted their independence. In response, Mahmud of Ghazna executed two prominent Ghur princes. This action incensed the Ghur tribes, and, in 1151, the Ghurs, led by Ala' al-Din (Auauddin) Husayn (r. 1149–1161), completely razed Ghazna and secured their independence.

In 1173, Husayn's nephew, Ghiyath al-Din (Giyasuddin) Muhammad (r. 1163–1203), rebuilt Ghazni and established the city as a key part of the Ghur Empire. He then appointed his brother Shihab al-Din (Shihabuddin), known as Muhammad of Ghuri, as governor of Ghazni. Muhammad used his position to strengthen the Ghur dynasty, and he immediately planned to invade the kingdoms of northern India.

Muhammad's initial attempt to invade India ended in failure. In 1178, he launched a massive attack against the kingdom of Gujarat but was repulsed. Eight years later, however, he conquered the entire Punjab region in India and extended Ghuri dominance to the basin of the Indus River. The agricultural richness of the region attracted Muhammad, and he determined to further expand his holdings, both to control the area's natural resources and to augment Muslim influence over the Hindu population.

In 1191, Muhammad led a major expedition deeper into India. The ruler of the Chauhan clan in Rajastan, Prithvi Raj (d. 1192), who controlled Delhi and its surrounding regions, united the Indian kingdoms and assembled an army. During the ensuing battle near Tarain, the Indians successfully halted Muhammad's progress, but the loss failed to deter him. In 1192, Muhammad reengaged the Indian forces at Tarain and emerged victorious. After slaughtering the opposing Hindu princes or rajas, including Prithvi Raj, Muhammad controlled northern India as far as Delhi. In 1197, Muhammad again attacked Gujarat. Although he raided the Gujarati capital at Anhilwara, the province once again withstood his invasion.

In 1203, Ghiyath al-Din Muhammad died, and Muhammad of Ghur assumed the throne as Mu'izz al-Din Muhammad III (r. 1203–1206). As ruler of the Ghur Empire, he controlled an area that included present-day Afghanistan, Pakistan, and much of India. His reign, however, was brief. In 1206, Khokar rebels, from a tribe in the Punjab region, ambushed and assassinated the powerful Ghur ruler. Muhammad III left no direct heir to rule his vast empire, and he was succeeded by a series of weak rulers. Without a strong central force to control the many disparate lands of the empire, the Ghur dynasty and its empire quickly crumbled.

See also: GHAZNAVID DYNASTY; INDIAN KINGDOMS; MAHMUD OF GHAZNA.

FURTHER READING

Bhattacharya, Sachchidananda. *A Dictionary of Indian History.* New York: George Braziller, 1967.

Smith, Vincent A. *The Oxford History of India.* 4th ed. Ed. Percival Spear. Delhi: Oxford University Press, 1981.

GLYWYSING KINGDOM
(400s–1000s C.E.)

Minor kingdom of early medieval Wales, located in the southern portion of the region. Although legend attributes the founding of Glywysing to a king named Glywys in the late fifth century, there is little historical evidence to confirm this. Little is known for certain about the early history of Glywysing, although historians suggest that the more typical pattern of inheritance by direct succession gave way at some point to a segmented pattern of succession in which cousins within the extended royal family could claim the right to inherit, with the different branches of the family assuming power from generation to generation. As this practice tended to give rise to violence as a means of seizing the succession, it may have been a factor in why Glywysing had little impact on events beyond its own borders.

Hywel ap Rhys (r. ca. 840–885) is one of the few rulers of Glywysing to have made an impact on history beyond the local level. He was one of five Welsh princes who sought the support of Alfred the Great of Wessex (r. 871–899) in 878, establishing friendly relations with the powerful king of Wessex as a means of increasing his own power and prestige at home. This is often considered the beginning of English (and later Norman) claims to overlordship of portions of Wales.

Around 930, Glywysing and the neighboring kingdom of Gwent were briefly united, along with some smaller territories, in the kingdom of Morgannwg under Morgan Hen (r. ca. 930–974). After the 970s, Glywysing reappeared as a separate kingdom, as did Gwent, but the name Morgannwg was sometimes used for Glywysing and the minor territories adjoining it.

In the eleventh century, the Normans, after their invasion of England, seized the region of Glywysing or Morgannwg. It became the lordship of Glamorgan under Robert fitz Hammo during the reign of King William II of England (r. 1087–1100). Although the more remote and mountainous portions of the region remained under Welsh control for some time, the kingdom of Glywysing ceased to exist at that time.

See also: ALFRED THE GREAT; GWENT KINGDOM; WELSH KINGDOMS; WILLIAM II (WILLIAM RUFUS).

GOLCONDA KINGDOM

(1518–1687 C.E.)

Kingdom in southern India ruled by the Qutb Shahi dynasty, one of five Muslim sultanates that came to power after the breakup of the Bahmani kingdom.

The founder of the Qutb Shahi dynasty was the Persian Quli Qutbul-mulk (r. 1518–1543), the governor of the eastern Bahmani province. He declared his independence from the Bahmani kingdom in 1518 and then ruled as Quli Shah until 1543. During his reign, Quli expanded the Golconda kingdom as far as Machilipatam, a seaport on the Bay of Bengal.

Quli's third son, Jamsheed, assassinated him and became the next sultan of Golconda. Jamsheed (r. 1543–1550) ruled for seven years, but he faced continual criticism from the nobles and others for killing his father. His youngest brother, Ibrahim, succeeded Jamsheed upon his death in 1550.

Ibrahim Qutb Shah (r. 1550–1580) was the true builder of the Golconda kingdom, which he ruled for the next thirty years. Ibrahim structured the central and provincial administrations so that they could work closely together, and he established a competent intelligence organization to keep him up to date on all important matters. He also made the kingdom safe for travel and commerce and was responsible for many public works. Militarily, Ibrahim was able to expand the kingdom as far south as Madras and Gandikota after the battle of Rakkasi Tangadi in 1565.

The Golconda kingdom was peaceful and prosperous for the next forty years under the rule of Ibrahim's successors. His son, Muhammad Quli (r. 1580–1612), was a scholar and poet famous for his writing as well as for his building projects. Muhammad Quli's nephew and son-in-law, Muhammad (r. 1612–1626), succeeded him in 1612. Like his uncle, Muhammad encouraged education and architecture. But he died prematurely in 1626 and was succeeded by a lazy son, Abdullah.

Abdullah Qutb Shah (r. 1626–1672) allowed the Mughals to penetrate the Golconda kingdom and make him a vassal. His much more able successor, Abul Hassan Qutb Shah (r. 1672–1687) (also known as Tana Shah), made a valiant effort against the Mughals. In the end, however, Golconda was captured by the Mughal ruler Aurangzeb (r. 1658–1707) and annexed as part of the great Mughal Empire.

See also: AURANGZEB; BAHMANI DYNASTY; MUGHAL EMPIRE.

GOLDEN HORDE KHANATE

(ca. 1240–1502 C.E.)

Muslim state, located in Central Asia, founded by Mongol and Turkish warriors, that controlled parts of present-day Russia and contributed to the decline of the Kievan Rus.

In the early thirteenth century, the Mongol warrior Genghis Khan (r. 1206–1227) brought the nomadic tribes of Mongolia under his rule. By 1240, a body of Turks and Mongols led by Genghis's eldest son, Juji, overran a large portion of Eastern Europe and founded the Mongol Jujid dynasty. The portion of this Mongol Muslim state, or khanate, in present-day Russia came to be known as the Empire of the Golden Horde.

The first capital of the empire, which also was known as the Kipchak khanate, was at Sarai Batu on the lower reaches of the Volga River. The capital was later moved to Sarai Berke, on the Volga near present-day Volgograd. The ascendancy of the Golden Horde khanate ended the rise of the Kievan Rus, as the Rus principalities became mere vassals of the Mongol khans. Although the Rus states kept their own rulers and administrations, the Mongol khans collected tribute and taxes. They also had a say in the princely successions of the Rus principalities.

Local Mongol leaders in the Golden Horde khanate were given the title of khan but were subject to the overall authority of the Grand (Supreme) Khan. When Genghis Khan died in 1227, the mantle of Grand Khan, or first emperor of the Mongol dynasty, fell upon the shoulders of his descendants, including his grandson Kublai Khan (r. 1260–1294), who ruled from the Mongol capital of Beijing in China. In the early 1300s, the Mongols of the Golden Horde adopted Islam as their official religion.

Meanwhile, internal strife between Mongol and Turkish groups, and attempts by Russian princes to end payments of tribute and gain greater autonomy, contributed to a decline in Mongol power beginning in the fourteenth century. The ravages of the Black Death (bubonic plague) and poor administration also caused the Mongol Empire to begin disintegrating.

In 1395, the Golden Horde capital of Sarai Berke was attacked and plundered by another great Mongol leader, Tamerlane (1370–1405), who absorbed part of the territory controlled by the khanate into his own empire. Upon his death in 1405, the empire split up into a number of smaller khanates. In the 1440s, the Golden Horde was again racked by civil war, and the local khans continued to grow weaker over time. By the 1550s, most of the small khanates formed after the breakup of the Golden Horde Empire had been absorbed into the growing Russian state.

See also: GENGHIS KHAN; KIEV, PRINCEDOM OF; KUBLAI KHAN; MONGOL EMPIRE; RUS PRINCEDOMS.

GÖTALAND MONARCHY

(ca. 150–1000 C.E.)

Monarchy that developed in the region of Sweden called Götaland or Götland, and that existed as a separate kingdom from about 150 to the early 1000s.

Before the union of most of Sweden under a single ruler in the late 900s, Götaland was the name of a territory located in the southern part of Sweden. The region was often divided into Östergötland and Västergötland, or East and West Götaland.

Very little is known for certain about the Götaland monarchy. The tribe from which the region took its name was the Götar, who were first mentioned by the Greek geographer Ptolemy around 150. At one time, some historians believed the Götar were the ancestors of the Goths, but this theory is no longer commonly held. Some scholars now identify them with the Geats mentioned in the Old English epic *Beowulf.* Others associate them with the Jutes of northern Jutland, a region on the peninsula that contains Denmark.

In the 900s, the Götar were absorbed into a unified Sweden. Before that time, their monarchy was probably similar to that of other Germanic tribes of the era—an elective kingship chosen from within a royal family by an assembly of free men of the tribe. The most important tribe in southern Sweden at this time was the Svear, who gave Sweden its name.

By 1000, the Svear had become the dominant group in Sweden. Swedish king Olaf Skötkonung (r. 995–1022), who came from the region of Västergötland ruled both the Svear and Götar as one kingdom, using the title "King of the Swedes and the Götar." After his rule, although Götaland remained a distinct region within Sweden, it had become, in effect, a province within the Swedish kingdom that retained its own laws and assembly.

See also: SWEDISH MONARCHY.

GRANADA, KINGDOM OF

(ca. 1238–1492 C.E.)

Moorish kingdom in Iberia founded in the early thirteenth century and comprising an area that included the modern Spanish provinces of Granada, Málaga, and Almeria.

From the time of the Moorish conquest of the Iberian Peninsula in the eighth century, Christian kings from the northern part of Iberia had attempted to retake the conquered lands to the south. By the thirteenth century, these attempts at reconquest, collectively called the reconquista, had succeeded in regaining control of much of the peninsula. After the defeat of the Moors by Alfonso VIII of Castile (r. 1158–1214) at the battle of Las Navas de Tolosa in 1212, the kingdom of Granada became the last bastion of Moorish rule in Spain.

Founded in the eighth century as a Moorish fortress, Granada became in 1238 the capital of what was left of Moorish rule in Iberia. Under the rulers of the Nasrid dynasty, founded by Abu ʿAbd Allah ibn Yusuf ibn Nasr al-Ahmar (Muhammad I, r. 1232–1273), Granada became an important cultural center, nearly rivaling the splendor of Córdoba, capital of the caliphate of Córdoba up to the early eleventh century.

Hoping to secure the safety of Granada, Muhammad I began paying tribute to Ferdinand III of Castile (r. 1217–1252) in 1246. The Nasrid kings remained vassals of Castile until 1492, when the kingdom was conquered by the Spanish forces of Castile and Aragon. Despite the lord–vassal relationship, Castile declared war on Granada many times over the 250 years of its existence, taking various cities but never conquering the Moorish capital itself.

In order to fight these wars, the kings of Granada asked for support and military aid from Morocco. Concerned that this aid might lead to a takeover by the Moroccans who came to fight, the Nasrid kings tried to maintain a delicate balance, never allowing large Moroccan forces to cross the Strait of Gibraltar. Nevertheless, the influx of Moroccan soldiers gradually led to what scholars have called the "arabization" of Granada. The kingdom also developed an absolutist form of government that depended on the military for its continued existence.

During the reign of Muhammad V (r. 1354–1391) of Granada, Castile temporarily lost interest in reconquest. The ensuing period of peace allowed Granada to reach its cultural and economic peak. The silk trade flourished, as did learning and the arts. The Alhambra ("red fortress") in the city of Granada, built as a royal palace and expanded over the years, is today one of the most beautiful and famous examples of Moorish architecture in the world. During this period the Moors of Granada also created the institution of *juez de la frontera* (judge of the frontier). These judges were Muslim officials charged with resolving disputes brought by Christians against Muslims. This institution did much to reduce border conflicts between the Moorish kingdom of Granada and the Christian kingdoms of the Iberian Peninsula.

In 1469, the marriage of Isabella of Castile and Ferdinand of Aragón united two major kingdoms of Spain. When Granada's ruler, Abu al Hasan ʿAli (r. 1464–1482), refused to pay Isabella tribute, she became determined to drive all the Muslims from Spain. By the time Isabella declared war against Granada in 1481, internal divisions had made Granada especially vulnerable. The last king of Granada, Muhammad XII (also known as Boabdil, r. 1482–1492), seized the throne from his father in 1482, an action that plunged the Moorish kingdom into a civil war just as the Castilians began their attack.

Muhammad XII surrendered Granada to the Spanish monarchs in January 1492, ending Moorish rule in Spain. As he rode from the city in tears, it is said that his mother reproached him, saying, "Do not weep like a woman for what you could not defend like a man."

See also: ARAGÓN, KINGDOM OF; CASTILE, KINGDOM OF; FERDINAND II AND ISABELLA I; MUHAMMAD XI; NASRID DYNASTY.

FURTHER READING

Collins, Roger. *Early Medieval Spain: Unity in Diversity, 400–1000.* 2nd ed. New York: St. Martin's, 1995.
Fletcher, Richard. *Moorish Spain.* Berkeley: University of California Press, 1993.

GREEK KINGDOMS, ANCIENT

(ca. 3000–500 B.C.E.)

Monarchies in the Aegean and eastern Mediterranean region that predated the democracies that arose in Greek city-states in the fifth century B.C.E.

When speaking of ancient Greek politics, democracy, especially Athenian democracy, is often recognized as the most important form of government. Nevertheless, not all Greek city-states practiced democracy, and, historically, democracy did not develop until after the so-called Dark Ages (ca. 1100–800 B.C.E.). In fact, prior to the Greek classical period (ca. 400s B.C.E.), monarchy was the dominant form of Greek government. Classical Greek philosophers thought much about political forms, and many, including Plato, noted the strengths of monarchical rule.

MYTHICAL KINGS OF KNOSSOS AND MYCENAE

The ancient Aegean civilizations of the Minoans and Mycenaeans were ruled by monarchs. The Minoans, whose civilization was centered on the island of Crete, governed their territories from palace-cities. The best known and largest of these was Knossos. Knowledge of Minoan civilization comes as much from legend as from historical fact. The civilization derived its name from the legendary King Minos, who ruled over a powerful kingdom that demanded tribute from its subject peoples. According to legend, every nine years, Athens paid tribute of seven young men and seven virgin women who were sent to Knossos to be sacrificed to a mythical beast called the Minotaur. The story of Theseus, son of the king of Athens who was able to kill the Minotaur, is also part of this legend.

The history of Minoan civilization rests primarily on archaeological evidence and the surviving art and architecture of the age. No decipherable writings of the period exist. Historians believe that Minoan kings also served as religious leaders and that their palaces were centers of religious worship.

Around 2000 B.C.E., the Mycenaeans, a group of Indo-European peoples also known as the Achaeans, invaded the Greek Peninsula, where they conquered and intermarried with the indigenous population. Around 1550 B.C.E., the Mycenaeans conquered the Minoans. Over the next four centuries, the Mycenaeans ruled over the Aegean Sea, waging war throughout the Mediterranean. Archaeological evidence and the epics, *Iliad* and *Odyssey,* by the Greek poet Homer provide much of what is known of Mycenaean civilization.

There were a large number of Mycenaean kingdoms. Among those mentioned by Homer are Ithaca, Argos, Sparta, Pylos, Arkadia, Olenos, Aitolia, Krete, Delos, and Messene. Scholars have located some of these kingdoms, but others remain a mystery. Homer's epics recount the story of the Trojan War and the adventures of Odysseus, the king of Ithaca.

The Mycenaean kings were warriors who ruled areas generally no larger than city-states and who usually relied on a ruling council of aristocrats to advise them. Ancient Greece developed a strong tradition of monarchical rule during this period, which was grounded to their epic literature and dignified by their philosophy.

PHILOSOPHICAL FOUNDATIONS OF GREEK POLITICS

The great political philosophers in the Greek tradition treated monarchy as a legitimate form of government; some even endorsed it. Plato, for example, identified the ideal form of government as monarchy, with philosopher-kings as rulers. Aristotle also discussed monarchy, viewing it as the most effective form of government because one ruler could act quickly and decisively, affecting rapid change and reform when needed. Monarchy also posed the greatest danger, however. The rule of one individual could quickly devolve into despotism if the ruler did not respect the needs of his kingdom and its people.

The ancient Greek city-state of Sparta enjoyed a reputation for military prowess, which was epitomized by its heavily armed foot soldiers or hoplites. Sparta's monarchical form of government put it in direct opposition to its democratic rival, Athens.

ROYAL RITUALS

THESEUS AND THE MINOAN BULL DANCE

The legendary King Minos imposed a penalty on the city of Athens as punishment for the murder of his son, Androgeus. Every nine years, fourteen Athenian youths were to be sent to Knossos to be sacrificed to the Minotaur in the famous labyrinth. Theseus, the son of Aegeus, king of Athens, volunteered to go to Knossos as one of the sacrificial victims. He planned to slay the Minotaur and end the suffering of his people. With the help of Ariadne, the daughter of Minos, Theseus succeeded. However, in a tragic twist of fate typical of Greek mythology, when Theseus sailed back to Athens, he forgot to change the ship's black sails to white, the prearranged signal indicating his success. Thinking that his son was dead, Aegeus threw himself out of a window and fell to his death.

On the whole, the philosophical debate over monarchy concerned two opposing notions of political rule: *monarchia* and *isonomia*. *Monarchia* emphasized the argument put forth by Aristotle—that rule by one individual was an effective and legitimate form of government. This was the more ancient philosophy, supported by the history and tradition seen in the works of Homer.

The latter term, *isonomia,* refers to a notion of equality within Greek society. Between 750 and 500 B.C.E., the ancient Greeks created a new form of political rule in response to the violence and war common to their society. They recognized that inequality often resulted in conflict, especially when a minority ruled over the majority. To combat this, the Greeks tried to ensure that legitimate rule would come from the "middle" of society or from between the political extremes. They accomplished this through democracy, in which a balance or equality of voices was ensured through the participation of all citizens.

THE GREAT CLASSICAL KINGDOM: SPARTA

Though not a total monarchy, Sparta represents the most advanced form of monarchical rule in classical Greece. Citizenship in ancient Greece was exclusive. In the case of Sparta, this meant that only those people of Spartan descent capable of bearing arms were considered citizens. Traditional Spartan government consisted of a dual monarchy (two kings at the same time), a council of aristocrats, and an assembly of citizens.

The legendary King Lycurgus (r. ca. 600s B.C.E.), who engineered one of the more remarkable social and political transformations in history, put the mature form of Spartan government in place. He reformed Spartan society by expecting all citizens to dedicate themselves to the interests of the state. This meant that government oversaw almost all aspects of Spartan life.

This type of monarchical control put Sparta in direct opposition to the great democracy of ancient Greece—Athens. The conflict and cooperation between the two great city-states of Athens and Sparta culminated with the story of ancient Greece's greatest triumph in the Persian Wars (500–449 B.C.E.) and their ultimate ruin in the Peloponnesian War (431–404 B.C.E.).

See also: ATHENS, KINGDOM OF; MINOAN KINGDOMS; MYCENAEAN MONARCHIES; SPARTA, KINGDOM OF; TROJAN KINGDOM.

FURTHER READING
Aristotle. *The Politics.* Mineola, NY: Dover Publishing, 2000.
Homer. *The Iliad.* Trans. Robert Fitzgerald. New York: Farrar, Straus & Giroux, 2004.
———. *The Odyssey.* Trans. Robert Fitzgerald. New York: Farrar, Straus & Giroux, 1998.

Plato. *The Republic.* Trans. Benjamin Jowett. Mineola, NY: Dover, 2000.

Willetts, R.F. *The Civilization of Ancient Crete.* Berkeley: University of California Press, 1978.

GREEK MONARCHY

(ca. 3000 B.C.E.–1973 C.E.)

Rulers of ancient and modern Greece, which includes a mainland territory on the southern part of the Balkan Peninsula and many large and small islands in the Aegean and Mediterranean seas.

Monarchs ruled the earliest Greek communities. According to tradition, the legendary King Minos of the island of Crete, son of Europa and the god Zeus, colonized the Greek Islands and rid them of pirates sometime between about 3000 and 1400 B.C.E. While Greek drama portrays Minos feeding children to a monster known as the Minotaur, scholars suggest that Minos was a term that described a dynasty of powerful, priestly, and just rulers of the Minoan civilization.

THE MINOANS AND MYCENAEANS

When the Minoan civilization spread to the Greek mainland, it gave rise to the Mycenaean civilization (ca. 1400–1200 B.C.E.) Powerful independent Mycenaean communities formed around palaces, where the head of the leading family was known as the *basileis* (interpreted as "chief," "lord," or "king"). The ancient Greek poet Homer described the *basileis* as priest, judge, and military leader. The Mycenaean kings were wealthy, powerful individuals known for their courage, piety, and wisdom, but major decisions required the approval of a council of the king's aristocratic equals, called *basileis,* or rulers.

THE DARK AGE

The Mycenaean civilization was destroyed around 1200 B.C.E. by Greek-speaking invaders from the north called Dorians. The Dorians established tribal settlements in the territories they conquered. These settlements eventually grew into small independent city-states dominated by a military aristocracy.

It was in the Dorian community on the Greek island of Cos, off the southwestern coast of Turkey, that the term *monarchos* first came into use to describe a single magistrate who ruled the community.

The monarch was also known as a *tyrannos* ("tyrant"), which derived from the Anatolian languages of western Asia Minor and meant "chief" or "master." The tyrant was not a violent despot, as the term means today, but rather a leader who considered himself a ruler above and not equal to the *basileis* or aristocracy.

ARCHAIC PERIOD

As early as the end of the eighth century B.C.E., communities on the Greek mainland sought to replace the monarchy with an oligarchy, or rule by a few members of the aristocracy. By 500 B.C.E., most Greek city-states were governed by oligarchies or democracies. Kings continued to rule but as magistrates or priests rather than monarchs.

According to the ancient Greek philosopher Aristotle, monarchs could be bad or good; *tyrannis* ruled for their own benefit or good; and *basileia* ruled according to the law and for the benefit of the subjects. The ideal king of the fourth century B.C.E. was a generous and pious military leader. Plato developed the idea of a philosopher-king who possessed absolute knowledge and goodness.

THE HELLENISTIC AGE

Monarchy took on new meaning for the Greeks after the Macedonian leader, Alexander III, the Great (r. 336–323 B.C.E.) conquered Babylon in 330 B.C.E. and became "king of Asia." Alexander ordered the Greek city-states to grant him divine honors because of his military achievements and his unlimited power.

After Alexander, royalty became dependent on the ability to lead an army to military conquest. This called for wealth and companions, called *philoi,* to form the royal establishment. The additional virtues of a Hellenistic king were generosity, philanthropy, justice, security, and peace.

UNDER FOREIGN RULE

There were no Greek monarchs from the fall of Actium in 31 B.C.E. until the Greek War of Independence (1821–1828). Throughout the centuries between those dates, Greece was effectively part of the Roman, Byzantine, and Ottoman empires. Emperors usually came to power following military victory and considered themselves chosen by God to rule the earth. They attempted to exercise unlimited power over all aspects of their society but had to give some consideration to the opinions of their court and the people who expressed their acclamation or dissent in the Hippodrome, or stadium, at Constantinople.

THE MODERN PERIOD

At the London Conference of 1830, Russia, France, and England recognized Greek independence and, in an effort to avoid power struggles among Greeks, they named Otto of Bavaria to be king of the Hellenes (Greeks). Otto I (r. 1832–1862) considered himself chosen by God and ruled with absolute authority until he was forced to accept the Greek constitution of 1844. In 1862 the Greek people revolted, sovereignty of the people was introduced, and Otto abdicated the throne.

Russia, France, and England then placed George of Denmark on the Hellenic throne. A popular and approachable monarch, George I (r. 1863–1913) often walked through the streets of Athens talking with people, and he introduced a democratic constitution. George's international stature grew as he coped with a wide range of military crises, including war with Turkey and challenges from the antiroyalist officers of the Military League. A mentally disturbed Greek assassinated King George in 1913.

King George's son and successor, Constantine I (r. 1913–1917), came to the throne only months before the outbreak of World War I. Constantine had spent some of his formative years in Germany and, because of this background, the British forced him to abdicate in 1917. The king's eldest son, Crown Prince George, had served with the German army, so he stepped aside in favor of his younger brother, Alexander, who declared war on Germany shortly after taking the throne.

King Alexander (r. 1917–1920) suffered an improbable accident in 1920. While walking in the private gardens near the palace, he was bitten by a monkey; he died of infection from the bite a few weeks after the incident. The Greek people then held a plebiscite and recalled King Constantine I (r. 1920–1922), who returned and continued the war with Turkey. During the last days of World War I, the army again asked King Constantine, his health failing, to abdicate. He assented and died just four months later.

The throne passed to Constantine's son, George II (r. 1922–1923, 1935–1947), whose grandson, Prince Phillip Mountbatten, would marry Queen Elizabeth II of England (r. 1952–present). However, hostility to George forced him to give up the Crown in 1923, whereupon the Greeks established a republic.

Restored to the throne in 1935, George appointed as prime minister General Ioannis Metaxas, who established a fascist dictatorship in Greece in 1936. When Greece fell to Nazi Germany in 1941, civil war erupted, lasting until 1947, when the royalists claimed victory and George II returned to the throne.

In 1947, George II died and was succeeded by his brother Paul (r. 1947–1964). During the post–World War II period, Greece experienced rapid social and economic development, but Paul's rule was right wing and authoritarian. King Paul continued to reign until 1964 when his son Constantine II (r. 1964–1973) came to the throne.

A military junta seized power in a coup in 1967 and established a dictatorship in Greece under Georgios Papadopoulos. As a result, King Constantine II went into exile. When a countercoup led by the king ended unsuccessfully in 1973, Constantine II was deposed by Papadopoulos and Greece was declared to be a republic. The country has been ruled as a parliamentary republic up to the present day.

See also: ALEXANDER III, THE GREAT; ATHENS, KINGDOM OF; MINOAN KINGDOMS; SPARTA, KINGDOM OF; TYRANNY, ROYAL.

FURTHER READING
Freemann, Charles. *The Greek Achievement.* New York: Viking, 1999.

Laistner, M.L.W. *A History of the Greek World from 479–323 B.C.* 3rd ed. New York: Barnes & Noble, 1962.

Sealey, Raphael. *A History of the Greek City States ca. 700–388 B.C.* Los Angeles: University of California Press, 1977.

GRIMALDI DYNASTY

(1297 C.E.–Present)

Rulers of Monaco, a tiny principality situated on a rocky promontory overlooking the Mediterranean coast between France and Italy. The Grimaldis continue to rule the oldest principality in Europe.

THE EARLY YEARS

In the thirteenth century, the seafaring Grimaldi family served as consuls in the Italian city of Genoa. During the political struggles between the papacy and Holy Roman Empire that wracked Italy in the 1200s, the Grimaldis took the Guelph, or pro-papacy, side.

After the victory of the Ghibelline, or pro-imperial, forces in 1295, the Grimaldis were expelled from Genoa and took refuge in France. In 1297, Francesco Grimaldi gained entrance to the Ghibelline stronghold of Monaco by disguising himself as a Franciscan friar. He and his comrades killed the unsuspecting guards and captured the fortress.

The Grimaldi family held Monaco intermittently for the next hundred years; they gained full control in 1419 and were recognized as *seigneurs* (lords) of the principality. In 1346, they acquired the lordship of the nearby towns of Menton and Roquebrune.

THE STRUGGLE FOR INDEPENDENCE

The Grimaldis struggled to maintain their independence in the midst of their powerful neighbors: France, Spain, the Republic of Genoa, and the French duchy of Savoy. Jean I (r. 1419–1454) of Monaco fought for this independence by securing the continued existence of his dynasty: he stipulated in his will that Grimaldi daughters could inherit if their husbands took the family name and coat of arms. Jean's strong-willed daughter Claudine (r. 1457–1458) forbade her descendants to cede any part of Monaco or do homage to any other power, on pain of losing their inheritance and being disqualified to rule.

From the beginning, the Grimaldis enjoyed an arrangement in which the French kings protected Monaco while allowing it sovereignty. In 1524, Augustin (r. 1523–1532) reversed this alliance by signing a treaty with Spain. In 1605, during the minority of Honoré II (r. 1604–1662), Spanish troops occupied Monaco. While keeping firm control of the territory, the Spanish granted the rulers of Monaco the title of prince in 1612. In 1641, in return for a promise of protection from Louis XIII of France (r. 1610–1643), Honoré II expelled the Spanish. Louis XIII then gave Honoré the duchy of Valentinois, the title to which passed to the eldest Grimaldi son.

With the death of Antoine I (r. 1701–1731), the male line of the Grimaldis died out. Antoine's daughter, Louise-Hippolyte (r. 1731–1733), married Jacques de Matignon (r. 1731–1733), count of Thorigny, founding the branch of the Grimaldi-Matignons. During the eighteenth century, the Grimaldi princes spent much of their time away from the principality at the French court. Monaco was annexed by France in 1793 during the French Revolution but was restored to the Grimaldis in 1814.

By the Treaty of Paris in 1815, the kingdom of Piedmont in northwestern Italy took over from France the protectorate of Monaco and established troops there. The towns of Roquebrune and Menton rebelled against Monaco in the revolution of 1848 and were claimed by Piedmont. The dispute over control of these towns continued until 1860, when Prince Charles III of Monaco (r. 1856–1889) ceded the towns to France and the Piedmontese troops withdrew. With this cession, the princes of Monaco lost a third of their territory. Some family members protested this violation of Claudine's will, but Charles III maintained that it had been necessary for Monaco to maintain its independence. During the 1860s, Charles III, looking for revenue to compensate for the loss of Menton and Roquebrune, built a casino in Monte Carlo, making Monaco a popular resort for the wealthy.

Since the late thirteenth century, the Grimaldi dynasty has ruled the principality of Monaco on the coast of the Mediterranean Sea. In 1956, this tiny nation became known throughout the world when its ruler, Prince Rainier III, married the American movie star Grace Kelly.

MODERN TIMES

The Grimaldis ruled Monaco autocratically until 1911, when Prince Albert I (r. 1889–1922) granted the principality a constitution with an elected council and universal suffrage. Albert was also a pioneer in the sciences of oceanography and paleography. His son and successor, Louis II (r. 1922–1949) helped Monaco survive the Depression by establishing the Grand Prix car race of Monte Carlo and building a sports stadium.

In 1920, a new branch of the family, the Grimaldi-Polignacs, was formed when Charlotte, the only child of Louis II, married Count Pierre de Polignac. Their son, Rainier III (r. 1949–) inherited the throne in 1949. Rainier worked to restore the casinos and hotels and once again made Monaco a prime tourist destination. He granted the country a new constitution in 1962, though he maintains strong authority and rules with a small group of ministers.

Prince Rainier's marriage to American movie star Grace Kelly in 1956 brought more glamour to the Grimaldi dynasty. They had three children: the heir, Prince Albert, and daughters Caroline and Stephanie. In recent years, the Grimaldi family has faced several tragedies and scandals, including the death of Princess Grace in an automobile accident in 1982, the unhappy marriages and divorces of Princess Caroline, and the scandalous personal life of Princess Stephanie. In 1997, the Grimaldi dynasty celebrated its seven hundredth anniversary.

See also: PIEDMONT KINGDOM.

FURTHER READING

Decaux, Alain. *Monaco and Its Princes: Seven Centuries of History.* Paris: Perrin, 1997.

GROOMS OF THE STOOL

An official of the English Privy Chamber who had responsibility for dealing with the monarch's excrement. The groom attended the monarch while he performed his bodily eliminations and, on the monarch's death, the groom received the chamber pots and commodes used by the sovereign. The groom of the stool also assisted the monarch in other aspects of daily life, such as dressing and eating.

The position of groom of the stool originated in the fifteenth century, with the introduction of the close-stool, a stool holding a chamber pot. The office of Yeoman of the Stool emerged in the reign of Henry VI (r. 1422–1471). The Groom of the Stool appears in the records around 1495, with the founding of the Privy Chamber by Henry VII (r. 1485–1509). The groom was head of the Privy Chamber, a group attending the monarch in his private rooms.

Although Henry VII's original Privy Chamber and Groom were low in social status, this changed following the accession of his son Henry VIII (r. 1509–1547). Henry VIII made the Privy Chamber a central component of his government. The groom, whose intimacy with the king made him well fitted to discreetly carry out special tasks, even controlled a separate treasury called the Privy Purse. Not all grooms had successful careers, of course. Henry Norris was one of the men executed for adultery with Queen Anne Boleyn. Sir Anthony Denny, on the other hand, was one of the most powerful men in England in the last years of Henry VIII's reign, amassing a large fortune and controlling access to the king's deathbed. The position of Groom of the Stool went unfilled for the remainder of the Tudor period, when the throne was occupied by the young Edward VI (r. 1547–1553) and two women, Mary I (r. 1553–1558) and Elizabeth I (r. 1558–1603).

James I (r. 1603–1625) of England revived the office of Groom of the Stool shortly after his accession to the throne in 1603. At that time, the Bedchamber, a group of courtiers attending on the king's most private rooms, was split off from the Privy Chamber, which had assumed more governmental functions. The Groom of the Stool was now head of the Bedchamber, and the position was sometimes held by nobles. The only case of a Groom of the Stool becoming a rebel occurred during the reign of Charles I (r. 1625–1649) in 1642, at the beginning of the English Civil War. Henry Rich, the first earl of Holland, was deprived of the office of Groom for joining the Parliamentarian side of the war.

The Groom of the Stool diminished in importance following the English Civil War, when the politics of the royal court became less central. One important holder of the office was Sarah Churchill, who served as Groom of the Stool under her friend Queen Anne (r. 1702–1714), although the two had a bitter quarrel shortly after the appointment. By this time, the office was often referred to as Groom of the Stole, and for that reason, the position was sometimes thought to be connected with the wardrobe. The office of Groom of the Stool was finally abolished in 1837 with the accession to the throne of Queen Victoria (r. 1837–1901).

See also: COURTS AND COURT OFFICIALS, ROYAL; SERVANTS AND AIDES, ROYAL.

GUDEA (d. 2124 B.C.E.)

Enlightened Sumerian monarch (r. ca. 2144–2124 B.C.E.) who ruled the ancient Mesopotamian city-state of Lagash and instituted a period of peace and social equality.

After the fall of the Akkadian Empire to the incursions of the barbaric Gutians around 2230 B.C.E., Mesopotamia fell into general turmoil. During this period, a Sumerian warrior named Gudea assumed the title of *ensi* (governor) and consolidated the city of Lagash and its surrounding lands into a secure community that flourished under his liberal rule.

The surviving records of Gudea's reign, which include many of the most important examples of classical Sumerian literature, do not detail his rise to power. The records do, however, reflect eloquently on a career devoted to the patronage of literature, religion, and public works. Found primarily on two large clay cylinders, the longest and most complex surviving Sumerian works, the records are unique among Sumerian writing in their organization and content.

These records detail the building of a temple at Eninnu as though it was begun and completed by Gudea. They also mention that Gudea established trade relations with the whole known world and had Elamite craftsmen to help build his temples. One of the few written passages dealing with Gudea's personal history suggests that before rising to rule in Lagash, Gudea was a priest of the Sumerian god Ningirsu. Certainly the remains of Gudea's public works support a vision of a deeply religious man. Over his twenty-year reign, Gudea built fifteen monumental temples in and around Lagash, and statues of the governor in devout posture remain as some of the most numerous examples of Sumerian sculpture.

Perhaps the most impressive of Gudea's accomplishments was the establishment of an advanced social policy in Lagash. In the second millennium B.C.E., Gudea was able to cite a social equality that

even some modern rulers have yet to emulate: "[In my town], the maidservant was the equal of her mistress, the slave walked beside his master, and . . . the weak rested by the side of the strong."

Sadly, this period of social equality did not survive past Gudea's death in 2124 B.C.E. After his death, Sumer once again became part of the general Mesopotamian culture.

See also: AKKAD, KINGDOM OF.

GUANG WUDI. *See* KUANG WU TI

GUANG XU. *See* KUANG HSÜ

GUISE, HOUSE OF. *See* LORRAINE DYNASTY

GUJARAT KINGDOM (1401–1583 C.E.)

North Indian Muslim kingdom dating to the fifteenth century that arose out of the destruction of the Delhi sultanate by the great Mongol conqueror, Tamerlane.

Tamerlane's invasions of the northern India and Delhi sultanate in the early fifteenth century, which hastened that state's decline, allowed areas under Delhi control, such as Gujarat, to liberate themselves and declare independence. The first moves toward independence were felt in the mid-fourteenth century, when the Delhi sultan, Firuz Shah III (r. 1351–1388), attempted to subdue Gujarat and the Sind (present-day Pakistan) in 1362. Once the sultanate had been fully destroyed a few decades later, the sultanate of the Gujarat was proclaimed.

The first sultan of Gujarat, Tatar Khan (r. 1403–1404), rose to power in 1403 after he imprisoned his father, Zafar Khan, who had been provincial administrator of the region under the Delhi sultans. In retaliation for being imprisoned, Zafar poisoned Tatar Khan the following year. This allowed Zafar Khan (r. 1404–1410) to become the second sultan of Gujarat, a title that he passed on to his grandson, Ahmad Shah I (r. 1410–1442), in 1410.

The period following the first two sultans helped to solidify Gujarat's independence. During his thirty-one-year reign. Ahmad Shah attempted to stabilize the kingdom by expanding its territory beyond the initial enclave of Asawal (present-day Ahmedabad) and its surrounding areas. He also defeated the armies of the neighboring kingdom of Malwa, which was located on a crucial trade route between Gujarat and the Ganges River. Ahmad played a crucial role in spreading Muslim hegemony in this region at the expense of Hinduism. His religious zealotry also cost the Hindus numerous temples, which were destroyed as a result of his expansionary plans.

Ahmad's death in 1442 brought his son, Muhammad Karim Shah (r. 1442–1451), to power. Muhammad Karim was followed on the throne by one of his sons, Qutbu-ud-din (r. 1451–1459). This period of relative dynastic stability was followed by the brief reign of one of Ahmad's other sons, Daud Shah (r. 1459), in 1459. Following Daud, the throne went to the young and strong-willed son of Muhammad Karim, Muhammad Bigahra (r. 1459–1511). Muhammad Bigahra became sultan at age thirteen and ruled without a protector. His reign was distinguished by his military prowess. Bigahra's military successes, such as overrunning the neighboring Cutch and the sultan of Ahmadnagar, combined with his young age when he took the throne, allowed him to reign for fifty-two years, longer than any other Gujarat ruler. Bigahra also distinguished himself for following in Ahmad's footsteps by continuing to spread Islam throughout the sultanate.

The sixteenth century brought Gujarat's first sustained contact with Europe. This contact took the form of the Portuguese attempt to establish trading posts along the coast of the Indian subcontinent. These moves by the Portuguese provided the most significant tests of Muhammad Bigahra's sultanate. The Portuguese intrusions into the Gujarat prompted the sultan to seek alliance with other kingdoms, such as Egypt and Calicut, to keep the Europeans at bay.

Despite a naval victory by Gujarat and its allies in 1507, the Muslim fleets were routed by the Portuguese in 1509. Two years later, in 1511, Muhammad Bigahra died and was succeeded by his son, Zafar Shah II (r. 1511–1526). During the reign of Zafar's son and successor, Bahadur Shah (r. 1526–1536), further Portuguese victories, and the subsequent establishment of trading posts, including Goa, along the coast, allowed the European invaders to take the small coastal enclave of Diu in 1535.

Despite the Portuguese threat, Bahadur managed to annex the Malwa kingdom in 1531. In 1535, however, he temporarily lost the important fortress of Champaner to Humayun Padshah, who was forced to give up his new conquest in order to keep other rivals at bay. These losses forced Bahadur to make difficult decisions, which resulted in a peace treaty with the Portuguese and the surrender of more land to the Europeans. During further negotiations, Bahadur was killed after falling off the deck of a Portuguese ship.

Bahadur left no successor to the sultanate. As a result, a succession of grandsons of Zafar Shah II held the throne between 1536 and 1553. By the early 1570s the Mughals, under the leadership of Akbar the Great (r. 1556–1605), forced the Gujarat to submit. The sultanate was fully absorbed into the Mughal Empire by 1584, just as the Delhi sultanate, the Mughal's predecessor, had done with Gujarat nearly two centuries earlier.

See also: AHMADNAGAR KINGDOM; AKBAR THE GREAT; DELHI SULTANATE; INDIAN KINGDOMS; MALWA KINGDOM; MUGHAL EMPIRE.

FURTHER READING

Duff, Mabel. *The Chronology of Indian History: From the Earliest Times to the 16th Century.* Delhi: Cosmo Publications, 1972.

Smith, Vincent A. *The Oxford History of India.* Ed. Percival Spear. 4th ed. New York: Oxford University Press, 1981.

Wolpert, Stanley. *A New History of India.* 7th ed. New York: Oxford University Press, 2003.

GUPTA EMPIRE (ca. 320–540 C.E.)

Empire that dominated the northern half of the Indian subcontinent, including much of the northern part of present-day India, nearly all of Pakistan, and part of Bangladesh. Classical Indian civilization reached its peak under the Gupta dynasty.

The founder of the Gupta Empire was Chandragupta I (r. 320–350), the grandson of a local *maharaja* ("great king") of the Gupta dynasty who ruled a small state in the Ganges River Valley. Around 320, Chandragupta conquered the Magadha kingdom in the region of Bihar and made it the center of a growing domain. Chandragupta expanded his realm by wedding a princess of the family that ruled Bihar (and perhaps Nepal). Under Chandragupta, the Magadha kingdom continued to grow and become more powerful.

When Chandragupta died in 350, his son and successor, Samudra Gupta (r. 350–376), began invading neighboring areas, expanding the kingdom into a great state that became known as the Gupta Empire. Samudra showed considerable skill in his military campaigns, and Indian legend portrays him as a musician and poet as well as a warrior. Indeed, a huge art revival took place while the Guptas ruled. Apparently, there was also a revival of Hinduism, as Samudra was a follower of the god Vishnu (known as the Preserver, and the second member of the triad that also includes Brahma the Creator and Shiva the Destroyer).

The next and best known ruler of the Gupta dynasty was Chandragupta II (r. 376–415). He was a forceful and dynamic king, and India was peaceful and affluent under his reign, which represented the height of the Gupta dynasty's dominance and cultural splendor. Chandragupta II encouraged education and the arts and received many scholars at his court, including the poet Kalidasa (sometimes referred to as the "Indian Shakespeare") and Aryabhata, the mathematician who discovered the laws of zero and taught how to calculate eclipses.

This period of Chandragupta II's reign also gave rise to a golden age of Indian culture, with thriving music, literature, painting, and drama, as well as cave art and classic Hindu temples and sculptures. The Guptas also standardized an image of Buddha that lasted hundreds of years. (The Guptan Buddha had a peaceful and pensive expression and twisting curls against the head, with a monk's robe around the body and a big halo in back of the head.) Guptan art forms spread from India to Central Asia, China, Japan, and Southeast Asia. Although Chandragupta II was a pious Hindu, he accepted Buddhism and Jainism in his kingdom, encouraging all three religions.

The peace and prosperity enjoyed during the reign of Chandragupta II began to be threatened under the rule of his son and successor, Kumara Gupta I (r. 415–455). During this period, the White Huns started to invade the empire from the north. Kumara was able to withstand the attacks, but his son and successor, Skanda Gupta (r. 455–470), and

Skanda's successors, could not resist the overpowering Hun assault, which ultimately ended the Gupta dynasty around 550 and placed a large part of India under the control of the White Huns.

See also: CHANDRAGUPTA MAURYA; INDIAN KINGDOMS; MAGADHA KINGDOM.

GURJARA-PRATIHARA DYNASTY (ca. 750–1000 C.E.)

Hindu dynasty that was the last of the powerful north Indian dynasties. At its height, the Gurjara-Pratihara dynasty reigned over nearly all of India north of the Vindhya mountain range (usually considered the dividing line between north and south India).

The Haricandra line of the Gurjara-Pratihara dynasty reigned in Marwar (now part of Rajasthan state) from the sixth through ninth centuries, mostly as feudatories. The Nagabhata line of the dynasty reigned first at Ujjain and later at Kannauj on the Ganges from the eighth through eleventh centuries. Although there were some other Gurjura lines of the dynasty also, they did not use the Pratihara family as well.

The origin of the Gurjara dynasty is unclear. Most historians formerly believed that members of the dynasty came to India just after the Hunas (the eastern, or White Huns) had forced their way into India in the fifth century, and were likely associated with the Khazars. Today, however, many historians believe that the Gurjaras were native to India. The first mention of the dynasty in ancient documents dates to the late sixth century.

The Nagabhata line of the Gurjara-Pratihara dynasty started with its founder, Nagabhata I (flourished ca. 750), in the eighth century. Evidence exists that his grandnephew, Vatsaraja (r. ca. 783–815), was king of Ujjain and that both Vatsaraja and his son, Nagabhata II (r. ca. 815–833), were defeated by the Rastrakuta dynasty and made their vassals.

During wars early in the ninth century, which involved the Rastrakutas, Palas, and Pratiharas, Nagabhata II took over the ancient city of Kannauj and became the strongest ruler in northern India. His son, Ramabhadra (r. ca. 833–836), acceded to the throne around 833, followed just three years later by his son, Mihira Bhoja I (r. ca. 836–893).

The Pratihara Empire attained the height of its power and wealth during the reign of Bhoja I and his successor, Mahendrapala I (r. ca. 893–914). During that time, the Pratihara realm was as large as the Gupta Empire, extending from Gurjarat and Kathiawar in the west all the way to northern Bengal in the east. Although the empire was vast, a large part of it was relatively insecure, with vassal kings.

The power of the Gurjara-Pratihara dynasty declined after the rule of Mahendrapala I, probably because of rivalries within the dynasty and also because of a strong attack from the Deccan region conducted by the Rastrakuta king, Indra I (r. 915–917), who overwhelmed Kannauj around 916.

The Pratiharas never managed to recover their power after the Rastrakuta victory. They lost the majority of their vassal states and retained control of only a small area. In 1018, Mahmud of Ghazna (r. 998–1030) forced the last significant king of the Gurjara-Pratihara dynasty, Rajuapala (r. ca. 975–1018), from Kannauj in 1018. A small principality controlled by the Pratiharas endured for about a generation after that in the area around Allahabad (in present-day Uttar Pradesh).

See also: GUPTA EMPIRE; INDIAN KINGDOMS; KHAZAR KINGDOM; MAHMUD OF GHAZNA; PALA DYNASTY; RASTRAKUTA DYNASTY.

GUSTAVUS I (VASA) (1496–1560 C.E.)

Founder of the Vasa dynasty of Sweden (r. 1523–1560), who ended the practice of electing Swedish kings and established a hereditary monarchy.

Born Gustavus Eriksson, Gustavus was the son of Erik Johansson, a Swedish senator and follower of Sten Sture, the regent of Sweden. In the early sixteenth century, Sweden was part of the Kalmar Union and was ruled by the king of Denmark and Norway acting through Swedish regents such as Sten Sture.

In 1518, Gustavus was taken to Denmark as a political hostage and imprisoned there after an uprising and civil strife in Sweden that involved Sture's party and a party led by the archbishop Gustav Trolle. This unrest eventually led the Danish king, Christian II (r. 1513–1523), to invade and conquer Sweden outright.

Gustavus escaped Denmark in 1519, returning to Sweden in 1520, the same year in which his father was killed in a massacre ordered by Christian II. By 1521, Gustavus had become the leader of a revolt against Danish rule. The Swedes pushed the Danes out of the country with the aid of Lübeck, a city of the Hanseatic League, and Gustavus was elected king in 1523.

Throughout the first years of his reign, Gustavus Vasa had to deal with uprisings led by adherents of the former regent's party. Simultaneously, he worked toward creating a strong central government. He recognized that one way to increase the power of the Crown was to increase its wealth; the rise of Protestantism could help in this objective, since the Catholic Church owned many estates. Gustavus ensured the support of Swedish nobles by offering them monastic lands as fiefs. By 1536, Sweden had broken ties with Rome and had installed a Lutheran archbishop. Gustavus also organized an army and established a navy.

In the early 1530s, Gustavus suppressed peasant rebellions and withstood a Danish invasion. In 1537, however, he allied with Denmark against Lübeck, and victory over that Hanseatic city helped to strengthen the Swedish economy. In 1544, Gustavus, with the approval of the Estates (a representative body comprised of the various classes of Swedish society), enacted the Pact of Succession. This new law instituted a system of hereditary succession rather than an elective one for the Swedish monarchy.

When Gustavus died in 1560, he was succeeded by his son, Erik XIV (r. 1560–1568). Gustavus left Sweden with a strong, almost autocratic monarchy. He had increased Sweden's foreign trade, encouraged improvements in farming and mining, and begun colonizing undeveloped regions in northern Sweden and Finland. Based on the foundation that Gustavus established, his successors began involving Sweden in European political affairs.

See also: KALMAR UNION; SWEDISH MONARCHY; VASA DYNASTY.

GUSTAVUS II (ADOLPHUS)

(1594–1632 C.E.)

King of Sweden (r. 1611–1632) of the House of Vasa and one of the most famous commanders during the Thirty Years' War (1618–1648).

Born in 1594, Gustavus Adolphus became king of

Sweden in 1611 on the death of his father, King Charles (Carl) IX (r. 1604–1611). During Gustavus's reign, Sweden was almost constantly at war. When he first came to the throne, Sweden was at war with Denmark; it was fighting Poland in Russia; and Sigismund III of Poland (r. 1587–1632) had been deposed as king of Sweden in 1599 but still claimed a right to its throne.

Gustavus made peace with Denmark in 1613 and ended the Russian war in 1617 with territorial gains for Sweden. At the end of another war in Poland, which lasted from 1621 to 1629, he forced Sigismund to renounce his claim to the Swedish throne and won lands in Livonia (now Estonia and Latvia).

Gustavus faced a greater challenge with the Thirty Years' War, which began in 1618 when Protestants in Bohemia revolted against the Catholic rule of the Habsburg dynasty. The war quickly engulfed all of Europe, becoming a conflict not only between Protestant and Catholic but also between those who wanted a weak Holy Roman emperor and the Habsburgs, who supported a strong empire. At first, Gustavus stayed out of the war, but events ultimately pulled Sweden into the conflict.

A strong Holy Roman Empire and a strong Germany would pose a threat to Swedish dominance on the Baltic Sea. This consideration, along with Gustavus's strong Protestantism, helped convince him to involve Sweden in the Thirty Years' War. Aided by a subsidy from Cardinal Richelieu of France, who believed that it was in his country's interest to keep the empire weak, Sweden invaded Germany in 1630. Over the next two years, Gustavus's campaigns gained the upper hand for the anti-Habsburg forces. But Gustavus was then killed in battle at Lützen in Germany in 1632.

While he reigned, Gustavus Adolphus made Sweden's armies a byword for efficiency, discipline, and valor. He enlarged Sweden's territories and sphere of influence, gaining control of most of the eastern Baltic. No other Swedish monarch made such an impact in European politics, and he left Sweden as an important power to be considered in the affairs of Europe.

Gustavus and his chancellor, Axel Oxenstierna, also created a strong central government for Sweden and ended the struggle for power between the nobles and the Crown. He also improved the educational system, establishing Gymnasia or secondary schools and

funding universities. Upon his death, Gustavus was succeeded by his daughter, Christina (r. 1632–1654).

See also: CHRISTINA; SWEDISH MONARCHY; VASA DYNASTY.

GWALIOR KINGDOM (ca. 700–1948 C.E.)

Former state in central India, located in the district of Malwa, centered on a strategic fort that helped guard the trade routes of northern India.

In the eighth century, a Rajput prince of northern India named Suraj Sen was cured of a deadly disease by a hermit-saint. In gratitude, Suraj Sen (r. 700s) built a city at the place of his cure and named it Gwalior, after his healer Gwalipa. The city became the capital of Suraj's Gwalior kingdom.

Over the years, Gwalior changed hands many times. The Pratihara king, Bhoja I (r. ca. 836–893), ruled Gwalior in the ninth century, followed by the Rajputs, who lost it to Muslim sultan Mahmud of Ghazna (r. 998–1030). In 1196, Gwalior was taken by Kutbuddin Aybeg (r. 1192–1210) of the Tughluq dynasty.

Recovered by the Hindu Rajputs in 1210, Gwalior was conquered by Sultan Iltumish (r. 1211–1236) of the Mu'izzi (Slave) dynasty of Delhi in 1232. In 1398, it was recovered once again by the Rajputs, this time the Rajputs of the Tanwar tribe.

Gwalior fell to Muslim sultan Ibrahim Lodi (r. 1517–1526) in 1518. Within a few years, however, the kingdom was occupied by Babur (r. 1526–1530), founder of India's Mughal dynasty. In 1558, Gwalior was conquered by Akbar the Great (r. 1556–1605) of the Mughal dynasty.

In 1726, forces from the Maratha Confederacy under General Ranoji Sindhia (r. 1726–1750) captured the district of Malwa, eventually taking the Gwalior fort in 1738. With help from foreign soldiers, including French mercenaries, Ranoji's son, Mahadji Sindhia (r. 1761–1794) extended the boundaries of Gwalior to include most of central India. He defeated the Rajputs, took the Mughal emperor of India, Shah Alam II (r. 1759–1806), under his protection, and defeated Holkar, the chief general of the Maratha, in 1793. The British recognized Mahadji as the de facto ruler of northwest India.

In 1794, Mahadji was succeeded by his adopted son, Daulat Rao Sindhia (r. 1794–1827). A period of unrest brought an intervention by the British, who stripped Daulat Rao of his extended lands and forts, leaving him in Gwalior. When Daulat died in 1827, he left no children. His wife, Maharani Baija Bai Sahib, adopted Mukut Rao, an eleven-year-old boy, to succeed Daulat as Jankoji Rao Sindhia (r. 1827–1843).

The nineteenth century was a time of weak rule and palace intrigue in Gwalior. When Jankoji died without a successor in 1843, the Sindhias, Gwalior's ruling family, asked the British for assistance. The British established a garrison staffed with British officers and Indian soldiers called sepoys. With British support, Jankoji's widow, Maharani Shrimant Akhand Soubhagyavati, adopted a boy, Tara Baj, to rule as Jayaji Rao Sindhia (r. 1843–1886).

After the pace of Westernization and British dominance throughout India increased dramatically in the middle of the nineteenth century, the Indian populace began to rebel against colonial rule. In 1857, sepoys from Gwalior joined in a large mutiny and killed the British officers at the garrison.

A frightened Jayaji Rao fled to the city of Agra, seeking British protection. After British order was restored in 1858, Jayaji Rao participated in campaigns against the mutineers. As a reward for these and other services, the British appointed him one of the first Indian generals of the British army.

When Jayaji died in 1886, the throne of Gwalior went to his ten-year-old son, Madhav Rao II Sindhia (r. 1886–1925), who contributed to the Allied effort during World War I. Upon his death in 1925, Madhav was succeeded by his nine-year-old son, George Jivaji Rao (r. 1925–1948). In 1948, the state of Gwalior was absorbed by a newly independent India and merged with Indore, Malwa, and other small states to form Madhya Bharat state. With this merger Jivaji Rao relinquished the throne, and the kingdom of Gwalior came to an end.

See also: INDIAN KINGDOMS; MARATHA CONFEDERACY; MU'IZZI (SLAVE) DYNASTY; TUGHLUQ DYNASTY.

GWENT KINGDOM

(ca. 400s or 500s–1000s C.E.)

Small medieval kingdom located in southeastern Wales that often served as a gateway between Wales and England. Gwent consisted of two regions, Upper Gwent and Nether or Lower Gwent. Gwent and the kingdom of Glywysing to the west were briefly united in the kingdom of Morgannwg around 930, but by the 970s at the latest, Gwent was once again a separate kingdom.

The kingdom of Gwent evolved from an earlier kingdom of Ewyas (later called Gwerthefyriwg), which was founded by Celtish Britons in the first century B.C.E. Around 470 C.E., this ancient kingdom split into Gwent and Ergyng, but the two were reunited briefly in the next century. Merged with the kingdom of Glywyssing in the early 600s, Gwent suffered from large-scale Saxon raids at that time, as the fall of other Welsh kingdoms opened up the border to Anglo-Saxon incursions.

Few rulers of Gwent made any impact on history. It was largely a territory through which armies passed on their way to campaign deeper into Wales. In 893 and 894 the region endured large Viking raids, while in 1055 Earl Harold Godwinson of Wessex conducted a military campaign against Gruffydd ap Llywelyn, king of Gwynedd and Powys in north-central Wales, and the fighting also raged throughout the southern Welsh kingdoms, including Gwent. After Gruffydd's death in 1063, Harold campaigned in Gwent against Caradog, the ruler of Morgannwg and Gwynllwg, a small territory adjacent to Gwent.

William fitz Osbern, the Norman earl of Hereford, annexed Gwent to his own rule shortly after the Norman Conquest of England in 1066. In the decades that followed, there was much Norman settlement in Gwent. Throughout the eleventh century, the eastern part of Wales, including Gwent, was ruled by Norman "Marcher lords." The Welsh Marches were the Norman-ruled border regions of Wales adjacent to England, and the Marcher lords were Norman barons to whom William I of England (r. 1066–1087) and his successors granted more autonomy than vassals holding more peaceful English fiefs were allowed. With the advent of Norman rule, Gwent played no further role as an independent kingdom within Wales.

See also: GLYWYSING KINGDOM; HAROLD II GODWINSON; NORMAN KINGDOMS; WELSH KINGDOMS; WILLIAM I, THE CONQUEROR.

GWYNEDD KINGDOM

(CA. 800s–1200s C.E.)

Medieval kingdom in northeastern Wales, from which much of the resistance to English and Norman rule emerged from the eleventh to thirteenth centuries.

The legendary founder of Gwynedd was Cunedda Wledig, a late fourth- or early fifth-century chieftain from northern Britain. Among the earliest historically attested kings of Gwynedd were Hywel ap Rhodri (r. 754–825) and his cousin's son Merfyn Frych, who ruled from 825 to 844 and was the father of Rhodri Mawr (r. 844–878). Rhodri Mawr inherited the Welsh kingdom of Powys through his mother, acquired the kingdom of Ceredigion by marriage, and came to rule much of Wales. Although the union of these kingdoms was temporary, Rhodri made Gwynedd an important power in Wales before fleeing to Ireland in 877 in the face of fierce Viking attacks. In the tenth and eleventh centuries, Gwynedd's influence declined as a result of disputes over the succession among Rhodri's descendants. But the kingdom rose to prominence again in the eleventh century.

Gwynedd was ruled by Gruffydd ap Llywelyn (r. 1039–1063) of Powys following the murder of Gwynedd's ruler, Iago ap Idwal (r. 1023–1039), by Iago's own men in 1039, possibly at Gruffydd's bidding. Gruffydd then spent the next fifteen years attempting to conquer the other kingdoms of southern Wales. In 1063, after being forced to retreat into central Wales by Harold Godwinson, earl of Wessex, Gruffydd was killed by his own men. The next ruler of Gwynedd, Bleddyn ap Cynfyn (r. 1063–1075), was in effect a client Edward the Confessor of England (r. 1042–1066). After the Norman Conquest, Norman lordships were imposed on much of Wales, although in the twelfth century Gwynedd maintained some degree of independence under Gruffydd ap Cynan (r. 1081–1137).

By the thirteenth century, when the word "prince" was used more often than "king" to denote the leading men of the royal Welsh families, a prince of Gwynedd became one of the most important figures in the history of Wales by uniting the Welsh against the English. Llywelyn ap Gruffydd (r. 1246–1282) succeeded in making himself overlord of much of Wales by 1257. He was acknowledged as "prince of Wales" by Henry III of England (r. 1216–1272) in 1267. But during the reign of Edward I (r. 1272–1307), he joined a rebellion against the English king begun by his brother Dafydd. The Welsh lost the war, and Llywelyn died in battle in 1282. His brother Dafydd was subsequently hanged, drawn, and quartered as a traitorous vassal the following year. In the aftermath of this revolt, Edward I covered Wales, including Gwynedd, with castles to prevent any further uprisings, and Gwynedd's existence as an independent state came to an end.

See also: ANGLO-SAXON RULERS; EDWARD I; HAROLD II GODWINSON; LLYWELYN AP GRUFFYDD; NORMAN KINGDOMS; POWYS KINGDOM; WELSH KINGDOMS.

GYGES. *See* LYDIA, KINGDOM OF

HAAKON VI (1339–1380 C.E.)

Second king (r. 1355–1380) of the Norwegian Folkung dynasty, whose hereditary claim to Sweden and marriage to Margrethe of Denmark paved the way for the Kalmar Union, by which the Scandinavian kingdoms of Sweden, Norway, and Denmark were united.

Haakon VI was the son of King Magnus VII of Norway (r. 1319–1355), who also ruled Sweden as King Magnus II (r. 1319–1363). Following revolts among nobles unhappy with the union between Norway and Sweden, Magnus agreed in 1343 to separate the two kingdoms. His older son Erik would be heir to the Swedish throne, while Haakon, the younger son, would become co-ruler of Norway, along with Magnus, until Haakon became of age to rule alone.

The Norwegians offered allegiance to Haakon in 1343, but he did not begin ruling on his own behalf until 1355. When Erik died in 1359, following a rebellion in which he was defeated by his father and brother, Haakon was designated his successor, and from 1362 he shared rule of Sweden with Magnus. Together, they warred unsuccessfully against Waldemar IV of Denmark (r. 1340–1375) over the region of Scania in southern Sweden. As part of a peace settlement of 1363, Sweden entered into an alliance with Denmark, and Haakon married Waldemar's daughter Margrethe.

In 1363, Swedish nobles, angered by the Danish alliance, revolted, deposed Magnus and Haakon, and chose Haakon's cousin Albert of Mecklenburg as king (r. 1363–1389). Magnus and Haakon invaded Sweden, but the attack failed. Magnus was captured and imprisoned in Sweden for six years, until Haakon was able to ransom him.

Haakon became sole ruler of Norway upon his father's death in 1374. He continued with unsuccessful attempts to retake Sweden and, allied with Denmark, became involved in wars with the Hanseatic League of German Baltic cities. These conflicts were resolved with a peace treaty in 1376, which granted trading concessions to Hanseatic merchants.

On the death of Danish king Waldemar IV in 1375, Haakon's young son Olaf was elected king of Denmark as Olaf II (r. 1376–1387); he also later ruled Norway as Olaf IV (r. 1380–1387). When Haakon VI died in 1380, Norway and Denmark were united under the rule of Olaf, with his mother Margrethe as regent. Margrethe then ruled as queen after Olaf's death in 1387. This union between Norway and Denmark lasted until 1814.

See also: DANISH KINGDOM; KALMAR UNION; NORWEGIAN MONARCHY; SWEDISH MONARCHY.

HABSBURG DYNASTY (900s–1918 C.E.)

Family that ruled various and extensive areas of Europe from the Middle Ages through the early twentieth century. Lords and owners of vast lands throughout Western and Central Europe, the Habsburgs possessed immense political power. As Holy Roman emperors, kings of Austria, and rulers of Spain, the different branches of the family ruled over kingdoms and empires on three continents. In the sixteenth through eighteenth centuries, the Habsburgs vied with France for European supremacy.

ORIGINS AND MEDIEVAL SUCCESS

The Habsburg dynasty's rise to power began in the Middle Ages, but its dominance in European politics came later. Yet, the dynasty enjoyed periodic successes in the medieval period as well, capturing the title of Holy Roman emperor twice in the thirteenth and fourteenth centuries.

Origins

The Habsburg family originated in Central Europe in modern-day Switzerland and Alsace in the tenth century. The dynastic name came from a castle in Aargau, Switzerland, whose owner was designated Count Otto of Habsburg. During the eleventh and twelfth centuries, the Habsburgs amassed both land and titles, accumulating vast estates in Alsace, Baden, and Switzerland. Although the Habsburgs would take part in many of the great wars of European history, their success came primarily through inheritance and marriage.

Holy Roman Emperors

In 1273, Count Rudolph von Habsburg (r. 1273–1298) was elected King Rudolf I (r. 1273–1298) of the Germans, and he soon solidified his claims to Austria and surrounding lands as well. The Habsburgs ruled Austria for the next six and a half centuries. Rudolph passed all his titles on to his son Albert I (r. 1298–1308), but the lands were eventually divided among family members in 1365 upon the death of Duke Rudolph IV of Austria (r. 1358–1365).

Over the next several generations, the Habsburg family added to its domains, with the Tyrol and Trieste coming under its control in 1363 and 1382, respectively. When Albert V of Austria (r. 1404–1439) married the daughter of Holy Roman Emperor Sigismund (r. 1433–1437), he inherited his father-in-law's titles as king of Bohemia and Hungary. Albert was then elected German king, as Albert II (r. 1438–1439) in 1438. With only one exception, Charles VII of Bavaria (r. 1742–1745), all subsequent Holy Roman emperors were Habsburgs.

FIFTEENTH-CENTURY RISE TO POWER

From the 1440s, then, the Habsburgs entered the elite of European royalty and politics. From that time, they were elected repeatedly as kings of Germany and Holy Roman emperors. Their rise to power did not come easily, however. Throughout the fifteenth cen-

One of the oldest and most distinguished dynasties of Europe, the Habsburgs originated in central Europe and established Austria as the center of their domain. Desiring a royal residence equal to that of their French rivals, the Habsburgs built Schonbrunn Palace in Vienna, beginning in 1695.

tury, the Habsburgs were forced into military conflict against the Hungarians. Ascendancy of the family, however, was ensured in the typical Habsburg manner, through marriage and inheritance.

Marriage and Expansion

Beginning in the fifteenth century, the Habsburgs entered into a series of marriages through which they acquired vast lands throughout Europe. Emperor Maximilian I (r. 1493–1519) began this tradition of making advantageous marriages. Through his marriage to Mary of Burgundy, the daughter and heiress of Charles the Bold (r. 1467–1477), Maximilian I acquired the Low Countries.

Maximilian's son Philip married Joanna of Castile, the daughter of Isabella I of Castile (r. 1474–1504) and Ferdinand II of Aragón (r. 1479–1516), and became Philip I of Castile (r. 1504–1506). Their

ROYAL RELATIVES

THE EMPRESS ELIZABETH

During the summer of 1853, Austrian emperor Franz Joseph met Bavarian princess Elizabeth, whom her family called "Sisi." Franz Joseph was slated to marry Helene, Elizabeth's older sister, but as soon as he saw the beautiful Sisi, he fell in love and announced their engagement. As empress, Elizabeth was known for her concern for the poor and for visits to hospitals and asylums, and enjoyed great popularity with the people of Austria and Hungary. Yet the empress's life was not without tragedy. Her first child, Sophie, died at the age of two, and her only son, Crown Prince Rudolf, committed suicide. Although she was an accomplished equestrian and exercised regularly, the empress was plagued by health problems, especially bouts of depression and perhaps anorexia. Elizabeth held many progressive political ideas and sided with Hungary in a struggle for autonomy that resulted in the 1867 division of the empire into two nations, both ruled by Franz Joseph and Elizabeth. The empress also traveled widely without her husband. While on a visit to Geneva in 1898, she was assassinated by an Italian anarchist.

son Charles, Maximilian's grandson, became Charles I of Spain (r. 1516–1556) and also Holy Roman Emperor Charles V (r. 1519–1558). Finally, Charles's younger brother Ferdinand married the daughter of Louis II (r. 1516–1526) of Bohemia and Hungary, bringing these lands into the Habsburg domain.

Charles V and the European Empire

By the reign of Emperor Charles V, the Habsburgs had assembled a large and polyglot empire. Through his father Philip I of Habsburg and his mother Joanna of Castile, Charles V inherited both the Habsburg domain of Central Europe and the kingdom of Spain. Crowned king of Spain in 1516 and elected Holy Roman emperor in 1519, Charles reigned over about one-quarter of the population of Europe, in addition to the Spanish Empire in the Americas.

Charles's reign marked the high point of Habsburg rule. However, his vast power came at a price. To fund his imperial enterprise, Charles levied extraordinary taxes and faced numerous tax revolts throughout his reign. Then as the Protestant Reformation swept through the Habsburg domains in Central Europe, Charles, a staunch Catholic, committed sizable resources to combating it. Charles V retired from his duties in 1556 and gave up his titles two years later.

The Habsburg succession did not follow the typical pattern of other European monarchies. The nature of the Habsburg Empire made it impossible to transfer the entire domain along a single family line. Charles's retirement also meant that he could pass on his territories and titles as he pleased. He chose to divide his lands between his son Philip II (r. 1556–1598) who inherited Spain, the Netherlands, parts of Italy, and the Spanish possessions in the Americas, and his brother Ferdinand I (r. 1558–1564), who inherited the Habsburg lands in Central Europe, including Austria. Ferdinand was also elected Holy Roman emperor. After this division of power, one ruler would never again unite the Habsburg domain.

THE MANY FACES OF HABSBURG POWER

Beginning in the reign of Charles V, Habsburg Europe faced dynastic and military threats from both inside and outside. The Ottoman Turks pressed in against the eastern Habsburg borders, forcing Charles V to expend resources on several fronts. In addition, the kingdom of France challenged Habsburg hegemony in Western Europe.

The Western Front

In the seventeenth century, the greatest and most enduring conflict faced by the Habsburgs was with France, especially under the French king Louis XIV (r. 1643–1715). During a series of wars against Louis, the Habsburgs lost Alsace, Franche-Comté, Artois, and part of Flanders, as well as control of the Spanish monarchy.

One of the more significant of these conflicts was the War of the Spanish Succession (1700–1713). In 1660, Louis XIV had married the daughter of King Philip IV of Spain (r. 1621–1665). When Philip's son, Charles II of Spain (r. 1665–1700), died without an heir in 1700, Louis used his wife's position to claim the Spanish throne and have his grandson crowned Philip V (r. 1700–1746).

The deceased Charles II had stipulated that the French Bourbon heir could inherit his title only if he renounced his claim to the French throne, which would have united France and Spain under one king. When Philip refused to do so, the Austrian Habsburg ruler, Emperor Leopold I (r. 1658–1705), pronounced Charles's will invalid and declared war on Spain and France. The possibility of a combined France and Spain brought England, Prussia, and the Dutch into the war on the side of Austria, making it a European-wide conflict.

The War of the Spanish Succession ended in a stalemate, and the Treat of Utrecht (1713) divided the contested territory among the rival powers. The Spanish lost the southern Netherlands and their Italian possessions to the Austrian Habsburgs; the Bourbon Philip V was recognized as king of Spain but was forced to renounce his claims on the French throne, and France ceded much of its North American territory to England.

In 1713, Holy Roman Emperor Charles VI (r. 1711–1740) issued the Pragmatic Sanction, an edict that changed the conditions of Habsburg succession, guaranteeing that in the event of no male heir, a daughter could inherit her father's titles and lands. This was important to Charles since the sole Habsburg heir to the Austrian throne was his daughter, Maria Theresa.

ROYAL PLACES

THE ESCORIAL OR THE MONASTERY OF SAN LORENZO EL REAL

Begun in 1563 under Philip II, the Escorial was one of the palaces of the Spanish Habsburgs. Located 27 miles northwest of Madrid, the enormous palace contains a cathedral-like church, a monastery, a library, and a school. Philip commissioned the palace to celebrate the battle of St. Quentin, which occurred on the feast day of St. Lawrence and at which the Spanish army defeated the French. Philip's intention was also that the building would serve as a royal burial place. The design reflects Philip's piety and Spanish royal power and might. The vast structure resembles a fortress at the main entrance, and its classic simplicity makes it seem austere. Although the royal apartments are modest, the church is huge and lavishly decorated. Taking over twenty years to complete, the palace has a perimeter of 3,000 feet and encompasses over 500,000 square feet. Within, there are 86 sets of stairs, 88 fountains, 1,200 windows, and 2,673 doors. The massive outer walls are 744 feet long and 72 feet high, with 200-foot towers at each corner. Since its construction, the building has been expanded several times, burned twice, and looted by French troops in 1807. Many Spanish monarchs, including Philip, are buried there. The building houses a great library, with a large number of fine Arabic manuscripts, as well as numerous Christian religious works, befitting the pious Habsburg monarchs. Escorial has not been a royal residence since 1861.

HABSBURG DYNASTY (900s–1918 C.E.)

Austrian Habsburgs

RUDOLPH I* (COUNT OF HABSBURG, DUKE OF AUSTRIA, KING OF GERMANY)	1273–1291
ALBERT I* (DUKE OF AUSTRIA, KING OF GERMANY)	1298–1308
ALBERT II (KING OF GERMANY)	1438–1439
FREDERICK III (EMPEROR)	1440–1493
MAXIMILIAN I* (EMPEROR)	1493–1519
CHARLES V* (EMPEROR)	1519–1556
FERDINAND I (EMPEROR)	1556–1564
MAXIMILIAN II (EMPEROR)	1564–1576
RUDOLF II (EMPEROR)	1576–1612
MATTHIAS (EMPEROR)	1612–1619
FERDINAND II (EMPEROR)	1619–1637
FERDINAND III (EMPEROR)	1637–1657
LEOPOLD I* (EMPEROR)	1658–1705
JOSEPH I (EMPEROR)	1705–1711
CHARLES VI (EMPEROR)	1711–1740
FRANCIS I (EMPEROR)	1745–1765
JOSEPH II* (EMPEROR)	1765–1790
LEOPOLD II* (EMPEROR)	1790–1792
FRANCIS II (EMPEROR)	1792–1835
FERDINAND I (EMPEROR)	1835–1848
FRANZ JOSEPH* (EMPEROR)	1848–1916
CHARLES I (EMPEROR)	1916–1918

Spanish Habsburgs

CHARLES I* (EMPEROR CHARLES V)	1516–1556
PHILIP II	1556–1598
PHILIP III*	1598–1621
PHILIP IV	1621–1665
CHARLES II	1665–1700

*Indicates a separate alphabetical entry.

Austrian Habsburgs and the East

When Maria Theresa (r. 1740–1780) assumed power, the Austrian Habsburgs faced a number of challenges from other European nations. During the War of the Austrian Succession (1740–1748), which resulted from Maria Theresa's accession, and the Seven Years' War (1756–1763), Austria lost some territory to Prussia but otherwise succeeded in defending its borders. While Maria Theresa could reign as Austrian archduchess and queen of Bohemia and Hungary, she could not be Holy Roman emperor. When Emperor Charles VII of Bavaria, a non-Habsburg, died in 1745, Maria Theresa's husband Francis I (r. 1745–1765) was elected emperor.

Maria Theresa launched a vast reform of the Aus-trian government. Her son, the future Holy Roman emperor Joseph II (r. 1765–1790), was sympathetic to the Enlightenment and favored liberalizing and centralizing the Austrian government. As emperor, he abolished serfdom, revised the penal code, enforced religious toleration, and lessened the power of the Catholic Church in Habsburg lands.

NINETEENTH- AND TWENTIETH-CENTURY DECLINE

Leopold II (r. 1790–1792) followed his brother Joseph II to the throne of the Holy Roman Empire. Leopold was not the reformer that Joseph had been. He reversed many of Joseph's reform measures and was an otherwise unexceptional ruler. Leopold's son and successor, Francis II (r. 1792–1835), had the misfortune of ruling Habsburg lands when Napoleon came to power in France, and Austria was overwhelmed by Napoleon's armies as they swept through Europe. However, Francis regained power in Austria after Napoleon's defeat and ruled until 1835.

Through the remainder of the nineteenth century, Habsburg hegemony was challenged on every front. The rise of Prussia meant that there was a rival power in Germany. The short-lived kingdom of Sardinia challenged Habsburg power in its Italian territories. And Russia's expansion into the Balkan region eroded Habsburg power there. The long reign of Emperor Franz Joseph (r. 1848–1916) witnessed further disintegration of Habsburg dominance. The dynasty lost Italy in 1859, and it ceded German leadership to Prussia in 1866.

In addition to the aspirations of other nation-states, the emotional stirrings of nationalism fueled hostility and resentment among many peoples within the Habsburg Empire itself. In 1914, the heir to the Habsburg titles, Francis Ferdinand, was assassinated by a Serbian nationalist—the spark that ignited World War I. Austria's defeat in the war forever dissolved the Habsburg Empire, and surviving members of the family were forced into exile.

The postcommunist nations of Eastern Europe repealed the Habsburg exile in 1996. However, despite the existence of Habsburg descendants, European nations today favor the development of democratic parliamentary governments, and the Habsburgs' dynastic claims to power are now a part of history.

See also: AUSTRO-HUNGARIAN EMPIRE; BOURBON DYNASTY; CHARLES V; HOLY ROMAN EMPIRE; JOSEPH II; LEOPOLD I; LEOPOLD II; MARIA THERESA; MAXIMILIAN I; SPANISH MONARCHIES.

FURTHER READING

Crankshaw, Edward. *The Fall of the House of Habsburg.* New York: Penguin, 1983.

Steed, Henry W. *The Habsburg Monarchy.* New York: Howard Fertig, 1969.

HADRAMAWT KINGDOMS

(ca. 1000 B.C.E.–628 C.E.)

South Arabian states of Saba (or Sheba), Ma'in, Qataban, and Hadramawt, which flourished in the first millennium B.C.E. and lasted until the seventh century C.E. Throughout much of their history, the kingdoms were noted for the production and sale of incense. They also developed complex irrigation systems in order to farm lands that were alternately parched and flooded. All four states were eventually absorbed into the Himyarite kingdom.

The kingdom of Saba, also known as Sheba, seems to have been the first of the four states to prosper. Located on the caravan route from the Indian Ocean to the Mediterranean Sea, Saba was rich as early as the tenth century B.C.E., when the legendary Queen of Sheba visited King Solomon of Israel (r. 970–931 B.C.E.). Rock inscriptions from later centuries praise the Sabean god Attar, who was supposed to bring twice-yearly rains. During these centuries, the rulers of Saba expanded the kingdom's territory through conquest. They also built temples, and, in the sixth century B.C.E., constructed a large dam at the capital city of Marib, which remained standing until 572 C.E.

The kingdom of Ma'in developed around a river oasis, now known as al-Gawf, located northwest of Marib. Ma'in began its existence as part of Saba, but it became an independent kingdom around 400 B.C.E. Thanks to its control over much of the trade route from south Arabia to the Mediterranean, the kingdom soon began to prosper economically. Ma'in established a colony at the Dedan oasis in northwestern Arabia and maintained relations with a number of foreign states, including Egypt and Ionia.

Like Ma'in, the Qataban state gained its independence from Saba in the late fifth century B.C.E. Within one hundred years, it had expanded as far south as the Indian Ocean and threatened Saba to the north. Its capital city was Timna.

The kingdom of Hadramawt remained tied to Saba until the fourth century B.C.E. According to legend, the kingdom took its name from the last words of the prophet Hud: "Hadara al-mawt," or "Death has come." Because Hadramawt's territory included frankincense-producing Dhofar, it held a key position in the international incense trade, a position it jealously guarded with strict laws regulating the harvest and sale of the costly aromatic resin of the frankincense tree, which was in great demand. Not coincidentally, Hadramawt's capital city, Sabwa, was located on a major trade route.

Between 125 and 100 B.C.E., Saba conquered and annexed Ma'in. Qataban also lost much of its western land to Saba and its southern territories to a breakaway province. By the middle of the first century C.E., Hadramawt had destroyed the Qataban capital, and both Hadramawt and Saba had annexed additional Qataban territory.

As Qataban declined, a new kingdom, the Himyar, began to gain influence in the region. The Himyarite rulers conquered land from both Saba and Qataban, established a capital city (Zafar) in what is now southern Yemen, and claimed the title "Kings of Saba and Du-Raidan." Meanwhile, Hadramawt had annexed what remained of Qataban. Saba, Himyar, and Hadramawt were now rivals for control of southern Arabia.

Saba held the upper hand for some time. Early in the third century, Saba's King Sarium Autar (r. first quarter of third century) captured the Hadramite ruler and sacked Hadramawt's capital city. The successors of Sarium Autar defeated the Himyarite king in 248 or 249 and ruled over much of modern Yemen.

Ultimately, however, both Saba and Hadramawt fell under Himyar domination. The Sabean dynasty died out soon after its triumph over Hadramawt. By 295, the Himyar ruler Sammar Yuharis (r. 295–328) was calling himself "King of Saba and Du-Raidan and Hadramawt and Yamanat." By the end of his reign, his military victories had justified his claim to the title.

Hadramawt enjoyed a brief period of independence in the late fourth century, but the Himyarites eventually conquered it. The Himyarite ascendancy lasted until the late sixth century, when all of southern Arabia became part of the Persian Empire. Hadramawt reappeared as an independent state at various times in the Islamic era. Echoes of the Hadramawt kingdoms still linger in southern Arabia in various place names and in the remains of old cities. Frankencense trees still grow in an area in Yemen known as the Wadi Hadramawt.

See also: SABAEAN KINGDOM; SHEBA, QUEEN OF; SOLOMON.

HADRIAN (76–138 C.E.)

Roman emperor (r. 117–138) noted principally for the many major public and defensive works constructed throughout the Roman Empire during his reign. Perhaps the most well known of these works is Hadrian's Wall in Britain.

The child of a politically important family, Hadrian (whose full name was Publius Aelius Hadrianus) was born in the Roman province of Hispania, or Spain. When his father died, Hadrian was taken into the family of the reigning emperor, Trajan (r. 98–117), who was the boy's nearest male relative. Educated as befitted his status, Hadrian showed a particular interest in the study of Greek. His noble lineage meant that he was guaranteed a position in the government upon achieving adulthood, and he made steady progress within the administration, ultimately becoming governor of the province of Syria.

Trajan died in 117, leaving the empire in need of a new emperor. His widow, Plotina, asserted that it had been Trajan's intention to make Hadrian his successor, but her claims were not popular among many influential people of Rome, who advanced candidates of their own. Nonetheless, Hadrian had the approval of the army, which proclaimed him emperor in 117. His opponents did not readily accept the judgment of the army, however. There was considerable dissent within the Senate, and to silence it, Hadrian charged four of the most outspoken senators with conspiring to remove him from the throne. He had these four arrested, and since conspiracy was a capital offense, the senators were executed. Rather than quiet his critics, however, Hadrian's action only served to increase senatorial hostility to his rule.

To strengthen his position, Hadrian set out to convert the Senate and the Roman citizenry to his side. His methods were direct: he gave outright grants of money to senators and sponsored lavish gladiatorial contests for the public. Aware that military success translated into popular support, he nonetheless did not seek to expand the territorial holdings of the empire. Instead, he concentrated on solidifying his control over the territories and provinces already claimed by Rome, thus bringing a measure of peace to the dangerous frontier regions of the empire.

A monument to Hadrian's goal is found along the border that separated the Roman province of Britain from the lands to the north (now Scotland), which were never successfully brought into the sphere of the empire. There Hadrian ordered a great wall to be built. The construction of this 73-mile-long wall, which took four years to build and was completed in 126, was built under Hadrian's personal supervision. With its forts, observation towers, and strong gates, the wall provided the province of Britain with secu-

The Roman Emperor Hadrian built many public works during his reign. Perhaps the most famous is Hadrian's Wall in England, constructed as a barrier between Roman Britain and the wild tribes of the north. Begun around 120 C.E., the wall spanned 73 miles and stood about 15 feet high.

rity and protection against raids from the north. Under Hadrian's orders, similar bulwarks against invasion by barbarian peoples were also constructed at other sensitive points on the imperial frontiers.

In Rome, Hadrian concentrated on governmental and tax reform. His policies, as well as his success in maintaining peace throughout the imperial territories, ushered in a period of great economic prosperity for the Roman Empire. Hadrian took advantage of the empire's increased wealth to finance the construction of temples, a mausoleum for his eventual burial, and other monumental buildings, some of which he designed himself.

Hadrian had no children, which meant that he had no natural successor to the throne. As he grew older and more infirm, he followed the custom of the time and looked among his relatives for a likely young candidate to adopt. He selected Antoninus Pius (r. 138–161), a mature man with family ties to his own adoptive mother, Plotina, and made him his heir. By 137, Hadrian's health had so deteriorated that he

could no longer rule, and he handed the throne over to Antonius Pius. When Hadrian died a year later, the success of his campaign to win the Senate's approval and loyalty was made completely clear: the Senate declared him a god.

See also: ROMAN EMPIRE; TRAJAN.

FURTHER READING

Grant, Michael. *The Roman Emperors.* New York: Charles Scribner's Sons, 1985.

Nardo, Don. *The Roman Empire.* San Diego: Lucent Books, 1994.

Starr, Chester. *A History of the Ancient World.* New York: Oxford University Press, 1991.

HAFSID DYNASTY (ca. 1229–1574 C.E.)

A Berber dynasty (also called Banu Hafs) that ruled in Tunisia and eastern Algeria (a combined area then known as Ifriqiya) until it was overthrown by the Ottoman Turks in 1574. Hafsid rule was the last of a succession of Muslim dynasties that began ruling in the seventh century.

The Hafsid dynasty was founded in 1222 by Abu Zakariya Yahya, a governor of the Almohad dynasty. The new dynasty was based in the city of Tunis, which prospered greatly and underwent a cultural revival under Hafsid rule. Abu Zakariya (r. 1229–1249) ruled for more than twenty years, keeping various tribal clashes and plots in check and assuring Hafsid affluence by means of trade agreements with Italy, Spain, and France. He also extended Hafsid control into the Iberian Peninsula and northern Morocco.

Abu Zakariya was succeeded by his son, Muhammad I al-Mustansir (r. 1249–1277), who brought the Hafsid kingdom to its height of power and status. Following his reign, however, internal strife and power struggles erupted, with various tribal factions competing for the throne. The Hafsid dynasty split up into minor tribal domains and city-states between 1277 and 1284. This era marked the height of external intrusion into Hafsid affairs—chiefly by the Christian kingdom of Aragon, which took advantage of the tribal split to gain trade and political concessions from the nominal Hafsid sovereigns.

Subsequently, Umar I (r. 1284–1295) and later Abu Yahya Abu Bakr (r. 1318–1346) restored Hafsid-controlled unity in Tunisia. Hafsid rule was still weak, however, with its power resting on insecure foundations. Its main support came from three broad groups: tribal leaders, who still held very high status because of their association with the former Almohad dynasty; refugees from Andalusia in southern Spain, who filled more and more important jobs in the administration; and local tribal and urban officials, who formed alliances with the central government without completely giving up their power. One of the most significant phenomena of the period between 1318 and 1346 was the development of a pirate fleet in some of the Hafsid ports. Piracy became a significant source of revenue in much of North Africa during the next four centuries.

The Hafsid kingdom became strong again under Ahmad II (r. 1370–1394), despite some Hafsid pirate activity that jeopardized international relations. Hafsid strength continued under Uthman (r. 1435–

1488) but started to weaken after his rule. First, Spaniards took control of the country. Eventually, fighting between Spain and the Ottoman Turks resulted in Turkish domination of the region, and Tunisia became an Ottoman province in 1574.

See also: ALMOHAD DYNASTY

HAIHAYA DYNASTY (ca. 1000–1745 C.E.)

A short-lived dynasty of India about which little is known beyond the reputed valor of its rulers.

The Haihaya dynasty, one of the many Rajput clans of ancient India, occupied the Nerbudda Valley in central India. The name of the dynasty, Haihaya, derives from the word *haya* ("horse")

According to a Hindu myth, Vishnu blessed the Haihaya prince, Kartavirya, and gave him a thousand arms instead of two. With this power Kartavirya set out to conquer the world. He decided to perform *digvijaya,* a symbolic conquest of the four corners of the earth, to prove his supremacy over the Kshatriyas, the warrior caste of the Aryan Hindus. Regardless of his best plans, Kartavirya was defeated and had his arms cut off by the Brahman hero, Parasurama, who appears in many Hindu legends.

More historical knowledge of the Haihaya dynasty does not appear until the tenth century. At that time, the Haihayas succeeded the Pandava dynasty of Chhattisgarh, and a member of the royal house named Kalingraja (r. 900s) became the first official leader of the Haihaya Dynasty. His grandson and immediate successor, Ratanraja (r. early 1000s), founded the city of Ratanpur, which continued as the capital of Chhattisgarh. The Haihaya dynasty ruled Chhattisgarh for six centuries.

In the fourteenth century, Chhattisgarh and the Haihayas split into two parts. The elder branch of the family continued to rule at Ratanpur, while the younger branch settled in the semi-independent state of Raipur. The Haihayas ruled Chhattisgarh until 1741, when they were overthrown by the Maratha Confederacy. In 1745, after conquering the region, the Marathas deposed Raghunathsinghji (r. ?–1745), the last surviving member of the Ratanpur branch of the Haihaya dynasty.

See also: INDIAN KINGDOMS; MARATHA CONFEDERACY.

HAILE SELASSIE I (1892–1974 C.E.)

Emperor of Ethiopia (r. 1930–1974) who worked to modernize his nation and increase its standing in the world.

Born Tafari Makonnen in the Ethiopian province of Harerge, the future ruler of Ethiopia was the son of a powerful member of the nobility. The young Makonnen was raised in an urban setting, educated at a French mission school, and attended Ethiopia's first modern educational institution, the Menelik School.

At a very young age, Makonnen was appointed governor of Harar and granted the title Dajazmach ("Commander of the Gateway"). At the time, Ethiopia was ruled by Emperor Menelik II (r. 1889–1913), who had taken the first steps to modernize the country and curb the powers of the feudal aristocracy. Within a decade, however, Menelik became debilitated by a series of strokes. Fearing that Ethiopia would pass to European control upon his death, Menelik named his twelve-year-old grandson, Lij Iyasu, as heir apparent, and he nominated a trusted subordinate, Ras Tassama Nadew, as regent.

Despite efforts to ensure an orderly transition of power, Menelik failed to achieve his goal. Ras Tassama Nadew died before the emperor did, and when Menelik died in 1913, the young Iyasu took the throne without a regent. The unprepared Iyasu alienated his grandfather's ministers and evicted from the capital all whom he perceived to be his political rivals. He also offended the nation's Christian elite by accommodating Ethiopia's Muslim community. A conspiracy of disaffected nobles formed to depose the young ruler, and among the plotters was Tafari Makonnen.

On September 27, 1916, the conspirators declared Iyasu deposed, and they replaced him on the throne with Menelik's daughter, Zawditu. They nominated Tafari Makonnen to serve as her regent, granting him the title of *Ras*, the highest rank of nobility. A far better administrator, politician, and diplomat than Zawditu, Ras Tafari monopolized the conduct of Ethiopia's foreign affairs.

In the eyes of the Western world, Ras Tafari was the real ruler of Ethiopia, and Europeans tended to ignore the empress. This situation was further exacerbated when, in 1923, Ras Tafari achieved a great foreign affairs coup by gaining his country's admis-

sion into the League of Nations. Ever a modernizer, Ras Tafari worked hard to engage Ethiopia with the wider world. Throughout the 1920s, he brought to his country several important reforms, from the introduction of the modern printing press to improvements in medicine. He also launched a major literacy campaign.

In his dealings with Europeans, Ras Tafari developed particularly warm ties with the French. This alliance proved decisive in helping Ethiopia escape annexation by the other European powers, most notably Britain and Italy, who sought to colonize Ethiopia. At home, Ras Tafari steadily consolidated his power and influence, ultimately gaining the trust and support of the empress herself. When Zawditu died in 1930, Ras Tafari assumed full imperial powers. Upon his coronation, he took the imperial name of Haile Selassie I.

As emperor, Haile Selassie introduced profound changes to Ethiopia. The most important of these were

Haile Selassie I, the last reigning emperor of Ethiopia, worked to bring his country into the modern world. This photograph of the emperor was taken in 1935, shortly before Selassie was driven into exile by Italian occupation. He was restored to the throne in 1941.

accomplished through the promulgation of the nation's first constitution (July 16, 1931). Among other things, this document established the legitimacy of Haile Selassie's claim to the throne by declaring him a direct descendant of Ethiopia's two most legendary figures, King Solomon and the Queen of Sheba. It also claimed divine status for the emperor.

Soon, however, the outside world impinged upon Haile Selassie's rule, for Italy had imperial designs on Ethiopia. In 1936, the Italian army attacked the country, overcame the emperor's forces, and drove him into exile, where he remained until 1941. While in exile in Europe, Haile Selassie gained the support of Great Britain, which had become Italy's enemy when Italy became Germany's ally in World War II. With Britain's aid and support, Haile Selassie was restored to the Ethiopian throne in 1941.

In the post–World War II era, Haile Selassie began a modernization campaign, funded by the prosperity of Ethiopia's coffee-based economy. However, in the late 1950s, the Ethiopian people became discouraged by government corruption and worsening economic conditions. In 1960, opposition leaders staged an abortive coup to eliminate imperial rule. Although the coup failed, the resentment it represented did not abate, and the aging emperor seemed incapable of responding to the growing anti-imperial sentiment. In 1974, the Ethiopian army seized control of the country. First stripped of his powers, Haile Selassie was finally deposed on September 12, 1974, and confined to house arrest in Addis Ababa, the Ethiopian capital. He died there on August 27, 1975.

See also: MENELIK II.

HAMMURABI (d. ca. 1750 B.C.E.)

Sixth king (r. ca. 1792–1750 B.C.E.) of the Amonte dynasty of ancient Babylon, an able administrator who established one of the first codes of law and unified Mesopotamia under Babylonian rule. Hammurabi's reign is considered a high point of Mesopotamian civilization, during which significant advances were made in science, mathematics, and the arts.

Hammurabi was the son of King Sin-muballit (r. ca. 1812–1793 B.C.E.) of Babylon. When Hammurabi inherited the Babylonian kingship upon the death of his father, Babylon was only one of a num-

ber of Mesopotamian city-states squabbling for access to water rights of the Tigris and Euphrates rivers. Ancient records from the time show that, during the first five years of Hammurabi's reign, he was concerned with religious duties and with building temples, improving irrigation systems, and strengthening Babylon's fortifications.

The Code of Hammurabi, written on the ancient stone pillar shown here, was one of the earliest legal codes in human history. This pillar, which shows the god Shamash dictating his laws to King Hammurabi, was discovered by archaeologists at the ruins of the city of Susa in 1901–1902.

Hammurabi's first military campaign came in 1787 B.C.E., when he clashed with Rim Sin (r. ca. 1822–1763 B.C.E.), ruler of the region of Larsa in southern Mesopotamia, over the cities of Isin and Uruk—traditional buffers between Larsa and Babylon. Both sides seem to have lost interest quickly, however, and Hammurabi soon turned his attention to strengthening the defenses of his northern cities.

The next twenty years were characterized more by frenetic building and breaking of coalitions among the more powerful Mesopotamian kingdoms—Babylon, Larsa, Mari, Ashur, and Eshnunna—than by significant military activity. In 1763 B.C.E., however, Hammurabi went to war once more against Rim Sin, this time conquering not only the area between Babylon and Larsa but Larsa itself. The conquest marked the beginning of a massive expansion. Over the next thirteen years, Hammurabi conquered all of the Mesopotamian states, including twenty-three cities. With these victories, Hammurabi secured Babylonian access to water as well as to important metal trade routes, and his kingdom became the dominant power in Mesopotamia.

As the empire grew, Hammurabi shifted away from the traditional Babylonian mode of legal governance, which had been developed for a city-state only fifty miles across. He developed a new set of laws, known as the Code of Hammurabi. For many years, the Code of Hammurabi was thought to have been the foundation for the development of Jewish Mosaic laws, but the unearthing of other ancient Mesopotamian law codes suggests that these ancient legal codes may merely have shared a common origin.

Discovered by French archaeologist Jean Vincent Scheil in 1901 in the ancient city of Susa, the Code of Hammurabi was divided into an epilogue and 280 judgments. These judgments dealt with both criminal and civil law and with topics ranging from murder, manslaughter, and bodily injury to the illegal removal of palm trees. Many of the judgments vary according to the participants in the case—that is, whether they were slaves, free citizens, or landowners. Yet, a common element in many of the judgments is the principle of an eye for an eye. Hammurabi described the law code as an aid to people in search of legal advice, and it is unclear how binding the judgments were when they were not adjudicated directly by the king. As his personal correspondence makes clear, Hammurabi took a personal and involved role in the daily administration of the government, eschewing a systematic bureaucracy.

During the last two years of his life, Hammurabi suffered from an unknown illness, and the governmental reins were handed to his son, Samsu-iluna (r. ca. 1749–1712 B.C.E.), who succeeded to the throne after his father's death around 1749 B.C.E. Unfortunately, without a supportive bureaucracy, Samsu-iluna was unable to hold the empire together, and it swiftly fell into decline.

See also: MIDDLE EASTERN DYNASTIES; SAMSU-ILUNA.

FURTHER READING

Edwards, I.E.S., C. J. Gadd, and N.G.L. Hammond, eds. *The Cambridge Ancient History.* 3rd ed. New York: Cambridge University Press, 1980.

HAN DYNASTY (206 B.C.E.–220 C.E.)

Chinese dynasty that established Confucianism as the central doctrine for imperial rule and continued to unify China under a strong centralized rule.

When the Han gained control of China in 206 B.C.E., the dynasty inherited a highly centralized bureaucratic state from their predecessors, the short-lived Ch'in dynasty (221–206 B.C.E.). Han rulers grafted Confucianism onto this system, creating a model for imperial government that endured for much of Chinese history. At the height of Han rule, Chinese troops ranged 2,000 miles from the capital city, surpassing the journeys of their contemporaries, the Romans.

WESTERN HAN

The Han dynasty was founded by Liu Pang (Liu Bang), also known as Emperor Kao Ti (Gaodi) (r. 206–195 B.C.E.), a village official turned rebel who came to power following the collapse of the Ch'in dynasty. Kao Ti declared the founding of the new Han dynasty with its capital at Chang'an, inaugurating the period known as the Western or Former Han.

Kao Ti kept the administrative system of the Ch'in, which relied on a centralized bureaucracy, but he eased many of the harsh laws and high taxes instituted by his predecessors. To win the support of aristocrats, Kao Ti granted them large landholdings to govern as feudal estates. He later abolished many of these feudatories, however, and by 154 B.C.E. most of them had been eliminated by his successors. The Western Han were menaced by constant invasion by the Xiongnu, a union of nomadic tribes to the north. To manage the Xiongnu threat, Kao Ti used diplomacy to avoid expensive military campaigns.

The Western Han reached its height under Emperor Wu Ti (Wudi) (r. 141–87 B.C.E.), who founded an imperial university that trained candidates for the bureaucracy in the Confucian classics. Wu Ti instituted a highly centralized government and established government monopolies to increase state revenue. His military campaigns drove the Xiongnu back to the north and doubled China's territory by expanding Han power into Manchuria, northern Korea, and the region of Xinjiang in the west. His envoy, Chang Ch'ien (Zhang Qian), traveled deep into Central Asia, bringing back China's first knowledge of other civilized states in the West.

A series of weak rulers followed Wu Ti, and the court was plagued by intrigue. In 9 C.E., the last emperor of the Western Han, the boy emperor Ju-tsu (Ruzi) (r. 6–9), was deposed by his regent, Wang Mang, who proclaimed the short-lived Hsin (Xin) dynasty (9–23). Rebellion broke out in 18 and Wang Mang was killed. According to tradition, the Hsin dynasty marks the division between the Western, or Early Han dynasty, and the Eastern, or Later Han dynasty.

EASTERN HAN

In 25, Liu Hsiu (Liu Xiu), a relative of the Han imperial family, reestablished Han rule. Known by his imperial name, Kuang Wu Ti (Guang Wudi) (r. 25–57), he moved the capital east to the city of Luoyang, inaugurating the Eastern Han period.

Under Kuang Wu Ti's successor, Ming Ti (Mingdi) (r. 57–75), the brilliant general Pan Ch'ao (Ban Chao) subdued the Xiongnu and extended Chinese control into Central Asia, giving China control over large portions of the trade routes that linked China with lands to the west. Foreign trade flourished, with Chinese merchants exchanging silks for ivory, linen, glass, and horses.

As the first century of Han rule drew to a close, ambitious regents took power by placing child em-

Western Han Dynasty		Eastern Han Dynasty	
KAO TI	207–195 B.C.E.	KUANG WU TI* (GUANG WUDI)	25–57
HUI TI	195–188	MING TI	57–75
LU HOU	188–180	CHANG TI	75–88
WEN TI	180–157	HO TI	88–106
CHING TI	157–141	SHANG TI	106
WU TI* (WUDI)	141–87	AN TI	106–125
CHAO TI	87–74	SHUN TI	125–144
HSUAN TI	74–48	CH'UNG TI	144–145
YUAN TI	48–33	CHIH TI	145–146
CH'ENG TI	33–7	HUAN TI	146–168
AI TI	7–1	LING TI	168–189
P'ING TI	1 B.C.E.–6 C.E.	SHAO TI	189
JU-TZU YING	6–9	HSIEN TI	189–220
		*Indicates a separate alphabetical entry.	

perors on the throne. Central control deteriorated and rebellion spread. In the ensuing chaos, three generals rose to power. One of them deposed the last Han emperor, Hsien Ti (Xiandi) (r. 189–220), in 220 and proclaimed the new Wei dynasty. Two rival dynasties also were established by other leaders, marking the end of the Han era and the beginning of the period known as the Three Kingdoms.

THE RISE OF CONFUCIANISM

The Han dynasty marks the ascendance of Confucianism as China's state philosophy. Han rulers found that Confucian ideals, based on the teachings of the Chinese sage Confucius (551–479 B.C.E.) and emphasizing ritual and obedience to authority, provided a useful moral and political philosophy for governing their large empire. Han scholars developed a view of the universe in which the emperor sat at the center of a divine order, linking heaven and earth.

Han rulers actively sponsored Confucian scholarship, establishing the study of Confucian classics as the basis for appointments to the bureaucracy. Confucian learning spread and became a unifying force among the scholarly elite throughout China. During the reign of Emperor Wu Ti, a scholar named Ssu-ma Ch'ien (Sima Qian), considered the father of Chinese history, compiled a general history of China.

ARTS AND TECHNOLOGY

The Han made important advances in science and technology. Han astronomers discovered sunspots and calculated the orbit of the moon. Other Han inventions included the sundial, the water clock, and the water-powered mill. Agriculture flourished under the Han with the introduction of crop rotation, improved harnesses and plows, and the invention of the wheelbarrow. The most famous Han innovation may be the invention of paper, which replaced the cumbersome wood and bamboo tablets used previously.

The Han were extremely interested in the supernatural; this passion was apparent in the magic, spirits, and myths that fill the art and literature of the period. Stone sculpture, associated with magical power, emerged in China at this time. A concern for the afterlife also predominated, evidenced by the elaborate tombs of Han rulers. These tombs contained luxurious provisions for the afterlife, including miniature sculptures of houses, servants, and amusements to replicate the lifestyle of the dead emperor.

See also: CH'IN (QIN) DYNASTY; KUANG WU TI (GUANG WUDI); THREE KINGDOMS.

FURTHER READING

Loewe, Michael. *Divination, Mythology, and Monarchy in Han China.* New York: Cambridge University Press, 1994.

HAN WUDI. *See* HAN DYNASTY

HANOVER, HOUSE OF (1714–1901 C.E.)

Ruling house of Great Britain that oversaw a period of great imperial expansion and industrial growth, and that restored royal power and prestige after years of violence and instability had threatened to undermine the monarchy. Though originally distrusted because of their German roots, the Hanoverians came to embody, especially in Queen Victoria (r. 1837–1901), the essence of British national identity.

ORIGINS

The House of Stuart, which held the throne of England for most of the seventeenth century, came to an end with the death of Queen Anne (r. 1702–1714) in 1714. In order to prevent a Catholic from gaining the throne, the British Parliament had passed the Act of Settlement in 1701 (which Anne signed), ensuring that the monarchy could pass only to a Protestant. At the time of Anne's death, the closest eligible Protestant heir to the throne was George, elector of Hanover, the great-grandson of King James I (r. 1603–1625). Although there were fifty-two other individuals—all Catholics or otherwise unfit to rule—between George and the throne, and despite the fact that he could speak no English, George of Hanover was crowned King George I (r. 1714–1727) in 1714, thus beginning the Hanover dynasty, or House of Hanover.

EARLY RULE

George paid frequent visits to Hanover and was never able to achieve any real popularity among the British people, who were distrustful of his German ancestry. A group of supporters of James II (r. 1685–1688), the Catholic king who had been exiled during the Glorious

The Hanover Dynasty of Great Britain ruled from the early eighteenth to the early twentieth century, a period of territorial expansion and economic growth. Its longest-ruling monarch, King George III, is remembered chiefly for losing the American colonies.

Revolution, mounted a series of uprisings throughout the early eighteenth century, but none of these was successful in removing George from the throne.

With the death of George I in 1727, the Crown passed to his only son, who reigned as George II (r. 1727–1760). More respected by the British public than his father due to his willingness to involve himself in England's affairs, George II had the good fortune to oversee England at a time of economic growth and military success, even leading troops personally into battle during the War of the Austrian Succession (1740–1748). Both George II and his father relied heavily on the political skills of Sir Robert Walpole, the chancellor of the Exchequer and first lord of the Treasury, who was the predecessor to the modern role of prime minister.

THE HEIGHT OF BRITISH POWER

George II, whose son Frederick Louis died before him, was succeeded at his death by his grandson, who reigned as George III (r. 1760–1820). During the long reign of George III, England underwent tremendous change, as the onset of the Industrial Revolution brought with it commercial growth and a population boom. The British Empire also began a long process of expansion, though it did lose its North American territory to the newly formed United States as a result of the American Revolution (1776–1783).

George III, the first ruler from the House of Hanover born in England, was both more powerful and more popular than his predecessors. He did not enjoy his popularity, however, because from the 1780s onward George was gripped by deepening bouts of apparent insanity. In fact, his mental aberrations were caused by porphyria, a blood disease. In 1811, with his mental faculties completely reduced and his eyesight nearly gone, George was stripped of his power by Parliament, though not his title. His eldest son was named prince regent and became king upon the death of George III in 1820.

Scandal and Setback

George IV (r. 1820–1830) was the opposite of his father in temperament, and his scandalous affairs and wasteful extravagance cost the monarchy much of its prestige, both at home and abroad. Aside from promoting culture, George did little as king, and though his reign coincided with a period of great literary achievement in Britain, he is remembered for his hedonism rather than for his governance. As George left no heirs, the Crown passed to his brother, William IV (r. 1830–1837), upon his death in 1830.

Only slightly more politically involved than his brother, and similarly touched by scandal, William IV oversaw several important changes in Britain, though

House of Hanover	
GEORGE I	1714–1727
GEORGE II	1727–1760
GEORGE III	1760–1820
GEORGE IV	1820–1830
WILLIAM IV	1830–1837
VICTORIA	1837–1901

he did little to support or hinder them. The most notable occurrence of his reign was the passage in 1832 of the first of three Reform Bills, which expanded the voting population significantly, though it retained the privileged status of the powerful landed gentry. William's reign also witnessed the abolition of slavery throughout the British Empire in 1833 and the first attempt to create an organized national system for assisting the poor. William was the first British monarch who resolved to cooperate with his prime minister, even if he disliked him.

PRESTIGE AND POWER RESTORED

At William's death in 1837, the Crown passed to his niece Victoria, the last of the Hanoverian monarchs. Victoria's reign saw the high point of Great Britain's power, and she was awarded more respect and admiration than almost any other monarch in English history. Over the course of her sixty-four-year reign —the longest of any British monarch—England experienced tremendous economic and social success, as imperial expansion and industrial growth filled the nation's treasury, and new laws doubled the size of the voting population. Scientific and technological advances occurred at a hitherto unseen rate, and many of the institutions and devices associated with modernity made their debut. Victoria's marriage to her cousin, Prince Albert of Saxe-Coburg-Gotha, united her family with that Germanic dynasty, thus making Victoria the last true Hanoverian monarch. Upon her death in 1901, the Crown passed to her eldest son, Edward VII (r. 1901–1910).

See also: ACCESSION AND CROWNING OF KINGS; ANNE; EMPIRE; GEORGE I; GEORGE II; GEORGE III; SAXE-COBURG-GOTHA DYNASTY; VICTORIA.

FURTHER READING

Redman, Alvin. *The House of Hanover.* New York: Coward-McCann, 1961.

Sinclair-Stevenson, Christopher. *Blood Royal: The Illustrious House of Hanover.* London: Jonathan Cape, 1979.

HARALD III HARDRAADE

(1015–1066 C.E.)

Viking king of Norway, surnamed Hardraade ("hardcounsel"), who claimed England and died at the battle of Stamford Bridge during the Norman invasion of England in 1066.

Harald Hardraade was the half-brother of King Olaf II of Norway (r. 1016–1030). In 1030, Harald supported his brother against the Danes at the battle of Stiklarstathir, in which Olaf was killed and Harald was wounded. Fleeing Danish-ruled Norway after that defeat, Harald took service as a mercenary, first with King Yaroslav the Wise (r. 1019–1054) in Russia and then in the Byzantine Empire, where he participated in campaigns against the Seljuk Turks.

After the death of Cnut the Great (r. 1019–1035) of Denmark in 1035, Norway returned to Norwegian rule under Olaf's son, Magnus I the Good (r. 1035–1046). Magnus and Cnut's son Harthacnut had agreed that each would inherit the other's kingdom if the other should die without a direct heir. Harthacnut ruled Denmark (r. 1035–1042) and became king of England (r. 1040–1042) when his half-brother Harold I Harefoot of England (r. 1037–1040) died in 1040. However, when Harthacnut died without an heir in 1042, the English chose Edward the Confessor (r. 1042–1066), Harthacnut's half-brother and son of King Aethelred II (r. 978–1016) of England, to be king.

Harald Hardraade became co-ruler of Norway with his nephew Magnus I in 1045 and sole king on Magnus's death in 1046. He spent the next two decades strengthening his position in the north. Under Harald, Norway once again became a great Scandinavian power. However, Harald did not forget Magnus's claim to inherit England, and on the death of Edward the Confessor in 1066, he asserted his right to the English Crown as Magnus's heir.

Harald invaded England in the autumn of 1066 and captured York, but was defeated and killed by King Harold II Godwinson (r. 1066) of England at Stamford Bridge shortly afterward. Harold II's need to ride south at once to oppose the invasion of William of Normandy (William the Conqueror), possibly leaving his footsoldier archers behind, may have been a factor in Harold's defeat at the battle of Hastings.

See also: CNUT I; EDWARD THE CONFESSOR; HAROLD II GODWINSON; NORWEGIAN MONARCHY; OLAF II (SAINT OLAF); WILLIAM I.

HARAPPAN STATES. *See* SOUTH ASIAN KINGDOMS

HAREMS

The section of homes or palaces set aside for women, especially in Muslim countries. In some harems, the women were there to give pleasure to the ruler. The founder of Islam, the prophet Muhammad, did not originate the idea of harems or of isolating or veiling women, but he did support these concepts and spread them along with Islam. Before that, the harem existed in pre-Islamic states of the ancient Near East, where it was a protected private lodging area for women. During that pre-Islamic period, women could be active in public life as well, however, which was not usually the case in Islamic harems. Harems with both similar and differing aspects have existed in many other parts of the world as well.

PRE-ISLAMIC HAREMS

In pre-Islamic Egypt, Persia, and Assyria, nearly all royal courts had a harem, which contained the monarch's wives and concubines, their female attendants, and eunuchs. These imperial harems had significant political as well as social functions. Rulers frequently acquired more wives for their harems in order to strengthen political ties. And since wives tried to gain the most influential positions for themselves and their sons, harems were the scene of much rivalry for dominance in the court and over royal successions. As the women in harems were generally from prominent families, harem plots often had far-reaching consequences, sometimes even leading to the collapse of ruling dynasties.

In ancient Egypt, the harem was solely the place where women resided in the home or palace. Kings had a number of palaces and many large harems. Each royal harem had its own estate, with money, land, and peasants to take care of food and other necessities.

Royal harems and private harems differed in size, economic independence, and marital status of the women. The harem in private homes was where single women lived, while the royal harem was the residence for the king's secondary wives and their servants and children. The secondary wives were well respected; some were Egyptian, whereas others were daughters of kings from other lands sent to Egypt as symbols of peace. Physically, the royal harem generally consisted of a group of mud-brick buildings surrounded by a high mud-brick wall. The homes generally encircled an open courtyard, and other buildings in the residential complex were used for storage and worship.

ISLAMIC HAREMS IN TURKEY

In the courts of Muslim Turkey, the sultan's harem was a complex organization with officers maintaining order and obedience. It was supervised by the sultan's mother, called the valide sultan. When Sultan Mehmet II (r. 1451–1481) conquered the Byzantine capital of Constantinople in 1453, he let the valide sultan arrange her house as closely as possible to the women's quarters of the Empress Helen, the widow of Byzantine emperor Constantine XI (r. 1449–1453). The women, who lived in the most secluded part of the palace, were divided up to perform various tasks and were guarded by a huge corps of male eunuchs.

The women in the Turkish harems included non-Muslim slave girls, who sometimes were sent to the sultan's court by their parents. Despite misgivings about their daughters becoming concubines, the parents were glad to send them to a life of luxury and ease. Once accepted into the harem, the slaves were converted to Islam and taught to be good concubines. The most beautiful and talented were trained to be concubines and learned to dance, play musical instruments, recite poetry, and perform erotic arts. Twelve of the best-looking and most gifted odalisques were chosen as the sultan's maids-in-waiting. They dressed and bathed him, did his laundry, and served his food and coffee.

ISLAMIC HAREMS IN INDIA

Harems in other Islamic countries had the same basic features as those in Turkey, with some of their own native characteristics. In India, harems were huge enclosed compounds with luxurious buildings inhabited by women. The average Muslim harem in India had about 2,000 women and was very sumptuous. The harem of the Mughal emperor Akbar the Great (r. 1556–1605) had about 5,000 women.

While women in the harems were there for the king to enjoy, there were also a large number of women besides queens and concubines who managed the harems. The harems were places of both amusement and tight security where everyone had to defer to the ruler's wishes. For instance, Sultan Ghiath-al-Din of Malwa (r. 1469–1500) had a harem of 15,000 women, which was organized like a small

ROYAL PLACES

TOPKAPI PALACE

About ten years after his conquest of Constantinople (present-day Istanbul), Mehmet II built the lavish Topkapi Palace on the sacred Seraglio Point, a splendid promontory between the Marmara Sea and the Golden Horn. Ancient legend had it that the Delphic Oracle named that spot as the finest for a new colony and it had become the Acropolis of ancient Byzantium.

The sultan's Seraglio was the seat of imperial power, and thousands of people lived there and worked in his personal and administrative service. The sultan's harem was the most private area of the Seraglio, effectively isolated from the rest of the palace. The harem first moved to the Seraglio in 1541, and it lasted until 1909, becoming the quintessential example of an Islamic harem.

With nearly four hundred rooms, the Seraglio was situated between the sultan's private apartments and those of the chief eunuch. Two houses linked the harem to the outside world, and they were guarded vigilantly. The eunuchs' quarters, and those of the valide sultan and the odalisques, were nearby. The lavishness of accommodations was based on the status of the occupants. Naturally, the sultan's quarters were the most sumptuous. Women of high rank had private apartments in the Seraglio, whereas new odalisques and eunuchs dwelled in dormitories.

In the fifteenth and sixteenth centuries, young princes received governorships and left the Seraglio with their own harems, decreasing the size of the Seraglio harem from more than one thousand to just a few hundred women. In the seventeenth century, however, when inheritance laws changed and princes were imprisoned in the harem pending succession, it grew again to almost two thousand inhabitants.

political state. It was guarded by two corps of women, each consisting of 500 slave girls from Africa and Turkey, whose function was to protect the chastity of the royal queens and concubines.

The harem of the king or emperor was headed by a eunuch who catered loyally to the king's needs, teaching the harem women how to be beautiful and how to satisfy the ruler sexually and in other ways. The women could spend an entire day adorning themselves with make-up, fragrances, and beautiful clothes.

NON-ISLAMIC HAREMS IN CHINA

Accounts indicate that by the eighth century B.C.E., kings in China kept one queen, three primary consorts, nine wives of second rank, twenty-seven wives of third, fourth, and fifth ranks, and eighty-one concubines of sixth, seventh, and eighth ranks—for a total of 121 women in a harem. Chinese imperial harems also could be much larger, with thousands of women. These huge harems had well-supervised rotating schedules for sex based on the women's menstrual cycles.

Women in the Chinese harems usually were selected from other royal families, unlike the women in the Turkish harems who were primarily prisoners of war or slaves. Nor did they learn the skills taught to the Turkish women, such as dancing, singing, playing musical instruments, and story-telling. However, like the valide sultan in the Turkish harems, the empress dowager in the imperial Chinese harem had considerable power. She chose the emperor's wives and concubines and could help select potential successors if the emperor died. As a member of the older generation, she also had some influence over the emperor's actions.

HAREM-LIKE ARRANGEMENTS IN THE NEW WORLD

Accounts by Franciscan friars in Mexico say that the Aztec emperor Montezuma II (r. 1502–1520) had 4,000 concubines and that each Aztec nobleman had as many women as he could afford, which often numbered in the hundreds for the noblest individuals. Similarly, in Peru, according to Spanish chronicler Garcilaso de la Vega (son of a Spanish governor and Incan princess), Incan kings had houses in every province that contained as many as 1,500 virgins.

HAREMS AS A SOURCE OF POWER

In smaller societies as well, the number of women in harems was clearly a measure of the power wielded by a ruler or chieftain. Successful hunters on the Kalahari Desert in South Africa might have two or three wives rather than just one. In the Amazon, native chieftains had up to ten wives, and in Polynesia—on the islands of Fiji, Samoa, and Tahiti—chiefs usually kept about one hundred women. Meanwhile, in numerous larger realms, the number of women in the royal harems reached into the thousands.

See also: CONCUBINES, ROYAL; CONSORTS, ROYAL; EUNUCHS, ROYAL; LEGITIMACY; MARRIAGE OF KINGS; POLYGAMY, ROYAL.

FURTHER READING

Coco, Carla. *Secrets of the Harem.* New York: Vendome, 1997.

Croutier, Alev Lytle. *Harem: The World Behind the Veil.* New York: Abbeville, 1989.

HAROLD II GODWINSON

(1020–1066 C.E.)

Last Anglo-Saxon king of England (r. 1066), who lost the battle of Hastings (at Senlac Hill) to William, duke of Normandy, in 1066. This defeat, one of the most famous battles in English history, was the first and most decisive event in the conquest of England by the Normans.

Harold was born in 1020 to Godwin, earl of Wessex, and his wife Edith. Although not of royal blood himself, Godwin came from a powerful noble family. He had been the first counselor to King Cnut (r. 1016–1035) and had connected his family through marriages to some of the most powerful families in Northern Europe. Godwin's daughter Edith married King Edward the Confessor (r. 1042–1066) of England, his nephew Sweyn became ruler of Denmark, and his son Tostig became the earl of Northumbria and married Judith, the daughter of the count of Flanders.

Godwin's political power angered and frightened the Norman advisers of Edward the Confessor, who persuaded Edward to depose Godwin from his seat in Wessex in 1051 and confiscate his properties. Godwin and Harold fled to exile in Flanders, but Harold returned in 1052, invading southwestern England. He defeated the king's armies and then was joined by his father in an advance on London.

Despite this action, Edward named Harold as earl of Wessex upon Godwin's death in 1053. Harold followed this honor by conducting a rapid and brilliant military campaign in Wales, ultimately presenting the head of the Welsh king, Gruffydd I (r. 1039–1063), to a frightened and diffident King Edward in 1063.

Just before his death, in January 1066, Edward named Harold as his successor, and the ruling body of Anglo-Saxon nobles—the witenagemot—crowned Harold within a month of the king's death. Meanwhile, Harold's brother Tostig, who had been exiled in 1051 along with Godwin and Harold but had not been called back by either his father or brother, made a secret alliance with Duke William of Normandy and persuaded King Harald III Hardraade of Norway (r. 1045–1066) to attack England in the north.

In a remarkable three-day march, the freshly installed Harold of England led his army from London to York, where they surprised and defeated Tostig's and Harald's forces at the battle of Stamford Bridge on September 25, 1066. During the celebrations following this victory, Harold learned that William of Normandy had landed in Sussex in southern England and was laying waste to the countryside there. Despite advice to rest his men, Harold force-marched to Hastings and met William's forces there.

Though rash and exhausted, Harold was not a foolish leader; he was an experienced and gifted military commander. He positioned his heavy infantry (he had no cavalry or missile weapons) along the top of a ridge named Senlac Hill and waited for William's heavy cavalry to attack. The battle that ensued on October 14, 1066, was long and hard-fought. At one point, a cry went up that William was slain, but this proved false. At another point in the battle, William's Breton infantry broke, but he was able to rally them. As night approached, it seemed that the battle might end in a stalemate—until one of William's archers struck Harold in the eye. Half-blind, Harold staggered through the enemy lines and was hacked to pieces by Norman swords. Harold's death at the battle of Hastings marked the end of over five hundred years of Anglo-Saxon dominion over the British Isles.

See also: ANGLO-SAXON RULERS; EDWARD THE CONFESSOR; ENGLISH MONARCHIES; HARALD III HARDRAADE; WESSEX KINGDOM; WILLIAM I, THE CONQUEROR.

HARUN AL-RASHID (766–809 C.E.)

Fifth caliph (r. 786–809) of the Abbasid dynasty, immortalized in *One Thousand and One Arabian Nights,* a classic of Arabic literature, who ruled the Islamic Empire at the peak of its power.

Harun was the second son of al-Mahdi (775–785), the third Abbasid caliph, and al-Khayzuran, a former slave girl. In 780 and 782, Harun led troops on his father's behalf to reconquer lands previously taken from the caliphate by the rulers of the Byzantine Empire. His campaign was so successful that the Byzantine ruler, the Empress Irene (r. 797–802), agreed as part of the peace treaty to pay a large annual tribute to Baghdad.

Al-Mahdi was so pleased with the military success that Harun came to be known as ar-Rashid (the Upright). While Harun's older brother, al-Hadi, had been named heir, al-Mahdi may have wished to make Harun heir designate. But whether that was the case will never be known, for Al-Mahdi died on a military campaign in 785 before he could do so. When al-Hadi (r. 785–786) died the following year, it was said that Khayzuran, the mother of both princes, had arranged for someone to smother al-Hadi with pillows. Upon the death of his older brother, Harun al-Rashid took the throne.

Upon succeeding to the caliphate, Harun al-Rashid appointed his mother's chief supporter and his own former tutor, Yahya the Barmakid, as his vizier, or chief adviser and administrator. Yahya and his sons held considerable sway in the empire, largely ruling in the name of the caliph, particularly between the death of al-Khayzuran in 789 and their fall from power in 803. As vizier, Yahya was a just and able ruler. Wise and effective, he saw that roads were built and that the provinces prospered.

Harun's large empire—spanning from the Indus River in the east to the Atlantic Ocean coast of North Africa in the west—saw considerable internal conflict. To relieve internal struggles, Harun began a policy of allowing regional dynasties to rule. However, this policy eventually weakened the unity of the empire and led eventually to the fall of the Abbasid dynasty.

Under Harun al-Rashid, the court in Baghdad became known for its lavishness. Learning was encouraged, and poets and musicians were rewarded with generous gifts. Baghdad came to be seen as the center of the civilized world, combining the splendor of great wealth with the flowering of Islamic culture.

In 803, Yahya and the Barmakids fell under Harun's displeasure, although the reason is unclear. Historians have suggested that perhaps Harun felt frustrated by the power of the Barmakids or that he coveted their wealth. Some suggest that the conflict may have involved different factions at court, with the Barmakids favoring a group that Harun wished to suppress. In any event, Harun had the Barmakids imprisoned, and the family's wealth reverted to the throne.

Harun died in 809, having fallen victim to illness while on a military campaign to put down a revolt in Khorasan. His son al-Amin (r. 809–813) succeeded him as caliph. Although Harun al-Rashid presided over a period of unparalleled wealth and culture, he left a kingdom restless with internal struggles that erupted into civil war not long after his death.

See also: ABBASID DYNASTY; CALIPHATES.

HASHEMITE DYNASTY

(ca. 200 C.E.–PRESENT)

Arab dynasty whose members have ruled various parts of the Arabian Peninsula and Mediterranean Middle East, including Syria, Iraq, and Jordan. The ruler of the Hashemite kingdom of Jordan is the only remaining Hashemite monarch.

ORIGINS AND EARLY HISTORY

The Hashemite dynasty originated in pre-Islamic Arabia and traces its origins back to the Arab chieftan Quraysh, supposedly a descendant of the prophets Ismail and Ibrahim (Abraham). Quraysh migrated to Mecca in the second century, and his descendant Qusayy became the leader of Mecca in 480. The dynasty's founder, Hashem, was the grandson of Qusayy and a great-grandfather of the Prophet Muhammad. The Hashemites (also known as the Bani Hashem) are directly descended from the Prophet Muhammad through his daughter Fatima and her husband Ali, the fourth caliph of Islam. The descendants of Ali and Fatima's elder son, Al-Hassan, are known as Sharifs, and it is this branch of the dynasty from which the modern Hashemite rulers are descended. The religious significance of this heritage has played a strong role in underpinning the Hashemite claim to rule large areas of the Islamic Middle East.

Throughout the tenth, eleventh, and twelfth centuries, a number of Sharifian families dominated the Hijaz region of Western Arabia. Although the Ottoman Empire conquered the Hijaz in 1517, the branch of the Hashemite family that had ruled Mecca since 1201 continued to play an important role in its governance as vassals of the Ottoman sultan. In the mid-1800s, the Hashemites were the most prominent and powerful family in Mecca. But by the early twentieth century, the Hijaz was beginning to chafe under the demands of Ottoman rule and Western imperialist expansion. When the Ottoman Empire allied with the Central Powers in World War I, the British Empire lent its support to an Arab nationalist uprising led by the Hashemite sharif Hussein bin Ali, emir of Mecca.

HASHEMITE ASCENDANCY AND MODERN-DAY RULE

The Arab Revolt of 1916 and the end of World War I led to victory for the Hashemites. Hussein's oldest son Ali remained in Mecca as his father's heir, while his second son Faisal, who had fought in the revolt alongside British army officer T. E. Lawrence, became viceroy of Syria and Jordan and then declared himself king of Syria in 1920. However, a secret French-British pact, the Sykes-Picot Agreement, had reserved Syria and Lebanon as areas of French colonial influence, and the French army drove Faisal from the Syrian capital of Damascus. With British support, Faisal later became king of Iraq (r. 1921–1933), and his younger brother Abdullah became the emir of Transjordan.

The Hashemite dynasty held sway over this large territory for only a short period, however. In 1925,

The rulers of modern Jordan are members of the Hashemite dynasty, which dates to the third century C.E. Abdullah II took the throne after his father, King Hussein, died of cancer in 1999. In this photograph, King Abdullah visits his father's grave, along with his wife, brother, and two children.

Ali was deposed as ruler of Mecca by the House of Saud, which still rules Saudi Arabia today. King Faisal I of Iraq died in 1933, and his son and successor, King Ghazi (r. 1933–1939), ruled for only six years. After Ghazi's death, Ali's son Abd al-Illah served as regent for Ghazi's young son, Faisal II, who reached his majority in 1953 and began to rule on his own. In 1958, however, Faisal II was assassinated in a military coup that put an end to the Iraqi monarchy.

The emirate of Transjordan gained full independence from Britain in 1946 and became the Hashemite kingdom of Jordan under the rule of King Abdullah I

Hashemite Kings of Jordan

ABDULLAH BIN AL-HUSSEIN	1921–1951
TALAL BIN ABDULLAH	1951–1952
HUSSEIN BIN TALAL	1952–1999
ABDULLAH II	1999–

(r. 1946–1951). On July 20, 1951, Abdullah was killed while attending prayers at the Dome of the Rock mosque in Jerusalem. His grandson Hussein (r. 1952–1999) narrowly escaped the assassin's bullet and became king in 1952, following a brief period of rule by his mentally unstable father, King Talal (r. 1951–1952).

At his death in 1999, King Hussein of Jordan was succeeded by his oldest son King Abdullah II (r. 1999–), the present ruler of the Hashemite kingdom of Jordan and the head of the Hashemite dynasty today. Abdullah's half-brother Hamzah, son of Hussein and his Arab-American wife Queen Noor, is the crown prince of Jordan and the current heir to the Hashemite throne.

See also: FAISAL I; HUSSEIN I; QURAYSH KINGDOM

FURTHER READING

Milton-Edwards, Beverly, and Peter Jordon. *A Hashemite Legacy.* New York: Brunner-Routledge, 2001.

HASMONEAN KINGDOM

(ca. 104–63 B.C.E.)

Short-lived kingdom of the land of Judea in ancient Palestine during the last century B.C.E.

In 168 B.C.E., the Seleucid king Antiochus IV (r. 175–164 B.C.E.) forbade the Jewish people of Jerusalem from practicing their religion and had altars to Greek gods erected in their temple. He was determined to promote the Hellenization of Judea and suppress Judaism. Antiochus's policies and actions outraged many Jews in Jerusalem, who chafed under Seleucid rule. Led by the Hasmonean family, later known as the Maccabees, some religious Jews left the city and began planning a revolt against Antiochus and the Seleucids.

The Hasmoneans were headed by the father of five sons, an old priest named Mattathias. When Mattathias died in 166 B.C.E., his son Judas, nicknamed Maccabeus ("Hammer-headed"), succeeded him as leader of the Hasmoneans. Judas was a superior general, and, though vastly outnumbered by the opposing Greek and Syrian troops, he managed to gain control of Jerusalem by 164 B.C.E. and became the de facto leader (r. 166–160 B.C.E.).

In 142 B.C.E., Simon (r. 143–135 B.C.E.), another son of Mattathias and a successor of Judas Maccabeus as head of the Hasmonean family, signed a treaty with the Seleucids that gained political independence for Judea. Far from maintaining the ideals on which the Hasmonean revolt had begun, however, the new state that evolved under Simon and his successors soon became as intolerant toward non-Jews as the Seleucids had been to Jews.

Simon's successor, his son John Hyrcanus (r. 135–104 B.C.E.), was an ambitious leader who extended the borders of his domain, conquering the regions of Samaria and Idumaea. He also moved into Galilee and east of the Jordan River. John forced all conquered peoples to convert to Judaism or be expelled from Judea. During John's rule, political factions began to divide the Jews, and the Pharisees, a powerful religious and political party, became the fiercest objectors to the Hasmoneans and Hasmonean rule.

By the time of the rule of Alexander Jannaeus (r. 103–76 B.C.E.), a son of John Hyrcanus, the Hasmonean leaders of Judea were calling themselves kings. Through conquest, Alexander extended his territory farther. He also began a policy of mass slaughter of his rivals. Upon his death in 76 B.C.E., his wife and successor, Salome Alexandra (r. 76–67 B.C.E.), tried to appease the Pharisees, but this tactic came too late.

After Salome Alexandra's death in 67 B.C.E., her sons Hyrcanus II (r. 67–63 B.C.E.) and Aristobulus II (r. ca. 67–63 B.C.E.) engaged in a civil war that lasted until 63 B.C.E. This conflict brought about the demise of Hasmonean rule. With the urging of the Pharisees, the Roman general Pompey entered the war and captured Jerusalem in 63 B.C.E. The Maccabees made a number of efforts to throw off Roman rule but were ultimately unsuccessful. Hyrcanus II, the last Hasmonean leader, was reinstalled as high priest by the Romans, but he was put to death in 30 B.C.E. on charges of treason.

See also: JUDAISM AND KINGSHIP; SELEUCID DYNASTY.

HASSAN II (1929–1999 C.E.)

King of Morocco (r. 1961–1999) who persistently strove to unify his country. Hassan was the son of King Muhammad V (r. 1955–1961), sixteenth ruler of the Alawite dynasty of Morocco. Muhammad named his son Moulay Hassan after his ancestor Hassan I, who ruled Morocco from 1873 to 1894.

The education of young prince Hassan was a blend of traditional and modern that included both Arab-Islamic training and Westernized studies. In 1934, he started religious classes at the Koranic school of the Royal Palace. After finishing primary school in 1941, Hassan studied with prominent Moroccan and foreign teachers at the Imperial College established by his father. Hassan earned the Baccalaureate degree in 1948 and advanced law degrees at the Institute of Higher Judicial Studies in Rabat (then part of the College of Law of Bordeaux, France).

In addition to his formal education, Hassan was introduced early on to royal politics, traditions, and national affairs. As a young prince he participated in several significant historic events, including a trip to Tangiers in 1947, where his father gave a speech to claim Morocco's independence from France. The prince spoke at the event, too, calling on the country's youth to mobilize for the independence of Morocco.

When French colonial authorities exiled his father and the whole royal family—first to Corsica in 1953 and then to Madagascar in 1954—Prince Hassan became his father's political adviser and participated in ensuing negotiations for independence. In 1955, the royal family returned from exile, and Morocco's independence was recognized by France. Hassan continued his political involvement in the newly independent nation, becoming chief of staff of the Royal Armed Forces in 1956. He was named official crown prince of Morocco in 1957.

Hassan became king of Morocco upon his father's death in 1961. Throughout the Cold War era, he pursued a neutral international policy, courting both the United States and communist nations. At the same time, he gained a reputation as a staunch Arab nationalist who focused on unifying the kingdom, even in the face of opposition and several attempted military coups. He was sometimes criticized internationally for his heavy-handed support of social inequality and suppression of popular unrest.

Hassan also is credited with more pacifying deeds. He participated in the Middle East peace process, which culminated in the 1979 peace treaty between Israel and Egypt. He later appeased some of its opponents by shifting Moroccan rule toward a constitutional monarchy and involving dissidents in government. In the early 1990s, Hassan released more than 800 political adversaries and commuted 195 death sentences, actions that helped to improve Morocco's relations abroad.

Hassan II died from a heart attack in 1999. Upon his death, his son, thirty-year-old Crown Prince Sidi Mohammed, a four-star general and coordinator of the Royal Armed Forces, succeeded to the throne as King Mohammed VII (r. 1999–).

See also: MUHAMMAD V

HATSHEPSUT (ca. 1540–1483 B.C.E.)

Wife of Pharaoh Thutmose II (r. 1518–1504 B.C.E.), who is known for pushing aside her husband and taking control of Egypt (r. 1503–1483 B.C.E.), even referring to herself as pharaoh or king.

Hatshepsut was the favored daughter of Thutmose I (r. 1524–1518 B.C.E.), third pharaoh of the Eighteenth dynasty of ancient Egypt, and Queen Ahmose. Well educated and intelligent, Hatshepsut showed a facility for handling affairs of state, and her father came to rely upon her advice and managerial skills during his reign. When Thutmose I neared death, he decided that Hatshepsut would be co-regent with his heir, her brother Thutmose II. Accordingly, she and her brother were wed, as was required by Egyptian pharaonic tradition. Hatshepsut gave birth to a daughter, Neferure, who died young. She produced no sons to inherit the throne.

Accustomed from her youth to exercising the judgment of a pharaoh and indulged in her administrative skills by her father, Hatshepsut was impatient with her assigned role as helpmeet to her husband. By the second year of Thutmose II's reign, she succeeded in shouldering him aside and taking full authority over the empire. When her husband died around 1504 B.C.E., there was no one of suitable age and royal status to succeed to the throne except Thutmose III (r. 1504–1450 B.C.E.), an infant son of Thutmose II and a secondary wife, Isis. Hatshepsut was named regent.

For a short while, Hatshepsut acted according to expectations, ruling the country but acknowledging that she was only acting in behalf of young Thutmose III. However, when he became old enough to challenge her right to rule, she took steps to retain power. She began making extravagant claims: that she was the actual daughter of Amun, the sun-god

One of the great female pharaohs of Ancient Egypt, Hatshepsut devoted much of her energy to building monuments, including her mortuary temple. Dramatically situated, it lies at the head of a valley, surrounded by high cliffs and a peak known as the "Lover of Silence."

and that Amun had decreed that she should be pharaoh. She sent Thutmose into the military, perhaps hoping that he would be distracted by the excitement of war and forget about claiming his throne. With Thutmose III out of the way, Hatshepsut began assuming the ritual responsibilities and the ritual attire of a male king. In 1503 B.C.E., she went so far as to formally declare herself pharaoh.

Hatshepsut had the backing of the priesthood dedicated to Amun, as well as the full support of the royal court. No doubt the religious hierarchy was gratified by her support of ritual and her aggressive policy of temple building. Indeed, Hatshepshut seems to have devoted a large proportion of her energies to a program of monument-building, most of which was directly aimed at glorifying her name and her rule. Her reign coincided with a period of internal stability within Egypt, but she was perhaps too inattentive to the needs of the larger empire. Imperial control over the more distant provinces was weakening, and it would later fall to Thutmose III to reclaim them.

Hatshepshut never willingly relinquished power to Thutmose III, and this may have been her undoing. Around 1458 B.C.E., she died unexpectedly, and some think that Thutmose III may have had a hand in hastening her death. It does appear that he strongly resented her long monopoly over the pharaohship, for immediately after she died he began an aggressive campaign to destroy all her monuments, replacing them with monuments celebrating his military prowess. The powerful queen was nonetheless buried with the honors owed to a pharaoh, and her mummified remains were laid to rest next to her father's in the Valley of the Kings.

See also: EGYPTIAN DYNASTIES, ANCIENT (EIGHTEENTH TO TWENTY-SIXTH); THUTMOSE III.

FURTHER READING

Breasted, James H. *A History of Egypt from the Earliest Times to the Persian Conquest.* New York: Bantam Books, 1964.

Gardiner, Alan Henderson, Sir. *Egypt of the Pharoahs.* Oxford: Clarendon Press, 1961.

HAWAIIAN KINGDOMS

Kingdoms on the Polynesian-populated archipelago of Hawaii in the eastern Pacific, ruled by numerous chieftains before being united in 1795.

Originally settled in the fifth century by Polynesians migrating from the Marquesas Islands, Hawaii experienced a wave of immigration from Tahiti in the ninth and tenth centuries. Skilled seamen, these early Polynesian immigrants navigated by observing nature, following the stars, sea currents, and migrating birds. Once established in the lush and secluded setting of the Hawaiian Islands, the new immigrants found little reason to return to their homelands, and they soon developed a thriving and individualized Hawaiian culture.

Although the islands were rich in food resources, material production was limited by the lack of metal deposits, clay for pottery, and land animals large enough to serve as beasts of burden. The Hawaiians ingeniously used the abundant shell, wood, stone, and bone, applying them to techniques for island navigation—the construction of double and outrigger canoes. A strong and inventive people, the Hawaiians honed their military skills through athletic contests, and they developed an advanced method of calendar-keeping.

Because early Hawaiians had no written language, current knowledge of the islands' history is limited to the rich Hawaiian oral tradition and to the scattered impressions of the Europeans, who first reached the islands in 1778. Captain James Cook, who explored much of the Pacific in the name of the British Crown, landed on Kauai Island in that year, and he communicated successfully with the local people, who treated him as a god. When Cook returned to Hawaii the next year, however, he was killed in a skirmish with the islanders at Kealakekua Bay.

UNIFYING THE ISLANDS

The Hawaii encountered by Captain James Cook was under the shifting control of various warring chieftains. As an archipelago, it was relatively easy for an ambitious chieftain to gain control of an island, but the conquest of the entire island chain was a task suitable only for a great conqueror.

In 1795, Kamehameha I the Great (r. 1795–1819) of the island of Hawaii emerged as this conqueror. Kamehameha swept swiftly with his troops across Maui and Molokai, and he then utilized European sharpshooters to defeat the king of Oahu. For the first time, Hawaii was a unified state, and the Hawaiian monarchy was definitively established.

Over the following years, Kamehameha strengthened Hawaiian autonomy even as the islands were faced with an onslaught of deadly foreign disease, religion, and trade interests. Although he maintained the traditional *kapu* legal system, which meted out harsh punishments, Kamehameha also worked to prevent the exploitation of the poor. He established Honolulu as Hawaii's leading trading center, and he shrewdly instituted a governmentally controlled sandalwood monopoly that soon generated a significant fortune for the newly united kingdom.

CONSTITUTIONAL GOVERNMENT AND FOREIGN RULE

By the 1820s, American and European whalers exploiting the rich resources of the Pacific had established outposts on the Hawaiian archipelago.

King Kalakaua was the next-to-last ruler of Hawaii. His attempts to revive various native practices, including the hula dance, were opposed by American settlers on the islands and only contributed to the weakening of the monarchy.

Kamehameha Dynasty

KAMEHAMEHA THE GREAT*	1795–1819
KAMEHAMEHA II	1819–1824
KAMEHAMEHA III	1825–1854
KAMEHAMEHA IV	1854–1863
KAMEHAMEHA V	1863–1872
LUNALILO	1873–1874
KALAKAUA	1874–1891
LILIUOKALANI*	1891–1893

*Indicates a separate alphabetical entry.

Christian missionaries soon followed, and they developed strengthening relationships with the royal family, which influenced the development of a constitutional government under the leadership of King Kamehameha III (r. 1825–1854).

Great Britain, France, and the United States soon made formal acknowledgments of Hawaiian independence. Foreign populations in the islands continued to grow, however, and with them foreign influence increased as well. Foreign-held corporations gained an increasing stronghold on the Hawaiian economy. In the late 1800s, King David Kalakaua (r. 1874–1891), attempting to limit foreign influence, revived a number of native Hawaiian practices, including the hula dance, which had been repressed by Christian missionaries because it was considered lewd and too sexual.

Powerful sugar barons, concerned with what they saw as Kalakaua's excesses, began to build private armies, uniting under the name of the Hawaiian League. In 1891, Kalakaua's sister, Liliuokalani (r. 1891–1917), succeeded to the Hawaiian throne and promptly prepared to proclaim a new constitution that would strengthen the power of the monarchy. Before she could do so, however, American businessmen seized control of the Hawaiian Supreme Court, declared a provisional American government, and named businessman Sanford Dole as governor. They appealed to the United States government for annexation, even as Queen Liliuokalani appealed to the U.S. government as well, seeking help against the

business interests on the islands. Responding to her appeal, U.S. President Grover Cleveland declared that the queen should be reinstated.

The sugar barons, unhappy with the order from the president, ignored it, and placed Liliuokalani under house arrest. To escape continued imprisonment, she signed a formal abdication in 1895, ending the Hawaiian monarchy. (Liliuokalani later claimed that her abdication was invalid because it was coerced.) Nevertheless, Sanford Dole continued as governor, and in 1900, as American interest in the Pacific increased, the United States formally annexed Hawaii.

See also: KAMEHAMEHA I, THE GREAT; LILIUOKALANI; SOUTH SEA ISLAND KINGDOMS.

FURTHER READINGS

Daws, Gavan. *Shoal of Time: A History of the Hawaiian Islands.* Honolulu: University of Hawaii Press, 1974.

HEALING POWERS OF KINGS

Kings have always been considered superior beings with powers and talents that separate them from the masses. In medieval Europe, many people believed that kings possessed the power to heal illness merely by touching the sick. This belief was shared by a number of European nations, including France, England, Hungary, and Spain.

In France, belief in the healing powers of the Royal Touch existed for at least 1,300 years, from the sixth to the nineteenth centuries. At coronations and on certain holy days, the sick would line up to receive a touch from the king. The French monarchs were believed to be able to cure numerous diseases, such as epilepsy and scrofula (tuberculosis of the lymphatic glands), which was known as the king's evil. The French practice was extremely widespread. For example, Louis XIV (r. 1643–1715) touched 1,600 people at Versailles in a single day.

In England, the practice of the king's touch dates back at least as far as Henry I (r. 1100–1135). The Norman conquest imported all things French to England—language, music, customs—including the belief in the healing powers of the king. English kings were believed to have the power to cure the king's evil. The practice continued throughout the Middle

Ages. In the sixteenth century, those who received the king's touch were given an angel coin, known as a touchpiece.

The king's touch was especially practiced by the Stuart monarchs of the seventeenth century—James I (r. 1603–1625), Charles I (r. 1625–1649), Charles II (1660–1685), James II (r. 1685–1688). The Stuarts were highly absolutist and believed strongly in the divine right of kings. Perhaps the height of Stuart healing came after the Restoration of Charles II in 1660. Although Charles supported scientific research through the Royal Society of England, he also administered the king's touch to enormous crowds of the sick within his realm.

The practice of the king's touch came to an end with the end of the Stuart dynasty. When the absolutist, Catholic monarch James II was forced out of England in the Glorious Revolution, a new era of British history was inaugurated. Kingship became less the choice of God and more the choice of the people, as the British people selected the Protestant William of Orange to take over the throne as William III (r. 1689–1702). William abolished the king's touch; it was resurrected briefly under another Stuart, Queen Anne (r. 1702–1714), but ended for good with the accession of the Hanoverian dynasty in the early eighteenth century.

See also: BOURBON DYNASTY; CHARLES I; CHARLES II; CURSES, ROYAL; DIVINE RIGHT; DIVINITY OF KINGS; JAMES I OF ENGLAND; JAMES II; LOUIS XIV; ROYAL CURSES; STUART DYNASTY; WILLIAM AND MARY.

FURTHER READING

Bloch, Marc. *The Royal Touch: Sacred Monarchy and Scrofula in England and France.* Trans. J. E. Anderson. New York: Dorset Press, 1990.

HEAVENS AND KINGSHIP

The idea that a ruler has a special relationship with the heavens. The idea of a relationship between the heavens and kingship is as old as humanity. In his 1936 anthropological study, *Kingship,* A. M. Hocart claimed: "The earliest known religion is a belief in the divinity of kings." Some scholars believe that earthly kingship developed in imitation of the rulership of the gods; others suggest that religions conceived of divine authority from the example of earthly kings. No matter which came first, the king

or the heavens, the relationship between the two has been expressed in many ways.

RULERS AND THE SKY

In the mythologies of many societies, royal dynasties trace their origin to a king born of a god. Sometimes the god takes the form of an animal to mate with a mortal woman. In Greek myth, for example, the god Zeus transformed himself into a swan to mate with Leda, who gave birth to Helen of Troy, the queen of Sparta.

Some kings are the result of a virgin birth, or a birth without human intervention. For example, the mother of Yu the Great, the legendary founder of China's first ruling family, the Xia dynasty (2205–1766 B.C.E.), was impregnated by swallowing a falling star that turned into a seed.

At times, the ruler is said to be born of a goddess. The Greek goddess Aphrodite had a son, Aeneas, by Anchises, prince of Troy. Aeneas married the daughter of the king of Latium and became the ancestor of the ancient Romans. For thousands of years, every Japanese emperor and empress has claimed descent from the first king, Nagini, who is said to be the grandson of the goddess Amaterasu.

Some kings claimed to be descended from the sun, moon, or planets. Beginning with the Fifth dynasty (ca. 2544–2407 B.C.E.), Egyptian pharaohs were regarded as sons of the sun-god Re. So strong was the relationship between heavenly bodies and kingship that in societies all over the world, kings determined the solar or lunar calendar and the seasons of the year.

Some rulers regarded as human during their lives were thought to become divinities after death. The Roman emperor Augustus (r. 27 B.C.E.–14 C.E.), for example, was called *Divi Filius,* or "son of the Divine," after his death. Many later Roman emperors were also declared gods.

RULERS AS PRIESTS AND INTERCESSORS

Not all kings were regarded as divine beings, but they all had divine sanction. In ancient Babylonia, kings interceded with the gods as leaders of the people. The people of ancient Mesopotamia believed that the moon-god Sin invested the king and gave him his scepter. The first rulers of ancient China and Japan were shamans who could communicate with spirits and act as mediators between the human and spirit worlds.

In some cultures there was a dual kingship, or partition between "sky kings" and "earthly kings." In ancient Sparta, for example, there were two kings: one king headed the cult of the celestial Zeus, and the other king headed the cult of the Lakedaimonian, or earthly Zeus. In many cultures, the sky king would be responsible for the creation of the calendar and giving of the law, while the earthly king executed the laws and acted as chief warrior.

Whether they were regarded as semidivine beings or representative of the people, kings frequently fulfilled a priestly function as intercessors between heaven and earth, even in societies that had a separate religious priesthood. The Egyptian pharaoh was the chief priest; the priests who actually performed the rites merely stood in for him. The Roman emperors served as *pontifex maximus*, or high priest.

In some cases, the priests themselves gave the king his power. At first, the ancient Israelites recognized God alone as their king, although they did have charismatic religious and tribal leaders in Abraham, Moses, the judges, and the prophets. The Israelites eventually asked the prophet Samuel to appoint a king for them "as other nations have." Samuel anointed first Saul (r. ca. 1020–1010 B.C.E.) and later David (r. ca. 1010–970 B.C.E.) as king.

In the Old Testament, the king, like the Israelite nation itself, was sometimes called son of God (understood symbolically), but more often was called his servant. The Israelites lived in expectation of the Messiah, or "Anointed One," a king who would bring in an age of peace. Christians came to regard Jesus Christ as the Messiah.

In Christian countries in medieval Europe, rulers became priest-kings after the example of Christ through anointing by a bishop. The association between kings and gods persisted in the Renaissance and later periods, although the understanding became symbolic rather than literal. For example, the popularity of Greek mythology and the sun-god Apollo led the French to call King Louis XIV (r. 1643–1715) the Sun-King.

See also: CHRISTIANITY AND KINGSHIP; EARTH AND SKY, SEPARATION OF; ENTHRONEMENT, RITES OF; MYTH AND FOLKLORE.

FURTHER READING

Benard, Elisabeth, and Beverly Moon, eds. *Goddesses Who Rule.* New York: Oxford University Press, 2000.

Perry, John Weir. *Lord of the Four Quarters: The Mythology of Kingship.* New York: Paulist, 1991.

HEBREW KINGS (ca. 1020–587 B.C.E.)

Rulers of three ancient Middle Eastern kingdoms, each of which was created on the basis of religious beliefs.

Much of what is known about the history of the Hebrews comes from the Old Testament of the Bible. Around 1100 B.C.E., a group of twelve Hebrew tribes, ruled by persons called judges, had settled in Palestine in the hills west of the Jordan River and formed a unified kingdom for security.

Hebrew kingdoms remained in the region of Palestine for nearly five hundred years, and throughout that time there were a total of forty-two Hebrew kings. Although the people of these kingdoms were united by a common belief in the god Yahweh, there was much that the different Hebrew tribes did not agree on, and divisions among them were common.

THE KINGDOM OF ISRAEL

Saul (r. ca. 1020–1010 B.C.E.), a leader of the Hebrew tribe of Benjamin, was appointed the first king of what was called the kingdom of Israel around 1020 B.C.E. Saul was seen by some as too weak to be a good leader, and he suffered periodically from depression. Throughout his reign, Saul dealt with the squabbling of those tribes dissatisfied with his rule. Yet, he created an army for Israel, kept the threat of the Hebrew enemy, the Philistines, at bay, and even managed to expand the kingdom's territory to include the highlands on either side of the Jordan River.

Saul was killed by the Philistines in battle and was succeeded by David (r. ca. 1010–970 B.C.E.) around 1010 B.C.E. David and his son, King Solomon (r. ca. 970–931 B.C.E.), reigned at the height of Hebrew power. David strengthened the army, eliminated the threat from the Philistines, and conquered more territory eastward and northward. He also captured the city-state of Jerusalem from the Jebusites, a rival hill tribe of the Hebrews. David had greater success than Saul at uniting all the Hebrew tribes into a cohesive kingdom.

With its position on the Mediterranean Sea coast, the kingdom of Israel controlled vital trading routes that brought it great wealth. David established a trading alliance between Israel and the Phoenician city-state of Tyre in the north, and Israel was given access to Tyre's talented shipbuilders.

David's son and successor Solomon continued and

expanded the work of his father. Under Solomon, the kingdom of Israel became a wealthy and powerful force in the region, and the king's leadership skills became firmly established. This is confirmed by the biblical story in which the queen of Sheba called upon Solomon to seek his wise advice.

Solomon doubled the size of the city of Jerusalem and turned it into a grandiose and sophisticated city with many new buildings. His largest construction project was a royal palace and temple on the top of Mount Zion, known as Solomon's Temple. By claiming this high site in Jerusalem for a temple to the God Yahweh, he was claiming the city for the Hebrew people.

To finance this ambitious growth, however, Solomon taxed the Israeli people heavily; this became a divisive issue in the kingdom. Upon Solomon's death around 931 B.C.E., his son Rehoboam (r. ca. 930–914 B.C.E) ascended the throne. However, when Rehoboam made it clear that he would continue his father's policies and not reduce the tax burden, many people not loyal to the Davidic dynasty revolted. The kingdom of Israel was then divided into two lesser kingdoms: the kingdom of Israel in the north, with Jeroboam I (r. ca. 931–910 B.C.E.) as its first king and the kingdom of Judah in the south, with Rehoboam as ruler. Neither was to regain the glory of the united kingdom of their predecessors.

THE SECOND KINGDOM OF ISRAEL

King Omri (r. ca. 885–874 B.C.E.) of Israel brought a period of stability to the land, during which peace was made with King Asa (r. ca. 911–871 B.C.E.) of Judah after years of fighting. Treaties also were signed with neighboring countries, and some expansion of Israel's territory was initiated.

Omri's son and successor, King Ahab (r. ca. 874–853 B.C.E.), maintained the stability brought about by his father, and the reigning years of Omri and Ahab marked the peak of power and glory for the second kingdom of Israel. Upon Ahab's death, the country would never again regain its footing and was subsequently defeated by the powerful Assyrian Empire in 722 B.C.E.

THE KINGDOM OF JUDAH

It was under King Uzziah (r. ca.766–740 B.C.E.) that the kingdom of Judah reached the height of its prosperity, largely as a result of coastal trade. The Babylonians finally conquered Judah under King Jehoiachin (r. ca. 598–597 B.C.E.) in 597 B.C.E. and then deposed the king and placed Zedekiah (r. ca. 597–587 B.C.E.) on the throne. When Zedekiah rebelled less than ten years later, the Babylonians responded by completely destroying Jerusalem and ended the kingdom of Judah.

See also: ASSYRIAN EMPIRE; DAVID; ISRAEL, KINGDOMS OF; JUDAH, KINGDOM OF; JUDAISM AND KINGSHIP; SOLOMON.

FURTHER READING

Alpher, Joseph, ed. *Encyclopedia of Jewish History.* New York: Facts on File, 1986.

Armstrong, Karen. *Jerusalem: One City, Three Faiths.* New York: Alfred A. Knopf, 1996.

Hitti, Philip K. *The Near East in History: A 5000 Year Story.* Princeton, NJ: D. Van Nostrand, 1961.

HEIAN PERIOD (794–1185 C.E.)

A golden period in Japanese history coinciding with the ascendancy of the Fujiwara family. The period dates from 794, when the imperial capital was moved from Nara to Heian-kyo (present-day Kyoto) under Emperor Kammu (781–806), to 1185, when Minamoto no Yoritomo (1192–1199) gained control of the Japanese imperial court and inaugurated the Kamakura period.

The Heian period is known as the classical period of Japanese culture—the fountainhead of art and literature and the zenith of artistic refinement. It was a period dedicated to form and perfection both intellectually and artistically. The period was also a glorious historic epoch that led to the rise of the equally historic shogunates, in which warrior lords ruled while emperors sat on the imperial throne.

The world's first novel, *The Tale of Genji* (ca. 1004), appeared during the Heian period. Written by Murasaki Shikibu, an educated and distinguished lady of the imperial court, the story celebrates the wealth and refinement of aristocratic life in Japan. It underlines the fact that the role of the imperial court was by that time limited to ceremonial and cultural affairs, and emperors had little political power.

From the ninth to eleventh centuries, Japan was largely at peace. The Fujiwara regents led lives of great brilliance at court, drawing immense wealth from their government posts. The Fujiwara sustained this brilliance by the stabilization of agricultural practices, including control over peasant labor; by cohesive social values derived from Buddhist and Shinto beliefs and aristocratic traditions; and by the established separation of the elite from other Japanese. This class distinction

The Heian Shrine in Kyoto, Japan, was built in 1895 to commemorate the founding of the capital there 1,100 years earlier. It is dedicated to the first and last emperors to rule from Kyoto, Kammu, and Komei. Shrine buildings replicate those of the ancient imperial palace in two-thirds scale.

was codified in the Taika Reforms of 645, which established a new government and administrative system largely influenced by the Chinese.

As China's T'ang dynasty (618–907) declined, the Japanese began to withdraw into themselves, believing they had nothing more to learn from China. They therefore ended diplomatic contacts with China in 894 and closed their foreign embassies. This withdrawal also removed potential destabilizing influences from abroad. Nevertheless, destabilizing forces were already at work within Japan. From 743 onward, newly reclaimed land had become the property of the reclaimer. During the Heian era, this practice supported the further creation of *shoen*, or large medieval fiefdoms. Absentee ownership became common, since aristocratic landowners preferred to be in the capital near the imperial court. Provincial families thus accrued power as local managers of the *shoen* and as designated tax collectors for landed families. At the same time, provincial branches of the aristocratic families, including the Fujiwara, built up their own private estates.

The expansion of the private estates by the elite discredited central government authority and encouraged territorial clashes. By the twelfth century, there was constant conflict among Japan's powerful families, and local power belonged to those who assembled the most armed men. The continuous civil warfare of that century was aggravated by the growing involvement of the *bushi* (warriors) or *samurai* (retainer) in the affairs of the imperial government. Many of these contending forces were controlled by offshoot branches of the powerful Fujiwara family or the imperial family.

During the late Heian period, two rival clans—the Taira and Minamoto—vied for control of Japan. As the powers of these clans grew, the Fujiwara began controlling the emperor more closely. In 1155, however, the succession to the throne fell vacant, and the naming of Go-Shirakawa (r. 1155–1158) set off a small revolution called the Hogen Disturbance, which was quelled by the Taira and Minamoto clans. This marked a turning point in Japanese history as the power to determine the affairs of state passed to the warrior clans.

In 1180, a samurai named Kiyimori forced the emperor Takakura (r. 1168–1180) from the throne and installed the emperor's son, Antoku (r. 1180–1185), as ruler. This action led to a civil war among powerful warrior clans and ushered in a feudal age in Japan. In a great battle in 1185, Antoku was killed. His death marked the end of the Heian period and the beginning of the Kamakura period, during which Japan was controlled by a military dictatorship centered at the city of Kamakura.

ROYAL PLACES

MOUNT HIEI

In 788, the Buddhist monk Saichō, now known as Dengyo-Daishi, founded a small temple on Mount Hiei located near present-day Kyoto. This temple was transformed from a small, quiet religious site in a remote area to one of the most powerful Buddhist monasteries of its time, influencing Japanese religion and politics for centuries.

Saichō studied Buddhism in Nara, then the imperial capital, and became a full monk at the age of nineteen. Soon after, he left for the remote area of Mt. Hiei to meditate and study with local holy men, where he built a small temple and lived in solitude.

The Emperor Kammu, weary of the political influence of the Buddhist monks in Nara, had moved the imperial court from Nara to Nagaoka in 784. Nagaoka proved unsuitable, and Kammu decided on Heian-kyo (Kyoto) as the new location for an imperial city, close to Mt. Hiei.

The ritual to purify the ground for the new capital took place in 793 and was performed by Saichō, as Kammu favored Buddhist monks who lived in the countryside and did not aspire to politics. Saichō so impressed the emperor that Kammu sent him to China to pursue his Buddhist studies there.

When he returned, Saichō brought the teachings of what would become known as the Tendai School of Buddhism, one of the most influential schools of Buddhism in the history of Japan. A monastery was established at Mt. Hiei and it soon flourished with the support of Emperor Kammu, who designated it as the empire's chief center of learning with Tendai Buddhism as the imperial religion.

Mt. Hiei's chief purpose was the training of monks, but that soon evolved as some monks returned to the imperial city and worked in positions in the government or the imperial court. At its peak, Mt. Hiei reached its greatest influence in the ninth through eleventh centuries, when it was made up of thousands of buildings and housed a university, also supporting its own standing army of militant monks.

In 1571, Oda Nobunaga, the unifier of Japan during the Warring States period, razed the monastery on Mt. Hiei, slaughtering its occupants and destroying its political influence. Mt. Hiei still exists today as a Tendai monastery and popular tourist attraction.

See also: FUJIWARA DYNASTY; KAMAKURA SHOGUNATE; NARA KINGDOM.

FURTHER READING

Brogan, Robert. *Sugawara No Michizane and the Early Heian Court.* Honolulu: University of Hawaii Press, 1994.

HELLENISTIC DYNASTIES

(ca. 312–30 B.C.E.)

Four Greek-based dynasties that ruled the ancient Middle East after the death of the Macedonian conqueror, Alexander the Great (r. 336–323 B.C.E.), and until the rise of the Roman Empire.

The first decades immediately following the death of Alexander the Great in 323 B.C.E. were combative ones in the Middle East. The period is called the Hellenistic Age because Greek culture was at the forefront in the Mediterranean and Middle East region. Since Alexander left no heir, his generals battled each other to gain control of his enormous empire.

By around 280 B.C.E., four dynasties controlled most of Alexander's former territory, with the former generals assuming the title of king for their region. The Ptolemaic dynasty of Egypt, the Seleucid dynasty of Syria, the Antigonid dynasty of Macedonia, and the much less influential Attalid dynasty of Pergamum held power almost continuously until the Romans began to gain control of the area in the late second century B.C.E.

Though always separate countries, the Hellenistic

dynasties of Egypt and the Middle East maintained a sense of unity through their shared Greek culture. Use of a common language, Greek, facilitated trade and cultural exchanges among the dynasties.

PTOLEMAIC DYNASTY

Founded in 306 B.C.E. by Alexander's loyal general Ptolemy I Soter (r. 306–282 B.C.E.), the Ptolemaic dynasty of Egypt was the longest-lived of the four dynasties, surviving more than two hundred and fifty years (ca. 306–30 B.C.E). Ptolemy established his capital at Alexandria, the city at the mouth of the Nile River founded by Alexander the Great, which became the epitome of a Hellenistic city.

The Ptolemaic dynasty ushered in many changes to the Egyptian way of life, including the transition to Greek as the language of the government. The Ptolemies were harsh in their treatment of the Egyptians for their own gain: they taxed the citizens heavily; they forced farmers to sell their crops to the state, which, in turn, sold them to other countries at huge profits; and they often treated native Egyptians as lower-class citizens.

The Ptolemaic kings of Egypt all took the name Ptolemy. They and a series of queens ruled the dynasty, sometimes separately and sometimes jointly. Much of the monarch's money was used to build an army and navy to maintain ongoing skirmishes over territory with the Seleucid and Antigonid dynasties.

In reaction to the harsh treatment of the Ptolemies, the people of Egypt mounted revolts on several occasions, disrupting the country and weakening the government. The last ruler of the Ptolemaic dynasty, Cleopatra VII (r. 51–30 B.C.E.), killed herself rather than submit to the Romans, and after her death in 30 B.C.E. Rome annexed Egypt as a Roman province.

SELEUCID DYNASTY

Another of Alexander's generals, Seleucus I Nicator (r. 312–281 B.C.E.), was the founder of the Seleucid dynasty (312–64 B.C.E.), which ruled over the easternmost area of the former Macedonian Empire. The Seleucid kings, most of whom took the name Seleucus or Antiochus, maintained a western capital in Antioch in northern Syria and an eastern capital in Seleucia on the Tigris River in Mesopotamia (present-day Iraq).

Although they had no city whose culture could match that of Alexandria in Egypt, the Seleucids actively recruited immigrants from Greece and Macedonia to colonize their territory in order to foster the development of Hellenistic culture. Since they treated these settlers with fairness, the Seleucid kings garnered their loyalty and were able to summon an army larger than any other of the Hellenistic states.

The territory controlled by the Seleucid dynasty grew and shrank over the years. At its height around 200 B.C.E., the Seleucid Empire stretched from the eastern Mediterranean coast to India. But the Seleu-

ROYAL RELATIVES

SISTER-WIVES

The last hundred or so years of the Ptolemaic dynasty were notable for the customary marriages between the king and his sister, often with the queen or the queen mother ruling with the king as co-regent. Most famous of these co-regents was Cleopatra, or more correctly Cleopatra VII, who consecutively married and shared the throne with two of her younger brothers (both of whom were killed) and then with her son. Intensely power-hungry, the Ptolemies were involved in frequent palace revolts and assassinations, with many kings moving out of power only to return again as king some years later. The later Ptolemaic period is thus confusing, and historians are not always in agreement on the order, duration, and sharing of the reigns of kings and queens.

cids were almost constantly at war, both with their own provincial leaders and with the other dynasties in the region. The one area they ruled continuously was northern Syria. Eventually, however, skirmishes with the Romans led to Syria's annexation as a Roman province in 64 B.C.E., bringing the Seleucid dynasty to an end.

ANTIGONID DYNASTY

Antigonus the One-Eyed, another of Alexander's generals, gained control of Macedonia after Alexander's death. As Antigonus I (r. 306–301 B.C.E.), he and his son Demetrius I (r. 306–287 B.C.E.) managed to retain their power and secure the founding of the Antigonid dynasty (ca. 306–168 B.C.E.). Since their territory had been through numerous battles and had lost many citizens who emigrated to other Hellenic countries, they ruled over a weakened and somewhat demoralized state.

The army of Macedonia was significantly smaller than either of the other two large Hellenistic powers in the region. Yet, the Antigonids had to fend off an invasion by the Gauls in 279 B.C.E. and several incursions by groups from the Balkans. They also had to exert considerable strength to maintain control over Greece, which resented the rule of the Macedonians.

The Antigonids were the first Hellenistic dynasty to fall to the Romans. In 168 B.C.E., after enduring three wars with the Romans, the Antigonid ruler, King Perseus (r. 179–168 B.C.E.), was overthrown and the dynasty was dissolved. Two years later, in 148 B.C.E., Macedonia was made a Roman province.

ATTALID DYNASTY

In 283 B.C.E., Philetaerus (r. 282–263 B.C.E.) of the Attalid family of Pontus seized the fortress of Pergamum in Asia Minor (present-day Turkey) and asserted his independence from the Seluecids. His son and successor, Eumenes I (r. 263–241 B.C.E.), proclaimed Pergamum a kingdom, but it was his son, Attalus I Soter (r. 241–197 B.C.E.), who was the first Attalid ruler to call himself king.

The kings of the Attalid dynasty (ca. 283–133 B.C.E.) added some Greek cities to their territory and eventually ruled much of western Asia Minor. They maintained a centralized power and taxed their subjects heavily to finance their army. But the Attalids also used their resources to expand the kingdom's culture, which they considered of great importance. They built an extensive library at Pergamum and encouraged art and other creative endeavors.

The Attalid dynasty never became a major power in the region. Throughout their reign, the Attalids felt threatened by the Seleucids, who wanted to regain control of all of Asia Minor. The last Attalid king, Attalus III Philometer (r. 139–133 B.C.E.), left Pergamum to the Roman Empire when he died in 133 B.C.E. It is thought that he did this in order to prevent a war with the Romans, which could not be won and which would cost many of his subjects' their lives.

See also: ALEXANDER III, THE GREAT; EGYPTIAN DYNASTIES, PERSIAN, HELLENISTIC, AND ROMAN; MACEDONIAN EMPIRE; PERGAMUM KINGDOM; PTOLEMAIC DYNASTY; PTOLEMY I; ROMAN EMPIRE; SELEUCID DYNASTY; SYRIAN MONARCHY.

FURTHER READING

Mostyn, Trevor, ed. *The Cambridge Encyclopedia of the Middle East and North Africa.* New York: Cambridge University Press, 1988.

Perry, Glenn E. *The Middle East: Fourteen Islamic Centuries.* 3rd ed. Upper Saddle River, NJ: Prentice-Hall, 1997.

HENRY II (1133–1189 C.E.)

King of England (r. 1154–1189), also known as Henry of Anjou and Henry Plantagenet, who founded the English Angevin dynasty, also known as the House of Plantagenet.

Henry II was a brilliant and passionate monarch who expanded the English realm and fathered two future kings of England—Richard I, the Lionheart (r. 1189–1199), and John (r. 1199–1216). He also was responsible for the murder of the archbishop of Canterbury (Thomas à Becket), and was married for thirty-seven years to one of the most remarkable queens in European history, Eleanor of Aquitaine.

EARLY LIFE

The young Henry was well educated by his parents, Matilda, the daughter of King Henry I of England (r. 1100–1135), and Geoffrey IV (r. 1129–1151), the count of Anjou. But Henry's tremendous energy and drive surpassed even his considerable intelligence. At age seventeen, he became duke of Normandy, and at age eighteen he inherited his father's title, count of Anjou. While still a youth, Henry came to the attention of the young queen of France, Eleanor of Aquitaine. In 1152, Eleanor received an annulment from her husband, the pious and unworldly Louis VII (r. 1137–1180), and married the nineteen-year-old Henry, thus making him duke of the enormously wealthy duchy of Aquitaine in southwestern France.

Together, Henry and Eleanor plotted a campaign to gain the English throne. In 1153, Henry invaded England and coerced his cousin, King Stephen (r. 1135–1154), into acknowledging him as heir. Stephen died within the year, leaving Henry, now twenty-one years old, monarch of a vast domain that stretched from Scotland across the English Channel and down the entire length of France to the Mediterranean Sea. In fact, Henry's holdings in France alone were roughly triple the area held by the king of France.

Henry proved himself a worthy ruler of this vast realm. He consolidated royal power, seeking a return of the influence held by Henry I, and established the primacy of his royal courts over local feudal courts. He defined and applied the foundation of what was to become English Common Law in his use of writs, application of juries, and replacement of trial by combat and ordeal with the less spectacular and more fair trial by law.

Henry's legal reforms were not, however, altruistic or far-sighted; they were implemented to strengthen royal power by whatever means at hand. In pursuit of this end, Henry also razed unlicensed castles and struggled with the Church over the power to appoint bishops and dispense other ecclesiastical privileges and benefits.

CONFLICT WITH BECKET

In 1164, Henry signed the Constitutions of Clarendon, which, in defining relations between Church and state, made clear his intent to usurp the Church's control over local ecclesiastical appointments (and Church property). Before the enacting of this law, his lifelong friend and adviser, Thomas à Becket, was his chief collaborator. Henry had even named Becket as archbishop of Canterbury in 1162, certain that he would have an even more potent advocate within the Church. Becket, however, took his new responsibilities (and his new chain of command to the papacy) seriously. With the passage of the Constitutions, Henry found that he had lost an advocate and gained an adversary.

In a moment of anger in 1170, Henry raged against Becket's unyielding stance and muttered "Will no one rid me of this troublesome priest?" Four knights, taking the king at his words, rushed to Becket and murdered the archbishop in his own cathedral in Canterbury. Henry mourned his friend and eventually did public penance for this murder, but his problems with Becket proved to be of little consequence compared to the woes visited upon him by his own family.

A REBELLIOUS FAMILY

Though eleven years his senior, Eleanor bore Henry eight children; the four sons who survived were all strong-willed, troublesome, and ungrateful to their father. Henry, the eldest son, crowned co-regent in 1170, stood to inherit the throne. He remained frustrated in his desire for the throne until his premature death in 1183, and on two occasions prior to that he rebelled openly and savagely against his father.

The founder of the Plantagenet dynasty, Henry II was a brilliant ruler who consolidated royal power and expanded the English realm. His successful administration and notable legal advancements set precedents that had an enduring impact on Western culture.

Geoffrey, to whom the king had given Brittany, likewise plotted with his brother Henry, with his mother, and sometimes with the king of France until he, too, predeceased his beleaguered father in 1186.

Richard, one day to be known as "Lionheart," was his mother's favorite, and, at her urging, Henry gave him the wealthy duchy of Aquitaine. In one of Richard's rebellions, in 1173–1174, he joined with his mother and with William the Lion of Scotland (r. 1165–1214). Henry quickly defeated his opponents and pardoned his son. In the aftermath of this rebellion, however, he chose to sequester his wife away from her sons and the temptations of the world. Eleanor remained locked away in confinement until Henry's death in 1189, when the dutiful Richard freed her.

Henry's youngest son, John Lackland, was his favorite. It was, in fact, Henry's attempts to secure a patrimony for John that caused much of the friction with his other fractious children. Even John, however, joined in a rebellion against his father in 1189, allying with the recently pardoned Richard and King Philip II (r. 1180–1223) of France (the son of Henry's long-time opponent and Eleanor's first husband, Louis VII). With this final betrayal, Henry's energy, fortune, and spirit were spent. Defeated in battle, he died near Tours in France in 1189.

HIS LEGACY

Henry's life and reign are among the most eventful and colorful of any English monarch. His remarkable early achievements, his affair and marriage with the redoubtable Eleanor, his relationship with the brilliant Becket, his tempestuous children—all of these events are rich in history and each of these portions of his story casts a long shadow on the history of Northern Europe. However, it is probably Henry's precedent-setting administrative and legal efforts that have made his reign of such enduring importance in English and, indeed, Western culture.

See also: ANJOU KINGDOM; COMPETITION, FRATERNAL; ELEANOR OF AQUITAINE; JOHN I; LOUIS VII; NORMAN KINGDOMS; PHILIP II, AUGUSTUS; PLANTAGENET, HOUSE OF; RICHARD I, LIONHEART.

FURTHER READING

Gilligham, John, ed. *The Angevin Empire.* 2nd ed. New York: Oxford University Press, 2001.

HENRY IV (ENGLAND)

(1367–1413 C.E.)

King of England (r. 1399–1413), who invaded England in 1399, forced his cousin Richard II (r. 1377–1399) to abdicate, and usurped the throne of England to become the first monarch of the House of Lancaster.

Born in 1367, Henry IV (also called Henry Bolingbroke) was the eldest son of John of Gaunt, the fourth son of King Edward III (r. 1327–1377) of England. John of Gaunt, duke of Lancaster, unscrupulously directed his father, the aging Edward III, for most of the last years of his life. In the process, he became the richest man in England and one of the wealthiest and most powerful men in Northern Europe. Gaunt's son, Henry, was raised in this environment and with expectations of greatness.

When Edward III died in 1377, Henry's ten-year-old cousin, Richard, was crowned king. However, John of Gaunt continued to rule in the young king's name while Henry, a year older than his cousin, remained in the background.

In 1387, however, Henry joined a group of lords who opposed the king and eventually forced him to submit to their rulings. The king, appeased by John of Gaunt, pretended to be reconciled to this humiliation. Henry took the cross and went crusading in Lithuania and Prussia from 1390 to 1392.

Richard II, however, had not forgotten the coercion from Henry and his supporters, and in 1398 he banished Bolingbroke from England for ten years. While Henry was in exile in France, John of Gaunt died, and King Richard confiscated the duke's vast holdings, disinherited Henry, and redistributed the Lancastrian possessions.

Richard II had made few friends among the aristocracy during his reign, and, while he was in Ireland in 1399, Henry returned to England with significant support from the English nobles. He forced Richard to abdicate the throne and imprisoned him. He then had himself crowned as Henry IV, with the approval of Parliament.

Henry faced a series of insurrections after taking the throne, and England remained in turmoil for the next ten years. He fought a succession of challenges from Owen Glendower of Wales, the Percys of Northumberland, and the duke of Norfolk. Even his own son, the future Henry V (r. 1413–1422), plotted to overthrow his father. Henry proved equal to all these difficulties until his health failed. Contemporaries assumed that the king had leprosy, but it may have been syphilis. In 1412, worn out by disease and endless strife, Henry IV reluctantly passed control of the kingdom to his son Henry and died the next year.

See also: EDWARD III; ENGLISH MONARCHIES; LANCASTER, HOUSE OF; RICHARD II.

HENRY IV (FRANCE) (1553–1610 C.E.)

King of France (r. 1589–1610), the first monarch of the Bourbon dynasty, who overcame violence between Protestants and Catholics to achieve peace, prosperity, and strong central government. One of the most popular of all French kings, Henry also ruled the kingdom of Navarre from 1572 to 1610 as Henry III of Navarre.

The son of Antoine of Bourbon and Jeanne d'Albret, the queen of Navarre, Henry was raised as a Protestant and became the leader of the persecuted Huguenots (French Protestants) in 1569. Religious unrest and violence against Protestants in France increased dramatically after the death of Henry II (r. 1547–1559) in 1559, culminating in 1572 with the St. Bartholomew's Night massacre, in which thousands of Protestants were killed by soldiers and angry Catholic mobs. In the aftermath of the massacre, Henry remained a prisoner of the courts of kings Charles IX (r. 1560–1574) and Henry III (r. 1574–1589) until 1576, when he managed to escape after several unsuccessful attempts. Henry then fought in the fifth of France's wars of religion, siding with Protestants and moderate Catholics against the more conservative Catholic forces.

In 1584, Francis, the duke of Anjou and brother of King Henry III, died. This made Henry of Navarre next in the line of succession. The French Catholic forces, led by Duke Henri of Guise, sought to overturn the order of succession. The issue was settled by the War of the Three Henrys, in which Henry of Navarre defeated the forces of King Henry III and then united with the king to defeat the Catholic League led by Henry of Guise.

When Henry III died in 1589, Henry of Navarre took the throne as Henry IV. Even after his succession, Henry continued to be plagued by the Catholic League and by violent unrest. After Protestant victo-

ries over the League's forces at Arques in 1589 and Ivry in 1590, the Catholics besieged Paris with aid from the Spanish.

Henry's conversion to Catholicism in 1593 enabled him to return to Paris, and the next year he began to reunite the kingdom. To unite the opposing religious factions, he used the more inclusive idea of allegiance to the French nation and loyalty to himself as their king. The idea of French nationalism also gained him support when he declared war on Spain (1595) in order to expel the Spanish from southern France. This ended in a French victory in 1598. That same year, Henry granted limited toleration, protection, and territory to the Protestants with the Edict of Nantes.

Henry then began the long process of rebuilding France after many years of religious violence, strengthening and centralizing his government in order to enforce his policies. He supported the development of infrastructure, agriculture, colonization in Canada, and domestic and international commerce (including trade agreements with Spain, England, and the Ottoman Empire). He worked to ensure that even the peasants shared in France's prosperity. During the final years of Henry's reign, France enjoyed the peace and prosperity brought about by these policies.

On May 14, 1610, Henry IV was stabbed to death by a Catholic fanatic who believed that God had appointed him to kill the king. There is some evidence and much speculation that this act was part of a wider conspiracy.

In 1572, Henry had married Margaret of Valois, the sister of King Charles IX, but the marriage was annulled in 1599. He later married Marie de' Medici (in 1600), and the couple had six children: his son and successor Louis XIII (r. 1610–1643); Elizabeth, who married King Philip IV of Spain (r. 1621–1665); and Henriette Marie, who married King Charles I of England (r. 1625–1649). Henry also had a number of illegitimate children by some of his many mistresses.

See also: BOURBON DYNASTY; CHRISTIANITY AND KINGSHIP; FRENCH MONARCHIES; NAVARRE, KINGDOM OF; VALOIS DYNASTY.

FURTHER READING

Greengrass, Mark. *France in the Age of Henri IV: The Struggle for Stability.* 2nd ed. New York: Longman, 1995.

Knecht, R. J. *The Rise and Fall of Renaissance France, 1483–1610*. 2nd ed. Malden, MA: Basil Blackwell, 2001.

Seward, Desmond. *The Bourbon Kings of France*. New York: Barnes & Noble, 1976.

HENRY IV (HRE) (1050–1106 C.E.)

German king (r. 1056–1105) and Holy Roman emperor (r. 1084–1105) who was a central figure in the dispute with the papacy over the issue of investiture, which involved the right to appoint individuals to offices within the Church.

When Emperor Henry III of the Holy Roman Empire and Germany (r. 1039–1056) died in 1056, his six-year-old son Henry was elected to the throne of Germany. Henry's mother, Empress Agnes, served as regent for her young son, but she lost control of the empire.

In Italy at this time, a controversy over investiture was brewing. The papacy objected to the fact that the pope was an appointee of the emperor. Thus the cardinals decided that they would select the pope, asking the emperor merely to approve their selection. Meanwhile, in Germany, the nobles increased their wealth and holdings at the expense of the monarchy. To secure a share of this wealth for the Church, Archbishop Anno of Cologne assumed the regency for Henry in 1062, and he shared it with Archbishop Adalbert of Hamburg-Bremen.

Henry IV came of age in 1066 and regained control of his country from the German nobles. As reigning king of Germany, he first attempted to recover his losses in Saxony, where he put down revolts but developed a reputation for tyranny in the process.

In 1075, Pope Gregory VII issued an investiture decree, which removed the papacy from secular control and claimed the power to appoint all bishops and abbots of the German church. Earlier, the emperor had always appointed these prelates, who served as the chief administrative officials of Germany.

Henry ignored the pope's decree and appointed and invested a new bishop of Milan in 1076. Annoyed by Henry's defiance of the ecclesiastical decree, Pope Gregory threatened to depose Henry, who promptly called a meeting at the German city of Worms and deposed Gregory. Gregory responded by excommunicating Henry from the Church and declaring him deposed. Rebellious German bishops immediately deserted Henry to seek the pope's forgiveness. The German nobles then threatened to depose Henry unless he could receive the pope's absolution by February 1077.

Pope Gregory did grant absolution to Henry, after Henry crossed the Alps in the dead of winter and stood barefoot in the snow for three days, a famous incident known as the Snows of Canossa. But the pope's absolution of Henry did not satisfy the German nobles, who elected Rudolph of Swabia (r. 1077–1080) to replace Henry as king. Civil war followed, during which Gregory recognized Rudolf's title (1080) and renewed Henry's excommunication. Henry, supported by a group of German and Italian bishops, deposed Gregory and elected an anti-pope, Clement III. When Rudolph died in 1080, Henry carried the war to Rome where he installed Clement III as pope and was crowned Holy Roman emperor.

In Germany, Henry stubbornly supported Clement III against Gregory's successors until his son, later Henry V (r. 1105–1125), rebelled against Henry in 1104. In 1105, Henry IV was imprisoned by his son and the rebels and was forced to abdicate. He died in 1106.

See also: CHRISTIANITY AND KINGSHIP; HOLY ROMAN EMPIRE; SALIAN DYNASTY.

FURTHER READING

Robinson, I.S. *Henry IV of Germany, 1056–1106*. New York: Cambridge University Press. 1999.

HENRY VIII (1491–1547 C.E.)

Strong-willed king of England (r. 1509–1547), a member of the house of Tudor, who broke with the Roman Catholic Church and established the Church of England.

The second son of King Henry VII (r. 1485–1509), known in his early years as "Good Prince Hal," was a popular youth, noted for his athletic ability and love of music. As a king, however, Henry was autocratic and unpredictable, often putting his personal desires above the welfare of his kingdom and its people.

Henry was not first in line to the throne, but he became prince of Wales and heir following the death of his elder brother Arthur in 1502. After succeeding to the throne in 1509 upon the death of his father, Henry married his brother Arthur's widow, Katharine of Aragón, the daughter of King Ferdinand II of Aragón (r. 1479–1516) and Queen Isabella of Castile (r. 1474–1504).

Henry reigned at a time when England had yet to become an imperial power. Instead, Spain and Portugal were masters of the seas, with growing empires in the New World, and the Holy Roman Empire was the major power in Europe. Henry sought to limit the influence of the Holy Roman Empire by allying with England's old enemy, France, in 1527, which led to diplomatic and economic reprisals. Meanwhile, domestically, Henry's imposition of new taxes, his heavy-handed rule, and his personal life made him increasingly unpopular as ruler.

PROBLEMS WITH MARRIAGE

Henry VIII is probably best known for his complicated marital history. Katharine of Aragón provided Henry with a daughter, Mary Tudor, in 1516, but she was unable to produce a male heir as well. Henry thus became determined to marry Anne Boleyn, who had been a lady-in-waiting to the queen. At first it seemed that Anne would become a royal mistress, as her older sister Mary had been, but she took advantage of the king's infatuation, insisting he would receive no sexual favors unless he married her. Motivated by passion, as well as a desire for a male heir, Henry sought a divorce from Katharine of Aragón.

Under the laws of the Catholic Church, however, divorce was out of the question. So Henry attempted to have his marriage to Katharine annulled on the grounds that the papal dispensation that had allowed him to marry his dead brother's wife had been illegal. Pope Clement VII established a commission to investigate Henry's request, but it failed to reach a decision. Henry then launched a parliamentary campaign, headed by Thomas Cromwell, the secretary to Cardinal Wolsey, to discredit the Catholic Church in England. Revenues earmarked for Rome were drastically reduced, and members of the English church agreed that all church decisions required royal approval.

Despite these pressures, the pope refused to grant Henry's divorce, but he did allow the appointment of Thomas Cranmer, an English churchman favorable to Henry, as archbishop of Canterbury in

One of the most formidable and influential of the English kings, Henry VIII was known for his strong will and fiery temper. He also is remembered for his rocky marital history and conflicts with the Roman Church. This painting, done in 1536, is one of a number of portraits of Henry VIII painted by the German Renaissance master Hans Holbein the Younger.

1533. Cranmer immediately annulled Henry's marriage to Katharine. Henry, who was already secretly married to Anne Boleyn, made Anne queen and was promptly excommunicated by the pope.

RELIGIOUS REFORMATION

In 1521, Henry had been given the title "Defender of the Faith" by Pope Leo X as a reward for Henry's support against Martin Luther and the Protestant Reformation. Now, however, as a result of Rome's refusal to grant Henry a divorce from Katharine, the king split completely with Rome.

Under the Act of Supremacy (1534), Henry was made head of the Church of England; two years later, in 1536, he also appointed himself head of the Church of Ireland. To minimize opposition to the religious changes from both the clergy and powerful nobles, Henry arranged to have an Act of Succession passed in 1534. Under the Act of Succession, Henry's marriage to Katharine of Aragón was declared retroactively null and void, and Anne Boleyn's offspring became first in line for the throne.

Also in 1534, Henry issued an Act of Treason, which declared that anyone who called the king "a heretic, schismatic, tyrant, infidel, or usurper of the crown" was guilty of high treason. Under this act, Henry was able to execute his former lord chancellor, Sir Thomas More, who objected to his break with Rome. To further limit opposition from English clerics and win support among the nobility, Henry closed the monasteries throughout England and granted some of the property to the landed gentry.

Meanwhile, Henry's marriage to Anne Boleyn did not last long. Anne provided a daughter, Elizabeth, but, like Katharine, failed to produce a male heir. Accused and convicted of committing adultery and of being involved in an incestuous relationship with her own brother, Anne Boleyn was executed in 1536. Within two weeks of her death, Henry married Jane Seymour, his mistress, who had been a lady-in-waiting to both Katharine of Aragón and Anne Boleyn. Much to Henry's pleasure, Jane produced the desired male heir, Edward VI, in 1537, but she died less than two weeks after giving birth.

DOMESTIC AND FOREIGN AFFAIRS

Since 1522, both France and England had been periodically battling the Holy Roman Empire. With a temporary peace established in 1538, it appeared that a Catholic campaign against Protestant England might begin. At the urging of Thomas Cromwell, Henry contracted a political alliance with Protestant German princes by marrying Anne of Cleves, the daughter of a powerful German prince.

Thomas Cromwell had led Henry to believe that Anne was attractive, but the king disliked her on sight, finding her both dull and unattractive. Although he went through with the marriage in January 1540, by July Henry had divorced Anne of Cleves and married his fifth wife, Catherine Howard, the niece of the powerful duke of Norfolk. Like her predecessors, Catherine did not last long as queen; she was executed in 1542 for committing adultery. The following year, Henry married Catherine Parr, a pious and scholarly widow who ultimately survived him.

Wars with Scotland and France occupied Henry through much of his reign. In France, Henry sought to expand territory and win security for the ports of southern England. Scotland was a particular threat, even though Henry's sister Margaret was married to the Scottish king, James IV (r. 1488–1513). When Henry, seeking glory, went to war with France in 1512, James sided with the French. Warfare between England and Scotland soon resulted in one of the legendary defeats in Scottish history, the battle of Flodden in 1513. In 1543, Henry again defeated the Scots at Solway Moss, near the English-Scottish border. From 1543 until 1546, Henry's army fought against the French alongside Holy Roman emperor Charles V (r. 1519–1558).

Despite Henry's personal problems and foreign challenges, England made notable advances during his reign. Social reform accompanied religious reform in the kingdom, and Parliament expanded its powers. Henry also established an effective navy that became the basis for British imperial power in the coming centuries. When Henry VIII died in 1547, he was succeeded by his children, each of whom ruled in turn: Edward VI (r. 1547–1553), his son by Jane Seymour; Mary I (r. 1553–1558), his daughter by Katharine of Aragón; and his daughter Elizabeth I (r. 1558–1603), whose mother was Anne Boleyn.

See also: EDWARD VI; ELIZABETH I; ENGLISH MONARCHIES; MARY I, TUDOR; TUDOR, HOUSE OF.

FURTHER READING

Starkey, David. *The Reign of Henry VIII: Personalities and Politics.* London: G. Philip, 1985.

HEROD (ca. 73–4 B.C.E.)

King of Judaea (r. 37–4 B.C.E.), often called Herod the Great, who was the last ruler of the Herodian dynasty.

Herod was born in Judea, a part of the Roman Empire. The son of a politically important family in the region, Herod was appointed governor of Galilee at age twenty-six, largely through the influence exercised by his father, Antipater. However, Herod failed to defend the territory from an invasion by the neighboring kingdom of Parthia around 37 B.C.E. Rather than be taken prisoner or killed, Herod fled to Rome, where he presented his case to the Roman Senate and was rewarded by being given rule over the kingdom of Judaea.

To help forge a better relationship with his new subjects, Herod selected a wife, a woman named Mariam, from one of the more powerful Judaean families living in Rome at the time. Herod then set out for Judea to claim his throne with the support of an army of Roman troops. He took control of Jerusalem in 37 B.C.E.

Herod was a capable administrator, and he left a legacy of many important buildings and improvements in Judea. He ingratiated himself with the religious leaders of Jerusalem by making repairs to the temple there. To better defend his territory, he ordered the construction of the great fortress of Masada in the deserts along the western shore of the Dead Sea. Herod also worked to maintain cordial relationships with the city-states of Greece, whose culture he greatly admired.

For all his attempts at good works, Herod was a deeply suspicious man, prone to acts of cruelty to those he felt were against him. His greatest fear was that his wife's family coveted the throne and was plotting against him. In retaliation for this perceived disloyalty, he had Mariam executed, along with many of her relatives. This was not enough to eliminate his fears, however; accordingly, when his sons by Mariam grew to maturity, he again suspected treachery. They were his designated heirs, but Herod was concerned that they would be unwilling to wait for his death to claim their birthright, so he had them executed in 7 B.C.E. The Roman emperor Augustus (r. 27 B.C.E.–14 C.E.), appalled by Herod's cruelty, exclaimed: "It would be better to be Herod's dog than to be one of his children."

Herod insisted on interfering with Judea's religious hierarchy and the conduct of ritual in the temples, thereby creating a great rift between himself and the leaders of the temple. In the Christian tradition, Herod is remembered for the "slaughter of the innocents." This tradition holds that Herod, fearing the rumors of a newborn child who would one day become "king of the Jews," ordered the murder of all male infants in the town of Jerusalem. Herod died in 4 B.C.E., and the kingdom of Judaea was divided among his surviving sons.

See also: AUGUSTUS; ISRAEL, KINGDOMS OF; ROMAN EMPIRE.

FURTHER READING

Grant, M. *Herod the Great.* New York: American Heritage Press, 1971.

Sandmel, Samuel. *Herod, Profile of a Tyrant.* Philadelphia: Lippencott, 1967.

HINDUISM AND KINGSHIP

Relationship of the Hindu religion on kingship and the way Hindu beliefs and rituals affected monarchs in Hindu societies.

The Hindu ideology of political authority began to exert strong influence on the concept and practice of kingship in much of South and Southeast Asia beginning in the third century C.E. Scholars generally agree that Hinduism should be distinguished from Brahmanism, which marked an earlier stage of religious thought. However, it is necessary to trace the beginning of Hindu ideology to the Brahmanical tradition, since Hindu ideology clearly appropriated much of Brahmanism's ideological and literary traditions. Initially, Hinduism and Brahmanism shared a common origin around 1000 B.C.E., when the oldest surviving Hindu texts, the "Vedas," were compiled.

EARLY PERIOD

During the Vedic age, two cults coexisted among the ruling Aryan clans in Asia: a popular cult with elements derived from indigenous culture and comparable to later Hinduism, and an esoteric ceremonial cult presided over by a priesthood, comparable to the priests of the succeeding brahmanical period. The Aryan focus on sacrifice gave way to brahminism in the late centuries B.C.E. Brahminism was a system of both ceremonial and social integration in which the Brahmans, or priestly caste, controlled the means to salvation. Early religious texts, including the Vedas, Brahmanas, and Upanishads, were studied only by those who had undergone initiation as Brahmans. The priests thus became entrenched as intermediaries between man and god.

Between the seventh and the first century B.C.E, Vedic and Brahmanical systems experienced competition from Buddhism, and during the early centuries C.E., from devotional Hindusim. The final form of devotional Hinduism, which appeared in the early second millennium C.E., emerged in the Dravidian region in the south of the Indian subcontinent.

BASIC HINDU CONCEPTS

Hinduism purported to make its scriptures available to all, including men of low caste and women. The main body of Hindu texts comprised the Ramayana and Mahabharata epics, the Puranas, and books of Sacred Law. Ramayana and Mahabharata epic literature emphasized the role of the *ksatriya,* or king. *Ksatriya* were the warrior caste. Theoretically, the brahmanical caste stood higher in social ranking, but in practice, *ksatriya* conducted day-to-day rule. The image of the Hindu ruler was more that of a war leader and protector than that of a priest or holy person.

Dharma was an important concept that influenced the actions of the *ksatriya* king, exemplified in the two epic heroes, Rama and Arjuna. Hindu gods played important roles in these epics. Rama was an incarnation of Vishnu, god of preservation, while Arjuna received instruction from Krishna, another avatar, or form, of the same god. In this context, *Dharma* implied the necessity of accepting one's role in the drama of human existence as determined by fate, justifying the use of force and even killing. Thus, when Arjuna hesitated on the eve of a climactic battle in which many men and animals would die, Krishna reminded him that it was his fate to lead the forces of good to victory. Because of the doctrine of reincarnation, those who were killed would be re-born into new bodies that would either be punished for their sins or rewarded for their good deeds.

The idea of the *chakravartin,* or "wheel-turner," was important in Hindu kingship. The "wheel-turner" was the person who became ruler by virtue of his goodness. The term conjures up an image of a person who remains stable at the center of the universe, anchoring the rest of the spinning cosmos. There could only be one cakravartin at any one time; thus, the virtuous ruler was justified in using force to bend his rivals to his will, for he was destined to benefit all beings by his just rule. Those who resisted his authority were by definition ruled by illusion and thus deserving of correction and chastisement.

In addition to the role of war leader, Hindu rulers were also expected to be spiritually potent. Power was achieved not merely by royal birth, though that was important; power could be increased almost infinitely through ascetic practices, particularly meditation. Hindu rulers needed the assistance of Brahman priests, who, through their ministrations to the gods on behalf of the rulers, could maintain the virtue of the ruler and the kingdom. This was done by glorifying the gods through establishing religious

The Hindu religion had a profound influence on the concept and actual practice of kingship in South Asia. This twelfth-century bas-relief sculpture from India depicts the Hindu trinity of the gods Brahma, Vishnu, and Shiva—the creator, the preserver, and the destroyer of the universe.

communities and the sponsoring of temple building, statue carving, and donations to holy men and monasteries. Large religious complexes were built and maintained by ambitious rulers. Conversely, when kings fought, the victor was pleased to capture the most important statues of gods erected by his defeated foe. The transfer of impressive statuary from one realm to another was a highly visible token of the favor of the gods themselves.

Theoretically, Hindu rulers owned all land in their kingdoms. Their virtue was thought to display itself in bountiful harvests and the absence of pestilence or other natural disasters. Earthquakes, floods, and poor harvests could be interpreted as omens signifying that the ruler was in danger of losing the gods' favor. Rulers often played parts in ceremonies meant to ensure fertility and good harvests.

Hindu rulers did not consider themselves incarnations of gods; rather, the institution of kingship was said to be divinely inspired. Secular works such as the *Arthasastra* were as important as religious texts in shaping the strategies of Hindu rulers. Since kings were born to be warriors, rather than priests, kingship in South Asian Hinduism had as many practical aspects as it did mystical aspects.

HINDUISM IN SOUTHEAST ASIA

When Hinduism spread to Southeast Asia in the early centuries C.E., adherents at first adopted the same relationship between gods and humans. Statues of Vishnu and Siva *linggas* (phallic symbols) began to appear in southern Vietnam, Cambodia, Thailand, Sumatra, and Java. The Ramayana and Mahabharata became well-known models of kingly behavior in the region.

Not all features of Hinduism were adopted in Southeast Asia, however. For example, no caste system was implanted there. Instead, rulers of Cambodia, for instance, conferred membership in "castes" (the three main *varnas*) upon favored subjects.

Hinduism in Southeast Asia presented several faces, varying from one region to another. Its relationship to the other major South Asian religion, Buddhism, also differed. Several Southeast Asian kingdoms espoused both Buddhism and Hinduism simultaneously. Buddhism eventually became the main religion of mainland Southeast Asia even as it was dying out in India, the land of its birth.

Surprisingly, Brahmans are still required participants in coronation ceremonies even in Buddhist kingdoms such as Thailand. It would be too simplistic to state that syncretism between Hinduism and Buddhism took place. When the Javanese ruler Kertanagara (r. 1268–1292) had himself commemorated in the mid-thirteenth century as both Siva and Buddha, two statues were erected, rather than one statue combining attributes of both deities. Hindu and Buddhist priesthoods were never combined, but always formed separate groups.

Southeast Asian rulers erected numerous religious complexes in honor of the Hindu gods Siva, Vishnu, and also Brahma, who was not normally so honored in South Asia. By the tenth century, rulers in Cambodia were beginning to claim semidivine status. The same tendency became pronounced in Java by the twelfth century. Thus, Southeast Asian rulers went much further than South Asian kings in claiming to be deified. Some statues of Siva in the form of the god Mahaguru are thought to have been portraits of kings.

Southeast Asians also had different ideas about the relationship between the living and their deceased ancestors, to which Hinduism accommodated itself. The idea of reincarnation was not important in the region. Instead, it was believed that the spirits of ancestors could descend into statues in Hindu or Buddhist sanctuaries, to be invoked for protection and guidance.

The position of royal preceptor was important in ancient Cambodia, and a complex hierarchy of priestly positions was established. The position of royal chaplain was hereditary, but chaplains were supposed to be celibate. The paradox did not pose a problem. In Cambodia as in much of Southeast Asia, descent in the female line was important in determining status, and the position of royal preceptor was handed down from maternal uncle to nephew. Preceptors were believed to be capable of initiating rulers into higher levels of religious awareness.

Between the thirteenth and fifteenth centuries, Hinduism was replaced by Buddhism in mainland Southeast Asia and by Islam in the Southeast Asian archipelago. Only one area remained Hindu: the island of Bali, where kingdoms that regarded themselves as Hindu persisted until 1906 when they were conquered by the Dutch. The population of Bali remains largely Hindu, but with numerous differences from Hinduism commonly practiced in South Asia. Because of the influence of the Sivasiddhanta sect, which arrived in the fifteenth century, the Balinese do not worship statues. The sun-god Surya occupies an important part in Balinese worship.

See also: BUDDHISM AND KINGSHIP; CAMBODIAN KINGDOMS; CASTE SYSTEMS; DIVINITY OF KINGS; INDIAN KINGDOMS; RELIGIOUS DUTIES AND POWER; SACRED KINGSHIPS; SOUTHEAST ASIAN KINGDOMS.

FURTHER READING

Aung-Thwin, Michael. *Pagan: The Origins of Modern Burma.* Honolulu: University of Hawaii Press, 1985.

Coedés, George. *The Indianized States of Southeast Asia.* Honolulu: University of Hawaii Press, 1971.

Drekmeier, Charles. *Kingship and Community in Early India.* Stanford, CA: Stanford University Press, 1962.

Gesick, Lorraine, and Michael Aung-Thwin, eds. *Centers, Symbols and Hierarchies: Essays on the Classical States of Southeast Asia.* New Haven, CT: Yale University Southeast Asian Studies, 1983.

Hall, D.G.E. *A History of South-East Asia.* 3rd ed. New York: St. Martin's Press, 1981.

Kulke, Hermann. *Kings and Cults: State Formation and Legitimization in India and Southeast Asia.* New Delhi: Manohar, 2001.

HIROHITO (1901–1989)

Japanese emperor (r. 1926–1989) who saw Japan's rise to world power and devastating defeat in the twentieth century. When Hirohito was born on April 29, 1901, his grandfather, Emperor Mutsuhito, ruled Japan from what was known as the Chrysanthemum Throne. His father, Crown Prince Yoshihito, was twenty-one years of age and chronically ill. Yoshihito's wife, Princess Kujo Sadako, was just sixteen when she gave birth to Michinomiya, which means "one who cultivates virtue."

Of all the infant's esteemed ancestors, the most important one was Amaterasu Omikami, the Shinto goddess of the sun, from whom 1,600 years of Japan's emperors traced their descent. As descendants of this goddess, Japan's rulers had a claim to authority that was divinely ordained.

According to Japanese imperial ritual, the newborn prince could not officially join the family until he was brought to the shrines of his ancestors. It was there, in a celebration known as *omiyamairi* ("shrine visiting"), that he received his family name, Hirohito.

CHILDHOOD

The imperial palace in Tokyo was home to the infant Hirohito for only seventy days. After that, tradition held that he be cared for not by his parents but by a trusted retainer of the emperor. This was Kawamura Sumiyoshi, a retired naval admiral. It was expected that Kawamura would teach the prince the values that were needed for assuming the throne. Hirohito's younger brother, Yasuhito, later joined the Kawamura household as well, and the two brothers were attended by a retinue of doctors, nurses, and servants.

Kawamura was sixty-six years old when he took on this responsibility. Upon his death in 1904, the young princes were returned to their parents, but Hirohito was now put under the care of a staff of servants, an arrangement that remained until he began formal schooling at age seven. Hirohito's education was rigidly defined by tradition. He was expected to

Hirohito, who ruled from 1926 to 1989, was the 124th emperor of Japan. A scholar in the field of marine biology, he ruled his country through the tumultuous events of World War II.

receive training in *bushido* ("the way of the warrior") and in Confucianism, then a prominent Chinese religion, as well as in academic disciplines. Chief among his early teachers was Maseruke Mogi, a general who had earned great honors for his service during the Russo-Japanese War (1904–1905).

In 1912, Emperor Mutsuhito died, and Hirohito's father took the throne. Hirohito, now eleven years old, became the heir apparent. Although still a boy, he was given an officer's rank in the Imperial army and navy. He continued his studies and graduated from elementary school in 1914. He then pursued advanced studies with private tutors. During this time he began studying marine biology, which became his lifelong passion.

CROWN PRINCE

In 1916, Hirohito was granted the title of crown prince, and the royal household began searching for a suitable bride of noble birth. The choice was too important to be left to the vagaries of romantic love. Court advisers chose Princess Nagako, one of Hirohito's distant cousins. This selection was not without controversy. Nagako was well bred, intelligent, and demure, but some considered her "imperfect" because some members of her immediate family were color-blind. Such objections were overcome, however, and the couple became formally engaged in January 1919.

Throughout most of its history, the Japanese imperial family ruled from seclusion; the emperor was rarely seen beyond the confines of the royal residences except on ceremonial occasions. This began to change after 1868, when Hirohito's grandfather led a group of samurai (military elite) in a modernization effort known as the Meiji Restoration. While the intensely private, strongly ritualized office of the emperor became more public, the ruler still remained a mysterious figure.

In 1921, when Hirohito visited England and met King George V, he became the first member of the Japanese imperial family to travel to the West. While he was gone, his father, Yoshihito, became very ill. The meningitis he contracted during his youth had profoundly affected his mental abilities, and he suffered from bouts of disorientation and disability. When it became apparent that Yoshihito could no longer lead, the crown prince was called home. On November 21, 1921, Hirohito was formally named regent (*sensho*), and a little more than a year later he wed Princess Nagako.

FROM CROWN PRINCE TO EMPEROR

Emperor Yoshihito lived for several more years, but his rule was effectively over and Hirohito took on the responsibilities of ruling the empire. When Yoshihito died on December 25, 1926, Hirohito became emperor of Japan. Following tradition, the installation

ROYAL RITUALS

DATING OF ERAS

In traditional Japan, the inauguration of a new emperor also marked the inauguration of a new era. Thus, events are dated by reference to the imperial era in which they occurred. For instance, the Russo-Japanese War, occurring during the reign of Emperor Mutsuhito, is dated to the Meiji period, whereas the Pacific War occurred during the Showa period. Currency issued during a particular era was marked accordingly, and an image of the reigning emperor was struck onto the faces of all coins. This traditional style of dating was forbidden by the new constitution imposed during the U.S. occupation of Japan after World War II. A change in law, however, is not always enough to force a break with tradition: the practice of reckoning dates, and of marking coins and other currency with the image and period of imperial rule, continues in Japan today.

of a new emperor was marked by the declaration of a new era, called *Showa* ("radiating peace" or "enlightened peace").

As emperor, Hirohito became the highest priest in the ancient Shinto religion; his authority came directly from the gods. In temporal matters, he was assisted by a large group of advisers and councilors. This diffuse style of rulership, called *nemawashi* ("prior negotiations leading to consensus") was codified in the Meiji constitution and sanctified by tradition.

Under Emperor Mutsuhito, Japan had begun a period of expansion. Its army and navy took Manchuria in China in 1931, and military campaigns continued throughout the early 1900s. Hirohito, as supreme commander of Japan's armed forces, continued this expansionist policy, ultimately leading to war with China in the late 1930s. Meanwhile, as Europe moved toward World War II, the Japanese began looking eastward at the islands of the Pacific, including Hawaii.

When war erupted in Europe in 1939, the United States hoped to remain uninvolved. However, when Hirohito, Adolf Hitler of Germany, and Benito Mussolini of Italy formed an alliance in December 1940, the United States could no longer remain wholly above the fray. Hoping to cripple its ability to wage war, the United States imposed an oil embargo on Japan that same year. Meanwhile, peace negotiations between the United States and Japan continued. Hopes for peace were dashed, however, when the Japanese launched a surprise attack on the U.S. fleet at Pearl Harbor on December 7, 1941.

FROM RULER TO FIGUREHEAD

Tales of atrocities committed by the Japanese during the war led to demands that its leaders be brought to trial for war crimes, and several high officials were brought before an international court. However, the United States believed that its occupation of Japan would be facilitated if the emperor remained on the throne.

Under the terms of the Potsdam Declaration (August 1945), which marked the official end of the war between the United States and Japan, Hirohito agreed to cooperate fully with the American occupation of Japan. In accordance with the provisions of a new constitution drawn up by the United States, Hirohito renounced his claim to divinity and divested himself of all but a purely symbolic role. This ritual role for the emperor suited the American occupying

forces well, providing the Japanese people with the appearance of continuity of tradition and helping to avoid the possibility of a popular uprising.

Hirohito remained emperor of Japan until his death from cancer on January 7, 1989. During the latter part of his reign, he occupied himself with his passion for marine biology. He also spent time traveling, particularly to Europe. From the end of World War II until his death, Hirohito became merely a symbolic figure.

Hirohito and Empress Nagako had seven children, the first four of whom were girls. This had caused great consternation, for one of the emperor's most important duties was to produce an heir to the throne. On December 23, 1933, the country experienced enormous relief with the announcement of the birth of Prince Akihito. When Akihito ascended to the Chrysanthemum Throne upon his father's death, he became the first Japanese emperor to reign as a purely symbolic figure and without invoking a divine right to rule.

See also: DIVINE RIGHT; EDUCATION OF KINGS.

FURTHER READING

Bix, Herbert. *Hirohito and the Making of Modern Japan*. New York: HarperCollins, 2000.

Hoyt, Edwin P. *Hirohito: The Emperor and the Man*. New York: Praeger, 1992.

Large, Stephen S. *Emperor Hirohito and Showa Japan: A Political Biography*. New York: Routledge, 1992.

HITTITE EMPIRE (ca. 1680–1220 B.C.E.)

Ancient empire in Asia Minor (present-day Turkey) that was one of the earliest and most powerful empires of the ancient Near East.

Around 1900 B.C.E., a group of Indo-European peoples entered Asia Minor, or Anatolia, from somewhere in the north. They claimed the territory as their own, called it Hatti, and converted the people they conquered to their Indo-European language and culture. Not all the local culture was lost, however. Most notably, these Indo-European people adapted cuneiform, the ancient method of writing using wedge-shaped strokes, to use in their own language.

By the seventeenth century B.C.E., these invaders, known to history as the Hittites, had founded what is now called the Old Hittite kingdom, which was centered in the Anatolian region of Cappadochiao. The first Hittite king was Labarna (r. ca. 1680–1650 B.C.E.), and the Hittites established a capital at Hattusa.

Soon after beginning his reign, Labarna started to expand his domain, and the Hittite kingdom soon grew to contain nearly all of central Anatolia. Labarna and his successors were all-powerful rulers, acting as chief priest, judge, and military commander. To help them administratively, they appointed provincial governors who enforced their ruling decisions.

Successors to the Hittite throne were ambitious and sought to gain more territory for themselves. King Hattushili I (r. ca. 1620–1600 B.C.E.) expanded the borders of the kingdom to the southeast and the southwest. Around 1595 B.C.E., Murshili I (r. ca. 1600–1590 B.C.E.) invaded northern Syria and then headed south to Babylon, withdrawing immediately after taking his fill from the Babylonian treasury.

When Murshili returned home to the capital at Hattusa, however, he was killed by his brother-in-law, Hantili I (r. ca.1590–1560 B.C.E.). His death led to an extended period of turmoil within the kingdom over who would succeed to the throne; this left the Hittite kingdom weak and vulnerable to attack.

While the Hittites were dealing with governmental instability, the neighboring kingdom of Mitanni in Syria and northwestern Mesopotamia was being formed and was growing strong. The Mitannis, wasting no time in taking advantage of Hittite weakness and vulnerability, began conquering some of the Hittite lands.

The Mitanni state became a continuing problem for the Hittites, who engaged in ongoing wars with the rival Mitannis over control of territory. The Mitannis captured northern Syria and much of Assyria, and by the end of the sixteenth century B.C.E., the size of the Hittite Empire had shrunk to its former area in central Anatolia as a result of Mitanni conquest.

Around 1525 B.C.E., King Telipinu (r. ca. 1525–1500 B.C.E.) came to the Hittite throne and brought about some stability to the kingdom. Among his accomplishments were new rules of succession aimed at preventing the problems that had disrupted the kingdom for decades. Telipinu proved unable to build up the Hittite strength sufficiently, however. In the late fifteenth century B.C.E., a series of inept successors once again left the Hittites weak and vulnerable.

By 1358 B.C.E., what is called the New Hittite kingdom, under a new ruling family, began with the reign of King Shuppiluliuma (r. ca. 1358–1323 B.C.E.), a former prince. Through the effective use of the horse and chariot in warfare, Shuppiluliuma beat back the Hittites' primary enemy, the Mitannis.

Shuppiluliuma then turned his attention to expanding the kingdom. A series of conquests extended Hittite borders and once again consolidated the kingdom's control over Anatolia and northern Syria. The Hittite Empire reached the peak of its power under Shuppiluliuma, and the Hittites rivaled the two other major empires of the time, Egypt and Assyria.

The power and strength of the Hittite Empire soon led to tensions with Egypt, and both empires sought to keep open trade routes between Africa and Asia. During the last half of the fourteenth century B.C.E., control of Syria and the trade routes along its coast became a major point of contention between the Hittites and the Egyptians. Around 1275 B.C.E., a great battle—the battle of Kadesh—was fought between the Hittite king Muwatalli (r. ca. 1285–1273 B.C.E.) and the Egyptian pharaoh Rameses II (r. ca. 1279–1212 B.C.E.). Although Rameses claimed a great victory, the Hittites continued to maintain control over Syria.

Finally, around 1258 B.C.E., the conflict between the Egyptians and Hittites was settled by a treaty signed by Rameses II and the Hittite ruler, Hattushili III (r. ca. 1266–1236 B.C.E.). The treaty, in which each side agreed to refrain from attacking the other and to come to the other's assistance if needed, marked the start of a short period of stability for the Hittites and their relations with Egypt.

Despite its powerful position in the region, the New Hittite kingdom lasted only about another century. It is not known for certain what caused the demise of the once-powerful empire. It is generally agreed that the appearance of a powerful new group known as the "peoples of the sea" or Sea Peoples led to the decline of the Hittite Empire and its eventual end. After centuries of constant warfare and political instability, the Hittites were unable to gather the strength to hold back a new force in the region.

See also: EGYPTIAN DYNASTIES, ANCIENT (EIGHTEENTH TO TWENTY-SIXTH); MITANNI KINGDOM; RAMSES II, THE GREAT; SYRIAN KINGDOMS.

HOHENSTAUFEN DYNASTY

(1138–1254 C.E.)

German princely family based in Swabia in southern Germany, which ruled Germany from 1138 to 1254 and the Holy Roman Empire from 1138 to 1208 and 1212 to 1250.

The Hohenstaufen family was descended from Duke Frederick I of Swabia (d. 1105) and took its name from his Staufen Castle, which he built in 1077 C.E.

The line of Hohenstaufen German kings and Holy Roman emperors began with Frederick's son, Conrad III (r. 1138–1152). During Conrad's reign, German colonists began settling in the Slavic lands to the northeast of the German kingdom. Conflicts between the Crown and rebellious nobles, which had been common during the rule of the Salian dynasty, also continued.

Conrad III's son Henry died before he could take the throne, so Conrad designated his nephew Frederick as his successor. Frederick I Barbarossa (r. 1152–1190) was crowned emperor in Rome in 1155. The most significant and successful of the Hohenstaufen rulers, Frederick maintained control over the German nobility, while asserting imperial rights in Italy. His involvement in Italy brought him into conflict with the papacy, which worked to cause the downfall of the Hohenstaufen dynasty. During Frederick I's reign, the term *Holy Roman Empire* was first used to denote the empire that was comprised of various German and northern Italian states.

Frederick Barbarossa drowned in 1190 while on Crusade in the region of Cilicia in Asia Minor. He was succeeded as German king by his son Henry VI (r. 1190–1197), who was crowned Holy Roman emperor in 1191. In 1194, Henry marched south through Italy and conquered the kingdom of Sicily, which he claimed through his wife, Constance, who was an heir to the Sicilian throne. During Henry's reign, he tried unsuccessfully to have the imperial succession declared hereditary in hopes of securing it for the Hohenstaufens. On Henry's death from a fever in 1197, Constance had their son Frederick crowned king of Sicily and cut Sicily's ties with the Holy Roman Empire. She died in 1198, and her ally, Pope Innocent III, became the official guardian of the young Sicilian king.

With Henry's son in Sicily, his brother Philip, duke of Swabia, was elected king in Germany (r. 1198–1208) instead. Philip also had imperial authority but not the actual title of Holy Roman emperor, since he was not crowned officially in Rome. Meanwhile, a rival faction of German nobles elected a different king, Otto IV, who was son of Duke Henry the Lion of Saxony (r. 1142–1180) and a member of the powerful Welf family, whose rivalry with the Hohenstaufen reached back to the election of Conrad III.

Pope Innocent III supported Otto's claim in return for concessions in Italy. A civil war broke out in Germany, which lasted until 1208, when Philip of Swabia and Innocent III negotiated a settlement. However, Philip was murdered in 1208, and Otto IV was elected undisputed king (1208–1212), bringing the Welf dynasty to the throne.

Otto IV was later crowned emperor in 1209, but when he attempted to retake Sicily the following year, the pope excommunicated him and persuaded the nobles of southern Germany to elect Frederick, the king of Sicily, as German king. The son of Henry VI and a Hohenstaufen, Frederick II (r. 1212–1250) had a prior claim to the German Crown, having already been elected king during the lifetime of his father as a means of ensuring the succession. Otto IV was defeated by Frederick's French allies in 1214 and lost control of most of Germany before his death in 1218.

Frederick II was crowned Holy Roman emperor in 1220, restoring the Hohenstaufen family to the throne. During his reign, the conflict between the Holy Roman Empire and the papacy over supremacy of lands in Italy continued. Toward the end of his reign, two anti-kings were elected with papal approval: Henry Raspe (r. 1246–1247) and William of Holland (r. 1247–1256).

When Frederick II died in 1250, his son, Conrad IV (r. 1250–1254), carried on the struggle with the pope, who was determined to end Hohenstaufen rule in Italy. In 1251, Conrad left Germany to try to retake lost Italian territories, leaving no effective government in Germany. On Conrad's death in 1254, his two-year-old son Conradin was left as heir to the throne of Sicily and Jerusalem, which his father had also ruled. However, Conrad's half-brother, Manfred, also claimed these Italian Crowns and made himself king of Sicily in 1258. But the pope granted that kingdom to Charles of Anjou, brother of the French king, in 1266. Manfred died in battle that same year trying to assert his claim.

Young Conradin attempted to recover his kingdom of Sicily in 1268, but was captured by the forces of Charles of Anjou and executed. His death marked the end of the Hohenstaufen dynasty's era of rule. In Germany, meanwhile, the period from 1250 to 1273 was called the Great Interregnum, as no single strong ruler emerged until Rudolf of Habsburg in 1273.

The period of Hohenstaufen rule in Germany was characterized by nearly continual conflicts between the Crown and the German princes who ruled quasi-independent territories, as well as by strife with the papacy, which felt threatened by a strong Holy Roman Empire. The most significant result of the unending conflict between the Hohenstaufens and their rivals was the failure to create a strong central authority at a time when other European kingdoms, particularly England and France, were doing so.

See also: Frederick I, Barbarossa; Frederick II; Holy Roman Empire; Papal States; Salian Dynasty; Sicilian, Kingdom of.

FURTHER READING

Hampe, Karl. *Germany Under the Salian and Hohenstaufen Emperors.* Trans. Ralph Bennett. Oxford: Basil Blackwell, 1973.

Haverkamp, Alfred. *Medieval Germany, 1056–1273.* 2nd ed. Trans. Helga Braun and Richard Mortimer. New York: Oxford University Press, 1992.

Holmes, George, ed. *The Oxford Illustrated History of Medieval Europe.* New York: Oxford University Press, 1988.

Riley-Smith, Jonathan. *The Crusades: A Short History.* New Haven, CT: Yale University Press, 1987.

HOHENZOLLERN DYNASTY

(1415–1918 C.E.)

Royal family of Germany that oversaw much of the five-hundred-year transition of that country from a loose collection of kingdoms to one of the most powerful industrial nations on earth.

One of the longest-running dynasties in history, the Hohenzollerns count among their members such figures as Frederick William, the Great Elector (r. 1640–1688); Frederick William I (r. 1713–1740); Frederick II, the Great (r. 1740–1786); and the powerful nineteenth-century German emperors Wilhelm I (r. 1871–1888) and Wilhelm II (r. 1888–1918). Along with the Habsburgs of eastern Germany and Austria, the Hohenzollerns dominated the evolution of Germany from the late Middle Ages until World War I.

ORIGINS AND EARLY RULERS

The Hohenzollern family name appears as early as the eleventh century C.E. during the reign of Holy Roman Emperor Henry IV (r. 1084–1105). Some historical evidence from that period suggests that members of the family acted as minor officials in or near the southern German city of Hechingen.

The family appears again in the late twelfth century, when Conrad Hohenzollern was appointed governor of the Bavarian city of Nuremberg by Holy Roman Emperor Frederick I (r. 1152–1190). The Hohenzollerns held this relatively minor position until the early fifteenth century, when Sigismund (r. 1387–1437), the Hungarian king and later Holy Roman emperor, rewarded Frederick Hohenzollern for his loyalty and support with the electorate of the state of Brandenburg in eastern Germany. Frederick, who had supported Sigismund in his wars against the Ottoman Empire, was named Frederick I of Brandenburg in 1415, thus beginning the reign of the Hohenzollern dynasty.

The reigns of the first several Hohenzollerns were largely uneventful, though family lands in Brandenburg expanded somewhat under Frederick's son and successor, Frederick II (r. 1440–1470). The latter Frederick's death in 1470 brought to power his younger brother, Albert Achilles, who issued a decree that all Brandenburg lands would pass to the eldest son of the ruling Hohenzollern, thus assuring the family's legacy. Albert's grandson, Albert of Brandenburg (r. 1525–1568), expanded the family's land dramatically when he became the first duke of Prussia in 1525. Although the second Albert was technically from a different branch of the family than the electors of Brandenburg, the two branches were reunited in 1618 under Elector John Sigismund (r. 1608–1620), making the Hohenzollern family one of the largest landholders in Germany.

CONFLICT AND FURTHER GROWTH

The Hohenzollerns managed to avoid some of the controversy over the rise of Protestantism in the late sixteenth century, despite high-profile conversions from ruling members such as Joachim II (r. 1535–

FRIDERICVS WILHELMVS
Marchio Brandenburgensis, Sacri Romani Imperii
Elector, et Archicamerarius Duc, Magdeburgi, Borussia,
Iulia, Clivia et Montium nec non Stetini et Pomerania
Dux, Princeps Halberstady, Mindæ, et Rugia, etc.

Frederick William, of the German Hohenzollern dynasty, was known as the Great Elector. Uniting various lands controlled by the Hohenzollerns, Frederick William established Brandenburg-Prussia as one of the most powerful states in seventeenth-century Europe.

1571) and John Sigismund. However, the outbreak of the Thirty Years' War (1618–1648) in 1618 desolated the Brandenburg lands, as John Sigismund's son and successor, George William (r. 1620–1640), was unable to preserve a position of neutrality in the face of invading forces from Sweden and elsewhere. George William effectively turned over the administration of Brandenburg to his ministers and left his lands in ruins. His death in 1640 brought his son, Frederick William, to the head of the family.

Frederick William, also known as the Great Elector, was one of the most important figures in the history of the Hohenzollern dynasty. Under his rule, the Hohenzollern lands, which had been badly wrecked by war and foreign occupation, became united into one of the most powerful states in all of Europe. Frederick William greatly improved the economy of Brandenburg with a series of administrative reforms and public works projects, including a canal on the Oder River that is still in use today.

The Peace of Westphalia (1648) and a 1657 Polish treaty secured Hohenzollern domain over Prussia and the eastern portions of Pomerania, and Frederick William's complete reconstruction of his national army ensured the family a position of great importance in subsequent European politics. Upon Frederick William's death in 1688, he was succeeded by his son, Frederick III (r. 1688–1701).

THE EMERGENCE OF PRUSSIA

Although Frederick III was not an especially gifted leader, he was able to use his military strength as leverage against Holy Roman Emperor Leopold I (r. 1658–1705) to have himself named King Frederick I of Prussia (r. 1701–1713) in 1701. The outbreak of the War of Spanish Succession (1701–1714) immediately thereafter, led ultimately to international recognition of the Hohenzollern claim to Prussia. Although Frederick succeeded in achieving true monarchial status for the Hohenzollern line, he was an ineffective ruler, undoing many of the advances made by his father. His death in 1713 brought his son, Frederick William I (r. 1713–1740), to the throne.

Frederick William I is regarded as the man who saved Prussia, as his father had left it teetering on the edge of bankruptcy. Frederick William streamlined the Prussian government and managed to pay off his father's creditors. He also practiced a strict protectionist economic policy, which led to great success for Prussian businesses. Although Prussia engaged in few military conflicts during Frederick William's reign, he expanded his army nearly threefold and turned it into one of the most well-equipped and well-trained forces in Europe. Despite his obvious political skills, Frederick William frequently quarreled with his son, the man who was to become one of the greatest leaders in European history, Frederick II (r. 1740–1786).

PRUSSIAN DOMINANCE

Generally known by the appellation "the Great," Frederick II began his reign in 1740 upon the death of his father. He continued the advances his father had made to astonishing ends. The Prussian military's success in two mid-century conflicts, the War of the Austrian Succession (1740–1748) and the Seven Years' War (1756–1763), made it the most powerful in all of Europe, and Frederick's political cunning allowed him to bring large portions of territory under

Prussian control. Frederick's internal policies were more progressive than his father's. He greatly modernized the Prussian legal system, set the economy on the road to industrialization, and initiated a series of civic projects, such as roads and canals, necessary for future growth. Frederick II, who had no direct descendants, died in 1786; his nephew, Frederick William II (r. 1786–1797) succeeded him on the throne.

YEARS OF MISRULE

The next eighty years did little to further the march of the Hohenzollern line begun by Frederick William I and Frederick the Great, as Prussia saw a series of weak and ineffective rulers take the throne. Frederick William II had the dubious distinction of returning the Prussian treasury to near-bankruptcy. His son

and successor, Frederick William III (r. 1797–1840), was forced to turn most of Prussia's affairs over to his ministers because he proved incapable of guiding the country through the Napoleonic Wars (1803–1815). Moreover, Frederick William III was not well liked, and his efforts to quash proto-democratic movements in Prussia only furthered his people's distrust. His death in 1840 brought his son, Frederick William IV (r. 1840–1861), to the throne.

The 1840s saw a series of revolutionary uprisings spread across Europe. Most were aimed, in one form or another, at achieving more popular representation in governmental affairs. The various German states responded by drafting a liberal constitution for unification that made Frederick William IV the head of a German empire. The Prussian king, however, had an immense dislike for the will of the people, and he re-

Electors of Brandenburg

FREDERICK I	1415–1440
FREDERICK II	1440–1470
ALBERT ACHILLES	1470–1486
JOHN CICERO	1486–1499
JOACHIM I	1499–1535
JOACHIM II	1535–1571
JOHN GEORGE	1571–1598
JOACHIM FREDERICK	1598–1608

Dukes of Prussia

ALBERT OF BRANDENBURG	1525–1568
ALBERT FREDERICK	1568–1618

Electors of Brandenburg and Dukes of Prussia

JOHN SIGISMUND	1608–1620, 1618–1620
GEORGE WILLIAM	1620–1640

FREDERICK WILLIAM, THE GREAT ELECTOR*	1640–1688
FREDERICK III	1688–1701

Kings of Prussia

FREDERICK I	1701–1713
FREDERICK WILLIAM I	1713–1740
FREDERICK II, THE GREAT	1740–1786
FREDERICK WILLIAM II	1786–1797
FREDERICK WILLIAM III	1797–1840
FREDERICK WILLIAM IV	1840–1861
WILHELM I	1861–1871

German Emperors

WILHELM I	1871–1888
FREDERICK III	1888
WILHELM II*	1888–1918

*Indicates a separate alphabetical entry.

fused to accept the Crown, causing the entire plan to fall apart. This political blunder was the blackest spot on Frederick William IV's otherwise unremarkable reign. A mental decline in his later years brought change to the Prussian government in the person of his brother, Wilhelm I (r. 1861–1871), who took control as regent in 1858. Wilhelm became king upon his older sibling's death in 1861.

TRIUMPH AND DEVASTATION

The reign of Wilhelm I was marked by the rebirth of Prussia as a fearsome military force and by the skilled statecraft of his prime minister, Otto von Bismarck. Wilhelm was a powerful figure, but Bismarck has historically received much of the credit for the rise of Germany in the late-nineteenth century. Shortly after Wilhelm took the throne, Bismarck began agitating for war with Austria, which would allow Prussia to unify Germany on its own terms. Although Wilhelm was not entirely supportive of this plan, Bismarck was able in 1866 to provoke the Austro-Prussian War, in which Prussia's military crushed Austrian opposition in just under two months.

GERMANY ASCENDANT

Following on the heels of the victory over Austria, Bismarck goaded France into the Franco-Prussian War of 1870. The Prussian military once more displayed its immense strength, marching all the way to Paris, this time with Wilhelm himself on the battlefield. The end of the Franco-Prussian War in 1871 saw the German princes unite behind Prussia, and Wilhelm was declared Emperor Wilhelm I. This is considered the birth of the modern German nation.

The Hohenzollerns continued to rise during the remainder of the nineteenth century, and Germany became the most powerful nation on the European continent, riding a wave of massive industrialization and nationalist sentiment. Upon Wilhelm I's death in 1888, the Crown passed to his popular but ill-fated son, Frederick III, who died just three months after being crowned emperor. Frederick was known for his liberal ideas, and his death was greatly lamented in some quarters, as it brought to power his militaristic son, Wilhelm II.

THE END OF THE DYNASTY

One of Wilhelm II's earliest political moves was to force the resignation of Bismarck, whom he felt had been exerting too much power over the royal house.

Wilhelm, however, lacked Bismarck's diplomatic talents and soon found himself embroiled in a series of international crises, all of which served to increase the growing tensions between the major powers of Europe—tensions that eventually led to World War I. Wilhelm exacerbated the situation by setting Germany on a rapid course of imperial expansion, largely in Africa and the Middle East, which threw it directly into conflict with the other major imperial powers, especially Great Britain and France.

A series of alliances eventually linked Germany with Austria-Hungary and most of Central Europe, in direct opposition to an Anglo-French alliance with Russia. The friction between these two immensely powerful groups continued to build until the summer of 1914, when World War I exploded across Europe. After four years of the most destructive fighting the world had ever seen, Germany, still standing but utterly exhausted, surrendered to the Allies, and Wilhelm II was forced to abdicate the throne. The last ruling member of the Hohenzollern dynasty fled to Holland, where he remained until his death in 1941.

See also: AUSTRO-HUNGARIAN EMPIRE; DIPLOMACY, ROYAL; DYNASTY; EMPIRE; FREDERICK II, THE GREAT; FREDERICK WILLIAM, THE GREAT ELECTOR; HABSBURG DYNASTY; IMPERIAL RULE; NATIONALISM; POWER, FORMS OF ROYAL; REGENCIES; ROYAL LINE; SIGISMUND; WILHELM II.

FURTHER READING

Nelson, Walter Henry. *The Soldier Kings: The House of Hohenzollern.* New York: Putnam, 1970.

HOLY ROMAN EMPIRE

(962–1806 C.E.)

Political body, composed of various states in Central Europe, that was formed in the Middle Ages and lasted up to the modern era. Intended to serve as the secular counterpart of the Roman Catholic Church, the Holy Roman Empire survived nearly one thousand years until it was dissolved by the last Holy Roman emperor, Francis II (r. 1792–1806), in 1806.

The Holy Roman Empire originated in form, but not in name, at the coronation of German king Otto

THE CHARLEMAGNE CONNECTION

Although some credit Charlemagne with the honor of being the first of the Holy Roman emperors, the political entity we know as the Holy Roman Empire in fact got its start more than 150 years later, in 962. In the years just prior, Pope John XII was facing a threat from King Berengar II of Italy, who sought to annex the Papal States. John turned to the powerful German king, Otto I, for assistance in repelling this threat. Once Berengar II was turned aside, the pope rewarded his collaborator by crowning him "Emperor of the Romans" and giving him authority over Italy and territory in the eastern portion of present-day France. This augmented Otto's German territories and formed the basis of the Holy Roman Empire. From the time of Otto's reign forward, the imperial office was based on German kingship, and the earlier connection to the Frankish Empire of Charlemagne and his Carolingian successors was broken.

I (r. 936–973) as emperor in 962. The name "Holy Roman Empire" did not come into common usage until several centuries later. The empire was, in essence, a successor to the empire established by the Frankish ruler Charlemagne (r. 800–814) in the 800s, which Charlemagne and his successors in the Carolingian dynasty saw as a continuation of the ancient Roman Empire.

SECULAR MIRROR OF CATHOLIC UNITY

The idea underlying the formation of the Holy Roman Empire was that there should be a secular, or nonreligious, equivalent to the Catholic Church. The emperors were intended to provide military and political support to the Church, uniting all Catholics into a single political state. In principle, this would have meant that once a king of Germany was crowned, he would travel to Rome to receive his imperial coronation directly from the pope.

In return for the imperial crown, the emperor was expected to spread the Catholic faith throughout his realm and into any new territories he might conquer. Equally important, he was expected to provide support and protection against all threats to the safety and authority of the pope. His civil courts were expected to prosecute all secular crimes against the Church, and he was obligated to provide military assistance, when needed, to protect the papal states should they be attacked.

In practice, this arrangement never really worked the way it was intended. Instead, the history of the Holy Roman Empire is one of power struggles between the emperors and the popes that crowned them. Rather than working together as two halves (secular and religious) of a single polity, the emperors and popes each sought ascendancy over the other.

SECULAR ASCENDANCY: 962–1250

During the first 300 years of the empire, the emperors clearly had the upper hand. The popes of this era were too dependent upon the protection of the emperors and their strong military capabilities to impose much control over the way the empire was run. In fact, the emperors were so strong that at times they would dismiss popes whom they deemed unsuitable and replace them with individuals more to their liking. Thus, for example, Otto III (r. 983–1002), the grandson of the first emperor, had a loyal friend installed as successor to Pope Gregory V. It was not until after the reign of Pope Innocent III (r. 1198–1216) that the papacy began to threaten the Hohenstaufen rulers of the empire.

During this period of secular ascendancy, the German kings exercised real control over all the territories of their empire, primarily through a form of indirect rule that relied upon local nobles and bishops to administer their cities and territories according to German edicts. Even in Italy this system was effective enough to ensure that the power of the kings was primary. By the end of the eleventh century, however, a series of popes took active steps to reduce their dependency upon the kings. Beginning with popes Gregory VII (r. 1073–1085) and Urban II (r. 1088–1099), the papacy asserted its authority more vigorously within the Papal States and then throughout Italy than papal predecessors had done.

The popes were aided in their assertion of authority by an accumulating weakness within the German territories, where excesses in taxation and falling revenues rendered the kings increasingly less able to refuse compliance with the newly invigorated papacy. By 1250, the German kings had become fully subordinate to the papacy, so much so that the popes began delaying the coronation ceremony when they were displeased with a particular king. At times they even refused to perform it at all, thus depriving the kings of the legitimacy that papal coronation normally bestowed.

AN EMPIRE OF DWINDLING POWER

Whereas the kings of the first three centuries of the Holy Roman Empire wielded true administrative and political control over their territorial possessions, the kings of the next 200 years were little more than figureheads. Not only was the papacy in ascendance, but the German nobility at home was also challenging the authority of the kings and establishing semi-independent hereditary dynasties. Moreover, the French were annexing parts of Burgundy from the empire, and some of the subject peoples of the empire were actively refusing to recognize the authority of the kings.

Further adding to the weakness of the German ruling house was the system by which kings attained the throne. The German kingship was not a hereditary office, but rather an elective one. A group of seven of the highest ranking nobles made their selection from among several important landowning families. The electors themselves were not averse to manipulating the system to gain benefits for their own houses, and during this period they began intentionally to choose weak kings, thus assuring for themselves the ability to manipulate the state to their

THE HOLY ROMAN EMPIRE

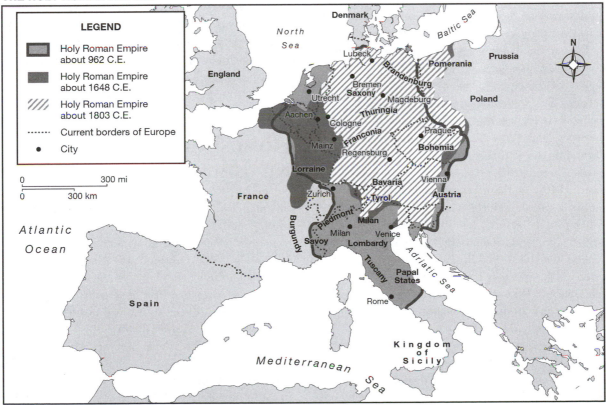

advantage. Not surprisingly, these weak kings lost their grip on the empire, and the once unified territory began to disintegrate, breaking up into a mass of independent or near-independent states and territories. By 1438, the empire was an empire only in name.

ATTEMPTS AT RECOVERY

Beginning in 1438, the kings of Germany began to be chosen almost exclusively from the ranks of a powerful Austrian noble family, the Habsburgs. These kings, determined to halt the steady dissolution of the empire that had begun in the preceding era, began to initiate a series of reforms designed to strengthen the state. Among these innovations was the institution of an assembly of nobles, each of whom represented an important city, district, or family. This assembly eventually evolved into a true legislative body.

The year 1500 saw further innovation in the empire when the first true administrative branch of government, called the *Reichsregiment*, was officially recognized. Soon a court system was also added to official governmental institutions, as was a board of taxation. These reforms might have succeeded in shoring up the power of the emperors, but internal resistance from noble families who refused to relinquish power to these new official bodies greatly impeded the progress that was being attempted.

Even if the nobles had gone along with the reform efforts, new pressures were working against the integrity of the empire. The weakness of earlier emperors had encouraged Germany's neighbors, particularly France, to make incursions into imperial territory, and Protestantism had gained significant ground in Germany's southwestern districts, as well as elsewhere in Europe.

In 1618, all these pressures culminated in the outbreak of the Thirty Years' War (1618–1648), which pitted Germany (and its Habsburg ally, Spain) against England, Denmark, Sweden, Germany, France, and the United Provinces (the Netherlands). In 1648, the war was finally brought to a close with the Treaty of Westphalia, which permanently ended the Habsburg attempt to regain power over the empire as a whole. Henceforth, the Habsburgs focused on building up their power in their hereditary lands—Bohemia, Austria, and Hungary.

The empire had insufficient resources and internal unity to withstand a concerted challenge by outside powers. Diplomacy and alliances through royal marriages were the only way that the once powerful Holy Roman emperors could maintain their standing in the community of European nations. But this was an uneasy period, throughout which the empire withstood threats from their powerful Ottoman neighbors to the east and continuing threats emanating from France, the traditional rival of the Habsburg rulers.

In the early 1800s, a new foe arose against whom the empire would ultimately prove powerless. Emperor Napoleon I of France (r. 1804–1815) began annexing German imperial lands, and encouraging other neighboring states to do the same. Within a few short years, on March 3, 1806, the last Holy Roman emperor, Francis II (r. 1792–1806), finally admitted defeat. He formally abdicated the imperial throne and dissolved the empire, remaining emperor of Austria only. The nearly thousand-year Holy Roman Empire was no more.

See also: CAROLINGIAN DYNASTY; FRANCIS I; FRANCONIAN DYNASTY; HABSBURG DYNASTY; HOHENSTAUFEN DYNASTY; OTTO I, THE GREAT; OTTONIAN DYNASTY; PAPAL STATES; SALIAN DYNASTY.

FURTHER READING

Barraclough, Geoffrey. *Crucible of Europe: The Ninth and Tenth Centuries in European History.* Berkeley: University of California Press, 1976.
———. *Origins of Modern Germany.* 3rd ed. Oxford: Basil Blackwell, 1988.

HOMOSEXUALITY AND KINGSHIP

The matter of homosexual inclinations and practices among monarchs is often difficult to disentangle from gossip and political slander. Concern with a monarch's sexual behavior was often not simply a matter of moral condemnation. In fact, at various times and places in history, personal affection between males was seen in a more positive light and was not viewed with as much suspicion or uncertainty as in more modern contexts. Gay male relationships involving a monarch often did provoke suspicion and concern, however, when it was feared that the monarch's male lover was exerting undue political influence. Although the same is true of heterosexual relationships, men in most societies have been able to wield greater institutional power than women, including royal mistresses.

A classic case of the male lovers' power is that involving King Edward II of England (r. 1307–1327) and his lovers, Piers Gaveston and Hugh le Despenser the Younger. Edward's favoring of these men, both of whom came from relatively low backgrounds, was only part of Edward's general political and military incompetence, but they provided a ready focus for his opponents. Edward and his two lovers all died violent deaths, Gaveston and Despenser because of their attempts to wield power, and Edward partly because of his poor judgment in allowing them to do so.

James I of Great Britain (r. 1603–1625) openly favored a succession of handsome young men, culminating in George Villiers, who was raised to the rank of duke of Buckingham by James and virtually led the royal government in the 1620s. This provoked both moral and political condemnation, although people had to be very cautious about expressing it. By contrast, Frederick II of Prussia (r. 1740–1786), who did not have a regular lover, endured nasty gossip but never allowed his sexual diversions to interfere with his political decisions.

Probably the most "high-profile" royal gay male relationship in Western history was that between the Roman Emperor Hadrian (r. 117–138) and the handsome youth Antinous. This relationship did not present a political problem inasmuch as Antinous did not exploit his position for political gain. However, after Antinous drowned in the Nile River in 130 while on a trip to Egypt, Hadrian built a city in Egypt named after the youth and promoted worship of Antinous as a god. These actions attracted great criticism as being excessive behavior.

In addition to fear of the royal favorite, homosexuality could adversely affect a king's reputation if expressed in particularly flamboyant cross-gender behavior, or "unmanly" activities. For example, Roman emperors with particularly bad reputations, such as Caligula (r. 37–41), Nero (r. 54–68), and Elagabalus (r. 218–222), were frequently portrayed as cross-dressing or taking a passive role in homosexual intercourse, something the Greeks and Romans thought degrading in an adult male. Henry III (r. 1574–1589) of France, an effeminate ruler who advanced the careers of handsome young noblemen

called his *mignons*, attracted similar criticism. All of these monarchs faced much political condemnation for other reasons, but their flamboyant homosexuality or bisexuality provided an especially easy target for their critics.

Christian Europe showed a higher degree of condemnation of same-sex erotic activity than most other civilizations. In societies that tolerate a greater acceptance of same-sex eroticism and lack exclusive social roles of "homosexual" and "heterosexual," homosexual behavior on the part of rulers was less objectionable and less problematic for the rulers. Many Chinese emperors, particularly in the Han dynasty (206 B.C.E.–220 C.E.), were known to have male or eunuch lovers, some of whom wielded considerable political power. The relationships of Duke Ling of Wei with Mixi Xia and the Han emperor Ai Ti (r. 7–1 B.C.E.) with Dong Xian are frequently referred to in Chinese literature. However, as the Confucian bureaucracy developed in later dynasties, it became more difficult for lovers of emperors to rise to political power.

Female rulers have generally had less sexual latitude than male ones, and there are far fewer known cases of lesbianism in rulers than male homosexuality. Queen Christina of Sweden (r. 1632–1654) engaged in a prolonged emotional affair with a court lady named Ebba Sparre, although it is not known if the relationship was also physical. Queen Anne of England (r. 1702–1714) was slandered as having the court lady Abigail Masham as a lover, an unproven allegation encouraged by Anne's rejected favorite, Sarah Churchill. Rumors about Marie Antoinette and her female favorites, the Princesse de Lamballe and the Comtesse de Polignac, date to the 1770s and flourished in pamphlets and pornographic images during the French Revolution, as part of an effort to depict her as an "unnatural" woman. Whether or not the rumors were based on fact, Antoinette, like Queen Christina, became a lesbian literary and artistic icon in the nineteenth and twentieth centuries.

See also: BEHAVIOR, CONVENTIONS OF ROYAL; EUNUCHS, ROYAL; GENDER AND KINGSHIP.

FURTHER READING

Bergeron, David. M. *Royal Family, Royal Lovers: King James of England and Scotland*. Columbia: University of Missouri Press, 1991.

Castle, Terry. "Marie Antoinette Obsession." In *The Apparitional Lesbian: Female Homosexuality in Modern*

Culture, 107–49. New York: Columbia University Press, 1993.

Hinsch, Bret. *Passions of the Cut Sleeve: The Male Homosexual Tradition in China.* Berkeley: University of California Press, 1990.

HONG BANG DYNASTY

(2879–258 B.C.E.)

A prehistoric and legendary dynasty said to have ruled over the first Vietnamese kingdom. The mythical dynasty was not recorded until the thirteenth century C.E., when the Tran dynasty commissioned the writing of a Vietnamese national history.

According to Vietnamese folklore, a Hong Bang ancestor by the name of Kinh Duong Vuong ruled an empire he named Xich Qui. Kinh Duong Vuong's son, Lac Long Quan, ruled Xich Qui through its golden age. He married Princess Au Co, who is said to have laid 100 eggs, each containing one son. After the eggs hatched, the two separated, and Au Co took half of the sons with her into the mountains while Lac Long Quan took the other half to the sea.

One of the sons of Au Co and Long Quan was elected the first of eighteen Hung kings who would rule the kingdom called Van Lang under the Hong Dynasty. The Vietnamese people consider the Hung kings as their patron saints and founders of their nation in the period preceding recorded history.

Few details have been passed down about the reigns of each of these legendary kings, and one can reason that the kingdom must have had more than eighteen kings, because with that number, each would have lived an average of 145 years to cover the dates of the dynasty. Au Co and Lac Long Quan are considered the ancestors of the Vietnamese people. The legendary kingdom of Au Lac followed the Hong Bang dynasty.

See also: TRAN DYNASTY; VIETNAMESE KINGDOMS.

HONGWU. *See* HUNG WU

HSIA DYNASTY (ca. 2205–1776 B.C.E.)

The first Chinese dynasty mentioned in China's historical record. Ancient Chinese texts describe the first three dynasties to rule China, the oldest of which is the Hsia, followed by the Shang and Chou.

Chinese histories referred to a series of god-like kings who ruled China before the first dynasty and who invented the arts and tools of Chinese civilization, such as silk and pottery production, metalworking, writing, and the domestication of animals. One of these rulers was Yu, the legendary founder of the Hsia dynasty. Yu is credited with taming China's waterways by implementing flood control and irrigation. He was said to be so virtuous and hard working that, although he passed his family's home multiple times during his years of work, he did not stop to visit them until he had accomplished his task of controlling China's rivers. Ancient texts reported that Yu's dynasty lasted for fourteen generations and seventeen rulers. After Yu, the dynasty deteriorated until its last king, an evil tyrant named Jie, was overthrown by the founder of the Shang dynasty in the 1700s B.C.E.

Although the Hsia are described in detail in Chinese histories, they were considered a mythical dynasty until archaeological findings in 1959 appeared to corroborate the ancient texts. Excavations at Erlitou, near the city of Luoyang, uncovered a city believed to be the Hsia capital, where archaeologists found bronze, jade objects, and pottery. Radiocarbon dating of the site placed it in the early second millennium B.C.E. While exact dates for the dynasty are not known, the Hsia probably lasted around 400 years, from the twenty-third century B.C.E. to the eighteenth century B.C.E.

Located in north-central China, the Hsia civilization was based on agriculture and appears to have been the first centralized state to rule over a large area. The dynasty probably marks the transition period from Neolithic to Bronze Age civilization in China. Archaeologists have uncovered ritual vessels made of bronze which they believe were used by shamans, or priests, to perform elaborate rituals. The rulers themselves may have officiated as the shamans in ceremonies that sought to communicate with the spirits of ancestors. Histories report that Hsia rulers passed the mantle of rule to their sons, and the Hsia are credited with introducing the practice of hereditary rule to China.

Although no written documents have survived from the Hsia period, archaeologists have found evidence of silk production, jade carving, pottery, and bronze casting. Excavations show urban communities that were home to skilled artisans and a stable social hierarchy.

See also: CHOU (ZHOU) DYNASTY; SHANG (YIN) DYNASTY.

HSUAN TSUNG (XUANZONG)

(685–756 C.E.)

Emperor of China (r. 712–756) during the T'ang dynasty (618–907), under whose rule China experienced a period of artistic and literary excellence. Hsuan Tsung, whose personal name was Li Lung-chi (Li Longji), rose to the imperial throne of China in 712 when he was twenty-eight years old. His father, Jui Tsung (r. 684–690), had ruled only a few years before dying in suspicious circumstances and was succeeded by his widow, Empress Mei, who may have had her husband poisoned. Mei's corruption eventually turned the government ministers against her. They revolted and installed her son Hsuan Tsung in her place.

EARLY YEARS

The reign of Hsuan Tsung began well. During the early years, the emperor was actively engaged in administrative duties. He is credited with making significant improvements in the conduct of government, pacifying the vast frontier regions of the empire, rationalizing the tax system, and ushering in a period of great cosmopolitanism, the likes of which the country had never previously known. Unfortunately, many of the changes he introduced would eventually contribute to his downfall.

Hsuan Tsung was also known by the name Ming Huang, which is variously translated as "Brilliant Monarch," "Enlightened Ruler," and "Radiant King." All of these epithets refer as much to Hsuan Tsung's support for the arts as to the wisdom of his rule. Indeed, his reign is generally understood to have been a glorious period of unprecedented flowering in the fields of art and literature. Under his patronage, two of China's greatest poets came to prominence: Li Po (Li Bo) and Tu Fu (Du Fu). Hsuan Tsung's commitment to intellectual pursuits is also reflected in his reign, for he founded China's first academies, in the capital city of Chang'an (Xian), and ordered schools to be built in every province in the empire between 725 and 738.

Hsuan Tsung is equally remembered for his affair with one of his sons' concubines, a woman named Yang Kueifei (Yang Guifei). This romance is perhaps the most famous in the history of China. Besotted with Yang Kueifei, the emperor became distracted from his duties and accorded her extraordinary influence, particularly in suggesting candidates for ministerial office. One such appointment was a young general named An Lushan, whom Yang Kueifei had adopted as a son. However, An Lushan was an ambitious man, not loyal to his sponsor, and Yang Kueifei would soon come to regret supporting him.

Yang Kueifei also led Hsuan Tsung into a deep study of Taoism, and soon the emperor became so absorbed in his studies that he virtually ignored his imperial duties. His inattention to his responsibilities did not go unnoticed by his generals, particularly those stationed on the frontier, and they became increasingly dissatisfied with Hsuan Tsung's withdrawal from the affairs of state. The generals were particularly upset that Hsuan Tsung did not seem to care that China's hold on the western borderlands was threatened by an uprising among one of the indigenous groups there, a Turkic people called the Uighurs.

DOWNFALL AND OVERTHROW

In 751, the Chinese army on the frontier lost a significant battle to these Uighurs, and this defeat was the last straw for Hsuan Tsung's disgruntled generals and ministers, most of whom blamed Yang Kueifei's seductive influence on the emperor for the troubles plaguing the empire. An Lushan saw an opportunity to seize power, and while Hsuan Tsung composed poetry to his concubine and pursued his philosophical studies of the Tao, the young general began amassing an army. In 755, An Lushan was ready to act. He led his troops in an insurrection and proclaimed himself the rightful new emperor of all of China.

Hsuan Tsung fled west toward Sichuan with his entourage, which included his beloved Yang Kueifei. As they fled, however, the emperor's guards decided that Yang Kueifei had to die. They killed her and dumped her body unceremoniously into a ditch. Soon after, Hsuan Tsung himself surrendered. An Lushan, did not profit from his insurrection, however. Hsuan Tsung designated his son Su Tsung (Suzong) as emperor, and imperial loyalists rallied around the new ruler (r. 756–762). A rather weak ruler, Su Tsung served well enough as a puppet for

China's powerful warlords, who restored some semblance of order and stability to the empire. Hsuan Tsung did not live long after abdicating his throne; he retired to one of his palaces and died in 762.

See also: T'ANG DYNASTY.

FURTHER READING

Johnson, David G. *The Medieval Chinese Oligarchy.* Boulder, CO: Westview Press, 1977.

Perry, John Curtis, and Bardwell L. Smith. *Essays on T'ang Society: The Interplay of Social, Political, and Economic Forces.* Leiden: E. J. Brill, 1976.

Wright, Arthur F., and Denis Twitchett, eds. *Perspectives on the T'ang.* New Haven: Yale University Press, 1973.

HUANG TI (HUANGDI) (YELLOW EMPEROR)

(ca. 2697–2597 B.C.E.)

One of the so-called Three Sovereigns and the first of the legendary Five Emperors of ancient China, who supposedly established the basic elements of Chinese civilization. According to traditional histories, the reign of this mythical ruler began in 2697 B.C.E.

The story of China's past and the life of Huang Ti (Huangdi) emerges through the works of ancient historians such as Sima Qian, who lived and wrote in the second and first centuries B.C.E. Although each of the legendary Five Emperors is believed to have enriched China's civilization, Huang Ti's myriad contributions shaped China to such an extent that many Chinese consider him to be the founder of the nation. His designation as the Yellow Emperor reveals Huang Ti's stature, since yellow in Chinese culture represents imperial authority and splendor.

Huang Ti is given credit for accomplishments in the practical, medical, cultural, and political spheres. According to tradition, he introduced wooden houses, boats, carts, the bow and arrow, ceramics, and the pottery wheel, and he encouraged his wife to teach people how to raise silkworms and weave beautiful silk cloth. Beginning in the third century B.C.E., Chinese physicians studied *The Yellow Emperor's Classic of Medicine,* an ancient text in which Huang Ti supposedly set down his medical wisdom. Huang Ti supposedly oversaw the invention of a system of writing, a particularly significant achievement because, to the Chinese, writing epitomizes all that is positive in their culture. Huang Ti is also regarded as the founder of the philosophical school of Daoism, while his victories on the battlefield secured China's dominion of the Yellow River plain and carved out a political identity for the nation.

Huang Ti is said to have died in an earthquake or shattering of the land, which legend attributes to nine dragons breaking up the town of Huangling. Interestingly, in the spring of 2002 C.E., the Chinese media reported that a meteorite over five thousand years old had been discovered in the province of Shaanxi in north-central China. The collision of this meteorite with earth may have been the event referred to in the ancient histories, leading some scholars to the conjecture that other elements of Huang Ti's life and history may be verified one day.

See also: MYTH AND FOLKLORE.

FURTHER READING

Loewe, Michael, and Edward L. Shaughnessy, eds. *The Cambridge History of Ancient China: From the Origins of Civilization to 221 B.C.* New York: Cambridge University Press.

HUARI (WARI) EMPIRE

(ca. 650–1000 C.E.)

Pre-Columbian empire that developed in the Andes Mountains of Peru in South America and believed by some scholars to have developed a tradition of aggressive empire building later adopted by the Inca. Archaeological evidence suggests that Huari brought other peoples under their control through military force and religious conversion.

The Huari, or Wari, Empire originated in the Ayacucho Valley of central Peru. At its height, it extended to the northern highlands as far as modern-day Cajamarca; along the central and southern coast as far as Moquegua; and to the southeastern highlands near Cuzco. The empire reached its peak of power around 900, but within the next century its authority began to wane as a result of increasing competition from other peoples and Andean states. Around 1100, the Huari were overthrown by these rivals, who established a number of regional states. Among these was the Chimu Empire.

The emergence of the Huari Empire was preceded by the appearance of several chiefdoms within the Ayacucho Basin. According to some scholars, the most influential of these was Huarpa, which laid the foundations for the Huari state. These early chiefdoms practiced an "archipelago system" in which colonies were established in different ecological environments, giving them access to a wide diversity of agricultural products.

The Huari state emerged from these chiefdoms around 650. While retaining many of the patterns and traditions begun by its predecessors, including the archipelago system, the Huari state also introduced the conscription of labor from subject communities. Such practices, accompanied by territorial expansion, allowed Huari to become the first known centralized state in Peruvian prehistory.

The capital city of the Huari Empire, also called Huari, was located on the eastern border of the Ayacucho Valley of southern Peru. The city grew steadily, eventually containing various administrative and ceremonial buildings, residential areas, and ceramic workshops where a distinctive form of pottery was produced. Massive stone walls divided Huari city into irregular sectors, but archaeologists have not found any indication of fortifications within the city. The lack of workshops dedicated to the manufacture of larger stone objects indicates that these were produced elsewhere.

At its peak, the city of Huari extended over 1,200 acres (about two square miles), and its estimated population ranged between 10,000 and 35,000 inhabitants. Huari provincial centers had similar architectural characteristics to the capital city, suggesting that their construction was centrally planned. The other major provincial sites of the empire were Jincamocco, Viracochapampa, and Pikillacta.

Huari culture shared some religious images and symbols with the Tiwanaku kingdom (ca. 500–1200), another pre-Columbian civilization that developed in the southern Andes of Bolivia and Peru. The nature of the relationship between Huari and Tiwanaku is still unclear. Some scholars believe they were parallel civilizations that shared similar cultural patterns. Other experts contend that Tiwanaku controlled Huari for a time during its early history, until Huari became an independent imperial power.

See also: CHIMU EMPIRE; SOUTH AMERICAN MONARCHIES; TIWANAKU KINGDOM.

HUASCAR (ca. late 1490s–1532 C.E.)

Last legitimate king (r. 1524–1532) of the Inca Empire in the period before the Spanish conquest of Peru.

The date of Huascar's birth is not known with certainty, but it must have been sometime between the late 1490s and the early 1500s because, according to accounts of the time, he was only about thirty-five years old when he died in 1532.

Huascar was one of the many sons of Huayna Capac (r. 1493–1524), ruler of the Inca Empire. The family of the Incan king was very large, for tradition permitted the ruler to take many wives and concubines, any of whom might bear his children. Only one of these relationships could yield a future Great Inca (king), however.

Of all a king's partners, only one was with a full-blooded member of his own lineage. This was the Inca's "true" wife, and only her eldest son could properly assume the throne. Huascar was not his father's favorite son—that distinction fell to one of his younger half-brothers. But as the eldest son of Huayna Capac's "true" wife, Huascar had special claim to the right of succession to the throne.

Unfortunately for Huascar, however, Huayna Capac was especially fond of one of his lesser wives. This woman was of noble rank and from the region of Quito. Huayna Capac even moved himself and his entire court to Quito in order to be closer to his beloved, leaving Huascar behind in the traditional Incan capital of Cuzco. This favorite, though lesser, wife bore Huayna Capac a son named Atahualpa.

As Huayna Capac lay dying, sometime in the mid-1520s, he sought to make one last gesture to show his love for his Quito-born princess. Although he could not break with Incan tradition and transfer successorship from Huascar to Atahualpa, he could do the next best thing. He ceded the lands of Quito to Atahualpa's rule, while leaving Huascar to inherit the Cuzco throne. His intent was for the two sons to rule separately but cooperatively.

The two brothers did manage to rule their kingdoms without friction for the first few years. But around 1530, a rift developed between them that was so great that Huascar and Atahualpa went to war. The cause of the conflict is disputed. Some say that Atahualpa was ambitious and simply wanted sole rule of the Inca Empire. Others say that the hostilities were triggered when Huascar claimed land that Atahualpa felt belonged to his own kingdom. Whatever the cause, a bloody civil war broke out and raged for more than a year.

In 1532, Huascar faced Atahualpa's advancing forces on the plain of Quipaypan, outside of Cuzco. The battle went decisively in Atahualpa's favor, and Huascar attempted to flee to safety. But Atahualpa's forces captured him, and Atahualpa had Huascar thrown into prison. With his rival out of the way, Atahualpa seized the Incan throne.

Huascar might have been allowed to live but for the arrival of the Spanish soon after his capture. The Spanish conquered the Incan capital but were unsure of how to administer so great a territory. Willing to turn over control of his empire in order to save his own life, Atahualpa offered the Spanish great sums of gold as well as his loyalty. He feared, however, that Huascar might put forward a competing claim in return for his freedom from prison.

To secure his own position, Atahualpa secretly ordered his supporters to assassinate Huascar. This was done in the latter months of 1532. Atahualpa did not long profit from his treachery, however. When the Spaniards learned of what he had done, they charged him with the crimes of fratricide and regicide (after all, Huascar was a king). For these crimes, Atahualpa was himself executed by the Spanish in 1533. He was replaced on the Incan throne by Topa Huallpa (r. 1533), one of the many other sons of Huayna Capac.

See also: ATAHUALPA; HUAYNA CAPAC; INCA EMPIRE.

FURTHER READING
Bauer, Brian S. *The Development of the Inca Sate.* Austin: University of Texas Press, 1992.

HUAYNA CAPAC (d. 1524 C.E.)

The eleventh Great Inca (r. 1493–1524) and the last to rule an undivided Incan Empire.

Huayna Capac died in 1524, eight years before the Spanish conquest of the Incan Empire. Because his life preceded the arrival of the Spanish, little information about him is available in the Western European historical record. His date of birth and the date of his ascension to the throne are uncertain. His father was Tupac Yupanqui, also called Topa Inca (r. 1471–1493). Huayna Capac succeeded his father on the throne in 1493.

As Great Inca, Huayna Capac was believed to be a direct descendant of the sun. Incan tradition tells the story of how the sun fathered two children: Manco Capac and Mama Ocllo Huaco. The sun ordered these two, who were also husband and wife, to travel the earth to gather all the humans they could find, and then to teach them how to create a civilized society. Their first-born son became the first Great Inca.

This tradition, though based on myth, provides information about certain Incan practices and customs. For one thing, although the Great Inca was expected to be polygynous (having multiple wives), one of these wives had to be his true sister, and only the first-born son of that sister could inherit the throne. The origin myth also provided a mandate for Incan imperialism: the sun-god himself ordered the "civilization" of the local peoples.

As the inheritor of this tradition, Huayna Capac was an exemplary Great Inca, even though his predecessors had already expanded the empire to nearly its fullest extent. Still, mindful of his mandate, Huayna Capac achieved a few more conquests, the final one being the conquest of Quito, in Ecuador. In the end, he ruled a territory in excess of three million square miles, incorporating all of what we now know as the countries of Peru and Bolivia, the southern portion of Ecuador, and the northern portion of Chile. These lands, gained through conquest, were frequently assimilated into the empire through relationships of marriage: the Great Inca and others of the royal house took wives and concubines from the ruling families of the conquered peoples. The children of such unions embodied the peaceful relationship established between the empire and its new subject peoples.

Like his predecessors, Huayna Capac married his sister, with whom he fathered two sons. His first-born, Huascar (r. 1524–1532), would be the legitimate heir of the empire, the other was Manco Capac, named after the founder of the Incan dynasty. Also like his predecessors, Huayna Capac took concubines from among the peoples he conquered. His final imperial victory was over the small Peruvian kingdom of Quito, and according to custom he took as his concubine a woman of Quito's former ruling family. With her he sired two more sons, the first of whom was named Atahualpa (r. 1532–1533).

Huayna Capac died suddenly in 1524 and, following traditional Inca practice, his body was mummified and entombed in the high mountains of the Andes. Although his official successor to the empire was Huascar, in the end four of Huayna's sons would briefly occupy the imperial throne. None, however, enjoyed a long or independent reign. Shortly after Huayna Capac's death, Huascar and Atahualpa fought a bloody civil war, and as soon as that war was concluded the Spanish conquistadors, led by Francisco Pizarro, arrived to conquer the empire and subject it to Spanish control.

See also: ATAHUALPA; HUASCAR; INCA EMPIRE; VIRACHOCHA.

FURTHER READING
Bauer, Brian S. *The Development of the Inca State.* Austin: University of Texas Press, 1992.

HULAGU. *See* IL-KHAN DYNASTY

HUN EMPIRE (ca. late 300s–400s C.E.)

Vast empire founded by a nomadic tribe of Central Asia which invaded Europe and attacked the Roman Empire during the fourth and fifth centuries, bringing both the eastern and western parts of the Roman Empire to the brink of destruction.

The origin of the Huns is not clear. It appears, however, that they originated in Asia and probably derived from the Hsing-nu (Xiong-nu) people of western China. The Hsing-nu seem to have split into two main groups after they were weakened by conflict with China. One group stayed in Asia and the other migrated westward, later becoming known as the Huns. Some modern-day states, such as Turkey and Laos, claim descent from Hunnic tribes, but these claims cannot be entirely verified.

MOVEMENT WEST
By the late fourth century, the Huns, possibly led by a semimythical king named Balamber (or Balamir), crossed the Volga River (in present-day Russia) and came into contact with the Alani people, who held the lands between the Volga and the Don rivers. After the Huns defeated them, the Alani provided some troops for future Hun campaigns.

The Ostrogoths (eastern Goths), a Germanic tribe, occupied the lands between the Dnestr and the Don rivers. They were the next tribe to be conquered and displaced by the invading Huns. As a result of Hun attacks, the Ostrogoths withdrew farther west and crossed the Danube River in Eastern and Central Europe. The Huns migrated farther west behind them.

As the Huns continued to move westward, they forced the Visigoths (western Goths), another Germanic tribe, to cross the Danube sometime around 376. The Visigoths sought protection from the Eastern Roman Empire. Within two years, the migration of the Visigoths into Roman territory led to one of the great disasters of Roman history. The Eastern Roman emperor, Valens (r. 364–378), allowed the Visigoths to settle on Roman lands. But unease among the Visigoths about their treatment by the Romans led to an open revolt around 378.

Valens led an army against a joint force of Visigoths and Ostrogoths at the battle of Adrianople in 378. The Goths formed an alliance with the Huns before the battle, and some sources speculate that Hun troops may have been on the battlefield that day, but this cannot be confirmed. The Roman army was annihilated and Valens was killed, while his western Roman counterpart, his uncle Gratian (r. 367–383), was just a few days' march away with an army from the Western Roman Empire.

ATTACKS IN EUROPE
Other than the legendary Balamber, the Huns appear to have been ruled by numerous chieftains rather than kings in the fourth century. By about 400, however, the various groups of Huns began to centralize under the leadership of a king named Uldin (r. dates unknown).

Uldin campaigned against the Goths around 400 and prevented them from crossing the Danube River. Around 404 or 405, he raided the Roman province of Thrace. Sometime in 405 or 405, the Goths attacked Italy, and Uldin and his Hun troops were recruited by the Roman general, Stilicho, to help defeat the Goth invasion. The combined forces of Romans and Huns destroyed the Gothic army near Faesulae in 406.

In 408, Uldin invaded the Balkan region, capturing the strategically important fortress of Castra Martis in the Roman province of Dacia. However, refusing to consider the peace overtures by the Roman commander of the province, Uldin found himself abandoned by his own men when the Romans successfully bribed his subordinates, inciting them to desert. Uldin was forced back across the Danube by the Romans the following year.

Uldin was eventually succeeded by Charaton (r. ca. 410–422) sometime between 410 and 420. Sources for this period are missing, and it is uncertain whether Charaton actually succeeded Uldin or whether they were contemporary kings who ruled different parts of the Hun Empire as co-regents.

RELATIONS WITH THE ROMANS
By 430, two brothers, Octar (r. ca 420s–430) and Ruga (r. ca. 420s–434) (also known as Roas, Rugilas, Rua, or Rugila), were kings of the Huns and ruling as co-regents. When Octar died in around 430, he was succeeded by Ruga, who ruled alone.

Ruga died around 434 and was succeeded as king by the brothers, Bleda (r. 434–445) and Attila (r. ca. 434–453), who also ruled as co-regents of the Hun Empire. These co-regents concluded a peace treaty with the Eastern Roman Empire that doubled the tribute paid by the Romans. The Romans agreed to this demand in order to avoid an attack.

Around 445, Attila murdered his brother and became the sole king of the Huns. Meanwhile, the Romans had failed to pay the agreed tribute, and in 441 Attila crossed the Danube River and invaded the Balkan provinces of the Eastern Roman Empire.

In 447, after a series of crushing defeats at the hands of the Huns, the Eastern Roman emperor, Theodosius II (r. 408–450), agreed to pay all arrears of tribute in exchange for a peace treaty. Such a comprehensive victory helped Attila consolidate his authority with his tribesmen.

The Huns invaded the Roman province of Gaul in 451, but they were defeated at the battle of the Catalaunian Plains by a combined force led by the Roman general, Aetius, and the Visigoth king, Theodoric (r. 418–451). But the Huns recovered quickly and, in 452, they invaded Italy. Several cities in Italy were sacked, and the Romans were forced to beg for peace, sending Pope Leo as an emissary to Attila and the Huns.

A combination of disease and famine forced the retreat of the Huns from the Roman heartland soon after. A small force of Huns was left behind to hold onto their newly acquired territory, but the Romans quickly routed these troops.

RAPID DECLINE
When Attila died in 453, his kingdom was split among his many sons rather than inherited by an appointed successor. His death threw the Huns into a state of disarray, and shortly after the division of the kingdom, war broke out between Attila's sons.

The civil war weakened the Huns and paved the way for a rebellion of the subject peoples. Around 455, an alliance of these peoples revolted against the Huns and defeated them decisively at the Nedao River in the region of Pannonia. The remaining Hun tribes fled to the east, and the Huns as a people eventually disintegrated. They were gradually assimilated into other tribes and lost their unique ethnic identity.

See also: ATTILA; OSTROGOTH KINGDOM; ROMAN EMPIRE; VISIGOTH KINGDOM.

FURTHER READING
Mänchen-Helfen, Otto. *The World of the Huns: Studies in Their History and Culture.* Berkeley: University of California Press, 1973.

Thompson, E.A. *The Huns.* Oxford: Blackwell Publishers, 1996.

HUNG WU (HONGWU)
(1328–1398 C.E.)

Chinese emperor (r. 1368–1398) who founded the Ming dynasty (1368–1644). Hung Wu began his life as Zhu Yuanzhang, the son of a peasant laborer.

Zhu grew up in poverty and lost most of his family to a massive famine in the 1340s. He was educated in a Buddhist monastery and later joined a rebel group that opposed the Yuan rulers, foreigners from Mongolia who had conquered China in 1279. Intelligent and a superb organizer, Zhu quickly rose through the ranks. He led his rebel troops in the capture of Nanjing in 1356, and in 1368, he proclaimed the Ming dynasty and adopted the name Hung Wu ("Vast Military Power"). By 1387 he had captured all of China from the Yuan, whose rulers fled to their native Mongolia.

Hung Wu built a great capital city at Nanjing, where he set to work restoring the Chinese customs that had been neglected by the Mongol rulers. He modeled his rule after the T'ang and Song dynasties, even wearing the clothing of these earlier eras.

Hung Wu revived agriculture, which had been devastated by natural disasters and years of warfare under the Mongols. He increased the amount of cultivated land, sponsored reforestation projects to prevent erosion, and ordered the building of dykes, canals, and reservoirs. Hung Wu kept taxes low and was frugal with government spending. To limit the state's expenses, he encouraged self-sufficiency throughout the empire, calling on villages to collect their own taxes instead of paying a government tax collector. He created a hereditary military that was to support itself by farming. However, there were drawbacks to this system. Government officials, who received very little pay, often turned to corruption to augment their salaries. The village system of collecting their own taxes also became riddled with corruption.

Hung Wu had thirty-six sons and sixteen daughters by his wife, Empress Ma, and his consorts. To prevent power struggles among his many sons, Hung Wu made them hereditary governors of the provinces. The sons possessed power in their respective regions but were forbidden to visit the capital.

Hung Wu issued frequent proclamations to the Chinese people promoting Confucian ideals and exhorting them to live moral lives. In his own administration, Hung Wu's high standards were not easy for officials to live up to. He nursed a paranoid fear of rivals, which led him to see disloyalty everywhere. Hung Wu created a secret police to spy on his own officials, and he ruthlessly punished any official he felt had questioned his imperial authority. In 1380, he executed his own prime minister, and as many as 100,000 people were killed in his frequent purges. Hung Wu eliminated the post of prime minister and established a highly centralized system in which all branches of the government were under his control. He also forbade the eunuchs—the castrated men who served the imperial family in the Forbidden City—from learning to read or being involved in politics.

The Ming founder died in 1398 at age seventy. In keeping with the Mongolian custom, Hung Wu's thirty-eight concubines were immolated with him. He was succeeded by his fifteen-year-old grandson, Jianwen (r. 1399–1402), who quickly lost the throne to his uncle, Yongle.

See also: MING DYNASTY; YUAN DYNASTY.

HUNTING AND KINGSHIP

A favorite leisure activity of rulers and their nobles throughout much of history. Royals and those with wealth have hunted for sport from the time of the ancient civilizations to modern aristocracy.

HUNTING AS AN ANCIENT SPORT

Huntsmen in ancient Egypt constituted an entire social class, hunting on their own as well as attending at the hunting of nobles. The pharaohs also occasionally went on fishing and hunting expeditions. The Assyrians and Babylonians also enjoyed the chase, as is shown by the hunting scenes depicted on the walls of their temples and palaces. Ashurbanipal of Assyria (r. 668–627 B.C.E.), sometimes known as the "Hunting King," had himself immortalized in a bas-relief with the accompanying boast: "I killed the lion."

A fifth-century silver dish showed the Sasanian king of Persia, Kavadh I (r. 488–496), galloping at full tilt after wild sheep. Hunting also began early among the ancient Greeks. A treatise by the Greek historian Xenophon, Kynegetikos ("On Hunting"), written in the fourth century B.C.E., was based on his own experience in hunting the hare but also describes boar and stag hunting.

FALCONRY

Falconry, the art and sport of training birds of prey to hunt in their natural habitat, has long been regarded as a noble art. The main objective of the falconer is to train a bird to return to the fist when called and then to train the bird to hunt with the falconer.

Falconry was a sport commonly practiced by the Arabic and Asian peoples, and it did not come to the Europeans until after 800 C.E. At that time, it was practiced primarily by the nobility, with each rank of nobility only able to use a certain species of bird.

References to falconry in China date from as early as 680 B.C.E. in the kingdom of Ch'u. One Japanese work states that falcons were used as gifts to Chinese princes during the Hsia dynasty (2205–1776 B.C.E.). Chinese emperor Teng's enthusiasm for falconry encouraged aristocrats to give falcons as gifts.

MEDIEVAL HUNTING

Frederick II of Hohenstaufen (r. 1194–1250), the Holy Roman emperor and king of Sicily and Jerusalem, was known as an avid hunter. He particularly enjoyed the noble art of falconry, and even devoted more than thirty years of his life to completing his book, *De Arte Venandi cum Avibus* (The Art of Falconry); his obsession with falconry interfered with his ability to lead his country effectively.

The idea of game preservation arose during the eleventh century, when the right to hunt became attached to the ownership of land. After the Norman conquest of England in 1066, England enacted stringent game laws, known as the Forest Laws, which made hunting the sole privilege of the king and his nobles. Other European feudal states had similar laws.

During the fourteenth century, drive hunts, in which game was driven into confined areas for shooting by the nobility, became very popular in parts of Europe. The English laws against hunting by commoners were progressively softened after the sixteenth century, until the nineteenth century, when hunting in England was open to everyone who obtained a license.

HUNTING IN THE SIXTEENTH CENTURY AND AFTERWARD

Hunting became increasingly popular among European nobility in the sixteenth century, as a result of which elaborate hunting castles were erected in areas where game was plentiful. Many of these castles, along with their trophies and artifacts, are still preserved today.

King Louis XIV of France (r. 1643–1715) was an ardent sportsman and was known to hunt or shoot every afternoon in the parks and forests surrounding his royal hunting lodge at Fontainebleau. His successor, Louis XV (r. 1715–1774), was so fond of hunting that on the very day of his coronation he stopped to chase stags in the Villers-Cotterets forest.

Elector John George II of Saxony (r. 1656–1680), also an avid hunter, is believed to have shot a total of 42,649 red deer in his lifetime. He refused the Crown of Bohemia, not for political reasons but because stags in Bohemia were smaller than the ones in Saxony. To protect his stags, he fenced the entire boundary between Saxony and Bohemia.

See also: PARKS, ROYAL; RIGHTS TO ANIMALS; RIGHTS, LAND; WILDERNESS, ROYAL LINKS TO.

HUSSEIN I (1935–1999 C.E.)

Third ruler (r. 1952–1999) of the Hashemite kingdom of Jordan, whose pro-Western political poli-

cies often brought him into conflict with other Arab leaders.

Hussein bin Talal was born on November 14, 1935, in Amman, in the then British mandate of Transjordan. At the time of his birth, his grandfather, Abdullah bin Al-Hussein (r. 1921–1951), was the emir of Transjordan, and his father, Talal (r. 1951–1952), was crown prince.

As a young prince with every expectation of inheriting the throne, Hussein received the best education available, attending schools in Egypt until he was in his teens. In 1945, his grandfather succeeded in winning his country's independence from Britain, and the newly formed nation received a new name: the Hashemite kingdom of Jordan.

As the first king of an independent Jordan, Abdullah began grooming his grandson for a life devoted to the needs of his people; when free of school responsibilities, the young Hussein spent much time in the company of his grandfather. Thus it was that Hussein was present in 1951 when a Palestinian assassin, angry over King Abdullah's close ties with the Western world, fired upon the two of them as they ascended the steps of the Al-Aqsa mosque in Jerusalem. The king was killed, but Hussein escaped injury. This would be the first of at least twenty-seven attempts on Hussein's life.

Hussein's father was next in line for the throne, and Hussein himself was proclaimed the new crown prince. Soon after, he was sent to England to complete his education at the prestigious Harrow School. Hussein had little time to adjust to his new status, however, for within a year it became painfully clear that King Talal, who suffered from schizophrenia, was unfit to rule. Hussein was swiftly called home for his own coronation as king on August 11, 1952. His father was committed to an asylum, where he remained until his death in 1972.

Because Hussein was too young to rule in his own right, a regency was appointed to conduct the affairs of government while the young king completed his studies in England. When Hussein reached the age of majority in 1953, the regency was dissolved and he assumed the full authority of his office.

Hussein was aware that far too often in the modern world, kings were deposed because they lost touch with their subjects. He vowed not to let that happen in Jordan, and he devoted his life to ensuring a responsive, benevolent government for his people. He also maintained close, cordial ties with the West, which did not please some of his subjects, particularly the large Palestinian faction that resented Western support for Israel. Nor did his pro-Western stance ingratiate him in the minds and hearts of some of his neighboring states. Syria, in particular, sponsored at least two attempts to assassinate Hussein in the late 1950s and early 1960s.

Hussein was married four times, twice to Western women, and he had a total of twelve children, plus one adopted daughter. His first two marriages ended in divorce, and his third wife, Alia Toukan, died in a helicopter crash in 1977. His fourth and final wife was Lisa Halaby, an American of part-Arab ancestry, whom Hussein married in 1978. She converted to Islam and took the name Queen Noor.

In the 1990s, Hussein was plagued with serious medical problems, requiring many trips to the United States for treatment. Diagnosed with non-Hodgkins lymphoma in 1998, he began failing fast. In order to assure an orderly transition of power upon his death, Hussein named his eldest son Abdullah as crown prince.

In early 1999, while in the United States receiving bone marrow transplants, Hussein fell into a coma; the family insisted that he be brought home to Amman. Clinically brain dead, the king was removed from life support on February 7, 1999, and died at the age of sixty-three. He was succeeded on the throne by his son Abdullah II (r. 1999–).

See also: HASHEMITE DYNASTY.

HYDERABAD KINGDOM

(1724–1947 C.E)

Kingdom located in the Deccan region of India, which came into existence as the capital of the Golconda sultanate and was formerly known as Bhagnagar.

The Hyderabad kingdom was formed in 1724, as the Mughal Empire was coming to an end, when Nizam-ul-Mulk (r. 1724–1748) of the Nizam dynasty established himself as an independent ruler at Hyderabad. As with previous Indian dynasties, such as the rulers of the Gupta Empire, the rise of the Nizam dynasty in Hyderabad encouraged the formation of a number of small regional kingdoms, such as those in the Bengal region of India.

Nizam-ul-Mulk remained on the throne at Hyderabad until 1748. As happened with many other dynasties, his death spawned an intense rivalry to control the throne. Unlike most other instances in Indian history, however, rival claimants were backed by European powers as well as by local supporters. Most significant in this respect were the British and French sponsorship of rival claims in the capital. Ultimately, the French candidate in Hyderabad gained power, although in other regional struggles, the French claimant in Arcot was defeated. This loss in Arcot split the young Hyderabad kingdom into two parts. It also instituted the French as de facto sovereigns over the kingdom of Hyderabad, with an Indian protégé to follow their lead.

French suzerainty in Hyderabad did not last, however. French commercial interests in India, which had been suffering because of these conflicts, led France to withdraw politically from the kingdom. In 1754, the French negotiated the transfer of Hyderabad to British control. The transfer of suzerainty did not provide the transfer of complete loyalty from the Indian population, however. This was demonstrated by the departure, in 1767, of the ruler of Hyderabad from the British campaign against Haider Ali Khan (r. 1755–1782), the ruler of Mysore.

This independent streak in Hyderabad rulers continued even though they were, at best, only nominally independent from European control. The princes of Hyderabad maintained their sense of autonomy by being one of the few states in the Indian subcontinent to be highly resistant to the Indian independence movement in the early twentieth century. One option proposed for the division of a soon-to-be independent Indian subcontinent was on the basis of religion. Dividing India in this way would have created a Muslim state, Usmanistan, out of the kingdom of Hyderabad.

By the time of Indian independence in 1947, the rulers of Hyderabad had refused to choose whether to accede to India or Pakistan. This act clearly expressed the self-determinant behavior of the kingdom's leader because, if the kingdom, whose population was mostly Hindu, remained independent of India and joined with Pakistan, Hyderabad would be surrounded on all sides by the new Hindu state of India. This lack of concern for the Hindu population by Hyderabad's Muslim leadership led to an invasion by the Indian police forces from Delhi and the subjugation of the kingdom within a week in 1947.

The kingdom of Hyderabad stands out for many reasons. Its history illustrates the intense regionalism that the governing bodies on the Indian subcontinent had to deal with on an ongoing basis. It also demonstrates the religious antagonism that has continually plagued relations within the subcontinent. The modern history of the Hyderabad kingdom provides insight into the complexity of the relationships between India and its neighbors, as well as an appreciation for the difficulty surmounted by everything that India, Pakistan, and Bangladesh have achieved and have yet to resolve.

See also: COLONIALISM AND KINGSHIP; GOLCONDA KINGDOM; HINDUISM AND KINGSHIP; INDIAN KINGDOMS; ISLAM AND KINGSHIP; MUGHAL EMPIRE; MYSORE KINGDOM.

FURTHER READING

Smith, Vincent A. *The Oxford History of India.* Ed. Percival Spear. 4th ed. New York: Oxford University Press, 1981.

Wolpert, Stanley. *A New History of India.* 7th ed. New York: Oxford University Press, 2003.

HYKSOS DYNASTY

(ca. 1663–1555 B.C.E.)

Ancient Near Eastern dynasty, apparently of Semitic/Asiatic origin, that ruled Egypt for some one hundred years during the so-called Second Intermediate Period.

Sometime during the eighteenth century B.C.E., large numbers of a migrating people from Asia, mostly of Semitic background, began settling in the Nile River Delta and northern Egypt, pushed west by population movements in Mesopotamia. Ancient Egyptian historians called the people the Hyksos ("rulers of foreign lands"). Their numbers and organization peaked at a time of internal weakness in Egypt, and by around 1663 B.C.E., the first Hyksos

pharaoh, Salitis (r. 1663–1655 B.C.E.), was able to take power.

The meager historical records that exist show the presence of concurrent dynasties in Egypt at this time—the Fifteenth dynasty, founded by Salitis, ruled most of Lower (northern) Egypt directly and the eastern sector through vassal pharaohs of the Sixteenth dynasty. A native Egyptian dynasty, the Seventeenth, ruled Upper Egypt from Thebes, though they too may have been vassals to the Hyksos.

Though of foreign origin, the Hyksos monarchs continued to rule Egypt through its existing political system, and they continued to support Egyptian religious institutions. They were active in construction and the arts, generally following preexisting styles and traditions. Some temples in the Syro-Palestinian style were built under the Hyksos, however, and the Semitic gods Baal and Astarte were worshiped alongside native Egyptian deities. From this point forward, Egyptian culture became less isolated and more open to foreign influences. The most striking changes introduced by the Hyksos, however, involved techniques of warfare: the use of harnessed horses, chariots, the compound bow, improved battle-axes, and advanced fortifications.

The last great Hyksos pharaoh, Apopis I (r. 1608–1567 B.C.E.), had to contend with increasing resistance from the native rulers at Thebes. His weaker successor, Apopis II (r. 1566–1555 B.C.E), was the last of the Hyksos line. The native pharaoh Ahmose (r. 1552–1526 B.C.E.) in Thebes succeeded early in his reign in conquering all of Egypt. The new Eighteenth dynasty that Ahmose founded dedicated major energies to invasions and conquests in Asia, perhaps to prevent a repeat of the humiliating Hyksos episode.

In light of the Semitic origin of the Hyksos pharaohs, some historians have speculated that the biblical children of Israel settled in Egypt during their rule and left after they were deposed. However, little evidence has been found to support this conjecture.

See also: EGYPTIAN DYNASTIES, ANCIENT (BEFORE EIGHTEENTH DYNASTY); EGYPTIAN DYNASTIES, ANCIENT (EIGHTEENTH TO TWENTY-SIXTH).

IBERIAN KINGDOMS (419–1492 C.E.)

Series of kingdoms established in the Iberian Peninsula between the early fifth century and the late fifteenth century, when the united kingdom of Spain began to emerge. Portugal was another Iberian kingdom that developed during this period.

THE VISIGOTHS

Around 419, the group of Germanic peoples known as the Visigoths migrated into the Iberian Peninsula from the north, and established a kingdom that straddled present-day France and Spain. This kingdom, with its capital at Toulouse, reached its greatest geographical extent during the reign of the Visigothic king, Euric (r. 466–484). At that time, the Visigothic kingdom incorporated most of Iberia along with southern France.

The Visigoths maintained control over most of Iberia for nearly three hundred years, until Arab Moors invaded the Iberian Peninsula from North Africa and conquered most of the peninsula in the early eighth century. The last Visigothic king, Roderic (or Rodrigo) (r. 710–711), was killed fighting the Arabs in 711. For the next seven centuries, much of the history of Iberia centered on the *reconquista* (reconquest) and the expulsion of the Moors by the Christian kingdoms that were established after the Moorish conquest.

MUSLIM KINGDOMS

The Muslim invaders established their own kingdoms in Iberia. The Muslim Umayyad dynasty ruled the Iberian Peninsula as part of the Islamic Empire from 756 to 1031. With the capital at Córdoba, the Umayyads developed a remarkable Islamic civilization in Iberia, one with a rich tradition of the arts, literature, architecture, and learning. The Umayyad caliphate of Córdoba reached its greatest period of splendor during the rule of Abd al-Rahman III (r. 912–961).

The Umayyad caliphate collapsed in 1031 and broke up into twenty-four separate Muslim territories, known as the Taifa states. Muslim Iberia remained divided in this way until around 1110, when a new Muslim dynasty, the Almoravids, restored political unity to Al-Andalus, the Muslim name for Iberia. Almoravid rule, however, was never entirely stable, and in 1174, another new dynasty, the Almohads, invaded Iberia from Morocco and ousted the last of the Almoravids.

Meanwhile, however, the small Christian kingdoms in northern Iberia had begun a slow reconquest of the peninsula from the Moors. As this *reconquista* spread, the Moors were confined to smaller and smaller territories. By 1238, the last remnant of Moorish power was confined to the kingdom of Granada, located in the southern part of the Iberian Peninsula, which was ruled by the Nasrid dynasty.

The end of Moorish rule in Iberia came in 1492, when the kingdom of Granada, the last Moorish stronghold on the peninsula, surrendered to Christian Spanish forces. The Christian conquest ended nearly eight hundred years of Muslim rule.

CHRISTIAN KINGDOMS

The first Christian kingdom established after the Moorish conquest of 711 was the kingdom of Asturias. Located in northwest Spain near the Bay of Biscay, it sheltered Christian nobles, Visigoth refugees who fled the Moorish invasion. Under King Pelayo (r. ca. 718–737), a Visigothic noble, Asturias defeated the Moors at the battle of Covadonga in 722. The Christian victory in this battle marked the beginning of the *reconquista*.

From 910 to 1230, the kingdom of Asturias was united with other areas of northwestern Spain as the kingdom of Asturias and León. At various times, this kingdom also included parts of the Basque region, Navarre, and Castile. Each of these areas enjoyed considerable autonomy and developed into separate, independent kingdoms.

The Christian kingdom of León had a complicated history. In the eighth and ninth centuries, the kingdom was controlled by Asturias, and from 910 to 1230, the two kingdoms were united as the kingdom of Asturias and León. At various times, however, León also was united with the kingdom of Castile. Indeed, by the end of the thirteenth century, the kingdom of Castile and León, which inclued Asturias, Córdoba, Extremurda, Galicia, Jaén and Seville, was one of the dominant kingdoms on the Iberian Peninsula.

The kingdom of Navarre was established in 824 under a Basque chieftain named Iñigo Aritza (r. 824–851). The kingdom reached the height of its power in the early eleventh century under Sancho III (r. 1004–1035), who ruled over nearly all of Christian Spain. Because of its size and power, Navarre played an important role in the *reconquista*. Navarre existed as a separate kingdom from 824 to 1589, when it was united with the kingdom of France.

At first, part of the kingdom of Navarre, the kingdom of Aragón, became a separate state in 1035 after the Navarrese king, Sancho III, divided his kingdom among his sons. At various times, the kingdom comprised Barcelona, Valencia, and the Balearic Islands, as well as Navarre. The kings of Aragón also ruled Sicily (1282–1410) and Naples (1443–1501). In the late 1400s, Aragón was united with Castile.

The kingdom of Castile, which eventually covered most of central Iberia, began with the settlement of the city of Burgos in 880. From 910 to 1029 it was a county of the kingdom of Léon. After a brief union with the kingdom of Navarre between 1029 and 1035, it was separated into a separate kingdom.

In the fifteenth century, Castile was united with the kingdom of Aragón by the marriage and rule of Ferdinand II of Aragón (r. 1479–1516) and Isabella I of Castile (r. 1474–1504). Although the two kingdoms were not officially united, the joint rule of Ferdinand and Isabella marked the beginnings of a united Spain. Their grandson, Charles I (r. 1516–1556), who also ruled as Holy Roman Emperor Charles V (r. 1519–1558), was the first ruler of a united kingdom of Spain.

PORTUGAL

Like Spain, the region of Iberia, now known as Portugal, was invaded by Muslims in the eighth century, and much of its subsequent history was also centered on the reconquest of the Iberian Peninsula.

Initially, Portugal was a county of the Spanish kingdom of Asturias and Léon. In 1139, Alfonso I of Portugal (r. 1139–1185) claimed the title of king, and the Spanish recognized the kingdom's independence in 1143. During the remainder of the twelfth century and throughout much of the next century, the kings of Portugal focused their attentions on re-

conquering territory from the Moors and consolidating their rule.

Under the Aviz dynasty (1385–1580), the kingdom of Portugal entered a period of great maritime expansion. Along with Spain, Portugal took the lead in the age of exploration and colonization that began in the late 1400s. Portugal established overseas trading centers and colonies in Asia, Africa, and Brazil.

The Aviz dynasty ended in 1580 with the death of King Henry (r. 1578–1580), who had no heir. King Philip II of Spain (r. 1556–1598) claimed the throne, and Portugal was ruled by the kingdom of Spain until 1640. After Portugal regained its independence, the two Iberian kingdoms continued to develop separately, never again to be united under one Crown.

See also: ALMOHAD DYNASTY; ALMORAVID DYNASTY; ARAGÓN, KINGDOM OF; ASTURIAS KINGDOM; AVIZ DYNASTY; CASTILE, KINGDOM OF; CHARLES V; CÓRDOBA, CALIPHATE OF; FERDINAND II AND ISABELLA I; GRANADA, KINGDOM OF; LEÓN, KINGDOM OF; NAVARRE, KINGDOM OF; PHILIP II; SANCHO III, THE GREAT; TAIFA RULERS; UMAYYAD DYNASTY.

FURTHER READING

Koenigsberter, H.G. *Medieval Europe, 400–1500.* Burnt Mill, England: Longman Group UK Limited, 1987.

Tierney, Brian, and Sidney Painter. *Western Europe in the Middle Ages, 300–1475.* 6th ed. Boston: McGraw Hill, 1999.

IBN SAUD (1880–1953 C.E.)

Founder and first ruler of the Kingdom of Saudi Arabia, who helped bring peace and stability to a land of warring clans and opened his country to oil exploration and production, bringing great wealth to the kingdom.

Abd al-Aziz ibn Saud, later known as Ibn Saud, was born into the ruling house of Saud as the eldest son of Abdul Rahman, sultan of the central Arabian province of Nejd. When the rival house of Rashid wrested control of Nejd from the house of Saud in 1891, Ibn Saud and his family were forced into exile in Kuwait. Unable to recapture the throne, Abdul Rahman abdicated to his son in 1900 and, in 1902, Ibn Saud and his supporters seized Riyadh in a surprise attack. Ibn Saud was proclaimed the ruler and religious leader of Nejd.

From this power base in Nejd, Ibn Saud began to use his considerable military expertise and diplomatic skills to expand his territory into a kingdom that, within thirty years, included most of the Arabian peninsula. Ibn Saud kept Ibn Rashid from regaining control over Nejd, drove the Turks out of eastern Arabia, and gained control of the western Arabian province of Hejaz, including the Islamic holy cities of Mecca and Medina. In 1926 and 1927 Ibn Saud was proclaimed King of Hejaz and Nejd. Then, in 1932, Ibn Saud consolidated the territories he controlled in the Arabian peninsula into the Kingdom of Saudi Arabia.

As king, Ibn Saud changed the lives of the Arabian people. He forced many nomadic people to adopt a settled way of life and abandon their tribal warfare. He protected Muslims as they made their yearly pilgrimages to the holy cities of Mecca and Medina. But the action that most transformed the region was when Ibn Saud granted oil concessions to two major United States oil companies in 1933. As Saudi Arabia's exports of its vast oil deposits grew during the 1930s and 1940s, so did the wealth of the king and his kingdom. Though Ibn Saud used some of the oil revenues for the betterment of his country, he spent much of it on his family and used this steadily increasing wealth as leverage for power within the Middle East and the world.

During World War II, Ibn Saud officially remained neutral, although he favored the United States and the other Allies. He also tried to limit his country's involvement in the Arab-Israeli war of 1948, taking only a minor part in the conflict. Upon his death in 1953, Ibn Saud was succeeded by his eldest son, Prince Saud (r. 1953–1964).

See also: ARABIA, KINGDOMS OF; ISLAM AND KINGSHIP.

Abd al-Aziz ibn Saud (seated) was the founder of the kingdom of Saudi Arabia. Under his rule, it was transformed from a backward tribal state into a prosperous modern nation with an economy based on oil exports. When Ibn Saud died in 1953, he was succeeded by Crown Prince Saud (standing).

ICONOGRAPHY

The conveying of meaning through symbolic images or image systems; the term *iconography* comes from two Greek works meaning "image-writing." In this form of representation, kings and queens are portrayed less as individuals than as monarchs.

Some of the symbolic iconography associated with rulers in art convey their divine or quasi-divine status, and others the idea of rule, conquest, or justice. Other images identify particular monarchs through personal objects associated with them or events from their reigns.

Often court painters have used images to convey an ideology of kingship to the public. Historians study the works of these artists to learn about the views that people had of their rulers and of the social and cultural history of the time.

SYMBOLS OF ROYALTY

Iconographic symbols of royalty associated with European monarchs include the crown, scepter, throne, and book of laws. For the Aztec rulers of Mexico, symbols of royalty found in art included a rattle staff, headdress, and nose plug.

The size and position of royal figures often reflected their importance. The king might be shown as bigger than others who surround him, as in the murals carved in stone from Edo in Africa. In other examples, the king might be seated above his court, reflecting his higher status, as in Aztec art.

Many types of images associate royalty with the divine. In ancient Egypt, for example, the pharaoh was often depicted with a falcon representing the god Horus (thought to have been the first ruler of Egypt), from whom the pharaohs derived the legitimacy of their rule. The Roman emperors, like many Asian rulers, were associated with the sun; the emperor Nero (r. 54–68), for example, was fond of having himself portrayed as the sun god Apollo riding in a chariot.

Other types of images portray the monarch not as a divine being but as a human ruler who embodies an important secular aspect of kingship. Many sovereigns in Renaissance Europe, for example, were depicted on horseback, indicating their strength and confidence. Manuscript illuminations from the reign of Akbar the Great (1556–1605) of India's Mughal dynasty depict him defeating his enemies or hunting wild animals to demonstrate his skill and courage.

ROYAL PORTRAITURE

Depictions of rulers in art may be either realistic or stylized, according to the artistic taste of the time. In either case, the societal conception of a ruler influences how their portraits are painted.

In humanist France, for example, from the fourteenth through sixteenth century, realistic portraits of kings and queens often showed them in ordinary dress without regalia, much like any other private citizen. Such is the case in the fifteenth-century painting of Charles VII (r. 1422–1461) of France by Jean Fouquet, and the anonymous contemporary portrait of Catherine de Medici, the wife of Henry II of France (r. 1547–1559).

During the consolidation of absolutist rule in France in the seventeenth and eighteenth centuries, portraiture was still realistic, but the image conveyed of monarchs was one of power and glory; they were always shown sumptuously dressed with all their regalia. The model for such portraits was Hyacinthe Rigaud's painting of Louis XIV (r. 1643–1715). The conception of royalty changed again after the French Revolution. When Louis-Philippe (r. 1830–1848) came to power in 1830, he was painted in simple military dress with his hand on France's new Charter, which indicated his intention of ruling as a constitutional monarch.

ROYAL ALLEGORIES

Sometimes the imagery associated with a monarch conveys a much more complex idea of the ruler to society. This was often done allegorically by portraying the king or queen using imagery associated with another famous figure. (An allegory is a story in which people, places, or events are given symbolic meaning.) For instance, one portrait of Ch'ien Lung (Qianlong) (r. 1735–1796), a Chinese emperor of the Ch'ing dynasty, shows him as the holy Buddhist layman Vimalakirti. The picture symbolized Ch'ien Lung's role as a religious man living in the world, distinct from the celibate Buddhist monks.

In Renaissance Europe, monarchs were often associated with figures from Greek and Roman mythology. One such ruler was Elizabeth I of England (r. 1558–1603), who remained unmarried and was often called the Virgin Queen. Elizabethan artists portrayed the queen as perpetually youthful (even in her old age), often in virginal white, or with flowers on her gown. These are the symbols of Astraea, the just virgin who heralded the new Golden Age, as described in the fourth *Eclogue* of the Roman poet Virgil. By depicting Elizabeth in this way, artists suggested that she had brought a Golden Age and perpetual springtime to England.

Today, especially in Europe, official photographs of monarchs, often in ordinary dress, have largely replaced iconographic representations of rulers. Nevertheless, the crown and other symbols of royalty still resonate strongly with people, as they have done universally in societies throughout the world and in all periods of history.

See also: HEAVENS AND KINGSHIP; REGALIA AND INSIGNIA, ROYAL.

FURTHER READING

Coquet, Michele. *Royal Court Art of Africa.* Trans. Jane Marie Todd. Chicago: University of Chicago Press, 1998.

Strong, Roy C. *Gloriana: The Portraits of Queen Elizabeth I.* New York: Thames and Hudson, 1987.

IEYASU TOKUGAWA. *See* TOKUGAWA IEYASU

IKHSHIDID DYNASTY (935–969 C.E.)

Muslim Turkish dynasty that came from Fergana in Central Asia and ruled briefly in Egypt and southern Syria in the tenth century.

The Ikhshidid dynasty was founded by Muhammad ibn Tughj (r. 935–946), a Turkish leader who was appointed governor of Egypt in 935, under the Abbasid caliphs. Four years later, in 939, Muhammad was named "Ikhshid" ("prince" or "ruler"). Muhammad's main achievements as ruler were defending Egypt against attacks by the Fatimids and reorganizing the government.

Upon Muhammad's death in 946, the throne passed to his sons, Unujur (r. 946–960) and Ali (r. 960–966). But the real power behind the throne during their reigns was Abu-al-Misk Kafur, a former Ethiopian slave belonging to Muhammad. Muhammad, recognizing Kafur's abilities, made him the tutor of Unujur and Ali. He also made Kafur a military officer, and the former slave proved to be an excellent leader. Before his death, Muhammad named Kafur guardian of Unujur and Ali, which gave him the real power in Egypt when they took the throne.

After the nominal reigns of Unujur and Ali, Kafur became ruler in his own right in 966. His court became famous for its lavishness, and Kafur also was known as a scholar and patron of the arts. The luxury of Kafur's court, however, was seen as a terrible excess at a time when Egypt experienced famine and plague, as well as destruction from a major earthquake.

When Kafur died in 968, he was succeeded by Ahmad (r. 968–969), the son of Ali. Ahmad ruled only briefly, however. He was deposed in 969, when the Fatimids conquered Epypt and established their rule, bringing an end to the short-lived Ikhshidid dynasty.

See also: ABBASID DYNASTY; FATIMID DYNASTY.

IL-KHAN DYNASTY (1265–1335 C.E.)

Ruling dynasty of the Mongol khanate of Persia, founded by the son of Hulagu (r. 1258–1265), who was the grandson of the great Mongol conqueror, Genghis Khan (r. 1206–1227).

In 1258, the Mongol warrior Hulagu razed Baghdad, the capital of Islamic culture and learning, and executed the last Abassid caliph, al-Mustasim (r. 1242–1258). The next year, Hulagu founded a new capital for this portion of the Mongol Empire at Maragha in northwestern Persia.

IMPORTANT RULERS

Upon Hulagu's death in 1265, his son Abaqa (r. 1265–1282) succeeded him as khan (lord), becoming known as the prince of Persia. Perhaps because of the enormous distance separating this portion of the empire from the seat of Mongol power in China, Abaqa's ties to the Great Khan, Kublai Khan (r. 1260–1294), were tenuous. Yet, his domain became known as the Realm of the Il-Khan ("lesser khan").

Abaqa's grandson, Ghazan (r. 1295–1304), was an energetic and enlightened ruler who took advantage of the great wealth and sophistication of the people and country he ruled. Ghazan converted to the Sunni sect of Islam, severed allegiance to the Great Khan, and moved his independent new capital to the growing city of Tabriz (in present-day Iran). There, he reformed the administration of the Il-kahn state and built mosques, colleges, hospitals, and libraries. By the late 1200s, Tabriz had become one of the great cities of the world, with a population estimated at around one million.

Ghazan died in 1304 and was succeeded by his brother, Uljaitu (r. 1304–1316). Although Uljaitu continued his brother's enlightened policies, in 1310 he converted to the Shi'ite form of the Islamic faith, a move that proved highly unpopular with his primarily Sunni subjects. Uljaitu's son, Abu Sai'd (r. 1316–1335), began his reign after his father's death in 1316 and soon reconverted to Sunni Islam. This conversion averted a civil war, which had been brewing during his father's Shi'ite conversion. However, internal factions continued to fragment the Il-khan realm and, when Abu Sa'id died in 1335 without an heir, the dynasty came to an end.

THE SCHOLARLY VIZIER

The most important and influential person in the Ilkhan dynasty was not a khan, but a government functionary, Rahshid-ud-al-Din. A member of the government, he first served as Abaqa's personal physician, and then he became Ghazan's vizier (a high government position similar to a minister of state). Upon the death of Ghazan, Rashid was appointed treasurer by Uljaitu Khan.

An impressive administrator and adviser, Rashid was also one of the great scholars of his day. He brought documents from all over the Mongol Empire to the royal court of Tabriz, and read them in their original Chinese, Arabic, Hebrew, Turkish, Persian, Mongolian, and Latin. He used this unique compilation of sources to write books on theology, medicine, and government as well as a remarkable seven-volume history of the world, the *Jam'ut-Tawarik* (*Compendium of Histories*).

In 1318, at the age of seventy, Rashid was denounced by a jealous co-treasurer during the reign of the last Il-Khan ruler, Abu Sa'id. In addition, the enormous university complex he had privately funded and built was destroyed.

See also: ABBASID DYNASTY; ISLAM AND KINGSHIP; REALMS, TYPES OF.

ILLYRIA KINGDOM (1225–167 B.C.E.)

Ancient kingdom in the Balkan region that, from the earliest period of its establishment, comprised a large area along the eastern coast of the Adriatic Sea and included the present-day regions of Dalmatia, Croatia, Bosnia, Herzegovina, Montenegro, northern and central Albania, and a large part of Serbia. The capital of the Illyrian kingdom was Scutaria, which is now the capital of northern and central Albania.

The earliest recorded king of Illyria was Hyllus (r. ?–1225 B.C.E), known as The Star, about whom little is known other than the year of his death in 1225 B.C.E. The kingdom reached the height of its power in the fourth century B.C.E. under King Bardhyllus (r. 385–358 B.C.E.), known as The White Star, who was one of the most prominent Illyrian kings.

Bardhyllus united the kingdom of Illyria with the Greek city-state of Molossia, or Epirus, as well as with a large portion of Macedonia, extending the realm from the port of Trieste to the Ambracic Gulf in the present-day Greek province of Arta. However, it was also during his reign that Illyria began to decline, when the kingdom came under attack by Philip II of Macedon (r. 359–336 B.C.E.), the father of Alexander the Great (r. 336–323 B.C.E.).

In 362 B.C.E. the Macedonian general Parmenion attacked and defeated Illyrian forces in order to recover land annexed by Bardhyllus. Upon succeeding his father Philip on the Macedonian throne, Alexander the Great declared war against the Illyrian kings. He emerged victorious, and in 334 B.C.E. the defeated Illyrian armies agreed to join Alexander in his expedition against the Persians, ultimately sharing in Alexander's triumph. Upon Alexander's death in 323 B.C.E. the Illyrian kings regained their independence.

In 232 B.C.E., the Illyrian throne was occupied by the celebrated Queen Teuta (r. 232–? B.C.E.), whom historians often call the Catherine the Great of Illyria. During her short reign, she expanded the Illyrian navy, whose raids on maritime commercial trading eventually brought Illyria into violent contact with Rome. The Roman Senate, seeking to protect its trading ships, declared war against Queen Teuta in 229 B.C.E and, after two years of conflict, Teuta sued for peace.

The last king of Illyria was Gentius (r. 168–165 B.C.E.), who ruled for only three years. In 165 B.C.E., Gentius was defeated by the Romans and brought to Rome as a captive. With the defeat of Gentius, Illyria became a Roman province and would never again regain its status as an independent kingdom.

See also: ALEXANDER III, THE GREAT; PHILIP II OF MACEDON; ROMAN EMPIRE.

FURTHER READING

Casson, Stanley. *Macedonia, Thrace and Illyria: Their Relations to Greece from the Earliest Times Down to the Time of Philip, Son of Amyntas.* Westport, CT: Greenwood Press, 1971.

IMPERIAL RULE

Means by which the subject nations of an empire are ruled.

Because an empire covers an extended area with different cultures and customs, its administration is inevitably complex. The system of imperial rule that evolves can have lasting consequences and may remain in place long after the empire has declined. Such effects are particularly true in the case of long-standing empires, such as Rome, or of empires that effected important reforms, such as the French Empire of Napoleon Bonaparte (r. 1804–1815). In such cases, common legal codes tend to become established throughout an empire over many years.

In some cases, an emperor or empress will permit a subject country's ruling monarch to rule in his or her stead as a puppet king. In other cases, however, the ruler may choose to appoint his own administrators. In either case, the vassal monarch is answerable to the emperor and is expected to enforce the legal code by which the empire is governed. In addition, the emperor normally exacts payment of tribute from subject nations. Although the subjects of an empire may resent such domination, it will almost always influence both language and government.

INFLUENCE OF LEGAL CODES

An empire can have a lasting influence long after it has ended, as was the case with the Roman Empire. Latin remained a universal language among the educated for more than a thousand years after Rome's decline, and the Roman legal system remains important even today.

Roman law, which was based on the Twelve Tables (written about 440 B.C.E.) and codified by Justinian in 529–534 C.E., was based on reason and natural law. The influence of the Roman legal system on our own legal code is perhaps noted most frequently in our vocabulary, but we are also indebted to their legal practices. In Roman practice, for example, a defendant was assumed innocent until proven guilty, two witnesses were required to prove a man guilty, and a recorder, or scribe, was required to take down the trial word for word. The jury's verdict also had to be unanimous.

Another example of the influences of imperial rule on the legal system is the *Code Napoléon,* or Napoleonic Code. The Code was established throughout much of Europe during the reign of Napoleon and remains the basis for much of civil code throughout the world today. Although the *Code Napoléon* reduced some of the privileges granted to French women under the First Republic, it was, nevertheless, a step forward for much of Europe, inasmuch as it abolished serfdom and granted equality of birth, instituted civil liberties, and established separation of church and state.

DIFFICULTIES OF IMPERIAL RULE

Imperial rule usually faces a number of obstacles, one of which is the long-term use of the military as an occupation force. As time goes on and an empire expands, more citizens become reluctant to perform military service. Ancient Rome, for example, encountered this problem and turned to conscripting soldiers from Germanic tribes to fill military requirements. This practice ultimately contributed to the decline and fall of Rome because Germanic soldiers learned Roman military strategies and counterstrategies, allowing them to fight more skillfully against their conquerors.

Similarly, the Napoleonic empire encountered difficulties as Napoleon spread his forces too thin and

as he attempted to extend his power beyond reasonable limits. Other kingdoms in Europe soon felt threatened by Napoleon and, consequently, formed an alliance against him. Moreover, his attempt to conquer Russia extended his army beyond that which he could successfully control and into a climate where his men were ill prepared to fight.

See also: CONQUEST AND KINGSHIPS; EMPERORS AND EMPRESSES; EMPIRE; KINGDOMS AND EMPIRES; MILITARY ROLES, ROYAL; REALMS, TYPES OF.

FURTHER READING
Durant, Will. *The Story of Civilization: Part III. Caesar and Christ.* New York: Simon and Schuster, 1944.

INCA EMPIRE (1200s–1572 C.E.)

South American empire centered in the area of present-day Peru. The Inca Empire was the largest and wealthiest empire to arise in the Americas, but it survived less than a century before being conquered by Spanish conquistadors led by Francisco Pizarro in 1525.

At its greatest extent, the Inca Empire stretched about 2,500 miles through South America: from the southern border of what is now Colombia south into present-day Chile, and eastward from the Pacific Coast into the Amazonian rainforest. At its peak, the Inca Empire boasted a population that may have exceeded 10 million. Although considered fabulously wealthy by the Spanish because of the abundance of gold and silver, it was the people within the empire, not precious metals, which constituted its real riches.

POSSIBLE ORIGINS

The people who came to be known as the Inca most likely originated in the region around Lake Titicaca, in Peru. The people who lived there from about 700 are known as the Tiahuanaco, who spoke an early form of the Quechua language and who worshiped, along with other, lesser gods, a creator god named Virachocha. The Tiahuanaco were driven from their settlements by a more powerful group, the Aymarans, who moved into the area around 1100. Fleeing northward, the Tiahuanaco eventually came to settle in the Valley of Cuzco, where they created a new society.

The fortress of Machu Picchu, located high in the Andes mountains of Peru, was likely built during the reign of the Inca ruler Pachacuti between 1460 and 1470. Deserted after the Spanish conquest of the early 1500s, this city of over 200 buildings was rediscovered in 1911.

Archaeological evidence supports this theory of Inca origins. So do the myths and legends that have been handed down by the Inca people, who survive today as the Quechua speakers of Peru and Ecuador. There is no written record of the Inca prior to the arrival of the Spanish in the 1500s because, unlike other civilizations in Central and Southern America, the Inca did not develop a system of writing. Archaeological excavations in the Lake Titicaca region have re-

vealed that the early peoples, the Tiahuanaco, mummified their dead, a practice that was also important to the Inca. In addition, the Inca recognized the god Viracocha as being the creator of their own most important god, Inti, who was revered as the sun-god.

EARLY INCAN KINGS

The name Manco Capac (who was believed to have been the son of the god Inti) heads the dynastic list of

Inca rulers. From Manco Capac, who lived perhaps in the 1200s, all other Inca rulers claim to trace direct descent. As a god, Manco had to have a wife of equal divinity, so he married his sister. All later Inca kings adhered to this form of royal marriage. Although the king could take many concubines, only the sons born of his marriage to his sister, who shared in the direct descent from Inti, could inherit the throne. In all, there were thirteen Incan kings, the last true Inca being Atahualpa (r. 1532–1533), who was conquered by the Spanish conquistador Francisco Pizarro in 1533.

Although Manco Capac gathered his followers in part through conquest, he was not a true emperor. In fact, the name "Capac" means "warlord" in Quechua. The kingdom he founded in the Valley of Cuzco was the first organized state in the region, and its strength was based on a system of tribute in which every able-bodied male was required to donate a set amount of labor to the service of the king. This labor requirement permitted the kingdom of the Incas to create a sophisticated system of irrigated agriculture that, in turn, supported rapid population growth. It also permitted the Inca to build an impressive army capable of overpowering and absorbing smaller settlements in the Valley of Cuzco.

There is no consensus as to the dates of rule for the first several Incas. The kingdom founded by Manco Capac was expanded and strengthened under the reign of the second king, Manco's son and heir, Sinchi Roca. Traditional accounts of this king describe him as a peaceful man. He was in turn succeeded by his son Lloque Yupanqui, who was followed by Maita Capac. This fourth Inca king is credited with finally succeeding in bringing the whole of the Valley of Cuzco under Incan control.

THE ERA OF EXPANSION

Maita Capac's successor, Capac Yupanqui, is believed to be the first Inca ruler to lead an army of conquest against peoples who lived beyond the borders of the Valley of Cuzco. Neither he nor his predecessors, however, took the title of Inca; the first to do so was Yupanqui's heir, Inca Roca. By the time of Roca's rule (he was the sixth Incan king), the supremacy of the kingdom was well established. During the reign of the seventh Incan king, Roca's son Yahuar Huacac, it is believed that the Inca reclaimed their putative homeland, the territory around Lake Titicaca that had come under the control of the Aymarans.

The first people to form a state powerful enough to pose a threat to the Inca kingdom arose in the region in the early 1400s, during the rule of Inca Viracocha (named for the Tiahuanacan creator god). At that time, a people called the Chanca organized themselves into a rival state and began to attack Inca

ROYAL RITUALS

BORN OF THE SUN-GOD INTI

The sun-god Inti was held to be the ancestral source of the lineage of Incan kings and later emperors. According to mythology, Inti sent his son, Manco Capac, and his daughter, Mama Ocllo, to earth in order to gather all of humankind together and teach them how to live as civilized beings. The two became husband and wife and arose from the waters of Lake Titicaca to walk the earth and carry out their task. They traveled north, gathering all the people they encountered along the way, stopping only when they reached the valley of Cuzco. There the golden rod that Manco carried was swallowed up by the earth, a detail that has been interpreted to mean that the land was suited for the cultivation of maize. Manco determined to build a city on the spot. Some variants of this myth claim that four brother-sister pairs were sent to earth, but events intervened to bar all the brothers but Manco Capac from successfully completing the journey to Cuzco.

THE INCA EMPIRE

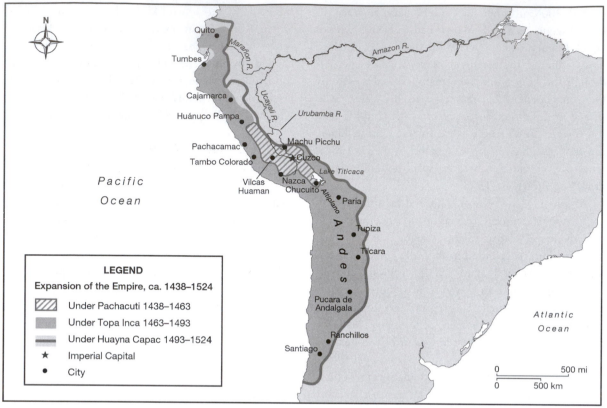

settlements. Inca Viracocha sent his sons Urco, Pachacuti, and Roca out to lead his armies into war against the Chanca. According to tradition, the eldest son, Urco, was a coward who fled to the mountains rather than risk his life in battle, whereas the other sons performed their duty and ultimately defeated the Chanca. Urco's cowardice earned him exile, and the next oldest son, whose full name was Pachacuti Inca Yupanqui (r. 1438–1471), inherited the throne around 1438 upon the death of Inca Viracocha. Pachacuti is the first Inca ruler whose dates of rule have been established with any degree of certainty.

THE FIRST TRUE EMPEROR

Pachacuti Inca Yupanqui was the first true emperor in the Inca dynasty. Like his father before him, he sent his sons and armies out to war, but this time the goal was territorial expansion, not merely defense. His son, Topa, spent his early adulthood advancing the borders of Incan territory, acquiring all the lands north of Cuzco into Ecuador and south to the Nazca Plains. When Pachacuti died, around 1471, Topa took

the royal name of Topa Inca Yupanqui (r. 1471–1493) and became the tenth Inca ruler.

By the time Topa Inca died, in 1493, nearly all the territory associated with the Inca Empire had been conquered. The reign of his son, Huayna Capac (r. 1493–1524), was largely devoted to consolidation and improvement. He did make one last, significant conquest, however, when he sent his troops north into Ecuador to conquer the kingdom of Quito, the last imperial conquest of Inca expansion.

Huayna Capac's proper heir was his son Huascar (r. 1524–1532), who eventually took the imperial throne in Cuzco. However, Huayna Capac had taken a concubine from among the ruling family of his latest conquest, Quito, and with her he fathered a son named Atahualpa. When Huayna Capac died in 1527, Huascar succeeded him, but Atahualpa (r. 1532) inherited the rule of Quito. This all but guaranteed the civil war that soon devastated the empire.

THE END OF AN EMPIRE

The early years of Huascar's reign as Inca were peaceful, but Atahualpa nursed ambitions of claiming the imperial throne. In 1532 he led an army against his brother, and in the same year he broke his half-brother's army, imprisoned Huascar, and declared himself Great Inca. Before he could march to Cuzco to claim his throne, however, Atahualpa was himself taken prisoner by a wholly unexpected enemy—the Spanish conquistador, Francisco Pizarro, who used a combination of trickery and superior military technology (cannons, muskets, and cavalry) to take the Atahualpa captive.

To secure his control over the Incan people, Pizarro intended to set up a puppet king, and he had to choose between Atahualpa and Huascar. To ensure that he would be chosen, Atahualpa ordered his supporters to assassinate Huascar in his prison cell. This strategy backfired, however, for it gave Pizarro a pretext to haul the Incan emperor before a court martial on the charge of fratricide. Atahualpa was executed, and Pizarro named Atahualpa's son Topa Hualpa (r. 1533) as the new Great Inca.

Topa Hualpa did not survive long in office. The Spanish found him insufficiently cooperative and had him killed. He was replaced by Huascar's younger brother, Manco Inca (r. 1533–1545). In 1536, Manco fled Cuzco to organize an army against Pizarro and his troops. Upon Manco's death in 1545, leadership of the resistance fell to his son, Saryi Tupac (r. 1545–1560). Although the Inca scored some isolated victories, the resistance forces could not hope to oust the Spanish, and in 1558 Saryi surrendered. The last descendant of the Great Incas, Tupac Amaru (r. 1571–1572), continued the tradition of resistance against the Spanish but was executed in 1572.

See also: ATAHUALPA; HUAYNA CAPAC; VIRACHOCHA.

FURTHER READING

Bauer, Brian S. *The Development of the Inca State.* Austin: University of Texas Press, 1992.

Loprete, Carlos A. *Iberoamerica: Historia de su civilizacion y cultura.* Upper Saddle River, NJ: Prentice Hall, 2001.

INCEST, ROYAL

The definition of incest varies from culture to culture. However, it generally refers to sexual intimacy and contact between relatives of the same nuclear family (mother, father, son, daughter) or between relatives sharing the same ancestors within two generations. Within royal houses, the focus of marriage between close relatives was often to keep the bloodline pure or the wealth and status within the royal family. Generally, other classes of society were forbidden from incestuous sexual contact or marriages, with the notable exception of first-cousin marriage, which was fairly common throughout history.

The children born of incestuous relationships (to people closely related) were observed to experience more health problems, if they survived birth at all. The child born from such a relationship tends to inherit more genetic traits that might have a detrimental effect on his or her health than a child born of two nonrelated people. The probability of detrimental effect is greatest in incestuous relationships between brothers and sisters. It is also very high in incestuous relationships between fathers and daughters, mothers and sons, uncles and nieces, and aunts and nephews. History shows that, in most cases, continuing this trend through multiple generations produces children that cannot survive or cannot reproduce.

Examples of incest among the royalty and the upper classes of societies are found in some of the earliest literature. The Hebrew scriptures, for example, tell of the marriage of the patriarch Abraham to his half-sister, Sarah. According to the ancient Greek historian Herodotus, King Chambyses of Persia (r. 529–522 B.C.E.) had incestuous sexual affairs with two of his royal sisters.

To ensure that the royalty of ancient Egypt was of the purest bloodlines, father–daughter and brother–sister marriages occurred quite frequently. When the royal wife of a pharaoh died, the next queen was chosen. This queen had to have the purest royal blood available, which often meant that a pharoah had to marry a daughter or a sister.

There are many examples of such forms of incest among the pharaohs of ancient Egypt. The pharaoh Sneferu (r. ca. 2613–2589 B.C.E.) married his eldest daughter, Nofretkau, and had several children by her. Pharaoh Khafre (r. ca. 2585–2566 B.C.E.) married his daughter, Rekhetre, and they had children. Akhenaten (r. 1350–1334 B.C.E.) married at least two of his daughters. Ramses II (r. 1279–1213 B.C.E.) married his daughter, Meryetamun, after the death of her mother Nefertari, as well as either his daughter or his sister, Hentmire. Tuthmose II (r.

1518–1504 B.C.E) married his sister, Hatshepsut (r. 1503–1483 B.C.E.), and they had one or two daughters. The Ptolemy dynasty of Egypt continued this ancient tradition. Cleopatra VII, in the seventh generation of brother–sister marriages among the Ptolemies, married her brother, Ptolemy XIII. Evidence exists that Ptolemy XIII may have had some type of mental deficiency, and he and Cleopatra had no children together.

Although royal incest between close family members did occur from time to time in classical Rome, the practice was legally forbidden. The Roman historian Suetonius wrote that the Emperor Caligula (r. 37–41 C.E.) had sexual relations with each of his three sisters. At one time, he was supposedly caught with his sister Drusilla by his grandmother Antonia. The emperor Claudius (r. 41–54) married his niece, Agrippina the Younger. Roman law stated that this marriage was incestuous, but Claudius had the law changed so that he could marry Agrippina. The emperor Nero (r. 54–68), Agrippina's son by a previous marriage, later had sexual relations with his own mother. The Emperor Domitian (r. 81–96) impregnated his niece, Julia Flavia, after he executed her husband. She allegedly died in 91 as a result of the abortion of Domitian's child.

An excellent example of the mental and physical disabilities created by extended, close inbreeding can be found in the Spanish royal family. The custom of uncle–niece and first cousin marriage had, over several generations in the fifteenth and sixteenth centuries, produced children who inherited several defective genes. For example, Charles II (r. 1665–1700), the fifth and only surviving son of Philip IV (r. 1621–1665), had an enormous head, misshapen jaw, and large tongue, which made both eating and speech difficult. He was mentally slow and did not learn to walk until nearly full grown, and then still tended to fall. Charles II became king of Spain at age three, and his mother, Mariana, ruled in his place. Although he was married twice, Charles was unable to father children. By age thirty-five, he was epileptic and lame, his hair and teeth had fallen out, and his eyesight was failing.

Early Hawaiian rulers before the nineteenth century provide another example of royal intermarriage. The *ali'i* (chiefs) of the highest Hawaiian lineages traditionally married brothers and sisters in order to keep the *mana*, or spirit of their divine ancestors, as pure as possible. The *mana* was considered to flow from this union of perfect lineage to the benefit of the entire community. Guards were placed on the bride until she conceived to ensure that her child could only be the offspring of her brother/ husband.

A child born to a brother-sister union in Hawaii would have a status equal to that of the gods. Hawaiian mythology tells of Haloa I, the first child of Wakea, who was born deformed and buried, giving rise to the first taro plant. Centuries later, Kauikeaouli, later King Kamehameha III (r. 1814–1854), fell deeply in love with his sister, Princess Nehi'ena'ena. Educated by Christian missionaries, they did not marry, but historians believe that they slept together as early as 1824. They were definitely together in 1827, although they had no children.

The leading chiefs of the Incas often married within the clan and were able to marry within the first degree of relations. This practice was forbidden to commoners, however. One of the last Inca rulers, Huayna Capac (r. 1493–1524), was married to his sister. Another Inca ruler, Sayri Tupac (r. 1545–1560), successfully petitioned Pope Julius III to consecrate his marriage to his sister, Cusi Huarcay. The Inca Empire fell to the Spanish conquistadors soon after, ending the ruling dynasty.

See also: BEHAVIOR, CONVENTIONS OF ROYAL; BLOOD, ROYAL; CONCUBINES, ROYAL; CONSORTS, ROYAL; GENEALOGY, ROYAL; HAREMS; MARRIAGE OF KINGS; ROYAL LINE; SIBLINGS, ROYAL; SOUL SIBLINGS AND CHILDREN.

INDIAN KINGDOMS

(ca. 600–322 B.C.E.)

The first recorded kingdoms in India's history, appearing during the sixth century B.C.E.

Around 1700 B.C.E., Aryan migrants from Central Asia crossed the Hindu Kush Mountains and settled in northern India. During the sixth century B.C.E. the Aryan tribes began to form distinct, independent kingdoms near the basins of the Ganges and Indus rivers. Sixteen kingdoms eventually emerged during this period: Anga, Magadha, Kasi, Kosala, Vriji, Malla, Chedi, Vatsa, Kuru, Panchala, Matsya, Surasena, Asvaka, Avanti, Gandhara, and Kamboja. These kingdoms occupy a significant position in Indian history because they bridge the divide between the earlier and more obscure Indian civilizations, such as the Harappan civilization of the Indus River Valley, and the series of great empires that began with the Maurya Empire in the fourth century B.C.E.

EARLY KINGDOMS

The earliest Indian kingdoms began as individual tribes, but as their populations increased, the rulers formed cohesive societies, built cities, and established primitive economies. Surprisingly, the sixteen kingdoms were originally republics rather than monarchies. Generally, assemblies called *gramakas* governed each community and oversaw all local affairs. Members of the assembly were divided among three categories: those who handled public affairs (the *sabbathaka*), those who decided legal issues (the *voharika*), and those who oversaw the military (the *senanayaka*). When a common threat or issue faced an entire kingdom, the local assemblies would convene at a meeting called a *mahavagga* to reach a joint response.

The kingdoms were relatively prosperous. Records show that northern kingdoms, such as the kingdom of Kosala, traded horses, furs, and finely woven blankets and tapestries. The southern kingdoms, such as Magadha, excavated gold, diamonds, and other gems and freely traded them for other goods. When the ambassadors of Alexander the Great (r. 336–323 B.C.E.) first visited the region, Indian rulers provided them with chariots, bundles of cotton, iron weapons, and even domesticated tigers and lions.

By the fourth century B.C.E., the Indian kingdoms had begun to issue currency to facilitate trade among themselves and with other kingdoms. Demand for the region's products increased, and artisans such as blacksmiths, weavers, and stonemasons sold their products to merchants from outside their communities. Most communities possessed a market for agricultural products and a bazaar for manufactured goods. Greek accounts indicate that foreign merchants frequented these markets and purchased goods to export to Europe.

DEVELOPMENT OF BUDDHISM AND JAINISM

The early Indian kingdoms were perhaps more widely known as the birthplace of two major religions, Buddhism and Jainism, during the sixth century B.C.E. Prior to these religions, Brahmanical Hinduism had been the dominant faith. However, many adherents of Hinduism in the kingdoms grew

ROYAL RITUALS

BRAHMAN SACRIFICES

The excesses of Brahman sacrifices helped precipitate the emergence of Buddhism and Jainism. The Brahmans claimed that the Vedas ("Books of Knowledge") were the sole guides to spiritual clarity and salvation. Because the Vedas called for sacrifices, the Brahmans instituted them as a major part of their religious ceremonies. The sacrifices occurred at the conclusion of lengthy and intricate ceremonies, when numerous animals would be viciously slaughtered. Because they occupied the highest caste, the Brahmans wielded great power, and they confiscated whatever animals they desired from individual families. Furthermore, the ceremonies became increasingly elaborate and greater numbers of animals were killed. The arrogance of the Brahmans, combined with their indifference to the needs of their followers, motivated both Buddha and Mahavira to form alternate religions. Both Buddhism and Jainism rejected the Vedas as the sole source of spiritual knowledge, and both religions forbade animal sacrifice.

disenchanted with the hierarchical class system imposed by the Brahmans and the elaborate rituals that they performed. The Brahman priests claimed that they alone possessed knowledge of how to attain salvation and gain enlightenment. Consequently, they adopted a highly condescending manner toward members of the other castes. They demanded that their congregations participate in lengthy, highly ritualized ceremonies that often culminated with blood sacrifices.

Both Gautama Siddhartha (the Buddha), a prince of the warrior caste of the Sakya clan, and Mahavira, a priest from the Indian Vriji kingdom, detested the arrogance and exclusiveness of the Brahmans. They argued that Brahmanical intervention was not necessary to achieve eternal life. Instead, they both advocated the pursuit of a moral life, urging their followers to shun things such as violence, material goods, or other impediments to a pure existence.

The religions they founded, Buddhism and Jainism, respectively, gained many adherents in the Indian kingdoms, and the influence of these religions gradually spread throughout Asia during the sixth century C.E. Yet, Brahmanical Hinduism continued to be the dominant religion in the Indian kingdoms. Historical records reveal a great deal of competition among the three religions. Hindu, Buddhist, and Jain histories list the names of their most prominent followers; frequently, the same names appear in each account. Most likely, leaders in the Indian kingdoms did convert, perhaps more than once, from one religion to another.

INDIA'S FIRST EMPIRES
The shape of the Indian kingdoms began to change in the fifth century C.E. For the first time, solitary monarchs reigned in both Kosala and Magadha. Consequently, they were able to consolidate their power, and the two kingdoms soon became the most powerful kingdoms in northern India. The rivalry between the two kingdoms exploded during the reigns of King Prasenajit of Kosala (d. 468 B.C.E.) and King Bimbisara of Magadha (r. ca. 603–541 B.C.E.), when Prasenajit conquered the neighboring kingdom of Kasi. Alarmed by Kosala's aggression, Bimbisara expanded his own kingdom through military conquest.

Bimbisara also sought a diplomatic solution. Around 594 B.C.E., he married a Kosala princess and temporarily strengthened ties between the two kingdoms. However, his oldest son, Ajatasatru, feared that the marriage would jeopardize his own position as heir. Ajatasatru (r. dates unknown) thus assassinated his father and took the throne. When Prasenajit learned of the murder, his forces attacked Magadha and defeated the new monarch. Prasenajit allowed Ajatasatru to retain his throne when the Magadha monarch pledged his loyalty to Kosala.

Another politically arranged marriage would soon topple the Kosala monarch. Prasenajit greatly admired Buddha, and he asked to marry a Sakya princess to join his kingdom with the Buddha's clan. The Sakyas abhorred the proposal, however, because they believed that Kosala was a socially inferior kingdom. But it was powerful militarily, so they could not reject the request. Instead, they tricked Prasenajit by sending him an illegitimate daughter of the Sakya chief. When the Kosala court learned of the deception, they demanded that Prasenajit attack the Sakyas to attain vengeance.

Because of his personal relationship with Buddha, Prasenajit refused. Led by the chief minister, the court rebelled and expelled Prasenajit. The beleaguered monarch pleaded with Ajatasatru for assistance, but the Magadhan monarch ignored him. Prasenajit died as an outcast, and the Kosala court officials placed his infant son, Virudhaka (r. dates unknown), on the throne as a puppet king.

BIRTH OF THE MAGADHAN EMPIRE
Ajatasatru quickly seized the opportunity posed by the situation in Kosala. While the Kosala army attacked the Sakyas, he invaded Kosala and easily assumed control of the capital. When the army returned, it tried to unseat him, but Ajatasatru's forces won a decisive battle. After this great victory, Magadha quickly became the most powerful kingdom in all of northern India.

Predictably, Ajatasatru next sought to subdue the remaining Indian kingdoms. Among them, Vriji was the most powerful. The Vriji kingdom was actually a confederacy of powerful clans, including the Lichchhavis, the Vajjis, and the Videhans. Ajatasatru used several petty border disputes to justify his attack upon the confederacy. But instead of immediately attacking the clans, he first created divisions among them by negotiating a series of false treaties. The strategy succeeded. Wary of each other, the clans failed to defend themselves and soon succumbed to the Magadhan army.

By 480 B.C.E., Magadha had gained control over

northern India, and the Indian kingdoms no longer existed as separate, autonomous states. The Magadha kingdom dominated the region until 324 B.C.E., when a military leader named Chandragupta Maurya assassinated the last Magadhan monarch, Dhanananda (r. ?–324 B.C.E.), and founded the Maurya Empire. Despite their eventual demise, the early Indian kingdoms had served as the birthplace for two great religions that would have a significant impact on world history.

See also: AVANTI KINGDOM; KOSALA KINGDOM; MAGADHA KINGDOM; MAURYA EMPIRE.

FURTHER READING

Raychaudhuri, Hemchandra. *Political History of Ancient India.* New York: Oxford University Press, 1996.

Thapar, Romila. *Early India: From the Origins to A.D. 1300.* London: Allen Lane, 2002.

INDO-GREEK KINGDOMS

(ca. 250–40 B.C.E.)

Kingdoms that arose from the remnants of eastern territories of the Hellenistic empire established by Alexander III, the Great (r. 336–323 B.C.E.).

When Alexander the Great died in 323 B.C.E., his generals divided his vast empire among themselves. A general named Seleucus gained control over the region that stretched east from Babylon into modern Afghanistan. Seleucus I Nicator (r. 312–281 B.C.E.) divided his domain into separate states and ruled the area for more than three decades.

CHALLENGE TO GREEK RULE

In 305 B.C.E., the Maurya Empire expanded rapidly from its nucleus in India. After Seleucus I suffered a major defeat at Kandahar that year, he signed a treaty with the Mauryas that divided Afghanistan equally between the Maurya Empire and the Seleucid kingdom.

But Seleucus also faced a severe threat in the west. While he battled the other Greek generals in the "Wars of the Successors" (ca. 322–275 B.C.E.), the Mauryas gradually overran the rest of Afghanistan. Under the leadership of Asoka (r. 268–232 B.C.E)., the most accomplished Maurya ruler, the Maurya Empire eventually extended over the entire

Indian subcontinent. When Asoka died in 232 B.C.E., Mauryan dominance steadily crumbled, and the Greek enclaves that remained in Afghanistan regained their autonomy.

RISE OF BACTRIA

One of these Greek states, Bactria, quickly became the most powerful of the group. Under the leadership of Diodorus I (r. ca. 256–248 B.C.E.) and his son, Diodorous II (r. ca. 248–235 B.C.E.), Bactria unified many of the former Seleucid states. These states were willing to accept Bactrian rule because they faced serious threats from other groups and required military protection. When the Mauryas retreated from the region after Asoka's death, Parthian raiders from the north invaded and plundered the area and exacted heavy tributes from the Greek communities there. Therefore, Bactria gained regional support by resisting the Parthians.

Diodorus II's successor, Euthydemus I (r. ca. 235–200 B.C.E.), utilized this newfound strength. During the 220s B.C.E., he achieved several decisive victories over the Parthians, conquered the city of Herat in the west, and expanded Bactria's eastern border into China's Xianjing province. Under Euthydemus's guidance, Bactria became a completely independent Hellenistic society, foremost among the Indo-Greek kingdoms.

While Euthydemus was consolidating his power, Antiochus III (r. 223–187 B.C.E.), one of the successors of Seleucus I, was attempting to reunify the former Seleucid holdings. In 209 B.C.E., he marched east and conquered all the areas up to the Bactrian border. A battle between the two Greek powers appeared imminent, but when Euthydemus and Antiochus met, they agreed to divide control of the region equally and protect one another from invasion. Soon after, however, Antiochus recognized the difficulty of maintaining such a vast empire. He focused upon his western territories, and Bactria again enjoyed complete independence.

ZENITH AND DECLINE

During the second century B.C.E., Bactria attained its greatest prominence. Euthydemus I's son and successor, Demetrius I (r. ca. 200–185 B.C.E.), spread Bactrian control over all of modern Afghanistan and across the rugged Khyber Pass into present-day Pakistan. In essence, the Bactrians were following the retreating Maurya Empire. As that empire crumbled, the

Bactrians advanced, seizing former Mauryan territories. Eventually, the Bactrian kingdom spread across the Indus River and all the way to Patna, the former Maurya capital, on the banks of the Ganges River.

Demetrius I established many Greek outposts throughout these new territories. A number of them, however, gradually loosened themselves from Bactrian control and gained independence. For decades, these Greek outposts remained as distinct communities, even as the empires surrounding them flourished and declined. As a result, centuries later, individuals with Hellenistic features could still be found throughout western India.

Bactria reached its zenith under the reign of Menander (r. ca. 155–130 B.C.E.), who assumed the throne in 155 B.C.E. and continued to fortify the Bactrian kingdom. Because of his affinity for Buddhism, Menander was given the Buddhist name Milinda. Menander led a large foray into central India, but was repulsed by a leader named Pushyamitra Sunga (r. ca. 187–151 B.C.E.), whose victory earned him the appellation "King of the Indians." Bactria's borders remained stationary for the remainder of Menander's reign.

Around 120 B.C.E., Bactria faced increasingly dangerous threats from the north. Nomadic invaders, consisting primarily of the Scythians, repeatedly pillaged the outlying Bactrian communities. After Menander died around 130 B.C.E., Bactria became increasingly fragmented as various leaders battled for control of the kingdom and sought to protect their own regions.

The last recorded Greek ruler of Bactria was Hermaeus (r. ca. 75–55 B.C.E.). During his reign, Hermaeus briefly restored Bactrian prominence by conquering the region between Kabul (in present-day Afghanistan) to the Indus River. After his death, the kingdom was briefly controlled by a series of Indian princes before it was subsumed by the Kushan dynasty in the last decades of the first century B.C.E.

See also: ANTIOCHUS III, THE GREAT; MAURYA EMPIRE; MENANDER; PARTHIAN KINGDOM; SELEUCID DYNASTY.

FURTHER READING

Smith, Vincent A. *The Oxford History of India.* Ed. Percival Spear. 4th ed. New York: Oxford University Press, 1981.

Tanner, Stephen. *Afghanistan: A Military History from Alexander the Great to the Fall of the Taliban.* New York: Da Capo Press, 2002.

INHERITANCE, ROYAL

The legacy of royal inheritance is a rather complicated and hardly universal matter. Intangibles such as title, prestige and rank, physical property, material wealth, and in some cases land and houses could be subject to inheritance by a royal. A monarch's coming to power could be inherited, especially for royal males under primogeniture. The act of assuming power, either to the throne or of a dynasty or empire, is called accession and is similar to, and can encompass, aspects of inheritance. The actual coming into power, that is, when royals attain actual ruling rank, is best understood by the study of royal accession.

For many royal cultures primogeniture was the norm; under this system, the eldest (almost always the son) would inherit the monarch's wealth, property, and throne. During the Warring States Period in China (403–221 B.C.E.), grown men were forbidden from living with their fathers in an effort to promote the cultivation of new agricultural land and to further increase tax revenues to the state. Following the Warring States Period, the Han dynasty (221 B.C.E.–220 C.E.) stipulated that inheritance was to be divided evenly among male heirs; to many outsiders, however, this practice seems to make little economic sense.

HAN DYNASTY (206 B.C.E.–220 C.E.)

The Han dynasty in China was founded by Liu Bang (r. 207–195 B.C.E.), who at the regime's commencement, ennobled his favorite relatives and friends. By 154 B.C.E., this line of princes had grown powerful and revolted against the Han dynasty's imperial authority. Emperor Han Wudi (r. 141–87 B.C.E.), seeking to quell the threat to his own authority and that of the dynasty's, enacted measures that required all princes to divide their property, Han Wudi also directed that princes could not give the bulk of their property to one son and significantly smaller shares to others. Through royal property inheritance, or *fenjia* mandates in Imperial China, it was ensured that the princes would never again gain too much power and pose a threat to the dynasty as they had in the early Han period.

LATER DYNASTIES FROM T'ANG

The T'ang dynasty (618–906 C.E.) held onto to some of the axioms established in the Han dynasty. Male heirs were to divide property evenly; if a brother

ROYAL RELATIVES

ELEANOR OF AQUITAINE

France's Eleanor of Aquitaine (1122–1204) was wife and mother to two kings and thoroughly a legend in her own right. When Eleanor was fifteen her father died and she inherited Aquitaine, the largest kingdom of France. That same year she wed King Louis VII of France; she later had the marriage annulled on the basis that they were related, though this would not have necessarily given pause to royals. She then married England's Henry II in 1154, who was scandalously eleven years her junior. Eleanor bore Henry seven children, two of whom went on to become kings of England: Richard and Henry. Henry sent Eleanor to her duchy of Aquitaine to restore order; she took an authoritative role. She was neither a figurehead queen nor the pawn of her husband the king. By 1173, having grown weary of Henry's philandering, she launched a rebellion against her husband, seeking to rule Aquitaine with her son Richard, without Henry's involvement. Henry responded by throwing her in jail for fifteen years. The shrewd Eleanor regained her duchy and lived to see her favorite son Richard I the Lionhearted (1157–1199) inherit the throne of England, very much against the late king's wishes and in line with her own. She was appointed Richard's regent while he fought against the Sultan Saladin (1138–1193) in the second crusade; Richard spent only about six months of his ten-year reign actually in England.

died, his son(s) inherited his share, unmarried sons were given additional property to cover marriage expenses, and a widow with a son would receive her husband's share of the property. Many of these edicts remained in place until the Communist revolution of the twentieth century.

The Song state in southern China, ruled by Mongols during the late thirteenth century, marked the only time in imperial Chinese history that an attempt was made to pass an inheritance tax. The purpose of the tax was to raise funds for military defense from invasions. The Song dynasty was ruled by Mongol invaders during the Yuan dynasty (1260–1368) and with foreign rule came new laws for inheritance. Mongols mandated a form of ultimogeniture wherein as each son came of age and married he was given a set amount of property for his own family. Chinese rule was reestablished in the Ming dynasty (1368–1644) with the first emperor Hung Wu (r. 1368–1398), and it was provided that sons were to inherit evenly whether they were born of a wife or a concubine.

Descent from God

Royals around the world and rulers from the earliest times often believed that they were descended from god(s). Many Greek and Roman nobles believed they came from demigods, whereas many kings claimed to rule by divine right. From the early medieval period to 900 C.E., the concept of royal blood, which only the monarch and relatives had running through them, prevailed. The need to pass the throne, property, and power on to another descended from the heavens often required that royals go to great lengths to secure an heir. Some royalty were thought to have magical, healing powers; King Edward the Confessor (r. 1042–1066), for example, is alleged to have healed hundreds at the touch of the hand. Primogeniture was the rule of thumb for European royalty, with all the wealth and the throne passed on to the eldest male heir, usually a son, (it was believed that women could not adequately lead military operations). However, royal women did play a central role in the primogeniture via the importance given to bloodlines and thus marriage. In royal marriage it was always assumed that the woman was a virgin, but the same did not hold for the king. Virginity was held in high esteem in order to ensure royal bloodlines and ultimately reduce heir confusion since children were to be born out of wedlock, prior to the royal union, and could lay claim to the throne and its wealth. Russia's Ivan IV known as the Terrible (r. 1533–1584) had his seventh wife drowned one day after discovering that his newest bride was not a virgin. The need to produce an heir, preferably a male one, often led to multiple wives and affairs with concubines if an heir could not be produced within marriage. Women fared better under the French king Chilperic (r. 561–584), who allowed them to inherit Salic land as long as they had no brothers.

See also: ACCESSION AND CROWNING OF KINGS; AQUITAINE DUCHY; CONCUBINES, ROYAL; FRANKISH KINGDOM; HAN DYNASTY; HENRY II; MARRIAGE OF KINGS; MONGOL EMPIRE; PRIMOGENITURE; ROYAL LINE.

FURTHER READING

Basch, Norma. *In the Eyes of the Law: Women, Property and Marriage in Nineteenth-Century.* Ithaca, NY: Cornell University Press, 1982.

IRELAND, HIGH KINGS OF.

See IRISH KINGS

IRENE (c. 750–803 C.E.)

Byzantine empress (r. 797–802) who served as a co-regent for her son, Constantine VI (r. 780–797) and who became sole ruler in 797. The first woman ever to hold the imperial throne of the old Roman and Byzantine empires, Irene ranks with Hatshepsut of Egypt (r. 1503–1483 B.C.E.) and Catherine II (the Great) of Russia (1762–1796) as a breaker of male-dominated dynasties.

Irene was born around 752 to a noble Greek family in Athens. In 769, she married the Byzantine crown prince, who later became Emperor Leo IV (r. 775–780). Their son, Constantine, became emperor upon his father's death in 780. But because Constantine was still a young boy, Irene ruled as his co-regent, effectively becoming the sole ruler.

When Constantine became of age to rule on his own, the ambitious Irene had her son deposed and blinded, taking the throne completely for herself in 797. Constantine died shortly afterward, and Irene became the first woman to hold the throne of the Byzantine, or Eastern Roman Empire.

Since Pope Leo III believed that no woman could legally become emperor, he considered the Roman throne of the empire to be vacant. To fill the seat, he turned to the Frankish king Charlemagne (r. 768–814), who ruled over most of Western Europe. In 800, the pope crowned Charlemagne as Roman emperor in the West. This act officially removed the Byzantine Empire from recognition in the West as being the heir of ancient Rome. Yet the Byzantine Empire lasted until 1453, always Roman in its own eyes.

During her reign, Irene was devoted to the Eastern Orthodox Church and sought to suppress iconoclasm, the worship of icons or images. In 784, she had Tarasius, one of her supporters, elected head of the Byzantine Church. Together, Irene and Tarasius convened a meeting of over three hundred bishops in 787, known as the Second Council of Nicaea, which refuted iconoclasm and declared that icons should be revered but not worshiped.

Irene was deposed by rebellious Byzantine nobles in 802 and taken to the Aegean island of Lesbos, off the west coast of Anatolia (present-day Turkey), where she died in exile in 803. As a result of Irene's fight against iconoclasm, the Greek Church later recognized her as a saint.

See also: BYZANTINE EMPIRE; CHARLEMAGNE; ROMAN EMPIRE.

IRISH KINGS (400s–1175 C.E.)

Elected tribal leaders of ancient and medieval Ireland who eventually assumed the title of kings.

The Song of Dermot and the Earl, an Anglo-Norman poem celebrating the English invasion of Ireland in the twelfth century, maintained that "in Ireland there were many kings." In fact, from the fifth to the twelfth centuries, as many as 150 kings might have reigned over individual territories in Ireland. Though their realms were small, these rulers played a large part in Irish legends and history.

EARLY LEGENDS

According to the legendary medieval saga, *The Book of the Taking of Ireland*, a people called the Fir Bolg invaded Ireland in the second millennium B.C.E. and divided the country into five provinces. Around 1900 B.C.E., the Fir Bolg were conquered by the Dé Danann, or "people of the goddess Danu." The names of some of the kings and heroes of the Dé Danann are identical with Celtic gods and goddesses.

In 1498 B.C.E., the Milesians, a Celtic people from Spain, came to Ireland, defeated the Dé Dannan, and banished them to the Otherworld or spiritual realm. That is the legend; the only certain facts are that Celts invaded Ireland about 200 B.C.E. and that the land was divided into five provinces: Leinster, Ulster, Connaught, Munster, and Meath.

With the beginning of the Christian era in the fifth century C.E., the history of Ireland is more certain. Medieval annals and genealogies contain lists of the Irish kings and the dates of their rule. Irish law texts from the seventh and eighth centuries recount how these kings of Ireland governed.

KINGS AND HIGH-KINGS

According to early Irish law tracts, there were three hierarchical levels of political kingship: the *ri* or leader of the *túaithe*, or tribal group; the *ruiri*, or overking, who was head of his own *túaithe* and overlord of one or more other tribal kings; and the *ri ruirech* or "king of overkings," who ruled over all the kings and overkings in a province.

The title *ard-ri* or "high-king" was given to the single king who ruled from his seat at Tara, a high hill near Dublin. The high-king's rule was religious rather than political. From the ninth century C.E. onward, however, the high-kingship of Tara often became a real political kingship as well as a position of religious leadership.

ROYAL PLACES

TARA: THE SACRED PLACE OF KINGS

The seat of the high-kings of Ireland, Tara was both a royal residence and a religious center. The name Tara (Temrai) means "Prospect Hill" in Gaelic. Some think this high hill near Dublin was named for an ancient Celtic goddess, Tea.

All that remains at Tara today are a few earthen mounds, one of which is a burial mound dating from the Neolithic period (3500–2000 B.C.E.). Within this mound is a stone passage with a slab decorated with images of the sun, moon, and stars. This might be a primitive calendar connected with religious feasts celebrated at Tara at the full moons in August (feast of Lughnasa), November (feast of Samain), February (feast of Imbolg), and May (feast of Bealtaine). Every year on Bealtaine all the fires in the surrounding area were lighted from the fire at Tara.

At his election, the high-king of Tara faced a series of ritual ordeals, which included running his chariot wheels over the phallic *Lia Fáil*, or Stone of Destiny. The stone would only cry out if he were the true king. During his inaugural feast of kingship at Tara at Samain, the king drank from a cup that symbolized his marriage with Maeve, the goddess of Ireland and Sovereignty. Although these rites declined with the rise of Christianity, Tara continued to be a symbolic seat of kings.

After the English invasion of Ireland in 1171, Tara became a rallying place for the cause of Irish independence. In 1798, the United Irishmen fought the battle of Tara against British forces. In 1843, the Irish patriot Daniel O'Connell called from Tara for the repeal of the union with Great Britain. In the early twentieth century, W. B. Yeats and other members of the Irish literary revival celebrated Tara as a sacred spot of Ireland's legendary past.

POWERS OF THE EARLY KINGS

In theory, each Irish king, even the *ri ruirech*, ("king of overkings"), exercised power only over his own *túaiche*. While an overking exercised a personal lordship over his sub-king, the overking did not have power over the sub-king's subjects. Each king was responsible for leading his *túaithe* in war and making political decisions. In practice, from the eighth century onward, the overkings began to subjugate other kings and their peoples, and they eventually established territorial lordships resembling those of feudal kings in the rest of Europe.

Ancient Irish kings did not generally make laws, for ancient Ireland was governed by traditional law, known as *brehon*. In judging cases, the king relied on legal experts trained in the schools of the druids, the priests of the Celtic religion. These *brehon* laws were codified with the help of the clergy in the early Christian era.

Like kingship in other ancient cultures, Irish kingship had a sacral character. Each king, overking, and high-king was symbolically married to the goddess of the local territory, to ensure the fertility and prosperity of the land.

SUCCESSION

The succession of Irish kings did not pass in a direct line from father to son. Primogeniture—inheritance of land and titles by the oldest son—was unknown in early Irish history. Instead, the kingship was elective. But family did play an important part in determining who would be elected king.

In order to be a candidate for kingship, or a *rigdomna*, a man had to be a member of a *derbfine*, a group of male kin, including first cousins, within five generations (father, son, grandson and great-grandsons) who had produced a previous king. The *derfine* elected the king from eligible candidates, based on the power and status of the candidate and the number of his followers.

Historians have long debated the meaning of the designation *tánaise ríg*, which can be translated as "expected king" or possibly "second king." Some scholars believe that this individual was appointed by the king as the designated successor, and that he was therefore the heir apparent. Many historians, however, regard the *tánaise ríg* as the man elected at the same time as the king, who would be ready to succeed him in case of sudden death. Other historians regard the *tánaise ríg* as a member of a branch of the family that was out of power for the moment, but was promised an eventual rise to the kingship.

LATER HISTORY

From the seventh century onward, various rulers claimed to be the high-king of Ireland. But these claims were dubious, although often supported by the Christian clergy in Armagh, the seat of the Irish church. The Viking invasions, beginning in 794–795, helped cement cooperation between the warring Irish dynasties. The first ruler to make the high-kingship a political reality was Máelsechnaill mac Máele Runnaid (r. 846–862), a member of the powerful Ui Neill dynasty of Ulster, whose members frequently held the high-kingship. Perhaps the most famous highking of Ireland was Brian Boruma mac Cennétig (r. 1002–1014), also known as Brian Boru, who called himself "emperor of the Irish."

In the twelfth century, the strongest high-kings were Turlough O'Connor (r. 1121–1156) and his son and successor Rory O'Connor (r. 1166–1186). In 1171, King Henry II of England (r. 1154–1189) landed in Ireland with the intention of subduing the Irish. In 1175, after Henry had conquered a great deal of Irish territory, high-king Rory O'Connor performed an act of fealty, accepting Henry as his overlord. Henry II also received fealty from several other Irish kings and proclaimed himself Paramount Lord of all Ireland.

King Rory O'Conner's half-brother, Cathal (r. 1186–1224), the last of Ireland's powerful high-kings, was required to acknowledge King John of England (r. 1199–1216) as his sovereign lord. However, even after the consolidation of English rule over Ireland, the provincial kings and sub-kings remained in power in some parts of the country until the end of the sixteenth century, when Henry VIII (r. 1509–1547) abolished all Irish royal and noble titles.

See also: BORU, BRIAN; CONNAUGHT KINGDOM; LEINSTER, KINGDOM OF; MEATH, KINGDOM OF; MUNSTER, KINGDOM OF; ULAID KINGDOM; ULSTER KINGDOM.

FURTHER READING

Byrne, Francis John. *Irish Kings and High-Kings.* 2d ed. Portland OR: Four Courts, 2001.

Jaski, Bart. *Early Irish Kingship and Succession.* Portland, OR: Four Courts, 2000.

ISLAM AND KINGSHIP

The relationship between religion and governance in Islamic thought and history. Islamic notions of kingship are multiple and complex and theological visions of Muslim government have often been at odds with the political reality. Nonetheless, religion has been essential to the image and reality of monarchy in Islamic societies. Rulers have often sought to frame justifications for their exercise of political power in terms of faith and have frequently based their actions on religious obligations. Likewise, Muslim opponents of particular rulers or of monarchy in general have couched their arguments in Islamic religious terms. In order to understand the history of the dynasties of the Islamic world, it is necessary to consider the relationship of Islam to kingship and the state.

ROOTS OF ISLAMIC GOVERNANCE

The Islamic religion originated in Arabia in the seventh century C.E., when the Prophet Muhammad received revelations from God which he proclaimed were a continuation and finalization of the earlier prophecies of the Judeo-Christian tradition. Muhammad preached a religion that emphasized strict monotheism, submission to God, and community values. Islam has been termed a religion of radical egalitarianism for its emphasis on the individual rights and obligations of each believer and the importance of the community of believers, or *umma*. While the prophet Muhammad was alive, he governed the growing *umma* himself, developing Islam into a unified religious and sociopolitical system.

After Muhammad's death in 632, the Islamic *umma* was ruled by a succession of four caliphs (an Arabic term for "successors"). In theological terms, the caliphs were vice regents of a sort, people who acted in Muhammad's place and governed a unified social, religious, and political community. During the rule of these first four caliphs, known as the "Rightly Guided caliphs," a blueprint for Islamic governance was created. The early caliphs were chosen by a process of nomination and election, and they controlled political, military, economic, legal, and religious affairs. In Islamic theology, the age of Muhammad and the Rightly Guided Caliphs is seen as a normative period in which God's community was ruled in a holistic and uncorrupted manner, in accordance with the laws written down in the Qur'an.

After the rule of the first four caliphs, a split developed between those who believed that political succession should be restricted to the Prophet's family, and those who favored a wider choice based on religious and political suitability. Furthermore, in 661 the establishment of the Umayyad dynasty, whose hereditary rulers called themselves caliphs, brought to the fore the difficulties of combining temporal and spiritual authority. The schism between the Shia (Shi'ite) and Sunni branches of Islam began at this time, as the Shia, followers of the fourth caliph Ali, denied the legitimacy of Umayyad rule.

Sunni and Shia Islam have very different visions of Islamic kingship: in Sunni Islam, the dominant branch of the faith, the caliph was the selected or elected political and military leader of the *umma*. His religious authority, however, was only partial—clerical scholars and learned men, called the *ulama*, and judges were responsible for religious interpretation and Islamic law.

In Shia Islam, on the other hand, political and religious authorities are closely knit together. The Shia believe that the rightful leader of the *umma* is an imam, who must be a descendent of both Muhammad and his son-in-law Ali, the fourth caliph and first imam. The imam is not only a political leader, but is also the divinely inspired interpreter of Islamic theology and law, a position reminiscent of the Catholic notion of papal infallability.

In both Sunni and Shia traditions, though, there is some degree of emphasis on the importance of the ulama's independence from the political leadership, although open revolt against an unjust leader was frowned upon unless the leader had directly violated religious principles. During Islam's formative years, the Sunni caliphs triumphed militarily over the Shia dissenters. As a result, Sunni Islam, along with Sunni ideas of Muslim rule, have dominated the majority of the Islamic world since. Notable exceptions to this are the Islamic empires of Persia and the Islamic republic of modern-day Iran, which were, and still are, Shia kingdoms.

MANIFESTATIONS OF ISLAMIC KINGSHIP

An old saying repeated by many early Islamic writers was that "religion and kingship are two brothers, and neither can dispense with each other." For the various Islamic dynasties that ruled over the centuries, the saying proved to be accurate. Islamic rulers

الوداع وانزل عليه ٥ انما النسى برمان يصل به فى الكفر يضل به الذين كفر وابلونه عاما
وحر مونه عاما ٥ نحطب عليه السلم ٥ وقال بان الزمان قد استدار كهئىة

For over a millennium, religion has played a vital role in the kingship of Islam. The intertwining of political and secular roles on the part of Islamic leaders goes back to the Prophet Muhammad himself, shown here preaching his last sermon in 632 C.E.

tended to use titles with religious connotations, such as caliph or sultan (from an Arabic word used in the Qur'an to denote power). Others, however, have used titles from non-Islamic traditions, such as shah (derived from a Persian work for ruler) or the English "king." Islamic rulers sought to balance their religious and secular roles, and an inability to maintain the balance could prove troublesome.

The revolt of the Abbasids against the Umayyad dynasty in 747 C.E. was partially rooted in a revivalist combination of Islam and politics, as Abbasid leaders claimed that the Umayyads had grown too aristocratic and wealthy and strayed from the communalist precepts of "true" Islam. This view was based partially in Islam's strong distaste for purely political kingly domination, or *mulk*. The Umayyads themselves had cloaked their political rule in religious language, with varying degrees of success. Both the Umayyad and Abbasid rulers used Islamic ideas and ideology to support their monarchical authority,

a trend continued by many other Muslim rulers across the centuries and continents.

Later Muslim empires, such as those of the Ottoman Turks, the Safavid dynasty of Persia, and the Mughal dynasty of India, also mixed religious ideology with worldly strength. The early Ottoman rulers were very much military leaders, but often cast their wars in a religious context, assuming the title "*ghazi*" or holy warrior. Some Ottoman rulers appropriated the title of caliph at times. However, in the Ottoman Empire there was actually a separate religious leader known as the chief mufti, a system mirrored in the Safavid and Mughal empires as well.

The rulers of all three of these empires incorporated Islamic law, or sharia, into their legal codes and considered their authority to be derived from God, carrying with it the obligation to defend Islam. Differences persisted, however: for example, the Shahs of the Safavid empire in the 1500s and 1600s ruled in the context of missionary Shia theology, which put them at odds with their Sunni Ottoman rivals to the west. The ideal of an Islamic community united politically and religiously under the role of a single caliph was long past.

Modern rulers of Islamic communities also draw on religious themes to justify their right to power. The Hashemite dynasty of modern-day Jordan places much emphasis on its direct descent from the Prophet Muhammad. The present-day Saudi monarchy is so closely tied to its religious functions that the first title of the Saudi ruler is not king, caliph, or sultan, but "Guardian of the Holy Places," the cities of Mecca and Medina.

Yet, as in earlier times, Islam also provides a critique against monarchs who are seen as insufficiently true to the precepts of early Islam. The Saudi monarchs face dissent and opposition from Islamic fundamentalists, while the last Shah of Iran was overthrown in 1979 in an Islamic revolution meant to restore the Shia ideal of government by the rule of an imam. In the Islamic context, kingship and religion are closely tied, but the relationship between them is fraught with ambiguity and has usually been subject to a broad gap between religious ideals and the reality of rule.

See also: ABBASID DYNASTY; HASHEMITE DYNASTY; MUGHAL EMPIRE; OTTOMAN EMPIRE; PAHLAVI DYNASTY.

FURTHER READING

Black, Antony. *The History of Islamic Political Thought: From the Prophet to the Present.* Edinburgh: Edinburgh University Press, 2001.

Esposito, John L. *Islam and Politics.* Syracuse, NY: Syracuse University Press, 1987.

ISRAEL, KINGDOMS OF

(ca. 1020–722 B.C.E.)

Two successive and short-lived ancient Hebrew kingdoms located on lands bordering the eastern Mediterranean in the ancient Near East.

Around 1100 B.C.E., twelve tribes of Hebrew people who shared a belief in the same god, Yahweh, settled in the hills of Canaan, west of the Jordan river in the region of Palestine. They formed their own kingdom with Saul (r. ca. 1020–1010 B.C.E.) anointed as the first king of Israel around 1020 B.C.E.

Saul created an army and set up an administration to rule the kingdom, but he was faced with dissension among the tribes and proved to be an ineffective leader.

EARLY KINGS

Saul was succeeded on the throne of Israel by King David (r. ca. 1010–970 B.C.E.) around 1010 B.C.E. David extended the boundaries of Israel and turned the kingdom into a powerful and stable entity. By controlling the major trade routes in the region, he was able to increase the prosperity of the kingdom of Israel. David conquered the city-state of Jerusalem from the Jebusites around 1000 B.C.E. and made it his capital. Jerusalem is still often called the "City of David."

Upon David's death in 970 B.C.E., his son Solomon (r. ca. 970–931 B.C.E.) succeeded him to the throne. Solomon used the wealth of the kingdom to turn Jerusalem into a sophisticated city with many grand buildings. The most grandiose of all was an enormous structure on the top of Mount Zion in Jerusalem that included a royal palace and a temple. By building a temple to Yahweh on a high point of the city, Solomon claimed Jerusalem for Yahweh's people, the Hebrews.

Solomon's costly building program required him to tax the people heavily, and he divided the kingdom into twelve districts to allow for easier tax collection. Despite the increased revenues, Solomon eventually overspent his funds and put the kingdom in a weak financial condition. Many people in the kingdom considered the excessive taxation an unnecessary hardship, and some began to rebel against Solomon's rule. When King Solomon died around 931 B.C.E., the divisions were irreparable.

When Solomon's son Rehoboam (r. 930–914 B.C.E.) succeeded his father as king, he was unable to repair the damage caused by Solomon, and the monarchy was divided into two separate kingdoms. The northern part of the country (with ten tribes) kept the name the Kingdom of Israel, while the southern part (with the two remaining tribes and the city of Jerusalem) was now called the Kingdom of Judah.

SECOND KINGDOM OF ISRAEL

This succeeding kingdom of Israel, facing warfare with the kingdom of Judah and general insurrection within its own borders, never managed to gain a truly stable footing. During the two hundred years of its existence (ca. 931–722 B.C.E.), the kingdom saw nine changes in dynasty, usually caused by internal rebellions.

The kingdom of Israel experienced only a few brief respites of peace and security. In the late ninth century B.C.E., King Omri (r. ca. 885–874 B.C.E.) managed to establish peace with Judah and with the neighboring Phoenician states of Tyre and Sidon. Later, in the mid-eighth century B.C.E., King Jeroboam II (r. ca. 781–754 B.C.E.) expanded Israel's borders during a temporary period of calm.

In 733 B.C.E., the Assyrian king Tiglath-pileser III (r. ca. 745–727 B.C.E.) defeated the Kingdom of Israel and annexed it as an Assyrian province. When King Hoshea (r. ca. 731–722 B.C.E.) of Israel refused to pay tribute, Assyria went to war against Israel. In 722 B.C.E., after a two-year siege, Israel's capital city, Samaria, was taken and the kingdom fell to King Sargon II of Assyria (r. 722–705 B.C.E.). Sargon deported the leaders of the tribes to remote regions of the Assyrian empire. These displaced Hebrews became known in legends as the "ten lost tribes" of Israel.

The kingdom of Judah fared somewhat better than the kingdom of Israel in that it lasted more than a century longer until finally being destroyed by the Babylonians. A rival of Israel's for years, Judah was beset by internal uprisings that weakened its power. In 605 B.C.E. Judah was made a vassal of Assyria, as the kingdom of Israel before it, and remained so until the Babylonians captured the kingdom in 587 B.C.E., destroyed Jerusalem, and deported the leaders of the country to other parts of the Babylonian empire.

See also: ASSYRIAN EMPIRE; DAVID; HEBREW KINGS; JUDAH, KINGDOM OF; JUDAISM AND KINGSHIP; SARGON II; SOLOMON.

ITSEKERI KINGDOM (1480–1884 C.E.)

Kingdom in West Africa, also known as Warri, which existed for more than five hundred years as an off-shoot of the kingdom of Benin.

The Itsekeri kingdom was founded around 1480 when Ginuwa, the son of the king of Benin, traveled to the western delta region of Nigeria with a group of followers in search of a place in which to settle.

Ginuwa (r. late 1400s), who is considered the first *olu,* or king, of the Itsekeri people, died before an appropriate settlement site could be found, however, and he was buried near the present site of Ijalla.

Ginuwa was succeeded by his son, Ijijen (r. late 1400s), who, according to tradition, consulted an oracle to determine the best place to found his kingdom. On the advice of the oracle, Ijijen led his party of followers to the site of present-day Warri, where he established his court. Almost immediately, the Itsekeri people established themselves as effective traders, brokering the exchange of goods between Europeans, who were beginning to appear on the Nigerian coast, and the inland peoples of Nigeria and beyond.

The wealth of the Itsekeri kingdom attracted immigrants from throughout the region. Some, like the original founding group, came from Benin; others came from the Yoruba states and from the lands of the Nupe people. By the 1500s, when the first European missionaries arrived, the Itsekeri kingdom was dominant in the region, maintaining at least reasonably peaceful relations with its neighbors in order to preserve the flow of trade. There were, however, challenges to Itsekeri dominance. Relations with the neighboring Ijaw people, for example, were often strained to the breaking point, and violence between the two sometimes erupted.

In 1597, the Itsekeri ruler, King Esigie (r. ca. 1570–?), converted to Christianity, and with his conversion came the nominal conversion of the entire kingdom, although many people still practiced traditional religion.

Meanwhile, the trade-based economy that provided the Itsekeri kingdom with its wealth and power remained vibrant up through the nineteenth century, although trading partners changed over the years, with the Portuguese eventually supplanted by the British in the early 1800s.

In 1848, the nineteenth and last Itsekeri king, Akengbuwa (r. 1807–1848), died, and no new *olu* was named to succeed him. Instead, the administration of the kingdom was left in the hands of a council of elders, who from time to time named a regent to represent the kingdom. In 1851, the elders entered into the first of several treaties with the British, a preliminary step to the absorption of the kingdom into the British colony of Nigeria. Under the terms of this and subsequent treaties, the Itsekeri retained the nominal status of a subject kingdom. In 1884 the kingdom became part of the larger British Protectorate of Nigeria.

See also: AFRICAN KINGDOMS; BENIN KINGDOM.

ITURBIDE, AGUSTÍN DE

(1783–1824 C.E.)

Leader of the Mexican independence movement who ruled Mexico briefly as Emperor Agustín I (r. 1822–1823).

Born to an upper-class family in the Mexican province of New Spain, Iturbide joined the Spanish-Mexican army as a very young man. By age fifteen, he was already an officer in his provincial regiment, and he quickly rose in rank. By 1810, Iturbide was a respected military leader, and he was offered a position in the rebel army of Miguel Hidalgo y Costilla. He refused, however. This decision proved fateful for the rebels when Iturbide's defense of the city of Valladolid decimated a large portion of rebel forces.

In recognition of his key leadership at Valladolid, Spanish colonial officials gave Iturbide command over two military districts under Spanish control, but this command was revoked in 1816 when Iturbide was charged with extortion and brutality. Four years later, however, he received another military commission to defeat the remainder of the weakened rebel forces, now under the command of Vicente Guerrero. A liberal political coup in Spain, however, left Mexican conservatives, including Iturbide, feeling disillusioned with the monarchy, and Iturbide promptly realigned his loyalties. He joined his forces with Guerrera's rebels, on the condition that Guerrera agree to three guarantees.

On February 24, 1821, Iturbide published his *Plan de Iguala,* which listed and explained the political guarantees he wanted from the rebels: Mexican independence from Spain, equality in the new Mexican state for Creoles and Spaniards, and a ban on all religions other than Roman Catholicism. Six months later, the viceroy of Spain signed the Treaty of Cordoba, acceding to Mexican independence.

After Mexico gained its independence, Iturbide separated himself from Guerrera and the rebels, and in May 1822, supported by his troops, he crowned himself Emperor Agustín I of Mexico.

Iturbide proved to be a tyrannical ruler, and he soon found himself without political allies. As a result, Mexico was once again threatened by revolutionary armies, this time led by Lieutenant Colonel Antonio Lopez de Santa Ana and a rebel leader who called himself Guadalupe Victoria. Santa Ana published a plan calling for Iturbide's exile, and on March 10, 1823, Iturbide abdicated, having served as emperor for less than a year.

After his abdication, Iturbide left Mexico and went to Italy and England. He later returned to Mexico, however, unaware that the Mexican congress had declared that his return would mean death. Captured by a military patrol on July 15, 1824, Iturbide was tried and shot by a firing squad four days later.

See also: AMERICAN KINGDOMS, CENTRAL AND NORTH; MEXICAN MONARCHY.

IVAN III, THE GREAT

(1440–1505 C.E.)

Grand Prince of Muscovy (r. 1462–1505) who united the principalities and territories of northern Russia into a single state.

Ivan Vasil'evich was the son of Grand Prince Vasily (Basil) II of Muscovy (r. 1425–1462) and Maria Yaroslavna. Defeated by the Tatar Khan of Kazan in 1445, Vasily was imprisoned and blinded by his cousin, Dmitri Shemiaka. However, Ivan and his younger brother eluded Dmitri's forces and escaped. Vasily was eventually freed and his power restored. But the Khan's victory and Shemiaka's treachery inspired Ivan to conquer the various principalities of northern Russia and end Muscovy's enforced allegiance to the Mongols.

When Vasily II died in 1462, Ivan became Grand Prince of Muscovy and immediately began pursuing his goal. In 1473 Ivan purchased the principalities of Rostov and Yaroslavl from their respective princes. He then sought to subdue the vast principality of Novgorod. In 1456, during his father's reign, Ivan had defeated the army of Novgorod and signed a treaty ensuring that Novgorod would maintain its allegiance to Moscow. But the leaders of Novgorod courted the support of Lithuania and Poland to protect them from Moscow's control. Consequently, in 1471, Ivan launched a military campaign against Novgorod. By 1478, he had subjugated the principality and formally annexed it as part of Muscovy. Once Novgorod fell, the principality of Tver, one of Novgorod's allies, also accepted Ivan's control.

After these successes, Ivan sought to free Muscovy from its allegiance to the Tatar Mongols. First, he formed an alliance with the Khanate of Crimea, an independent Mongol state that also wished to eliminate its obligations to the Tatars. In 1478, assured of Crimean support, Ivan refused to supply the annual tribute to Akhmat, the Tatar Khan. Akhmat responded by marching towards Moscow, but Ivan and his forces blocked the Tatar's progress at the Urga River. Surprised by the boldness of the Muscovites, Akhmat avoided battle and retreated. Although Muscovy would be threatened by future Tatar invasions, Ivan had effectively ended Mongol domination. This victory inspired the posthumous title of "Ivan the Great."

After consolidating the state, Ivan reformed Muscovite society. He decreased the power of the Orthodox Church, instituted mandatory military service for all classes, and renovated the city of Moscow. In Novgorod, he severely curtailed the nomadic habits of the farmers, causing a new landowner class to develop. This class helped stabilize the emerging Russian society that was now freed from Mongol oppression. Ivan's most significant achievement, however, was the establishment of a united and independent Muscovy.

See also: GOLDEN HORDE KHANATE; RUS KINGDOMS; RUSSIAN DYNASTIES.

IVAN IV, THE TERRIBLE

(1530–1584 C.E.)

Russian tsar (r. 1533–1584) of the Riurikid dynasty who reformed government and greatly expanded the territory ruled by Moscow. He became a feared and brutal despot, earning him the epithet "Iran the Terrible."

The son of Grand Duke Vasily (Basil) III of Moscow (r. 1503–1533), Ivan was born in 1530, becoming ruler of Russia at age three upon his father's death in 1533. His mother, Grand Dutchess Yelena Glinskaya, shared the regency with the boyar duma, or council of nobles, until her death in 1538, possibly a result of poisoning by political enemies. The regency then alternated among various boyar families, all of whom were vying for power. Ivan thus grew up surrounded by intrigues and feuds among the boyars.

In 1546, Ivan began to exercise power himself. The follow year, in 1547, he assumed the title of tsar ("caesar," or emperor). In doing so, Ivan became the first Russian ruler to take the title formally, although it had been used occasionally by his father and grandfather and had also been applied by Russians to the khans of the Golden Horde Khanate, a Muslim state that ruled a large area of Russia. In 1547, Ivan also married Anastasia Romanova of the Romanov family, whose relatives would found Russia's second great dynasty.

REFORM AND MILITARY CONQUESTS

Ivan IV instituted many changes in Russia's system of government and in Russian society. The first *zemsky sobor*—a two-level assembly that included boyars, churchmen, and elected representatives from all free classes of society—met in 1550. Ivan intended the *sobor* to be a check on the power of the boyars.

Among the reforms he made with the approval of the *sobor* were changes giving local districts more control over their own administration, a new law code, and the reorganization of the army, including the creation of a standing army of musketeers. However, Ivan also limited the freedom of peasants, passing laws that forbade them from moving between landholders' estates in certain years. This began the process of permanently binding Russian peasants to the land as serfs.

Ivan's first military venture was the conquest of the Tatar khanate of Kazan in 1552. In 1556, his forces conquered the khanate of Astrakhan. These two military ventures launched Russian expansion eastward. Seeking access to the Baltic Sea, Ivan then turned his attention to the west. In 1558, Ivan launched a war against the state of Livonia (which included parts of present-day Estonia and Latvia) and its ally Lithuania. By the time this war ended twenty years later, it had also drawn in Sweden and Poland against Russia, which, in the end, failed to make any substantial gains.

Back in the east, the Stroganov family of merchant–adventurers, with a force of Cossacks (peasant soldiers), conquered a Tatar khanate in western Siberia between 1581 and 1584. The Cossack leader, Yermak, offered the conquered territory to Ivan just before the tsar's death; the government in Moscow

The grand prince of all the Rus, Ivan the Terrible was the first Russian ruler to claim the title of *tsar,* or emperor. Portrayed in this sixteenth-century engraving, Ivan IV was a brutal tyrant, whose reign degenerated into political and economic turmoil.

finished what the Cossacks had begun, annexing western Siberia in 1585.

A FEARED DESPOT

Ivan had always had a stern and rather unforgiving character, perhaps forged, in part, by the intrigues and feuds that he witnessed during his childhood and by the murders of both his mother and his wife Anastasia, who was also poisoned and died in 1560. By the 1560s, however, Ivan's behavior had become increasingly arbitrary, irrational, and tyrannical. Fits of rage alternated with periods of prayer and repentance.

During the Livonian war, Ivan accused defeated commanders of treason, leading one general to change his allegiance to the Lithuanians rather than face Ivan's anger over a lost battle. The tsar also suspected conspiracy and treason everywhere.

Late in 1564, Ivan announced that he would abdicate the throne because of treason on the part of the boyars. When the people of Moscow protested, Ivan demanded what was in effect absolute power. He formed a new special court, the *oprichnina,* which had none of the checks and limitations of traditional Russian assemblies. The *oprichnina* eventually numbered as many as six thousand men, supported by numerous confiscated boyar estates. This force acted as Ivan's secret police, executing those who opposed him.

In 1566, Ivan had the *oprichnina* torture 300 boyars who had spoken out against his persecutions. In 1567, the head of the Russian Orthodox church was executed for preaching a sermon against the *oprichnina.* Members of the *oprichnina* sacked the city of Novgorod in 1570, killing thousands, because Ivan believed the townspeople were conspiring against him. Ivan disbanded the *oprichnina* in 1572 because the terror and disorder were undermining the country. This disorder may have contributed to Russia's failure in the Livonian war.

LEGACY

Ivan IV and his first wife, Anastasia, had two sons, Ivan and Feodor. After Anastasia's death in 1560, Ivan IV married at least six more times; the seventh wife bore him another son, Dmitri. Ivan killed his eldest son and namesake during a fit of rage in 1582. The tsar himself died of natural causes in 1584. Dmitri was murdered in 1591, possibly on the orders of Boris Godunov, the acting regent for Ivan IV's son and successor, Feodor I (r. 1584–1598). When Feodor died childless in 1598, the ancient Riurikid dynasty, which had ruled Russian duchies and princedoms since around 910, came to an end.

Despite his despotism and cruelty, Ivan IV left Russia a strong, centralized country that was able to withstand the disruption of the "Time of Troubles" that followed the death of Feodor I. Ivan's policies were continued by those who followed him: serfdom became the dominant form of agricultural labor; Russia expanded to the east and resumed attempts to gain access to the Baltic Sea and the west; and the rule of the tsars became increasingly autocratic.

See also: GOLDEN HORDE KHANATE; IVAN III, THE GREAT; KIEV, PRINCEDOM OF; RIURIKID DYNASTY; ROMANOV DYNASTY; RURIK; RUSSIAN DYNASTIES.

FURTHER READING

Carr, Francis. *Ivan the Terrible.* Newton Abbott: David & Charles, 1981.

JAGIELLO DYNASTY (1386–1572 C.E.)

Series of seven kings who ruled the dual state of Poland-Lithuania from the late Middle Ages through the early modern era. The Jagiello rulers presided over the emergence of a stable constitutional monarchy.

In 1385, the Polish magnates (major lords, church prelates, and merchants) invited Grand Duke Jogailo of Lithuania to fill the vacuum left by the death of King Louis (r. 1370–1382). A pagan, illiterate, but capable ruler of the sprawling Lithuanian domains, Jogailo agreed to accept the conditions: conversion to Latin Christianity, perpetual union of Poland and Lithuania, and marriage to Louis's twelve-year-old daughter Jadwiga, crowned temporary "king" the previous year. Jogailo took the name Wladislaw II Jagiello (r. 1386–1434), giving the dynasty its name.

Selecting Jogailo was a stroke of genius by the Polish magnates. By including Lithuania in the monarchy, the magnates swelled the borders and resources of a small, vulnerable country. Furthermore, by adopting the Lithuanian political tradition of weak central rule, they were able to protect and expand their rights and privileges at the expense of king and peasants alike.

In 1410, at the battle of Tannenberg, the country inflicted a crushing defeat on the Teutonic Knights of Prussia, who had been a perpetual threat on Poland's Baltic frontier. Wladislaw II's son and successor, Wladislaw III (r. 1434–1444), added the Crown of Hungary to his titles in 1440 and then promptly launched a crusade against the expansionist Ottoman Turks. Wladislaw III's death in 1444 at the hands of the Turks at the battle of Varna brought his brother Casimir IV (r. 1446–1492) to power.

PEAK OF POWER

Casimir's fifty-five-year reign saw the pinnacle of Jagiello's power and prestige, as the dual state of Poland-Lithuania dominated the region. His wife, Elizabeth of Habsburg, gave Casimir six sons and seven daughters. Five of the daughters married into Germany's most illustrious courts, where they kept the family's prestige alive for generations. Their son Wladyslaw became King Wladyslaw II of Bohemia (r. 1471–1516) and of Hungary (r. 1490–1516).

Perhaps learning a lesson in caution from his unlucky brother Wladislaw III, Casimir IV tried to maintain good ties with both the Ottomans and the tsars of Muscovy. However, he was unable to mount a consistent defense against the latter's territorial growth at the expense of Lithuania, which continued with little pause for 300 years. Casimir did stake one claim to military glory: the final submission of the Teutonic Knights in 1466. Half of Prussia was annexed outright, and the other half became a vassal state.

Three of Casimir's sons followed him to the Polish throne: John Albert (r. 1492–1501), Alexander I (r. 1501–1506), and Sigismund I (r. 1506–1548). The first two left little mark on history, but Sigismund was perhaps the most capable and accomplished of the Jagiello monarchs. Sigismund I preserved most of the country's borders by diplomacy and occasional military victories (against Muscovy in 1514 and 1535, and Moldavia in 1531). However, he was unable to offer much help to his nephew Louis II (r. 1516–1526), the last Jagiello king of Bohemia and Hungary, who was killed fighting the Turks at the battle of Mohacs in 1526.

Sigismund, lacking resources of his own, sought financial and manpower assistance from the *szlachta* (the nobility). In exchange for their help, he was forced to make repeated concessions of power. Sigismund imposed fiscal and monetary reforms on his country, using the experience he garnered as the margrave (military governor) of Silesia (1499–1506). He also integrated the Mazovia region and its capital Warsaw into the kingdom after the last duke of its Piast dynasty died in 1529.

Sigismund and his second wife, Bona Sforza of Milan, presided over a flourishing Renaissance court in his capital city of Krakow, livened by Italian sculptors and architects. The introduction of printing stimulated a large literary output in Latin and Polish; the first printed Polish and Lithuanian books date from this period. Their policies helped reinvigorate the university at Krakow, while the city of Koenigsburg in the north became an early site of intellectual life focused on the Protestant Reformation.

Lutheran, Calvinist, and radical Protestant ideas spread rapidly under Sigismund, who decided that tolerance was the most politic response to the Reformation. A devout Catholic himself, he nevertheless reaffirmed the rights of the large Jewish and Orthodox Christian communities.

DECLINE

The reign of Sigismund's son and successor, Sigismund II Augustus (r. 1548–1572), saw political struggles between the king, the magnates in his council (cabinet), and the numerous lesser nobles of the kingdom. A permanent House of Envoys (representing the entire nobility) competed for influence with the king's council. The Sejm (national parliament) assumed more powers at its periodic sessions, while local and regional *sejmiki* remained hotbeds of ferment.

In 1569, the Union of Lublin, long sought by the nobles, consolidated the legal and administrative systems of Poland and Lithuania. The Polish nobility soon came to dominate Lithuania. Both lands remained overwhelmingly agricultural and farm output grew, but the peasants were gradually driven into serfdom. Sigismund II had no male heirs, and upon his death in 1572, the Jagiello dynasty came to an end.

See also: CASIMIR IV; LITHUANIA, GRAND DUCHY OF; PIAST DYNASTY.

FURTHER READING

Davies, Norman. *God's Playground: A History of Poland.* New York: Columbia University Press, 1982.

Lukowski, Jerzy, and Zawadzki, Hubert. *A Concise History of Poland.* New York: Cambridge University Press, 2001.

JAHAN, SHAH (1593–1666 C.E.)

Mughal emperor of India (r. 1628–1658) who had an appetite for military expansion and became best known as builder of the Taj Mahal in the city of Agra.

Shah Jahan was born as Khurram Shihab-ud-din Muhammad, the third and favored son of the Mughal emperor of India, Jahangir (r. 1605–1627). To ensure that the prince would be the next ruler of the Mughal dynasty, Jahangir changed the boy's name from Prince Khurram to Shah Jahan ("King of the World") in 1616, after the prince helped to subdue rebellious states in the south.

Khurram did not consider this a sufficient guarantee of succession, however, so he had his older brother, Khusran, murdered. Jahangir and his nobles understood the need for a contender to the throne to eliminate rivals, but they felt that Shah Jahan was becoming too treacherous. Recognizing their disapproval, Shah Jahan kept his distance from them and the imperial forces for four years before reconciling with his father, just eighteen months prior to Jahangir's death.

After Jahangir died in 1627, Shah Jahan ordered the death of his brothers, Dawar Bakhsh and Gurshasp Shahriyar, and several cousins. He then took the throne as the fifth ruler of the Mughal dynasty.

Like Jahangir, Shah Jahan attempted to emulate the empire-building activities of his grandfather, Akbar the Great (r. 1556–1605). He had the requisite personal qualities: he was a brave and competent

Mughal Emperor Shah Jahan was a farsighted leader who sought to follow in the footsteps of his ancestors by expanding the empire. His greatest legacy, however, is the magnificent Taj Mahal in Agra, a mausoleum built to honor his wife, Mumtaz Mahal, who died during childbirth in 1631.

commander, a generous master who treated his servants with respect, and a far-sighted leader with a strict sense of justice. But neither he nor his father ever achieved the imperial expansionism of Akbar.

Shah Jahan did, however, manage to expand imperial control into northwestern India and to penetrate deep into the region of southern India known as the Deccan. In 1638, his forces took the city of Qandahar (in present-day Afghanistan), and by 1646 the Mughals occupied the neighboring cities of Badakhshan and Balkh. However, Shah Jahan lost the province of Balkh (in Afghanistan) in 1647, and attempts to retake it in 1649, 1653, and 1653 cost manpower, time, and money. With his empire nearly bankrupt, Shah Jahan needed the wealth of southern India to restore his fortunes.

By 1636, Shah Jahan had annexed the kingdom of Golconda and most of the kingdom of Bijapur, agreeing not to fight with those states in return for the conquest. This permitted the remaining forces of those states to war successfully against the rich Hindu states to their south. By 1656, however, Shah Jahan needed money, so he invaded Bijapur and Golconda, gaining control of their wealth and access to several active trading ports on the Arabian Sea. Shah Jahan then returned north to concentrate on building the city of Shahjahanabad (the new Delhi) while his son, the young prince Aurangzeb, became commander-in-chief of Mughal forces in the Deccan.

Under Shah Jahan, Muslim India experienced a Golden Age of architecture and the climax of Indo-Persian culture. Shah Jahan built mosques, temples, many opulent monuments, and magnificent gardens. In the city of Agra, he built the Pearl Mosque, so called because of the translucent white marble used on the interior. In 1638, Shah Jahan moved his capital to Delhi and built a palace with a magnificent jeweled throne, which became the principal residence of emperors for the rest of Mughal reign.

Shah Jahan's greatest architectural legacy was the Taj Mahal, built in the city of Agra as a mausoleum, or tomb, for his wife, Mumtaz Mahal, who died in 1631 while giving birth to their fourteenth child. Completed in 1643, the Taj Mahal is considered one of the great wonders of the world.

When Aurangzeb heard that his father had become ill in Delhi, he immediately returned from the Deccan to stake a claim to the throne. In 1658, Aurangzeb seized the Mughal throne and confined his father to the palace in Agra. It was there that Shah Jahan spent the last few years of his life, looking out on the tomb of his beloved wife. Shah Jahan died in 1666.

See also: AHMADNAGAR KINGDOM; AKBAR THE GREAT; AURANGZEB; JAHANGIR; MUGHAL EMPIRE.

FURTHER READING
Patnaik, Naveen. *A Second Paradise*. New York. Doubleday & Company, 1985.

JAHANGIR (1569–1627 C.E.)

Fourth emperor (r. 1605–1627) in the Mughal dynasty of India, known primarily for his artistic and cultural contributions as a patron of the arts.

Born as Prince Salim to the Mughal ruler Akbar the Great (r. 1556–1605), Jahangir was next in line for the throne. He could not wait to attain power, however, and revolted in 1599 while his father was at war in the Deccan region of India.

Akbar sent a loyal lieutenant, Abu-1 Fazl, to deal with his rebellious son, but Fazl was killed attempting to quell the revolt. Nevertheless, Akbar remained ruler until the 1605, when he suddenly died—possibly from a dose of poison dispensed by his son. Thus, the ambitious Jahangir began his twenty-two-year rule. The empire that he inherited was perhaps the strongest in the world at that period.

Jahangir ably carried on where Akbar left off, but he was not a great ruler or daring warrior like his father. Jahangir allowed things to remain basically as they had been in the Mughal Empire. He managed the central administration and occasionally extended the empire's borders slightly, but these were minor accomplishments. He also governed his people fairly and impartially, regardless of their religion.

Jahangir's greatest contribution to the Mughal Empire was not administrative or military; it was artistic. During his reign, the art form of pietra dura (mosaic inlay of precious stones of different hues) became highly developed. Painting, which Jahangir loved, reached its height as well. The Persian influence that had dominated Indian painting up to that time was replaced by a more distinctive Indian and Mughal style, and a number of schools of miniature painting emerged in India.

Jahangir is perhaps most famous for being the father of his successor, Shah Jahan (r. 1628–1658), who constructed many large and beautiful buildings in India, including the famous Taj Mahal at Agra. The years of Jahangir's rule were a transition period in Mughal architecture between its two great stages that occurred under Akbar and Shah Jahan.

During Jahangir's reign, two English envoys visited India seeking to increase trade opportunities. The first was Captain William Hawkins, who arrived in 1609. Although Hawkins came with 25,000 gold pieces and a letter to Jahangir from King James I of England (r. 1603–1625), he was disappointed to find that India had no need to trade with England and had little interest in goods from Western countries.

By the time James I sent another ambassador, Sir Thomas Roe, in 1616, Jahangir welcomed him more cordially. Jahangir now hoped to count on British ships for transportation (previously provided by the less seaworthy and more bigoted Portuguese) for the important yearly pilgrimage to Mecca. In 1619, Roe reached an agreement with Jahangir to allow the English East India Company to build a factory at Surat, the main port city of the Mughal Empire. Roe knew well enough to be satisfied with the profits from that venture and not try to gain territory in India.

After 1611, Jahangir was greatly influenced by his Persian wife, Nur Jahan, and her relatives, as well as his third son, Prince Khurram (who later became Shah Jahan). Those individuals virtually controlled government affairs until 1622. After that, Jahangir faced frequent rebellions by Prince Khurram. Jahangir died in 1627 while traveling to Lahore from Kashmir. Prince Khurram, or Shah Jahan, succeeded in claiming the throne the following year after overcoming the claims of various rivals.

See also: AKBAR THE GREAT; JAHAN, SHAH; MUGHAL EMPIRE.

JAMES I OF ARAGÓN

(1208–1276 C.E.)

King of Aragón (r. 1213–1276), renowned for his expansion of Aragónese territory.

Born in Montpelier in the area of Toulouse (in present-day southwestern France), James was the son of Peter II of Aragón (r. 1196–1213), who fought and died with the Albigensians, a heretical Christian sect that emphasized the duality of good and evil, light and dark, soul and body.

James had a tumultuous childhood. The death of his father in 1213 left the young James hostage to and in the care of Simon de Montfort, a military leader of the anti-Albigensian forces who had defeated Peter II and his allies. It was with some difficulty that Aragonese nobles persuaded Montfort to release the boy hostage in 1214.

In the meantime, James's uncle, Count Sancho of Roussillon had been appointed regent, but Sancho and other relatives plotted to overthrow James after his release. Opposed by nobles of both Aragón and Catalonia, Sancho resigned as regent in 1218, an act that led his supporters to rebel. James spent much of his youth fighting against various factions, but by 1227 he had effectively gained control of his kingdom.

After leaving the care of de Montfort, James was raised and educated by the Knights Templar, a wealthy and powerful religious-military order that combined both military and monastic traditions. With their apparent assistance, James eventually restored order in Aragón and consolidated royal power before launching campaigns to regain Christian control of Iberia from the Moors in the so-called reconquista, or reconquest. James seized the Balearic Islands from the Moors between 1229 and 1235, drove Islamic forces from Valencia in 1238, and helped end Moorish control of Murcia in 1266.

In 1258, under the Treaty of Corbeil, James relinquished the Aragónese claim to lands in southern France. In reciprocation, Louis IX of France (r. 1226–1270) abandoned long-standing French claims to Barcelona, which was part of Aragón's realm.

With the conquest of the Balearic Islands, James opened the way for increased Catalan and Aragónese trade in the Mediterranean and, with it, increased prosperity for the kingdom. A supporter of arts and letters, he made Catalan the official language of Aragón and introduced a variety of reforms. In 1247, for example, he promulgated his legal code, the Customs of Aragón, a long overdue legislative reform. During James's reign, the *Libre del Consulat de Mar* (Book of the Consulate of the Sea), an important compilation of maritime laws and customs, was also created. Upon James's death in 1276, he was succeeded by his son, Peter III (r. 1276–1285) while another of his sons ruled as James II of Majorca (r. 1276–1311).

See also: ARAGÓN, KINGDOM OF; LOUIS IX; SPANISH MONARCHIES.

JAMES I OF ENGLAND (JAMES VI OF SCOTLAND) (1566–1625 C.E.)

King of Scotland (r. 1567–1625) and England (r. 1603–1625) whose accession to the English throne led to a union of the Crowns and the creation of a unified Great Britain. James was the first of the Stuart monarchs of England and one of the most memorable eccentrics ever to sit on the throne.

A TURBULENT CHILDHOOD

Born in Scotland, James was the only son of Mary, Queen of Scots (r. 1542–1567), and Henry Stewart, Lord Darnley. When James was just a baby, the house his father was staying in to recuperate from an illness was blown up and his father killed. Suspicion fell immediately upon Mary and her next husband, the earl of Bothwell, although the event remains a mystery to this day.

Because of suspicions about her possible role in Darnley's death, Mary fled, but was captured by rebellious Scottish nobles who had gone to war against her. She agreed to turn the throne over to her one-year-old son, who became King James VI in 1567. James never saw his mother in his adult life, and he became a devout Protestant in contrast to her Catholicism. Mary was eventually executed by her arch-rival, Elizabeth I of England, on grounds of plotting in a scheme to murder the English queen. James registered only a token disapproval of his mother's execution.

James was in danger for much of his youth— Scotland was in turmoil and previous Stuart monarchs had been assassinated. James was thus kept protected and given a good education. After James fell under the influence of the Catholic duke of Lennox, the Protestant earl of Gowrie kidnapped James in 1582 and forced him to renounce Lennox. The young king was able to escape, and from then on he relied less on advisers and began to rule in person.

ADULTHOOD AND KINGSHIP OF ENGLAND

In 1589, James married Princess Anne of Denmark. She gave birth to their first son, Henry, in 1594, and to Charles (the future Charles I of England, r. 1625–1649) in 1600. In the late 1500s and early 1600s, one of James's prime concerns was the English succession. The Tudor monarch of England, Elizabeth I (r. 1558–1603), never married and had no surviving siblings.

As Elizabeth advanced in years, speculations ran rampant about whom she would choose as her successor among her many distant relations who were eligible for the throne. One of these relatives was James, who was the great-grandson of Margaret Tudor, the daughter of Elizabeth's grandfather, King Henry VII (r. 1485–1509).

Perhaps because of James's many flattering gestures and conciliatory policies toward England, Elizabeth eventually chose James as her successor.

When Elizabeth died in 1603, James made his way south to assume his new role as king of England, Scotland, and Wales. This journey became notorious for the number of titles he bestowed along the way. His accession also became legendary because, at nearly the same moment that he united the Crowns of England and Scotland under one monarch, a

The only son of Mary, Queen of Scots, King James I of England (James VI of Scotland) was named as successor to the English Crown by Queen Elizabeth I before her death. The first ruler of England's Stuart Dynasty, James fought with Parliament throughout his reign.

bloody rebellion in Ireland ended because the Irish were pacified at having a Celtic, even if Scottish, king. Eventually James thus became known as the British Solomon, a learned peacemaker.

James was well known both for his real learning and his pretensions to greater knowledge than he actually possessed. During his lifetime, he published many works on topics as diverse as the divine right of kings, witchcraft, and the evils of tobacco, as well as a large body of poetry. He was known to take great pride in displaying his skills in Latin, often unaware of his errors in the language. His most lasting literary achievement was his commissioning of a new English translation of the Christian Bible, completed in 1611, which is known as the King James Bible. Another landmark of James's reign was the founding in 1607 of Jamestown, the first permanent British settlement in North America.

James became equally notorious for his alleged homosexuality. He lavished titles and riches on a number of handsome male favorites, such as George Villiers, the first duke of Buckingham, and he was known to fondle the codpieces of male courtiers.

James was much less memorable as a ruler than for his eccentricities. His conflicts with Parliament over state finances and his absolutist tendencies paved the way for his son Charles's similar disputes and, eventually, civil war. James spent the state's funds liberally on such luxuries as elaborate court masques by the dramatist Ben Jonson and others.

The religious conflict between Catholic and Protestant that haunted James's childhood in Scotland intensified during his reign as king of England. One of the first manifestations of this was the Gunpowder Plot, a failed attempt by Guy Fawkes and other conspirators to blow up the Houses of Parliament in 1605. Fawkes, a Catholic, was motivated by anger over the reimposition of heavier fines and taxes upon Catholics than Protestants.

James also repeatedly attempted to forge an alliance with Catholic Spain, to the dismay of Parliament, which was staunchly Protestant and experiencing a strong influx of Puritan members. In 1621, James dissolved Parliament over its criticisms of his policies with Spain. His dissolution of Parliament over religious and policy disagreements did not solve the problem; on the contrary, the power struggle between king and Parliament intensified in the next reign, leading to civil war in 1642.

James died in 1625, leaving the Crown and his troubles with Parliament to his son Charles I, who had already been running the country for the last year of James's life during his father's last illness.

See also: CHARLES I; ELIZABETH I; HOMOSEXUALITY AND KINGSHIP; MARY, QUEEN OF SCOTS; STUART DYNASTY; TUDOR, HOUSE OF.

FURTHER READING

Bergeron, David M. *Royal Family*, *Royal Lovers: King James of England and Scotland.* Columbia: University of Missouri Press, 1991.

Fraser, Antonia. *King James VI of Scotland, I of England.* New York: Alfred A. Knopf, 1975.

Lee, Maurice, Jr. *Great Britain's Solomon: James VI and I in His Three Kingdoms.* Urbana: University of Illinois Press, 1990.

Scott, Otto J. *James I.* New York: Mason/Charter, 1976.

JAMES II (1633–1701 C.E.)

King of England (r. 1685–1688) whose Catholicism led to his deposing in the Glorious Revolution.

James was the second son of Charles I (r. 1625–1649) and Henrietta Maria, the sister of King Louis XIII of France (r. 1610–1643). While James was only a child, his father became involved in a bitter conflict with Parliament, leading to the English Civil War and eventually to Charles's execution in 1649.

During the first part of the Civil War, between 1642 and 1646, James was sent to Oxford, which was a Royalist stronghold. The city ultimately surrendered to the Parliamentary armies and James was ordered to return to London. In 1648, he escaped to the Netherlands and from there he made his way to France. James remained in exile on the Continent until 1660. During his time in exile, he served in the French and Spanish armies.

RESTORATION

The death in 1658 of Oliver Cromwell, Lord Protector of England, in the period known as the Interregnum (between kings), left a void in the leadership of the nation. Cromwell's son Richard ruled as Lord Protector for a brief and disastrous period (r. 1653–1658), but Parliament then asked James's older brother Charles to return to England from exile in France and assume the throne. He was crowned

Charles II (r. 1660–1685) in 1660. The period of his reign is termed the Restoration.

Under Charles, James served as Lord High Admiral and became involved in colonial trade projects. (New Amsterdam was renamed New York in his honor after England took that American colony from the Dutch.) In 1660, James married Anne, daughter of the earl of Clarendon. Some eight or nine years later, he converted to Catholicism, an act that would ultimately lead to his downfall; his daughters Mary and Anne, however, were raised in the Anglican faith.

In 1673, James's wife Anne died, and he married Mary of Modena, a staunch Catholic. Because Charles II had no legitimate heirs, his brother James was next in line for the throne. However, this troubled many English Protestants, who did not want any possibility of a Catholic reassuming the throne after the bitter religious conflicts of the sixteenth century. This led Parliament to attempt to pass legislation between 1679 and 1681 that would exclude James from the throne because of his religion.

REIGN

Parliament's efforts to exclude James from the line of succession failed, and when Charles died in 1685 without a legitimate heir, James was crowned James II (r. 1685–1688). But almost immediately after James took the throne, the duke of Monmouth, an illegitimate son of Charles II and a staunch Protestant, led an unsuccessful attempt to oust James in the name of the Protestant cause. James's bloody reprisals against Monmouth and his followers fueled Protestant hatred of the new king.

James's reign was brief and turbulent. He was already highly unpopular because of his religion, his autocratic tendencies, and his lack of respect for parliamentary authority. But he intensified the opposition to his rule by establishing a policy of religious toleration of Catholicism (the Declaration of Indulgence, 1687), filling many high-ranking government posts with Catholics, and eliminating laws that penalized Roman Catholics and other nonmajority religious groups. As a result of such actions, many feared that James wanted to reestablish Catholicism as the official religion of England.

A crisis developed in 1688, when James's Catholic wife, Mary of Modena, gave birth to a son. The threat of a Catholic heir and dynasty in Protestant England was too great for many people to bear. High-ranking English noblemen called on William of Orange, ruler of the Netherlands, to step in. William was married to James's daughter Mary, which made his claim to the throne of England not entirely illegitimate. More importantly, William and Mary were both Protestant, and William was a staunch defender of Protestantism against Catholic France.

REVOLUTION AND AFTER

In the fall of 1688, William of Orange prepared to invade England and forcibly take the throne from James. Force proved unnecessary, however, as James's Protestant soldiers refused to fight for him and defected to William's side, leaving James without forces to defend his Crown. Because the accession of William (r. 1689–1702) and Mary (r. 1689–1695) ensured a Protestant line on the throne and was accomplished without violence, it became known as the Glorious Revolution.

James fled to Ireland in 1689 and tried to consolidate his power with the support of the Irish. But William's armies defeated him at the battle of the Boyne (1689). Catholic Ireland suffered harsh punitive measures for most of the eighteenth century because of its support for James, who escaped to France with his wife and children and established a court in exile there.

James died in France in 1701. The supporters of his cause and the cause of a Stuart restoration became known as Jacobites (after Jacobus, Latin for James). They staged two unsuccessful invasions of England in the eighteenth century in an attempt to restore James's son and grandson, and thus the Stuart line, to the English throne.

See also: CHARLES I; CHARLES II; STUART DYNASTY; WILLIAM AND MARY.

JAMES II OF ARAGÓN

(1260–1327 C.E.)

King of Aragón (r. 1291–1327) and count of Barcelona (r. 1291–1327), who defended his kingdom's claims to Sicily until that island was later relinquished in exchange for rule over the islands of Sardinia and Corsica.

The grandson of James I of Aragón (r. 1213–1276) and son of Peter III of Aragón (r. 1276–1285), James became king of Sicily on his father's death in

1285. At the same time, his older brother Alfonso succeeded to the throne of Aragón as Alfonso III (r. 1285–1291). For several years, James defended Sicily from King Charles II of Naples (r. 1285–1309), who also claimed the island kingdom with support from both Pope Nicholas IV and James's own brother, Alfonso III.

When Alfonso III died in 1291, the nobles in Aragón invited James to take the throne of that kingdom. He accepted, appointing his younger brother Fadrique to serve as governor of Sicily during his absence. Although there were objections to his taking the Aragónese throne, partly because the pope had forbidden it, James retained power in Aragón. After negotiations with Pope Boniface VIII and Charles II, he gave up the throne of Sicily in exchange for control of Sardinia and Corsica.

To further pacify Charles and the Angevin dynasty—long-time enemies of his family and chief rivals for the control of Sicily—James II married Charles's daughter, Blanche.

James did not press his claim to Sardinia for several years, waiting until he was able to conduct a successful military campaign for control of the island. Sardinia was finally joined to his kingdom around 1323, but he never took possession of Corsica.

During the reign of James II, the Act of Union of 1319 joined the kingdoms of Aragón and Valencia with the county of Barcelona and feudal territories of the island of Mallorca. The act stipulated that none of these territories could be divided through bequests or gifts, although the king was empowered to donate individual castles and properties.

When James died in 1327, he was succeeded as king of Aragón by his son, Alfonso IV (r. 1327–1336), who had played an important part in the conquest of Sardinia in 1323.

See also: ARAGÓN, HOUSE OF; ARAGÓN, KINGDOM OF; IBERIAN KINGDOMS; NAPLES, KINGDOM OF; SICILY, KINGDOM OF; SPANISH MONARCHIES.

JANGGALA KINGDOM

(ca. 1000s–1200s C.E.)

Buddhist kingdom located in east Java that flourished from the eleventh to thirteenth centuries.

Early in the eleventh century, King Airlangga of Java (r. ?–1041) reunified several independent states to create a unified Java kingdom. However, before his death in 1041, he divided his realm into two, forming the kingdoms of Panjalu (Kediri) and Janggala. According to a fourteenth-century Javan source, the *Nagarakrtagama,* Airlangga did this for his two sons, "both of whom were kings." However, an inscription on a Buddha statue called the *Joko Dolok* (literally "fat man") in Surabaya says that the existence of these two kingdoms stemmed from enmity between two princes, who may or may not have been related.

Of the two kingdoms, Janggala is always mentioned first in ancient sources, which may indicate that it was more important. The story of the drawing of the boundary between the two kingdoms is steeped in legend. According to tradition, a learned Buddhist monk named Bharada, who was a master of yoga, went to Bali by walking over the water. The Joko Dolok inscription says he divided the two kingdoms by means of "magic water in a crock."

Early twentieth-century Dutch archaeologists found the remains of a stone wall that once ran from Mount Kawi in eastern Java to the south coast. This wall was called the Pinggir Raksa, or Giant Border. Some scholars believe that the wall marked part of the mythical boundary between the kingdoms of Janggala and Panjalu. The boundary thus may have run more or less from north to south, with Janggala controlling the land to the east of the boundary, and Panjalu the land to the west, theoretically bounded on all other sides by the sea. Another theory holds that the Brantas River formed the rest of the boundary between the two kingdoms.

Other scholars believe that the idea of the division of the kingdom corresponds to ancient Javanese ideas of the importance of the four quarters of the universe, and that Bharada corresponds to the Naksatraraja, the king of the constellations. This idea is based on the assumption that all Indonesian thought once stressed divisions into two, such as high–low, male–female, light–dark, sea–mountain, and so on, which were then further divided into four. Similarly, the magic water in Bharada's water pot can be seen as a manifestation of the importance of water in contemporary Balinese culture.

If this theory about the old wall as part of the boundary between Janggala and Panjalu is correct, then the kingdom of Janggala would have included the province of Malang and the Brantas River Delta. It is possible that Janggala corresponds to Sukitan, a place name mentioned in thirteenth-century sources.

If this is the case, then Janggala would have controlled the ports on the north coast of Java.

The location of Janggala's capital is unknown. Some scholars suggest that it was located at Bakong, a town on the Porong River. Tenth-century inscriptions found near there are important because they show a strong Javanese cultural orientation rather any heavy Indian influence, suggesting the Janggala kingdom had not been heavily influenced by India.

See also: JAVAN KINGDOMS; PANJALU KINGDOM; SOUTHEAST ASIAN KINGDOMS.

JAUNPUR KINGDOM (1398–1500 C.E.)

Muslim kingdom in north-central India that was ruled by the Sharqi dynasty from 1398 to 1479.

In the eleventh century, the kingdom of Jaunpur was no more than a frequently flooded strategic crossing point on the banks of the Gomati River in the Uttar Pradesh region of north-central India. In 1194–1197, the Muslim forces of Muhammad of Ghur (r. 1163–2003) captured the region from the Hindu Ghadavala dynasty.

After the murder of the sultan of Delhi, Qutbuddin (r. 1316–1320), in 1320, Ghazi Malik Ghiyasuddin Tugluq I (r. 1320–1325) came to the throne of the Delhi sultanate. It was Malik's descendant, Firoz Shah Tughluq (r. 1351–1388) who built the city of Jaunpur in 1359, naming it after his immediate predecessor, Muhammad bin Tughluq (r. 1325–1351), who was also known as Juna Khan.

To maintain control of Jaunpur in the face of increased attacks from the forces of the Mongol invader Tamerlane, Firoz Shah sent his eunuch slave, Malik Sarwar Khwaja (r. 1394–1399), to govern Jaunpur and the surrounding area. Malik took the title Sultanus Sharq ("eastern emperor"). In the confusion that followed Firoz Shah's death in 1388 and Tamerlane's sack of Delhi in 1398, Malik Sarwar Khwaja declared independence and founded the kingdom of Jaunpur in 1398.

Jaunpur maintained its independence under the Sharqi dynasty for eighty-one years. The kingdom became as strong as Delhi and developed into a center of Islamic art and culture under Ibrahim Shah (r. 1402–1440). It also developed a distinctive type of architecture, reflected in several great mosques with imposing gateways.

The Sharqi dynasty was defeated in 1483, when the ruler of Jaunpur, Husain Shah (r. 1458–1495), lost a fierce struggle with a confederacy of Afghan and Turkish chiefs held together by the emperor of Delhi, Ibrahmin Bahlul Lodi (r. 1451–1489). At the time of Sikandar Lodi (r. 1489–1517,) Jaunpur was permanently annexed to the Delhi sultanate.

The Lodi dynasty (1451–1526) held Jaunpur and other northern kingdoms, including Malwa and Bengal, until the Maratha Confederacy dissolved in the face attacks from the Mughal ruler of Kabul, Babur (r. 1526–1530), in 1526. The northern region fell under the control of the Mughal Empire's Akbar the Great (r. 1556–1605) in 1559 and was gradually taken over by the British starting in 1775.

See also: AKBAR THE GREAT; BABUR; DELHI KINGDOM; INDIAN KINGDOMS; LODI KINGDOM; MARATHA CONFEDERACY; MUGHAL EMPIRE; TAMERLANE (TIMUR LENG); TUGHLUQ DYNASTY.

JAVAN KINGDOMS (800s–1700s C.E.)

Hindu, Buddhist, and Islamic kingdoms located both on the coast and in the interior of Java; there were at least twenty different kingdoms, both large and small, throughout the whole island of Java.

Javanese history can be divided into the early classic, middle classic, late classic, and Islamic periods. This historical breakdown is based on cultural changes reflected in inscriptions, monumental remains, and textual sources, both Chinese and Indonesian.

EARLY CLASSICAL KINGDOMS OF CENTRAL JAVA
The early classic period of Javan history, from the eighth to tenth centuries, coincided with the dominance of the Hindu Sanjaya and Buddhist Sailendra dynasties in the Kedu plains of central Java. This period was marked by the integration of the Javanese people into an international trading network and by the application of Indian models for Javan sculpture and temple architecture.

The earliest evidence of a kingdom in central Java is an inscription dated 732 found on Mount Wukir, which contains a hymn of praise to a Sanjaya king. People claiming to be his descendants were responsible for constructing Hindu complexes of the Dieng Plateau, Gedong Songo, and Prambanan.

JAVAN KINGDOMS (800s–1700s C.E.)

Early Mataram Kingdoms—Sailendra and Sanjaya Dynasties

SIMO	674–732
SANJAYA, RAKA MATARAM	732–778
PANCAPANA, RAKA	
PANANGKARAN	778–829
RAKA GARUNG	829–864
RAKA PIKATAN	864–879
RAKA KAYUVANGI	879–882
RAKA VATU HUMALANG	886–898
BALITUNG, RAKA VATUKURA	898–910
DAKSA, RAKA HINO	915–919
TULODONG, RAKA LAYANG	919–921
VAVA, RAKA PANGKAYA	924–928

East Javanese Kingdoms I—Janggala, Panjalu, and Kadiri

SINDOK	929–947
SRI ISANATUNGGAVIJAYA	947–991
DHARMAVAMSA	
ANANTAVIKRAMA	991–1007
AIRLANGGA	1019–1049
JURU	1049–1060
JAYAVARSA OF KEDIRI	1060–1104
KAMESVARA I	1115–1130
JAYABHAYA	1135–1157
SARVVESVARA	1160–1171
ARYYVESVARA	1171–1181
KRONCARYYADIPA, GANDRA	1181–1185
KAMESVARA II	1185–1190
SARVVESVARA II	1190–1200
KERTAJAYA	1216–1222

East Javanese Kingdoms II—Singosari and Majapahit

RAJASA (KEN ANGROK)	1222–1227
ANUSAPATI	1227–1248
TOHJAYA	1248
VISHNUVARDHANA	1248–1268
KERTANAGARA	1268–1292
JAYAKATWANG	1292–1293
KERTARAJASA	
JAYAVARDHANA	1293–1309
JAYANAGARA	1309–1329
TRIBHUVANA	1329–1350
RAJASANAGARA	
(HAYAM WURUK)	1350–1389
VIKRAMAVARDHANA	1389–1429
SUHITA	1429–1447
KERTAVIJAYA	1447–1451

West Java—Bantam Sultanate

SUSUHUNAN GUNUNG JATI	1526–1550
MAULANA HASANUDDIN	1550–1570
MAULANA MUHAMJAD	1570–1580
SULTAN ABDUL	
ABDUL KADIR	1580–1596
ABDUL FATAH, SULTAN	
AGUNG	1596–1651
ABDUL KAHAR, SULTAN	
HAJI	1682–1687

Central Java— Mataram Kingdom

SUTAVIJAYA SENOPATI	1582–1601
MAS DJOLANG	1601–1613
SULTAN AGUNG	1613–1645
PRABU AMANGKURAT I	1645–1677
AMANGKURAT II	1677–1703
AMANGKURAT III	1703–1705
PAKUBUWANA I	1705–1719
AMANGKURAT IV	1719–1727
PAKUBUWANA II	1727–1749
PAKUBUWANA III	1749–1788

(Mataram split into Surakarta and Yogyakarta in 1755)

Surakarta Sultanate

PAKUBUWANA III	1749–1788
PAKUBUWANA IV	1788–1820
PAKUBUWANA V	1820–1823
PAKUBUWANA VI	1823–1830
PAKUBUWANA VII	1830–1858
PAKUBUWANA VIII	1858–1861
PAKUBUWANA IX	1861–1893
PAKUBUWANA X	1893–1939
PAKUBUWANA XI	1939–1945
PAKUBUWANA XII	1945–

Yogyakarta Sultanate

AMANGKUBUWANA I	1755–1792
AMANGKUBUWANA II	1792–1810
AMANGKUBUWANA III	1812–1814
AMANGKUBUWANA IV	1814–1822
AMANGKUBUWANA V	1822–1855
AMANGKUBUWANA VI	1855–1877
AMANGKUBUWANA VII	1877–1921
AMANGKUBUWANA VIII	1921–1939
AMANGKUBUWANA IX	1939–1988
AMANGKUBUWANA X	1988–

*Indicates a separate alphabetical entry.

Around 780 another ruling dynasty, the Sailendras, rose to challenge the Sanjayas for power in central Java. The Sailendras sponsored Buddhist architecture such as Candi Kalasan, built around 778, and the monumental temple complexes of Borobudur, Mendut, and Pawon, completed in the mid-ninth century.

The last written record of a central Javanese kingdom is dated 919. For the next 500 years, all evidence of political activity in Java is limited to the eastern and western parts of the island. Scholars have posed various theories to explain the move to east Java. The most plausible include a volcanic eruption, an epidemic outbreak of disease, and an attack by the kingdom of Srivijaya in Sumatra.

MIDDLE CLASSICAL PERIOD— MOVE TO EAST JAVA

The end of the ninth century marks a major watershed in Javanese history. No temples of stone or brick were built for the next 350 years, although literary activity and sculpture continued in east Java.

For most of the eleventh and twelfth centuries, east Java was divided into a number of kingdoms. Kadiri is the best known of these kingdoms because of its literary remains. Another of these states was Janggala, a prominent trading kingdom. Although this period did not produce any great architecture or sculpture, it marked a time when major social changes were taking place in Java, such as the expansion of commercial networks, rapid urbanization, and the arrival of Chinese immigrants in both Java and Sumatra.

The kingdom of Kadiri was eventually eclipsed in 1222 by the kingdom of Singasari. This kingdom, which lasted until 1292, represents the formative phase of the largest empire in Indonesian history. The kings of Singasari were inclined toward Buddhism. They revived architecture in brick and stone at the sites of Jago and Kidal.

A Mongol invasion and attack of Singasari in 1292 led to the rise to power of Raden Wijaya (r. 1292–1306) (also known as Kertarajasa Jayavardhana), a Singasari prince, who succeeded in driving Mongols out of the kingdom. Two years later, in 1294, Raden Wijaya became the ruler of the powerful new Hindu kingdom of Majapahit.

LATE CLASSICAL PERIOD AND THE KINGDOM OF MAJAPAHIT

The late classic period, from the fourteenth to sixteenth centuries, coincided with the rise and fall of Majapahit, the largest and most powerful Hindu empire in ancient Southeast Asia. During the fourteenth century, Majapahit's capital, present-day Trowulan, grew into the largest city in the Indonesian archipelago.

Majapahit exhibited many sophisticated features, such as occupational specialization, the use of money, and increased production of art, including mass-produced art objects. Details about the kingdom's founding and expansion are contained in the *Nagarakrtagama* (1365), a court text that describes a cosmopolitan court, a complex system of religious rituals, and diplomatic relations with other countries.

Following the death of Hayam Wuruk in 1389, Majapahit gradually lost control of its territories on the outer islands, and it no longer constructed major monuments. Nevertheless, the kingdom remained in existence until the 1520s.

ISLAMIC KINGDOMS

The first major Islamic kingdom of Java, Demak, rose on the north coast of the island in the early 1500s. It only lasted for about fifty years, however. Thereafter, the Muslim sultanate of Bantam, in northwestern Java, developed into a powerful state. It dominated the spice trade until the 1680s, though its territorial extent was relatively limited.

In the mid-sixteenth century, several new kingdoms arose in the interior of central Java. One of these, Pajang, was absorbed by a state named Mataram. Founded around 1582, the sultanate of Mataram subjugated most of the ports in north-central and northeastern Java and came to dominate the island. Soon, however, Mataram came under increasing pressure from the Dutch, and in 1755 it was split into two states, Surakarta and Jogjakarta. Both of these states were eventually absorbed into the Republic of Indonesia, when it gained its independence from Dutch colonial rule in 1949.

See also: JANGGALA KINGDOM; MAJAPAHIT EMPIRE; MATARAM EMPIRE; SAILENDRA DYNASTY; SOUTHEAST ASIAN KINGDOMS.

FURTHER READING

Miksic, John, ed. *Indonesian Heritage: Ancient History*. Vol. 1. Singapore: Archipelago Press, 1995.

Reid, Anthony, ed. *Indonesian Heritage: Early Modern History*. Vol. 3. Singapore: Archipelago Press, 1995.

Ricklefs, M.C. *A History of Indonesia Since c. 1200*. Stanford, CA: Stanford University Press, 2001.

JEANNE D'ALBRET. *See* BOURBON DYNASTY; HENRY IV (FRANCE)

JIMMU (ca. 40–10 B.C.E.)

The semilegendary direct descendant of the Japanese sun-goddess, Amaterasu, who founded Japan's ruling dynasty and ruled as first emperor of Japan. Jimmu is also known as Jimmu Tenno, the posthumous name of the reign by which he is commonly known. Jimmu is the ancestor of an unbroken imperial line of Japanese emperors, a dynasty that claims to have survived more than 2,500 years.

Jimmu's story is told in the colorful *Kojiki* and *Nihon Shoki*, chronicles that were solicited from scholars during the reign of Emperor Temmu (r. 673–686) in order to establish and exploit the divine heritage of the imperial line. These lively and heroic chronicles report that, with the inspiration of the sun-goddess, Amaterasu, and following a years-long campaign of conquest along the Inland Sea, Jimmu succeeded in establishing his imperial capital in the

Yamato province of central Japan, south of Kyoto. Described as brave, wise, pious, hardy, and clever, Jimmu united the Japanese people under his rule.

Traditionally, unification of the country is said to have taken place in 660 B.C.E. Modern historians cannot substantiate the legendary accounts, but they point out that the Yamato clan did establish territorial control in the first century B.C.E. and also founded the imperial line of Japan that survives to this day. Some scholars speculate that if there was a real Jimmu, he probably ruled around the beginning of the Christian era.

Jimmu is reputed to be the great-great-grandson of the Shinto sun-goddess, Amaterasu, ruler of the heavens. Amaterasu's brother is Susano-o, the god of storms who rules over the seas. After a quarrel, Susano-o tormented Amaterasu with various angry pranks, which included destroying her rice paddies. After these pranks, Amaterasu shut herself away in a cave, plunging the world into darkness. The other gods and goddesses lured her out with songs and laughter. Susano-o was then banished and went to Izumo province in western Japan, where he sired many children, had many adventures, and made peace with Amaterasu.

Susano-o's heroic son, Okuninushi, pacified the wild lands of Izumo, and eventually his sons acceded to Amaterasu's request to let her descendants rule the land. Her great-great-grandson Jimmu thus became the first earthly emperor of Japan.

Jimmu's dynasty survived for more than 2,500 years because those who held real power in Japan—shoguns, dictators, and warlords—never actually overthrew the emperor. Instead, men ruled in the name of the sovereign emperor of divine descent. These leaders traditionally based their right to rule upon the legitimacy of positions sanctioned, however circuitously, by the imperial office.

See also: NARA KINGDOM; YAMATO DYNASTY.

JOÃO (JOHN) VI (1767–1826 C.E.)

King of Portugal (r. 1816–1826) who also ruled as first king of the former Portuguese colony of Brazil after the royal court fled there following the invasion of Portugal by the forces of Napoleon Bonaparte in 1870.

A member of the Bragança dynasty, João VI was one of seven children born to Queen Maria I and King Pedro III (r. 1777–1786) of Portugal. Only João and two of his royal siblings survived into adulthood. His family had a long history of madness, and João ended up attaining the throne prematurely when dementia struck his own mother.

The first ten years of João's life were a time of great tribulation in Portugal. His maternal grandfather, King Jose I (r. 1750–1777), was a weak and probably disturbed man who left the running of government to a powerful court noble, the marquis of Pombal. Pombal's approach to administration was bloodthirsty, and the execution of troublesome nobles was common. It was only with the death of King Jose that Pombal could be dislodged from power.

Maria I (r. 1777–1816) succeeded to the throne of Portugal upon the death of her father in 1777, when João was ten years old. As a prince in the royal household, João was in line for succession, but he was not the probable heir to the throne. In the event of Maria's death, succession would pass to her husband, King Pedro III (r. 1777–1786), who would hold the reigns of power until their eldest son, Jose, was deemed old enough to take the throne. In the late 1780s, however, the royal family suffered twin tragedies: the death of Pedro III in 1786 and the untimely death of Jose from smallpox. Suddenly, João found himself next in the line of succession.

Maria was only thirty-two years old when her husband died. Under normal circumstances, João would have had a long wait before becoming ruler of Portugal. However, Maria shared the family problem of dementia, and by 1792 her ministers recognized that she was no longer fit to govern. In 1799, after a quick education in the responsibilities of a king, João was officially named prince regent and was charged with the care of the kingdom while his mother remained unable to discharge her duties.

João's years as regent were devoted largely to restoring Portugal to some semblance of peace and stability after the damage done during Pombal's usurpation of power. João's policies earned him the reputation as a benevolent ruler (he was called "the forgiving"). However, he was much troubled by the spirit of revolution sweeping through Europe at the time, leaving much devastation in its wake; this no doubt prompted much of his benign policy. João's work was interrupted by the expansionist aims of Napoleon.

In 1801, French and Spanish troops invaded and defeated Portugal, and João was forced to sign the

Treaty of Badajoz, which placed him totally under Napoleon's control. Even so, Napoleon invaded again in 1807. When attempts to enlist military support from Britain failed, the entire Portuguese royal family fled to Brazil in 1808. The British did at least assist in this regard, by providing ships of the British Navy to conduct the family to safe harbor in Rio de Janeiro.

In exile in Brazil, João established a new seat of Portuguese government. He elevated the colony to the status of kingdom, although he intended it to remain subordinate to Lisbon once he was able to return to his ancestral home. While in Brazil, in 1816, Maria died and João attained full sovereign powers. He was reluctant to return to Lisbon, even after Napoleon's forces were ultimately driven out of Portugal in 1811. Instead, João continued to rule from Rio de Janeiro and left the day-to-day management of Portugal to a regency established by the British.

In 1821, João was called home to Portugal when the Cortes, the Portuguese legislature, became alarmed at a movement that had arisen to challenge the monarchy and establish a constitution. With no choice but to comply, João left the Brazilian throne in the hands of his son Pedro. If he was relying on his son's sense of duty to keep Brazil subordinate to the Portuguese Crown, however, he was mistaken. Within a year, Pedro declared Brazil independent and took the title Emperor Pedro I (r. 1822–1831).

João was able to retain the throne of Portugal, but only briefly, for he died in 1826. His death sparked a civil war because his policies had favored a constitutional monarchy, which angered more absolutist elements within the government. João's son, Pedro I of Brazil was made King Pedro IV of Portugal, but he relinquished the Crown to his daughter, Maria II (r. 1834–1853).

Problems in Brazil finally led Pedro to abdicate the Brazilian throne in favor of his son, Pedro II (r. 1831–1889), and he returned to Portugal. Pedro's presence did nothing to reduce political tensions there, however, for he favored a constitutional monarchy. The so-called Miguelist Wars (named for Pedro's brother Miguel, the leader of the absolutist faction) that ensued raged for eight years, ending with victory for the faction led by Pedro and his daughter Maria, who was restored to the throne.

See also: BRAGANÇA DYNASTY; BRAZIL, PORTUGUESE MONARCHY OF; PEDRO I; PEDRO II.

JOÃO THE GREAT

(1357–1433 C.E.)

Ruler of Portugal (r. 1385–1433), also known as John of Aviz and João the Bastard, who founded Portugal's Aviz dynasty (1385–1580).

The illegitimate son of Pedro I (r. 1357–1367), João acceded to the throne after a convoluted dynastic struggle between Castilian and Portuguese royalty. João's half-brother Ferdinand I (r. 1367–1383) was the last of the legitimate Portuguese line descended from Henry of Burgundy, the father of Afonso I (1112–1185). Following Ferdinand's death in 1383, his widow Leonor and her Galician favorite, João Fernandes Andeiro, promoted the claim of Juan I of Castile, who was betrothed to Leonor's daughter Beatriz.

The people of Lisbon rioted against the unpopular Leonor. Meanwhile, a young Portuguese noble, Nuno Alvares Pereira, recruited João to murder Leonor's lover. Supported in Lisbon and Porto by the merchants and guilds, and helped by an outbreak of the plague, João and his forces drove out the Castilian pretender in September 1384. In April 1385 the Portuguese Cortes, or parliament, at Coimbra elected João king, declaring no other heir legitimate.

João and Nuno Alvarez, now João's constable, ended the two years of civil war with victory at the battle of Aljubarrota in August 1385, establishing Portuguese independence from Spain. Over 2,500 Castillians died there, although the Spanish greatly outnumbered the Portuguese forces. Joao I confiscated the lands of pro-Castilian nobles and established a new landed aristocracy among his own supporters.

João inherited a merchants' alliance established with England in 1353, and supported John of Gaunt, duke of Lancaster, in his claim through marriage to the Castilian throne. The two signed the Treaty of Windsor in May 1386, pledging peace and friendship between England and Portugal in what is still the oldest unbroken sovereign treaty in the world. João later married John of Gaunt's daughter, Philippa, who became a very popular queen.

John of Gaunt pressed his claim only half-heartedly. He lost his claim to the Castilian throne, but married another of his daughters, Catherine, the heir to the throne of Castile and returned to England in 1387. João made a ten-year truce with Castile in 1389 that, despite intermittent skirmishing, led to peace in 1411. Catherine, now the widowed queen

The founder of the Aviz Dynasty of Portugal, João I won independence from Spain in the 1385 Battle of Aljubarotta, where he defeated Juan I of Castile. His victory is depicted in this fifteenth-century history by Flemish author Jean Batard de Wavrin.

of Castile, formally recognized the house of Aviz in 1431.

João and his sons captured the Moroccan port of Ceuta in 1415 and made it a colony. It proved to be a costly colony, however, since much of its wealth was already looted and the garrison had to be supplied from Portugal across the water.

The reign of João I is especially noted for launching the Age of Discovery. João's son, Prince Henry the Navigator, led numerous explorations far from Portugal. In 1418–1419, Portuguese sailors explored the islands of Madeira in the Atlantic, and in 1427 they discovered the Azores Islands. During the mid-1400s, Prince Henry and his navigators explored the west coast of Africa.

See also: IBERIAN KINGDOMS.

FURTHER READING

Anderson, James M. *The History of Portugal.* Westport, CT: Greenwood Press, 2000.

Kaplan, Marion. *The Portuguese: The Land and Its People.* New York: Viking, 1991.

Livermore, H.V. *A New History of Portugal.* 2nd ed. New York: Cambridge University Press, 1976.

Marques, A.H. de Oliveira. *History of Portugal.* New York: Columbia University Press, 1976.

Payne, Stanley G. *A History of Spain and Portugal: Antiquity to the Seventeenth Century.* Vol. 1. Madison: University of Wisconsin Press, 1973.

Robertson, Ian. *A Traveller's History of Portugal.* New York: Interlink Books, 2002.

Wheeler, Douglas L. *Historical Dictionary of Portugal.* Metuchen, NJ: Scarecrow, 1993.

JODHPUR KINGDOM (1459–1947 C.E.)

Kingdom in northwestern India, strategically located on the trade routes between Delhi and the Arabian Sea, that was one of India's many Rajput states.

The city of Jodhpur in Rajasthan was founded in 1459 by Rao Jodha (r. 1458–1488), a chief of the Rajput clan known as the Rathors. The Rajput clans were landowners from central and northern India. Jodhpur prospered because of its location on a strategic trading route between the city of Delhi and the Arabian Sea. Over the years, the people of Jodhpur benefited from the traffic in opium, copper, silk, sandalwood, dates, and coffee.

The Rathor dynasty controlled a large part of the Rajasthan region in northwestern India, especially during the reign of Rao Udai Singh (r. 1581–1595). The rulers of the Mughal Empire coveted the Rathors' riches, and the easiest way to gain them was through an arranged marriage between the Mughal emperor, Akbar the Great (r. 1556–1605), and the sister of Rao Udai Singh. This marriage alliance ensured that the Rathors received military support from the Mughals for their campaigns on the southern India plain and into the kingdom of Gujarat, the state located between Jodhpur and the Arabian Sea coast.

Problems arose in the mid-seventeenth century when the Rathor Maharaja of Jodhpur, Jaswant Singh I (r. 1638–1678), supported forces loyal to Akbar's grandson, Emperor Shah Jahan (r. 1593–1658), in the Mughal war of succession. Jaswant Singh promised to help the emperor's loyal son, Dara Shikoh, defeat Shah Jahan's rebellious son, Aurangzeb.

At the last minute, however, Jaswant Singh withdrew his support for Dara Shikoh and Aurangzeb defeated and then killed his brother at the battle of Deorai in 1659. Now emperor, Aurangzeb (r. 1659–1707) turned his attention to Jaswant Singh. The Mughals pillaged Jodhpur, and Aurangzeb attempted to force the kingdom's Hindu citizens to convert to Islam. Jaswant Singh's son and heir, Ajit Singh, was murdered, and the Mughals staked their claim to the Jodhpur throne. Ajit's infant son, Ajit Singh II (r. 1707–1724), was taken underground by a Rathor noble, Durga Das, to a tiny Himalayan village, where he was hidden for thirty years. He eventually returned to Jodhpur after Aurangzeb's death in 1707 and recaptured it.

The eighteenth century saw many bloody battles between Jodhpur and other princely states in the regions of Rajasthan, Jaipur, and Udaipur. The successor of Ajit Singh II, Maharaja Abhai Singh (r. 1724–1749), captured Ahmedabad, and later, in 1818, Jodhpur signed a treaty with the British. Although the Rathors lost some of their honor, the treaty ensured that Jodhpur would enjoy relative peace and prosperity. Jodhpur became part of the Republic of India in 1947 under its last ruler, Maharaja Umaid Singh (r. 1918–1947).

See also: AKBAR THE GREAT; AURANGZEB; MUGHAL EMPIRE; RAJASTHAN KINGDOM.

JOHN I (1167–1216 C.E.)

King of England (r. 1199–1216), a member of the Plantagenet dynasty, whose aggression, tyrannical acts, and paranoia made him extremely unpopular. He was nicknamed John Lackland because his father's land was divided among his older brothers.

John was the fifth son of King Henry II (r. 1154–1189) and Eleanor of Aquitaine. The two oldest sons of Henry and Eleanor—Henry and Geoffrey—died before their father, so it was the fourth son, Richard I (r. 1189–1199), nicknamed the Lionheart, who became king upon his father's death in 1189. Richard had no legitimate heir, and instead of his brother John, he chose Duke Arthur of Brittany to succeed him. As John was a rival for the throne, and had been given extensive holdings in France, Richard forbade John access to England while Richard was away on the Third Crusade. In defiance of his brother, however, John not only traveled to England, but also attempted to usurp Richard's rule.

After Richard's death in 1199, John maneuvered to succeed him with the assistance of his mother, Eleanor of Aquitaine, and King Philip II Augustus of France (r. 1180–1223). Philip Augustus, however, then took advantage of the first opportunity to reclaim English holdings in France. In the ensuing war with France (1204–1206), England lost the regions of Normandy, Anjou, Maine, and Poitou. A costly attempt to recover these territories ended in an English defeat in 1214.

John's reign was also marked by conflicts with English barons. In order to pay the costs of military engagements against France, John demanded exorbitant taxes from his subjects. This and other tyrannical acts alienated the English nobles. To curb his abuses, the English barons forced John in 1215 to sign the Magna Carta, a document that clearly delineated the limits of his power. John's refusal to honor the document initiated a civil war, the first Barons' War (1215–1217), during which John died.

John also engaged in conflicts with the church. He angered Pope Innocent III when he refused to accept the elected archbishop of Canterbury. As a result, in 1209 the pope excommunicated John in order to reestablish papal authority. Then, in 1213, the pope further extended papal authority by forcing John to make England a fief of the Holy See.

John married his first wife Isabella, the daughter of William, earl of Gloucester, in 1189. Their ten-year marriage produced no children and was annulled. His second marriage, in 1200, was to Isabella, the daughter of the count of Angoulême. They had five children: Henry, Richard, Joan, Isabella, and Eleanor. John also had at least twelve illegitimate children. One of these, Joan, married Llywelyn the Great (r. 1194–1240), the ruler of all Wales. It was from their union that the Tudor Dynasty arose. John died of an illness in 1216 during the first Barons' War. He was succeeded on the throne by his son, Henry III (r. 1216–1272).

See also: BRETAGNE DUCHY; ELEANOR OF AQUITAINE; ENGLISH MONARCHIES; HENRY II; PHILIP II, AUGUSTUS; RICHARD I, LIONHEART; TUDOR, HOUSE OF.

JOHN III (JOHN SOBIESKI)

(1630–1696 C.E.)

King of Poland (r. 1674–1696) who led the armies of Poland and Austria in the defeat of the Turks at Vienna in 1683. Although he is now revered in his native country as the savior of Europe, his reign was plagued by legislative and diplomatic disappointments.

The son of lesser Polish nobility, John Sobieski early distinguished himself as a gifted military leader, first with the invading Swedish king, Charles X (r. 1654–1660). Then, as grand marshall of the Polish army, John led successful campaigns against the Russian Cossacks in 1665 and against the Turks from 1670 to 1673. These last victories secured John election as king in 1674, despite opposition by members of the powerful Habsburg dynasty.

Arriving in Cracow for his coronation in 1674, John (or Jan) Sobieski was a highly experienced military leader. He had been married for nineteen years to Maria Kazimiera, a noblewoman of royal French blood who had planned, plotted, and assisted her husband's career at every step. Together, John and Maria had seen Poland invaded by Charles X of Sweden and participated in the revolt that made Poland independent again. They had also endured the ineptitude of Sobieski's predecessors on the throne, John Casimir (r. 1648–1668) and Michael Wisniowiecki (r. 1669–1673), who had ceded sovereignty of the western Ukraine to the Turks.

Poland in the late seventeenth century suffered other problems as well. Russia coveted the eastern Polish Palatinates as far west as the Vistula River; Prussia looked for any chance to take the northwestern marches; and the Austrian Empire was enticed by the wealth of Cracow. After taking the throne, John III Sobieski made his foreign policy very clear: expulsion of the Turks from Europe. At Lvov in the Ukraine in September 1675, Sobieski defeated a Turkish army four times larger than his own and compelled the Turks to sign the Treaty of Zuravno, which abolished Ottoman claims to the Ukraine.

Sobieski was disappointed, however, in his many attempts to engage Louis XIV of France (r. 1643–1715) and Holy Roman Emperor Leopold I (r. 1658–1705) in diplomatic alliances against the Turks. He finally did negotiate a mutual protection treaty with Leopold, however, and when the Turks once again besieged Vienna in 1683, Sobieski mobilized the entire Polish army and moved to break the siege. His counterattacks were brilliant, and the Polish victory over the Turks at Vienna on September 12, 1683, marks one of the most important military events in European history.

Unfortunately, Sobieski's luck in personal negotiations did not mirror his skill on the battlefield. Although John III helped liberate Vienna from the Turks, an ungrateful Leopold I would not pledge his daughter in marriage to Sobieski's son despite attempts to persuade him otherwise. Nevertheless, John III returned from the battles in Austria to an adoring Polish nation.

Though admired, even revered, for his military accomplishments, culture and intelligence, and legendary romance with his wife, Sobieski was never able to overcome the narrow interests of the *Szlachta,* the Polish nobility, and their intransigence in the Polish parliament, the *Sejm.* Any one of these feudal lords could exert a veto over any of the king's orders or the Sejm's laws and, most often, one did. Nevertheless, a frequently disappointed Sobieski continually attempted reforms until his death in June 1696.

The death of John III Sobieski marked the virtual end of Polish independence, although the final dismemberment of the nation would not be complete for another hundred years. Poland still reveres John III as a savior and as Poland's greatest military hero.

See also: AUSTRO-HUNGARIAN EMPIRE; LEOPOLD I; LOUIS XIV; OTTOMAN EMPIRE.

JOSEPH II (1741–1790 C.E.)

Emperor of the Holy Roman Empire (1765–1790) and king of Hungary and Bohemia (1780–1790), who sought to reform and modernize the ancient Habsburg regime.

Joseph Benedict Augustus John Anthony Michael Adam of Habsburg was born in 1741, the son of Maria Theresa of Austria and Holy Roman Emperor Francis I (r. 1745–1765). One of the foremost members of the Habsburg dynasty, his mother made sure Joseph was thoroughly groomed for the throne and family legacy by providing him with a complete education. Taught languages and other liberal arts, Joseph became most interested in political philosophy, including many of the innovative and revolutionary ideas of the eighteenth-century Enlightenment.

Much to his mother's consternation, Joseph's future as a political reformer was evident from an early age. Maria Theresa was a European monarch of a past era—she was authoritarian, elitist, and devoutly religious. Accordingly, the Enlightenment ideas of tolerance and equality were anathema to her. During the fifteen years (1765–1780) when she and Joseph ruled as co-regents of the Habsburg Austrian domains, they disagreed often on policy and reform.

MARRIAGE AND DEATH OF HIS FATHER

At age nineteen, Joseph married Princess Isabella of Bourbon-Parma, the daughter of an Italian duke and granddaughter of King Louis XIV of France (r. 1643–1715). The marriage, which was a happy one for Joseph, also cemented Austria's new alliance with France and furthered its influence in Italy.

A beautiful and intelligent noblewoman, Isabella gave birth to a daughter in 1762, but she died the next year of smallpox. After Isabella's death, Joseph fell into a deep depression and never again allowed himself a close relationship with a woman. In 1765, Joseph remarried for dynastic reasons only, wedding a German princess, Maria Josepha of Bavaria. In 1770 Joseph's unhappiness deepened with the death of his daughter, also named Maria Theresa, from pneumonia.

After the death of Joseph's father, Francis I, in 1765, Joseph and his mother were often in conflict in their joint rule of the Habsburg lands. Maria Theresa maintained most of the authority and relied heavily on her closest adviser, Prince Wenzel Anton Kaunitz. The prince was a fastidious and exacting minister of state who had engineered the diplomatic revolution of 1756 that allied Austria with its traditional enemy, France.

FOREIGN POLICY AND REFORMS

As emperor, Joseph was largely ineffective in his foreign policy efforts, failing to annex Bavaria in the War of the Bavarian Succession (1778–1779) or in securing the exchange of the Austrian Netherlands for Bavaria in 1785. From 1787 to 1792, Austria joined Russia in fighting against the Ottoman Empire, but this effort was also unsuccessful.

While he ruled jointly with his mother, Joseph became impatient with her resistance to political reform. However, a series of religious and political crises in the late 1770s and early 1780s, coupled with his mother's death in 1780, allowed Joseph to institute many of the reforms his mother had opposed.

In spite of his political tolerance, Joseph was a strong exponent of absolutism and often used despotic means to push through his reforms. He was also a faithful Roman Catholic. Nevertheless, in 1781 he issued an Edict of Toleration that allowed minority religions, including Judaism, to be practiced in Austria.

Concern for the poor prompted Joseph to abolish serfdom and feudal taxes, enabling tenants to buy land and giving peasants greater freedom to marry and to move. In addition, he founded orphanages, hospitals, and poorhouses. Joseph also modernized Austrian government by abolishing redundant offices and restructuring state finances. He overhauled the military, state-run agriculture, and education as well. By the time of Joseph's death in 1790, Austria's government had been completely transformed. Joseph's reforms were not permanent, however. Most of his changes were rescinded during the reign of his brother and successor, Leopold II (r. 1790–1792).

See also: HABSBURG DYNASTY; HOLY ROMAN EMPIRE; LEOPOLD II; MARIA THERESA.

JUAN CARLOS (1938–Present)

King of Spain (r. 1975–) who presided over Spain's transition to democracy after decades of authoritarian rule under the dictator Francisco Franco.

Born in Italy on January 5, 1938, Juan Carlos was the oldest son of Juan Carlos de Borbón y Battenberg and María de las Mercedes de Borbón y Orleans. His grandfather, King Alphonso XIII (r. 1886–1931), relinquished the throne of Spain in 1931 and went into exile upon the proclamation of the Second Spanish Republic.

Juan Carlos lived in Italy until 1947, when he went to Spain because his father wanted him to be educated there. He was placed under Franco's care as a possible successor to the dictator. After receiving his bachelor's degree from San Isidro School in 1954, Juan Carlos studied at the Spanish military academies and received commissions in the army, navy, and air force. He also studied law and economics at the University of Madrid. In 1962 he married Princess Sofia of Greece, with whom he had three children—Elena, Christina, and Crown Prince Felipe.

In 1939, Spanish dictator Francisco Franco abolished the Spanish Republic and declared Spain a representative monarchy. During his reign as dictator, however, Spain had no monarch. In 1969, the aging Franco named Juan Carlos as his successor and the future king of Spain. When Franco died in 1975, Juan Carlos ascended the Spanish throne. He quickly proved to be much more liberal in his politics than the right-wing Franco. With the help of Adolfo Suárez, whom Juan Carlos named as prime minister in 1976, the king led the way to many reforms, including a new constitution that established Spain as a parliamentary monarchy, and democratic elections. Juan Carlos granted amnesty to many political prisoners and revived political parties. Other reforms included a more liberal divorce law in 1981 and the legalization of independent trade unions.

These reforms angered many conservatives in Spain, and in 1981 a group of conservative leaders attempted a military coup. As the coup attempt unfolded, Juan Carlos appeared on television and called on Spaniards to support the democratic government. He also contacted military leaders to inform them that he intended to support democracy. Juan Carlos's deft handling of the coup solidified his position and increased his popularity, especially among liberals and other supporters of democracy. It also helped legitimize the monarchy in the eyes of the Spanish people.

Juan Carlos has traveled extensively during his reign, becoming the first Spanish king to visit the Americas and China. A strong supporter of the European Union, he received the Charlemagne Award in 1982 for his personal cooperation with European states, his role in maintaining peace, freedom, democracy, and human rights in Europe, and his support for the expansion of the European Union."

See also: Spanish Monarchies.

Judah, Kingdom of

(ca. 928–587 b.c.e.)

An ancient Hebrew state, formed when the kingdom of Israel was divided in two after the death of King Solomon (r. 970–931 b.c.e.).

Around 930 b.c.e., when the kingdom of Israel was divided in two, the northern part of the old kingdom retained the name the kingdom of Israel. The southern part, which included the city of Jerusalem, became known as the kingdom of Judah and retained the dynasty of kings established by David and Solomon. Solomon's son, Rehoboam (r. ca. 930–914 b.c.e.), was the first king of Judah.

For about the first fifty years after the division of the two kingdoms, Judah and Israel retained their old animosities and regularly warred with each other. Finally, around the mid-ninth century b.c.e., King Jehoshaphat of Judah (r. ca. 871–847 b.c.e.) signed a peace treaty with King Omri of Israel (r. ca. 885–874 b.c.e.), which allowed Judah to begin to stabilize and prosper. Jehoshaphat built up his kingdom's army, devised a better system for tax collections, and established a supreme court in Jerusalem.

The kingdom of Judah enjoyed its height of stability and prosperity in the eighth century b.c.e. during the reign of King Uzziah (r. ca. 766–740 b.c.e.). Uzziah brought trade revenues into the kingdom through the coastal lands he controlled. He also extended his territory by adding settlements in Transjordan (in present-day Jordan).

During the reign of Uzziah's grandson, Ahaz (r. ca. 730–715 b.c.e.), a new threat loomed to the east—Assyria, which was building an empire and expanding west. The Assyrians initially bypassed tiny Judah and invaded nearby Israel and Damascus. Eventually, however, King Tiglath-pileser III of Assyria (r. ca. 745–727 b.c.e.) forced Judah to pay tribute, and the kingdom became a vassal state of the Assyrian Empire.

Ahaz was succeeded by his son, King Hezekiah (r. ca. 714–686 b.c.e.), who, around 701 b.c.e., rebelled against the Assyrians and refused to pay tribute. The Assyrian king Sennacherib (r. 704–681 B.C.E.) marched with his army to Jerusalem and laid siege to the city. Although Sennacherib destroyed much property in Jerusalem, he did not take the city. Nevertheless, Hezekiah, chastened by Assyria's might, began to pay tribute again.

When Babylonia defeated Assyria and Egypt around 605 B.C.E., Judah became a vassal of Babylonia. King Jehoiachin of Judah (r. ca. 598–597 B.C.E.) attempted to rebel against Babylonia and align his kingdom with Egypt. But the Babylonian ruler, Nebuchadrezzar II (r. 605–562 B.C.E.), quickly quashed the rebellion and, in 597 B.C.E., destroyed much of Jerusalem, deporting many of Judah's leaders to Mesopotamia. Yet, Babylonia left Judah independent.

Under King Zedekiah (r. ca. 596–586 B.C.E.), Judah again attempted to rebel against Babylonia. This time King Nebuchadrezzar showed no mercy toward Judah or Jerusalem. He and his army burned Solomon's temple, destroyed homes, exiled more Hebrews, and, by 586 B.C.E., had completely conquered the kingdom of Judah.

See also: ASSYRIAN EMPIRE; DAVID; HEBREW KINGS; ISRAEL, KINGDOMS OF; JUDAISM AND KINGSHIP; NEBUCHADREZZAR II; SENNACHERIB; SOLOMON.

JUDAISM AND KINGSHIP

The significance of monarchy in the Jewish religion, and the practical role of kings in the life of ancient Israel (ca. 1000 B.C.E.–44 C.E.).

In the earliest stage of Jewish history, as depicted in the biblical books of Joshua and Judges (ca. 1300–1020 B.C.E.), the Israelites had no king. Instead, the twelve tribes of Israel maintained a loose confederation, united by the common worship of one God. In times of danger, the tribes temporarily united behind a military leader or a prophet (who would interpret God's will), but they reverted to tribal autonomy once the threat passed.

The Israelite religious and legal tradition, as recorded in the first five books of the Bible, made no provision for kings, apart from a single unclear reference in Deuteronomy to future kings. The commandments and laws were supposed to be enforced by judges and leaders chosen by tribal elders or recruited directly by God (as were Moses and Joshua).

ORIGIN OF THE MONARCHY

Recurrent attacks by Philistines and other enemies eventually convinced many Israelites that a national monarchy was needed as a defensive measure. But the Bible seems to find the idea irreligious. When Israelite leaders asked the military hero Gideon to become their king, he replied, "I will not rule over you myself, nor shall my son rule over you; the Lord alone shall rule over you." Similarly, when the people later asked the prophet Samuel to appoint a king "to govern us like all other nations," Samuel at first refused. God even told him, "it is Me [the Israelites] have rejected as their king" by asking for a human monarch. Nevertheless, God ordered Samuel to do what the people requested.

This negative attitude toward kings was to remain a common theme throughout the later books of the Bible and subsequent Jewish writings, alongside other, more positive attitudes. Saul (r. ca. 1020–1010 B.C.E.), the very first Israelite king, whom Samuel anointed (poured sacred oil over), ignored the prophet's spiritual advice and acted according to reasons of state. According to the Bible, God rejected Saul, who died in battle with his son, who could not inherit the throne once his father was delegitimized.

KINGSHIP'S NEW RELIGIOUS ROLE

Saul's successor, also anointed by the prophet Samuel, was the popular hero David (r. ca. 1010–970 B.C.E.). The positive attitudes toward monarchy within later Jewish writings all point back to David.

David added many spiritual and religious elements to the Israelite monarchy. He performed sacrifices, serving as a mediator between God and the Israelites. He brought the Ark of the Covenant, containing the Ten Commandments, to Jerusalem and planned a temple to house it, later built by his son and heir, King Solomon (r. ca. 970–931 B.C.E.). The books of Samuel relate several cases in which David repented his sins, reinforcing the idea that only a just king can be a legitimate ruler of Israel.

Tradition cites David as author of the intensely spiritual book of Psalms. God eventually promised David, through the prophet Nathan, that all legitimate future Jewish kings would come from his descendants. Unlike most rulers of Egypt or Mesopotamia, however, David was never deified, or turned into a God. No prayers were addressed to him, and no statues in his image were fashioned.

The kingdom of Israel broke into two after the

reign of King Solomon. Both kingdoms were eventually destroyed, the northern kingdom of Israel in 721 B.C.E. and the southern kingdom of Judah in 586 B.C.E. The next Jewish kings, the Maccabees or Hasmoneans (166–37 B.C.E.), came from a family of priests, and made themselves hereditary high priests as well as kings.

KINGSHIP LOSES ITS PRACTICAL ROLE

The Romans' conquest of Judea, as the entire country was now called, in 63 B.C.E., put an end to an independent Jewish monarchy. The Herodians, who ruled as puppets of the Romans from 37 B.C.E.–44 C.E., were considered illegitimate rulers by the rabbis of the Talmudic era (100–600 C.E.).

After the destruction of Jerusalem by the Romans in 70 C.E., Jewish ideas of kingship became bound up with the hope for a messiah, or savior (literally, the "anointed one"). The messiah was to be a descendant of King David; he would restore Jewish political sovereignty and establish a just order for Israel.

Jesus was said by Christians to be from "the stem of Jesse" (David's father), and was regarded by some as the new "king of Israel." Similarly, during the last Jewish rebellion against Rome in 131–135, the revered Rabbi Akiba proclaimed the rebel leader Bar Kochba to be the "King Messiah." Although that rebellion failed, many Jewish scholars, such as the medieval philosopher Maimonides (1135–1204), kept the idea of a king messiah alive.

Nevertheless, during the centuries of Jewish existence without a state, the idea of earthly monarchy lost its appeal. In Jewish prayers, kingship refers almost exclusively to God, and not to man. When Jewish nationalism revived in the nineteenth century through the Zionist movement—at a time when most of the world was led by Christian, Moslem, Hindu, Buddhist, or Shinto monarchs—no Jewish monarchist party or faction ever arose.

See also: DAVID; HEBREW KINGS; ISRAEL, KINGDOMS OF; JUDAH, KINGDOM OF; SOLOMON.

JULIAN THE APOSTATE

(331–363 C.E.)

Roman emperor (r. 360–363) who attempted to reinstate the traditional gods of Rome after they had been replaced by Christianity during the reign of Constantine I (r. 307–337).

Julian was born Flavius Claudius Julianus during the reign of his uncle, Emperor Constantine I. His father was Julius Constantius, an important man in Constantinople, which was then the capital of the Eastern Roman Empire. Being related to the emperor was not always an advantage in the Roman Empire; this was especially true when an emperor died and there was doubt as to his legitimate successor.

Julian and his family discovered this at the death of Constantine I in 337. The emperor's son, Constantius II (r. 337–340), inherited the imperial throne but was fearful of rivals. Hoping to secure his claim to the empire, he had all his adult male relatives executed, attempting in this way to secure his claim to the throne. Julian was just six years old at the time and constituted no threat to his imperial cousin, so his life was spared. Instead, he was sold into slavery and was taken to Asia Minor.

During the reign of Constantine I, Christianity had become the favored religion of the Roman Empire, and Julian was brought up in that faith. Even as a child, however, he was fascinated by the traditional Roman gods and the classical Roman and Greek literature and philosophy of the pre-Christian era. While in Asia Minor he also had the chance to learn about the religions of the East. He became particularly interested in the Greek goddess Demeter and in the Persian cult known as Mithraism.

Julian might have passed into obscurity had it not been for his cousin's thoroughness in eliminating rivals. In 355, Constantius II found it necessary to appoint a successor, but he had no sons or other male relatives upon whom to confer this honor, except for his exiled cousin Julian. Julian was duly recalled to Rome and given command over the Roman legion stationed in the provinces of Gaul and Britain. Although he only served in this capacity for five years, Julian proved very popular with the troops under his command. The same could not be said for his cousin, the emperor. In 360, the Roman military revolted against Constantius II and proclaimed Julian the new emperor.

Julian is called "the Apostate" because of one of his first actions upon becoming emperor. An apostate is a person who renounces his religion, and Julian did precisely that, not just for himself but for the entire empire. He demoted Christianity from its privileged status as state religion, banished Christians from positions of power within the government, and restored the temples and rituals of the pre-Christian era. Julian had little time to do much more as emperor, however. Soon after taking power he attempted to conquer Persia, and personally accompanied the troops into battle. He died on the battlefield in 363. His apostasy died with him: Christianity was reinstated as the state religion shortly after his death.

See also: CONSTANTINE I, THE GREAT; ROMAN EMPIRE.

JULIANA (1909–2004)

Queen of the Netherlands (r. 1948–1980), known for her social concerns and work on behalf of children.

The daughter of Queen Wilhelmina (r. 1890–1948) and Hendrik, duke of Mecklenburg-Schwerin, Juliana received her early education from her devout mother, who told her a ruler carried out God's will. Juliana then studied literature, philosophy, and law at the University of Leyden. In 1937, she married German prince Bernhard of Lippe-Biesterfeld. The royal couple had four daughters: Beatrix, the heir to the throne, and Irene, Margriet, and Christina.

The German invasion of the Netherlands in May 1940 forced the royal family to flee to England, where they supported the resistance. Princess Juliana spent part of the war years in Canada, where her daughter Margriet was born. In April 1945, Juliana and her mother, Queen Wilhelmina, returned to the liberated part of the Netherlands and joined the relief operations for the victims of the Nazi occupation.

Immediately after World War II, the Dutch colony of Indonesia began agitating for independence, and the Dutch government sent troops to quell the uprising. Queen Wilhelmina, unwilling to give Indonesia its independence, abdicated in favor of her daughter in 1948 after celebrating the fiftieth anniversary of her reign. By abdicating, Wilhelmina was following a precedent set by William I (r. 1813–1840), the first king of the Netherlands, who had abdicated in 1840.

In 1949, Queen Juliana signed documents giving Indonesia its independence. Five years later, in 1954, she signed a new charter for the Netherlands that regulated relations between the three remaining parts of the kingdom: the Netherlands and the colonies of Surinam in South America and the Netherlands Antilles in the Caribbean. (Surinam later became an independent republic in 1975.)

Juliana's strong religious beliefs led her to work for social justice. In 1952, she told the U.S. Congress that countries should spend less on defense and more on social concerns. In 1966, Juliana provided the International Union for Child Welfare with financial support for a project to study child care and child protection measures to be applied as part of local or regional development plans. The queen also supported cultural and social service organizations in the Netherlands through the Juliana Welfare Fund. Although Juliana, a constitutional monarch, did not take a public role in promoting government legislation, she often intervened with government bureaucracy to help individuals. She also intervened on behalf of immigrants from Indonesia in the 1970s.

Although Queen Juliana was shy and reserved, the Dutch people loved her for her social concerns and her unpretentious manner. Even the revelation in 1976 that her husband had accepted bribes from Lockheed Corporation did little to diminish her popularity. Nevertheless, in 1980 Juliana followed the precedent of her mother: she abdicated the throne in favor of her eldest daughter, Beatrix (r. 1980–).

See also: NETHERLANDS KINGDOM; WILHELMINA.

JULIO-CLAUDIANS (27 B.C.E.–68 C.E.)

First through fifth rulers of the Roman Empire, beginning with Augustus (27 B.C.E.–14 C.E.) and ending with Nero (54–68 C.E.), all of whom were related as members of the Julian and Claudian families.

Gaius Julius Caesar Octavianus, born Gaius Octavius, was born in 63 B.C.E. to a prosperous senatorial family. His grandmother was the sister of Julius Caesar (r. 49–44 B.C.E.), a member of the Julian *gens,* or clan, one of the oldest patrician (saristocratic) families of Rome. Curiously, the Julian *gens* did not originate in Rome but in Rome's earliest rival city, Alba Longa. According to legend, Rome's third king, Tullus Hostilius (r. ca. 673–642 B.C.E.), conquered Alba Longa and asked its citizenry, which included the Julian clan, to join as equals with the Romans.

Not producing a son of his own, Julius Caesar

showed a keen interest in Octavian who, when only eighteen, learned that his great-uncle had been assassinated and that he had been named Caesar's heir. Despite the obstacles presented by his inexperience and by Caesar's chief lieutenant, Mark Antony, who thought himself the appropriate successor to the Roman dictator, Octavian was determined to pursue his inheritance.

In 31 B.C.E., after thirteen years of political intrigues, Octavian defeated Antony at the battle of Actium, thus securing his hold on Roman power. When he returned to Rome, he named himself *princeps*— First Citizen—of Rome and thus began the Roman Empire (though, technically, referred to as the principate). Shortly thereafter he was named "Augustus" by the Senate, which roughly translated as "great father." In 38 B.C.E., Augustus married Livia Drusilla, a member of the Claudian clan, Rome's oldest patrician family.

Augustus ruled Rome for forty-five years, and most of his reign was remarkable for its efficiency and prosperity. His political and military successes were not echoed in his family life, however. A succession of his chosen successors met with untimely ends, and he was finally left with his adopted son, Tiberius, the son of his wife Livia, as his reluctant choice for an heir.

As the son of Livia Drusilla, Tiberius Claudius Nero (r. 14–37 C.E.) was a member of the Claudian *gens* by birth. Of Sabine origin, the wealthy Claudians were considered one of the founding patrician families of Rome. As the adopted son of Augustus, he claimed descent from the Julian clan.

Tiberius began his reign with the full coffers and relative peace left him by Augustus. Although he became reclusive, paranoid, and increasingly tyrannical, Tiberius passed on a prosperous empire to his grandnephew Caligula (r. 37–41), who was also a Claudian.

Caligula's peculiarities, excesses, and strange appetites would probably have had a detrimental effect on Rome had he reigned for a great deal longer than he did. However, Rome's fortunes were saved by his assassination in 41, at which time his uncle Claudius (r. 41–54) was surprisingly placed on the throne by the temporarily leaderless Praetorian Guards.

Claudius's ties to the Julian line were more tenuous than those of his predecessors, since those ties did not even include a direct adoption. He was, however, the grandson-by-marriage of the emperor Augustus (through Claudius's grandmother, Livia). Of course, Augustus himself was Julian only by adoption.

Claudius managed the empire well, expanding it through the conquest of southern Britain, peacefully absorbing client states, and organizing the imperial bureaucracy. He passed to his successor a Rome even more prosperous than the state inherited by Tiberius.

Unfortunately, Claudius passed the empire to his adopted son, Nero (r. 54–68). Nero's pedigree was perhaps the most noble of all the Julio-Claudians. His mother was the daughter of Claudius's revered brother, Tiberius Claudius Germanicus, and the great-granddaughter of the emperor Augustus. Nero's father was the great-grandson of Julia, the sister of Julius Caesar. He was, therefore, the only Julio-Claudian of direct descent (not adoptive) in both the Julian and Claudian lines.

The purity of Nero's bloodlines, however, did not affect his profligacy or inattention to state business. He spent more money (almost entirely on personal indulgences) than any of his predecessors. He is also commonly thought to have been responsible for the great fire of Rome in 64, a conflagration that he blamed on the Christians. Whatever the causes of the fire, Nero used the devastation as an excuse for massive construction projects, replacing "a city of wood with a city of marble."

Nero's complete negligence of public responsibilities provided fertile ground for the seeds of discontent. He had misused the power that was his, and it was inevitably seized by another, General Galba. In 68, as Galba's troops searched the streets for the emperor, Nero found himself unable to effect his own suicide. He persuaded his slave to hold his sword and ran himself through, thus ending the dynastic line of the Julio-Claudians.

See also: AUGUSTUS; CAESARS; CALIGULA; CLAUDIUS; JULIUS CAESAR; NERO; ROMAN EMPIRE; TIBERIUS.

FURTHER READING

Grant, Michael. *History of Rome.* New York: History Book Club, 1997.
Graves, Robert. *The Claudius Novels.* New York: Penguin, 1999.

JULIUS CAESAR (ca. 100–44 B.C.E.)

Military hero, statesman, and ultimately dictator of Rome (r. 49–44 B.C.E.) in the final years of the Roman Republic; after his death, struggles for power culminated in a change from a republic to an empire, and the era of the Roman Empire began.

Gaius Julius Caesar was born in Rome to a family of great heritage but little wealth. An ambitious man, he knew that there was one sure route to success and fortune: to marry into a powerful family. Accordingly, when he was still only sixteen years old, he married Cornelia, whose father played an important role in the political life of the Roman republic. Unfortunately, this marriage angered the dictator Lucius Cornelius Sulla, against whom Cornelia's father had conspired. Sulla ordered Caesar to divorce Cornelia, but the young man refused. To escape Sulla's wrath, Caesar found refuge in the military, accepting a posting to the campaigns being waged far to the east.

Upon Sulla's death in 78 B.C.E., Caesar returned to Rome and began preparing for a career in politics. To further his ambitions, he traveled to the island of Rhodes to study the art of oratory. While there, he also distinguished himself as a military man of great ability. By 73 B.C.E. Caesar decided that he was ready to embark on a political career. He accepted a commission into the officer's ranks of the army and allied himself with the new ruler of Rome, Pompey. Within four years, Caesar had so established his reputation that he was elected to his first political office, as military tribune. However, he also experienced a great personal loss, when his wife, Cornelia, died. Caesar's funeral oration for her is credited with earning him a reputation as a public speaker, which helped him achieve further political offices.

By 61 B.C.E., Caesar had become a well-established politician, but the cost of maintaining his position was immense. It was with relief, then, that he accepted an appointment as governor of the province of Spain, where he could embark on military campaigns. Success in war would provide the opportunity to confiscate the riches of the people he conquered, and Caesar soon became wealthy. A year later, in 60 B.C.E., he again returned to Rome, this time to run for the office of consul. He had the support of Pompey and other powerful men of the city, and his election was all but assured.

After becoming consul, Caesar entered into a political alliance with Pompey and another powerful man, Crassus, in 60 B.C.E., forming what was known as the First Triumvirate. As part of their alliance, Caesar was placed in charge of governing the provinces of Illyricum and Gaul, which added to his wealth. To further strengthen this political alliance, he married a relative of Pompey, a woman named Pompeia, but this union proved to be unsatisfactory. He soon divorced Pompeia and married a woman named Calpurnia.

Over the next decade, Caesar made a name for himself on the battlefield. He pacified Gaul, which had up to this time been only tenuously held by Rome. His success in Gaul, and his subsequent invasion of Britain, earned him the loyalty of the army and the adulation of the Roman people. However, the Roman Senate began to fear that he held too much power. They worried that his popularity would lead to a loss of power for the Senate itself. Several senators secretly met with Pompey, urging him to withdraw his support of Caesar. They succeeded and set into motion a plan to reduce Caesar's power.

The first step of this plan was to order Caesar to return to Rome. The Senate ordered this in 49 B.C.E., insisting that he leave his troops behind. Instead, Caesar marched his forces to the banks of the Rubicon River, which marked the border between Gaul and Italy. On January 19, Caesar led his troops across the river into Italy, launching a civil war. With his powerful and loyal troops, Caesar's victory was all but assured, and his opponents were forced to flee. Knowing that there was likely to be resistance, Caesar then sent his armies to subdue rebellions in Spain and even invaded Greece, to which his opponents, including Pompey, had fled in exile. Within a year, Caesar had conquered Greece and driven Pompey into Egypt. Pompey tried to raise support in Egypt but was killed. While pursuing Pompey into Egypt, Caesar met the Egyptian ruler Cleopatra VII (r. 51–30 B.C.E.) and made her both his governor and his consort.

On his return to Rome, Caesar ruled as tribune and dictator, passing various reforms to improve living conditions for ordinary Romans. In 44 B.C.E., Caesar was elected consul and had himself named dictator for life. During his reign, he instituted reforms of the administration and the military, and consolidated control over Rome's overseas holdings, including those as far away as Britain. His popularity among the citizens soared, but his political opponents grew increasingly restive. Their greatest fear, that Caesar would declare himself king, seemed confirmed when one of his allies, Marcus Antonius (Mark Antony), proposed that he accept a crown. Caesar also outraged noble families by his increasingly open dalliance with Cleopatra.

Although Caesar turned down the honor of kingship, several of his political rivals conspired to remove him from office. When he arrived to address the Senate on March 15, 44 B.C.E., he was overpowered by a mob of conspirators and assassinated. As Caesar left no designated heir, Rome was plunged into a war of succession. When it was over, a great-nephew of Caesar's emerged victorious and became the first true emperor of Rome. This was Caesar Octavianus Augustus, better known as the Emperor Augustus (r. 27 B.C.E.–14 C.E.).

See also: AUGUSTUS; CLEOPATRA VII; ROMAN EMPIRE.

FURTHER READING

Grant, Michael. *The Roman Emperors: A Biographical Guide to the Rulers of Imperial Rome, 31 B.C.–A.D. 476.* New York: Barnes & Noble, 1997.

Nardo, Don. *The Roman Empire.* San Diego: Lucent Books, 1994.

Starr, Chester. *A History of the Ancient World.* New York: Oxford University Press, 1991.

JURANE-BURGUNDY KINGDOM. *See* BURGUNDY KINGDOM

JUSTINIAN I (483–565 C.E.)

Eastern Roman emperor (r. 527–565) whose reign is perhaps best remembered for the codification of Roman law, commonly called the Corpus Juris Civilis.

The nephew and successor of Emperor Justin I (r. 518–527), Justinian was given responsibility for administering imperial policy during much of his uncle's reign. Upon Justin's death in 527, Justinian succeeded to the throne of the Eastern Roman, or Byzantine, Empire.

Justinian I gained fame as both a strong ruler and an extremely competent administrator. Among his most valuable contributions was his codification of Roman law, popularly known as the Justinian Code. Seeing many discrepancies and inconsistencies in the Roman legal system, Justinian gathered together the best legal scholars of the empire and authorized them to take Roman laws dating back from the time of the Emperor Augustus (r. 27 B.C.E.–14 C.E.) and condense them into a single uniform code.

Justinian also attempted to restore much of the territory of the old Roman Empire. From 533 to 554, Justinian's troops, under the guidance of his loyal generals, Belisarius and Narses, took back many of the western and North African provinces that had been lost to the Goths, Vandals, and Franks earlier in the fifth century. However, when Belisarius, who had won brilliant military success, began to overshadow Justinian in popularity, the emperor became jealous of his top general. That jealousy, coupled with a lack of funds in the imperial treasury, contributed to Justinian's failure to send reinforcements to retake Italy from the Ostrogoths. Justinian also had little success against the Persians.

Justinian taxed his people heavily in order to finance his military gains. He also began to collect taxes that people had been evading either through legal loopholes or by bribing government officials. Many people lost their fortunes when imperial tax collectors came to calculate and collect back taxes.

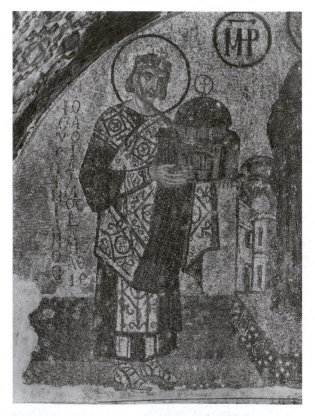

Emperor Justinian I was a strong ruler of the Eastern Roman Empire in the sixth century C.E., known for his codification of Roman law, the Justinian Code. He also rebuilt the Hagia Sophia in Constantinople, and its many treasures include this mosaic depicting Justinian's dedication of the church to Christ and the Virgin Mary.

Justinian used tax revenues not only to finance military campaigns, but also to expand construction in Constantinople, the capital of the Eastern Roman Empire, which had lost many of its most magnificent buildings to fires during the Nika Revolt in 532.

Justinian used this destruction as an excuse to spend large sums of money rebuilding the lost structures, replacing them with much grander buildings, such as the church of Hagia Sophia.

One of Justinian's strongest supporters was his highly intelligent wife, the empress Theodora. The empress played an instrumental role in helping Justinian govern his ever-expanding empire. Her bravery and quick thinking saved his throne, and possibly his life, during the Nika revolts, which arose because of public discontent over Justinian's fiscal policies and religious orthodoxy. When the emperor's generals and court advisers urged him to flee after the revolt started, Theodora convinced him to stay and fight, and she gave a moving public speech that convinced Justinian to offer resistance.

Justinian introduced a policy called caesaropapism, in which the emperor was supreme over the Christian church. This policy included supremacy over not only church organization but also Christian dogma. In 553, hoping to reconcile competing Christian factions, Justinian called a church council, the Second Council of Constantinople. The council accomplished nothing, however, and religious heresies continued to divide the faithful.

When Justinian died in 565, he was succeeded by his nephew, Justin II (r. 565–578). Because of his strong rule, but especially as a result of his codification of Roman law, Justinian I is often known by the epithet, Justinian the Great.

See also: BYZANTINE EMPIRE; THEODORA I.

FURTHER READING
Browning, Robert. *Justinian and Theodora.* New York: Thames and Hudson, 1987.
Moorhead, John. *Justinian.* New York: Longman, 1994.

JUTLAND KINGDOM

(ca. 700–900 C.E.)

Early medieval kingdom on the Jutland Peninsula of Denmark, which emerged from history at about the time that Denmark was becoming united.

Very little is known for certain about the kingdom of Jutland. The kingdom of Denmark has its roots in a number of smaller kingdoms of the Viking era (ca. 700–1000) and earlier centuries. Little historical record of these pre-Christian kingdoms exists, since literacy and written histories in Northern Europe tended to follow conversion to Christianity, by which time the deeds of earlier generations had become legends.

It is probable that the Jutland Peninsula, like other regions inhabited by Northern European and Scandinavian groups, had an elective monarchy in which kings were chosen from among a royal family by an assembly of free men of the tribe. The tradition of elective monarchy persisted in both Scandinavia and Germany through the Middle Ages in at least a formal aspect, despite the tendency of kings themselves to encourage hereditary succession.

Little record exists of any specific kings of Jutland, and what little information there is lacks reliability. The medieval Danish historian Saxo Grammaticus (ca. 1150–1220) wrote a history, *Gesta Danorum*, much of which deals with early Danish history in a colorful but not necessarily factual manner. The story of Hamlet (given its most famous form in Shakespeare's tragedy) is found in Saxo as the adventures of Amleth, who briefly ruled Denmark and died in Jutland in battle against a governor of Scania and Zealand. Saxo also mentions a king Vermund of Jutland, although no other record of him exists.

History rather than legend emerges for Jutland only in the late 800s, just as the various regions of Denmark were merging into one kingdom. Gorm the Old (r. ca. 883–940) is considered the traditional founder of the Danish kingdom and the ancestor of Danish kings down to the present day. Gorm ruled from Jelling in Jutland. His son, Harald Bluetooth or Harald I (r. 940–986), ruled Denmark from Hedeby in Slesvig in the southern part of the Jutland Peninsula. The first to rule the larger area of Denmark, Harald moved his capital to the island of Zealand, a more central position from which to dominate Denmark, which by then included Scania, now the southern part of Sweden.

Jutland has always been an important region of Denmark, but it was never a stable political entity on its own. In 1146, during the civil wars that ended when Waldemar (Valdemar) I (r. 1157–1182) became king, Denmark was briefly divided into three districts, each ruled by a contender for the throne.

Waldemar had Jutland, Svend Ericson ruled Scania and Bornholm, and Knud Magnusson controlled Zealand and the neighboring islands. This division did not last, however. Svend murdered Knud and was then himself killed, leaving Waldemar to rule over a once more united Denmark. With the reunification of Denmark under Waldemar, the kingdom of Jutland again ceased to exist.

See also: DANISH KINGDOM; WALDEMAR I, THE GREAT.

FURTHER READING

Jones, Gwyn. *A History of the Vikings.* 2nd ed. New York: Oxford University Press, 2001.
Toyne, Stanley M. *The Scandinavians in History.* 1948. Reprint, New York: Barnes & Noble, 1996.

KABAREGA (1850–1923 C.E.)

Twelfth ruler (r. 1869–1899) of the Nyoro kingdom of western Uganda, remembered as a fierce defender of Nyoro independence during the colonial era.

Kabarega was a younger son of King Kyebambe IV Kamurasi, who ruled Nyoro from 1852 to 1869. Kabarega spent much of his childhood away from the center of Nyoro power, living in western Zaire during an uprising that threatened to topple his father. When the uprising was finally put down, Kabarega returned to Nyoro, where he came of age.

The death of King Kamurasi in 1869 triggered a war of succession that was fought between two competing factions. Kabarega had the support of the military and the people, but his elder brother, Kabigumire, was favored by the nobility. With the power of the military behind him, Kabarega was able to force his brother to withdraw from the contest.

Upon taking the throne, Kabarega immediately launched a policy of expansion. Intending to create a great empire, he created an impressive army that was charged with conquest as well as with raiding for slaves and other resources. Within six years, Kabarega had established control over dozens of neighboring peoples and had expanded his territory to include a wide variety of ethnic groups. With so vast an empire, he found it necessary to create a mechanism by which to ensure loyalty among his highly diverse subjects.

Kabarega ruled the heart of his empire directly, but in the more distant regions he adopted a different strategy. He appointed governors from among his trusted counselors, giving each a district to oversee in the king's name. Kabarega attempted to consolidate his rule even further by encouraging intermarriage between the various clans and peoples of his empire, thus breaking down tribal-based loyalties. In this, he enjoyed only limited success.

Kabarega's rule coincided with the encroachment of European colonial powers in Africa. In his region, it was Great Britain that sought to gain control. The British were quick to exploit factionalism within the indigenous kingdoms, the better to weaken the powers of the local kings. Kabarega was forced to fight a series of wars, as formerly conquered peoples rose up with the assistance of the British. These wars culminated with an alliance struck between chiefs of the Ganda people, who resented Nyoro power, and the British East Africa Company, which represented British interests. With the encouragement and support of the British, the Ganda declared war on Kabarega and his kingdom.

In January 1894, the Ganda captured Mparo, the capital of the Nyoro kingdom, and Kabarega was forced to flee into the countryside. He gathered his supporters and embarked upon a guerrilla war against the Ganda and the British, but he never managed to muster enough support to prevail over the superior military might of the British-led alliance. Kabarega was ultimately captured on April 9, 1899, and sent into exile to the Seychelles Islands, where he remained until 1923. In that year, he gained permission from the British to return, but the ailing king died aboard ship as he sailed for home.

See also: GANDA KINGDOM.

KAFA KINGDOM (ca. 1370–1897 C.E.)

Former kingdom located in what is now southwestern Ethiopia; also spelled Kaffa.

Although not as numerous, powerful, or historically renowned as the Amhara who dominated the lands that now comprise Ethiopia and much of Somalia, the people of the Kafa region nonetheless managed to retain autonomy throughout their history. The kingdom is credited with being the first to cultivate the coffee bean, which has long been, and remains, a centerpiece of the regional economy. In fact, the word "coffee" is believed to be derived from the Kafa, who were the first to cultivate this crop.

Kafa was one of three "border kingdoms" that occupied the lands now roughly incorporated in Ethiopia's Oromo District. The other two, the Konta and Dauro, may well be related to the Kafa, but they were independent entities by the late fourteenth century, with their own royal lineages. The Kafa rulers expanded their territory through wars with neighboring lands and built their first city, Shadda, around 1500. The Oromo, another native people, migrated north into Kafa lands in southern Ethiopia in the early 1600s, and intermarried with the original population.

Although the Kafa region is said to have become a kingdom in 1390, the lists of Kafa kings usually do not begin until 1675. All the Kafa kings were called *kafi atio*, but their identities seem to have been lost. In 1700, Gaili Ginocho (r. 1675–1710) proclaimed the transformation of the Kafa kingdom into an empire.

From Gaili Ginocho's reign to the incorporation of the Kafa into the larger Ethiopian polity in 1897, there were eleven Kafa rulers. With the reign of Kaye Sherocho (1854–1870), the royal title was changed from *kafi atio* to *kafi atiojo*, a title bearing connotations of semidivinity and enhancing the king's authority. Kaye was succeeded by Gaili Sherocho (r. 1870–1890), who was followed by Gaki Sherocho (1890–1897). By the time of Gaki's reign, however, Menelik II (1889–1913) had become emperor of Ethiopia and had begun an expansion that resulted in his conquering surrounding kingdoms, including Kafa to the southwest, Harar in the east, and Sidamo in the south.

See also: AMHARA KINGDOM; DIVINITY OF KINGS; MENELIK II.

FURTHER READING

Huntingford, G.W.B. *The Galla of Ethiopia: The Kingdoms of Kafa and Janjero.* London: International African Institute, 1969.

KALACURI DYNASTIES

(ca. 500s–1400s C.E.)

Series of Indian dynasties that ruled at unrelated times and locations. Besides the name of the dynasty and possibly a common lineage, there is hardly any evidence linking these various groups.

The first known Kalacuri dynasty (ca. 550–620) reigned in the regions of Gujarat, Maharashtra, Malwa, and areas of the western Deccan. The three rulers of this dynasty—its founder, Krsnaraja (r. ca. 550–575), Sankaragana (r. ca. 575–600), and Buddharaja (r. ca. 600–620)—have been identified from ancient epigraphs and coins.

Another Kalacuri family reigned in the Deccan region of India from 1156 to 1181. Its power was established in the state of Karnataka by Bijjala (r. 1156–1168), a former vassal of the Chalukya dynasty of Kalyana. This Kalacuri family also ruled only briefly, but it was historically significant because its rule coincided with the emergence of the Lingayat, or Virasaiva, a Hindu sect whose followers worshiped Siva (Shiva Linga) as their only god.

The most famous Kalacuri dynasty reigned in central India, based at Tripuri (current-day Tewar). Although the dynasty probably began in the early eighth century, not much is known about it until the time of Kokalla I (r. ca. 850–885). Between his reign and that of Kokalla II (r. ca. 990–1015), the Kalacuris of Tripuri consolidated their power. A number of marriages cemented relations between the Kalicuris and the Rastrakutas, one of the most powerful dynasties in India, and the politics of the two families were sometimes intertwined.

From the mid-ninth to the early eleventh centuries, the Kalacuris of Tripuri consistently opposed the kingdoms of Kosala, Kalinga, Gauda, and Vanga. They also found themselves at odds with the dynasties of the Gurjaras, Chandellas, and some of the Calukyas. The Kalacuris did not achieve any great military success, however, until the reign of Gangeyadeva (r. ca. 1015–1041).

Gangeyadeva defeated many rivals and took over the Varanasi area to the north of the Kalacuri domain. His son and successor, Karna (r. 1041–1073) was particularly successful, expanding control in the Varanasi-Allahabad area and carrying out sweeping military operations in other regions of India. Despite such successes, the Kalacuris gradually lost their power between the reigns of Yasakarna (r. 1073–1123) and Vijayasimha (r. 1188–1209). Beginning around 1211, much of the Kalacuri kingdom was incorporated under the rule of the Chandellas.

Two other Kalacuri dynasties were those of Sarayupara and Ratanpur. The Sarayupara branch of the dynasty ruled an area on the banks of the Sarayu River (now the Ghaghara) in the region of Uttar Pradesh from the late 700s to late 1000s. The Ratanpur were distant relatives and vassals of the Kalacuris of Tripuri. Their rule began in the early eleventh century and reached its peak during the reign of Jajalladeva I (r. early 1100s) in the early twelfth century. By the fifteenth century, the Ratanpur had divided into two branches, Ratanpur and Raipur.

See also: CALUKYA (CHALUKYA) DYNASTY; CHANDELLA DYNASTY; GAUDA KINGDOM; INDIAN KINGDOMS; KALINGA KINGDOM; KOSALA KINGDOM; RASTRAKUTA DYNASTY.

KALINGA KINGDOM

(ca. 500s B.C.E.–1593 C.E.)

A kingdom in southern India on the Bay of Bengal that was a wealthy bastion of Hindu culture.

Kalinga was one of the nine ancient kingdoms of southern India. Its borders shifted over the years, but its territory generally included the eastern Madras coast from Pulicat to Chicacole, and extending inland from the Bay of Bengal to the Eastern Ghats mountain range. At one time, Kalinga included the region known as Orissa, and its influence may have extended as far north as the Ganges River Valley.

EARLY HISTORY

By the sixth century B.C.E., Kalinga was already a well-known kingdom throughout much of India. Its first recorded king was Brahmadatta (r. dates unknown), who ruled during the time of Buddha in the sixth century B.C.E. According to tradition, a monk gave King Brahmadatta a relic of the Buddha, a tooth, to preserve at Kalinga.

In the fourth century B.C.E., the Nanda dynasty of the Magadha kingdom gained some degree of hegemony over Kalinga, but its control was not deep-rooted. When Chandragupta Maurya (r. 321–297 B.C.E.), the founder of the Maurya Empire, overthrew the Nandas and conquered the Magadha kingdom around 325 B.C.E., Kalinga remained an independent state, as well as a powerful rival to the newly founded Maurya Empire.

By the mid-third century B.C.E., Kalinga was the greatest maritime power on the eastern coast of India, with overseas colonies and a thriving foreign trade. Around 260 B.C.E., the Mauryan emperor, Asoka (r. 268–232 B.C.E.) fought a bloody war against Kalinga in an attempt to gain control of the land and sea routes to southern India. Asoka conquered Kalinga, but the bloody horrors of the war troubled the emperor so much that he renounced war and adopted the Buddhist ideals of peace and nonviolence.

DEVELOPMENT OF AN EMPIRE

In the second half of the first century B.C.E., after the decline and fall of the Maurya Empire, King Kharavela (r. dates unknown) of the Chedi dynasty took control of Kalinga. One of the greatest rulers of ancient Kalinga, Kharavela was a devoted follower of the Jain religion.

According to historical records, which may have been exaggerated by the religious fervor of his court historians, Kharavela conquered vast territories in Magadha and southern India, leaving outposts and garrisons throughout the land. Kharavela built a mighty and far-flung empire, but after his rule, the kingdom fragmented into a number of smaller, little-known principalities. Even so, Kalinga continued to enjoy international trade and economic prosperity for at least two more centuries.

From the middle of the fourth century C.E., Kalinga suffered from several invasions and changes of leadership, as various Indian emperors and kings sought Kalinga's wealth and access to ocean trading routes. In 795, King Mahasivagupta Yayanti II of Kalinga (r. dates unknown) invited 10,000 learned Hindu Brahmins from Kanauj to settle in Kalinga. Mahasivagupta also united Kalinga with the kingdoms of Kangoda, Utkala, and Kosala.

In the mid-eleventh century, Kalinga was ruled by the eastern branch of the Ganga dynasty, whose strength consolidated the kingdom. In the thirteenth and fourteenth centuries, when much of India was overrun by the Muslims, Kalinga remained independent. Very prosperous from its income from international trade, Kalinga became a stronghold of Hindu religion, philosophy, art, and architecture.

DECLINE AND FALL

The decline of Kalinga began in 1206, when the kingdom was captured without a battle by the Muslims of Bengal. A generation later, in 1264, Kalinga's Hindu forces regained their kingdom and captured Bengal. Sixty years later, in 1324, Kalinga was captured by the ruler of the Delhi sultanate, Tughluq (r. 1320–1325). But after receiving a gift of many elephants from Kalinga, Tughluq left the kingdom to its own Hindu leadership. The ancient kingdom of Kalinga finally came to an end in 1592, when it was conquered and absorbed into the Mughal Empire by Akbar I, the Great (r. 1556–1605).

See also: AKBAR THE GREAT; ASOKA; CHANDRAGUPTA MAURYA; DELHI KINGDOM; GANDA KINGDOM; KOSALA KINGDOM; MAGADHA KINGDOM; MAURYA EMPIRE; UTKALA (ORISSA) KINGDOM.

KALMAR UNION (1397–1523 C.E.)

Union of Denmark, Norway, and Sweden under one Crown, which lasted from the late fourteenth century to the early sixteenth century.

The Kalmar Union was largely the work of Queen Margaret of Denmark (r. 1375–1412), a powerful and intelligent ruler whose efforts to hold the vast Scandinavian Empire together were not enough to stave off eventual collapse. Despite the eventual failure of the Kalmar Union, its three member nations have been linked through a variety of alliances continuing to the present day.

TANGLED RELATIONSHIPS

The histories of Denmark, Norway, and Sweden had been interrelated for centuries, but it was not until 1319 that an official union began to develop. It was then that a group of Swedish gentry elected Magnus VII (r. 1319–1363), heir to the Norwegian throne, as king of Sweden. Magnus felt much stronger ties to Sweden than to his hereditary kingdom, and consequently he virtually abandoned Norway. This greatly displeased the Norwegian people, who compelled Magnus to name his son, Haakon VI (r. 1355–1380), his successor to the Norwegian throne.

Meanwhile, the Swedes grew tired of what they perceived as Magnus's poor leadership and supported Albert of Mecklenburg, a German noble, in a bid for the throne. The Swedes deposed Magnus, and

Albert (r. 1364–1389) took the Crown in 1364. The previous year, Haakon VI had married Margaret, the heir to the Danish throne. Their marital union laid the foundations for placing Norway and Denmark under the same rule, a development that immediately put Sweden on the defensive, since Haakon was also mounting a bid to take back his father's former kingdom.

Haakon attacked Sweden in 1371 and spent much of the remainder of his life in battle or negotiation with the Swedes under Albert of Mecklenburg. Haakon's absence left Margaret the de facto ruler of Norway and Denmark, a position further assured by the death of her father, Danish king Waldemar IV (r. 1340–1375), in 1375. Although the Danish Crown passed to Haakon and Margaret's son, Olaf II (r. 1376–1387), the prince was barely an infant. Margaret thus took control of the kingdom as regent. Haakon's death in 1380 left Margaret in virtual control of both Denmark and Norway, and she pushed to have young Olaf named the king of Sweden as well. When Olaf died in 1387, Margaret continued to rule Denmark and Norway.

The Swedish nobility, chafing against the increasingly brutal rule of Albert of Mecklenburg, began to make overtures to Margaret for assistance. In 1388, the Swedish nobles named Margaret the rightful ruler of Sweden and granted her the power to choose her successor there, moves that precipitated war between Margaret's forces and those of Albert. Faced with an overwhelming number of Danish and Norwegian troops and a lack of internal support, Albert was forced to surrender in 1389, effectively leaving Margaret the head of the three kingdoms.

FORMATION OF THE UNION

In 1397, Margaret convened a meeting of the nobility of the three kingdoms at Kalmar, Sweden, at which she forced the election of her teenage grandnephew to the joint Crowns of Denmark, Norway, and Sweden. Eric of Pomerania (r. 1412–1439), the newly named king, was not yet of age to rule, thus leaving Margaret as regent in control of the Kalmar Union. The nobility had pledged to honor the Union, but tensions quickly arose as Margaret favored Denmark in her decision making, following traditional Danish policies and staffing royal offices with Danish nobles. Margaret's skills as a politician, however, were enough to hold the empire together until her death in 1412, at which time Eric took full control.

Margaret's death precipitated a crisis for the Kalmar Union, especially in Sweden, where the nobility had begun to agitate against foreign rule. In the 1430s, a mine-owner named Engelbrecht Engelbrechtson initiated a series of uprisings in Sweden that forced Eric to send Danish troops into battle, a very unpopular move in Denmark. Although Engelbrecht was murdered in 1436, the pro-independence movement he spearheaded continued to grow, culminating in the election of Engelbrecht's compatriot, Karl Knutsson, to the Swedish throne as Charles VIII (r. 1438–1441, 1448–1457, 1464–1465, 1467–1470). This threw Denmark into controversy; the nobility voted no confidence in Eric and elected his nephew, Christopher of Bavaria (Christopher III, r. 1440–1448), to the throne in 1440. Norway followed suit in 1442, replacing Eric with Christopher III.

DECLINE AND END OF THE UNION

The rest of the fifteenth century saw the slow breakup of the Kalmar Union. The untimely death of Christopher III in 1448 led Norway to affirm its allegiance to Charles VIII of Sweden, and led Denmark to place Christian of Oldenburg on its throne as King Christian I (r. 1448–1481).

Shortly thereafter, Christian I pressured the Norwegians to abandon Charles and to side with him, a move that led to war between the Danes and the Swedes. Charles VIII was ousted in 1457, and Christian took control of the three kingdoms, only to see Charles return to power in 1464 and again in 1467. Charles's death in 1470 led Christian to attack Sweden once more. The next half-century saw a series of battles between the two countries, with the Crown of Sweden changing hands numerous times.

The succession of Christian II (r. 1513–1523), son of John of Denmark (r. 1481–1513), to the throne of Denmark and Norway in 1513 signaled the end for the Kalmar Union. Determined to capture Sweden by any means necessary, Christian II ordered the massacre of much of the Swedish nobility in 1520, a move that turned all of Sweden against him and allowed Gustavus Vasa, a pro-independence leader, to rise up and expel the Danes from Sweden.

Three years later, the young leader was named King Gustavus I of Sweden (r. 1523–1560), thus permanently ending Swedish participation in the Kalmar Union. Denmark and Norway remained united until the end of the Napoleonic Wars (1803–1815), when Norway came under the nominal control of Sweden, though it was, in effect, granted independence. Denmark retained its autonomy into the twentieth century.

See also: DANISH KINGDOM; ELECTION, ROYAL; GUSTAVUS I (VASA); MARGARET OF DENMARK; NORWEGIAN MONARCHY; REGENCIES; SWEDISH MONARCHY.

FURTHER READING

Butler, Ewan. *The Horizon Concise History of Scandinavia.* New York: American Heritage, 1973.

KAMAKURA SHOGUNATE

(1192–1333 C.E.)

The first Japanese shogunate, established at Kamakura (about thirty miles from modern-day Tokyo) by Minamoto Yoritomo in 1192 to legitimize his governance. The Kamakura shogunate marked the beginning of the medieval period in Japan, which established feudal military rule under a samurai warrior class. Under shogunal rule, the shogun warlords held the real power while the emperors were mainly figureheads.

The Kamakura government established by Yoritomo was known as the *bakufu* (temporary military "field tent headquarters"), a term that came to designate the shogunate itself. The *bakufu* rewarded supporters with strategically located estates and administrative offices, establishing the personalized lord–vassal relationship that characterized Japanese society for almost 700 years. Japanese feudalism represented not so much a sharp break with the past as a new form of dual government, with the military warrior-state functioning alongside the imperial-aristocratic institutions in the imperial capital of Kyoto.

The administrative reforms that Minamoto Yoritomo established in Kamakura relied on personal loyalty. The reforms were designed primarily to control conflicts between the military lords and the court aristocrats, as well as to contain the power and influence of the wealthy temples and shrines.

The Minamoto vassals served as *jito* (stewards) or *shugo* (constables), governing the provinces according to local traditions, which further weakened the centralized institutions of the imperial court. *Shugo* were in charge of judicial and police proceedings, while *jito*

Kamakura Shogunate

MINAMOTO YORITOMO*	1192–1195
YORIIE	1202–1203
SANETOMO	1203–1219
KUJO YORITSUNE	1226–1244
KUJO YORITSUGU	1244–1252
MUNETAKA	1252–1266
KOREYASU	1266–1289
HISAAKI	1289–1308
MORIKUNI	1308–1333

*Indicates a separate alphabetical entry.

levied taxes and managed *shoen* (estates). In a variation on the tradition established by the Fujiwara clan—ruling as hereditary regents for the emperor—the Hojo clan added a new level of government in the thirteenth century by ruling as *shikken*, or hereditary regents for the Kamakura shoguns.

The Kamakura shogunate inspired lively movements in religion and art that reflected the prominence of the warrior class. Zen Buddhism fostered the culture of military virtue, and the Kamakura samurai directly inspired the *bushido* codes of conduct and honor that were later followed by sixteenth-century warlords as well as the military zealots of the twentieth century. Kamakura artists displayed heightened realism in painting, depicting in stirring detail the battles and exploits of the warriors and the noble families. The economy of Japan also expanded somewhat during the Kamakura era, with improved productivity on the *shoen* (estates), underwriting the prosperity of traders who plied the coastlines delivering rice and goods.

Two massive invasions by the Mongol forces of Kublai Khan—in 1274 and 1281—were repulsed by the spirited resistance of the Hojo and shogunal forces, aided by two enormous storms that engulfed the Mongol fleets. The typhoons were called *kamikaze*, "divine winds," and reinforced the enduring Japanese belief that their island-nation was protected by the gods.

After the death of Minamoto Yoritomo in 1199, his widow, Hojo Masako, usurped ruling power from the Minamoto clan for her own clan, the Hojo. Although the Minamoto remained shoguns by title, the real power was now in the hands of the Hojo, who ruled through puppet shoguns and titular emperors. The emperor tried to regain power in 1221, but the imperial rebellion failed to wrest power from the shogunate.

Another imperial attempt to gain primacy occurred in 1331, when the emperor, Go-Daigo (r. 1318–1339), attempted to regain power. This rebellion was more successful, since the most powerful general of the shogunate, Ashikaga Takauji, decided to side with the emperor. In 1333, Ashikaga and his forces defeated the Hojo clan, and the Hojo shogunal regent committed suicide. This marked the end of the Kamakura *bakufu*, but shogunal rule was suspended only temporarily. In 1338, Ashikaga Takauji received the title of shogun and established the Ashikaga shogunate.

See also: ASHIKAGA SHOGUNATE; FUJIWARA DYNASTY; MINAMOTO RULERS.

KAMEHAMEHA I, THE GREAT

(ca. 1755–1819 C.E.)

First king (r. 1795–1819) of the Kamehameha dynasty of Hawaii, and the first Hawaiian monarch to unify all the islands under a single ruler.

The actual date of Kamehameha's birth is uncertain, but most scholars place it between 1752 and 1761. When he was born, the islands of Hawaii were politically fragmented, with each island under the control of one or more chiefs. Kamehameha's father was the ruling chief of a territory that comprised approximately half of the so-called Big Island of Hawaii, and it is this territory that Kamehameha inherited when his father died in 1795.

CONQUEST AND RULE

Kamehameha was raised with the expectation that he would inherit this chiefdom, and he was thus educated in the arts of war and in traditional ritual practices. By all accounts, he was a powerful man, intelligent, and ambitious. Not content to accept the territorial limitations of his inherited chiefdom,

Kamehameha led a series of invasions against neighboring islands, and within a few short years of becoming chief, he conquered the islands of Maui, Lanai, and Molokai. His campaign of conquest, however, was interrupted when he received word that his territory on his home island of Hawaii was under attack by the chief who controlled the other half of the island.

Kamehameha returned home to deal with this threat, and by 1791 he had succeeded in bringing all of the Big Island under his rule. With this consolidation of power, Kamehameha set out once again, this time to conquer the island of Oahu. After successfully subduing the Oahu chiefs, he remained on that island for a time. Meanwhile, another powerful chief, Kaiana, had left his own island of Kauai to take advantage of Kamehameha's absence from the Big Island, launching an invasion there in 1796. Kamehameha returned home again to deal with this new challenge, but Kaiana proved a difficult adversary, and it was a year before Kamehameha succeeded in capturing and killing him.

With the defeat of Kaiana, Kamehameha had brought all but two main islands—Kauai and Niihau—under his control. These islands, formerly controlled by Kaiana and now under the control of Kaiana's successor, Kaumaulii, remained independent for another fourteen years, but in 1810 they, too, became a part of Kamehameha's kingdom.

All the islands were ruled directly by Kamehameha except Kauai, which was permitted to retain a degree of autonomy, but acknowledged the sovereignty of Kamehameha and paid him an annual tribute. Notwithstanding the special arrangements afforded to Kauai, all the Hawaiian islands were unified for the first time in their history.

EUROPEANS IN HAWAII

Throughout this period of conquest and consolidation, Kamehameha also was forced to deal with Europeans who had been stopping at the island ever since Captain Cook's fleet arrived in 1778. Once Kamehameha had become established in power, he became more willing to learn from these outsiders, although he was selective in the influences he was willing to adopt. For instance, he was quick to appreciate the British style of political organization, and as his island holdings grew, he adopted the practice of appointing loyal followers as governors of the newly conquered territories. However, Kamehameha retained traditional features of rule as well, particularly in his retention of members of former chiefly families as advisers and in his use of the *kapu* (taboo) system to maintain order and control.

Kamehameha's unified Hawaii soon became recognized by all the European powers, and its harbors became important trade and refueling stops for the many ships passing through on whaling voyages. Among those visiting Hawaii's ports were Spanish ships, one of which brought the first pineapples to be planted on the islands. This new crop, along with sugarcane, became an important trade item and attracted European and American settlers, who established plantations, as well as missionaries intent on bringing Christianity to the islands. Kamehameha insisted that these newcomers were only visitors, however. He refused to grant them the status of citizens, and he rejected Christianity in favor of traditional beliefs and practices.

HIS SUCCESSORS

Kamehameha ruled for another nine years after unifying the islands. In 1818 or 1819 he fell ill, and neither local healers nor European medicine could cure him. Kamehameha I died on May 8, 1819, and was succeeded by his son, Liholiho, who took the dynastic name of Kamehameha II (r. 1819–1824). Liholiho ruled for just five years before he died in 1824 from a case of the measles, which he contracted during a visit to Britain earlier that year.

Liholiho's younger brother, Kauikeaouli, was next in line to assume the Hawaiian throne, but because he was only eleven years old, he was guided by regents. The first of these regents was Kaahumanu, his father's favorite wife. At her death, the responsibility of regent fell to Kinau, Kauikeaouli's half-sister and a granddaughter of Kamehameha I. Upon reaching his majority in 1839, Kauikeaouli assumed the name Kamehameha III (r. 1825–1854). Among his first acts after gaining independence from his regent was the introduction of the first written laws in Hawaii. Kauikeaouli was also the first Hawaiian monarch to welcome Christian missionaries, who had been persecuted under his predecessors. In 1840, Kauikeaouli enacted Hawaii's first written constitution.

Kauikeaouli died in 1854 and was succeeded by his nephew, who was the first of Hawaii's rulers to have been baptized as a child and given a Christian name: Alexander Liholiho. He assumed the throne as Kamehameha IV (r. 1854–1863) at the age of twenty. He ruled with his queen, Emma, who was of British descent. Kamehameha IV and Queen Emma had only one child, who died of meningitis at the age of four. Over the years, the Hawaiian people had suffered greatly from foreign diseases such as measles, meningitis, and smallpox, against which they had no immunities. Kamehameha IV was inspired by the death of his son to establish the first Western-style hospital in Honolulu in 1859 and to encourage the spread of Western medicine throughout the islands.

Kamehameha IV died in 1863, his health weakened by a lifelong battle with asthma. He was succeeded by the last of the Kamehameha dynastic line, his brother Lot Kapauiwa, who took the dynastic name Kamehameha V (r. 1863–1872). A lifelong bachelor and Westernized playboy, Kamehameha V spent most of his reign away from Hawaii, traveling often to the United States and Great Britain. When he died while visiting San Francisco, he left no successor.

To avoid a potential battle for succession between William Charles Lunalilo and David Kalakaua, both of whom had roughly equivalent claims of kinship with Kamehameha I, the Hawaiian legislature stepped in. Lunalilo (r. 1873–1874) was given the throne, becoming Hawaii's first elected king. He ruled only two years, however, before dying of tuberculosis, and David Kalakaua (r. 1874–1891) was elected to replace him. When Kalakaua died in 1891, his sister Liliuokalani (r. 1891–1893) took the throne. But she was deposed by American plantation owners in Hawaii in 1893, ending the nearly 100-year line of monarchs begun by Kamehameha I.

See also: HAWAIIAN KINGDOMS; LILIUOKALANI.

FURTHER READING

Daws, Gavin. *Shoal of Time: A History of the Hawaiian Islands.* New York: Macmillan, 1968.

Wisniewski, Richard. *The Rise and Fall of the Hawaiian Kingdom: A Pictorial History.* Honolulu: Pacific Basin Enterprises, 1979.

KANDY KINGDOM (1500s–1818 C.E.)

Singhalese kingdom located in the central highlands of the island of Ceylon (present-day Sri Lanka), off the southeastern coast of India, that remained independent in the sixteenth century as the rest of the island fell under Portuguese and Dutch colonial rule.

Founded early in the sixteenth century, the Kandy kingdom was one of three kingdoms to emerge out of internal strife on the island of Ceylon. The other two kingdoms, the Singhalese kingdom of Kotte and the Tamil kingdom of Jaffna eventually fell to Portuguese colonial power at the end of the sixteenth century.

The Kandy kingdom was centered on the city of the same name, which was established as early as the fifth century B.C.E. by Singhalese peoples. It did not become the capital of the Singhalese kingdom, however, until 1591, after the Singhalese population split into two separate kingdoms—Kandy and Kotte. The first ruler of the kingdom of Kandy was the Singhalese leaader, Vimala Charma Surya I (r. 1591–1604).

The Portuguese first invaded the island of Sri Lanka in 1505 and quickly annexed the Jaffna kingdom and the Kotte kingdom. But the Kandy kingdom, located in the rugged central highlands, escaped Portuguese control. The Portuguese sought access to the spices of the East Indies, and they utilized the sophisticated trade networks that already existed between those islands and Sri Lanka. They also became inextricably involved in the local politics and power struggles on the island.

Intolerant of Islam, Hinduism, and Buddhism, the Portuguese converted many of the Singhalese and Tamils populations on the island to Roman Catholicism. As the only kingdom to remain independent of Portuguese control, the Kandy kingdom thus became an important center of Buddhist Singhalese power.

The foundation of the Dutch East India Company in 1600 was designed to wrest control of Asian markets from Spain and Portugal, the two main rivals of the Dutch Republic. The Dutch enlisted local allies, in particular the kingdom of Kandy, in an effort to counter Portuguese power. In return, the rulers of Kandy, such as King Senarat (1604–1635), sought Dutch support against the Portuguese and other enemies. But, like the Portuguese, the Dutch were never able to control the whole of the island. Kandy, in the inaccessible, mountainous, and heavily forested interior, was able to maintain its independence.

Like the Portuguese, the Dutch also were attracted by the spice trade, and Sri Lanka was also an important staging point on the Dutch East India Company's trade routes to the East Indies, China, and Japan. When the Dutch Republic declined at the end of the eighteenth century, its overseas possessions became natural targets for Great Britain, whose power was on the rise.

The British were more successful than the Portuguese and Dutch in subduing Sri Lanka. In the early nineteenth century, Britain invaded the island and forced the Dutch to surrender the island. Sri Lanka, except for Kandy, which remained independent, became a British colony in 1802. Kandy continued to resist attempts by Britain to gain control until 1815, when British troops invaded the kingdom, deposed the king Sri Vikrama Rajasinha (r. 1798–1815), and abolished the Kandy monarchy. Three years later, in 1818, the British annexed the entire island of Sri Lanka, ending all remnants of Kandy's independence.

See also: SOUTH ASIAN KINGDOMS.

KANEMBU-KANURI KINGDOM

(ca. 1100–1901 C.E.)

Powerful African kingdom that initially flourished on the northwestern shores of Lake Chad beginning about 1100; around 1400 the original capital, at Kanem, was abandoned when the ruling clan moved their capital south to the former tributary state of Bornu.

FOCUS ON TRADE

By 900, the Lake Chad region was beginning to be drawn into the trans-Saharan trade, which was forever seeking new sources of goods—particularly ivory and slaves. The Kanuri-speaking nomadic people of the Lake Chad region were among many in the region to offer goods to the visiting traders.

In the twelfth century, a strong local leader of the Saifawa clan of the Kanuri, named Hummay, saw a way to increase the wealth that flowed from this trade. Hummay convinced several of the neighboring clans to unite under his leadership, correctly judging that this would permit him to dominate other, smaller groups and gain a monopoly over the flow of trade goods northward. With the forging of this alliance, he founded the great Kanuri kingdom of Kanem.

Hummay was a follower of Islam, which no doubt helped him in his dealings with the predominantly Muslim trans-Saharan traders. He created a capital city at a place called Njimi, the exact location of which is presently unknown. The kingdom of Kanem grew in wealth and strength by acting as broker between the trans-Saharan traders to the north and the peoples to their south, who offered ivory, slaves, and ostrich feathers.

In return for facilitating trade, the Kanem rulers (called *mai*) exacted a tariff, paid in horses and weapons, which gave them a great advantage in might over their neighbors. The rulers of Kanem also sought to expand their territory through conquest, resulting in the acquisition of growing numbers of captives that could be sold directly onto the trans-Saharan market. By the reign of *Mai* Dunama Dibalami (r. 1210–1248), the kingdom of Kanem was the preeminent power in the region.

AN EXPANDED KINGDOM

Kanemi expansion reached its limits in the fourteenth century, in part because the territory had become too vast for centralized control, in part because the ruling Saifawa clan had incurred the resentment and envy of another powerful family, the Bulala. The Saifawa family opted for prudence over confrontation and vacated the Kanem capital, moving their base of power southward to one of their client states.

This client state was Bornu, the location of which permitted the Saifawa *mais* to retain their monopolistic control of trade from the south, effectively cutting Kanem off from the flow of goods and thereby maintaining their economic supremacy in the region. Again, the Saifawa rulers set about subduing their new neighbors, and within a matter of years, even Kanem paid tribute to Bornu.

The Bornu incarnation of the Kanembu-Kanuri kingdoms achieved far greater success than its predecessor state. It grew so quickly that it soon controlled nearly all of the regional trade destined for the trek across the Sahara to Tripoli and Egypt. It achieved such dominance that it drained away the trade previously monopolized by the great Songhai Empire, contributing to the ultimate decline of that legendary state.

During the era of Bornu preeminence, the greatest of the Saifawa *mais* was Ibn Idrisi III Aloma (r. 1571–1603), who came to power around 1571. Idrisi succeeded in uniting all the people of the savannah region under his rule, threatening even the powerful kingdom of Darfur to the east and encroaching on the territory claimed by the powerful Hausa states to the west.

END OF THE KINGDOM

As a conquest-based state, the Kanembu-Kanuri kingdom was faced with the problem of creating a sense of unity among culturally and even linguistically disparate groups. The *mais* solved this problem through the spread of Islam, which respected traditional differences but provided common ground in the areas of law, religion, and the language of the scholars (Arabic).

Until the late 1800s, the state itself was feudal in structure, with a landed nobility whose fields and herds were tended by commoners and slaves. The Bornu kingdom endured successive invasions during the seventeenth century, first by the Fulani and later, more disastrously, by a great Sudanese militarist named Rabih ibn Fadl Allah (r. 1893–1901), who conquered the kingdom in 1893. Rabih did not have long to enjoy his conquest, however, for he was killed in 1901 by French forces. The French annexed the Bornu territory, bringing the kingdom of Bornu to an abrupt end.

See also: AFRICAN KINGDOMS; FUR KINGDOM; SONG-HAI KINGDOM.

FURTHER READING

Cohen, Ronald. *The Kanuri of Bornu.* New York: Holt, Rinehart & Winston, 1967.

KANEMI, MUHAMMAD AL-AMIN AL (ca. 1775–1837 C.E.)

Ruler (r. 1808–1837) of the kingdom of Bornu in North Africa and founder of the Kanemi dynasty.

The child of a Kanembu father and an Arab mother, Kanemi was born in southwest Libya. He received a classical education in Islam, attending schools in North Africa and Hejaz, Arabia. When he was in his early to mid-twenties, Kanemi left school and began to travel throughout those areas of northern and Sahelian Africa where there were strong Muslim communities, seeking a greater understanding of the Islamic faith. He finally settled in the kingdom of Bornu, located west and south of Lake Chad, where he developed a reputation as a scholar and began gathering a large following.

Kanemi's scholarly reputation and leadership qualities brought him to the attention of Mai Ahmad (r. 1793–1810), who was then the ruler of Bornu. Ahmad was struggling with the problem of controlling the Fulani people of the Sokoto caliphate, who had declared a jihad and whose expansionist ambitions threatened to destabilize the Bornu kingdom. Kanemi was able to assist Ahmad, not only by providing willing defenders from among his followers, but also by more diplomatic means. Among these was his initiation of a dialog between the leaders of Bornu and Sokoto, in which he called into question the justice of the jihad.

Ahmad's reign ended in 1808, by which time Kanemi had earned the admiration of the people of Bornu for having saved the kingdom from the Fulani jihad. He became the de facto ruler of the kingdom, even though he was not a member of the previous ruling dynasty. With the successful transition of power from himself to his own son, Shehu Umar ibn al-Kanemi (r. 1837–1853), in 1837, a new dynastic line was firmly established in Bornu.

See also: SOKOTO CALIPHATE.

KANG XI (1654–1722 C.E.)

Chinese emperor (r. 1661–1722), second emperor of the Ch'ing dynasty, whose long reign earned him a reputation as one of China's greatest rulers. Kang Xi was the first of three remarkable Ch'ing rulers who gave China over a century of prosperity and internal peace.

The son of Emperor Shunzhi (r. 1644–1661), Kang Xi assumed the throne at the age of eight in 1661 on the death of his father. A regent, Oboi, ruled in his place until Kang Xi was 14, when the teenaged emperor ordered Oboi removed and took power.

In 1673, Kang Xi triumphed in a revolt known as the War of the Three Feudatories, defeating rebellious generals who had seized much of southern and western China. In 1683, his armies conquered Taiwan, and in 1720, he brought Tibet under Ch'ing control. Kang Xi also consolidated Ch'ing power in Central Asia, leading expeditions in the 1690s against the tribal leader Galdan, who was attempting to take power in the region.

Since capturing China in 1644 from their base in Manchuria, the Ch'ing rulers had passed many laws persecuting the Chinese population, including banning intermarriage between Manchus and Chinese and forcing Chinese men to adopt the Manchu hairstyle of a shaved head in front with a long braid in the back. Kang Xi ended and eased many of these discriminatory practices. He lowered taxes, revived agriculture by banning the Ch'ing practice of confiscating land, and reduced government corruption by raising official salaries. While he installed Manchus in the most powerful positions, Kang Xi also recruited Chinese scholars to serve in his government.

An admirer of the Chinese classics, Kang Xi gained the support of intellectuals by commissioning scholars to write lengthy histories and sponsoring the *Kang Xi Dictionary*, a vast compilation of classical texts totaling 5,020 chapters. The Manchu ruler further cemented his image as a supporter of Chinese tradition when he issued the "Sixteen Moral Principles." These pronouncements, which celebrated ancient Confucian virtues such as obedience to authority, were read throughout the empire. At his court, Jesuit scholars from Europe taught him about Western science and served as astronomers, mapmakers, and doctors.

Kang Xi worked hard, rising early in the morning to begin managing the government. In the afternoons he read, painted, or went hunting, but in the evenings he went back to work, sometimes until late in the night. To make sure he received accurate information about all corners of his vast empire, Kang Xi established a secret system of communication in which provincial officials sent reports directly to him, bypassing government officials. He also traveled on several grand tours of the empire, meeting the people and inspecting local conditions.

Troubles arose at the end of Kang Xi's reign over who would succeed him as emperor. His son Yingreng, as the emperor's only son among his fifty-six children to be born to an empress, was the only legitimate heir. When Yingreng proved to be mentally unstable and was caught in a conspiracy against his father, Kang Xi revoked the son's right to succeed him. The distraught Kang Xi named no other heir before his death in 1722. In the confusion that followed, Kang Xi's fourth son, Yongzheng, claimed the throne.

See also: CH'IEN LUNG (QIANLONG); CH'ING (QING) DYNASTY.

KANVA DYNASTY (ca. 75–30 B.C.E.)

An early Indian dynasty, successors of the Sunga dynasty, that ruled remnants of the Maurya Empire in the first century B.C.E.

Scholars know very little about the Kanva dynasty or its rulers. Most information is based on a few ancient coins, on accounts of the history of the geographical area, and on the *Puranas*, an ancient account of the Hindu religion that is more useful for genealogical information than for political history.

According to the *Puranas*, the Kanva dynasty had four kings—Vasudeva (r. ca. 75–66 B.C.E.), Bhumimitra (r. ca. 66–52 B.C.E.), Narayana (r. ca. 52–40 B.C.E.), and Susarman (r. ca. 40–30 B.C.E.)—who ruled for a total of only forty-five years. Power was passed from father to son in the Kanva dynasty. The founder of the dynasty was Vasudeva Kanva, an adviser of King Devabhuti (r. ca. 85–75 B.C.E.) of the Sunga dynasty, which had supplanted the last ruler of the Maurya dynasty, Brihadratha (r. 187–180 B.C.E.), in the second century B.C.E.

Before coming to power, the members of the Kanva dynasty had served as advisers and administrators for the Sunga dynasty, which controlled a large territory in central India. In the early first century B.C.E., the Sungas came under military pressure from invading Indo-Greeks, who occupied the western part of their territory, known as the Punjab. Pressure also came from the Mitra kings, a short-lived dynasty that ruled the ancient kingdoms of Kosala and Panchala, and gradually gained control of a large part of the plains around the Ganges River. Scholars believe that as the Sunga dynasty became weak from external attacks, the Kanvas usurped power from within, not removing the Sunga dynasty completely but leaving them as sovereigns in name only.

By the time the Kanva dynasty officially came to power around 75 B.C.E., the Sungas held the ancient town of Vidisa, now known as Bhilsa, leaving only the city of Magadha under Kanvas control. Magadha is in the southern part of the modern province of Bihar.

According to the *Puranas*, the Kanva dynasty was overthrown by the Andhra, or Satavahana, dynasty. However, no archaeological evidence, coins, or inscriptions, have been found to substantiate the *Puranas* account, and the *Puranas*, at another place, indicates that the Andhra dynasty was founded two centuries before the overthrow of the Kanvas. In any event, the short-lived Kanva dynasty left little mark on the history of India.

See also: ANDHRA KINGDOM; INDIAN KINGDOMS; MAURYA EMPIRE; SATAVAHANA DYNASTY; SUNGA DYNASTY.

KAO TSUNG (GAOZONG)

(1107–1187 C.E.)

Chinese emperor (r. 1127–1162) who founded the Southern Sung dynasty. Kao Tsung was the ninth son of Hui Tsung (Huizong) (r. 1101–1125), emperor of the Northern Sung dynasty. In 1126, Jurchen invaders from the north swept into northern China, seizing the Northern Sung capital at Kaifeng and imprisoning much of the imperial family, including Huizong and Kao Tsung's brother, Emperor Ch'in Tsung (Qinzong). The Jurchen established the Jin dynasty in north China, which ruled from 1127 to 1234.

Kao Tsung managed to escape capture by the Jin, fleeing south and declaring himself emperor in 1127. Jin armies pursued Kao Tsung until 1135, when they withdrew to the north. Their withdrawal allowed Kao Tsung to establish a capital in the southern city of Hangzhou in the lower Yangtze River Valley. In 1141, he signed a treaty with the Jin, making the Sung a vassal state and agreeing to pay a large annual tribute in silk and silver.

A skilled and conscientious ruler, Kao Tsung presided over the reestablishment of the Sung dynasty in the south of China. He faced the difficult task of rebuilding the Sung army, which had completely disintegrated as a result of the Jin invasion. However, his government was plagued by infighting between those satisfied with the southern empire and those determined to reconquer the north. In addition, the military remained weak, forcing Kao Tsung and his successors to pay tribute to border states to stave off invasion.

Kao Tsung's rule ushered in a great age for China. The Southern Sung period was a time of cultural renaissance and thriving trade. The Southern Sung had the most advanced technology and the largest cities in the world. Learning and the arts flourished, and the city of Hangzhou became a thriving center of culture and commerce.

Kao Tsung's father, Emperor Hui Tsung, had been a skilled painter who founded an academy of the arts in the northern capital of Kaifeng. Kao Tsung continued his father's tradition of artistic patronage. He reestablished the academy in the new capital of Hangzhou, and under his patronage, Chinese landscape painting reached its pinnacle. Kao Tsung also oversaw a renaissance in classical learning. The Sung, cut off from contact with the West by hostile neighbors, began to look to their own past, reviving and reexamining ancient texts.

In 1162, Kao Tsung abdicated in favor of his adopted son, Xiaosong, and retired from political life. He spent his final twenty-five years enjoying an imperial lifestyle in his palace at Hangzhou.

See also: SUNG (SONG) DYNASTY.

KASHMIR KINGDOM (1339–1589 C.E.)

Muslim kingdom in northwestern India dating to the fourteenth century, whose history has made the region a source of continuing conflict between the modern nations of India and Pakistan.

The first kingdom of Kashmir was a Hindu state that dates to the seventh century. The geography of Kashmir, surrounded by towering mountains, prevented this kingdom from playing a significant role in the early history of India. This earliest recorded period of the kingdom's history is littered by accounts of tyrannical leaders and an oppressed peasantry.

The Muslim kingdom of Kashmir, also known as the sultanate of Kashmir, came into existence in 1339. During this phase of Kashmir's history, the populace of the region had Islam thrust upon it and was forced to give up Hinduism. The kingdom arose in tandem with a series of other regional sultanates, including Bengal, Malwa, and Gujarat. The Muslim Kashmir kingdom came to an end in 1586, when it was annexed by the Mughal emperor Akbar the Great (r. 1556–1605). However, the annexation and absorption of Kashmir into the Mughal Empire did not occur before the local regional dialect had matured and ingrained itself into Kashmiri culture.

The first decade of the Muslim kingdom of Kashmir was rather unstable in terms of leadership, having three kings within its first five years of existence. The first Kashmiri sultan was Shah Mir (r. 1339–1342), who usurped the throne from the Hindu raja. Mizra then married the raja's widow to help secure his control. His hold on the kingdom was finally secured by implementing a generous taxation policy to maintain the allegiance of the populace. These policies were continued and improved on by his sons, who ruled the kingdom until 1356.

Kashmir's geography prevented it from actively influencing the early history of the Indian subcontinent. Its geography also provided the kingdom with fortuitous protection. Such protection showed its usefulness when the great Mongol conqueror Tamerlane swept into India from the Central Asian steppe but did not turn his attention to this small mountainous domain.

Sikander Shah (r. 1393–1413) was Kashmir's sultan while Tamerlane moved through India. History has labeled Sikander the Idol-Breaker, a name he earned because of his religious zeal which, though it attracted numerous learned Muslim scholars, found expression in a streak of religious intolerance that led to the destruction of many Hindu temples and idols. One other effect of Sikander's religious zeal was the conversion of the Kashmiri populace to Islam at the tip of Sikander's sword, which killed many Brahmin priests when they proved unwilling to convert.

The intolerance of Sikander's reign contrasted with that of Zain-ul' Abidin (r. 1420–1470), who succeeded to the throne within a decade of Sikander's death. The fifty-year reign of Zain-ul' Abidin was characterized by complete religious toleration, particularly to those Brahmins who had gone into exile while Sikander ruled. Zain-ul' Abidin's willingness to allow alternative religious doctrines within the kingdom led to the reconstruction of Hindu temples. One other effect of this new tolerance was an artistic and literary revival. Ironically, in terms of his outlook and actions toward religion, philosophy, and the arts, Zain-ul' Abidin resembled the individual who eventually took over and ended the Kashmir kingdom, Akbar the Great.

The century following the reign of Zain-ul' Abidin was characterized by a seemingly endless succession of short-lived monarchs, only a couple of whom reigned for a decade or more. In 1589, Kashmiri independence came to an abrupt end when Akbar the Great, the Mughal emperor, conquered the kingdom, along with other territories including Kandahar, Sind, and parts of the Deccan plateau. Although the Kashmir kingdom was no longer independent, its history continued to shape and prepare the region for its place in the struggle between Pakistan and India after these countries gained independence in the twentieth century.

See also: AKBAR THE GREAT; INDIAN KINGDOMS; MALWA KINGDOM; MUGHAL EMPIRE.

FURTHER READING

Duff, Mabel. *The Chronology of Indian History: From the Earliest Times to the 16th Century.* Delhi: Cosmo Publications, 1972.

Kulke, Hermann, and Dietmar Rothermund. *A History of India.* 3rd ed. New York: Routledge, 1998.

Smith, Vincent A. *The Oxford History of India.* Ed. Percival Spear. 4th ed. New York: Oxford University Press, 1981.

KASSITES (flourished ca. 1729–1155 B.C.E.)

Ancient people of the Near East, best known for their conquest of Babylonia in the eighteenth century B.C.E.

First mentioned in ancient Elamite texts, the Kassites were unknown in Babylonian texts until about 1741 B.C.E., during the reign of Samsu-iluna (r. 1749–1712 B.C.E.), the son of Hammurabi (r. 1792–1750 B.C.E.). The Kassites made their first offensive movements against Babylon around that time but were only able to secure a few holdings along the northern border of Babylonia while Samsu-iluna was alive.

Lists of Kassite kings suggest that by the early seventeenth century B.C.E., these northern holdings had multiplied. Gandash (r. 1729–1700 B.C.E.), the first Kassite king, and the first king of the second Babylonian dynasty, probably ruled over this northern area of Babylonia contemporaneously with one of the later kings of the first Babylonian dynasty, who still held Babylon. However, the dynasty founded by Gandash did take control of all Babylon around 1600 B.C.E. and ruled until the Elamites conquered them around 1155 B.C.E.

The Kassite innovation of the *kudurru,* a boundary stone that recorded a royal grant of land, was important as both a means of record-keeping and as a source for Kassite art, since the stones were often beautifully decorated. Unfortunately, neither kudurru stones nor any other Kassite documents have been found written in Kassite. All that is known of the Kassite language has been reconstructed from about three hundred words found in Babylonian documents. These words suggest that the Kassites were Indo-European in origin. Kassite religious objects show that they had a polytheistic religion, and they seem to have worshiped the horse, which they probably introduced to Babylonia.

After about 1380 B.C.E., the Kassites gradually became less militarized and more focused on the priorities of trade, commerce, and agriculture that had interested their Babylonian dynastic predecessors. At the same time, they became more troubled by external military threats. During the reign of Kashtiliash

IV (r. ca. 1232–1225 B.C.E.), Kassite Babylonia was attacked by both Assyria and Elam, and the city of Babylon was destroyed.

It was a decade before the Kassites restored the state under Adad-Shuma-asur (r. ca. 1216–1187 B.C.E.), but peace was short-lived. The Elamites under their king Shutruk-Nahhunte (r. ca. 1185–1155 B.C.E.) attacked once more, and in 1155 B.C.E., the Kassite dynasty was destroyed. After this defeat, the Kassites withdrew to the Zagros Mountains in present-day Iran. There they retained their independence—except for a brief conquest by Alexander the Great (r. 336–323 B.C.E.) until Christian times, when they disappear from the historical record.

See also: ALEXANDER III, THE GREAT; ASSYRIAN EMPIRE; HAMMURABI; SAMSU-ILUNA.

KATHIAWAR KINGDOM

(ca. 700–1297 C.E.)

Also known by its ancient Hindu name Saurashtra, a kingdom that occupied the peninsula in western India (part of the present-day state of Gujarat) that lies between the Gulf of Kutch and the Gulf of Cambay.

Kathiawar was first consolidated as part of the Maurya Empire in the late fourth and early third centuries B.C.E. Several hundred years later, in the fourth century C.E., it passed to the control of the Gupta Empire. Kathiawar achieved its greatest independence in the early eighth century, when several minor dynasties divided the kingdom among themselves. The most prominent of these clans was the Saindhavas, who inhabited the Barda Hills.

In 739, the first ruler of the Saindhava dynasty, Pushyadeva (r. dates unknown), gained widespread recognition by defeating an invasion by Muslims from Sindh, a state in present-day Pakistan. During the reign of Agguka I (r. dates unknown), Pushyadeva's grandson, the Sindh Arabs launched two more invasions, but on both occasions the Kathiawar kingdom repelled the invaders.

The Saindhava dynasty maintained its prominence for more than two centuries. As the most powerful dynasty on the Kathiawar Peninsula, they allowed the other dynasties in the region to exist as feudatory clans. In 915, however, the status of the dynasty diminished when its last ruler, Jaika II (r. dates unknown), died without leaving an heir.

Among the other regional dynasties, the Calukyas (Chalukyas) controlled eastern Kathiawar. Two brothers, Kalla and Mahalla, founded that dynasty in Kathiawar in the late eighth century. Their autonomy lasted only a very brief time, however. Around 825, the Pratihara Empire conquered the Kathiawar region and forced the Calukyas to sign a treaty of obeisance. The Calukyas remained as local vassals of the Pratihara Raja.

After the Saindhava dynasty crumbled in the early tenth century, two dynasties, the Abhiras and Chapas, struggled for control of western Kathiawar. Neither achieved supremacy, however, and repeated Pratihara invasions weakened both dynasties. In 942, Mularaja (r. 942–997), the most famous Chapa monarch, won control of the peninsula, but his domination was fleeting in the unstable region.

A massive Muslim invasion in 1024 made the petty dynastic struggles of Kathiawar seem inconsequential. Sultan Mahmud of Ghazni (r. 998–1030) avenged the earlier Arab defeats and invaded the peninsula from the north, ravaging the Kathiawar kingdom. Mahmud's army took vast amounts of treasure but did not permanently occupy Kathiawar.

After the Muslim invasion by Mahmud of Ghazni, Kathiawar experienced several centuries of lawlessness before the region became part of Gujarat under the sultan of Delhi around 1297. The region of Kathiawar later came under the control of the Mughal Empire in the sixteenth century. Kathiawar briefly regained its independence after the Mughals left India in the mid-1800s, but soon after it was made part of the British colony of India. Today, the region of Kathiawar is revered as the homeland of Indian political and spiritual leader, Mohandas (Mahatma) Gandhi.

See also: CALUKYA (CHALUKYA) DYNASTY; DELHI KINGDOM; GUJARAT KINGDOM; GUPTA EMPIRE; INDIAN KINGDOMS; MAHMUD OF GHAZNA; MAURYA EMPIRE; MUGHAL EMPIRE; SOUTH ASIAN KINGDOMS.

KENNETH I (KENNETH MACALPIN) (ca. 810–858 C.E.)

Also known as Kenneth MacAlpin, the first monarch of a united Scotland. Kenneth's reign, from around 843 until 858, has been the focus of many myths. He was born Cinaed MacAlpin on the Scottish isle of Iona around 810. His father, Alpin, was a king of the

Scots—Gaelic-speaking tribes that had migrated from northern Ireland to western Scotland around 500, founding the kingdom known as Dalriada. After Alpin's death in 834, Kenneth succeeded him as ruler of Galloway, and around 840 he became king of all the Dalriadic territory, ruling over a disorganized collection of tribal chiefs.

Kenneth's reign was significant because he was the first monarch to rule jointly over the Scots and, after 842, over the Picts, a Celtic people of northern Britain. Traditional accounts have claimed that Kenneth inherited both kingdoms—the patrilineal Dalriadic line through his father, and the Pictish matrilineal crown through his mother. Some medieval accounts suggest that he captured or consolidated his rule over the Picts by means of treachery. According to these writings, he invited Pictish nobles to a banquet at which he had them ambushed.

Kenneth's reign was marked by war—especially against the English, Norse, and Danes—and by close association with Christian strongholds of the time, especially the Scottish sites of Scone, Dunkeld, and Iona. He is said to have promulgated the so-called laws of MacAlpin, which consisted of criminal and civil codes with harsh penalties. Kenneth is credited in myth as the king who brought the famous "stone of destiny" to Scone, where it played a highly symbolic role in Scottish royal coronations. Kenneth was succeeded by his brother, Donald (r. 858–862), and then by his own sons Constantine (r. 862–876) and Aed (r. 876–878). Through them, his dynasty ruled Scotland until the death of Malcolm II (r. 1005–1034) in 1034.

See also: PICTS, KINGDOM OF THE; SCOTTISH KINGDOMS.

KENT, KINGDOM OF (450–860 C.E.)

The oldest of the Anglo-Saxon kingdoms, occupying the same territory in southeastern England as the modern county of Kent.

According to semilegendary accounts, two brothers, Hengist and Horsa, from the Anglo-Saxon people known as the Jutes, arrived in Britain in 449 to help British king Vortigern battle the Picts who occupied northern Britain. Paid for their services with money, supplies, and land, the brothers nevertheless led a revolt against Vortigern within a few

years. The Jutes (who probably originated in what is now Denmark) then established the kingdom of Kent in 450. Hengist (r. 449–488), whose son Oisc (r. 488–512) succeeded him as king, established a dynasty that lasted more than three centuries.

During the first century of its existence, the kingdom of Kent was ruled jointly by two rulers, with the stronger in East Kent and the weaker in West Kent. The East Kentish capital was established at the Roman city of Durovernum Cantiacorum, referred to by the Jutes as Cantwarabyrig, or "fortress of the Men of Kent" (modern-day Canterbury).

By 595, Æthelbert I of Kent (r. 560–616), had become *Bretwalda*, or overlord, of the Anglo-Saxon kingdoms, the only Kentish king to achieve that title. A pagan, Æthelbert was married to a Frankish princess, Bertha, a Christian who insisted on the right to practice her faith as a condition of marriage. In 597, Æthelbert welcomed a delegation of Christian missionaries led by St. Augustine of Canterbury. Although he initially refused to convert to Christianity himself, Æthelbert gave the missionaries land for a church as well as permission to preach in his kingdom. Within four years, thousands of people in Kent had been converted and Æthelbert himself was baptized as well.

Æthelbert was also known for his legal reformers. During his reign, the oldest surviving code of laws in the Anglo-Saxon vernacular was created. Based partly on Roman law, and probably drawn up with the assistance of St. Augustine, this legal code stipulated fines for various offenses and outlined a social hierarchy headed by Christian bishops.

The Saxon rulers of the kingdoms of Wessex and Mercia were the chief rivals of the Kentish kings. Around 686, Kent was occupied by Caedwalla of Wessex (r. 685–688). Nearly a century later, Offa (r. 757–796), the king of Mercia, made Kent a province of his kingdom. A powerful king, Offa signed the first recorded commercial treaty in English history with the Frankish ruler Charlemagne (r. 768–814) in 796. Offa also introduced a new coinage, the silver penny, on which the system of English currency was based for more than seven hundred years.

Following Offa's death in 796, the people of Kent revolted against Mercian rule but were defeated. In 825, following the battle of Ellandon, King Baldred of Kent (r. 823–825) was deposed, and possession of the kingdom was transferred from Mercia to the kingdom of Wessex. By 860, Wessex had completely absorbed Kent into its domain, ending centuries of Kentish independence.

Although subject to frequent raids by Danish invaders, the kingdom of Kent, at its peak, enjoyed an economic and cultural life that surpassed that of neighboring Anglo-Saxon kingdoms. Its economic and political leaders maintained close ties with the European continent, while the presence of the bishopric of Canterbury made Kent one of the most important Christian centers in Britain. There is evidence as well that remnants of Roman culture survived in the kingdom.

See also: ANGLO-SAXON RULERS; MERCIA, KINGDOM OF; WESSEX, KINGDOM OF.

KERTANAGARA EMPIRE

(1268–1292 C.E.)

Empire of Kertanagara, the last king of Singhasari in eastern Java. He is still revered by the Javanese as one of their greatest leaders.

What little information exists about Kertanagara comes mainly from two Javanese chronicles, the *Pararaton* (Book of Kings) and *Nagarakertagama* (the epic of Majapahit), which tell very different stories about this king. According to *Pararaton,* Kertanagara was often drunk and loved good food. He sent away his capable chief minister Raganatha (Kebo Arema) and hired Aragani (possibly the same as Kebo Tengali) instead because Argani was able to provide good food every day. According to this account, the king's death was a result of all his wine drinking and orgies because his enemies killed him at one of his rowdy parties. On the other hand, *Nagarakertagama,* the account best supported by historical evidence, tells of the king's greatness and wisdom. It portrays him as an ardent disciple of Tantric Buddhism, which involved magic and evil spirits and *ritualistic* rather than pleasure-seeking drinking and orgies. He was venerated as a Siva-Buddha who had called upon demonic powers in himself to eliminate the demons who wanted a divided Java. According to *Nagarakertagama,* Kertanagara believed he was living in a time of fear, confusion, and disaster and that it was his duty as king to save the world. Since he knew that was impossible, he tried to fight evil by reinforcing Buddhism.

Statues of Kertanagara support the belief that he was a very religious king, but he also was very capable in politics and government—frequently using religion to help him achieve political goals. According to *Nagarakertagama,* Kertanagara was the first Javanese leader to foresee a unified Indonesia. Actually, his *birth* did unify the two halves of Java since he was born of a princely family from each half—King Vishnuvardhana of Janggala and a princess of Kadiri. His own vision of unity, however, was not totally accomplished until about fifty years after he died, when King Hayam Wuruk of Majapahit ruled. King Kertanagara may have been too ambitious with his expansionist foreign policy, which was a reaction to the growing threat of the Mongol emperor of China, Kublai Khan. In 1284, Kertanagara led an ineffective expedition into Bali and sent his army to conquer the kingdom of Malayu in lower Sumatra, leaving him vulnerable to rebellion at home.

Some powerful officials who had loyally served his father, Wishnuwardhana, but were subsequently demoted to inferior positions, started a revolt that resulted in Kertanagara's death in 1292. His brother-in-law, Jayakatwang, who claimed he was descended from royalty and thought the throne should be his rather than Kertanagara's, also became Kertanagara's enemy. Kertanagara's ministers tried to warn Kertanagara about his vulnerability, but he failed to recognize it and died trying to defend his palace against Jayakatwang's overwhelming forces.

See also: JANGGALA KINGDOM; KUBLAI KHAN; MAJAPAHIT EMPIRE; MONGOL EMPIRE.

KHALJI DYNASTY (1290–1320 C.E.)

Short-lived Muslim dynasty that ruled the Delhi sultanate of India in the late thirteenth and early fourteenth century.

The Khalji dynasty was the second dynasty of the Muslim sultanate of Delhi. The origin of the Khalji family was probably Turkish, but they had lived a long time in Afghanistan. The dynasty had three sultans, who successfully fought their way into the Hindu south.

The first Khalji ruler of Delhi was Jalal-ud-Din Khalji (r. 1290–1296). An esteemed army officer, Jalal founded the Khalji dynasty after the collapse of the Mu'izzi (or Slave) dynasty in 1290. Jalal-ud-Din, also known as Firuz Shah II, was a clever and peaceable ruler who loved learning and avoided bloodshed. During his reign, the Delhi sultanate withstood a forceful Mongol invasion in 1292, after which approximately three thousand Mongols surrendered and adopted Islam.

Jalal-ud-Din was unpopular in India, however, both because the Khaljis were believed to be Afghan and because he eschewed violence. However, his son-in-law and nephew, Juna Khan, led an invasion of the Hindu Deccan region around 1294. Two years later, in 1296, he murdered his uncle Jalal-ud-Din, deposed his cousin Ibrahim (Jalal's son), and became sultan of Delhi. He ruled for the next twenty years as Ala-ud-Din Khalji or Muhammad I (r. 1296–1316).

A cruel ruler but a capable general and administrator, Muhammad I seized the states of Ranthambhor (in 1301), Chitor (in 1303), and Mandu (in 1305). The first Muslim king to attempt to extend Delhi rule over the whole of the Deccan, he also annexed the affluent Hindu kingdom of Devagiri and resisted attacks from the Mongols. From 1308 to 1311, his lieutenant, Malik Kafur, led successful raids in the south, taking over the state of Warangal, bringing down the Hoysala dynasty south of the Krishna River, and occupying the state of Madura in the far south. Muhammad received significant booty from his military ventures, and the rulers he defeated had to pay substantial tribute.

Eventually, nearly all of India was then ruled by the Delhi sultanate under Muhammad I. His achievements, however, were not all military. He maintained strict separation between religion and government, and regulated the cost of goods. He also supported the arts, bringing specialists and masters, such as the Persian poet Amir Khusru, to his court.

Over time, however, the Khalji dynasty began to weaken. When Muhammad I died in 1316, Malik Kafur deposed Muhammad's son, Umar, and usurped the throne. But Malik managed to hold power for only a month before he was overthrown. The throne then went to Muhammad I's other son, Qutb-ud-din, who ruled as Mubarak I (r. 1316–1320). In 1320, Mubarak was killed by his chief minister, Khusraw Khan (r. 1320), who ruled only briefly before being overthrown by Ghiyas-ud-Din Tughluq, the founder of the Tughluq dynasty.

See also: DELHI KINGDOM; INDIAN KINGDOMS; TUGHLUQ DYNASTY.

KHAMA III (ca. 1835?–1923 C.E.)

Also called Khama the Great, African king (r. 1872–1923) who was sponsored by the British as ruler of the Sotho-Tswana in what is now Botswana in south-central Africa.

Khama was born into one of the royal lineages of the Sotho-Tswana people in the town of Shoshong in the Transvaal, in the region that is now present-day Botswana. Had Khama been born prior to the advent of European imperialism in Africa, he might have risen to the status of local chieftain like his father, who had been chief of the Ngwato people. Instead, he became a powerful king, ruling a far more extensive territory than would have traditionally been possible.

While Khama was still a child, his homeland in the Transvaal was plagued with violence and outlawry as European slave raiders, mercenaries, and refugees overran local settlements. With these disrupting influences came another—missionaries from Great Britain. Khama's family converted to Christianity, as did many others in the region.

In 1872, Khama succeeded his father to the chieftaincy of the Ngwato. Along with other leaders of the region, he accepted British assistance in stabilizing the unsettled region, making the Sotho-Tswana territory a protectorate of Great Britain. This opened the door to an influx of British colonials and more missionaries, and in appreciation of Khama's cooperation, his new British allies essentially created a kingdom for him to rule.

Khama carefully cultivated his reputation as a loyal supporter of the British Empire, which enabled him to call upon his sponsors for help in expanding his realm. He aligned himself with the missionaries so that as they evangelized throughout his realm they brought word not only of Christianity, but also of Khama's rule, thus creating a network of loyalists throughout the territory. His rule was largely supportive of British colonial policies, but he made a noteworthy trip to England in 1895 in an attempt to keep the British South Africa Company from encroaching upon his kingdom's territory. Khama III died in 1923. His grandson, Seretse Khama, became the first president of Botswana when that country attained independence in 1966.

See also: TSHEKEDI KHAMA.

KHATTI KINGDOM. *See* HITTITE

EMPIRE

KHATTUSHILI I (d. ca. 1600 B.C.E.)

Also known as Hattushili, Hittite king (r. ca. 1650–1620 B.C.E.) who is credited with founding the Hittite Old Kingdom and who was responsible for the early expansion of Hittite influence throughout Anatolia (present-day Turkey) and other parts of the ancient Near East.

Khattushili was a prince of the royal house of Kussara, who established his capital at the city of Khattusha around 1620 B.C.E. When the remainder of the Kussaran kingdom fell as a result of rebellion and invasion by the Hurrians, Khattushili was left ruler of a new independent kingdom.

Khattushili adopted his ruling name, which means "man of Khattusha," upon founding his new kingdom. He also appears to have adopted the name "Labarna," a royal title conferred upon all later Hittite kings. Much of what scholars know about Khattashili is drawn from just three ancient Hittite documents—the *Annals,* the *Testament,* and the *Proclamation.*

A warrior-king, Khattushili spent much of his reign conquering or raiding other territories, extending Hittite power from the capital at Khattusha to the Cilician Gates, a mountain pass in southern Anatolia. In the process of conquest, he destroyed a number of cities, including the ancient trading center of Alalakh in Syria. Khattushili also pushed further into Syria, crossed the Euphrates River, and even recaptured the old capital of Kussara. While he was on campaign against the kingdom of Arzawa in western Anatolia, the Hurrians invaded the old Hittite kingdom, conquering much of its territory with the exception of the capital of Khattusha. Khattushili cut short his conquests and returned to retake his kingdom.

A strong ruler, Khattushili consolidated Hittite power, providing a basis for later rulers to extend Hittite influence even further throughout the ancient Near East. While on campaign against Aleppo around 1600 B.C.E., it appears that Khattushili received a wound from which he later died. His grandson, Murshili I (r. ca. 1600–1590 B.C.E.), succeeded to the throne.

See also: HITTITE EMPIRE.

FURTHER READING

Bryce, Trevor. *The Kingdom of the Hittites.* New York: Oxford University Press, 1998.

Macqueen, J.G. *The Hittites and Their Contemporaries in Asia Minor.* Rev. ed. New York: Thames and Hudson, 1986.

KHAZAR KINGDOM

(flourished 600s–900s C.E.)

Turkish kingdom in the steppelands of Central Asia, located between the Caspian and Black seas and bordered by the Caucasus Mountains in the south. The Turkic-speaking Khazars established a successful commercial empire by the end of the eighth century. In the middle of that century, the leaders of the nation imposed Judaism as the state religion.

EARLY HISTORY

Sometime in the seventh century, the Turkic tribes known as the Khazars (sometimes also known as the Khabars or Kadars) traveled across the Caucasus Mountains and settled in the broad lands between the Dnieper River and the Caspian Sea. Within the next hundred years, the Khazars built a capital city, Itil, on the banks of the river of the same name (the modern-day Volga River). They also began to build a commercial empire on the fertile and relatively unpopulated lands north of the Caucasus, enjoying the cultural vigor nurtured by their diversity.

The Khazars first appeared on the world stage around 627 as allies of the Eastern Roman (Byzantine) emperor Heraclius (r. 610–641), to whom their *kagan* (king) lent 40,000 cavalry to assist in the destruction of the Persian Empire. At this time, however, the Khazars had not yet established dominion north of the Caucasus region, and they were just one of many Turkic-speaking nomadic tribes.

Early in its history, the Khazar kingdom faced many military challenges from the rising power of Islam. Within thirty years of the Prophet Muhammad's death in 622, the Arabs were attacking the great land barrier of the Caucasus—at the same time that they were attacking the equally formidable barrier of the Pyrenees Mountains on the Iberian Peninsula far to the west. Unlike the Pyrenees, however, the Caucasus boasted two fairly accessible paths through the mountains—a pass known as the Darband Gate and a narrow passage along the western shore of the Caspian Sea.

The Arabs succeeded in breaching Darband at least twice and made incursions deep into the Khazar region, once as far as the Dnieper River. However, the young and vital Khazar kingdom forced the Muslim invaders back each time after great battles involving thousands of soldiers.

In 652, the highly skilled Muslim leader, Abd al-Rahman, was defeated by the Khazars on the banks of the Caspian Sea, bringing the first wave of Islamic invasions to a close. This defeat of the Muslims also—and almost incidentally—saved the Byzantine Empire as well by preventing the Arabs from crossing the Caucasus Mountains and approaching Byzantium from the north.

BUILDING THE KINGDOM

After stopping the initial Muslim threat in the mid-600s, the Khazars consolidated their empire, defeating the Bulgars, Magyars, and various seminomadic tribes that occupied the trans-Caucasus region. It was also during this time that the Khazars built their soon-to-be magnificent capital on the banks of the the River Itil.

In 722, seventy years after the last Arab incursion, the Khazars struck back at the Muslims, invading Anatolia (present-day Turkey) and reaching as far south as Mosul (in present-day Iraq). Unable to hold their advance, however, the Khazars retreated back behind the safe wall of the Caucasus Mountains. Thus began fifteen years of invasions and retreats, as the Khazars would move south but then retreated, and the Arabs moved north in retaliation but then also retreated.

This second period of warfare against the Muslims came to an end in the mid-700s. Soon after taking the throne, Marwan II (r. 744–750), the Muslim caliph of the Ummayad dynasty, successfully crossed the Caucasus Mountains, and persuaded the Khazar *kagan* to accept Muhammad as God's Prophet. The Khazar conversion to Islam seems not to have been wholly sincere, however. Sometime in the following sixty years, an even more remarkable religious-political event occurred in Khazaria—the Khazars converted to Judaism.

CONVERSION TO JUDAISM

One of the best contemporaneous sources for information about the Khazar conversion to Judaism is the Muslim historian and chronicler al-Masudi, who reported that the king of the Khazars and all his court were converted to Judaism during the caliphate of Harun al-Rashid (r. 786–809) of the Abbasid dynasty.

Although this Jewish conversion of a monarchy

ROYAL RITUALS

LEGACY OF THE KHAZAR CONVERSION

Although the Khazar conversion to Judaism began with only the royal family and court in the eighth century, by the end of the tenth century, Arab chroniclers were describing the Khazars as "all Jews."

As the kingdom of Khazaria succumbed to pressures from the Rus kingdoms from the north and then to invasions by the Mongols from the east, they migrated into Hungary. At the end of the kingdom, accompanying the outbreak of bubonic plague in the mid-1300s, most of the remaining Khazars fled what was left of their ravaged homeland and settled in the Ukraine and Poland.

These migrations, involving vast movements of people, helped to shape the future of Jewry in Europe by populating Eastern Europe with large numbers of migrant Jews. As a result, some scholars contend that the majority of non-Sephardic Jews today could eventually trace their ancestry back to these same peoples.

had no precedent in the medieval world, it made a good deal of political sense for the Khazars. The Khazars had long enjoyed a good relationship with the Christian Byzantine court, occasionally even supplying a royal wife and heir. But the sometimes belligerent creed of the Byzantines always posed a potential threat. Despite occasional periods of warfare, the Muslim Arabs of Georgia, Armenia, and the Trans-oxus region were important trading partners of the Khazars and not to be angered unnecessarily. Both the Muslims and Khazars had attempted religious proselytization numerous times and would probably take conversion to the "other" religion as reason enough for war.

On the other hand, Khazaria had long been a refuge for Jews escaping persecution by the papacy in Rome and the patriarch of Byzantium. The Judaic community was wealthy and influential in Itil long before the *kagan* accepted Muhammad as his Prophet. Conversion to Judaism—a religion that shared elements with both Islam and Christianity—seemed a good solution to a sticky problem.

Coming originally from the culturally diverse Anatolian Peninsula, the Khazars embraced the many customs and cultures that surrounded them. A complex seven-court system was established, which included two courts for Muslims, two for Christians, two for Jews, and one for heathens. Appeals to the judgments of these courts were handled by one of the Muslim courts, as Islamic jurisprudence was considered the most effective of that time. As might be inferred from this unusually open-minded judicial system, freedom of religion was encouraged throughout Khazaria.

The unique religious tolerance of Khazaria benefited the kingdom. This tolerance, together with the strategic geographical position of Khazaria—Russians and Vikings to the north, Islam to the South, Byzantium (Christians) to the southwest, and Asia to the east—contributed to making the kingdom, and particularly the capital of Itil, enormously prosperous by the late eighth century.

LAST DAYS OF THE KINGDOM

After their conversion to Judaism, the Khazars enjoyed more than a century of prosperity and peace. As the tenth century wore on, however, raids by the Rus principalities increased. In 965, the now-wealthy and sophisticated Khazars suffered a decisive defeat at the hands of the ruler of the Kievan Rus.

After this defeat, Khazaria began a long and steady decline. For the next 200 years, the relatively cultured and refined state of the Khazars suffered numerous defeats and reverses on all fronts. The Kievans continued pushing from the west, and the Viking Rus struck all along the length of the Volga River to the Caspian Sea. The Khazars also faced renewed raids by Arabs across the Caucasus and from the southeast, and even their sometime allies, the Byzantines, did whatever they could to weaken Khazaria.

By the time the bubonic plague struck the area in the mid-fourteenth century, there had not been a coherent Khazar kingdom for more than a hundred years. Nevertheless, this remarkable state had made its mark on history, both by halting the eastern advance of the Muslims into Byzantine lands and by contributing to the future of the Jewish people.

See also: BYZANTINE EMPIRE; CALIPHATES; KIEV, PRINCEDOM OF; RUS PRINCEDOMS.

FURTHER READING

Frazer, Sir James George. *The Golden Bough: A Study in Magic and Religion.* Abridged ed. Mineola, NY: Dover Publications, 2002.
Soucek, Svatopluk. *A History of Inner Asia.* New York: Cambridge University Press, 2001.

KHMER EMPIRE (500s–1400s C.E.)

Ancient kingdom of Southeast Asia that once ruled most of the Indochinese Peninsula. The kingdom flourished from the ninth to the fifteenth century, with its capital at Angkor.

RISE OF THE EMPIRE

During the sixth century, the Cambodians, or Khmers, created an empire in the general area of present-day Cambodia and Laos. It was split during the eighth century and reunited early in the ninth century under King Jayavarman II (r. 802–834). During the next six centuries, a period sometimes referred to as the "golden age" of the Khmer Empire, its area expanded in the east to where Thailand is today, in the south to the Mekong River delta, and in the north into Laos. The capital was set up at Angkor (which actually means "capital"), in northwestern Cambodia, under the rule of King Yasovarman I (r. 889–900).

Angkor Thom, one of the notable architectural achievements of the Khmer Empire, served as its last capital. Built in the twelfth and thirteenth centuries during the reign of Jayavarman VII, Angkor Thom included residences for priests and officials, a number of temples, and other public buildings. The fortified city was enclosed by a wall that measured 26 feet high and a moat 328 feet wide.

ANGKOR ERA

The Khmer culture and religion were largely influenced by Indian and Buddhist practices, both of which deified the king. During the Angkor era, from the ninth to the fifteenth century, the arts blossomed as the Khmer court attracted a large number of Indian scholars, artists, and religious teachers, and supported Sanskrit literature.

The most significant cultural accomplishments of the Khmer Empire were in sculpture and architecture. Sculpture evolved to include far more than statues in the round—sculptures standing freely to be viewed from all directions. Bas-reliefs—sculptures carved from a flat surface so that they project a little from the background—became very important, portraying Khmer life vividly and in rich detail on nearly every wall of later Khmer monuments.

Angkor Wat

From the late 800s to early 1200s, many big construction projects were completed. As a result, Angkor had one of the greatest complexes of buildings in the world. Perhaps the most renowned example of Khmer architecture was the temple of Angkor Wat ("wat" means "monastery"), built as the state temple under Suryavarman II (r. 1113–1150) and considered the most beautiful Khmer monument, both architecturally and ornamentally. The area around Angkor Wat, on the plain of modern-day Siemreap province north of the Tonle Sap Great Lake, became the center of Khmer civilization.

Angkor Thom

A few miles north of Angkor Wat—and also famous for its architecture—was the town of Angkor Thom, whose elaborate monuments were erected under Jayavarman VII (r. 1181–1218). Before he became king, Jayavarman VII won the country back from Champa (a kingdom within present-day Vietnam), which had sacked Angkor in 1177. Jayavarman was a strong king, whose rule started a new era of Khmer conquests as well as significant advances in architec-

ROYAL PLACES

ANGKOR THOM

Built around 1200, the Khmer town of Angkor Thom—with its temple, the Bayon, at the exact center—is the masterpiece of Jayavarman VII's reign. Sometimes referred to as the "walled city," it was a vast rectangular complex (over 2,000 acres) surrounded by more than seven miles of walls and a moat. It had five roads that led to five gateways in the city walls.

The name *Angkor Thom* means "Angkor the great," and indeed it was seen as the source of all the Khmer Empire's treasures, blessings, and opulence. It is thought that more than 100,000 people lived there at its peak. Irrigated rice fields bordering the city were a source of food, and large reservoirs provided drinking water.

The Bayon temple at Angkor Thom was very complex. Consisting of as many as 200,000 enormous blocks of stone formed into flowing sculptures, it was apparently built without mortar or cement. The rich symbolism of its sculptures established it as a temple devoted to Buddhism and dedicated to all the other divinities of the Khmer Empire.

The Bayon also portrayed aspects of day-to-day human life through bas-reliefs on its inner and outer walls. These sculptural reliefs illustrated historical events, such as the Khmer combating an enemy, as well as everyday scenes, such as a man fishing and people preparing meals. Although many of the bas-reliefs are in poor condition today, enough of the scenes remain visible to offer a dynamic and poignant view of the Khmer civilization.

ture and sculpture. He also was a religiously devout ruler, who declared a new form of Buddhism, called Mahayana, to be the state religion. Its main purpose was to appeal to more followers and expand religious authority to a greater number of people. Apparently very moved by the suffering of his people, Jayavarman VII ruled with great compassion, and this was reflected in some of the Buddhist art of the period.

Jayavarman VII constructed numerous monuments—probably more than those of all his predecessors combined. They included many temples in both the capital of Angkor and the provinces. There is also evidence that Jayavarman had more than 100 hospitals built, another indication of how much he cared about the well-being of his people.

DECLINE OF THE EMPIRE

Because of all his accomplishments, Jayavarman VII is considered the greatest of the Khmer rulers. However, his zeal to vanquish and build may have over-whelmed and sapped the energy of his kingdom and its people. While the empire reached unprecedented heights during his reign, no significant monuments were constructed in Angkor afterward, and some people who opposed his imposition of Mahayana Buddhism as the state religion destroyed images of the Buddha on his monuments during the rule of Jayavarman's successors.

The Khmer Empire eventually weakened, as new powers with expansionist aims emerged in Southeast Asia as threats to the Khmer. After the creation of the Ayuthaya kingdom in nearby Thailand, the Thais attacked Angkor repeatedly and weakened Khmer power in the eastern part of the empire. In 1434, the Thais captured Angkor, and the Khmers moved their capital moved south to Phnom Penh, signaling the end of the golden age of the Khmer Empire. After that, the Thais and Khmers deserted Angkor, leaving much of the formerly booming capital to be taken over by the jungle.

See also: AYUTTHAYA KINGDOM; CAMBODIAN KINGDOMS; CHAMPA KINGDOM

FURTHER READING

Dagens, Bruno. *Angkor: Heart of an Asian Empire*. New York: Abrams, 1995.

Zephir, Thierry. *Khmer: The Lost Empire of Cambodia*. New York: Abrams, 1998.

KHUFU (ca. 2600 B.C.E.)

Egyptian king (r. ca. 2640–2615 B.C.E.) of the Fourth Dynasty, known as Cheops in Greek, who built the Great Pyramid at Giza.

Khufu inherited the throne of Egypt from Sneferu (r. ca. 2680–2640 B.C.E.), the founder of the Fourth dynasty, when he was already a middle-aged man. Nevertheless, he chose to embark upon a building project unparalleled in scope, even among the massive funerary structures of Egypt—a huge pyramid at Giza on the west bank of the Nile River.

Khufu's vizier, Hemiunu, was responsible for ensuring that the king's tomb was properly prepared, and it is likely that a whole village of skilled workmen and craftspeople grew up around the enormous building site. These workmen may also have labored on Khufu's lesser-known building projects, including a fleet of massive boats over 120 feet long, built of precious cedarwood, that were to be used by the king in the afterlife.

Little is known of Khufu's life. Soon after his death, his pyramid was looted, leaving little evidence of his reign. Remaining tomb inscriptions indicate that he probably led military expeditions into the Sinai, Libya, and Nubia. Khufu ruled for perhaps twenty-three or twenty-four years, and the ancient Greek historian Herodotus described him as a merciless despot. However, there is no evidence to suggest that Khufu employed any massive slave force to build his own enormous pyramid, his boats, or any of the three smaller pyramids that were erected for Khufu's queens. Rather, it seems likely that descriptions such as that of Herodotus, made 2,000 years after Khufu was laid in his monumental tomb, were merely reactions to the Great Pyramid's awesome size. Herodotus also credits Khufu with writing the Sacred Books, but no document or record of these has survived in any form.

Khufu had at least four wives and many children.

Two of his probable sons, Radjedef (r. 2615–2605 B.C.E.) and Khafre (r. 2605–2580 B.C.E.), succeeded him as pharaoh.

See also: EGYPTIAN DYNASTIES, ANCIENT (BEFORE EIGHTEENTH DYNASTY).

KHWARAZM-SHAH DYNASTY

(1157–1231 C.E.)

Central Asian dynasty that first came to power as Seljuk governors but then ruled independently, eventually controlling central and eastern Iran, Transoxiania, and much of Afghanistan.

In 1098, the Seljuk sultan of Iran, Barqyaruq (r. 1094–1105) appointed Qudbaddin Muhammad as governor of the province of Khwarazm. The first governor of the Khwarasm-Shah dynasty, Qudbaddin (r. 1098–1128) died in 1128, and his son, Atsiz (r. 1128–1156), was made governor by Seljuk Sultan Sanjar (r. 1118–1157).

Financed by heavy taxation, Atsiz began conquering strategic cities. Concerned by Atsiz's heavy-handed rule, Sanjar fought him three times. Although Atsiz's forces were defeated, Sanjar let Atsiz continue ruling because the Kara-Khitai people were invading the province. The Kara-Khitai destroyed Sanjar's army and took the Suljuk ruler prisoner. Soon after, in 1141, Atsiz declared independence. When Sanjar later escaped the Kara-Khitai, Atsiz resubmitted to Seljuk rule.

Atsiz died in 1156 and was succeeded by his son Il-Arslan (r. 1156–1172). In 1157, Il-Arslan again proclaimed independence from the Seljuks. He defeated the Kara-Khitai and the Qarakhanids, a Central Asian Turkish dynasty, and captured the cities of Bukhara and Samarkand.

Upon Il-Arslan's death in 1172, his son, Alaeddin Tekish, assumed the throne. Alaeddin Tekish (r. 1172–1200) again defeated the Kara-Khitai, as well as the Kipchaks, another Central Asian group. In 1183, he captured the province of Khorasan and several years later, in 1194, he overthrew the Iraqi Seljuks. Tekish then took the fort of Arslan-Gusha, one of the vital forts of the Assassins, a violent Muslim group that terrorized parts of Central Asia. When Alaeddin Tekish died in 1200, his son, Alaeddin Muhammad (r. 1200–1220) took the throne.

In 1214, Alaeddin Muhammad destroyed the Kara-Khitai Empire and, soon after, the Gurid sultanate of India. He also signed a treaty with the Mongol ruler, Genghis Khan (r. 1206–1227), in 1218. As a peace gesture, Genghis sent a caravan to Khwarazm, but the merchants were murdered and the emissaries humiliated on the way by a provincial governor in the Khwarazm state. Infuriated, Genghis invaded Khwarazm in 1219 and the next year, he captured the cities of Bukhara, Samarkand, Jend, Khokand, and Urgench.

Alaeddin Muhammad died in exile in 1220. Jalal-al-Din Mangubarti (1220–1231) came to the throne, but the Seljuk sultan, Alaeddin Qaykubad I (r. 1219–1237) defeated his forces in 1230 at the battle of Yassi Chemen. Jalal-al-Din was murdered in 1231, thus ending the Khwarazm-Shah dynasty.

See also: ASIAN DYNASTIES, CENTRAL; GENGHIS KHAN; SELJUQ DYNASTY.

FURTHER READING

Seaman, Gary, and Daniel Marks. *Rulers from the Steppe: State Formation on the Eurasian Periphery.* Los Angeles: Ethnographics Press, Center for Visual Anthropology, University of Southern California, 1991.

Soucek, Svatopluk. *A History of Inner Asia.* New York: Cambridge University Press, 2000.

KIEV, PRINCEDOM OF

(ca. 910–1240 C.E.)

Medieval principality that dominated the region in Russia around the Dnieper and Volga rivers from the ninth to the thirteenth century; also referred to as Kievan Rus or Kievan Russia.

In the tenth century, the city of Kiev on the Dnieper River became an important commercial center for a region dominated by the Riurikid dynasty. The Riurikids were descendants of Rurik, a Rus prince who founded the dynasty in Novgorod in the late 800s and quickly came to dominate the Slavic tribes of the region. Oleg, regent for Rurik's son or descendant Igor, seized Kiev around 910 and established a new state, the Kievan Rus. Oleg (r. 910–941) united the eastern Slavs and freed them from control by the nomadic Khazars. Upon Oleg's death, Rurik's son Igor (r. 941–945) became prince of Kiev.

Rurik's great-grandsons, Vladimir (r. 978–1015) and Iaropolk (r. 972–978), ruled as princes of Novgorod and Kiev, respectively, in the late 900s and early 1000s. War between the brothers resulted in Vladimir becoming prince of Kiev as well in 980. Vladimir continued his conquest of the region, becoming sole ruler of the Kievan Rus within a few years.

During Vladimir's reign, the Kievan Rus changed from a tribal-based system to one of princely rule. He established his sons as governors of the various regions under his control, and he regarded the entire land as belonging to his family. Vladimir also introduced Greek Orthodox Christianity to Kievan Russia, after an initial failed attempt to unify worship of the various Norse, Slavic, Finnish, and Iranian gods worshiped by the disparate peoples of his principality. By 988, Byzantine clergy were active in Kiev, and missionaries traveled to all parts of Vladimir's domain.

Vladimir did not establish a unified country under a single ruler. Each of his sons inherited a part of the realm, and as the family expanded, so did the number of principalities, although the idea of the Kievan Rus as a single entity was never lost. Among the chief principalities were Kiev, Chernigov, Smolensk, and Novgorod. The last named was a city of great commercial importance to the Baltic region, conducting trade with Scandinavia and northern Germany.

Vladimir's son Yaroslav (r. 1019–1054), called Yaroslav the Wise, inherited Novgorod but seized Kiev from his brother Svyatopolk (r. 1015–1019) and presided over the high point of Kievan culture. He made Kiev a political, religious, and cultural capital, building a cathedral, ordering books translated from Greek into Slavic, and revising the law code. During his reign, relations between Russia and the Byzantine Empire worsened for a time. In 1043, Kiev even sent an army and a fleet to attack Constantinople, but the expedition failed and friendly relations were established again by 1052. Yaroslav left his realm to his sons as a group, and although there were periods of peaceful shared rule, they also fought among themselves.

Despite such internal conflicts, Kiev remained the center of the realm. Throughout the eleventh century the princes were capable of uniting under Kiev's leadership against external threat. Within the Riurikid dynasty, the senior member of the eldest generation was supposed to hold the throne of Kiev.

This system led to dynastic conflict in the twelfth century, which continued through the thirteenth and eventually weakened the Kievan Rus.

The instability in Kievan Russia left it vulnerable to threats from outside. In 1237, the Mongols launched an invasion of Russia and sacked a number of cities, including Moscow. A besieged Kiev fell to the Mongols in December 1240. The Mongols devastated Kievan Russia, destroying its agricultural and commercial base, and leaving many cities in ruin.

Kiev's era of dominance ended with the Mongol sack of the city, which also marked the end of the Kievan Rus. The Riurikid dynasty remained the rulers of Russia, however, and continued the custom of giving precedence to the senior prince, who thereafter ruled the city of Vladimir as grand prince. The khans of the Golden Horde (as the Russian Mongol realm was called) regarded the Riurikid princes as their subordinates, confirming or denying their right to rule. In the fourteenth century, the princes of Moscow and Vladimir held the title of grand prince and the dominant position in Russia, both under the Mongols and afterward.

See also: MONGOL EMPIRE; RIURIKID DYNASTY; RUSSIAN DYNASTIES.

FURTHER READING

Freeze, Gregory L., ed. *Russia: A History.* New York: Oxford University Press, 1997.

Riasanovsky, Nicholas V. *A History of Russia.* 6th ed. New York: Oxford University Press, 2000.

Vernadsky, George. *Kievan Russia.* New Haven, CT: Yale University Press, 1973.

KILLING. *See* REGICIDE

KINGDOMS AND EMPIRES

Areas of land that are governed by a common ruler. The term *empire* has its origins in ancient Rome, but today it refers to any realm containing several subject kingdoms ruled by vassals who were answerable to an emperor. For example, King Herod the Great of Judaea (r. 37–4 B.C.E.) was a vassal to Augustus (r. 27 B.C.E.–14 C.E.), the emperor of Rome. The common people usually held such vassal kings in great con-

tempt because they profited from imperial domination by dictating laws that were often unpopular and at odds with tradition. In addition, they often imposed harsh taxation to exact tribute. In some cases, as in that of Herod, the vassal king was not even from the kingdom that he ruled and was thus regarded as an intruder as much as was the emperor.

Some kingdoms were entirely independent from an empire; these included many medieval and Renaissance kingdoms such as Spain. The monarchs who ruled these kingdoms often needed to be strong or faced the danger of being overrun by other kingdoms and empires. Such was the case with eighteenth-century Poland. By the early eighteenth century, the power of Poland's kings had become so limited by the nobility that they could not provide even the basics of defense. Consequently, Poland eventually became a satellite of other nations, in particular Russia, and in the late eighteenth century it was annexed piecemeal by Russia, Prussia, and Austria.

See also: EMPERORS AND EMPRESSES; IMPERIAL RULE; KINGS AND QUEENS.

KINGLY BODY

The physical body and its biological processes both unite monarchs with the humblest of their subjects and provide many opportunities for reinforcing the special nature of monarchs and monarchies. Those who serve a ruler's bodily needs often wield political power, particularly in polities that do not have a governmental bureaucracy. A biblical example is Nehemiah, who went from being a cupbearer to the Persian king to an appointment as governor of the Jewish territory. Early modern English rulers employed their Grooms of the Stool, servants charged with the monarch's excretions, as confidential agents and even treasurers.

BEAUTY AND UGLINESS IN MONARCHICAL BODIES

Physical perfection can be important in a ruler. Some societies have barred persons with conspicuous physical defects from rulership. (Eunuchs, in particular, have been banned from formal rule.) When Byzantine emperors were overthrown, if they were not killed they were often blinded or otherwise mutilated. When Justinian II (r. 685–695) was overthrown in 695, his nose was cut off to signify his loss of power (though he regained the throne in 705 and ruled to 711).

Kings with poor reputations (like other people with poor reputations) were often said to be physically deformed or inadequate. The alleged physical deformities of Richard III of England (r. 1483–1485), "Crookback Dick," were exaggerated after his death. Condemned for murdering his nephews and usurping the throne, he became the royal monster par excellence for English writers under the succeeding Tudor dynasty.

Good kings, by contrast, were often presented as models of physical perfection. The Byzantine princess and historian Anna Comnena, the daughter of Emperor Alexius I (r. 1081–1118), wrote about the father she idolized, emphasizing the effect his physical qualities had on those who met or beheld him and the links between his physique and his power to command:

Alexius was not a very tall man, but broad-shouldered and yet well proportioned. . . . when one saw the grim flash of his eyes . . . he reminded one of a fiery whirlwind, so overwhelming was the radiance that emanated from his countenance and his whole presence. . . . The man's person indeed radiated beauty and grace and dignity and an unapproachable majesty.

Conventions of royal art have often treated monarchs' bodies in an idealized fashion. The Egyptian pharaoh Akhenaten (r. ca. 1350–1334 B.C.E.) broke with conventions of Egyptian art, which portrayed the pharaoh in a standardized and ideal way, to have himself portrayed as a pot-bellied, thin-legged, slightly grotesque man. Ironically, this became a new physical standard, and Akhenaten's courtiers had their own appearance recorded to resemble the appearance of the pharaoh.

THE GENDERED ROYAL BODY

Gender affected the royal body in many ways. Both male and female royal bodies were often associated with the fertility of the land. In early modern Europe, monarchical art often discreetly stressed the monarch's penis, particularly when depicting royal infants. In this case, the penis signified both fertility and membership in the ruling political gender.

Fertility was even more important for queen consorts, central to whose responsibility was the bringing forth of heirs. Queens sometimes emphasized their (clothed) breasts in portraiture, displaying themselves as "nursing mothers" of their families and kingdoms. The virgin queen, Elizabeth I of England (r. 1558–1603), followed a different strategy, presenting herself in a famous speech during the Spanish Armada crisis of 1588 as androgynous. Elizabeth

ROYAL RITUALS

THE FUNERAL OF HENRY VII OF ENGLAND

After the death of Henry VII in 1509, his body was embalmed, encased in lead, and placed in a coffin. The king's body was represented during the ceremonies by an effigy, or statue, in a recumbent position on top of the coffin. The effigy held the symbols of kingship, the orb and scepter, all under a cloth of gold. After a processional involving knights carrying banners and a throng of over fourteen hundred mourners and nearly seven hundred torchholders, the king's coffin and effigy were placed in St. Paul's Cathedral in London with a solemn requiem and then removed the next day to Westminster Abbey, where the final interment took place. After the coffin was lowered into a vault, heralds cried (in French, the formal language of state occasions in England at that time): "The noble King, King Henry the Seventh is dead! Long Live the noble king Henry VIII!" Henry's successor, his son Henry VIII, was not present at his father's funeral. This was common protocol, for the old king was not viewed as being fully dead until burial.

claimed to combine the body of a woman with the "heart and stomach of a king."

ROYAL CORPSES AND THEIR POWERS

A ruler's dead body could be honored or execrated. Kingly bodies were usually buried or otherwise disposed of with honors, but in some cases they received the opposite treatment. The usurping Byzantine emperor Phocas (r. 602–610) had the bodies of his predecessors, the emperor Maurice (r. 582–602), his sons, and closest followers dragged through the streets and burned.

A ruler's remains were sometimes considered unworthy of representing him or her at the last rites. Many European medieval or early modern monarchical funerals used an effigy placed on top of the coffin containing the remains to represent the kingly body. (This custom was not restricted to monarchs.)

The parts of a dead ruler's body were sometimes claimed to have magical or religious powers. The blood of the "martyr king" of England, Charles I (r. 1625–1649), beheaded in 1649, was sopped up in cloths that Royalists then claimed had healing powers.

Some West African Yoruba communities practiced ritual cannibalism to create a physical continuity between an Oba, a local ruler, and his predecessor. Obas are elected monarchs, and the new Oba is not the son of the old one. Igemo chiefs, a priestly group, removed the tongue and heart of the Oba soon after his death, and they were served to the new Oba as part of the accession ceremony. The dead Oba's head was also removed, and in some communities the new Oba drank maize gruel from the skull. This led to controversy in 1960, where the old Oba of the community of Orangun was the first Muslim to serve in the position. His family, also Muslim, claimed that the cutting off of his head violated Islamic law. In a compromise, the head was not removed from the body, but other traditional Yoruba ceremonies took place.

See also: BEHAVIOR, CONVENTIONS OF ROYAL; BODIES, POLITIC AND NATURAL; FUNERALS AND MORTUARY RITUALS; GENDER AND KINGSHIP; GROOMS OF THE STOOL; HEALING POWERS OF KINGS; SACRAL BIRTH AND DEATH.

FURTHER READING

Anglo, Sydney. *Images of Tudor Kingship.* London: Seby, 1992.

Bertelli, Sergio. *The King's Body: Sacred Rituals of Power in Medieval and Early Modern Europe.* Trans. R. Burr Litchfield. University Park: Pennsylvania State University Press, 2001.

Comnena, Anna. *The Alexiad of Anna Comnena: Being the History of the Reign of Her Father, Alexius I, Emperor of the Romans, 1081–1118 A.D.* Trans. Elizabeth A. S. Dawes. New York: Kegan Paul, 2003.

Finer, S. E. *The History of Government from the Earliest Times.* New York: Oxford University Press, 1997.

Pemberton, John, and Funso S. Afolayan. *Yoruba Sacred Kingship: A Power Like That of the Gods.* Washington, DC: Smithsonian Institution Press, 1996.

KINGS AND QUEENS

The rulers of a particular region, or realm. Often, these rulers are believed to be appointed by God, or their right to rule is hereditary. Kingship is an ancient form of rule, going back thousands of years in societies such as those in ancient Mesopotamia and China. Many cultures have had kings or queens at some time, although both ancient Greece and ancient Rome had a history of representative government.

EARLY EVIDENCE OF KINGSHIP

Among the earliest surviving documents of antiquity are king-lists—rosters of kings with occasional notes on their achievements. Such lists are found in numerous cultures around the world, from the king-lists of ancient Sumeria in Mesopotamia, which date from the early second millennium B.C.E., to lists of the Pictish kings of ancient and early medieval Scotland.

King-lists are often unreliable as sources of dates, citing impossibly long reigns for the earliest kings, but they are important for noting a ruler's important achievements, and they provide some sense of what each culture valued. The Sumerian king-lists cite five dynasties before a Great Flood, and many of the kings named are possibly legendary. The listings of later rulers, however, note reigns of more reasonable length, and the Sumerian king-lists become more credible as a source of historical information. Similarly, an early historian at the court of the Han dynasty (207 B.C.E.–220 C.E.) in China, Suma Qian, provides only a skeletal listing of the rulers of the semi-legendary Xia dynasty and only occasionally provides important information about them.

HEREDITARY BASIS OF KINGSHIP

Throughout history, monarchs have generally come from the ruling class or aristocracy of a society. In some cases, kings or queens are chosen by the aristocracy in an election of some sort, but in most countries, the right of succession to the throne is hereditary. Some societies may practice matrilineal inheritance, in which the king inherits through the maternal line. In most cases, however, inheritance and succession to the throne are patrilineal, through the male line; if there is no son to inherit, the throne may go to the king's brother or a male cousin.

RELIGIOUS BASIS OF KINGSHIP

In many cultures, kingship has a religious basis. In ancient Sumeria, for example, kingship was said to have descended from heaven. Similarly, both the Egyptian pharaohs and the emperors of Rome were exalted as gods. God also appointed the kings of ancient Israel; the Old Testament tells how the prophet Samuel first anointed Saul (r. 1020–1010 B.C.E.), and then David (r. 1010–970 B.C.E.), as king of the Israelites.

In ancient China, although the state did not impose any particular religion, the emperor was nonetheless perceived as an intercessor between the ordinary people and heaven. As late as World War II, the Japanese emperor was still considered a god, and even today, a Shinto-oriented, war museum in Japan claims that the emperor Hirohito (r. 1926–1989) never renounced his divinity, as Westerners believe, and remains a divine being. In Christian Europe, from the early Middle Ages to today, the anointing and coronation of a monarch are performed by a bishop, signifying the bond between religion and kingship.

MILITARY BASIS OF KINGSHIP

In earliest times, a monarch needed to have strong military skills as well as the ability to govern. For example, with the invasions of Europe by Germanic tribes beginning in the first centuries C.E., European monarchs needed to be able to defend their country, and much of a monarch's legitimacy was based on his qualities as a warrior. This remained true throughout Europe during the Middle Ages and, in some countries, well into the Renaissance. In contrast, a king who would not, or could not, fight when necessary risked being deposed or conquered by a stronger warrior.

Because monarchs led their armies into battle and frequently conquered the countries they ruled, a king often held more power than a queen, who may have served only as a consort. Women, however, also ruled in their own right, and in some cases, they even rode with their armies, as did Eleanor of Aquitaine in the twelfth century and Isabella I of Spain (r. 1474–1504) in the sixteenth century.

WOMEN RULERS

With the establishment of the European nation-state beginning in the Renaissance, women rulers became more accepted, if infrequent. From the sixteenth to eighteenth centuries, Europe saw a number of powerful queens, including Elizabeth I of England (r. 1558–1603); Maria Theresa of Austria, Bohemia, and Hungary (r. 1740–1780); and Catherine the Great of Russia (r. 1762–1796). Although female rulers were rare in the Near East and Asia, China saw two great female rulers, the Empress Wu (r. 690–705) and Dowager Empress Tz'u Hsi (Cixi) (r. 1874–1908), and Japan had several women rulers in the early periods of its history.

See also: DYNASTY; KINGDOMS AND EMPIRES; QUEENS AND QUEEN MOTHERS; REALMS, TYPES OF; ROYAL FAMILIES; SUCCESSION, ROYAL.

FURTHER READING

Miller, Townsend. *The Castles and the Crown: Spain 1451–1555.* New York: Coward-McCann, 1986.

Weir, Alison. *The Wars of the Roses.* New York: Ballantine, 1996.

KIPCHAK KHANATE. *See* GOLDEN HORDE KHANATE

KNUT. *See* CNUT I, THE GREAT

KOGURYO KINGDOM

(ca. 37 B.C.E.–667 C.E.)

The first of Korea's three early native kingdoms.

Koguryo was established in 37 B.C.E. when a tribe from the Puyo state in Manchuria forcefully occupied a large region of land that extended from Manchuria's eastern border to the northern Korean Peninsula. Initially, the settlers did not develop a cohesive economy or society, but instead staged repeated raids on neighboring China to obtain food and material goods. These raids fostered a permanent enmity between Koguryo and China.

AN EMERGING POWER

During the first century C.E., King Taejo (r. 53–146) emerged as Koguryo's first major ruler. He aggressively expanded the borders of the kingdom, first by conquering Okcho to the southeast and then by annexing Chinese holdings in the northwest part of the Korean Peninsula. Taejo allowed local leaders in these regions to retain authority in return for large tributary payments of rice and other agricultural products. These tributes were essential to Koguryo because much of the kingdom's mountainous terrain was not arable.

Taejo also consolidated his power. Before his accession, the rulers of Koguryo were elected from among a few elite families. However, Taejo decreed that the throne would pass from brother to brother and remain within his family, the Kyeru-bus. To preserve his authority, Taejo also instituted a system of regional governors, who answered directly to him and collected local tributes. During Taejo's reign, the first formal laws of Koguryo were enacted. These laws provided harsh penalties for murder, assault, theft, and female adultery. Wives could also be punished for overt acts of jealousy.

When King Kogukchon (r. 179–197) assumed the throne in 179, he revised Taejo's rule of succession; the Crown would now pass from father to son rather than from brother to brother. He also divided Koguryo into five distinct provinces dependent upon the central government. Most significantly, under Kogukchon, Koguryo again sought to absorb additional land.

In 313, under King Michon (r. 300–331), Koguryo conquered the Chinese military outpost at Lolang. During this period, the rival Korean kingdom of Paekche also overthrew the Chinese fortification of Taifang. With the conquest of these two outposts, China was expelled from the Korean Peninsula, and both Koguryo and Paekche emerged as the region's major powers.

CONFLICT AND RECOVERY

Conflict between Koguryo and Paekche erupted in 371, when Paekche invaded Koguryo, captured the

Kings of Koguryo

TONG-MYONG	37–19 B.C.E.
YU-RI	19–18
TAE-MU-SIN	18 B.C.E.–44 C.E.
MIN-JUNG	44–48
MO-BON	48–53
T'AE-JO	53–146
CH'A-DAE	146–165
SIN-DAE	165–179
KO-GUK-CH'ON	179–197
SAN-SANG	197–227
TONG-CH'ON	227–248
CHUNG-CH'ON	248–270
SO-CH'ON	270–292
PONG-SANG	292–300
MI-CH'ON	300–331
KO-GUG-WON	331–371
SO-SU-RIM	371–384
KO-GUG-YANG	384–391
KWANG-GAE-T'O	391–413
CHANG-SU	413–492
MUN-JA	492–519
AN-JANG	519–531
AN-WON	531–545
YANG-WON	545–559
PYONG-WON	559–590
YONG-YANG	590–618
YONG-YU	618–642
PO-JANG	642–668

city of Pyongyang, and killed King Kogugwon (r. 331–371). The defeat severely weakened Koguryo, but it also allowed the society of the kingdom to be transformed. In 372, Kogugwon's successor, King Sosurim (r. 371–384), adopted Buddhism as the state religion and used it to unify Koguryo spiritually. Sosurim also adopted many Confucian principles, and he modeled a new bureaucracy after the overriding Confucian belief in fidelity. In addition, Sosurim negotiated peace with the rival Paekche, providing the Koguryo army with an opportunity to recover from its devastating loss to that rival kingdom.

Koguryo's recovery occurred during the reign of King Kwanggaeto (r. 391–413). Kwanggaeto conquered the eastern Chinese province of Liao-tung, subjugated the Manchurians in the north, regained the territory lost to Paekche, and repelled a Japanese invasion of Silla, a neighboring Korean kingdom and Koguryo's ally. His son, King Changsu (r. 413–492), maintained these conquests by negotiating with the rival Sui and Tang dynasties in China and preventing them from mounting a unified invasion of Koguryo.

During Changsu's reign, Koguryo experienced its greatest prosperity. Pyongyang, the kingdom's new capital, quickly became an active commercial center, and a number of families in the city achieved great power and formed the highest level of society. Many were given government positions based on wealth and heredity. In this manner, a social system emerged that was parallel to Silla's "bone-rank," in which birth determined one's social position.

Areas beyond Pyongyang were tightly controlled. Changsu divided Koguryo into administrative districts, each with its own fortress and governor to command the local military and bureaucracy. Appointed officials within these districts headed local villages, collecting taxes from the peasantry and arbitrating minor disputes.

Although China posed a constant military threat to Koguryo, the kingdom—along with Paekche and Silla—enthusiastically imported Chinese goods and culture. But Koguryo also developed its own cultural institutions during its period of prosperity in the late 400s and 500s. The monarchy commissioned written national histories, while Buddhist monks wrote the *hyangga*—poetic songs that called for divine intervention in earthly events. Gilt bronze sculptures produced in Koguryo were also highly prized throughout the region.

CONFLICT WITH CHINA

Conflict with China eventually interrupted Koguryo's prosperity. In the late sixth and early seventh centuries, Koguryo sought an alliance with the Central Asian Turks to counter the growing power of China's Sui dynasty. In response, the Sui emperor, Yang Ti (r. 604–617), launched a widespread inva-

ROYAL RITUALS

KOGURYO BURIALS

Because wood was the primary building material in Koguryo, examples of Koguryo architecture no longer exist. However, Koguryo's tombs reveal the great importance its monarchs placed on death and the afterlife. These tombs were elaborate rooms with vaulted ceilings carved into the earth. Each tomb was given a specific name, and the walls of each tomb were carefully painted to reflect its name. For example, the Tomb of the Four Spirits contains dazzling renditions of the azure dragon of the East, the white tiger of the West, the red phoenix of the South, and the tortoise and snake of the North. These paintings are often highly detailed and extremely realistic. Artists specialized in tomb painting, and several developed such widespread reputations that they traveled to Japan to paint both tombs and temples.

sion of Koguryo. In 612, Yang Ti led nearly a million soldiers in an attack upon Liaotung. When the attack failed, he ordered 300,000 of his soldiers to attack Pyongyang, but the Koguryo general Mundok ambushed the Chinese forces at the Salsu River. The Koguryo victory over the Sui forces was overwhelming; only 2,500 Chinese soldiers survived. After this defeat, the Sui dynasty rapidly dissolved.

With the decline of the Sui dynasty, the Tang dynasty assumed control of China. Under the Tang emperor Tai Tsung (r. 626–649), the Chinese again prepared for a massive invasion of Koguryo. This renewed threat caused a severe political upheaval in Koguryo in 642. During this turbulence, general Yon Kaesomun seized control and assassinated the king of Koguryo, Yong Yu (r. 618–642). When the Chinese attacked in 645, they successfully destroyed several of the provincial fortresses, but Kaesomun's forces defeated the Chinese at Anshih Fortress and the invaders were once again repelled.

The costly victory, however, left the Koguryo forces irreparably weakened. Recognizing an opportunity to become the preeminent power on the Korean Peninsula, the kingdom of Silla joined forces with the Tang dynasty, and together, they eliminated Paekche in 660. Seven years later, they reunited and attacked Koguryo. Unable to resist this formidable alliance, the Koguryo forces crumbled and the area fell under Chinese and Silla control. Although refugees from Koguryo fled north and founded the Parhae kingdom, the Koguryo kingdom was effectively ended.

Despite its final defeat, Koguryo had stubbornly repulsed two previous massive Chinese invasions. If either of these invasions had succeeded, China would have absorbed the Korean Peninsula into its empire. Instead, Koguryo's resistance allowed Silla to develop its military strength. Although Silla used this strength against Koguryo, it also enabled Silla to preserve Korea's autonomy.

See also: PAEKCHE KINGDOM; SILLA KINGDOM; SUI DYNASTY; T'ANG DYNASTY.

FURTHER READING

Eckert, Carter J., et al. *Korea Old and New.* Cambridge, MA: Harvard University Press, 1990.
Lee, Ki-baik. *A New History of Korea.* Trans. Edward W. Wagner, with Edward J. Schultz. Cambridge, MA: Harvard University Press, 1984.

KONDAVIDU KINGDOM

(ca. 1336–1518 C.E.)

Kingdom located near the mouth of the Krishna River on the eastern coast of India, which struggled to attain independence during the decline of the Tughluq dynasty.

The Kondavidu kingdom was founded in the 1300s by a local leader named Prolaya Vema (r. 1324–1353), who took advantage of the declining power of the Tughluq dynasty to seize territory in northern and central India. During his reign, Vema struggled to distance his kingdom from the incessant warfare between Bahmani and Vijayanagar, two powerful empires that emerged after the Tughluqs lost power. Kondavidu was constantly threatened because it occupied a strategic position between the two hostile empires. When Prolaya died in 1353, his successors, Anapota Vema (r. 1353–1364) and Anapota Reddi (r. 1364–1386), could no longer prevent external aggression.

In 1365, after defeating the Bahmanis in a crucial battle, Vijayanagar eagerly annexed significant portions of Kondavidu territory. Vijayanagar invaded Kondavidu again in 1382. Desperate to preserve some semblance of autonomy, the Kondavidu monarch, Anapota Reddi, formed an alliance with Bahmani. The enmity between Bahmani and Vijayanagar had religious origins; Bhamani was a Muslim kingdom while Vijayanagar was Hindu. Although Kondavidu was also a Hindu kingdom, it joined Bahmani because the Bahmani sultans had been less overtly aggressive toward Kondavidu.

Because of its alliance with Bahmani, Kondavidu experienced two decades of relative security. In 1402, however, internal strife devastated the kingdom. Upon the death of the Kondavidu monarch, Kumaragiri (r. 1386–1402), two of his relatives, Peda Komati Veda and Kataya Vema, both claimed the throne. Kataya quickly seized two major cities and allied himself with Vijayangar. Consequently, Bahmani and Vijayanagr were once again drawn into a bloody war. Kataya was eventually defeated, Peda Komati Veda (r. 1402–1420) assumed the throne, and Kondavidu enjoyed twenty more years of autonomy under Bahmani protection.

Vijaynagar's urge to control Kondavidu could not be assuaged, however. By 1427, Vijayanagar forces had again invaded Kondavidu, this time successfully holding the kingdom and repelling the Bahmani army. Kondavidu thus became a completely sub-servient territory of the Vijayanagar Empire.

In 1454, Kondavidu gained one last chance for au-tonomy. The kingdom of Orissa, which straddled the northeastern border of the Vijayanagar Empire, in-vaded Kondavidu and expelled Vijayanagar from the kingdom. The Kondavidu people hoped that the Orissans would adopt the Bahmani position and allow them conditional independence in return for allegiance. But Orissa merely assumed Vijayanagar's position and took full control of Kondavidu.

Vijayanagar regained control of the region in 1518 after a power struggle with Orissa, and Kon-davidu ceased to exist as an autonomous kingdom. Despite its aspirations of independence, Kondavidu ultimately failed to maintain its autonomy because it was coveted by more powerful empires.

See also: BAHMANI DYNASTY; INDIAN KINGDOMS; VI-JAYANAGAR EMPIRE.

KONGBAUNG DYNASTY. *See*

ALAUNGPAYA DYNASTY

KONGO KINGDOM

(ca. 1480–1700s C.E.)

First of the powerful kingdoms to emerge in west-central Africa, as European explorers began making contact with the peoples of Africa south of the Sahara.

Located in what is now the nation of Angola, the kingdom of Kongo arose in west-central Africa during the late 1400s from a collection of several smaller, in-dependent states. These member states joined to-gether under a king who was elected from among the various chiefly families and, with their combined strength, came to dominate the region. An adminis-trative capital was established at Mbanza Kongo.

Rule of the Kongo kingdom was coordinated through the offices of provincial governors, who were appointed by the king and served wholly at his plea-sure. These officials were usually drawn from the fam-ily of the king himself in order to ensure their loyalty to the throne. Kongo rulers maintained a standing

army in the capital to secure the peace. By 1600, the origins of the Kongo kingdom as a loose confedera-tion of small states were largely obscured, and it had become a fully integrated, centralized state.

Early in the history of the Kongo kingdom, the first Europeans arrived in west-central Africa. The first Eu-ropean contact was with a Portuguese expedition that arrived in 1483 seeking permission to cross Kongo territory on their way to the coast. The ruler of Kongo at that time was Nzingu Kuwu (r. 1484–1506), who welcomed the arrival of the Portuguese. He saw these newcomers as potential allies in his efforts to consoli-date his power. In a gesture of goodwill, Nzinga Kuwu accepted conversion to Christianity and received the baptismal name of Joao I.

Joao I, however, quickly grew disillusioned with his new European allies. He was angered by what he saw as their greed and corruption, and he was par-ticularly displeased with the aggressive missionary activities carried out by the religious order of Jesuits. In his anger, he rejected Christianity and encouraged all his subjects to return to the religion of their an-cestors. Toward the end of his reign, Joao summoned the power of his military and ordered the Portuguese to leave his kingdom.

The break with the Portuguese was short-lived, however. When Nzingu Nkuwu (Joao I) died, his son, Mvemba Nzinga (Afonso I, r. 1506–1543) assumed the throne and once again welcomed the Europeans. Under Afonso's rule, Christianity spread rapidly throughout the Kongo kingdom. He hoped to keep the Portuguese as his exclusive allies, thus keeping for his kingdom a monopoly over the lucrative trade develop-ing between Portugal and the region. In this, however, he failed, and Portugal soon forged strong ties with Afonso's regional rival, the kingdom of Ndongo.

This turned out to be an unexpectedly good thing for the Kongo kingdom, however. The Portuguese annexed the Ndongo territory during the 1600s, whereas Kongo retained its autonomy during that period. It remained independent even during a civil war that erupted out of a succession dispute upon the death of King Antonio I (r. ca. 1660–1665) in 1665.

This war was but the first of many civil insurrec-tions that ravaged the Kongo kingdom over the next several years. These struggles involved three primary factions, each laying claim to the throne and each con-trolling roughly a third of the kingdom. The violence of these insurrections, and the practice of selling captured adversaries as slaves to European traders, devastated Kongo for decades.

Finally, King Pedro IV of the Kongo (r. 1709–1718) succeeded in restoring the monarchy and establishing some semblance of order in the kingdom. Nonetheless, the days of Kongo dominance in the region were over, for the Portuguese had gained ascendancy. The kingdom's independence did not long survive as an independent entity. Soon after Pedro's rule, the kingdom became a constituent part of the larger Portuguese colonial enterprise in the region.

See also: AFONSO I, NZINGA MBEMBA; AFRICAN KINGDOMS; LUNDA KINGDOM.

FURTHER READING

Hilton, Anne. *The Kingdom of the Kongo.* New York: Oxford University Press, 1985.

KORYO KINGDOM (918–1392 C.E.)

Korean kingdom that bridged the gap between Korea's earlier civilizations and the powerful Yi dynasty, which ruled Korea from 1392 to 1910.

The Koryo kingdom emerged during the tenth century when it conquered the kingdom of Silla, becoming the only kingdom on the Korean Peninsula. Extreme civil unrest, fueled by unbearable taxes on the peasantry and barriers that prevented the aristocratic class from gaining high government positions, contributed to Silla's collapse. During this unrest, a military commander named Wang Kon assembled displaced peasants into a formidable military force. Initially, he protected the kingdom of Silla against other rebellious peasants. But in 918, Wang Kon seized the throne and changed the kingdom's name to Koryo, a variation of the name Koguryo, an earlier Korean kingdom.

Wang Kon (r. 918–943) eliminated the rigid system that had prescribed social position in Silla and invited members of aristocratic families and descendants of the fallen Koguryo nobility to join the new government. Still, before his death in 943, Wang Kon failed to suppress the large groups of bandits that continued to terrorize the outskirts of Koryo and threatened the newly formed kingdom.

CHANGES IN KORYO SOCIETY

In 949, King Kwangjong (r. 949–975) stabilized Koryo by creating civil service examinations for both the bureaucracy and the Buddhist clergy. These exams, which based promotion upon merit, created new opportunities for Koryo citizens and helped to staunch the possibility of rebellion. Kwangjong also instituted Confucianism as the official state religion, although most Koryo citizens still adhered to Buddhism.

Kwangjong's reforms did not permanently erase civil unrest, however. Although the exams were open to everyone, only wealthy citizens could afford the education necessary to pass them. Consequently, an extremely small group of bureaucrats, called the literati, achieved complete control of the government. During their ascendancy, Koryo society became highly stratified, much like Silla's had been.

In 1170, the Royal Guard Regiment, the best-trained unit in the Koryo army, deposed and executed nearly all of the literati. But the generals who led the coup badly mismanaged the government, and Koryo endured three decades of near anarchy. In 1196, General Choe Chunghon slaughtered his rivals and established a dictatorship. Chunghon created an elite military force to protect his authority, installed the Koryo king as a mere figurehead, and re-created the literati class to run the government.

DICTATORSHIP AND FOREIGN RULE

Under the Choe dictatorship, Koryo society assumed an almost feudalistic structure. Chunghon and his successors seized large amounts of land and enslaved thousands of peasants to farm it. Many leading military leaders also created huge estates. At the same time, however, Chunghon based military and civil promotion solely upon merit, which enabled a new nobility to emerge among the literati.

A foreign threat eventually crippled the Choe dictatorship. In 1219, Koryo joined the Mongols to defeat the Khitan. But in 1224, the Mongols demanded a huge annual tribute from Koryo. The ruling Choe dictator refused, and, in 1231, he retreated to Kanghwa Island off the mouth of the Han River. For years afterward, the Mongols repeatedly ravaged Koryo, slaughtering countless citizens and razing the country's major cities until, in 1258, a small group of officials assassinated Choe Ui, the final Choe dictator, and surrendered to the Mongols.

The Mongols were harsh rulers. They exacted an exorbitant tribute from Koryo, held the Koryo king prisoner, annexed most of the northern part of the kingdom, and squandered Koryo's navy during two

Wang Dynasty

T'AE-JO	918–943	MYONG-JONG	1170–1197
HYE-JONG	943–945	SIN-JONG	1197–1204
CHONG-JONG	945–949	HUI-JONG	1204–1211
KWANG-JONG	949–975	KANG-JONG	1211–1213
KYONG-JONG	975–981	KO-JONG	1213–1259
SONG-JONG	981–997	WON-JONG	1259–1274
MOK-CHONG	997–1009	CH'UNG-YOL	1274–1308
HYON-JONG	1009–1031	CH'UNG-SON	1308–1313
TOK-CHONG	1031–1034	CH'UNG-SUK (I)	1313–1330
CHONG-JONG	1034–1046	CH'UNG-HYE (I)	1330–1332
MUN-JONG	1046–1083	CH'UNG-SUK (2)	1332–1339
SUN-JONG	1083	CH'UNG-HYE (2)	1339–1344
SON-JONG	1083–1094	CH'UNG-MOK	1344–1348
HON-JONG	1094–1095	CH'UNG-JONG	1348–1351
SUK-CHONG	1095–1105	KONG-MIN	1351–1374
YE-JONG	1105–1122	WI-JU	1374–1388
IN-JONG	1122–1146	CH'ANG	1388–1389
UI-JONG	1146–1170	KONG-YANG	1389–1392

failed invasions of Japan. For the next century, the Mongol influence significantly altered Koryo's language and culture.

REGAINED POWER AND FINAL COLLAPSE

In 1351, King Kongmin (r. 1351–1374) struggled to reassert Koryo's independence. Taking advantage of a rebellion within the Mongol court, Kongmin eliminated the Mongol administration in Koryo and regained the annexed lands. He also attempted to confiscate the large estates that the Mongols had granted to Koryo aristocrats sympathetic to Mongol rule, but a group of these aristocrats assassinated Kongmin before he could achieve that goal.

Under Kongmin, the literati regained control of the Koryo government and exerted the power they had possessed before the Choe dictatorship. However, between 1374 and 1388, foreign dangers again disrupted Koryo's stability. During that time, Japanese pirates repeatedly ravaged Koryo's eastern shores, and the newly formed Ming dynasty in China threatened Koryo's northern region. Yi Songgye, a Koryo general, achieved much influence by repulsing the Japanese raids. In 1388, he assumed control of the army; four years later he deposed the last Koryo king, Kongyang (r. 1389–1392), and changed the country's name to Choson. Yi's actions marked the beginning of the Yi dynasty and the end of Koryo.

Despite its downfall, the Koryo kingdom had fundamentally altered Korea's history. The literati class, formed at the beginning of the Koryo period, maintained a permanent influence in Korean society. Furthermore, Koryo's successes against Mongol, Japanese, and Chinese invaders allowed a distinct Korean culture to continue to develop.

See also: CHOSON KINGDOM; SILLA KINGDOM; WANG KON; YI SONGGYE.

FURTHER READING

Lee, Ki-baik. *A New History of Korea.* Trans. Edward W. Wagner, with Edward J. Schultz. Cambridge, MA: Harvard University Press, 1984.

KOSALA KINGDOM

(ca. 600–468 B.C.E.)

Kingdom located near present-day Oudh, a province in northern India, which was one of the sixteen states of ancient India.

Aryan tribes first migrated into northern India during the third millennium B.C.E. During the succeeding centuries, these tribes gradually split and established sixteen separate states. One of these, the kingdom of Kosala, extended from the Gandak River in the east to the Panchala River in the west, and from the Sarpika River in the south to the foothills of the Himalaya Mountains in Nepal in the north. The city of Sravasti served as the kingdom's capital.

During the sixth century B.C.E., Kosala conquered the neighboring state of Kasi, temporarily making Kosala one of the most powerful of the sixteen Indian states. Because of its increased strength, the kingdom developed a bitter, unappeasable rivalry with the Magadha kingdom, another powerful state located southeast of Kosala. Constant warfare between the two threatened to eventually eradicate both kingdoms. Finally, King Prasenjit (d. 468 B.C.E.), the most famous Kosala monarch, achieved peace with Magadha when his daughter married Bimbisara, the Magadhan king.

But Bimbisara's adult son, Ajatasatru, murdered his father and stepmother and seized the throne. Enraged by his daughter's murder, Prasenjit invaded Magadha and defeated the young usurper. In order to keep his throne, Ajatasatru pledged loyalty to Kosala and paid an immense tribute. He also asked Prasenjit's permission to attack the kingdom of Lichchhavi, promising to divide his spoils with Kosala.

Foolishly, the Kosala monarch agreed. Ajatasatru successfully subdued the Lichchhavis, but he used the resources from his conquest to reengage the Kosala army. Unprepared for such an attack by its ally, the Kosala army crumbled, and Prasenjit was forced to accept a treaty that now made his kingdom subservient to Magadha.

Prasenjit's perceived devotion to Buddhism also undermined his kingdom. The monarch and Siddhartha Gautama (the Buddha) were contemporaries. Although he never converted to Buddhism, Prasenjit frequently visited the seer and his clan, the Sakyas. These visits upset his Hindu subjects. Moreover, Prasenjit even requested that a princess from the Sakya clan marry a Kosala prince. The Sakyas were angered by the request, but they feared Kosala's military power. The Sakyas offered an illegitimate princess to Prasenjit instead, but they concealed her illegitimacy. The marriage took place, but the princess's status was soon discovered.

When Prasenjit refused to disinherit the princess, the Kosala people rebelled and crowned a new monarch. Prasenjit begged Magadha for support, but King Ajatasatru ignored him. When Prasenjit died in 468 B.C.E., Ajatasatru reinvaded Kosala, defeated the new monarch, and ended Kosala's independence.

See also: INDIAN KINGDOMS; MAGADHA KINGDOM.

KOTA KINGDOM (1627–1771 C.E.)

Kingdom in northwestern India, located in the region known as Rajputana ("country of the Rajputs"), that was established by a branch of the Chauhan dynasty, a Rajput clan, in the early seventeenth century.

In 1625, Shah Jahan (r. 1628–1658), heir to the Mughal Empire, rebelled against his father, Jahangir (r. 1605–1627) because Jahangir was apparently planning to name another successor to the throne. The conflict divided kingdoms throughout India. The Raja of the state of Bundi supported Jahangir, but his youngest son, Madho Singh, defied his father and fought for Shah Jahan. Although Shah Jahan's rebellion was suppressed, he later reconciled with his father and remained heir. In 1627, when Shah Jahan assumed the Mughal throne, he created the Kota kingdom and bequeathed it to Madho Singh (r. 1625–1656) to reward his loyalty.

During the early years of its existence, the Kota kingdom was highly unstable. To create the kingdom,

Shah Jahan had merely issued a royal dictate and he ignored the indigenous Bhil tribe of the region. Madho Singh was left to subdue the Bhils. He was largely successful, but when he died in 1656, his five sons struggled for the throne. Their dispute threatened to dissolve the infant nation. Eventually, the eldest son, Mokund Singh (r. 1656–1657) gained control.

Bhim Singh (r. 1707–1719), who took the title *Maha Rao* ("Great King"), was the most powerful Kota monarch. Drawing upon his alliance with the Mughals, he first attacked the neighboring Amber kingdom and then proceeded to assault his relatives in Bundi. During Bhim Singh's reign, Kota expanded its borders well beyond its originally territory.

After Bhim Singh's death in 1719, however, Kota's influence in the region began to decline. In 1723, when Durjan Sal (r. 1723–1756) assumed the throne, Mughal control over India was waning and the Marathas of the Western Deccan region were rapidly expanding across the Indian subcontinent. To ensure Kota's continued existence, Durjan Singh swiftly switched his allegiance from the Mughals to the Marathas. The Marathas did not try to occupy or incorporate states under their control; they only wanted to ensure the fealty of the various Rajput states. As a result, they exercised minimal control over the region.

Initially, this autonomy benefited the Kota kingdom. But without a strong Maratha presence, the other Rajput states united to avenge the earlier incursions against them by Bhim Singh. In 1761, Kota was nearing collapse when Zalim Singh, a distant relative of the royal family, rallied the Kota army and defeated the Rajput invaders. Zalim's victory gained him an elevated position at court. In 1771, when ten-year-old Umed Singh (r. 1771–1819) inherited the throne, Zalim was appointed as his regent. Embracing the opportunity, Zalim executed both Umed and the entire royal family. The remaining nobility fled Kota, and Zalim (r. 1771–1826) assumed control.

In 1817, under Zalim's leadership, Kota became one of the first Rajput states to sign a treaty with the British, making it part of British India. In return, the British agreed that Kota would be divided and a separate kingdom carved out of it for Zalim's descendants. This resulted in the formation of the new kingdom of Jhalawar in 1838.

See also: BUNDI KINGDOM; INDIAN KINGDOMS; JAHAN, SHAH; JAHANGIR; MARATHA CONFEDERACY; MUGHAL EMPIRE; RAJASTHAN KINGDOM.

KUANG HSÜ (GUANG XU)

(1871–1908 C.E.)

Chinese emperor (r. 1875–1908) of the Ch'ing (Qing) dynasty, whose attempts to modernize China were thwarted by the Empress Dowager T'zu Hsi (Cixi).

Named Ts'ai T'ien (Caitian) at birth, Kuang Hsü (Guang Xu) became the ninth Ch'ing emperor at age four, when his aunt, the Empress Dowager T'zu Hsi, placed him on the throne. Having ruled China as regent to the previous emperor, Tz'u Hsi wished to retain control by serving as regent to Kuang Hsü, the son of her younger sister. Controversy surrounded the succession. Because Kuang Hsü was of the same generation as the previous emperor, his cousin T'ung Chih (Tongzhi) (r. 1861–1875), he could not by law properly perform the required Confucian rites to honor his predecessor. Tz'u Hsi appeased angry Confucian scholars by promising that Kuang Hsü would perform these rites in honor of T'ung Chih.

Kuang Hsü was a sickly individual, plagued by lung problems. As a child, he was frightened of his aunt Tz'u Hsi, and continued to be dominated by her for most of his life. Though he came of age in 1887, the manipulative Tz'u Hsi stayed on as regent for another two years.

Unlike his aunt, Kuang Hsü was well educated and conscientious. The young emperor studied English and sought solutions to the crises that threatened the empire. He was aware that the Chinese people were angry at increasing foreign dominance of China, especially in trade and industry. Foreign nations also laid claim to ever-larger areas of Chinese territory.

In response to these challenges, Kuang Hsü turned to the reformer K'ang Yu Wei (Kang Youwei), who supported modernization of China's institutions. In 1898, Kuang Hsü issued the "Hundred Days' Reforms," a series of edicts that called for sweeping changes to the educational system, the military, the economy, and the bureaucracy. Empress Dowager Tz'u Hsi, siding with more conservative forces, opposed these changes. In the power struggle that ensued, Tz'u Hsi triumphed, and Kuang Hsü was detained in the summer palace. He remained Tz'u Hsi's prisoner for the rest of his life.

Kuang Hsü died in 1908 at age thirty-seven. Suspiciously, his death came one day before that of Tz'u

Hsi, who had appointed his nephew, the three-year-old Pu Yi, to succeed him.

See also: CH'ING (QING) DYNASTY; T'ZU HSI (CIXI).

KUANG WU TI (GUANG WUDI) (5 B.C.E.–57 C.E.)

Chinese emperor (r. 25–57) who founded the Eastern Han dynasty (23–220). Kuang Wu Ti ("shining martial emperor") was a wealthy landowner and a cousin of the Han imperial family. Originally named Liu Xiu, he reunited China and reestablished the Han dynasty after the fall of the brief Xin dynasty (9–23). Kuang Wu Ti inherited a China devastated by two years of civil war in which the Western Han capital at Chang'an was destroyed. The emperor established a new capital to the east at the city of Luoyang, and the new dynasty is therefore known as the Eastern or Later Han.

A talented leader, Kuang Wu Ti instituted Confucianism as the state doctrine, suppressed rebel groups, and restored Chinese territory lost since the Western Han period. His reign brought peace and prosperity to China. Kuang Wu Ti strengthened the economy, reducing the tax burden on China's peasants and reestablishing the state monopolies on salt, iron, and liquor instituted by earlier Han rulers. He promoted Confucian rituals and education, establishing government-sponsored schools to train candidates for the civil service in the classical texts. Kuang Wu Ti also increased the number of officials who won posts through the examination system. The first record of an official visit from Japan comes from Kuang Wu Ti's reign.

Kuang Wu Ti's reign was marred by the growing power of the families of imperial consorts, a trend that would cause the dynasty's decline in succeeding generations. Kuang Wu Ti was succeeded by his son, Mingdi (r. 57–75).

See also: HAN DYNASTY.

KUBA KINGDOM

(ca. 1600s C.E.–Present)

Kingdom established by Bantu immigrants on the Sankuru River in what is now the Democratic Republic of Congo.

In the late 1400s, the Sankuru River of southeastern Congo (Zaire) was occupied by a people called the Twa. Into this region came a group of Bantu migrants called the Bushoong (or Shoong) who had traveled from the far north and who chose this fertile land as their new home.

Over the next hundred years, these immigrants absorbed the Twa peoples into their own society. As their settlements grew in size and territory, the Bushoong did the same with many other peoples living in the region, including the Ngeende, Kel, Pyaang, Bulaang, Ilebo, Kaam, and Ngongo.

The territory controlled by the Bushoong came to include more than fifteen ethnic groups, but only the founding group, the Shoong themselves, could produce a king. This was dictated by their creation myth, which also provided the basis for divine claim to the kingship.

Around 1600, a dynamic Bushoong leader named Shyaam declared himself the first *nyim,* or king, of Kuba, as the kingdom became known. Shyaam established his capital at a settlement named Musheng. Legend holds that his right to rule was absolute, conferred upon him by god. Shyaam, however, was a practical leader, so he created a powerful army to ensure that his rule would be obeyed. Shyaam's army had other uses as well. The Kuba kingdom was surrounded by powerful neighbors, among them the Chokwe, Luba, and Lele, but the power of the army was enough to keep these potential threats at bay for about two hundred years.

The Kuba kingdom achieved the height of its power in the middle of the nineteenth century. At that time, just prior to the arrival of the European traders seeking slaves, the Kuba kingdom was finally invaded successfully by a rival regional power, the Nsapo, and much of the Kuba territory was lost to these newcomers. The Kuba kingdom survived this assault, although in much reduced form. Moreover, it was spared the devastation that more accessible peoples suffered with the rise of the slave trade in the region.

Today the Bushoong people number between 50,000 and 100,000 in Zaire. Although the Kuba kingdom continues to exist, the king serves more as a cultural icon than as a political force. The current king of Kuba is the twenty-sixth member of the royal line, tracing descent back to the founding king, Shyaam.

See also: AFRICAN KINGDOMS; LUBA KINGDOM; LUNDA KINGDOM.

KUBLAI KHAN (ca. 1215–1294 C.E.)

Mongol leader (r. 1260–1294) who succeeded his brother Mongke as ruler of the Mongol Empire. Grandson of Genghis Khan (r. 1206–1227), he was also the founder of the Yuan (or Mongol) dynasty of China (1206–1368).

Kublai was the fourth son of Tolui, who was in turn the fourth son of Genghis Khan. Little is known of his childhood and youth; it was not until 1251, when he was already in his mid-thirties, that his brother Mongke, the fourth ruler of the Yuan dynasty, gave him the military assignment of subduing southern China. Kublai spent most of the rest of his life in that country. After fighting in southern China for eight years, he inherited the position of khan, or lord, from his brother but chose to rule from China. This led to growing friction with some of the more traditional Mongols, who saw in a China-centric state the dissipation of the Mongol culture. Throughout Kublai's reign, he was plagued with hostility from that political faction. Further tension was caused by questions of Kublai's legitimacy as khan.

In 1279, when Kublai Khan finally defeated the ruling Sung (Song) dynasty, the Mongol Empire reached its greatest extent. Later attempts to incorporate Japan, Indonesia, Vietnam, and Myanmar all met with failure. Kublai's victory over the Sung marked the first time since the T'ang dynasty (618–907) that all of China was unified under one ruler. Kublai eventually discovered, however, that there was little support within Mongol society for the complicated statesmanship needed to maintain control of such a vast, ancient, and highly stratified China. The Mongols, after all, were nomads, not administrators. Kublai was thus heavily influenced by his Chinese advisers, and he developed a system of government that was, for its time, remarkably humane and liberated.

Although Kublai himself was probably a Tibetan Buddhist, he allowed religious freedom to the vast majority of his subjects. (He did persecute Taoists,

Kublai Khan developed a remarkably humane and progressive government for the era in which he ruled. Much of our knowledge of him comes from Marco Polo, who traveled to China in 1266 C.E. and became a confidant of the Mongol ruler. This scene from a fifteenth-century illustrated manuscript shows Kublai Khan giving his seal to Marco Polo at the new capital of Cambuluc (modern-day Beijing).

though not to the degree they were persecuted by other contemporaries.) Kublai insisted that his generals show mercy and clemency to conquered peoples—an outlandish proposition to many in the thirteenth century. He allowed men of all nationalities to participate in government civil service, and he embarked on a system of public works, extending highways, constructing and repairing public granaries, and rebuilding the Chinese Great Canal.

Kublai Khan also constructed the great city of Cambuluc (modern-day Beijing) and encouraged the establishment of foreign trade. An important source of Western knowledge concerning Kublai's reign is Marco Polo, who enjoyed a position at the king's palace for seventeen years before returning to his native Venice and writing his memoirs. Marco Polo, although an admirer of Kublai Khan, described him as an extravagant and sometimes over-emotional ruler, who indulged himself with elaborate food, expensive hunts, and an active sex life.

Through the adoption of Chinese philosophy, customs, and traditions, Kublai proved to be a successful emperor. But his continued battles with warring Mongolian factions within the empire proved to be a fatefully bad example for his less capable successors. After Kublai's death in 1294, the Yuan dynasty entered a long period of decline and, eventually, the Mongols retreated to the steppes of Central Asia, retiring from the stage of world politics.

See also: EAST ASIAN DYNASTIES; GENGHIS KHAN; MONGOL EMPIRE; YUAN DYNASTY.

FURTHER READING
Soucek, Svatopluk. *A History of Inner Asia.* New York: Cambridge University Press, 2001.

KULASEKHARA DYNASTY. *See*

CERA DYNASTY

KUMAON KINGDOM

(ca. late 1500s–1805 C.E.)

Kingdom that existed in the lower Himalayas, bordered by India, Nepal, and Tibet, and flourished in the seventeenth century.

The Kumaon kingdom stretched across the central portion of the Himalayas and was bordered on the east by Nepal and on the north by Tibet. The region has always been important in the Hindu religion because it contains the traditional wellspring of the sacred Ganges and Jumna rivers and is the burial ground of the Pandavas, the five great heroes of the Hindu epic, the *Mahabharata.* Consequently, Kumaon contains numerous ancient temples and for centuries has been a frequent destination for Hindu pilgrims.

The area that became the Kumaon kingdom was originally inhabited by a large number of Hindu clans, each controlling a small area and protecting it with a fortress. These fortresses were scattered across the western portion of Kumaon, where fertile cropland was more readily available. Because of these fortresses, western Kumaon was referred to as Garwhal, the "country of fortresses."

During the fifteenth century, the tribes in the Kumaon region began to consolidate. One leader, Ajaiya Pala, successfully subdued the majority of the clans, and his descendants maintained sporadic control over the region for over a century. But it was not until the final years of the sixteenth century that Kumaon emerged as a distinct kingdom ruled by a recognized Raja.

Because of its crucial strategic position and its religious significance, Kumaon's existence was always tenuous. In the sixteenth century, the sultans of Bahmani launched several expeditions into Kumaon, both to conquer the region and to attack enemies in Nepal. But the Mughal Empire posed the greatest threat to the Kumaon kingdom. In 1635, the Mughal emperor, Shah Jahan I (r. 1628–1658), launched a massive invasion of Kumaon. When Kumaon successfully repelled the Mughals, Shah Jahan increased the size of his force and attacked again. Finally, in 1654, the Raja of Kumaon signed a treaty with the Mughal ruler, promising his allegiance.

Kumaon regained its independence when Mughal control over India declined in the eighteenth century. Yet the kingdom's location, nestled among the powerful kingdoms of India and Nepal, again proved to be a serious weakness. In 1803, Nepal attacked the Kumaon kingdom and attempted to annex it. Under Pradhuman Shah (r. ?–1805), the last Kumaon Raja, the kingdom vigorously resisted the Nepalese invasion for two years. In 1805, however, the Nepalese forces achieved victory, and Kumaon permanently lost its autonomy.

Nepal's control of the region was brief. In 1815, the British defeated the Nepalese army and occupied Kumaon. The kingdom remained under British control until 1947, when India gained its independence and incorporated Kumaon within its new borders as part of the state of Uttar Pradesh.

See also: JAHAN, SHAH; MUGHAL EMPIRE.

KUSANA DYNASTY (ca. 40–375 C.E.)

Dynasty thought to be of Chinese origin that conquered much of present-day Afghanistan and parts of Pakistan.

The Kushans were initially a clan of the Yueh-Chi (Yuezhi) tribe, which is thought to have originated in the Gansu region of China. Military defeats gradually pushed the tribe westward to the Oxus River (the present-day Amy Darya River) in the region known as Transoxania. Around 100 B.C.E., the Yueh-Chi invaded Bactria (in present-day Afghanistan) and divided it into five confederated territories.

Around 30 C.E., a warrior named Kadphises, the commander of the Kushan territory, subjugated the other Yueh-Chi territories and founded the Kusana dynasty, ruling as Kujula Kadphises I (r. ca. 30–78). Kadphises next conquered lands south of the Hindu Kush Mountains as far as Kabul and east of the Indus River to Taxila. By his death in 78, the Kushans had expelled the Indo-Greeks and Indo-Parthians from much of the Indian borderlands. Kadphises's successor, Kadphises II (r. 78–103), had larger goals. During his reign, he conquered most of northern India and extended Kushan dominance to the Indus River basin.

The Kusana dynasty experienced its greatest prosperity during the reign of Kanishka I (r. ca. 143–162). Continuing the pattern begun by his predecessors, he conquered Kashmir, Bihar, and the Turkistan region of the Chinese Empire. These acquisitions gave the Kushans two major economic advantages. First, they now possessed valuable agricultural regions along the Oxus, Indus, and Ganges rivers. Second, they controlled a major portion of the silk trade route between China and Central Asia. All traders paid a hefty tribute when passing through the Kushan territory.

Kanishka donated much of this wealth to Buddhism. He summoned the major Buddhist theologians to the Fourth Buddhist Council to settle their doctrinal disputes. He erected numerous temples and shrines, and he enlarged a number of Buddhist schools. Because of these activities, Kanishka is regarded as the second greatest Buddhist patron, following only the emperor Asoka (r. 268–232 B.C.E.) of the Maurya Empire of India. Yet Kanishka also respected and practiced tolerance toward those who practiced other religions, thus preventing religious unrest in the Kushan Empire.

Aside from religious tolerance, the expansive Kushan Empire was difficult to maintain. During his reign, Kanishka faced frequent rebellions from the indigenous inhabitants of lands under Kushan control. During one especially arduous campaign, disgruntled military officers assassinated the aging ruler in 162. Control of the Kushan dynasty passed to his son Huvishka II (r. 162–166).

Huvishka and his successors gradually lost the outlying portions of the empire. These areas were either annexed by rival empires or simply seceded. In 226, the Sasanian (or Sassanid) dynasty of Persia conquered most of the Kushan Empire. Although the Kushans continued to rule small regions for nearly two hundred more years, Kushan dominance had ended. The Kusana dynasty itself ended with the death of Kipunada (r. ca. 350–375), the last ruler who was a Kusana descendant.

See also: SASANID DYNASTY.

KUSH, KINGDOM OF

(ca. 1700 B.C.E.–ca. 350 C.E.)

An African kingdom to the south of Egypt that played a major role in ancient Egyptian history.

At the dawn of history along the southern reaches of the Nile River, in a region called Nubia, a civilization gradually emerged in parallel with Egypt, its more famous neighbor to the north. Both the people and culture of this civilization seem to have been an amalgam of Egyptian and black African elements. A large-scale exchange of goods and labor (free and slave), periodic migrations, and long episodes of military conquest in both directions make it difficult to decipher the record of cultural influence and exchange between Egypt and its southern neighbor.

The powerful pharaohs of the Egyptian Middle

Kingdom (ca. 2100–1720 B.C.E.) established a series of military bases along the Upper Nile to protect their trade routes, thus asserting control over much of Nubia. These bases were abandoned during the Hyksos era (1700s–1600s B.C.E.), when northern Egypt was ruled by foreign invaders known as the Hyksos. Freed from Egyptian control, an independent kingdom became established in Nubia with its capital at Kerma, a trading center south of the Third Cataract on the Nile. Kerma was situated at the southern end of the caravan routes that linked the oases west of the Nile. The Kerma state became known in Egypt as the kingdom of Kush.

Kush was a centrally ruled state. Large mud-brick palaces, temples, and administrative buildings dotted the capital, which was protected by massive fortifications. The economy was based on cattle breeding; trade routes reached as far north as the Nile Delta.

With the revival of native Egyptian power after around 1570 B.C.E., northern Kush became a province of Egypt under a viceroy. Tribal chiefs as far south as the confluence of the Blue and White Nile rivers and as far east as the Red Sea, became vassals to the Egyptian pharaoh. This era saw the greatest degree of Egyptianization of Kush, as large numbers of civilian and military officers, priests, merchants, and artists settled in the region.

Egyptian religion also took hold in Kush, centering on temple and burial complexes at Napata. The temple to the sun-god Amun, possibly established by Egyptian refugees from Thebes during the Amarna period (late 1300s B.C.E.), remained the religious anchor of all of Kush for over a millennium. Although elements of local culture remained, the Kushite elite, whether of Nubian or Egyptian origin, became devoted to traditional Egyptian values, even as Egypt itself came under increasing foreign influence (Asian and, later, Greek).

After Egyptian power and unity waned in the eleventh century B.C.E., a new Kushite kingdom emerged with its capital at Napata to the south of Kerma. The first known prince was named Alara (r. 785–760 B.C.E.); the dynasty itself may have descended from leading priests of Amun, possibly deriving ultimately from Thebes in Egypt. The Kushite kingdom prospered from its position on the North-South and East-West trade routes, from agriculture, and from gold and emerald mines.

Around the middle of the eighth century B.C.E., King Kashta (r. 760–747 B.C.E.) was able to incorpo-rate much of Upper (southern) Egypt into the kingdom. His son Piye (r. 747–713 B.C.E.) completed the task of conquest, seizing the Nile Delta and reigning as the first pharaoh of Egypt's Twenty-fifth dynasty. When Piankhy returned to Napata after his military campaigns, the Nile Delta may have regained effective autonomy, but Upper Egypt remained firmly in Kushite hands.

The Kushite pharaohs of the Twenty-fifth dynasty considered themselves to be the defenders of ancient Egyptian religious and cultural practices, which they believed had been ignored in the previous period. They undertook military campaigns in Syria, which provoked an Assyrian invasion of Egypt. The Assyrians forced Taharqa (r. 690–664 B.C.E.), the last Kushite pharaoh of Egypt, back to Napata in the mid-600s B.C.E. Abandoning his Egyptian ambitions, Taharqa turned his attention to expanding Kush's southern borders.

Future Egyptian attempts to reconquer Kush uniformly failed, although an invading army in 590 B.C.E. captured and laid waste to Napata. For four centuries, the Kushite kings continued to call themselves pharaoh, worship the Egyptian god Amun, speak the Egyptian language, and use Egyptian hieroglyphic writing, even as such practices were being abandoned in Egypt itself.

Around 275 B.C.E., the kingdom of Kush moved its capital several hundred miles farther up the Nile to Meroe, where a magnificent capital was built. Meroe was adorned with pyramids, temples, palaces, and baths. Complex irrigation systems fed an expanded population. Iron foundries supplied an indigenous metalworking industry, which may have been instrumental in spreading such technology to West Africa. Art and architecture showed Hellenistic and Indian influences. Trade routes were maintained with Egypt, which was by then under foreign rule (Persian, Greek, and Roman in succession).

Over time, the Meroitic kingdom gradually lost its old Kushite character, as local languages replaced Egyptian, and local styles in sculpture took over. In the early centuries of the Christian era, the Meroitic kingdom began to lose ground. A succession of nomadic groups from east and west of the Nile gradually detached the northern districts, while the Ethiopian kingdom at Aksum encroached from the southeast. Around 350 C.E., Meroe was destroyed by the Axumites, putting an end to a kingdom that had lasted, in one form or another, for some fourteen hundred years.

See also: AFRICAN KINGDOMS; ASSYRIAN EMPIRE; EGYPT-IAN DYNASTIES, ANCIENT (EIGHTEENTH TO TWENTY-SIXTH); HYKSOS DYNASTY.

FURTHER READING

Grimal, Nicolas; Shaw, Ian, trans. *A History of Ancient Egypt.* Oxford: Basil Blackwell, 1994.

Nelson, Harold D., ed. *Sudan: A Country Study*, 3rd ed. Washington, DC: Foreign Area Studies, American University, 1982.

LABOR, FORMS OF

Livelihoods derived from the hierarchical class systems operating in society. In ancient monarchies, the lowest and most difficult menial labor was typically performed by slaves; slightly less dangerous or difficult tasks were done by peasants or the poor; warfare was conducted by the royal and aristocratic class; and professional occupations—if there were any—constituted a middle class of skilled laborers.

FOUNDATIONS OF LABOR

The earliest divisions of labor, in hunting and gathering societies, found the men hunting and practicing the skills of warfare and the women accomplishing everything else: all domestic chores, the healing arts, and child care and education. Slavery was unknown in purely hunting and gathering societies. It took the development of agriculture to create the need for regular, repetitive menial labor and, therefore, the practicality of enslaving others to perform this tedious work.

Ultimately, a labor hierarchy was encouraged by those who were able to apply the most aggressive force, the warrior kings. Thus, the most common hierarchical breakdown of labor groups in ancient and medieval society were monarchs, patricians or aris-tocrats, priests (scholars), professionals and artisans, free peasants and workers, serfs (attached to institutions or land), and finally slaves.

ALTERNATIVE LABOR SYSTEMS— ANCIENT EXAMPLES

Not all ancient and medieval societies were large or complicated enough to include either the priest-scholar or the professional class as separate from the other classes. The first example to possess the entire hierarchy of labor was Pharaonic Egypt (beginning around 3100 B.C.E.). As was often the case in pre-Christian times, the ruler himself was also the head of the priestly class. In ancient Egypt, this coalescence of the sacerdotal with the royal roles lent a certain credibility and authority to the priestly class and fostered its temporal power.

Similarly, the serfs, as a class, were not always differentiated from slaves in the ancient or medieval world. For example, in ancient Greece of the seventh century B.C.E., the Spartans conquered the neighboring Messenians on several occasions and then used these unhappy peoples as their general labor force. These Messenians, called helots by the Spartans, were required from birth to contribute a minimum of half their goods and half their labor to Sparta. Not surprisingly, the relations between the two peoples remained violent and strained for 300 years.

Near the beginning of its founding in 753 B.C.E., the city-state of Rome (after a 200-year period of monarchy) adopted a form of representative government. It remained an agrarian culture with patrician (noble) and plebeian (freemen) farmers as its main constituents—with some slaves. However, by the time of the late Roman Empire (around 350 C.E.), Rome had developed a complex class structure with the emperor at the top followed by the patrician and plebeian senatorial class (which labored only politically and militarily); the equites (who were merchant princes); the professional class; free Roman citizens; domestic, or "house" slaves; free peasants; and agricultural slaves, who evolved into the late Imperial and Byzantine "coloniae" and serfs of the Middle Ages.

AN EARLY EXPERIMENT IN LABOR REFORM

During the Middle Ages, while William the Conqueror (r. 1066–1087) transformed Anglo-Saxon society and took control of England, a new experiment in labor reform began in China. During the Liao dynasty, Wang An Shi, the chief magistrate of the emperor T'ai Tsu (r. 907–926), held that government had a responsibility to protect its less-advantaged citizens from the predatory practices of the wealthier class. He abolished the forced labor to which essentially all Chinese peasants had previously been subject. He gave free seed to the unemployed and offered low interest loans for them to purchase their own farms.

Wang set up commissions to regulate wages for labor and set price controls for certain goods. He nationalized most commodities, having the government buy and store these items in order to prevent profiteering. He also created a formal budget system and maintained pensions for the old, the unemployed, and the ill.

Unfortunately, a series of floods and the appearance of a comet in the sky (an ill omen in Chinese society of the time) enabled Wang's conservative political enemies to persuade the emperor to relieve Wang of his duties. The brave experiment in labor and social reform dissolved quickly into the previous labor system of feudal serfs and their aristocratic masters.

FORMATION OF GUILDS AND THE BIRTH OF DEMOCRACY

Prosperity and a new spirit of liberalism spread across Europe in the eleventh and twelfth centuries. Triggered by cultural contact with the vibrant Islamic cultures encountered during the first Crusades, the professions, crafts, and mercantile systems of the European Continent teemed with new life and enthusiasm. During this time in Central and Western Europe, the merchants and crafts guilds were formed, and several towns began to experiment with political autonomy from their traditional feudal lords.

This led to the creation of a new middle class of workers and signaled the beginning of great changes in the political and economic structure of Europe. By the mid-nineteenth century, these changes would culminate in the complete abolition of slavery and serfdom; the creation of capitalism, socialism, and communism; and the great rise of the middle class.

See also: RIGHTS, LAND; SLAVERY, ROYAL.

LAKHMID DYNASTY

(late 200s–602 C.E.)

Pre-Islamic tribal Bedouin dynasty that helped the Sasanian rulers of Persia (present-day Iran) fight the Byzantine Empire. The Lakhmids encouraged the development of some of the first Arabic poetry.

With its capital at the then prominent Christian city of al-Hirah in southern Iraq, the Lakhmid kingdom was basically an Arab vassal state of Sasanian Persia. Al-Hirah was the diplomatic, political, and military center of Persia, the Byzantine Empire, and the entire Arabian Peninsula. Its strategic location helped protect the Sasanians against raids by Arabian nomads, and it was a principal station on the main caravan route between Persia and the Arabian Peninsula.

At the peak of their power in the sixth century, the Lakhmids contributed significantly to the pre-Islamic cultural history of the Arabs. They enhanced the city of al-Hirah with palaces and castles. Arabic script apparently was developed in the city, too, and the Lakhmid kingdom was the first to make Arabic its official language.

Al-Hirah played an important part in the emergence of Arabic poetry, with the Lakhmid court welcoming some of the most famous poets of pre-Islamic Arabia; among them were Tarafah and an-Nabighah adh-Dhubyani. Al-Hirah also had a significant role in promoting Arab Christianity, as the seat of the bishop for Nestorian Christians was located there and helped spread Christian monotheism to the Arabian Peninsula.

The strongest and most famous Lakhmid ruler was Mundhir III (r. 503–554), who attacked Byzantine Syria and confronted the Arab pro-Byzantine Ghassan kingdom, which defeated Mundhir in 554. The Lakhmid dynasty came to an end when its last ruler, Numan III (r. 582–602), a Nestorian Christian, died in 602. Nearly three decades later, in 633, the city of al-Hirah yielded to the Muslims.

See also: BYZANTINE EMPIRE; SASANID DYNASTY.

LANCASTER, HOUSE OF

(1399–1471 C.E.)

English dynasty that ruled England for much of the 1400s—Henry IV (r. 1399–1413), Henry V (r. 1413–1422), and Henry VI (r. 1422–1461, 1470–1471)—and fought the War of the Roses against the house of York.

The house of Lancaster, a branch of the Norman house of Plantagenet, began when Edmund "Crouchback," the youngest son of Henry III (r. 1216–1272), was named the first earl of Lancaster in 1267. The title passed to Edmund's son Thomas, earl of Lancaster, and then to another son, Henry, earl of Lancaster, upon Thomas's death. Henry's son Henry became the first duke of Lancaster. Duke Henry of Lancaster left no male heirs, so the title eventually went to the husband of Henry's daughter Blanche, John of Gaunt, a son of Edward III (r. 1327–1377). When John of Gaunt died in 1399, the Lancaster title and lands went to his eldest surviving son, Henry, who was known as Henry Bolingbroke.

Henry Bolingbroke was a member of a group of nobles who opposed Richard II (r. 1377–1399) as a weak and ineffectual ruler. In 1398, Richard banished Henry and the following year seized the estates that should have passed to Henry upon John of Gaunt's death. Henry used this betrayal as an opportunity to assert his rule in opposition to Richard. In July 1399, Henry invaded England from abroad and forced Richard to hand the Crown over to him, becoming Henry IV. He claimed his right to rule England through his descent from Henry III.

For much of his reign, Henry IV had to wage war against opponents of his rule, the supporters of Richard. But by the time the Crown passed on to his son, Henry V, this opposition to the Lancastrian dynasty had lessened. One of the most powerful and popular kings of the medieval period, Henry V is perhaps best remembered today as the title character in Shakespeare's play, *Henry V.* His major accomplishment was victory over France in the battle of Agincourt (1415), which raised England to new heights of power. As a result of the Treaty of Troyes (1420)—an agreement between Henry, King Charles VI of France (r. 1380–1422), and Philip the Good of Burgundy (r. 1419–1467)—Henry was betrothed to Charles's daughter, Catherine, and named heir to the French throne, but he died two years later without becoming ruler of France.

The next and last Lancastrian monarch, Henry VI, became king upon his father's death, when he was less than a year old. During his reign, the Yorkists attempted to take back the throne lost by Richard II, even though their claim was no more valid than that of the Lancastrians. Both houses derived from the sons of Edward III, and there was much dispute over which house was legally entitled to the kingship. The Yorkists succeeded in 1461, when they defeated the Lancastrians in battle, deposed Henry, and Edward IV (r. 1461–1470) became the first member of the house of York to sit on the throne. Henry was briefly restored to the throne in 1470, but the following year he was taken prisoner by the Yorkists and murdered in the Tower of London. Through the Beauforts, descendants of an illegitimate child of John of Gaunt, Lancastrian claims passed to the house of Tudor.

See also: HENRY IV (ENGLAND); PLANTAGENET, HOUSE OF; RICHARD II; RICHARD III; TUDOR, HOUSE OF; YORK, HOUSE OF.

FURTHER READING
Weir, Alison. *The Wars of the Roses.* New York: Ballantine, 1996.

King Henry VI of England succeeded to the throne at the age of nine months upon the death of his father, King Henry V. The last ruler of the House of Lancaster, Henry VI struggled for power throughout his reign and was eventually deposed by the Yorkists and executed.

LANDHOLDING PATTERNS

Terms under which property is distributed or owned within a country or society.

The history of landholding patterns is much the

same in both Eastern and Western civilizations; sovereign rulers and aristocrats have controlled the land cultivated by poor laborers. Land ownership has been persistently linked to power and status for royalty and commoner alike.

LANDHOLDING IN EARLY ASIA

In ancient China, the first emperor of the T'ang dynasty, T'ang T'ai-tsung (Taizong) (r. 626–649), attempted to equalize landholding through land reform. He took possession of all land with the express purpose of redistributing it to those best qualified to manage the land. Instead, the emperor was forced to give land back to the wealthy aristocrats who protested his reform efforts. Later during the T'ang dynasty, however, more land reforms were instituted that allowed individual farmers to purchase property of their own.

In feudal Japan, the warrior class, which owned the land, was distinct from the farmer class. Farmers could register the land they occupied and cultivated, but they were required to produce crops and pay taxes to the owners. Prohibited from owning weapons, the farmers were essentially serfs on the land they tended.

FEUDAL LANDHOLDING IN EUROPE

During the Middle Ages in Europe, the ruler was viewed as the ultimate owner of property; land was the monarch's to bestow or appropriate at will. Although many estates were handed down through families, their ownership was not always guaranteed or held without condition. In European feudal society, an element of service to the sovereign was tied to possession of land.

To retain ownership to land, the feudal lord might be required to pay taxes, supply men for the army, or give his own service in battle to the king or overlord. Rulers often made grants of fiefs in recognition of some favor done for king or country. In William Shakespeare's play *Macbeth,* King Macbeth receives the title and lands of Cawdor as a reward for his service in war after they were taken from the treacherous previous thane.

Under tsarist rule in Russia, the pattern of land ownership was much like that of medieval Europe. Barons and other nobles owned great estates that were populated by serfs, peasant laborers who were not citizens and who had few rights. Tsar Alexander II (r. 1855–1881) abolished this landholding system and freed Russian serfs, issuing the first Emancipation Law in March 1861. Unfortunately, this law did not successfully end the call for land reform, and ultimately terrorists assassinated the tsar.

CHANGES IN ENGLISH LANDHOLDING

During the seventeenth century, many English farmers were the owners of small properties or were tenants on large estates, and on the surface it seemed that land distribution was becoming more equitable. In the mid-1600s, however, the Acts of Settlement greatly restricted the movement of the poor from one area to another and banned the public from deer parks and forests, making it more difficult for working-class individuals to support themselves and their families. Laws of primogeniture also kept estates in the hands of a few aristocrats.

Despite attempts to preserve and tighten aristocratic land ownership, English lands in the eighteenth century were still owned in part by lords of vast estates and in part by small farmers. Soon, however, greedy aristocrats in Parliament began passing a series of Enclosure Acts (between 1760 and 1830) that allowed estate owners to examine the ownership of small nearby farms, many of which had been cultivated by the same family for generations. When the farmers could not prove ownership, the lords were allowed to enclose the farms, taking the land from the yeoman farmers and forcing them to become tenants or to migrate to towns and cities. As a result of the Enclosure Acts, land ownership in Great Britain was consolidated in the hands of a few wealthy aristocrats.

Even after several land reforms were instituted in England beginning in the late 1800s, the oppressive system of aristocratic land ownership continued in Ireland. Absentee English landlords owned estates rented by poor Irish tenants. If the often exorbitant rents could not be paid, it was an easy mater to evict the tenants. In the early 1900s, the Irish Land League was successful in bringing about passage of a series of Land Acts that curbed some of the excesses of English landlords.

Throughout history, the unequal distribution of land has been a major source of conflict between monarchs and their subjects in both Eastern and Western cultures. Not only did unequal land distribution have a significant impact on the social structure of society, but it also was the cause of numerous uprisings against rulers.

See also: CASTE SYSTEMS; FEUDALISM AND KINGSHIP; LABOR, FORMS OF; RIGHTS, LAND; TAXATION.

LE DYNASTY (1428–1802 C.E.)

Vietnamese dynasty that flourished from its founding until the 1500s, when it entered a slow period of decline that culminated in its final collapse in 1788.

The Le dynasty was founded in 1428, when rebel leader Le Loi formed a resistance movement to overthrow control of his country, An Nam, by the Ming dynasty of China. After twenty-one years of Chinese occupation, Le Loi restored independence to An Nam and became the first ruler (r. 1428–1433) of the Le dynasty (sometimes called the Later Le dynasty).

To defeat the Ming, Le Loi employed guerrilla warfare tactics, often relying on surprise attacks and avoiding direct combat with larger enemy forces. The Vietnamese would continue to use such tactics throughout its history, including modern times, during the Vietnam War in the mid-1900s.

When Le Loi took the throne, he ruled using the name Le Thai To and changed the name of the country from An Nam to Dai Viet. Dai Viet flourished for the next hundred years, while the dynasty Le Loi founded lasted for more than 350 years. When Le Thai To died in 1433, his young son, Le Thai Ton (r. 1433–1442), succeeded to the throne.

Under the leadership of Le Thanh Ton (r. 1460–1497), a son and later successor of Le Thai, the country experienced one of the most successful periods in Vietnamese history. Le Thanh Ton established a legal code that was unique from the Chinese system previously used. He also encouraged the spread of Confucianism, spurred the growth of foreign trade, promoted the arts and architecture, and supervised the writing of a national history.

In 1471, following decades of conflict with their southern rivals, the kingdom of Champa, the Vietnamese under the leadership of Le Thanh Ton captured the Cham territory. After invading the Cham capital of Vijaya, the Vietnamese massacred many of the Cham people and forced many of the survivors to flee south.

The glory days of the Le dynasty came to an end during the sixteenth century as rival families and groups within the kingdom struggled for power. With its power in decline, the Le dynasty began losing control of both its northern regions and the southern territory it had acquired from the Chams.

In 1545, the Le kingdom was divided into two territories; the rival Trinh and Nguyen families controlled the northern and southern regions, respectively. Although the Le monarchs remained kings in name, they exercised very little real authority from this point forward. By the end of the eighteenth century, the Le dynasty was in serious decline as a result of the growing power of its rivals. In 1788, the Nguyen dynasty took control of the entire country, and the last ruler of the Le dynasty, Le Man Hoang De (r. 1786–1788), fled north to China.

See also: NGUYEN (HUE) DYNASTY; TRINH DYNASTY; VIETNAMESE KINGDOMS.

LEGITIMACY

The basis on which a government establishes its right to rule. Legitimacy of rule has been based on military strength, religion, heredity, and other claims to power.

RELIGIOUS BASIS

The earliest sovereigns based their rule on divine order, claiming to be divine, as in ancient Egypt, or claiming to be descended from the gods, as in ancient Rome. Similarly, the ancient Sumerians believed that kingship came from heaven and that kings were the representatives of the gods and stood in for them as their intermediary.

In ancient China, the kingship was seen as an intermediary position between heaven and earth. This concept goes back to the overthrow of the Chang dynasty by the Chou dynasty between about 1025 and 1050 B.C.E. The Chou justified their power by claiming that the last Chang ruler was corrupt and indifferent to the people's needs. They believed that their dynasty, the Chou, had been given a mandate from heaven to rule China. This mandate long remained a central political concept in establishing the legitimacy of Chinese rulers.

Similarly, when Europe became Christianized during the early Middle Ages, monarchs grounded their legitimacy in claims to be the anointed chosen of God. They were crowned in churches and anointed by archbishops with the oil used in baptism and confirmation, giving their coronations sacramental undertones.

ABSOLUTIST BASIS

As the Catholic Church's authority declined and nationalism increased in the late Middle Ages and the Renaissance, rulers established themselves as absolute monarchs. In some cases, this idea of absolutism was blended with divine right to bolster claims of legitimacy and the right to rule.

In 1534, with the Act of Supremacy, King Henry VIII (r. 1509–1547) of England made the English church a national institution, putting himself at its head.

Later, James I (r. 1603–1625) of England, himself a theologian, wrote *The Trew Law of Free Monarchies and Basilikony Doron*, a treatise that established and supported the divine right of kings. In eighteenth-century France, Louis XIV (r. 1643–1715), the "Sun-King," claimed absolute authority over the Church as Henry VIII did a century earlier. Louis required the French nobility to remain at court where their purpose was to render him honor. "The state is myself!" he declared.

OTHER BASES OF LEGITIMACY

In addition to claims of divine right and absolutism, a dynasty may need to establish its legitimacy through other means. A ruler whose economic or political policies are failing may lose his or her legitimacy altogether, as happened with Louis XVI of France (r. 1774–1792) during the French Revolution.

Similarly, the Yuan (or Mongol) dynasty, which conquered China in 1279, evicted thousands of farmers and occupied their lands, causing famine among the Chinese. Ming Hung-Wu, who led the resulting rebellion (1359–1368) and was proclaimed emperor in 1368, recognized the need to restore the Chinese economy at once and to establish his legitimacy as the new emperor. His agricultural policies, though reactionary, were popular; moreover, he also tried to eliminate corruption in his government.

MONARCHY AND REVOLUTION

By the eighteenth century, particularly in Western Europe and in North America, people had begun to question absolute power and divine right. Increasingly, subjects demanded more voice in the government, and the king's legitimacy became based on his ability to rule justly rather than absolutely or by divine right.

In 1649, Charles I of England (r. 1625–1649) was beheaded when he refused to call Parliament and tried to force the Scots to worship according to Anglican rites. In the bloodless Glorious Revolution of 1688, William of Orange, a prince of the Netherlands, accepted the English Crown as William III (r. 1689–1702) based on The Declaration of Right, which, together with the precepts established in Magna Carta (1215), became the basis for constitutional monarchy in England. Similarly, Louis XVI of France was beheaded in the French Revolution because he could not solve, or even understand, the impoverishment of the French people.

As the success of American democracy became apparent after the American colonies gained their independence from Great Britain, some people began to question the need for a monarch altogether. The nineteenth century saw a number of political upheavals, chiefly in Western Europe, in which monarchies were discarded.

FIGUREHEAD MONARCHY

Today, most countries retaining a monarch are ruled by a prime minister, and the monarch serves only as a figurehead symbolizing national pride. The legitimacy of these monarchs comes from a combination of tradition and constitutional laws. Figurehead monarchies are found throughout Western Europe and in Japan. Though less intrusive in people's lives than the monarchies of the past, even such figurehead monarchies may not be secure. In countries such as Great Britain, for example, scandals in the royal family have led people to question the legitimacy even of figurehead monarchy, and some have called for its abolition altogether.

See also: BLOOD, ROYAL; CONQUEST AND KINGSHIPS; DESCENT, ROYAL; DETHRONEMENT; DIVINE RIGHT; DIVINITY OF KINGS; INHERITANCE, ROYAL; MONARCHY; POWER, FORMS OF ROYAL; ROYAL FAMILIES; ROYAL LINE; SACRED KINGSHIPS; SUCCESSION, ROYAL.

LEINSTER KINGDOM (400s–1603 C.E.)

Ancient and medieval kingdom of Ireland (known also as Laighin), located in the middle and southeast of the country, which was isolated from the rest of Ireland by the Slieve Bloom Mountains on its western border.

EARLY HISTORY

In the fifth century, the rulers of Leinster were from a dynasty called the Dál Mesin Corb, and one of the earliest kings was Bressal Belach (r. ca. 436–444). In the seventh and eighth centuries, the overkings of Leinster came from two dynasties, the Uí Máil and the Uí Dunlainge. The last king of the Uí Máil dynasty, Cellach (Kelly) Cualann (r. 693–715), died in 715.

Later in the eighth century, two powers contended for supremacy in Leinster, the Uí Cheinselaig in the south and the Ui Dúnlainge in the north. The Ui Cheinnselaig, like the Uí Neill and the Ui Bríuin dynasties of Ireland, traced their descent from Eremon, one of the legendary brothers who divided the island of Ireland between them in the eleventh century B.C.E. By the end of the eighth century C.E., the Ui Dúnlainge had gained supremacy over the Ui Chennselaig, and they effectively excluded other groups from the kingship until 1042.

By the tenth century, the powerful Uí Neill kings in Ulster had long held the high kingship of Ireland. In 956, the Irish high king, Congalach Uí Neill (r. ca. 944–956) attacked Leinster and forced its kings to acknowledge his overlordship. However, the Uí Neill were soon battling among themselves, and the Leinster kings became more powerful.

Yet, Leinster still faced a serious threat from the

ROYAL RELATIVES

ARTHUR MACMORROUGH KAVANAGH (1831–1889)

Although the Irish kings were driven from power by the English in the sixteenth century, their descendants continued to bear their royal titles proudly. One of the most noteworthy, both for his accomplishments and the adversity he had to overcome, was Arthur MacMorrough Kavanagh, a nineteenth-century member of Parliament who was born without arms or legs.

His parents, Squire Thomas Kavanagh and Lady Harriet Le Poer Trench, named him for his ancestor, Art Oge MacMorrough (1375–1415), king of Leinster, who had successfully defied Richard II. The Kavanagh family possessed the ancient charter and Royal Crown of Leinster at their estate, Borris House, in County Carlow. By then, the family was staunchly Protestant and a supporter of the English Crown.

The energetic Lady Harriet was determined that her son should succeed in life despite his disability. Arthur, who possessed only six-inch stumps for arms and legs, learned not only to ride and shoot like any other gentleman, but also to draw and paint, a talent he inherited from his mother. As a young man, he traveled to Cairo and the Holy Land, Europe, Russia, Persia, and India. In 1855, he married a distant cousin, Frances Forde Leathley, and fathered six children.

After the early deaths of his two older brothers, Arthur inherited the family estates and the duties of landlord. At that time, the peasants of Ireland were suffering from the effects of the potato famine. Unlike many of the callous absentee landlords in Ireland at this time, Kavanagh was an enlightened, though somewhat paternalistic, landlord, rebuilding the homes of the peasants in the village of Borris at his expense and encouraging the local cottage industry of lace-making. In 1866, he ran for and won a Unionist seat in Parliament, which he kept for thirteen years, attending sessions in London in a wheelchair. Unlike many Unionists and Conservatives, he supported Gladstone's Land Act, which sought compensation for dispossessed tenants. In private, Kavanagh believed that the government should give credit to the peasants to buy their own land. His opinions on Irish questions were also followed in the United States. In 1880, agitation by the Irish nationalist Fenians turned sentiment in his district against him and he lost his re-election bid. He died a saddened man in 1889.

powerful O'Brien high kings and the O'Connor clan. The rulers of Leinster thus turned to military alliances, first with other kings of Ireland and then with the Viking invaders, as a means of protection. In 1014, for example, Leinster allied with the Vikings at the battle of Clontarf against the Irish high king, Brian Boru (r. 1002–1014).

In 1042, Diarmait mac Mael na mBo (r. 1042–1072) of the Ui Dunlainge dynasty became king of Leinster. His descendants, known as the MacMorroughs, succeeded him on the throne and ruled Leinster for the next 500 years.

THE COMING OF THE ENGLISH

Dermot IV MacMorrough (r. 1126–1171) is perhaps the most reviled of Irish kings because he is blamed for the English invasion of Ireland. After being driven from his kingdom in 1169 by high-king Rory O'Connor (r. 1166–1186) and O'Connor's allies, Dermot went to England to seek allies there.

King Henry II of England (r. 1154–1189) granted Dermot letters patent to seek help from his knights. As a result, Dermot was able to enlist the aid of Richard de Clare, the earl of Pembroke, popularly known as Strongbow. Dermot gave Strongbow his daughter Aoife in marriage, perhaps allowing Strongbow to think that he would inherit the throne of Leinster, though this was not according to the Irish law of succession.

Strongbow came to Ireland with his forces and captured Waterford in 1170. Dermot died in 1171, and later that year, Henry II landed in Ireland. He granted Richard de Clare the lordship of Leinster, making it the first Irish kingdom to come under Norman rule. Dermot's chosen successor, Dohmnall Caermanach, immediately opposed Strongbow but was slain by the Normans in 1171.

LATER HISTORY

The Leinster kings continued to fight English domination. Donal V (r. 1171–1175), an illegitimate son of Dermot IV, raised his family's claim to the kingship and took up arms against the English. Nicknamed Caomhinach (Kavanagh) ("The Handsome"), he founded the MacMorrough Kavanagh branch of the dynasty.

By the fourteenth century, the Norman barons in Leinster had either died or moved away, and the Leinster kingship was revived. Art Mor Mac Airt MacMorrough Kavanagh (r. 1375–1417) restored much of the kingdom's pre-Norman strength and even obtained tribute from the English colonists.

Art Mor Mac Airt married a Norman woman, Elizabeth Veele, and concluded an agreement with King Richard II of England (r. 1377–1399) over the restoration of his wife's lands, which had been confiscated by the Normans on her marriage. But the agreement did not last, and Richard II soon landed in Ireland with his army but was unable to prevail over King Art, who ruled until his death in 1417.

The English subsequently sought to set up a puppet king in Donnchad Mac Airt Mhoir MacMorrough (r. dates unknown), but soon he, too, took up arms against them. However, Donnchad eventually signed an agreement with King Henry IV of England (r. 1399–1413) in which he received tribute in exchange for the English-occupied territory in his kingdom.

In 1553, Caothaoir Ma Airt of Leinster (r. 1547–1553) surrendered his kingdom to King Edward VI of England (r. 1547–1553) in exchange for becoming Baron of Ballyanne in Wexford. However, his descendants continued to resist English domination. In 1595, during an attempt to drive out the English, Dohmnall Spainneach Mac Donnchadha (Donal) IX (r. 1595–1603), who had been in exile in Spain, was acclaimed as king of Leinster. He commanded the kingdom's forces against the armies of Elizabeth I (r. 1558–1603), but surrendered and abdicated in 1603, ending the long-lived kingship of Leinster.

See also: BORU, BRIAN; IRISH KINGS.

FURTHER READING

Byrne, Francis John. *Irish Kings and High-Kings*. 2nd ed. Portland Or: Court Courts Press, 2001.

Ellis, Peter Beresford. *Erin's Blood Royal: The Gaelic Noble Dynasties of Ireland*. New York: Palgrave Macmillan, 2002.

McCormick, Donald. *The Incredible Mr. Kavanagh*. New York: Devin-Adair, 1961.

LEO III. *See* BYZANTINE EMPIRE

LEÓN, KINGDOM OF (910–1230 C.E.)

Historic kingdom in northwest Spain, originally part of the kingdom of Asturias.

In the tenth century, the rulers of the kingdom of Asturias shifted their capital from Ovideo to León, and the city gave its name to the surrounding territory. The first ruler to hold the title king of León was Garcia I (910–914).

By the early eleventh century, rulers of the kingdom of Asturias and León had gained control of the Iberian regions of Galicia, Navarre, the Basque provinces, and parts of Castile. But their involvement in the *reconquista* (the campaign to recapture the Iberian Peninsula from the Moors), as well as rivalries and insurrections among nobles, made it impossible to retain complete authority over all their holdings. As a result, some of these areas splintered into separate kingdoms. The independent kingdom of Navarre was established in 905 under Sancho I (r. 905–925), and an independent kingdom of Castile was established in 1035 under Ferdinand I (r. 1035–1065).

In 1037, Ferdinand I of Castile conquered León, and for nearly three decades the kingdom was joined with Castile and ruled by the House of Navarre. León separated again Ferdinand's death in 1065, with his eldest son Sancho (r. 1065–1072) inheriting Castile and the second son, Alfonso (r. 1065–1109), inheriting León. Following Sancho's assassination in 1072, the two territories again merged, and Alfonso ruled as King Alfonso VI of Castile and León.

Separated again in the twelfth century, León joined Castile once more in 1230 during the reign of King Ferdinand III of León (r. 1217–1252). León remained part of Castile until the dual kingdom merged with Aragón in 1479, forming the greatest state on the Iberian Peninsula. With the reign of Charles I (r. 1516–1556), the grandson of Isabella I of Castile (r. 1474–1504) and Ferdinand II of Aragón (r. 1479–1516), the three formerly independent kingdoms—León, Castile, and Aragón—became the foundation of the modern kingdom and nation of Spain.

See also: ARAGÓN, KINGDOM OF; ASTURIAS KINGDOM; CASTILE, KINGDOM OF; IBERIAN KINGDOMS; NAVARRE, KINGDOM OF; SPANISH MONARCHIES.

LEOPOLD I (1640–1705 C.E.)

Holy Roman emperor (r. 1658–1705) and inheritor of the Austrian Habsburg titles, who faced serious challenges from both France and the Ottoman Empire. During his reign, Leopold I consolidated many of the disparate lands of Germany into a series of larger and more effective states. In addition to his title as Holy Roman emperor, he was duke of Upper and Lower Silesia, count of Tyrol, archduke of Upper and Lower Austria, king of Bohemia (elected in 1656), and king of Hungary and Croatia (elected 1655). While Leopold held the imperial throne, the city of Vienna became a center for culture and the arts.

Born in 1640, Leopold was the second son of Holy Roman Emperor Ferdinand III (1637–1657). Educated for a position in the Church, he became heir to the throne after the death of his older brother Ferdinand in 1654. When Leopold took to the throne after the death of his father, the political situation in Europe saw the great rival powers of France and the Ottoman Empire competing for supremacy.

Leopold inherited an Austria weakened by the costly Thirty Years' War (1618–1648) and facing an advancing threat from the Ottomans Turks in the east. Austria, therefore, found itself in the middle of a precarious situation both politically and geographically. In order to compete and survive, Leopold instituted sweeping reforms of the Austrian military and government. He replaced the unreliable mercenaries common to early seventeenth-century armies with professional soldiers trained and paid by the state, and he expanded state authority by organizing and enlarging bureaucratic oversight of government action. Leopold also helped create a powerful German ally to the north by granting the title of king to Frederick I (r. 1701–1713) of Prussia, who was continuing the state-building efforts of his father, Frederick William (1640–1688), elector of Brandenburg.

Leopold's leadership was not always admirable. In June 1683, a vast Turkish army of approximately one hundred thousand soldiers lay siege to the city of Vienna. Leopold fled the city and left its defense to his advisers. After several months, Poland, Venice, and Russia sent troops to aid the beleaguered city, driving off the surprised Turks. The defeat of the Turks at Vienna is considered a decisive moment in the eventual fall of the Ottoman Empire.

Leopold's efforts continued to be divided as he struggled against both the French and the Turks. In 1686, he formed the League of Augsburg, an alliance among European nations to defend the German Palatinate. England joined the League in 1689, and the coalition became known as the Grand Alliance. The ensuing conflict between these powers and

France was known as the War of the Grand Alliance (1688–1697). The Treaty of Ryswick (1697) settled the war and temporarily halted the expansionist policy of the French king, Louis XIV (r. 1643–1715).

The Turkish conflict was also resolved in 1697 by the Treaty of Karlowitz, which granted Leopold most of Hungary. These treaties did not end Leopold's hostilities, however. In 1700, after the last Habsburg king of Spain, Charles II (r. 1665–1700), died without an heir, Leopold claimed the Spanish throne for his second son Charles, while Louis XIV of France demanded that his grandson Philip be recognized as king of Spain. Fighting began, and the War of the Spanish Succession lasted from 1701 to 1714.

Leopold did not live to see the end of this conflict. He died in 1705 of a series of debilitating heart attacks, leaving his titles to his son, Joseph I (1705–1711), who continued the modernizing efforts of his father as well as the war over the Spanish throne.

See also: FRENCH MONARCHIES; HABSBURG DYNASTY; HOHENZOLLERN DYNASTY; HOLY ROMAN EMPIRE; LOUIS XIV; OTTOMAN EMPIRE.

LEOPOLD II (1747–1792 C.E.)

Short-reigning but influential Habsburg ruler of the Holy Roman Empire (r. 1790–1792), whose earlier position as Grand Duke Leopold I of Tuscany earned him a reputation as a strong and progressive ruler. Though frequently unpopular with his people, Leopold, who also ruled Hungary and Bohemia in addition to other Habsburg lands, swept away much of the waste and corruption that had plagued Tuscany before his rule. In doing so, he left a legacy of intelligent, productive, and profitable governance. As Holy Roman emperor, however, Leopold was forced to repeal many reforming policies in order to maintain domestic peace and was caught up in the international turmoil leading to the French Revolutionary Wars.

Born into the powerful Habsburg dynasty, Leopold was the third son of the Austrian archduchess Maria Theresa and emperor Francis I (r. 1745–1765) of the Holy Roman Empire. As part of the settlement that made him his father's successor to the Grand Duchy of Tuscany, Leopold married Maria Louisa, daughter of King Charles III of Spain (r. 1759–1788).

The couple had sixteen children, including Leopold's successor, Francis II (r. 1792–1806).

Leopold became grand duke of Tuscany upon his father's death in 1765, at which time his older brother became Emperor Joseph II (r. 1765–1790) of the Holy Roman Empire. As ruler of Tuscany, Leopold quickly began undoing the corrupt systems put in place by the Medici family, who had ruled Tuscany for centuries before his father's time. Leopold loosened many of the restrictions placed on Tuscan industry and instituted a fair tax system, which helped generate widespread economic growth. His actions, however, created resentment among the powerful families in Tuscany who had benefited from the corrupt policies that Leopold abolished. As his brother, Emperor Joseph II, did in his own domains, Leopold did much to fortify the civil rights of his people, such as putting a stop to capital and corporal punishment.

Upon the death of his brother Joseph II in 1790, Leopold became Holy Roman emperor as well as king of Hungary and Bohemia, inheriting subjects who were deeply divided over Joseph's progressive reforms. In order to prevent civil insurrection, Leopold rescinded many of Joseph's reform policies. Leopold's main role as Holy Roman emperor, however, was international. He secured his borders with Turkey, put down a rebellion in the Netherlands, and attempted to secure an alliance with Prussian king Frederick William II (r. 1786–1797) in order to prevent the French Revolution from spreading throughout Europe.

In 1791, Leopold and Frederick William issued the Declaration of Pillnitz, which claimed their intent to restore Louis XVI (r. 1774–1792), France's recently deposed king, to the throne by force, provided that the other major powers in Europe joined them. This declaration incensed the French revolutionaries, and actually hastened the advent of war.

Leopold died suddenly in 1792, not knowing that the peace he believed he had helped to secure would end in just a month's time, as the wars of the French Revolution engulfed nearly all of Europe.

See also: AUSTRO-HUNGARIAN EMPIRE; CHARLES III; DIPLOMACY, ROYAL; FREDERICK WILLIAM, THE GREAT ELECTOR; HABSBURG DYNASTY; HOLY ROMAN EMPIRE; JOSEPH II; MARIA THERESA; MEDICI FAMILY; SIBLINGS, ROYAL.

LIANG DYNASTIES

(502–557 C.E., 907–923 C.E.)

Two Chinese dynasties that ruled briefly during the Southern and Northern Dynasties era and the Five Dynasties period. The first Liang dynasty was one in a series of small, short-lived kingdoms that ruled southern China during the period known as the Southern and Northern dynasties (386–589). Falling at the end of the 300 years of chaos that followed the disintegration of the Han dynasty, the Southern and Northern dynasties era saw China divided politically between north and south. Although the southern dynasties did not control the north, Chinese historians have generally considered them to be China's legitimate rulers.

The Liang dynasty was the third of four dynasties that followed the collapse of the Eastern Jin dynasty at their capital at Jiankang (present-day Nanjing). These four dynasties were the Liu Sung dynasty (420–479), the Southern Ch'i dynasty (479–502), the Liang dynasty (502–557), and the Ch'en dynasty (557–589). The Liang founder, Xiao Yan, served as

Liang Dynasty

Wu Ti	502–549
Chien Wen Ti	549–551
Yu-chang Wang	551
Yuan Ti	552–555
Ching Ti	555–557

Later Liang Dynasty

T'ai Tsu	907–912
Ying Wang	912–913
Mo Ti	913–923
Chuang Tsung	923–926
Ming Tsung	926–933
Min Ti	933–934
Fei Ti	934–937

regent to Hedi, the teenage emperor of the Qi dynasty (479–502). When Hedi killed Xiao Yan's brother, a minister at his court, Xiao Yan attacked the capital, seized the throne, and proclaimed the new Liang dynasty. Known as Liang Wudi (r. 502–549), he was a scholar and a devoted Buddhist. During his long, stable rule he established schools for the study of the Confucian classics. As a Buddhist, Liang Wudi opposed the use of violence, and on several occasions left the throne to live as a Buddhist monk. Liang Wudi's eldest son, Xiao Tong, compiled China's most famous anthology, *Literary Selections.*

The reigns of Liang Wudi's successors were bloody and brief, beginning in 548 when his son, Jian Wendi (ruled 550), staged a rebellion against him. In 557 Liang Wudi's grandson was deposed by the founder of the Chen dynasty. The last of the southern dynasties, the Chen would soon fall to the Sui dynasty, which would reunite China under a single rule.

The Liang name was revived in 907 when Zu Wen, also known as Liang Taizu (r. 907–912), established the Later Liang dynasty (907–923) at Luoyang after the fall of the T'ang dynasty. This Later Liang dynasty marks the beginning of the Five Dynasties period, an era of constant warfare in which five different dynasties succeeded each other in northern China in the space of fifty years. In 923, Liang Taizu's son, Modi, was overthrown by Zhuangzong, the son of a Turkish general who founded the Later T'ang dynasty.

See also: FIVE DYNASTIES AND TEN KINGDOMS; HAN DYNASTY; SUI DYNASTY; T'ANG DYNASTY.

LIANG WU TI (464–549 C.E.)

Chinese emperor (r. 502–549) of the first major Liang dynasty (502–556), one of the southern dynasties in a period of disunion in Chinese history that lasted from 265 to 589. Liang Wu Ti's reign was the longest and most stable of the period.

Born with the name Xiao Yan, Liang Wu Ti was a cousin of the emperor Gaodi (r. 479–482) of China's Southern Qi dynasty. As a member of a powerful aristocratic family, he had a strategically located fiefdom and held a number of senior posts in the imperial administration before becoming regent to Emperor Qi Hedi (r. 501). In 502, Xiao Yan launched an attack on the Qi capital of Nanjing and seized power for himself, becoming emperor and founder of the Liang dynasty. He took the imperial name Liang Wu Ti, or "martial emperor of the Liang."

A first-rate scholar, Emperor Wu Ti presided over a period of tremendous cultural progress. During his reign, literature, philosophy, and art flourished, and Buddhism spread extremely rapidly, fueled by the emperor's conversion to the religion around 511 and his great devotion to it. Contributions to Buddhist monasteries grew to enormous proportions, with Wu Ti the most generous donor. The emperor spent vast sums to build Buddhist temples, monasteries, and statues in the vicinity of the capital of Jiankang and farther away. He even arranged to be held hostage at temples until members of his court paid huge amounts of ransom. Wu Ti's focus on spiritual matters often deflected his attention from other urgent matters. Several times during his rule, the armies of the Wei kingdom to the north launched attacks into southern China and threatened Liang rule.

As a devout Buddhist, Wu Ti apparently lived and ate very simply. He did not allow meat or wine at the royal table and is credited with starting a custom of vegetarian meals in China. Using both his royal power and Buddhist principles, he also prohibited wine and meat in the monasteries. Although some Buddhist leaders objected, Wu Ti insisted that it was not possible to be compassionate if one drank wine or ate the flesh of animals. From that time on, monks and nuns ate only vegetarian meals. Ironically, the emperor died of starvation at the age of eighty-five—not because of his eating habits, but as a result of a revolt in his capital that cut off the food supply. A few years after Wu Ti's death in 549, the Liang dynasty collapsed, largely because of internal conflicts among the emperor's descendants and heirs.

See also: LIANG DYNASTIES.

LIAO DYNASTY (907–1125 C.E.)

Foreign dynasty that ruled a large empire centered in northern China after the fall of the T'ang dynasty. The Liao dynasty was founded by the Khitan, a semi-nomadic people originating in Manchuria. Khitai, a variant of Khitan, was the basis for the word Cathay, the medieval European term for northern China. The Khitan, who practiced agriculture, hunted, and bred cattle in the steppes northeast of China, sent tribute to their powerful southern neighbors, the T'ang (618–907). As the T'ang dynasty collapsed in the early tenth century, a Khitan leader, Abaoji, united several Khitan tribes and proclaimed himself emperor of a new dynasty.

In 926, the Liao extended their domain east to the shores of the Yellow Sea. That same year, Abaoji died and was succeeded by his son, establishing a system of hereditary succession modeled after the Chinese. In 936, the Liao gained territory around Beijing in exchange for helping the Later Jin (937–947) dynasty defeat the Later T'ang (923–937). Beijing, which had previously been an insignificant frontier city, became the Liao dynasty's southern capital.

The Liao military, with its massive cavalry of mounted archers, posed a potent threat to neighboring states. In 1004, the Liao defeated armies of the Song dynasty, winning a treaty that forced the Song to pay a large annual tribute in silk and silver. Similar treaties were forced on other states bordering the Liao Empire, including the Western Xia state in the northwest. At its height, the Liao domain reached across parts of Mongolia, Manchuria, and north China, from the Yellow Sea to Central Asia.

The Liao employed a dual system of governing. In the southern portion of their realm, they ruled according to the Chinese system inherited from the T'ang, with a bureaucracy staffed by Chinese officials, a limited examination system, and a Confucian political philosophy. In the vast plains to the north, they employed the traditional Khitan tribal system of rule. The highly mobile Liao government moved seasonally between five capitals.

At the peak of Liao rule, about 750,000 Khitans ruled over some two to three million Chinese. Unlike most foreign rulers of China, the Liao successfully avoided absorption into Chinese culture. Nobles who endeavored to assimilate into the Chinese system were punished, and a script was created for the Khitan language. While the elite became well versed in both Khitan and Chinese culture, the majority of Khitan subjects maintained their traditional culture.

In 1125, the Liao were defeated by an alliance of the Song and the Jurchen, a rival northern tribe that later forced the Song south and founded the Jin dynasty (1125–1234) in northern China.

See also: FIVE DYNASTIES AND TEN KINGDOMS; SUNG (SONG) DYNASTY; T'ANG DYNASTY.

LILIUOKALANI (1839–1917 C.E.)

Last reigning monarch of Hawaii (r. 1891–1893), remembered for her efforts to maintain the dignity and independence of the Hawaiian people and for her musical compositions, including the well-known song, "Aloha Oe."

The daughter of high chief Kapaakea and his wife Keohokalole, Liliuokalani was born on September 2, 1838, in Honolulu, on the Hawaiian island of Oahu. Shortly after her birth, she was baptized into the Christian religion and given the baptismal name Lydia. The reigning Hawaiian king at the time was Kamehameha III (r. 1825–1854).

In order to strengthen ties of loyalty and support with other high-born families, Liliuokalani's parents followed Hawaiian tradition by having their children adopted out to other important families. Accordingly, Liliuokalani was raised by one of Kamehameha III's royal advisers, Abner Paki, and his wife Konia. The couple already had a daughter of their own, Bernice, who became like a sister to Liliuokalani, and with whom the future queen of Hawaii maintained close ties throughout her life.

Because Liliuokalani was in line to inherit the throne, she was educated at the Royal School, which was run by American missionaries. There she became fluent in English and was instructed in the Christian faith. She also studied music, becoming proficient at several instruments, and during her school years she began writing songs—something she continued to do for the rest of her life.

In her adolescence, Liliuokalani became a member of the inner court of King Kamehameha IV (r. 1854–1863) and his wife, Queen Emma. She was thus exposed to the day-to-day conduct of life in Iolani Palace, the royal residence, and she remained a member of the court throughout the reigns of Kamehameha IV and his successors. From this privileged position, Liliuokalani was able to witness growing American influence in the Hawaiian court, led by U.S. sugar-plantation owners who wanted to wield greater power over local policies.

Kamehameha IV died after ruling nine years, a victim of a lifelong battle with asthma. He was succeeded by his brother, who took the royal name of Kamehameha V (r. 1863–1872) and was the last truly hereditary king of the islands. Kamehameha V's reign no doubt had a great influence on certain of Lili-

Queen Liliuokalani was the last monarch to reign over the Hawaiian kingdom. She attempted to maintain Hawaiian independence but was deposed in 1894 by American settlers who advocated the formation of a republic. During the last years of her life, Liliuokalani worked to preserve the traditions of her people.

uokalani's own beliefs, for he identified strongly with European culture and prejudices, and during his rule he attempted to suppress such traditional Hawaiian practices as the hula. Liliuokalani spent much of her own reign trying to restore Hawaii's rich cultural tradition.

On the death of Kamehameha V in 1872, the succession to the throne was thrown into doubt. The king had left no children, and there were several claimants to the throne who could trace roughly equivalent descent from Kamehameha I. The Hawaiian legislature stepped in and ordered an election, which was won by William Charles Lunalilo (r. 1873–1874). Lunalilo's reign was too brief to effect much change, however, for he died of tuberculosis within a year.

Once again, there were many claimants to the throne, among them Liliuokalani's brother, David Kalakaua (r. 1874–1891). Kalakaua won the election and began his reign by attempting to restore Hawaiian traditions, which had been eroded over the years under pressure from American missionaries. However, his enjoyment of high living and of travel caused him to spend much of his time away from Hawaii. During his absences, Liliuokalani served as regent.

By 1887, Kalakaua had become largely ineffective, unable to withstand pressure from American interests and the pro-U.S. faction on the Big Island. He was forced, under threat of mass insurrection, to sign what became known as the Bayonet Constitution, which turned over extraordinary power to non-Hawaiian (mostly American) interests and rendered the monarchy nearly powerless. Shorn of responsibilities, Kalakaua threw himself into his playboy lifestyle, and on a visit to San Francisco in 1891 he died.

Liliuokalani, having served as regent during much of her brother's rule, was the logical choice for Hawaii's next ruler, and she took the throne in January 1891. Her first order of business was to undo the damage that the Bayonet Constitution had done to the power of the monarchy. She proposed a new constitution in 1893, only to rouse the ire of U.S. business interests and their local allies within the Hawaiian legislature. Realizing that these factions would never agree voluntarily to a restoration of royal authority, she began to rule by edict, bypassing the legislature and even ignoring her ministers.

The queen's independence did not sit well with the increasingly powerful U.S. sugar-growing interests and their allies among the native Hawaiians. These dissidents called upon John L. Stevens, the resident U.S. minister of Hawaii, who called in U.S. troops to depose the queen and establish a new government. U.S. President Benjamin Harrison supported the insurrection and annexed the island-nation, making Liliuokalani's deposition official. She was kept under house arrest because it was feared that she might inspire a rebellion among the indigenous people.

While under arrest, Liliuokalani remained in contact with her supporters, and brought the fight to regain her throne all the way to the office of the new U.S. president, Grover Cleveland. He reversed the order of annexation, fueling hope that Liliuokalani would soon regain her position as Hawaii's queen. The entrenched U.S. interests on the island, however, had no intention of relinquishing their control. They defied the presidential order and declared Hawaii a republic in 1894, naming one of the powerful plantation owners, Sandford Dole, as their new president.

Liliuokalani's supporters were outraged, raising fears in Hawaii's American community that the deposed queen was fomenting rebellion. Dole had her rearrested and confined to her private residence in 1895. Later that same year, soldiers forcibly entered her home and conducted a search, turning up a cache of arms. It is not known whether these arms were hidden there by supporters or planted by the searchers, but the discovery served as a pretext for stripping Liliuokalani of all freedom of movement, and she was imprisoned in the Iolani palace.

Liliuokalani was finally granted limited freedom in 1896, and she set out to personally petition the U.S. president and Congress for the restoration of the monarchy. By this time, however, Hawaii had become too important to U.S. interests, for the islands were considered to be strategically necessary for the protection of U.S. naval interests in the Pacific. Congress, therefore, decided to support the so-called republic. Four years later, Congress once again approved annexation of Hawaii, ending all hope for the restoration of the monarchy.

Liliuokalani, no longer considered a threat, was finally set free to live as a private citizen in Honolulu. She put aside all further attempts to restore the monarchy, and spent the next two decades trying to protect and preserve the traditions of her homeland, devoting much of her time to public service. Before her death, on November 11, 1917, she established the Liliuokalani Trust for the support of Hawaiian orphans.

See also: HAWAIIAN KINGDOMS; KAMEHAMEHA I, THE GREAT.

FURTHER READING

Daws, Gavin. *Shoal of Time: A History of the Hawaiian Islands.* New York: Macmillan, 1974.

Wisniewski, Richard. *The Rise and Fall of the Hawaiian Islands.* Honolulu: Pacific Basin Enterprises, 1979.

LITERATURE AND KINGSHIP

The varying portrayal of kings and queens in literature reflects the changing ideas that societies have had of their rulers throughout history. Literary works present monarchs, real and imaginary, in many different lights: the king may be portrayed as an ideal, used to give a warning about tyranny, or made into a scapegoat for political frustrations.

THE IDEAL KING

Literary descriptions or discussions of ideal kingship can be either prescriptive or descriptive. Prescriptive literature often takes the form of moral essays, or "Mirrors for Princes," which contain advice for rulers. A Muslim example, the *Nasihat al-Muluk* (Book of Advice for Princes), by the twelfth-century Persian philosopher and mystic, Mu'allafat al-Ghazali, urges Muslim sultans to beware of eternal punishment if they rule unjustly. In a more practical vein, it also tells rulers to avoid counselors who flatter them.

Similar works in medieval Europe advised rulers to practice Christian virtues. But in the secularized society of the Renaissance, a more cynical attitude developed. The advice in *The Prince* (1513), a treatise of an "ideal" ruler by Florentine statesman Niccolo Machiavelli, actually reverses many of the precepts of the earlier Mirrors for Princes. Writing for the ruling Medici family of Florence, Machiavelli proposed that since human beings are imperfect, attempts to govern solely by practicing virtue will inevitably fail. Therefore, a ruler might sometimes resort to means that are morally evil in order to preserve the state and prevent the greater evil of foreign conquest.

An ancient and widespread monarchical ideal is the sage-king. In his classic work, *The Republic,* the Greek philosopher Plato describes his ideal monarch as a philosopher-king. Two of China's greatest humanist philosophers, Confucius and Mencius, idealized mythical god-kings of China—the Yellow Emperor (Huang-ti), Yu, Yao, and Shung—as sage-kings of a former Golden Age. Confucius advised rulers to imitate them in the practice of the virtues of benevolence, loyalty, and moderation, for only a ruler who is worthy will be entitled to receive the Mandate of Heaven, or authority to rule.

Another ideal monarch is the king who is both a warrior and a religious ruler. The medieval epic poem, *The Song of Roland,* written by an unknown author in France in the twelfth century, was inspired by the Christian struggle against the Muslims during the Crusades. The poem looks back on the Frankish king Charlemagne (r. 768–814) as an ideal king who was both a pious religious man and a courageous warrior. In the Indian epic, *The Mahabharata,* compiled around 350, Prince Arjuna is a warrior king who receives sacred revelations from the god Vishnu.

One of the greatest kings of myth is King Arthur of Britain. His legend is based on the exploits of a Romanized Celtic general in fifth-century Britain who fought the Anglo-Saxon invaders. Medieval writers, such as Geoffrey of Monmouth in England and Chrétien de Troyes in France, portrayed Arthur as the ideal of medieval chivalry. So important was the cult of Arthur that King Henry II of England (r. 1154–1189) sought to attach himself to it by proclaiming his discovery of Arthur's burial place at Glastonbury in southwestern England around 1183. Four years later, Henry named his recently born and youngest son Arthur in honor of the legendary ruler.

More recent rulers have also been made into idealized symbols of their nation and its view of itself. In nineteenth-century England, for instance, the ideal of a woman as a "domestic queen" developed

Throughout the centuries, the lives of kings and queens—both real and imaginary—have been detailed and interpreted in works of literature and philosophy. Some works portray monarchs as they truly were; others present idealized views. Perhaps the best-known Renaissance treatise on the ideal ruler is *The Prince* (1513) by Florentine statesman Niccolo Machiavelli, shown in this sixteenth-century portrait.

from the image of Queen Victoria, who was celebrated by poets and novelists as a middle-class monarch whose main concern was with husband and home.

CHANGING PORTRAYALS

Few people have written about as many rulers as the great English playwright, William Shakespeare. For many years, critics have debated his political intentions in the portrayal of monarchs. Some have seen a single thread running through his English history plays of a fatal curse resulting from the deposition of King Richard II (r. 1377–1399) by Henry Bolingbroke (Henry IV, 1399–1413), an action that haunted Henry's successors. Some have seen Shakespeare's play, *Richard III,* as a defense of the position held by the Tudor dynasty that Richard was evil and Henry VII (r. 1485–1509), the first Tudor king, was right to depose him.

The same Shakespearean work often receives different interpretations. For example, in a 1944 film version of *Henry V,* that king is portrayed as a perfect monarch and military hero who achieved a miraculous victory over the French at the battle of Agincourt in 1415. This portrayal was intended to give England hope in the ongoing struggle against the

ROYAL PLACES

THE GREEK THEATER

Myths about kings and queens formed much of the basis of the ancient Greek theater, which reached its height in Athens in the fifth century B.C.E. The great tragedies of Aeschylus, Sophocles, and Euripides dramatize the Greek conceptions of monarchy and the role of kings.

The first Greek dramas were rituals enacting the myths of the death and resurrection of the ritual god-king. The theater in Athens started as songs and dances at the *Dionysia,* the feast in honor of Dionysius, the god of wine. These eventually became dramatic plays with actors answering a chorus that recited narrative.

Many Greek tragedies deal with the role of kings in regard to the city and the gods. At a time when Athens was engaged in a struggle for democratic government, the tragic poets often criticized tyrannical kings. In the play *Agamemnon* by Aeschylus, Clytemnestra, the wife of King Agamemnon, murders the lawful king, her husband, and allows the tyrant Aegisthus to seize the throne.

In *Antigone* by Sophocles, the heroine Antigone defies the impious king Creon to seek burial for her brother, who had been killed in battle. Creon's disobedience of the divine laws by which the city should be governed results in tragedy. In another play by Sophocles, *Oedipus the King,* the city of Thebes is inflicted with plague. When Oedipus eventually learns the truth—that he unwittingly killed his father and married his mother—he blinds himself, and his wife Jocasta kills herself. But the city is saved, an echo of the ancient idea that the purging of a bad king will restore health to the people.

In his *Bacchae,* the Greek playwright Euripides describes Pentheus, the ruler of Thebes, as little more than a wild beast because of his violence and arrogance. Pentheus ends up being torn apart by the female devotees of the god Dionysius. These plays are not meaningful only for fifth-century Athens. They are still compelling today because of their moral themes about fate and the responsibility of human rulers.

William Shakespeare dramatized the lives of a number of monarchs in his history plays. Perhaps the most infamous was Richard III, whom he depicted as a villain of monstrous proportions. This engraving by William Hogarth shows the eighteenth-century actor David Garrick performing the role of the evil king in Shakespeare's *Richard III*.

Nazis in World War II. In a more recent film version of the same play (1990), Henry V (r. 1413–1422) is portrayed as a more human and flawed monarch.

Different authors have portrayed the same ruler according to the beliefs of their own times. In *Antony and Cleopatra*, Shakespeare, in accordance with his idea of tragedy, portrayed Cleopatra as a passionate woman whose flaws helped destroy her and her Roman lover. In early nineteenth-century France, Theophile Gautier, in his short story "One of Cleopatra's Nights," portrayed the queen as a decadent aristocrat who kills her peasant lover and uses her feminine wiles to increase her power. Gautier's image of Cleopatra was colored by his feelings about the aristocracy of pre-Revolutionary France.

Sovereigns often become scapegoats for their kingdom's ills and are made the objects of satire. For instance, cartoonists and satirists in the eighteenth century criticized the sexual excesses of King Louis XV of France (r. 1715–1774), while others in the late nineteenth and early twentieth centuries found fault with the relationship of Empress Alexandra of Russia, the wife of Tsar Nicholas II (r. 1894–1917), to the alleged holy man, Rasputin.

THE PRESENT AND FUTURE

The mystique of kingship has come to seem outdated in modern democratic societies, as is reflected in twentieth-century literature in the West. But ideals of kingship have also been kept alive in literary works. One of the most resonant is the portrayal of King Arthur in the novel *The Once and Future King* (1958), by English author T.H. White. In this work, King Arthur struggles to rule Camelot by justice and right, only to see his kingdom fall because of violence, which White called "the mental illness of humanity." In the end of the novel, Arthur finds comfort in the fact that the ideal of Camelot will live on in stories. This idea was especially relevant in the twentieth century and was reflected by the response of American audiences to the Broadway musical *Camelot,* based on White's work, which came to be identified with the ideals of the vibrant and idealistic administration of President John F. Kennedy.

Another work that captures kingly ideals and resonates with modern audiences is the trilogy *Lord of the Rings,* written by English author J.R.R. Tolkien, first published in 1954–1955 and named "Book of the Century" by a readers' poll in England in 1997. Tolkien portrays the kingly character, Aragorn, in powerful archetypal images. He is the true king who comes to his rightful throne, forges his sword anew, and acts as a healer for his kingdom. Tolkien's notion of an ideal king, similar to that handed down from ancient pre-Christian mythology, remains popular today as a link with rulers found in the literature of the past.

See also: ARTHUR, KING; CHRISTIANITY AND KINGSHIP; HINDUISM AND KINGSHIP; MYTH AND FOLKLORE.

FURTHER READING

Homans, Margaret. *Royal Representations: Queen Victoria and British Culture, 1837–1876.* Chicago: University of Chicago Press, 1998.

Lagorio, Valerie M., and Mildred Leake Day, eds. *King Arthur Through the Ages.* New York: Garland, 1990.

LITHUANIA, GRAND DUCHY

OF (ca. 1230–1569 C.E.)

A large, ethnically diverse duchy that covered much of present-day Lithuania, Poland, Belarus, Russia, and the Ukraine. The Lithuanian grand dukes presided over the last pagan state in Europe, finally merging with the kingdom of Poland between the fourteenth and sixteenth centuries.

ORIGINS

People speaking a Baltic language (whose only surviving descendants are Lithuanian and Latvian) lived around the southeastern shores of the Baltic Sea more than 4,000 years ago. They eventually were challenged by Germanic and Slavic tribes who moved into the area. The struggle for power and territory among these three ethnic groups has long defined the flow of Lithuanian history.

Early Russian and German chronicles mention Lithuanian dukes as early as 1040. Pagan landowners and warriors, the dukes devoted much of their energies to expansion into Slavic territories. They ruled the new lands they conquered in accordance with local traditions, tolerating Orthodox Christians as well as small communities of Latin Christians and Jews. Official documents were written in the language known as Old Byelorussian; for that reason, and because much of the population was Slavic-speaking, some Russian historians refer to the medieval Lithuanian duchy as "West Russia."

A 1219 treaty with the duke of Volynia mentions twenty-one Lithuanian dukes under an informal chieftain named Mindaugas (r. ca. 1235–1263). A growing threat from the Latin West by two Germanic military-religious orders—the Livonian Order in Latvia and the Teutonic Knights in Prussia—pushed the dukes closer together at this time. Apparently led by the same Mindaugas, the Lithuanians defeated the Livonians at the battle of Saule in 1236.

Mindaugas accepted Latin Christianity in 1253 and, with Livonian support, was crowned king two years later. He set up a Lithuanian diocese, but his attempts to convert the population to Christianity proved unpopular with most nobles. The king was assassinated ten years later; a pagan temple was built on the ruins of his cathedral in Vilnius.

EXPANSION

Mindaugas's successors maintained the unity that he had achieved, but they declined to use the title of king, calling themselves grand dukes instead. A series of conquests and opportune marriages, especially under Grand Duke Vytenis (r. 1295–1316), expanded Lithuania's control over present-day Belarus. His brother and successor, Gediminas (r. 1316–1341), gave his name to the dynasty—the Gediminian dynasty. Their clan's ancestral base, the town of Vilnius, became the country's capital.

The Lithuanian nobles remained powerful as the source of the Gediminian military strength. However, most ethnic Lithuanians, perhaps half a million people, remained serfs. Gediminas himself invited merchants, artisans, and intellectuals from the German Baltic cities and from religious orders in Saxony to settle in his lands. He also invited the core of what became a thriving Jewish community in Vilnius by the end of the fourteenth century.

Gediminas's son Jaunutis (r. 1341–1345) ruled briefly but was deposed. His successor, his brother Al-Girdas (r. 1345–1377), kept up a steady pace of military campaigning that gradually extended the rule of the Lithuanian dukedom to the south and east. Al-Girdas was able to leave his son Jogaila (r. 1377–1392) a dominion that stretched nearly to Moscow in the east and all the way to the Black Sea in the south. Al-Girdas remained a devoted pagan; after his death in battle, he was cremated together with eighteen warhorses. However, in his marriage and his appointments to high offices, he favored Orthodox Christians.

Jogaila tried to continue his father's eastward expansion, siding with the Mongols of Central Asia against Russia, their common enemy, in the late 1370s. However, after the 1380 Russian victory at Kulikovo against the Mongol Khan Mamai and his Golden Horde, Jogaila was forced to turn westward. However, as long as Lithuania remained a pagan state, it was considered a legitimate military target of crusades by the Germanic religious-military orders.

UNION WITH POLAND

When the Polish nobles offered their country's vacant throne on the condition of conversion to Christianity, Jogaila accepted. In the Kreva Union Act of 1385, he pledged to accept Latin baptism (with the new name Wladyslaw Jagiello) and promised to keep Lithuania and Poland united in perpetuity. The next year, Jogaila personally supervised a mass baptism in Vilnius.

The new Lithuanian churches established under Jogaila were staffed by and dependent on Polish bishops. In the political sphere, however, Jogaila agreed to allow the grand duchy of Lithuania to survive as a distinct political entity within the kingdom of Poland under the leadership of his cousin Vytautas (r. 1392–1430). Together, the two rulers delivered a decisive blow against the Teutonic Knights at the battle of Tannenberg in 1410.

Vytautas died three days before his scheduled coronation as grand duke in 1430, but his successors managed to preserve some legal and political autonomy for the duchy. Only in 1569 did Polish noblemen under the last Jagiello ruler of Poland, Sigismund II (r. 1548–1572), succeed in imposing the Union of Lublin, which effectively ended Lithuanian independence for 350 years.

See also: JAGIELLO DYNASTY; PIAST DYNASTY.

LIU PANG (GAO TI) (247–195 B.C.E.)

Chinese emperor (r. 207–195 B.C.E.) who founded the Han dynasty and became one of the great heroes of Chinese history.

Born a peasant, Liu Pang was a minor village official under the Ch'in (Qin) dynasty (221–207 B.C.E.). He later became a bandit and then a rebel leader in the period of civil war that followed the disintegration of Ch'in rule. Liu Pang defeated rival warlords and established a base of power in the Han River region. After reconquering Ch'in territory, ending five years of civil war between rival states, he proclaimed himself emperor of the new Han dynasty in 206 C.E., taking the name Gao Ti. The new emperor established the Han capital at Chang'an. His reign marks the beginning of the Western or former Han dynasty.

Because of his humble beginnings, Liu Pang was not well educated, but he was intelligent and a conscientious ruler. One of his first tasks as emperor was to reestablish the unity of the empire, which he accomplished by replacing the rulers of all but one of the provinces and kingdoms under his rule with members of his own family. To win support from powerful families, he gave them large landholdings to govern as feudal estates. However, he later eliminated many of these estates after realizing the mistake of sharing power with the aristocracy. Having inherited an economy crippled by war, Liu Pang took pains to restrict government spending. He avoided the high cost of military campaigns by using diplomacy to deal with the dynasty's biggest menace, the Xiongnu. A federation of nomadic tribes to the north of China, the Xiongnu engaged in constant raids on their richer southern neighbor. Liu Pang kept the peace by arranging strategic marriages and alliances and giving generous gifts.

Liu Pang continued the highly centralized system of bureaucratic administration established by the Ch'in dynasty, but he eased the harsh practices of Ch'in rule by reducing taxes and instituting more humane punishments. In place of the Ch'in rulers' legalist philosophy, which relied on fear and punishment to maintain control, Liu Pang introduced Confucianism as his governing philosophy. Confucianism stressed the moral responsibility of the ruler to his people and the maintenance of a carefully defined social order based on obedience to authority. Confucian scholars filled the Han bureaucracy and predominated at court, where they tutored Liu Pang's heir.

Liu Pang died in battle on the frontier in 195 B.C.E. and was posthumously given the name Gao Ti (or Gaodi). He was succeeded by his young son, Huidi, whose mother, Empress Lu, ruled China for sixteen years as his regent.

See also: CH'IN (QIN) DYNASTY; HAN DYNASTY.

LLYWELYN AP GRUFFYDD

(d. 1282 C.E.)

Welsh prince who ruled the principality of Gwynedd in northeastern Wales from 1246 to 1282 and led a rebellion against King Edward I of England (r. 1272–1307).

Llywelyn ap Gruffydd and his brothers inherited the rule of Gwynedd from their childless half-uncle, Dayfdd ap Llywelyn (r. 1240–1246) in 1246. At first, Llywelyn and his older brother Owain (Owen) divided Gwynedd between them. But in 1255 Owain allied with Dafydd, a younger brother, against Llywelyn, who defeated them in battle, took them prisoner, and ruled the kingdom alone.

With Gwynedd firmly under his control, Llywelyn set out to restore the kingdom's power and independence. To do this he sought to dominate the other Welsh principalities, as the former kingdoms of Wales were often termed in this period. In 1256 and 1257, Llywelyn conquered a number of other Welsh regions, including Powys and Glamorgan in the south. In 1258, he began styling himself "prince of Wales," and gained the support of many other Welsh princes.

Following war between the English monarch Henry III (r. 1216–1272) and Simon de Montfort in England in 1264–1265—in which Llywelyn aided de Montfort (he later married de Montfort's daughter)—the prince of Wales was able to negotiate a beneficial treaty with the victorious Henry. In the Treaty of Montgomery (1267), Llywelyn gained recognition of his title, along with lands and castles, although English overlordship of Wales continued. In 1274, his brother Dafydd conspired to assassinate Llywelyn, but upon discovery of the plot Dafydd fled to the protection of Edward I of England.

Llywelyn repeatedly refused to do homage to Edward I as his overlord, and in 1276–1277 Edward made war on Llywelyn and defeated him. Llywelyn retained his title as prince of Wales but was required to do Edward homage, give hostages, and make financial payments. When his brother Dafydd, ambitious for power, rebelled against Edward in 1282, Llywelyn joined Dafydd, perhaps to retain his claim as overlord of the Welsh, which would be threatened if Wales rose up and followed Dafydd. Llywelyn was killed in a skirmish against the English late in 1282; Dafydd was executed by Edward I in 1283.

While he ruled, Llywelyn restored Gwynedd to unity and strength at a time when many Welsh principalities were disintegrating. He briefly united enough of the Welsh princes to make the region once more a problem for the rulers of England. However, it is highly unlikely that Llywelyn would ever have been able to rule a truly independent Wales, or even that he aspired to do so. He remains a romantic figure in Welsh history and an icon of Welsh nationalism.

See also: EDWARD I; GWYNEDD KINGDOM; WELSH KINGDOMS.

FURTHER READING

Holmes, George, ed. *Oxford Illustrated History of Medieval Europe.* New York: Oxford University Press, 1988.

Powicke, Sir Maurice. *The Thirteenth Century: 1216–1307.* 2nd ed. New York: Oxford University Press, 1998.

Walker, David. *Medieval Wales.* New York: Cambridge University Press, 1990.

LOBENGULA (ca. 1836–1894 C.E.)

Last ruler (r. 1870–1894) of the Ndebele kingdom (now part of Zimbabwe), who struggled unsuccessfully to overcome the threats to his kingdom from European colonists.

Lobengula was the son of Mzilikazi (r. ca. 1820s–1868), a warrior who fought alongside Shaka Zulu (r. 1816–1828) during the campaign to create the Zulu nation. Rather than remain part of the Zulu nation, however, Mzilikazi ultimately broke away and founded the Ndebele kingdom. Lobengula's mother was a member of the royal house of the Swazi kingdom and was related to the Swazi king, Sobhuza I (r. ca. 1780–1834).

Like his father before him, Lobengula had a reputation as a fine warrior and hunter, and he grew up to be a man of impressive size and bearing. His strength, and the wisdom for which he was highly respected, were much needed, for his inheritance of the throne was by no means guaranteed.

When Mzilikazi died in 1868, the Ndebele kingdom was riven by civil war. The Ndebele were comprised of many different peoples who had come together under Mzilikazi's rule, but whose loyalty was given to the man, not necessarily to the Ndebele state. Even before Mzilikazi died, factions had begun to form within the kingdom, and upon his death these factions clashed in open violence.

It took Lobengula two years to form a group of followers that was powerful enough to secure his claim to the throne. In the end, however, he succeeded and assumed rulership of the Ndebele in 1870. The years of Lobengula's reign were difficult. Though respected as a leader, he did not possess the power or the charisma of his father, and he never fully eliminated the factional strife that rocked his kingdom.

In addition, Lobengula was forced to deal with the increasing numbers of European settlers, both British and Boer (of Dutch ancestry). The Boers wanted farmland, while the British were drawn by something much more precious—gold, which had been discovered in Ndebele territory in 1867. Lobengula was soon nearly overwhelmed by European demands for mineral rights in his territory.

In 1888, hoping to eliminate the constant incursions of would-be miners and settlers onto his lands, Lobengula decreed that only the British would be granted such rights. This led to the formation of the British South Africa Company, headed by Cecil Rhodes (who later founded Rhodesia). Lobengula's decision was intended to increase stability in the region by restricting access to mining rights in Matabeleland (as the Ndebele kingdom was then known). Instead, the decision resulted in the downfall of both his reign and his kingdom.

In 1890, the British South Africa Company mounted an expedition to search for additional mineral deposits in Matabeleland. The peoples of the area, resenting this intrusion, sent raiders to attack one of the company's settlements. Lobengula called for peaceful negotiations to deal with the situation, hoping to avert a disastrous war. The British South Africa Company, however, saw opportunity in the tragedy: a war could end its dependence on Lobengula's approval and open up the entire territory to mining.

Thus, with a ready-made pretext for war, the British South African Company mustered an army and, in 1893, attacked the Ndebele capital of Bulaweyo. The city was burned to the ground, and Lobengula was forced to flee. With a small group of followers, Lobengula spent a year trying to regain his kingdom, but he failed. In 1894, this last king of the Ndebele contracted smallpox and died, leaving Matabeleland under the complete control of the British.

See also: CETSHWAYO; DINGISWAYO; MZILIKAZI; NDEBELE KINGDOM; SHAKA ZULU; SOBHUZA I; SOBHUZA II; ZULU KINGDOM.

FURTHER READING

Oliver, Roland, and G. N. Sanderson, eds. *Cambridge History of Africa: From 1870 to 1905.* New York: Cambridge University Press, 1985.

LODI KINGDOM (1451–1526 C.E.)

Short-lived kingdom in India that arose in the mid-fifteenth century, but fell to the Mughal dynasty in the early sixteenth century.

The Lodis, a tribe of Afghan descent, gradually rose to prominence during the rule of the Tughluq dynasty, which ruled the Delhi sultanate of India from 1320 to 1414. Eventually, Malik Kala, an influential Lodi merchant, became the administrator of the region of Daurala. In 1451, his son, Bahlul (r. 1451–1489), acquired the governorship of Panjab. Utilizing his new power, Bahlul quickly attacked Delhi and seized control of the entire sultanate from the Sayyid dynasty, establishing the Lodi dynasty. Bahlul then invaded the region of Jaupur and also subjugated it.

Bahlul integrated Afghan tribal principles into Delhi government and society. He eliminated the rule of hereditary succession and insisted that the nobility elect his heir. He also extended many of the sultan's personal social privileges to all members of the nobility. Finally, Bahlud divided the main army among the different provinces under his control. Afghan leaders whom he placed in control of individual regions were granted a great deal of autonomy. Although required to pay an annual tribute and provide troops when Bahlud declared war, these local leaders were largely free to control their respective provinces.

When Bahlud died in 1489, the nobility elected his son, Sikandar (r. 1489–1517), to be his successor. To solidify his power, Sikandar banished his brother, the governor of Jaupur, and assumed direct control of the sultanate. As ruler, Sikandar was extremely benevolent to the Muslim inhabitants of the Delhi sultanate. He built numerous Muslim schools and converted several highly sacred Hindu sites into Muslim mosques. He also persecuted Hindu religious leaders. Consequently, Hindu unrest spread across the kingdom and threatened the dynasty's continuation.

A combination of Hindu rebellion and Afghan dissent finally doomed the Lodi dynasty. After Sikandar's death in 1517, the nobility elected his son, Ibrahim (r. 1517–1526), to succeed him. But they demanded that an independent member of the dynasty again be appointed governor of Jaupur. Ibrahim refused and viciously punished the nobles who opposed him. His actions had a predictable backlash. As Hindu revolts became increasingly serious, the Afghan governors refused to lend Ibrahim any military support.

Babur, the Timurid ruler of Transoxiana, exploited the weakness of the Lodi dynasty. In 1526, with the consent of many Afghan nobles, Babur invaded Delhi and defeated Ibrahim at the battle of Panipat. Ibrahim died during the battle, and the Lodi dynasty abruptly ended. The victorious Babur (r. 1526–1530) established the Moghul dynasty in India and went on to create the Moghul Empire, which incorporated the Delhi sultanate. The Lodis had established the first Afghan sultanate in Delhi, but they were unable to maintain control because they were unable or unwilling to reconcile the Muslim and Hindu cultures within their domain.

See also: BABUR; DELHI KINGDOM; MUGHAL EMPIRE; TUGHLUQ DYNASTY.

LOMBARD DYNASTY (569–774 C.E.)

Dynasty of Germanic origin that established the Lombard kingdom in northern Italy, a dynasty that reigned until the late eighth century.

The Lombard dynasty formed a bridge that linked two of the great empires of Western civilization, the Roman Empire and the Holy Roman Empire. The origins of the dynasty began with the movement of the Germanic tribe called the Lombards (or Longobards) into the Italian Peninsula beginning in the first century C.E. The dynasty ended in 774, when the Lombards were defeated by the Frankish empire of Charlemagne (r. 768–814).

The Lombard dynasty was briefly led by a king named Alboin (r. 569–572), who invaded and conquered the region of Pavia in northern Italy in 569. This conquest began a nearly two-hundred-year period during which the Lombard dynasty expanded into and gained control of much of northern Italy, leaving the south to the Byzantine Empire.

The reigns of Alboin, which abruptly ended with his assassination in 572, and his successor Cleph (r. 572–574), were important for developing the Lombard kingdom from a nomadic monarchy to one established in a fixed locale. The assassination of Cleph in 574 brought a brief end to the new Lombard kingdom. In the decade following his death, the kingdom was divided into thirty-five duchies, each based in a city that the Lombards had conquered.

The ten-year interregnum (period "between reigns") was ended by the acclamation of Cleph's son, Authari (r. 584–590), as the new king of the Lombards. Authari spent part of his reign shoring up the kingdom, and he attempted to make peace with the Franks. Peace with the Franks allowed the Authari to wage war on those who entered alliances with the Franks against him.

In 588, when the Franks refused to link themselves to the Lombards by marriage, a union was arranged with Theudelinda, the sister of the Bavarian king. This was done despite the fact that she was previously committed to the Frankish king, Childebert II (r. 575–595). Upon Authari's death in 590, Agiluif (r. 590–615), the duke of Turin, became the Lombard king, with Theudelinda as his queen. Scholars dispute whether this transfer of power was violent or consensual. Upon Agilufo's death in 615, his son Adaloald (r. 615–626) took the throne. He reigned under the regency of his mother, Theudelinda, until 624, when he was deposed by his sister's husband, Arioald (r. 626–636).

As in other early dynasties, after the reigns of the initial monarchs, a great degree of conflict developed among various members of the noble classes, who sought greater powers. The Lombard dynasty was no exception. On countless occasions, the Lombard kings felt pressured to exercise their power and encourage loyalty by deposing subordinate aristocrats who appeared less than faithful.

Furthermore, the lack of entrenched traditions in the Lombard dynasty in this period was evident in the transition of power between sovereigns. One method of transferring power was the remarriage of queens who were related by bloodlines to the first monarchs. An example of such a remarriage occurred when the Lombard king, Rotari (r. 636–652), married Adaloald's sister Gundeberga after she was widowed by Arioald.

Another means of transferring power was the development of blood connections to previous monarchs for whom there was a sense of primacy. This familial attachment was then made more concrete through religious and political affiliations. This can be seen in the elevation of Ariperto I (r. 653–661), a nephew to Theudelinda as well as a Catholic with pro-Roman sentiments, to the throne in place of other family members, who may have held anti-Roman views or been Arian Christian, as were the early Lombard kings.

This dynastic infighting and scheming continued through the reigns of Aripert's sons, Perctarit (r. 661–662, 672–688) and Godepert (r. 661–662). These descendants of Theudelinda's family were soon overthrown by Grimoald (r. 662–671), the duke of Bene-vento, who was assassinated a decade later. Upon Grimoald's death, Perctarit returned to the throne to be followed by his sons and the sons of his brothers. Pertarito's return also made the Lombard dynasty much more of a Bavarian dynasty, because of the influence of Theudelinda's line.

After the reigns of the offspring of Perctarit and Godepert, kings from various royal houses ruled the Lombard Kingdom until the kingdom's final conquest by the Franks in 774.

See also: CHARLEMAGNE; FRANKISH KINGDOM; LOMBARD KINGDOM.

FURTHER READING
Hodgkin, Thomas. *Italy and Her Invaders, 376–814.* New York: Russell & Russell, 1967.

LOMBARD KINGDOM (568–774 C.E.)

Kingdom in northern Italy established in the sixth century by the Lombards, one of the Germanic tribes that migrated into Europe after the collapse of the Roman Empire.

The Lombard kingdom began when the Lombard king, Alboin (r. 568–572), invaded northern Italy around 568. The kingdom was later taken over by the Franks, led by Charlemagne (r. 768–814), in 774.

ESTABLISHMENT OF THE LOMBARD DYNASTY
The kingdom of the Lombards (or Longobards) originated in the Germanic region of Pannonia. The Lombards initially entered the Italian Peninsula under the leadership of Alboin and took the province of Venice. The Lombards next conquered the province of Liguria in the northwestern part of the Italian Peninsula. Lombard conquests quickly absorbed most of Italy north of Tuscany, with the exception of a few seaside fortifications and Ravenna.

With the deaths of Alboin in 572 and his successor, Cleph (r. 572–574), in 574, the Lombard territories were divided into a series of duchies. This interregnum of duchies, which was marked by periodic raids on neighboring territories, was ended by the elevation of Authari (r. 584–590) as Lombard king in 584. Authari's accession to the throne marked a definite end to the initial period of instability that characterized the Lombard realm.

Up to the reign of Alboin, the Lombard domains had been subject to successive migrations, and Lombard territory did not have well-defined borders. The regions conquered by Albion and Cleph in Italy became the core territory of the future Lombard kingdom, but later kings expanded this territory to create a more viable kingdom.

CREATION OF THE LOMBARD KINGDOM
The accession of Authari to the Lombard kingship marked the point at which regional differences among the Lombard nobility were subjugated enough to allow a workable state to emerge. However, the sovereignty of this kingdom of the Lombards would be challenged repeatedly over the next two centuries, most significantly by the Franks. At the same time, the Lombard realm expanded as the Lombards conquered important Italian cities, including Padua, Genoa, Calabria, Taranto, and Brindisi.

By the death of the Lombard king, Grimoald I (r. 662–671), in 671, the kingdom of the Lombards had reached its peak of power. The expansionary zeal of the Lombards had not subsided completely, however.

In 712, the Lombards besieged Rome, a rival state that had been a constant irritant. The siege of Rome occurred during the reign of Liutprand (r. 712–744). The other major Italian center that had managed to avoid Lombard invasion was Ravenna, which was finally captured by the Lombards in 751 under King Aistulf (r. 749–756).

FRANKISH CONTROL OF THE KINGDOM

Despite Aistulf's success in Ravenna in 751, his reign spelled the end of Lombard control of their kingdom. Four years later, in 755, the Frankish ruler, Pepin the Short (r. 751–768), led the Franks to victory over the Lombards at the battle of Pavia.

In terms of political independence, with the Frankish victory at Pavia, the Lombard kingdom was now under the authority of the Franks, and the Lombards were forced to recognize Pepin's suzerainty over them. Pavia, the Lombard capital, was surrendered to Pepin's son and successor, Charlemagne, in 774 by the last Lombard king, Desiderius (r. 757–774). This fully incorporated the kingdom of the Lombards into the Frankish kingdom.

See also: CHARLEMAGNE; FRANKISH KINGDOM; HOLY ROMAN EMPIRE; PEPIN THE SHORT (PEPIN III).

FURTHER READING

Foulke, William Dudley, trans. *The History of the Lombards: Paul the Deacon.* Philadelphia: University of Pennsylvania Press, 2003.

LORDS OF THE ISLES

(ca. 1300s–1493 C.E.)

The Lordship of the Isles was a quasi-kingdom in northwestern Scotland, based in the Hebrides or Western Isles. The Clan Donald chieftains who styled themselves "Lords of the Isles" claimed descent from Somerled, a twelfth-century ruler of mixed Gaelic and Scandinavian ancestry who was supposedly descended from the dynasty of the Scots-Gaelic Dalriada kingdom. After the death of Scottish king Robert the Bruce (r. 1306–1329), the MacDonald clan chiefs became increasingly powerful and independent. Able seafarers, they dominated the waters of northwestern Scotland with their fleet, since the

kings of Scotland lacked a navy until the rule of James III (r. 1460–1488) in the 1400s.

The Gaelic-speaking Lords of the Isles had a fractious relationship with their Scottish overlords, whose roots stemmed from the Anglo-Scots-speaking community of the southeast. The Lords ruled a large area of territory in northern Scotland with near-independence, acknowledging the authority of the Scottish king in Edinburgh, yet largely ignoring him. John MacDonald, the first Lord of the Isles, became leader of his clan in 1325, and his son, grandson, and great-grandson all carried the lordship title. At the battle of Harlaw in 1411, the second Lord of the Isles, Donald MacDonald, led a number of Gaelic clans into battle against Scotland's Stewart dynasty, fighting over the claim to the earldom of Ross. King James I of Scotland (r. 1406–1437) tried to subdue Alexander MacDonald, the third Lord of the Isles, but succeeded only in provoking successive rebellions from the Isles.

John MacDonald, the fourth and final Lord of the Isles, was defeated in battle by King James III of Scotland in 1476. Nonetheless, MacDonald's son Angus Og and other Gaelic chieftains continued to trouble the Stewart dynasty in the years that followed, despite their forfeiture of the lordship to the Scottish Crown in 1493.

See also: SCOTTISH KINGDOMS

LORRAINE DYNASTY (1496–1675 C.E.)

A French dynasty formed from a branch of the ruling house of Lorraine, noted for its violent attacks on Protestants and intrigues to gain power. Of the seven generations of the dynasty, the second and third dukes of Guise were the most powerful. They founded the Holy League, were leaders in persecuting the Huguenots (French Protestants), and were instrumental in causing the European Wars of Religion.

The founder of the Guise dynasty was Claude de Lorraine (1496–1550), who married into the French royal family with his marriage to Antoinette de Bourbon in 1513. As a reward for his services in the Italian Wars and as governor of Champagne, King Francis I of France (r. 1515–1547) made Claude the duke of Guise in 1527. Claude's daughter, Mary of Guise, married King James V of Scotland (r. 1513–1542).

The second duke of Guise was Claude's son, François (r. 1519–1563). During the Italian Wars,

François led an unsuccessful campaign against King Philip II of Spain (r. 1556–1598), but he won Calais from the English in 1558. His niece, Mary Stuart (daughter of James V of Scotland), married the young King Francis II (r. 1559–1560), and after 1559, François and his brother Charles de Guise, the cardinal of Lorraine, shared control of the French government.

François and Charles abused their power, viciously persecuted Protestants, and scorned the royal family and nobles. After Francis II died in 1560, they lost their power under the regency of Catherine de Medici, the mother of Charles IX (r. 1560–1574), and formed an independent political and military party in opposition to both the Huguenots and the Crown. François was assassinated in 1563, but his brother Charles continued his intrigues and persecution of the Protestants until 1570. During that time, Charles sought Spanish support for the Catholic cause in France.

François's son Henri, the third duke of Guise (r. 1550–1588), was instrumental in the Saint Bartholomew's Day massacre of 1572, in which perhaps as many as 25,000 Protestants were murdered by soldiers of the Crown and Catholic mobs. Henri founded the Catholic League, which opposed the appointment of the Protestant Henry of Navarre (Henry IV, r. 1589–1610) as heir presumptive to the throne of France. By this time, the Guises were virtually in the pay of Spain. Fearful of Henri's power, Henry III (r. 1574–1589) had him assassinated in 1588, along with his brother Louis, the cardinal of Guise.

The remaining dukes of Guise were much less powerful than the first three. The fourth duke, Charles (r. 1571–1614), was the son of Henri. The fifth was Charles's son, Henri (r. 1614–1650), who also served as archbishop of Reims and as grand chamberlain to the Crown. The sixth duke was Henri's nephew, Louis Joseph (r. 1650–1670), whose son, François Joseph de Lorraine (r. 1670–1675), was the last duke of Guise. With his death in 1675, the Guise dynasty came to an end.

See also: CHRISTIANITY AND KINGSHIP; FRANCIS I; FRENCH MONARCHIES; HENRY IV (FRANCE).

LOTHAIR I (795–855 C.E.)

Grandson of the Frankish ruler Charlemagne (r. 768–814) and eldest son and successor of Louis I, the Pious (r. 814–840), as emperor of the West (r. 840–855).

At the death of Charlemagne in 814, Lothair's father, Louis, inherited the Frankish Empire. To ensure an orderly succession, Louis had Lothair crowned co-emperor in 817 and installed his other two sons, Pepin and Louis the German, as subkings. This system worked well until the death of Louis's first wife Ermengard, the mother of Lothair, Pepin, and Louis. Louis the Pious married again to a powerful noblewoman, Judith, who gave birth to a son, Charles the Bald, in 823.

Angered by this threat to their inheritance, the sons of Ermengard rebelled against their father twice, in 830 and 833. In both instances, the inability of the brothers to overcome their own rivalries resulted in failure to depose their father.

Pepin died in 838, and after the death of Louis I in 840, Lothair, Louis, and Charles waged war against one another for control of the empire. In 843, the three brothers signed the Treaty of Verdun, which divided the Frankish Empire into three parts. This division had an enormous impact on the future shape of Europe: the western portion of the former empire would become the kingdom of France, and the eastern portion, Germany.

Lothair received the central portion of the divided Frankish Empire, which ran from the North Sea south into Italy. He also retained the imperial title as emperor of the West. Before his death, Lothair divided his realm among his three sons, one of whom, Louis II (r. 855–875) later became emperor. His brother Lothair gave his name to the region known as Lotharingia, or Lorraine; parts of this territory retain the name today. Lothair abdicated his throne in 855 and became a monk. He died shortly afterward.

See also: CAROLINGIAN DYNASTY; CHARLEMAGNE; HOLY ROMAN EMPIRE; LOUIS I, THE PIOUS; MEROVINGIAN DYNASTY; PEPIN DYNASTY.

LOUIS THE GERMAN. *See*

CAROLINGIAN DYNASTY

LOUIS I, THE GREAT (1326–1382 C.E.)

King of Hungary (r. 1342–1382) and Poland (r. 1370–1382) who campaigned successfully against the Ottoman Turks and brought Hungary to the peak of its power while promoting the flowering of art, literature, and learning.

Louis was born in 1326 to King Charles I of Hungary (r. 1307–1342), the first Hungarian ruler of a branch of the French Angevin dynasty. Louis succeeded to the throne of Hungary upon his father's death in 1342. Charles I had played an important role in restoring the power of the Hungarian monarchy and in uniting the country. Louis devoted his own long reign to ceaseless military campaigns and expansion, enlarging Hungary's borders to perhaps their greatest extent.

A man of great personal courage, Louis launched military campaigns virtually every year during his reign, aimed at enforcing Hungarian suzerainty over the various Croatian, Serbian, Bosnian, Bulgarian, Wallachian, and Moldavian lords and petty rulers under the hegemony of Hungary. His own nobles won glory and a steady income in the spoils of war. Louis also directed his military actions against other threats, including the Ottoman Turks and states in Italy.

By the time Louis took the throne in 1342, Byzantine power was quickly waning, but the Ottomans had not yet penetrated far into the Balkan region. Thus, no major counterforce existed to check Louis's imperial ambitions. Nevertheless, his only permanent conquests were in Croatia, all of which were absorbed into Hungary, along the Dalmatian coast. Repeated campaigns against Venice, in alliance with the Italian city-state of Genoa, forced the Venetians to cede control of Dalmatia to Hungary in 1358 and to grant Hungary and the cities of Dalmatia freedom of passage in the Adriatic Sea. In 1377, Louis turned his attention to the Ottomans, whom he campaigned against successfully.

Louis's brother Andrew was married to Joanna I of Naples (r. 1343–1381). When Andrew was murdered in 1345, possibly at the behest of Joanna, Louis broke Hungary's alliance with that branch of the Angevin dynasty. In 1347, Louis mounted a campaign in Italy in support of his family's claim to the kingdom of Naples, but this action was less productive than his other military ventures. Although Louis occupied Naples in 1348, he was forced to leave there soon after because of an outbreak of plague, and his campaign against Naples resulted in no lasting political gains.

Perhaps Louis's greatest achievement was to unite the Crowns of Poland and Hungary. By aiding his uncle, the heirless King Casimir III of Poland (r. 1333–1370), in his battles against the Lithuanians, Louis assured himself election as king of Poland when Casimir died in 1370. The union between the two kingdoms proved short-lived, however. After Louis's death, Poland became united with Lithuania under the Jagiello dynasty rather than with Hungary.

Louis's French background and contact with the Italian Renaissance during his campaigns in Italy led to his patronage of the arts and learning, which flourished in Hungary during his reign. Ruling during the age of European chivalry, Louis was styled "the Great" immediately after his death in 1382. His martial achievements proved ephemeral, however, as the power vacuum of the Balkans was soon filled by the growing power of the Ottoman Empire.

Louis had no male heir, and upon his death the throne of Hungary went to his daughter, Mary (r. 1382–1385), the wife of future Holy Roman Emperor Sigismund (r. 1410–1437). Mary was deposed in 1385, after which a period of turmoil followed. Restored to the throne in 1386, Mary then ruled Hungary jointly with Sigismund. Poland, which refused to continue the union of Crowns, broke away from Hungary and allowed Louis's younger daughter, Jadwiga (r. 1383–1399, to rule along with her husband, Wladyslaw II Jagiello (r. 1386–1434).

See also: ANGEVIN DYNASTIES; HOLY ROMAN EMPIRE; JAGIELLO DYNASTY; NAPLES, KINGDOM OF; SIGISMUND.

LOUIS I, THE PIOUS (778–840 C.E.)

King of Aquitaine (r. 781–840), Holy Roman emperor (r. 814–840), and only legitimate, surviving son of Charlemagne (r. 768–814), the founder of the Carolingian dynasty. When Louis died in 840, the Carolingian Empire was divided between his sons.

Although intelligent, well educated, and capable as a ruler, Louis was not a good military leader, which weakened his government and caused the nobles of his realm to lose respect for him. Many nobles took the opportunity to increase their own power and wealth at Louis's expense and, well before his death, even Louis's own sons challenged him.

Louis found a strong ally in the Church by supporting Benedict of Aniane in attempts to reform the church and restore the monasteries to religious rule and discipline. In 816, Louis appointed Benedict director of all the monasteries in the Frankish realm, and he established Benedict in a monastery near the royal residence.

Louis had three sons by his first wife: Lothair, Louis "the German," and Pepin of Aquitaine. In 817, Louis decreed that his eldest son, Lothair, would succeed him as emperor and that his other two sons would become kings within the empire. By tradition, the sons should have inherited equally, but Louis hoped that this decision would preserve the unity of the empire.

This partitioning of the empire was thrown into question in 823 when Louis had a fourth son, Charles (later known as "The Bald"), by his second wife. Louis wanted to secure a kingdom for this son also, but his other sons refused. The resulting challenges lasted until Louis's death, greatly weakening the monarchy. Louis was deposed by his three older sons in 833, but he was restored to power in 834 by his sons Louis and Pepin, who feared Lothair's power. When Louis I died in 840, the empire built by Charlemagne was dissolved into three kingdoms split between Lothair I, Louis the German, and Charles the Bald. Louis's son Pepin had already died in 838.

See also: AQUITAINE DUCHY; CAROLINGIAN DYNASTY; CHARLEMAGNE; FRANKISH KINGDOM; LOTHAIR I.

LOUIS IV, THE BAVARIAN

(1283–1347 C.E.)

German king (r. 1314–1347) and Holy Roman emperor (r. 1328–1347,), a member of the house of Wittelsbach, who was a controversial monarch who defied the pope.

Louis IV was the son of Duke Louis II of the house of Wittelsbach of Upper Bavaria. After his father died in 1294, Louis, now duke of Upper Bavaria, and his mother Mechthild, a member of the Habsburg dynasty and daughter of Holy Roman Emperor Rudolf I (r. 1273–1291), went to Munich to live with Louis's older brother, Rudolph.

Tensions arose in the family at this time, as Mechthild supported the attempt of her brother, Albert I of Austria (r. 1282–1308), to take the German throne from Adolph of Nassau (r. 1292–1298),

whom Rudolph supported. Adolph had been placed on the throne by an assembly of German princes, called electors, who feared the growing power of the Habsburgs.

Because of the increased tensions, Louis was sent to live in Vienna with his Habsburg relatives. Meanwhile, Albert I of Austria defeated Adolf of Nassau at the battle of Göllheim in 1298, making himself king of Germany and forcing Rudolph to accept Louis's legal right to govern.

Following the assassination of Albert I in 1308, the German electors chose Henry VII of Luxembourg (r. 1308–1313) as Albert's successor. Wanting to restore the ancient Holy Roman Empire, Henry VII marched with his troops into Italy in 1312 and was crowned emperor by a reluctant Pope Clement V.

In Germany, meanwhile, Louis and Rudolph divided Upper Bavaria. Louis also gained control of Lower Bavaria when Duke Stephen I (r. 1290–1309) died and left Louis as regent for his sons. However, the traditional anti-Austrian attitude of Lower Bavaria led to a quarrel with Frederick III of Austria (r. 1298–1330), which Louis won in a decisive victory at the battle of Gammelsdorf in 1313. Rudolph objected to Louis's rise in power, and Louis turned to the Habsburgs for military support. A peaceful solution was reached in 1314 after the two sides negotiated with the archbishop of Salzburg acting as mediator.

When Henry VII died suddenly in Italy in 1313, the German electors rejected the succession of his son, John of Bohemia, because of the boy's young age. Four of the electors chose Frederick III of Austria to be the new German king, but five other electors, voting a few days later, chose Louis instead, setting the stage for a political and military struggle.

In 1322, Louis defeated and captured Frederick, but the problem of shared rule was not fully resolved until Frederick's death in 1330. With the support of Philip V of France (r. 1316–1322), Pope Clement V and his successor, Pope John XII, claimed the right to govern the Holy Roman Empire, including Germany, until the election could be resolved.

Tired of papal interference in their political affairs, the six German electors at Rhense declared that election by a majority of electors automatically conferred the royal title of Germany and rule over the Holy Roman Empire, with or without papal support. The pope then excommunicated Louis.

In 1327, Louis took his army to consolidate

northern Italy and to convince Pope John XXII to crown him emperor. The pope refused. But in 1328, Louis was crowned emperor by Sciarra Colonna, the leader of a group of Italian nobles. Louis returned to Germany in 1330 because of instability at home and the death of Frederick III of Austria.

Throughout his reign, Louis sought to establish the house of Wittelsbach on the same level as the house of Luxembourg and the Habsburg dynasty. To this end, he kept adding to the possessions of his family, and annoying everyone else. In 1342, he acquired the Tyrol by voiding the first marriage of Margaret Maultasch, the countess of Tyrol, to a Luxembourg husband and marrying her to his son, Louis of Brandenburg, thus alienating the house of Luxembourg. In 1346, he further antagonized the German princes by conferring Holland, Zeeland, and Friesland upon his wife.

Pope Clement VI, the successor of Pope John XXII, took advantage of the hostility toward Louis and set out to depose him. Clement was sensitive to the feelings of the German electors, who deserted Louis one by one, and encouraged Charles of Luxembourg to seek the throne. In 1346, the electors declared Charles IV (r. 1346–1378) as king of the Germans (as a rival to Louis) by a majority vote. Later that year, while preparing to mount resistance to Charles, Louis IV died of a heart attack during a bear hunt.

See also: HABSBURG DYNASTY; HOLY ROMAN EMPIRE; LUXEMBOURG DYNASTY; SALIAN DYNASTY.

FURTHER READING

Heer, Friedrich. *The Holy Roman Empire.* New York: Praeger, 1968.

LOUIS VII (1120–1180 C.E.)

King of France (r. 1137–1180), also called Louis the Younger, who played an important role in strengthening the French monarchy. The son of Louis VI (r. 1108–1137) and member of the Capetian dynasty, Louis married Eleanor of Aquitaine shortly before becoming king. An intelligent and skillful strategist and adviser to her husband, Eleanor was also heir to the wealthy and powerful duchy of Aquitaine in southwestern France.

Between 1147 and 1149, both Louis and Eleanor,

with full support from the French nobility, participated in the Second Crusade. The Crusade, initiated by Saint Bernard of Clairvaux, was a complete failure, ending in military defeat for the Christian forces. The marriage of Eleanor and Louis was a further casualty of the campaign. She was arrested for disobedience, and Louis had their marriage annulled. As a result, not only did France lose Aquitaine, but also the duchy to a dangerous rival when Eleanor later married Henry Plantagenet, the future Henry II of England (r. 1154–1189). Conflict over a variety of issues led to recurring warfare between the two monarchs.

During his forty-three-year reign, Louis greatly strengthened the French monarchy, reduced the power of feudal lords, and furthered the development of French towns. The king's personal strong religious devotion also helped improve his relations with the church. As a result, both the royal government and the Church gained power at the expense of local lords.

Louis's heir, Philip II, Augustus (r. 1180–1223), was the son of his third marriage, to Adela of Champagne. Because of Louis's failing health, and to avoid any possible disagreements over succession—such as from the English children of Eleanor of Aquitaine—Philip was made co-ruler in 1179. Philip succeeded to the throne upon his father's death the following year.

See also: AQUITAINE DUCHY; CAPETIAN DYNASTY; CRUSADER KINGDOMS; ELEANOR OF AQUITAINE; FRENCH MONARCHIES; HENRY II; PHILIP II, AUGUSTUS.

LOUIS IX (ST. LOUIS)

(1214–1270 C.E.)

King of France (r. 1226–1270) and member of the Capetian dynasty who led the seventh and eighth Crusades. Canonized in 1297 by Pope Boniface VIII, Louis was known for his piety, fairness, and desire for peace.

Louis was the fourth son of Louis VIII (r. 1223–1226), but his three older brothers all died before their father. Upon his father's death in 1226, Louis became king at age twelve. His mother, Blanche of Castile, the granddaughter of Eleanor of Aquitaine, ruled as regent from 1226 to 1234.

Blanche was a very capable ruler, and her accomplishments included gaining the Languedoc region by the Treaty of Paris (1229).

Louis traveled to Egypt on the Seventh Crusade (1248–1254), but his capture by Muslims at El Mansura in 1250 necessitated the payment of a large ransom for his release. He remained in the Holy Land until 1254, helping to strengthen Christian defenses there. Louis then returned to France, where he negotiated a number of favorable territorial agreements with the rulers of England and the kingdom of Aragón in Spain. Louis embarked on the Eighth Crusade in 1270. Although initially successful in capturing Carthage in North Africa, Louis died of disease (possibly plague or dysentery) soon after his arrival there.

On domestic issues, Louis continued the efforts at reform begun by his grandfather, Philip II (r. 1180–1223). His legacy included prohibiting private warfare, instituting a more equitable tax system, stabilizing the currency, and attempting to reduce abuses of power. By granting the universal right of appeal to the Crown, Louis diminished the power of both the ecclesiastical courts and the feudal lords. His fame for giving impartial justice helped strengthen the Crown's repute. Internationally, Louis achieved peace with England in 1258, assisted the Christian cities in Syria in their struggle against the Muslims, and served as a mediator for Henry III of England (r. 1216–1272) in Henry's disputes with English barons.

Louis married Margaret of Provence, and they had eleven children. Their son succeeded Louis on the throne as King Philip III (r. 1270–1285).

See also: CAPETIAN DYNASTY; CHRISTIANITY AND KINGSHIP; CRUSADER KINGDOMS; ELEANOR OF AQUITAINE; FRENCH MONARCHIES.

LOUIS XI (1423–1483 C.E.)

King of France (r. 1461–1483), a member of the Valois dynasty, who continued to centralize authority under the Crown, and added the valuable duchy of Burgundy to the French domain. Louis was a clever and unscrupulous ruler known as the "Spider King" because of the network of paid spies who helped carry out his various intrigues.

The son of King Charles VII (r. 1422–1461) of France, Louis had an austere and isolated childhood,

and his ongoing conflicts with his father began early. In 1437, at age fourteen, Louis fought with his father against the English. Frustrated at his father's unwillingness to act decisively to end a siege at Chateau-Landon, Louis led the attack that broke the eleven-day siege. He was merciless to the defeated enemy, killing all captured English soldiers and their allies.

After Louis had made repeated plots and attempts to seize power or the Crown itself, in 1447 the king banished him to exile in Dauphiné in southeast France, which Louis governed as if it were an independent state. Continued defiance of the Crown resulted in his banishment to the Netherlands. Louis did not return to France until 1461 following the death of his father, when he was crowned at Reims. The new king released his allies and imprisoned those who had been loyal to his father, causing a great tumult in the government. Many of those Louis included in his government were from the middle classes, as Louis rewarded not noble birth, but unquestionable loyalty to himself. This struck a decisive blow at the feudal system.

As king, Louis's throne was challenged by Charles the Bold of Burgundy (r. 1467–1477) and the League of the Public Weal, an organization of dissatisfied nobility. Louis eventually triumphed in 1477, when Charles the Bold died without a male heir and Louis secured treaties of alliance with Switzerland and with King Edward IV (r. 1461–1470) of England. As a result of these treaties, Louis was able to increase French lands with the addition of Burgundy, Picardy, Franche-Comte, and Artois. His methods of acquisition made him so unpopular with the former landowners that he withdrew for safety to a self-imposed exile in the castle of Plessis-les-Tours, where he remained until his death.

Although his methods of imposing his will relied on spying, broken promises, and treaties, imposing punitive taxes to obtain money to buy allies, and the ruthless punishment of enemies, Louis's legacy was to create a strong, efficient, centralized government. This was created at the expense of the nobles, the courts, the feudal system, and the Church, but helped raise the standard of living of the common people. His policies of expanding domestic and foreign trade and encouraging industry also helped improve the economy of France.

Louis was married in childhood to Margaret, the daughter of James I (r. 1406–1437) of Scotland, who died childless in 1444. Louis had a son, Charles, and a daughter, Anne, by his second wife, Charlotte of Savoy. His son succeeded him as Charles VIII (r. 1470–1498).

See also: Burgundy Kingdom; Charles VII.

Louis XIV (1638–1715 C.E.)

King of France (r. 1643–1715), the longest-reigning monarch in French history, who was also known as the "Sun-King" because of the brilliance of his royal court.

The future Louis XIV was born in 1638, the first child of King Louis XIII (r. 1610–1643) and Anne of Austria, the daughter of King Philip III of Spain (r. 1598–1621) after more than twenty years of marriage. The French people, who had given up hope of an heir, hailed the birth of the child as a miracle, earning the young prince the nickname *dieudonné,* or "God-given."

Louis's family, the Bourbons, had held the French Crown since 1589, when his grandfather, King Henry IV (r. 1589–1610), took the throne after years of religious war and the failure of the reigning Valois dynasty to produce an heir. Louis's father, Louis XIII, had succeeded in consolidating royal power with the help of his chief adviser, Cardinal Richelieu. Louis's inheritance thus gave his reign a powerful foundation. Yet, France still faced mounting challenges from an entrenched aristocracy and other European powers suspicious of French hegemony.

CHILDHOOD

Louis's parents were never close. His father preferred hunting and the company of close advisers to his family. His mother, Anne of Austria, was a Spanish princess of the Austrian Habsburg dynasty, who left her homeland to marry at the age of fourteen. During the early seventeenth century, France and Spain were continual enemies, often at war. The marriage of Louis and Anne was an unsuccessful attempt to ease the relationship between the two countries.

Continuing hostility between Spain and France after Louis and Anne's royal wedding resulted in a variety of accusations and suspicions that Anne was a spy. None of these allegations was true. Nonetheless, Anne remained a stranger in France and in her own household until the 1640s. The birth of two sons, Louis, and later Philippe, improved her position by transforming her from a foreign princess to the queen mother.

Louis XIII died only five years after his son's birth. Although Louis XIV was technically the inheritor of the Crown, his mother and her minister of state, Cardinal Mazarin, ruled as regents during Louis's childhood. Anne and Mazarin gave little thought to Louis's education and environment through much of his early childhood, being more concerned with the growing threats to their power and the increasing financial difficulties facing the royal household. Because of these difficulties, Louis grew up in a very relaxed and informal manner. He had an intimate knowledge of his servants' lives, and he and his brother often played unsupervised in the kitchen or garden.

The tranquility of Louis's life changed in 1648 with the outbreak of rebellion in France. Two elements of French political culture contributed to a growing discontent among aristocrats and government bureaucrats. In need of cash during the Thirty Years' War (1608–1648), Louis's father had created and sold many new government offices.

This practice was common in most European governments prior to the late eighteenth century and

A member of the Bourbon Dynasty, Louis XIV was the longest-reigning monarch in French history. The concept of absolute monarchy, epitomized by his phrase *"l'état c'est moi"* ("I am the state"), is said to have reached its peak during his 77-year reign.

ROYAL PLACES

VERSAILLES

Louis XIV's childhood had given him an antipathy for Paris. After Mazarin's death in 1661, Louis set out to plan and build an elaborate palace of his own. He chose to expand an old royal hunting lodge about fifteen miles from Paris near the town of Versailles. Between 1668 and 1682, Louis constructed the most extravagant palace in all of Europe. With endless gardens and its ornate decoration, Versailles became the center of French politics and society during Louis's reign. An anecdotal story illustrates Versailles' grandeur and Louis's control over it. In the 1680s, Louis dined with an aristocratic woman in the garden. As they walked to the gazebo where lunch was to be served, the woman noted the white flowers along the path, and mentioned how she preferred red. On their return, all the flowers were red. Louis had arranged for all the white flowers in his garden to be replaced by red ones.

More important than its size or beauty were the political goals that Versailles represented. Using his power, wealth, and social status as king, Louis gathered the aristocracy of France about him at Versailles, making them dependent upon him in many ways. The independent and dangerous aristocracy of Louis's youth disappeared amid the pomp and pageantry of Versailles.

is known as venality, or the buying and selling of offices. The number of new government offices created by Louis XIII inflated the prices of existing offices and created increased competition for authority among officeholders, since the existing offices were also open to the highest bidder.

Under the able oversight of Cardinal Richelieu, Louis XIII had also created a new governing philosophy—absolutism. This theory of monarchical rule sought to establish unchallenged royal authority by undercutting traditional aristocratic power. In 1648, officeholders and aristocrats fought back against these policies in a series of revolts commonly known as the Fronde, a French word referring to a type of slingshot used by commoners in the streets of Paris. Over the next five years, Louis and his family wandered from one loyal city to another while royal troops besieged Paris and put down the revolt.

Louis XIV learned several lessons from his childhood. From his informal youth in the royal kitchens and gardens, he realized the worth of servants and commoners. This was especially evident in his personal life as an adult. It was well known that he preferred his personal servants to the fawning aristocrats of court. Although this sentiment never translated into notions of social or political equality, Louis respected the honesty of common life.

Louis's most important and profound lessons came during the Fronde. The rebellion instilled in him a deep mistrust of Paris and the aristocracy. As a result, he moved out of Paris and transformed a hunting lodge at Versailles, several miles outside the city limits, into the greatest royal palace in Europe.

When Cardinal Mazarin died in 1661, Louis proclaimed himself his own minister of state. Louis took on the day-to-day responsibilities of ruling his kingdom, signing all royal correspondence personally, and ruling over his splendid and socially complicated court at Versailles. The combination of Louis's power, ability, and image resulted in a powerful cult of the king, best articulated by the contemporary French churchmen Jean-Bénigne Bossuet as the "divine right" of kings. Louis happily accepted the appellation "Sun-King," derived from a Bourbon family symbol of the Greek god Apollo.

RELIGION AND WAR

Louis XIV spent much of his reign dealing with religious issues within France and fighting wars. France's great power during Louis's reign made it a favorite target for rival powers; therefore, the nation was rarely at peace, fighting a series of wars over dynastic succession and territorial expansion while Louis held the throne.

MATTERS OF FAITH

In terms of religion, Louis fought on two fronts—against Protestantism and against the papacy's efforts to exert authority in the national or political matters of France. Although France was officially Catholic, a sizable number of French Protestants, or Huguenots, lived in the western and southern provinces of the country.

Louis's grandfather, Henry IV, had been a Protestant prior to converting to Catholicism upon his coronation. In 1598, Henry issued the Edict of Nantes, which gave Protestants the legal right to exist and practice in France. Henry did not, however, pass his religious beliefs on to his descendants. Louis XIII vigorously sought to curtail Protestant rights and independence. After an uprising in protest of the policies of Louis XIII, the Peace of Alais (1629) stripped Protestant Huguenots of all political rights but still allowed them freedom of worship.

When Louis XIV gained the throne, he continued his father's anti-Protestant efforts, finally outlawing Protestantism in the Edict of Fontaineblemu in 1685.

Despite his devout Catholicism, Louis XIV also fought to maintain French independence from the papacy. In 1666, one of his advisers advocated reducing the number of priests and monks in France by reestablishing a legal age for ordination. This resulted in the Church admonishing Louis against taking the advice of laypersons on matters of Church authority.

The battle between pro-papal Catholics and advocates for an independent French church divided Catholic France. Louis strongly advocated a position that promoted limits on the pope's authority in favor of that of the French bishops and the king, and he saw himself as the director of most religious matters within his realm. The Declaration of the Clergy of France, written in 1682, clearly argued the king's and the bishops' position on papal authority.

FRANCE AT WAR

In European affairs, France's position had been strengthened by restraints on its main rival, the empire of the Habsburgs, in the Treaty of Westphalia (1648), which ended the Thirty Years' War. Louis pressed his advantage over the Habsburgs through marriage, legal claims, and war.

Between 1667 and 1713, Louis waged war on a variety of Habsburg lands. The brief War of Devolution (1667–1668) pursued Louis's claim to the Spanish Netherlands through his first wife, Maria Theresa, a Habsburg princess. France gained possession of several northern cities as a result.

Only a few years later in the Dutch War (1672–1678), Louis again invaded the Netherlands. Although the French were much more powerful, they were thwarted by the heroic actions of the Dutch, who flooded their territory, halting the advance of the French army.

Louis then turned his attention east, annexing the region of Alsace without a fight in 1681 and battling the Austrian Habsburgs for Cologne and the Palatine in the Nine Years' War (1689–1697), which ended in a stalemate. Finally, Louis also pursued the Spanish throne by claiming inheritance rights in the War of the Spanish Succession (1702–1713). Louis's wars were rarely successful; worse, they drained his treasury and created animosity for France throughout Europe.

Although Louis never lost his mental faculties and continued to rule his kingdom to the end, his death in 1715 from gangrene was slow and agonizing. Upon his death, his great grandson Louis XV (r. 1715–1774), inherited the throne of France.

See also: BOURBON DYNASTY; DIVINE RIGHT; EUROPEAN KINGSHIPS; FRENCH MONARCHIES; HABSBURG DYNASTY; HENRY IV (FRANCE); LOUIS XV; VALOIS DYNASTY.

FURTHER READING

Birn, Raymond. *Crisis, Absolutism, Revolution: Europe.* Fort Worth, TX: Harcourt Brace Jovanovich, 1992.

Bluche, F. *Louis XIV.* New York: Watts, 1990.

Lewis, W.H. *The Splendid Century: Life in the France of Louis XIV.* Prospect Heights, IL: Waveland Press, 1999.

LOUIS XV (1710–1774 C.E.)

King of France (r. 1715–1774), also called Louis "the Well-Beloved," whose long reign was influenced by a series of powerful advisers. Taking the throne at the age of five, Louis was a much-loved child-king who was among the most reserved monarchs of the Bourbon dynasty. Although his reign was relatively peaceful and prosperous at home, it was beset by a series of unsuccessful foreign wars and domestic power struggles. When Louis died nearly sixty years after taking the throne, the government of France was almost bankrupt, the monarchy was greatly weakened, and France had lost most of its foreign territory.

When Louis was born in 1710, he was far down the line of succession. The great-grandson of the ruling monarch, Louis XIV (r. 1643–1715), he was the youngest of three sons born to Louis XIV's grandson, Duke Louis of Burgundy, and Marie Adelaide of Savoy. Before Louis XV was two years old, his parents and brothers had all died in an epidemic that claimed many lives in France. A few years later, in September 1715, Louis XIV died and the five-year-old Louis XV, now next in line to the throne, became king of France.

In 1725, Louis XV married Maria Leszczynska, the daughter of King Stanislas I of Poland (r. 1704–1736). The marriage was carried out by proxy since Louis was only fifteen and Maria was twenty-two at the time. Although not from a powerful family—or perhaps because of it—Maria was deemed an appropriate match for Louis. The most important criterion was that she be able to quickly provide an heir, which she did in addition to nine other children. However, Louis's son and heir, the dauphin, died before his father, leaving Louis's grandson heir to the throne (he later ruled as Louis XVI from 1774 to 1792). Two other grandsons of Louis XV—Louis XVIII (r. 1814–1824) and Charles X (r. 1824–1830)—also ruled as kings of France.

Perhaps because Louis XV took the throne at such a young age, and more likely because he lacked the desire to govern, he allowed others to either rule in his place or strongly influence him throughout his reign. The first of these regents and advisers was his cousin Philippe, the duke of Orléans. In his will, Louis XIV had appointed the duke, his nephew, to be regent, and Philippe ruled for the young Louis XV from 1715 to 1723.

Once Louis achieved legal majority in 1723, Louis remained content to let his ministers govern, especially the elderly Cardinal André Hercule de Fleury and the duke of Bourbon. After Fleury died in 1743, Louis took a more active part in governing France. Yet, he was heavily influenced by his mistresses, most notably Madame de Pompadour, who held sway from the 1730s to 1764, and Madame Du Barry, who wielded a great deal of power from 1768 until Louis's death in 1774.

During Louis's final years, from 1771 to 1774, France was governed by a number of high government advisers, including the chancellor, the controlleur general, and the secretary of state for foreign affairs. These advisers accomplished some much needed reforms, including ending the sale of government offices, limiting the power of the Parlement of Paris (not a true parliament but a court), and attempting to define judicial authority.

The reign of Louis XV was marked by a series of foreign wars. When Stanislaus I of Poland, Louis's father-in-law, became embroiled in a struggle for his throne, France became involved in the War of the Polish Succession (1733–1735). When the war ended, the resulting negotiations for territorial exchanges lasted until 1738. The most significant result for France was that Stanislaus received the duchy of Lorraine, which Louis later inherited in 1766. A few years later, France entered the War of the Austrian Succession (1740–1748) in support of Prussian claims to the Austrian Crown. That expensive conflict not only damaged France's finances, but also had significant military and diplomatic costs.

The most damaging conflict for France was the Seven Years' War (1756–1763) in North America, also known as the French and Indian War. This conflict among the major European powers over colonial supremacy in North America ended with the Treaty of Paris in 1763, in which France lost nearly all its imperial possessions in the New World, as well as territory in India. France was also required to remove troops from Germany, and its prestige in Europe reached a low point.

Repeated wars, along with the extravagant lifestyle of the royal court and resistance to the Crown's authority to impose taxes, resulted in increasing debts throughout much of Louis's reign. Because of his lack of leadership, the aristocracy and upper bourgeoisie of France were able to increase their power at the expense of the monarchy. His legacy of neglect and profligacy left France in a worsened condition that ultimately led to revolution during the reign of his successor, his grandson Louis XVI.

See also: BOURBON DYNASTY; FRENCH MONARCHIES; LOUIS XIV; LOUIS XVI; LOUIS XVII; STANISLAUS I.

FURTHER READING

Bernier, Olivier. *Louis the Beloved: The Life of Louis XV.* Garden City, NY: Doubleday, 1984.

Roche, Daniel. *France in the Enlightenment.* Cambridge, MA: Harvard University Press, 2000.

Seward, Desmond. *The Bourbon Kings of France.* New York: Harper and Row, 1976.

LOUIS XVI (1754–1793 C.E.)

King of France (r. 1774–1792) whose apathy regarding political and economic affairs contributed to his overthrow and execution during the French Revolution. Louis XVI maintained a difficult marriage with the controversial and unpopular Marie Antoinette, a relationship that, in some ways, hastened his downfall. The actions and inactions of Louis and Marie Antoinette certainly furthered the uprising that brought their lives to a violent close. However, it is uncertain whether any monarch could have maintained effective power amidst the complicated social problems that gripped France during the 1780s and 1790s.

EARLY YEARS

Born in 1754 to Louis, the dauphin (crown prince) of France, and Marie Josèphe of Saxony, Louis Augustus became heir to the throne at his father's death in 1765, and was crowned king upon the death of his grandfather, King Louis XV (r. 1715–1774), in 1774. Louis's marriage four years earlier to Marie Antoinette, the daughter of Austrian archduchess Maria Theresa and Emperor Francis I (r. 1745–1765) of the Holy Roman Empire, was intended to create an alliance between France and Austria. Ultimately, however, this had the opposite effect, because Marie's sympathies for Austria incurred the ire of many powerful French political figures.

Louis's reign began with an attempt to enact economic and social reforms favorable to the middle and lower classes in France. This reform movement was led primarily by Anne Robert Jacques Turgot, a French economist who served as comptroller general of finances in the early years of Louis's rule. Turgot's reforms, though beneficial to many, outraged the French nobility, including Marie Antoinette. As a result, Louis was forced to ask for Turgot's resignation in 1776, appointing the wealthy banker Jacques Necker to take his place.

TROUBLE BEGINS

Though popular with the public and with more democratic leanings than most nobles, Necker inadvertently worsened France's financial situation by borrowing money to support the American colonies in their rebellion against Britain. These loans came at very high rates of interest, and the money the French government had been able to save as a result of the domestic reforms of both Necker and Turgot was absorbed in their repayment. Much like his predecessor, Necker outraged the upper classes, and he resigned in 1781 after failing to gain support from the royal court.

Throughout the next decade, France's economic situation grew worse as the kingdom's debt and its interest accumulated. Louis's indecisiveness and indifference in the face of rising troubles began to galvanize public opinion against him. With hunting and lock-making as his most passionate interests, Louis was a poor leader at a time when France desperately needed a strong one. His apathetic approach to government allowed the national debt to increase drastically while the court spent extravagantly.

By 1787, France's financial troubles were so bad that Louis was forced to act. He called into session the Assembly of Notables, a group of powerful aristocrats and religious figures, to try to push forward a plan for taxing the wealthy. The Notables, however, would not concede. Necker, who had been restored to power by Louis in 1788, helped convince the king to use his weapon of last resort—the States-General, a kind of parliament—which Louis called to assemble in 1789.

REVOLUTION

After prolonged infighting within the States-General, and indecisiveness on Louis's part, the Third Estate (made up of commoners) broke away from the nobility and clergy and declared itself the National Assembly in June 1789, an action that marks the beginning of the French Revolution. Louis dispatched troops to Versailles to monitor the actions of the National Assembly, and this, coupled with Necker's discharge, led to an attack by a Paris mob on the ancient fortress and prison, the Bastille, on July 14, 1789.

Louis seemed to support the reforms of the National Assembly and the Revolution, but he also supported attempts by Marie Antoinette and others to begin a counterrevolution. Fearing that a coup was imminent, Louis began negotiations with foreign

King Louis XVI of France was unprepared to deal with the economic and political troubles that plagued his reign, which ultimately led to the outbreak of the French Revolution in 1789. Deposed and imprisoned by the revolutionaries, Louis was executed at the guillotine in 1793.

governments to secure his safety but to no avail. The royal family was detained by revolutionaries in Paris in October 1789 and was recaptured in June 1791 while attempting to escape France in disguise. Shortly after his second capture, Louis was forced to take the oath of kingship under a new constitution, which severely limited his powers.

Louis's surrender of power was not enough for the increasingly radical revolutionaries, however. He and his family were once again imprisoned in August 1792 after France had gone to war with Prussia and the Holy Roman Empire. From this arrest and incarceration there would be no reprieve. After abolishing the monarchy in September 1792, the National Convention tried and convicted Louis of treason in January 1793. He was summarily executed by the guillotine later that month. Marie Antoinette met the same fate the following year.

See also: CLASS SYSTEMS AND ROYALTY; DETHRONEMENT; FRENCH MONARCHIES; LOUIS XV; MARIE ANTOINETTE; REGICIDE.

FURTHER READING

Hardman, John. *Louis XVI: The Silent King.* New York: Oxford University Press, 2000.

LOUIS-PHILIPPE (1773–1850 C.E.)

The last king of France (r. 1830–1848), whose unpopular reign is known as the July Monarchy. The sixty-five years between 1785 and 1850 produced some of the most remarkable and violent changes in European history, and Louis-Philippe received both the pleasures and pains of these transformations, riding a wave of violence to and from the throne.

A member of a cadet branch of the French royal family, the Bourbons, Louis-Philippe was born in Paris in 1773 to Philippe Égalité, the duc d'Orleans, and Louise Marie Adelaide de Bourbon. Philippe Égalité was an extravagant and controversial figure, and his actions as a French Revolutionary ultimately cost him his life in the Reign of Terror during the French Revolution. Louis-Philippe, though he joined the Revolutionary Army, could not maintain his father's commitment to the cause and deserted to Austria in 1793, remaining exiled from France for twenty years.

While in exile, Louis-Philippe married Princess Maria Amelia, the daughter of Ferdinand IV of Naples (r. 1759–1816) (later Ferdinand I of the Two Sicilies, r. 1816–1825). Returning to France in the wake of Napoleon's flight to Elba and a reconciliation with the new French king, Louis-Philippe found himself a wealthy man, given a high military rank and the remaining Orleans estates that he had inherited from his father. His popularity grew over the next few years, especially among influential liberal writers and upper-middle-class citizens, who led the short but violent July Revolution in 1830. This series of street battles between royalists and antiroyalists ended with King Charles X (r. 1824–1830) exiled to England and Louis Philippe named "citizen-king" of France.

The most notable foreign policy decisions made by Louis-Philippe during his reign included an armistice with England after decades of sporadic fighting and the expansion of the French Empire into North Africa. However, Louis-Philippe's role as an international leader was overshadowed by France's internal turmoil.

A constitutional monarch, Louis-Philippe courted unpopularity by attempting to consolidate more power for himself, mostly through the promotion of weak-willed, conservative lackeys to important government posts. His failure to respond to the needs of the lower classes generated more dissatisfaction with his domestic policies, which favored the upper classes. This discontent and frustration on the part of the masses eventually led to the 1848 February Revolution, the first in a series of revolutions that spread across Europe that same year. A few short bursts of violence were enough to drive Louis-Philippe from the throne and allow France to set up a republican government. Louis-Philippe fled to England, where he died in exile in 1850.

See also: CLASS SYSTEMS AND ROYALTY; FRENCH MONARCHIES; NAPOLEON I (BONAPARTE); POWER, FORMS OF ROYAL.

LOVEDU KINGDOM

(ca. 1600 C.E.–Present)

Small kingdom of southern Africa said to be ruled by direct descendants of the rulers of Great Zimbabwe.

Oral tradition holds that the Lovedu kingdom was founded around 1600, the result of a family dispute within the household of King Mambo, ruler of Great Zimbabwe (in present-day Zimbabwe). The king discovered that his sister was pregnant, but she refused to tell him the name of the father. (According to tradition, her lover was Mambo's own brother.)

Fearing that Mambo would harm her for refusing to tell him what he wished to know, the girl stole an important talisman dedicated to the rain and fled to the south. There she gave birth to a son whom she named Muhale, and together they founded the Lovedu kingdom. When Muhale grew older, he is said to have traveled back to Great Zimbabwe, where he invited many to return to Lovedu with him. Although much of this origin tale may be myth, the Lovedu do share cultural and linguistic links with the Zimbabwean people.

Muhale was succeeded by three further kings. During the reign of the last one, Mugodo, a crisis arose and his legitimacy was cast into doubt. (This is also the subject of numerous legends, but civil unrest was probably at the root of the trouble, and drought and famine may have been factors as well.) In 1800, Mugodo was forced to abdicate in favor of one of his daughters, Mujaji (Modjadji) (r. 1800–1854), who became known as the Rain Queen.

Although never married, Mujaji gave birth to a daughter. Legend holds that Mugodo fathered this child. From this time forward, only queens would rule the Lovedu. Up to the most recent ruler, Mujaji VI (r. 2003–present), the queenship has passed from mother to daughter in an unbroken line of succession, and no one knows who the fathers of these queens might be. A custom of Lovedu queenship that survives to the present day is the system of "woman marriage," in which the Lovedu queens maintain a harem of wives whom they may marry.

Mujaji I, and all the Lovedu queens who followed her, were credited with the power of controlling the rain—an important gift in a region often plagued by drought. This gift is believed to be handed down along with the Crown through the royal female line.

Mujaji I ruled from seclusion, rarely seen by her subjects. She was succeeded by one of her daughters (Mujaji II, r. 1854–1895), for whom power over the rain was not enough. Throughout her reign, Lovedu and its people were threatened by invading Europeans on the one hand and Zulus on the other. She is said to have attempted to turn back the Zulu by afflicting their pasturelands with drought, but this failed. In the face of the powerful forces on her borders, Mujaji II retreated into hiding.

In 1981, Mujaji V (r. 1981–2003) ascended to the Lovedu throne. Toward the end of her reign, she often complained that few people came to her for the rain-making ritual. She died in 2003, but her daughter, who should have inherited the throne, had died just two days earlier. Thus her granddaughter, Mujaji VI, was installed as Rain Queen in April 2003. At age twenty-five, she is the youngest queen ever to rule the Lovedu people.

See also: AFRICAN KINGDOMS; QUEENS AND QUEEN MOTHERS; ZIMBABWE KINGDOMS, GREAT.

LOZI (OR ROTSE) KINGDOM

(late 1800s C.E.–Present)

One of several Bantu states to arise in what is now Zambia in south-central Africa. The territory of the Lozi kingdom encompasses the floodplain of the Zambezi River.

The Lozi kingdom had its origin in an earlier state, the Luyi kingdom, which existed at least from the early 1800s and from which the Lozi rulers have always traced their descent. In the 1830s, the Luyi kingdom, located in present-day Zaire, was conquered by a rival state called the Kololo kingdom, led by a king named Sekeletu.

The Kololo held their newly conquered lands for only about thirty years, until a leader of the Lozi people named Lewanika launched a war against them. Lewanika successfully expelled the Kololo invaders in 1864 and set himself up as king (r. ca. 1864–?). The Lozi kingdom he established continues, in reduced form, even today.

During the colonial period, the Lozi kingdom retained nominal independence by cooperating fully with the desires of the British South Africa Company. However, even this degree of political autonomy ended in the mid-1960s, when the kingdom became subordinate to the larger national polity of the nation of Zambia.

Traces of the original hierarchical structure of the Lozi monarchy remain in the kingdom today. The Lozi king rules by divine right, according to traditional religious beliefs that include reverence for ancestors. The king is supported by a class of ministers drawn from high-ranking clans in society. Succession to office, including that of the king, is through selection by the family head, not through primogeniture (the principle of inheritance by the first-born son). The lowest rungs of Lozi society are occupied by commoners and a class of laborers called "slaves" (although they are not slaves in the western sense of being owned).

Perhaps the most important of the Lozi royal traditions to survive today is the *kuomboka,* which involves a ritual change of residence. The Lozi king maintains two palaces, one for the dry season and one for the rainy season. In March, when the rainy season begins, the king and his retinue board the royal barge to travel to the rainy-season palace. Accompanying the royal family onboard are a multitude of royal attendants, and the barge is propelled by 100 rowers. To set the pace for the rowers there are three royal bands, comprised of drums and xylophones. These royal bands accompany the king at all his public appearances, and the drums are themselves ritually identified with the king.

See also: AFRICAN KINGDOMS; LUBA KINGDOM; LUNDA KINGDOM.

LUANG PRABANG KINGDOM

(1707–1975 C.E.)

Kingdom of northern Laos that was founded in the early eighteenth century and survived into the modern era. The capital of the kingdom was the city of Luang Prabang (also Louangphrabang), which also served as the capital of French colonial Laos after 1893.

With the demise of the Lan Sang (Xang) Empire around 1700, Prince Kingkitsarat, the grandnephew of the last Lan Sang king, fled to the city of Luang Prabang and established a new kingdom in 1707. Kingkitsarat ruled the kingdom from 1707 to 1713. By the end of his reign, Laos was divided into three kingdoms—Vientiane, Luang Prabang, and Champasak (Champassak).

Luang Prabang maintained complete autonomy for nearly sixty years. Then, from 1771 to 1791, the kings of Luang Prabang were vassals to the more powerful kings of Siam. The Siamese kings, however, failed to effectively protect the Luang Prabang kingdom from Chinese invasions in the 1870s and 1880s. As a result, King Un Kham (r. 1870–1891) finally asked the French for assistance, and Laos became a French protectorate in 1893.

Beginning in 1904, the French exercised indirect rule of Laos through the kings of Luang Prabang, giving the French resident adviser final authority in the region. In 1946, the French made King Sisavangvong (r. 1904–1959) ruler of a unified Laos under the French Union, and Luang Prabang was absorbed into the larger state. The next year, a constitution was signed to create an elected legislature, and in 1953 the French gave Laos full independence.

For the next twenty years, various factions fought to gain control of the Laotian government, and the monarchy became increasingly unstable. In 1975, communist victories in Cambodia and Vietnam gave the Laotian Communist Party, the Pathet Lao, the power to take over the government. The declaration of the Lao People's Democratic Republic in 1975 led to the abdication of the last Luang Prabang king, Savangvatthana (r. 1959–1975), who is believed to have died three years later.

See also: CAMBODIAN KINGDOMS; CHAMPASSAK KINGDOM; SIAM, KINGDOMS OF; VIETNAMESE KINGDOMS.

LUBA KINGDOM (ca. 1400s–1800s C.E.)

One of several powerful kingdoms to dominate the territory of what is now modern-day Democratic Republic of Congo; the founders of the Luba kingdom are thought to have migrated to their territory from the lands south of Lake Chad.

The kingdom of the Luba grew out of a population that appears to have been settled in the territory south of Lake Chad since at least the fifth century. As early as the eighth century, there is evidence that these people began moving further south into what is now Zaire and began to coalesce into small states as Luba settlements grew.

By the fifteenth century, these communities had begun producing goods, particularly copper, for the Indian Ocean trade. With the wealth from this enterprise, several fully formed Luba kingdoms arose up in the area, which in the early 1500s came to be consolidated under the rule of a single king, called Kongolo.

The Luba became one of several important powers in the region, along with their neighbors the Lunda and Kuba. The Luba and Lunda kingdoms formed an alliance around 1600, when a son of the Luba ruling family married the daughter of the Lunda king. This provided the Luba with a degree of territorial security that fostered the kingdoms' continued growth and expansion.

The Luba king, called the *mulopwe,* retained rights of ownership over the more valuable of locally produced trade goods, such as salt and copper, and claimed the revenues they brought in trade. The king's authority was sanctioned by the creation tales at the core of traditional Luba religion, and the rituals of his installation on the throne recalled the divine origin of his authority over the people.

As the Luba kingdom expanded its territory, the king faced increasing difficulties in exerting control over his domain. To deal with this situation, he delegated authority over local matters to subordinate rulers. These positions were hereditary, and the local leaders were supervised by agents handpicked by the king. The agents were also charged with collecting tribute and ensuring that these revenues were sent back to the king.

In the late 1700s, the Luba kingdom experienced a period of great expansion. The king during this period, Ilungu Sungu (r. 1780–1810), claimed territories to the east all the way to Lake Tanganyika. His expansionist policies were continued during the reign of his successors, King Kumwimbe Ngomba (r. 1810–1840) and King Ilunga Kabale (r. 1840–1870).

By the reign of Ilunga Kabale, however, European and Arab slave raiders had entered the region, and the Luba king found it increasingly difficult to protect his subjects from capture and enslavement. By the time of Kabale's death in 1870, these slave raiders had wrested control over many of the peoples who once paid tribute to the Luba kingdom; without a stable source of revenue, the king fell into decline. Soon after, Belgian colonizers arrived in the region. They divided the Luba kingdom into two units, effectively ending the kingship.

See also: AFRICAN KINGDOMS; KUBA KINGDOM; LUNDA KINGDOM.

LUNDA KINGDOM (ca. 1400s–1800s C.E.)

African kingdom that once occupied territory extending from Congo (present-day Zaire) into western Zambia and northern Angola. The Lunda kingdom was founded sometime in the fifteenth century, when Bantu migrants came into the region from the north. The kingdom was the dominant power in that region from the early seventeenth century to the late nineteenth century. At the end of that period, one of the kingdom's powerful rivals, the Chokwe, succeeded in displacing the Lunda Empire and gaining ascendancy.

The Lunda kingdom reached the height of its powers and territorial expansion after the ruling family formed an alliance with the neighboring Luba kingdom by arranging a marriage between the Lunda king's daughter and a son of the Luba royal house. Soon thereafter, a wave of migration occurred, as people from the central portion of the Lunda kingdom set out to establish settlements and small tributary states. At its peak in the 1700s, Lunda could more properly be considered an empire, with client states and kingdoms covering all the lands stretching from Lake Tanganyika in the east almost to the Atlantic coast in the west.

The Lunda king bore the title *Mwaat Yaav*, and he traditionally held absolute authority over his realm, although he maintained a large council of advisers drawn from the various groups that made up his empire. In practical terms, however, he ruled indirectly, relying on local leaders, particularly in the more far-flung reaches of his territory, to handle day-to-day administrative duties. He maintained authority with the aid of royal appointees who oversaw the collection of tribute and kept an eye on the local political leaders.

The king's authority was rooted in a divine charter, bestowed on the Lunda monarchy by a creator god named *Nzambi*. In a way, the king's rule and his relationship with his subjects was modeled upon the relationship thought to exist between *Nzambi* and his believers. Like the god, the *Mwaat Yaav* was not to be petitioned directly, but through intermediaries. For the god, these intermediaries were the spirits of ancestors; for the Lunda king, they were local authorities or members of the royal court.

See also: AFRICAN KINGDOMS.

LUSIGNAN DYNASTY (1192–1489 C.E.)

French dynasty that played an important role in the Crusades and, through that role, became rulers of Cyprus. Kingdoms of the Holy Roman Empire viewed the Crusades as a means both to extend the power of the Roman Church and also to capture the richness of the near Middle East. Lusignans from the Frankish kingdoms participated and eventually came to rule Cyprus.

During the Crusades, Richard the Lionheart of England gained control of the island of Cyprus in the eastern Mediterranean. Before returning to England, he left Cyprus in the charge of two nobles who had joined him on the Crusade, Richard of Camville and Robert of Tornham. When his nobles were faced with revolt from the Cypriot people, however, Richard the Lionheart sold the island to the Knights Templar, a military order. When the Templars also had to face the revolts, they begged Richard to cancel their purchase. He then offered Cyprus to Guy of Lusignan, who had been king of Jerusalem. Guy accepted the offer and thus began the Lusignan dynasty of Cyprus, which lasted 300 years. Upon his death in 1194, Guy was succeeded by his brother Amaury, who obtained a Crown from the Holy Roman emperor, remained the king of Cyprus, and became the first Lusignan king of Cyprus.

The Lusignan dynasty, in terms of art, marked one of the most brilliant and significant eras in the history of Cyprus. Gothic churches, abbeys, and crusader castles all remain the legacies of Frankish art sponsored or encouraged by the Lusignans. The Seventh Crusade, which developed after the fall of Jerusalem in 1244, brought many talented architects, artists, and stone masons to Cyprus, who would play an instrumental role in the Gothic art of the period.

In 1267, Hugh of Antioch came to the throne and, after he took action against plague and famine, Cyprus prospered. In 1291, with the Muslim conquest of Palestine, Cyprus became the Christian outpost of the East. Merchants from Genoa, Venice, and other cities came to Famagusta, which became a major trading center between the East and the West. In the 1300s, the city was one of the wealthiest in the Mediterranean. However, the bubonic plague of 1349 brought trade to a halt, and in its aftermath, Cyprus began to decline. During the 1400s, the Lusignan rulers had little power, most of it having been ceded to the Genoese in the century before. The dynasty died out in 1474 with the death of James III of Cyprus, and fifteen years later the island was taken over by Venice.

See also: BYZANTINE EMPIRE; CRUSADER KINGDOMS; HOLY ROMAN EMPIRE; RICHARD I, LIONHEART; SALADIN.

LUXEMBOURG DYNASTY

(1308–1437 C.E.)

European dynasty based first in Luxembourg and then in Bohemia, which provided kings of Germany and Holy Roman emperors in the fourteenth century.

Count Henry VII of Luxembourg (r. 1288–1310), a vassal of the French king, was elected king of Germany in 1308 as a result of a compromise between candidates for the throne from the Austrian house of Habsburg and the French Valois dynasty. At the Diet of Frankfurt in 1310, Henry also gained the disputed Crown of Bohemia for his son John, in return for confirming Habsburg rights in Austria and Styria.

John married Elizabeth, sister of king Wenceslas III of Bohemia (r. 1305–1306), the last Bohemian king from the Premysl dynasty. John ruled Bohemia until 1347, and his successors in the house of Luxembourg continued to rule that kingdom until 1437.

Meanwhile, Henry VII was crowned Holy Roman emperor in Rome in 1312, but he died the following year while trying to reassert imperial rights in Italy. Civil war followed his death, as German princes elected two rival kings—Louis IV of Bavaria (r. 1314–1347) and Frederick of Austria (r. 1314–1330)—for the imperial throne.

In Bohemia, John of Luxembourg increased that kingdom's territory, gaining the regions of upper Lusatia and Silesia. He also supported the Teutonic Knights in the wars against Lithuania. John died in 1346 at the battle of Crècy, fighting alongside the French against the English in that important battle of the Hundred Years' War (1337–1453). Upon John's death, his son Wenceslas inherited the Bohemian throne, ruling as Charles IV (r. 1346–1378). During the reign of Charles IV, the Bohemian capital of Prague became a great cultural center, attracting scholars and artists from all over Europe.

The Luxembourg dynasty regained the Crown of Germany when Charles IV of Bohemia was elected German king in 1346. He was later crowned Holy Roman emperor in 1355. Charles IV's most significant achievement as emperor was the Golden Bull of 1356, an edict intended to clarify and reform the electoral process by which German kings and Holy Roman emperors were chosen.

The Golden Bull reaffirmed the requirement of a majority vote among the electors, and it made the territory of the electoral princes inheritable only by the eldest son, and indivisible to prevent quarreling over the status of elector. The edict also confirmed that the archbishop of Mainz held the right to convene electors and cast the deciding vote in the event of a tie, and it set the number of German electors at seven. During Charles IV's reign, the German princes gained in power and autonomy.

Charles IV died in 1378 and was succeeded in Bohemia by his son Wenceslas IV (r. in Germany 1378–1400; r. in Bohemia 1378–1419). In Germany, Wenceslas had been elected king in 1376 while his father still ruled, a means of ensuring the succession.

Wenceslas's reign was a time of great unrest in Germany. Conflicts grew between the nobility and the cities over matters such as taxes and the flight of rural laborers to the cities. The Swabian League of 1376 was formed by a number of cities for mutual protection. Although allied with similar leagues in other parts of Germany, the Swabian League was defeated by the forces of the nobility in 1388. Wenceslas had initially supported the cities, but in 1389 he ordered all city leagues to disband. Neither the princes nor the cities trusted him, however, and German electors deposed Wenceslas in 1400.

Wenceslas's reign in Bohemia also was marked by conflict; in this case, with the Bohemian nobles. He was twice imprisoned by the nobles and released after granting concessions to the power of the nobility. Despite his problems with the nobility, Wenceslas remained king of Bohemia until his death in 1419, when he was succeeded by his brother, Sigismund (r. 1419–1437). Sigismund had already been elected king of Hungary in 1387, and as king he led an unsuccessful Crusade against the Turks in 1396.

Throughout Sigismund's reign as king of Bohemia he was at war with the Hussites, followers of the Bohemian religious reformer Jan Hus. Under their leader, Jan Zizka, the Hussites repelled repeated attacks by Sigismund, who came to terms with them only in 1436, the year before his death.

Also prior to gaining the throne of Bohemia, Sigismund had been elected king of Germany in 1410. Much later, in 1433, he was crowned Holy Roman emperor. During his reign in Germany, conflicts between the cities and the princes continued, and the lack of effective central authority hampered attempts to resolve these conflicts. Sigismund's death in 1437 marked the end of Luxembourg rule in Bohemia, Hungary, and the Holy Roman Empire.

In general, the rule of the Luxembourg dynasty was not successful. In Bohemia, the Luxembourgs oversaw a period of territorial expansion, but they also struggled with great social and religious upheaval during the Hussite rebellion. In Germany, territorial expansion under the early Luxembourg rulers was followed by an era of lawlessness and disorder, as German princes and electors gained power at the expense of the Crown. Germany became more disunited and provincial, as each territory became more concerned with its own affairs. The Luxembourg dynasty was followed by a period of Habsburg rule in Germany, Bohemia, and Hungary, and by nearly four hundred years of Habsburg rule of the Holy Roman Empire.

See also: CHARLES IV; ELECTION, ROYAL; HABSBURG DYNASTY; HOLY ROMAN EMPIRE; SIGISMUND; VALOIS DYNASTY; WENCESLAS IV.

FURTHER READING

Barraclough, Geoffrey. *The Origins of Modern Germany.* 3rd ed. Oxford: Basil Blackwell, 1988.

Holmes, George, ed. *The Oxford Illustrated History of Medieval Europe.* New York: Oxford University Press, 1988.

LYDIA, KINGDOM OF (680–547 B.C.E.)

Ancient kingdom of western Anatolia, known for its great wealth and the invention of metallic coinage; its most famous ruler was King Croesus.

In the late 600s and early 500s B.C.E., the kingdom of Phrygia in Anatolia was conquered and destroyed by the Cimmerians, a people who invaded from the region north of the Black Sea. The fall of Phrygia left a power vacuum in western Anatolia that was filled by Lydia. The founder of the new kingdom was Gyges (r. ca. 680–648 B.C.E.), whose Mermnad dynasty lasted until about 550 B.C.E.

The oldest Lydian settlement, the city of Sardis, had easy access to rich gold, silver, and electrum deposits in the surrounding Anatolian countryside. It was in Sardis that gold and silver coins were first minted in the seventh century B.C.E. Early in their history, the Lydians were in contact with the Greeks, and the use of coinage quickly spread to Greece and Greek city-states on the coast of Anatolia. The use of coinage contributed to the rise of Greek commercialism and thus to the cultural revolution that altered Greek civilization in the sixth century B.C.E. The ancient Greek historian Herodotus also ascribed the innovation of permanent, stationary retail shops to the Lydians. Whether or not this is true, archaeological evidence shows that Lydia was a wealthy commercial state.

Herodotus, though not particularly impressed with Lydia, recorded one major building project there: the tomb of Alyattes. This tomb, the ruins of which still exist in west-central Anatolia, was constructed of massive stones and packed earth and was, according to Herodotus, "built by men of the market and the craftsmen and the prostitutes." Herodotus also explains that lower-class Lydian women often worked as prostitutes to gather a dowry before marriage. Some scholars have seen a religious significance in the Lydian custom of prostitution. However, there is no evidence to suggest that the practice was common to Lydian women other than those of lower classes or that prostitution was carried out in a ritual context.

Herodotus also claims that the Lydians were the originators of many ancient leisure activities, including ball-playing. These games were allegedly invented to amuse the Lydian populace during a long famine. Despite the distraction of sport, however, the famine—which lasted eighteen years—took its toll on the Lydian people, and eventually the prince Tyrrhenus decided to lead a part of the population to found a new state. Herodotus claims that the Lydian refugees found their way to Italy, where they became the Etruscans. However, archaeological evidence has provided only limited support for this assertion.

The relationship between Greece and Lydia was a complicated one. Although the Greeks benefited from cultural and economic trade with Lydia, and individual Greeks seem to have traveled freely within the country, part of Lydian wealth was based on the looting of Greek cities. These raids were common even under the first Lydian ruler, King Gyges. It seems, however, that the goal of these raids was commercial gain rather than conquest, and no evidence suggests that Lydian troops were permanently garrisoned in Greek cities. This is true even during the reign of Croesus (r. ca. 560–546 B.C.E.), under whom many Greek cities were forced to pay tribute.

Herodotus writes that Croesus was made so confident by his successes over Greek cities in the west that he began to consider attacking the Persians to the east. The king consulted the famous oracle of Apollo at Delphi on the Greek mainland, inquiring as to the outcome should he attack Persia. The oracle answered: "If Croesus crosses into Persian territory, he will destroy a great kingdom." Croesus, emboldened by this guarantee, attacked the Persians in 546 B.C.E. But Croesus' forces were crushed by those of Cyrus the Great of Persia (r. 559–529 B.C.E.), who by 547 B.C.E., had destroyed the great kingdom of Lydia.

See also: CROESUS; CYRUS THE GREAT; PERSIAN EMPIRE; PHRYGIA KINGDOM.

MACCABEES. *See* HASMONEAN KINGDOM

MACEDONIAN EMPIRE

(359–323 B.C.E.)

Short-lived empire, ruled by Philip II of Macedon (r. 359–336 B.C.E.) and his son, Alexander the Great (r. 336–323 B.C.E.), that included the part of modern-day Greece northeast of the Gulf of Thermai.

The word *Macedonia* comes from a tribe of tall (*maekos*) Greek-speaking people from the north of Greece who lived outside the cultural and political developments of the southern city-states. The Athenians looked upon them as barbarians.

ARGEAD DYNASTY

Under the Argead dynasty (700–310 B.C.E.), the kingdom of Macedonia spread to the southeast, developing an aristocratic class of landlords and an army of landowning soldiers. When Macedonian interests began to overlap with those of Athens in the fourth century B.C.E., Athens attempted to colonize eastern Macedonia and destabilize the ruling dynasty. The Macedonians resisted but took an active interest in

Athenian art, philosophy, and literature. They even switched from their Macedonian dialect to the Attic dialect common in the southern cities of Greece.

PHILIP II OF MACEDON

The Macedonian Empire was established when King Philip II of Macedon set out to unify the Greek city-states and defeat the Persian Empire through war and diplomacy. Philip was able to combine Greek and Macedonian soldiers into a powerful fighting machine through war and diplomacy.

Imperial Ambitions

As a young man, Philip spent time as a hostage in the Greek city of Thebes, where he was able to observe Epaminondas, a Greek tactician who led the best army in Greece. On his return to Macedonia and accession to the throne in 359 B.C.E., Philip reestablished the kingdom's army, training six brigades (9,000 men) and adapting a fighting formation known as the phalanx. In the phalanx, soldiers with shields stood shoulder to shoulder, sixteen deep. They were armed with *sarissa,* thirteen- to twenty-one-foot spears that were longer and stronger than Greek spears. Archers and heavy cavalry carrying javelins and swords protected the formation's sides. Not even Athens' powerful military could stop Philip's phalanx.

In addition to his military might, Philip used political marriages and diplomacy to extend the Macedonian kingdom. He stabilized his northwestern frontier in 359 B.C.E. by marrying Olympias, a Molossian princess of Epirus and mother of Philip's child, Alexander the Great. Philip waited six years without using force to gain control of Hermopylae, a strategically important pass on the east coast of central Greece, through diplomacy. Afterward, in 352 B.C.E., he was elected president of the Thessalian League. Within a few years, Philip controlled most of the small states in Greece, and his power extended as far north as the Danube River.

Winning Support from Greece

In 338 B.C.E., Philip II took his army south, winning a decisive victory at Chaeronea, which gave him control of the city-state of Thebes, located northwest of Athens. Philip replaced Theban democracy with a Macedonian government and established a military garrison there. Scholars argue that Philip could have taken Athens at this time, but he did not because he needed Athens' military, especially its navy, to fight against Persia.

In 337 B.C.E., the Greek city-states and the Macedonians met near a Macedonian garrison in Corinth to discuss an attack on the Persian Empire. They made Philip II the military commander of their combined forces. Unfortunately, Philip was assassinated in 336 B.C.E. by an irate Macedonian noble, and the attack was delayed until another meeting at Corinth handed the military power to Philip's son and successor, Alexander the Great.

ALEXANDER THE GREAT

Alexander had grown up with the passion to destroy Persia and rule the world. Immediately on taking the throne, he executed everyone thought to be behind his father's assassination and anyone who might be opposed to him. Then he consolidated the Macedonian kingdom, stopped a revolt at Thebes, burned the city to the ground, killed about six thousand of its inhabitants, and sold the survivors into slavery.

Imperial Expansion into Asia Minor

In the spring of 334 B.C.E., Alexander left one of his generals, Antipater, in charge of Macedonia, ordering him to protect the northern frontiers and keep order among the Greek states. Alexander's army, consisting of 35,000 Macedonian, Thessalian, and Greek soldiers, marched into Asia Minor (present-day Turkey) and won major victories against the Persian army at the Granicus River and near the Sea of Marmara. In 333 B.C.E., they defeated the Persians at Gordian, Ankara, and along the Pinarus River.

Most of the cities of Asia Minor simply opened their gates to Alexander, who expelled their rulers, established Greek-style democracies, and left Macedonian officers in charge of their armies. The Persian king, Darius III (r. 336–330 B.C.E.), who had not been prepared for Alexander's advance, attempted a counterattack in the late fall of 333 B.C.E. But Darius was forced to flee when Alexander routed the Persians in a battle along the Pinarus River.

Control of the Eastern Mediterranean

As Alexander marched south into Syria and Phoenicia, the cities of those regions fell to his soldiers with little or no resistance. Darius twice made offers for peace, which Alexander rejected. Alexander's greatest battle was at the island city of Tyre, where a siege of seven months over the winter of 333–332 B.C.E. ended in the death of 6,000 of the city's citizens. The survivors were sold into slavery.

Continuing south, Alexander encountered resistance at Gaza but was looked upon as a liberator once he reached Egypt. During the winter of 332–331 B.C.E., Alexander founded the city of Alexandria just west of the Nile River. Again, he left local governors in administrative control of their country, with Macedonians in control of their armies. With the conquest of Egypt, Alexander was now in control of the entire eastern Mediterranean coast, and he prepared to advance into Mesopotamia.

Advance into Mesopotamia

Alexander fought the decisive battle against the Persians when he defeated them on the plain of Gaugamela, located between Nineveh and Arbela, in 331 B.C.E. However, Darius escaped. Alexander left one of Darius's commanders, Mazaeus, to administer the city and province of Babylon with the support of a Macedonian military commander.

Alexander then crossed the Zagros Mountains into Persia and entered the city of Persepolis, where he burned the great palace built by Xerxes (r. 485–465 B.C.E.). From Persepolis, he moved north into Media, where he captured its capital, Ecbatana. With the Persians defeated, Alexander sent his Thessalian and Greek soldiers home.

Years of fighting his formidable Persian enemies had started to change Alexander's concept of empire. In the past, he had created democratic city-states, modeled on those of Greece, whenever possible. Now, however, he started to envision an empire ruled jointly by Macedonians and Persians.

Move Toward Central Asia

After his conquest of Persia, Alexander continued his rapid move eastward toward Central Asia in 330 B.C.E., discovering that Darius had been deposed and killed by Bessus, Darius's administrator of Bactria. After taking Bactria, Alexander captured Bessus and arranged for a public execution in Ecbatana. He arranged for Darius to be buried with full royal honors.

Continued successes at the eastern edge of the former Persian Empire led Alexander to an attitude of absolutism. Wearing Persian dress, he attempted to make people prostrate themselves before him. It was a Persian custom to treat their rulers as gods. However, when the Macedonians and Greeks openly laughed at Alexander, he abandoned the idea.

Taking the Empire to India

In 327 B.C.E., Alexander left Bactria through the Khyber Pass and eventually reached Taxila, located

THE MACEDONIAN EMPIRE OF ALEXANDER THE GREAT

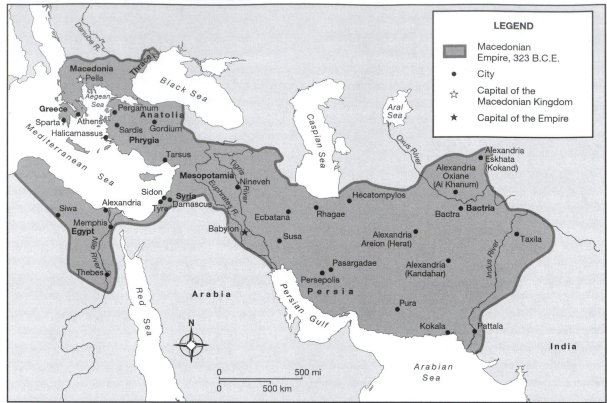

on the banks of the Indus River, in 326 B.C.E. Taxiles (r. ca. 320s B.C.E.), the ruler of Taxila, gave Alexander elephants and soldiers in return for aid against his chief rival, Porus, a powerful Indian warlord. Alexander's last great battle was against Porus on the banks of the Hyphasis River in 326 B.C.E.

The victorious Macedonian army, now weary in body and spirit, convinced Alexander to turn back and proceed no further into India. By land and on the water, the soldiers fought their way down the Hyphasis and the Indus to the Persian Gulf. Some of the army set out for home by sea, while Alexander attempted to march through Gedrosia, an area on the border between India and Pakistan. The march over arid desert was a mistake that resulted in much suffering among Alexander's troops. Eventually, Alexander rejoined his fleet at Amanis and headed home.

Attempt to Consolidate the Empire

During his remaining years, Alexander sought to consolidate his empire. Everyone who betrayed him or was guilty of poor administration was executed.

Alexander also developed of policy of trying to merge the races of Macedonia and Persia at Susa, the capital of Elam, in 324 B.C.E. He and eighty of his officers took Persian wives, and 10,000 of his soldiers married to native wives were given generous dowries. Worthy soldiers from across the Persian Empire were taken into his army, and Persian nobles were accepted into the royal bodyguard. This policy bothered the Macedonians, who felt that they were being sidelined in the new empire and that the power was shifting toward Persia. Although Alexander was able to reassure the Macedonians, he continued in his own megalomania to consider himself a god.

In 323 B.C.E., Alexander was in Babylon planning to improve the irrigation of the Euphrates Valley and arrange for settlement along the Persian Gulf. Suffering from a fever, he died suddenly after a prolonged bout of drinking.

DECLINE OF THE MACEDONIAN EMPIRE

Alexander's death was untimely, since there was no appointed heir and he died before he could consolidate his empire into a political entity. This resulted in years of chaos and suffering. Wars of succession pitted general against general, and civil wars and ambitious leaders appeared in all parts of the Macedonian Empire. By 168 B.C.E., the glorious empire begun by Philip II and brought to fruition by his famous son, Alexander the Great, had been reduced to the status of a Roman province.

See also: ALEXANDER III, THE GREAT; CONQUEST AND KINGSHIPS; GREEK KINGDOMS, ANCIENT; PHILIP II OF MACEDON.

FURTHER READING

Bosworth, A.B. *Conquest and Empire.* New York: Cambridge University Press. 1988.

Hammond, Nicholas G.L. *The Miracle that Was Macedonia.* New York: St. Martin's Press. 1991.

MACEDONIAN KINGDOM

(658–168 B.C.E.)

Kingdom in the region of Macedonia, in northeastern Greece, centered on the coastal plain of the Chalcidice Peninsula. The plain was fertile and productive, and there were important silver mines in the eastern part. The population of the region was very diverse and included Anatolian peoples as well as several Hellenic (Greek) groups.

The first influence of Greek culture in Macedon came from Greek colonies along the shore that were founded in the eighth century B.C.E. Macedon was a Persian tributary in 500 B.C.E. but took no real part in the Persian Wars. Alexander I (r. 495–464 B.C.E.) was the first Macedonian king to enter into Greek politics, and he began a policy of imitating features of Greek civilization. For the century after his reign, Hellenic influences grew and the Macedonian state became stronger.

These processes reached their culmination with Philip II (r. 359–336 B.C.E.), who created an excellent army that his son, Alexander III, the Great (r. 336–323 B.C.E.), used to forged a mighty empire. That empire, though resulting from Macedonian conquest, was the personal creation of Alexander the Great.

After Alexander's death in 323 B.C.E., his Macedonian generals carved up the empire. These generals, the successors (the Diadochi) of Alexander—including Antipater, Perdiccas, Ptolemy, Seleucus, Antigonus, and Lysimachus—founded a number of states and dynasties, including the Ptolemaic dynasty of Egypt and the Seleucid dynasty of Syria. Alexander's successors had largely Macedonian and Greek armies, and most of them founded cities with colonies of their soldiers. Thus began the remarkable spread of the Hellenistic (Greek, rather than Macedonian) civilization.

Macedon, with Greece as a dependency, was one of the states carved out of Alexander's empire. Almost immediately, however, a struggle began for control of Greece and even over Macedon itself. Cassander (r. 304–297 B.C.E.), the son of Antipater and an officer under Alexander the Great, took Macedon and held it until his death in 297 B.C.E.

After a number of short-lived attempts by Demetrius I (r. 294–287 B.C.E.), Pyrrhus of Epirus (r. 287–285 B.C.E.), Lysimachus (r. 285–281 B.C.E.), and others to hold Macedon, Antigonus II (r. 277–239 B.C.E.) established himself as king. Antigonus fought off invaders from the region of Galatia in Asia Minor (present-day Turkey) and used his long reign to restore Macedon economically.

The Macedonian kingdom faced almost constant trouble with the Greek city-states. Many of them regained independence, but Antigonus III (r. 229–221 B.C.E.) reestablished Macedonian hegemony during his reign. Under his son and successor, Philip V (r. 221–179 B.C.E.), Macedon engaged in war against Rome. Although the First Macedonian War (215–205 B.C.E.) ended favorably for Philip, he was decisively defeated in the Second Macedonian War (200–197 B.C.E.) and was forced to give up most of his fleet and pay a large indemnity. By collaborating with the Romans, however, he was able to reduce the indemnity.

Philip's son and successor, Perseus (r. 179–168 B.C.E), foolishly aroused Roman fears of Macedonian rebellion and lost his kingdom in the Third Macedonian War (171–168 B.C.E.). After the war, Rome divided Macedon into four republics and annexed it, making Macedon a Roman territory.

See also: ALEXANDER III, THE GREAT; PHILIP II OF MACEDON; ROMAN EMPIRE.

FURTHER READING

Ashley, James R. *The Macedonian Empire: The Era of Warfare under Philip II and Alexander the Great, 359–323 B.C.* Jefferson, NC: McFarland, 1998.

MADAGASCAR KINGDOMS

Series of kingdoms that ruled on Madagascar, a large island off the southeastern coast of Africa. By the time Arab traders had begun to visit the island of Madagascar in the 900s C.E., a number of these kingdoms had long been firmly established, and over the next several centuries, the power of the kingdoms waxed and waned.

The island of Madagascar was settled by several waves of immigrants. Perhaps the earliest of these were Malayo-Polynesian peoples who sailed across the Indian Ocean from Indonesia sometime between 1,500 and 2,000 years ago. These newcomers spread out over the island, establishing settlements and, presumably, intermarrying with whatever indigenous groups might have been living there already.

These early immigrants to Madagascar were joined by, and intermarried with, later immigrants who came from the eastern coast of Africa, from India, and from Arabia. With very few exceptions, all these groups intermingled and intermarried within their settlement areas, but over time, individual groups laid claim to defined territories on the island.

Historians identify eighteen different territorially defined settlements, and these constitute the officially recognized traditional kingdoms of Madagascar. The kingdoms include Antaifasy, Antaimoro, Antaisaka, Antambahuaka, Antakarana, Antanosy, Antandroy, Bara, Betsilio, Betsimisaraka, Bezanozano, Mahafaly, Merina, Sakalava, Sihanaka, Tanala, Tsimihety, and Vezo. Of these, the most powerful by far was the Merina kingdom, which in the late eighteenth century succeeded in absorbing most of kingdoms in the central portion of Madagascar under the their rule. In the nineteenth century, the Merina kingdom absorbed most of the remaining kingdoms on the island, unifying it under one rule.

Beginning in the late 1700s, European missionaries and traders became very active in Madagascar, and France and Britain, in particular, began vying for control of the island. Initially, the Merina kingdom welcomed the Europeans, but later Merina rulers tried to drive them from the island as European interests began to clash with Merina power.

The European rivalry ended in 1895, when Britain recognized a French protectorate over Madagascar. One year later, in 1896, Madagascar was made a colony of France, and the sole surviving kingdom, that of Merina, came to an end.

See also: AFRICAN KINGDOMS; MERINA KINGDOMS; RADAMA I; RADAMA II; RANAVALONA I.

FURTHER READING

Kottak, Conrad P. *Madagascar: Society and History.* Durham, NC: Carolina Academic Press, 1986.

MAGADHA KINGDOM

(ca. 600 B.C.E.–1200 C.E.)

Kingdom in India that was the birthplace of Buddhism and Jainism, as well as the power base of the Maurya dynasty, which established the first Indian Empire.

Bounded in the north and west by the Ganges and Son rivers, in the east by the Champa River, and in the south by the Vindhya Mountains, Magadha was in a strategic location to control food production on the Ganges plain and trade on the Ganges River. Abundant forests and rich iron deposits gave those who controlled Magadha a technological advantage over their competitors.

The first real growth of the kingdom of Magadha, previously known as the city of Rajagrha, began under the rule of King Bimbisara (r. ca. 603–541 B.C.E.) of the Haryanka dynasty. Bimbisara ruled 80,000 villages with India's first administrative system and an iron hand. He had 500 wives to insure political alliances with all possible opponents. During his reign, Bimbisara annexed the kingdom of Anga, taking control of the Ganges Delta and its ocean trading ports.

Bimbisara was a great supporter of Gautama Siddhartha, who became known as the Buddha. The first Buddhist texts were written in the language called Pali, a dialect spoken in Magadha, and many sites in the early kingdom of Magadha were sacred to Buddhists. It was also in sixth-century Magadha that the Hindu holy man, Mahavira, developed the Jain religion.

Anxious to inherit the throne, Bimbisara's son, Ajatasatru (r. 541–519 B.C.E.), had his father imprisoned. As king, Ajatasatru extended his influence into the neighboring kingdoms of Kosala and Kasi, winning control over the trade routes to the Deccan region, an extensive plain that comprised most of southern India.

For the next two centuries, life in the Magadha kingdom was uneventful and poorly documented, but the region maintained its strength, mainly because of its wealth and effective administration. Fear of the strong army developed by the kingdom's Nanda dynasty stopped the advances of Alexander the Great (r. 336–323 B.C.E.) in 327 B.C.E., keeping Greek forces in the Punjab region.

The Nanda dynasty's hold on Magadha was broken by the Indian leader Chandragupta, also known as Chandragupta Maurya (r. 321–297 B.C.E.), who became the founder of the Maurya Empire. Educated in military tactics, Chandragupta gathered mercenary soldiers and public support to defeat the Nandas and control Magadha in 321 B.C.E. Chandragupta made Magadha the nucleus of his growing empire.

Taking the advantage after the death of Alexander the Great, Chandragupta captured the Punjab region from the Greeks around 321 B.C.E. He then expanded into Persia and took his army from Magadha across the Vindhya mountain range to control most of southern India. The formation of the Maurya Empire of Chandragupta marked a turning point in the history of India as, for the first time in history, most of India was united under one rule.

Chandragupta's grandson, the emperor Asoka (r. 268–232), left excellent records and helped Buddhism expand throughout Asia. After Asoka's reign, however, the Mauryan Empire began to collapse as a result of invasions and internal dissension. With the decline of the empire, Magadha ceased to be a place of political significance, and the former kingdom was overrun by the Muslims in the late twelfth century.

See also: ALEXANDER III, THE GREAT; BUDDHISM AND KINGSHIP; CHANDRAGUPTA MAURYA; GUPTA EMPIRE; INDIAN KINGDOMS; MAURYA EMPIRE.

MAHARASHTRA KINGDOM. *See*

YADAVA DYNASTY

MAHMUD OF GHAZNA

(971–1030 C.E.)

Sultan (r. 998–1030) of the Central Asian kingdom of Ghazna, which consisted initially of present-day Afghanistan and northeastern Iran, and founder of the Ghaznavid dynasty. Under Mahmud's rule, Ghazna grew to include northwestern India and most of Iran.

Mahmud was born to a Turkish slave who became ruler of the Ghazna kingdom in 977. Upon his father's death, Mahmud fought and defeated his older brother in a struggle for the throne. When Mahmud took the throne at age twenty-seven, he already had acquired great political skills and was determined to enlarge the kingdom he had inherited.

Between around 1001 and 1026, Mahmud launched seventeen successful military expeditions into India. By 1008, he had acquired the Punjab region of India and was able to progress farther to the south. His final expedition was against the state of Somnath on the Arabian Sea. During the last years of his rule, Mahmud fought successfully to contain the Central Asian tribes that were menacing Ghazna.

The wealth Mahmud gathered from his military expeditions helped him consolidate the huge empire that gradually became his, and he turned Ghazna into a great cultural center. He reconstructed the capital and promoted the arts, inviting artists and scholars to his court, founding colleges, laying out gardens, and building palaces, mosques, and caravansaries (inns for caravans crossing the desert).

A staunch Muslim, Mahmud also was the first invader of India to bring Islam into the Indian subcontinent, but he did not compel his subjects to adopt his faith. Nevertheless, his expeditions were successful in introducing Islamic culture into India. Mahmud died in 1030 and was succeeded by his sons, Muhammad (r. 1030, 1040–1041) and Masud I (r. 1030–1040). The dynasty he founded lasted until 1186.

See also: GHAZNAVID DYNASTY; INDIAN KINGDOMS.

MA'IN KINGDOM

(flourished 300s–100s B.C.E.)

Peaceful ancient kingdom located in the southern Arabian Peninsula, supported primarily by trade and ruled by an early form of democracy.

The people of the Ma'in kingdom, the Minaeans, were, unlike most of their contemporaries on the Arabian Peninsula, primarily a trading people, and their social system reflected the importance of trade. Indeed, the Roman historian Pliny suggests that the Ma'in kingdom was founded by the Hadramites to secure the route through northern Yemen for the trade of frankincense and spices.

Minaean communities were organized around

trading groups or tribes, which controlled various townships and trading posts throughout the kingdom. Important members of these communities were typically called "elders" and became part of the king's council. This council and the king himself, along with representatives from all levels of Minaean society, worked together to enact new legislation. The Minaean kingship was likely hereditary, although the brother of a king occasionally inherited the throne before the Crown passed to the next generation.

Although Minaean inscriptions indicate that their trade routes extended throughout Arabia to Egypt and the Greek island of Delos in the Aegean Sea, there is no record of a Minaean king or the Minaean state entering into conflict with any foreign state. Perhaps this is an indication that Minaean trade caravans bringing desired items to other kingdoms enjoyed safe passage through much of the area.

The Minaeans seem to have experienced some sort of cultural rivalry with the Sabaeans of Yemen, the main military power in the area at the time. However, details of the rivalry have been lost. Nevertheless, it is clear that they shared similar religious practices and related linguistic features. It is difficult to know when military skirmishes between the Minaean and Sabaean kingdoms began, but by the late second century B.C.E., the Ma'in kingdom had fallen under Sabaean rule.

See also: Arabia, Kingdoms of; Sabaean Kingdom.

MAJAPAHIT EMPIRE (1200s–1500s C.E.)

Powerful Hindu Empire based in Java, whose rulers exercised control over parts of Sumatra and Borneo at the peak of their power. The Majapahit Empire was the last Hindu state in Java.

The Majapahit Empire was initially founded in the thirteenth century C.E. as a kingdom that ruled Bali, Madura, Malayu, and Tanjungpura. The first ruler of the dynasty was Vijaya (Kertarajasa Jayavardhana) (r. ca. 1292–1309), a prince of Singhasari, then a powerful Malay kingdom of eastern Java. The Majapahit Empire reached its peak of power in the fourteenth century under King Hayam Wuruk (r. 1350–1389) and his prime minister, Gajah Mada, who was an early national hero in Indonesia.

Before Wuruk's rule, a commoner named Gajah Mada had proved his intelligence, bravery, and loyalty to King Jayanagara (r. 1309–1329) and was made a minister. His loyalty vanished, however, when Jayanagara stole his wife. In 1328, as Jayanagara was ailing, Gajah Mada told the court physician to kill the king while operating on him. The king died, and the physician was held responsible and put to death.

Since Jayanagara had no sons, his daughter, Tribhuvana (r. 1329–1350), became the next ruler of Majapahit. During her reign, Gajah Mada became increasingly powerful. In 1331, he put down a revolt in Sadeng (eastern Java), after which he was named prime minister. In 1343, Gajah Mada led an invasion that conquered Bali.

When Tribhuvana stepped down from the throne in 1350, she was succeeded by her son, Hayam Wuruk. King Wuruk was only too glad to leave the affairs of state to the capable Gajah Mada. Majapahit became a very important power in the area, with control over the entire Indonesian archipelago and regular relations with China, Cambodia, Champa, Annam, and Siam (Thailand).

The golden age of Majapahit was brief, however. After Gajah Mada died in 1364, the empire started to decline, and it continued to weaken after the death of King Hayam Wuruk in 1389. The Majapahit Empire collapsed and came to an end late in the fifteenth or early sixteenth century, as Muslim rule spread over Java and the Muslim sultanates of Bantam and Demak arose and overthrew Hindu leaders and states.

See also: Javan Kingdoms; Southeast Asian Kingdoms.

MALI, ANCIENT KINGDOM OF (1200–1600 C.E.)

Former West African Empire located along the interior floodplain of the Niger River, second and most widespread of three great empires that included Ghana and Songhai.

The rise of the kingdom of Mali is tightly bound up in the history of the trans-Saharan trade. It was formed in the thirteenth century through the leadership of one man, Sundiata Keita (r. 1210–1260), whose life and legend remain a cherished part of the traditions of the Malinke people. The rapid rise of Mali could not have occurred, however, without the great lust for gold, and later for slaves, that powered the numerous trading caravans across the desert to North Africa and Egypt.

THE RISE OF GHANA SETS THE STAGE

The trans-Saharan trade developed over centuries, giving rise to powerful Muslim states along the North African littoral. Traders brought salt from the north down to the communities that lay south of the Sahara and exchanged it for local goods. In western Africa, the most coveted trade article was gold, which was first mined along the Senegal River. The markets of North Africa grew wealthy controlling the flow of gold to Europe and the Arab world, and as the northern African states grew wealthy, so did those in the gold-producing region. The Soninke, who founded the empire of Ghana, were the first of the sub-Saharan peoples to prosper from the gold trade. As Ghana grew in wealth and power, it sought to control more land and trading outposts. Among the peoples over whom Ghana asserted authority were the Malinke, the people from whom the great empire of Mali would ultimately arise.

SUNDJATA KEITA AND THE RISE OF MALI

The Sosso tribes, who had contributed greatly to the decline of the Ghana Empire, also considered the primarily agricultural Malinke chiefdoms of the upper Niger River region to be their vassals. Sosso raiding parties swept down upon Malinke settlements with increasing frequency through the late 1100s and early

The ancient kingdom of Mali was at the crossroads of the Arab-Muslim civilization of North Africa and the traditional native cultures of sub-Saharan Africa. Trade in slaves and gold brought wealth to Mali's trading cities, such as Timbuktu (shown here in an 1830 engraving), which became a center of Islamic culture.

1200s. The Malinke farmers were ill equipped to stand up to the efficient Sosso raiders. Sundjata Keita was the leader of a small Malinke state called Kangaba, and with judicious planning, he was able to eventually gain control of the vast region that would become the Mali Empire.

Before Sundjata, each Malinke settlement was autonomous, ruled by a chief who bore the title of *mansa*. This leader based his claim to local authority on his descent from the ancestor who founded the settlement that he ruled. The legitimacy of authority was based on traditional beliefs that the assistance and goodwill of ancestral spirits was essential to the well-being of the community, to the success of the harvests, and to the fertility of the people. The *mansa* served as intercessor with the ancestral spirits, and to fulfill this role, he was required to belong to their clan.

Sundjata traveled throughout Malinke territory during the late 1220s, enlisting the *mansas*, one by one, to join with him to end Sosso domination. As each chief agreed to join with him, he assumed that chief's claim to the title of *mansa*. With each acquisition of the title, he effectively multiplied his ritual and political importance, until he could symbolically lay claim to descent from all the founding ancestors of the Malinke settlements. His authority thus legitimized, he was able to call up a powerful army, drawn from throughout Malinke territory, and to lead this force against the Sosso ruler, Sumaguru. In 1238, Sundjata defeated Sumaguru at the battle of Kirina and laid claim to the lands that had been controlled by the Sosso. He created a capital at the city of Niane and set out to build an empire.

Over the next few years, Sundjata not only consolidated his new kingdom but dramatically expanded its territories through conquest. His successors built upon his work, and ultimately the kingdom of Mali extended from the Atlantic Ocean in the west to the city of Gao, far to the east, and from the southern fringes of the Sahara in the north to the Bure goldfields in the south. The empire, which rose so quickly to regional dominance, endured as the greatest power in West Africa for nearly four centuries, achieving the height of its glory in the latter half of the 1300s.

MALI CONFEDERATION

At its pinnacle in the fourteenth century, Mali was an alliance of twelve provinces and the three states of Mali, Mema, and Wagadou. The right to administer justice and control of trade, however, remained the privilege of the king.

When Mali's ruler Mansa Musa (r. 1312–1337) made a pilgrimage to Mecca in 1324 and 1325, he took with him samples of the great wealth of Mali, including hundreds of camels transporting gold and a retinue of 500 slaves. Musa's pilgrimage spread Mali's reputation for wealth and power throughout the Muslim world and created new markets for trade. Under Musa, commercial centers such as the cities of Timbuktu and Djenne were founded, and African gold made its way to Europe. Mali cities also became centers of religion and learning that attracted scholars from throughout the world. Musa built mosques, libraries, and Islamic universities, especially in Timbuktu, which held its position as a center of culture even after the Mali Empire collapsed.

MALI DECLINES

Mali began its decline in the fifteenth century. The empire had grown so large that its military, however impressive, could no longer successfully protect its borderlands from raids by neighboring peoples such as the Tuareg Berbers to the north and the Mossi to the south. Internally, subject communities such as the Sosso and Gao began to assert claims to autonomy around 1400, and palace intrigues over the line of succession further weakened the power of the kingdom. The crowning defeat of the empire occurred in 1433, when Tuareg raiders swept into Timbuktu. The *mansa*'s armies could not regain Timbuktu, and from that time forward the empire lost more and more of its subject peoples. By the 1600s, even the core Malinke chiefdoms had reasserted their autonomy, and the Songhai Empire began its rise.

See also: GHANA KINGDOM, ANCIENT; MANSA MUSA; SONGHAI; SUNDJATA KEITA.

FURTHER READING

Jackson, John G. *Introduction to African Civilizations.* Secaucus, NJ: Citadel Press, 1970.

Levtzion, Nehemia. *Ancient Ghana and Mali.* New York: African Publishing, 1980.

Martin, Phyllis, and Patrick O'Meara. *Africa.* 3rd ed. Bloomington: Indiana University Press, 1995.

Niane, D. T. *Sundiata: An Epic of Old Mali.* Trans. G. D. Pickett. London: Longman, 1965.

MALWA KINGDOM (ca. 1401–1562 C.E.)

Provincial kingdom in central India, pivotal to the development of local political structures, that was later absorbed into the Mughul Empire by Akbar I (r. 1556–1605).

In 1310, Sultan Ala-ud-Din Muhammad Shah (r. 1296–1316) of the Khalji dynasty conquered the kingdom of Malwa and made it a province of the Delhi sultanate. A provincial governor ruled Malwa until the late 1300s. The last Delhi governor, Dilavar Khan Husain Ghuri (r. 1390–1405), declared himself independent of the Delhi sultanate around 1300. In 1405, Dilawar Khan was poisoned by his son, Alp Khan Hushang (r. 1405–1435), who took the throne of Malwa under the name Hasam al-Din Hushang Shah.

Hasam Shah moved the capital of Malwa to the city of Mandu, which he renamed Shadiabad (City of Joy). During his reign, Hasam built splendid monuments, improved the city's fortress, and founded the town of Hushangabad. He also fought Muzaffar Shah I (r. 1391–1411), the ruler of Gujarat, and other regional rulers, occasionally winning new territory for the Malwa kingdom. Hasam Shah died in 1435, and his ornate mausoleum in Mandu still survives today.

Hasam Shah's son and successor, Ghazni Khan Muhammad (r. 1435–1436), ruled for only a short time. He began his reign in bloodshed, killing his three brothers and several relatives. He also handed over daily government to his second cousin, Mughith, and Mughith's son, Mahmud Khalji. Muhammad Shah was poisoned in 1436 and was succeeded by Mas'ud Khan (r. 1436). But various uprisings quickly led to Mahmud Khalji being proclaimed Sultan Mahmud Shah I (r. 1436–1469).

During the reign of Mahmud Khalji, Malwa conquered the enemy fortresses of Ranthambor and Mandalgarh as well as the Mandasor district and the city of Ajmir. Mahmud Khalji overcame several attempts to overthrow his kingship, both led by the sons of his predecessor, Muhammad Shah. He invaded the regions of Gujarat, Deccan, and Chitor several times, but was unsuccessful in claiming them for his kingdom. An able administrator, he fostered trade and established a hospital at Mandu supported by state funds.

Ghiyath Shah (r. 1469–1500), Majmud Khalji's son, succeeded to the throne upon his father's death in 1469. A mild, religious man, he worked to consolidate his father's conquests and left the daily governing of Malwa to his son and heir, 'Abd al-Qadir, better known as Nasir Shah.

In 1500, two of Giyath's sons, Nasir Shah and Shuja'at Khan, began battling openly for the throne. Nasir Shah won and imprisoned his brother as well as his father, Ghiyath Shah. Soon afterward, Ghiyath Shah formally abdicated, making Nasir Shah (r. 1500–1511) the new sultan.

Immediately after taking the throne, Nasir Shah had to crush an uprising from disaffected nobles in the kingdom. Ten years later, his son, Shihab al-Din, led a revolt against his father as well. Nasir put down the revolt and tried to win over his son but failed.

In 1511, Nasir Shah's third son, Mahmud, was crowned Mahmud Shah II (r. 1511–1531). Shihab al-Din contested for the throne but died attempting to wrest it from his brother. Mahmud then proceeded to defeat the nobles of the kingdom with help from the Rajputs, opening a new era of Rajput influence in the politics of the Malwa kingdom. Rajput nobles replaced those in Malwa, and Medini Rai, a Rajput leader, become an adviser to Mahmud.

An assassination attempt against Medini Rai's son, Salibahan, and Salibahan's subsequent death, led to distrust between Mahmud II and Medini Rai. This distrust led to civil strife and, eventually, to the alienation of the powerful Rajputs and the partial destruction of the Malwa sultanate. Mahmud II retained control of the region of Sarangpur, where he reigned until 1526, when Bahadur of Gujarat invaded Malwa.

By 1531, Bahadur (r. 1531–1536) had conquered Mandu, and Mahmud II and his sons were killed that year. However, the fact that Bahadur sheltered Mughal rebels and refugees led to conflict with the sultan of Delhi. With the help of the Rajputs, Delhi gained control of Mandu but failed to consolidate gains in the region. Just before his death in 1536 or 1537, Bahadur named Mallu Khan the governor of Mandu.

Mallu Khan came to the throne as Qadir Shah (r. 1536/1537–1542). He restored the peace and gained back the allegiance of the Rajputs. Then, in 1542, an Afghan leader named Sher Shah Suri conquered Mandu without a fight after Qadir Shah fled to Gujarat. Sher Shah (r. 1542–1544) appointed a follower, Shuja'at Khan, as governor. Shuja'at reorganized the administration and made Sarangpur the seat of government.

When Shurja'at died in 1544, another Afghan, Miyan Bayazid, took power. Miyan Bayazid assumed the throne as Baz Bahadur Shah (r. 1544–1561). Baz Bahadur Shah ruled Malwa until 1561, when the Mughal emperor, Akbar I, invaded and conquered the kingdom, ending its independence.

See also: AKBAR THE GREAT; GUJARAT KINGDOM; INDIAN KINGDOMS; MUGHAL EMPIRE; RAJASTHAN KINGDOM.

FURTHER READING

Bombay Subaltern, A. *History of Mandu: The Ancient Capital of Malwa.* Bombay: Education Society's Press, Byculla, 1879.

Day, Upendra Nath. *Medieval Malwa: A Political and Cultural History.* Delhi: Munshi Ram Manohar Lal, 1965.

MAMLUK DYNASTY (1250–1517 C.E.)

A dynasty of sultans that arose from a Turkish slave caste, and ruled Egypt and Syria for more than 250 years during the late Middle Ages.

In the thirteenth century, a strong and industrious dynasty emerged in Egypt from the corps of slave soldiers known as the Mamluks (an Arabic word for slave). These Turkish (and later Circassian) rulers built a powerful state in Egypt and Syria. With this sultanate as their base, the Mamluks went on to rescue the Arab world from the threat of Christian Crusaders, while holding off the destructive Mongols until the latter could be assimilated into Muslim civilization.

ORIGINS AND EARLY RULE

As early as the ninth century, Arab Muslim rulers of the Abbasid dynasty came to rely on slave soldiers to control their newly conquered lands. A caste of slave soldiers soon developed, with their own officers and generals. Use of the Mamluks, as these slave soldiers were called, spread throughout the Muslim world. From the twelfth century onward, they served the rulers of the Ayyubid dynasty, but they eventually became powerful enough to challenge their masters.

The last Ayyubid sultan of Egypt and Syria, al-Salih Ayyub (r. 1240–1249), used the Mamluks almost exclusively to defend and expand his realm. When al-Salih died in 1249 during the Sixth Cru-sade, his son and heir, Turan Shah, was murdered by the Mamluk troops, who proclaimed one of their generals, al-Mu'izz Aybak (r. 1250–1257), the new sultan.

Although Aybak and his first two successors had the title of sultan, they were only figureheads. The power behind the throne was Baybars (r. 1260–1277), a Kipchak Turk captured by Mongol raiders and eventually sold to al-Salih. Baybars commanded the force that defeated King Louis IX of France (r. 1226–1270) at al-Mansura in Egypt in 1250. He also led the conspiracy that murdered Turan Shah.

In 1260, Baybars imposed a crushing defeat in Syria on the Mongols, whose attacks had devastated much of the region. Flushed with victory, he proceeded to murder the third Mamluk sultan in Cairo, al-Muzaffar Qutuz (r. 1259–1260), and assume formal power himself as al-Zahir Baybars I (r. 1260–1277). In fierce military campaigns over the next seventeen years, Baybars effectively destroyed the remaining Crusader principalities in the Near East. He also kept the Persian Mongol Empire in check and launched attacks against Christian Armenia and Nubia.

Among his domestic accomplishments, Baybars suppressed the fanatic Assassin sect in Syria, whose killings of officials had undermined public safety and stability for 150 years. He also maintained a vigorous program of military and civil construction. In 1261, Baybars invited a relative of the last caliph of Baghdad, the nominal religious leader of all Muslims, to move to Cairo. The caliph and his descendants bestowed religious legitimacy on Mamluk rule in the eyes of Arabs and other Muslims.

POLICIES AND ACHIEVEMENTS

The Mamluk state was ruled by a highly organized dual administration of civil and military departments. Slave officers led civilian staffs in both branches of the government. Agricultural land was divided into lifetime grants (nonhereditary) to other Mamluk officers, or *amirs*, who used the income to maintain military units.

Many of the *amirs* integrated into Arab society. But on their death, they were replaced by other slave officers, so that the ruling strata remained Turkish-speaking throughout the first period of Mamluk rule (the Bahri era, which lasted until 1382). In the Burji era that followed, the ruling classes spoke Circassian.

The sultanate itself was hereditary in the Bahri era, but during the Burji era, the most powerful Mamluk commander would take over upon the death of the previous sultan.

Forceful government, trade pacts with European states, efficient mail systems, and public works assured Mamluk control of trade routes on the Mediterranean and the Red seas. A flourishing trade provided customs duties and profits for middlemen. The revenue from trade financed a flowering of the arts and literature, especially history; it was an age of lengthy chronicles and encyclopedias.

The Mamluks favored the Sunni branch of Islam, especially its more orthodox form. They built mosques and schools throughout their realm, fostering Islamic legal studies. They persecuted religious minorities that had flourished in the mountains of Lebanon and Syria, including Druze, Maronites, Isma'ilis, and Alawites. The status of the Coptic Christian minority in Egypt also took a turn for the worse under the Mamluks, with occasional purges of Copts from the ranks of the bureaucracy.

The fall of Acre, the last remaining Christian Crusader stronghold in Palestine, in 1291 was a crowning achievement for Mamluk sultan al-Ashraf Khalil (r. 1290–1293). But the peak of Mamluk power came during the reign of his successor, al-Malik al-Nasir (r. 1293–1341), under whom the Mamluk Empire reached its greatest extent. The reign of al-Nasir was also a time of great opulence and luxury, but this extravagance only helped to undermine the state and led to the end of the Bahri era.

DECLINE AND END OF THE MAMLUKS

The Burji era that followed was a time of great challenges for the Mamluks, as well as a period of bloodshed and treachery. The Mamluks had built a strong state, able to withstand challenges such as the Black Plague, which reached Cairo in 1348 and returned frequently thereafter, and attacks by the Mongol chieftain Timur (Tamerlane), who sacked and burned Damascus and Aleppo in 1400. But the loss of the India trade to Portuguese control by 1500 struck a heavy blow to state finances. The fate of the Mamluk state was sealed by the rise of a new power in the region. In 1517, the Ottoman sultan, Selim I (r. 1512–1520), conquered Egypt, initiating a period of Ottoman Turkish rule that lasted for more than 300 years.

Mamluk power did not entirely disappear, however. Major military units remained under the Mamluk system, continually refreshed with new slave purchases. Mamluk *amirs* gradually built up their own power base within the ruling bureaucracy, even regaining a large degree of autonomy after the mid-1700s when Ottoman power began to decline. In 1769, the Mamluk leader Ali Bey even proclaimed himself sultan and declared his independence from Constantinople, the seat of Ottoman rule. But this minor resurgence of Mamluk power was short lived. The invasion of Egypt by Napoleon in 1798 put a final end to the Mamluk power that had played such a major role in Egyptian life for more than 500 years.

See also: ABBASID DYNASTY; AYYUBID DYNASTY; OTTOMAN EMPIRES; SULTANATES; TAMERLANE (TIMUR LENG).

FURTHER READING

Nicolle, David. *The Mamluks, 1250–1517.* London: Osprey, 1993.

MAMPRUSI KINGDOM

(ca. 1450 C.E.–Present)

African kingdom founded around 1450 in what is now present-day northern Ghana.

The Mamprusi kingdom is one of three states that were founded more or less contemporaneously by peoples who came into northern Ghana from the northeast. The other two kingdoms founded at about this time are the Dagomba (also of Ghana) and the Mossi (of present-day Burkina Faso). Tradition holds that the Mamprusi, Mossi, and Dagomba share a common founding ancestor, Ouedraogo.

The Mamprusi came as invaders, and, by virtue of their superior military might, they successfully conquered the indigenous peoples, who were predominantly Akan-speakers. The Mamprusi quickly became involved in the lucrative trans-Saharan trade in gold and slaves, upon which they built their wealth and power. By the end of the 1500s, they had become one of the most powerful kingdoms in the region.

The paramount leader of the Mamprusi, equivalent to a king, was the nayiri, who served as supreme authority over the people. The nayiri was assisted by a high council, which worked in concert with the leaders of the local communities under Mamprusi control. Local stability and prosperity were greatly enhanced by the fact that the Dagomba and the Mossi, who were the nearest potential rivals for territory and power, shared a probable common origin with the Mamprusi. This allowed all three to develop in relative peace.

Kingly authority among the Mamprusi was based on reverence for ancestors, and the king himself owed his position to his descent from the founding ruler. Rights to all land were held by the king. This ultimate authority justified the king's imposition of taxes, which he collected in the form of food, craftwork, and gold. He used these resources to enhance the kingdom's power within and beyond the region, through trade. Some of it went to purchase arms and horses, strengthening the military. The rest was sold into the trans-Saharan trade. In addition, taxes were used to support craft specialists, including leatherworking and weaving, for which the Mamprusi became renowned.

Traditional Mamprusi society was heterogeneous, divided into three distinct social groups. At the top were descendants of the peoples who had originally invaded the region, presumably of Mande origin. Next were the traders, drawn from a specialist caste of Mande known as Dyula, who were early converts to Islam. The Dyula became famous throughout West Africa for their great trading skills. The lowest social class was made up of descendants of the indigenous peoples, who were primarily farmers.

As was true of many kingdoms of West Africa, the fortunes of the Mamprusi were closely linked to their participation in trade—first the trans-Saharan trade and, later, the Atlantic slave trade. When the Atlantic slave trade gained precedence in the region, the Mamprusi were poorly situated to compete with the Asante, whose control of the Ghanaian coastal ports gave them greatest access to the European slave buyers. Thus, by the mid-1600s, when the slave trade was at its peak, the Mamprusi's regional influence began to decline.

The kingdom never utterly failed, however. Its line of kings continued, unbroken, throughout the colonial era and into the present, but its territory is much reduced and the kings are subordinate to the Ghanaian government. The most recent king is Gamni Mohamadu Abdulai (r. 1987–present), who ascended to the throne in 1987.

See also: AFRICAN KINGDOMS; DAGOMBA KINGDOM; MOSSI KINGDOMS.

FURTHER READING

Drucker-Brown, Susan. *Ritual Aspects of the Mamprusi Kingship.* Leiden: Afrika-Studiecentrum, 1975.

MAMUN, AL- (786–833 C.E.)

Seventh caliph (r. 813–833) of the Abbasid dynasty, who ruled the Muslim caliphate from Baghdad. Al-Mamun furthered the cause of the arts and education, yet he was never a popular ruler, having risen to power after a civil war that left a partisan military unwilling to support either Mamun or his immediate successors.

Al-Mamun was the son of the fifth Abbasid caliph, Harun ar-Rashid (r. 786–809). Under Rashid, the Muslim army was divided into groups led by different commanders. The soldiers were recruited from the ranks of slaves and Turkish-speaking tribes rather than local landowners; thus, they had little stake in the country itself and maintained fierce allegiance to their commanders. This situation contributed to the outbreak of civil war after the death of Rashid in 809.

When Harun ar-Rashid died, Mamun's brother, al-Amin, was declared caliph. Mamun also claimed the throne, however, and both brothers were able to back claims to the caliphate with considerable military force. More successful than Amin in the alliances he made, Mamun was able to stage a siege of Baghdad that lasted from April 812 until September of the following year. When the city finally fell, Amin was killed, apparently despite his own wish to surrender and Mamun's orders that he be spared. Mamun thus succeeded to the throne of the caliphate, although he was unable to enter Baghdad until 819 because of continued opposition to his rule among many Muslims.

In matters of religion, Mamun furthered the cause of his own sect, the Mutazilites, at the expense of other Muslims, some of whom he persecuted with vigor. His reign was particularly noted for its cultural achievements. In Baghdad, Mamun established the House of Wisdom, an institution that evolved, under his patronage, from a caliphate library (originally built by his father) into a remarkable library and university. Scholars at the House of Wisdom translated texts from Greek and other languages, making scientific and philosophical works available to academicians throughout the Muslim world.

One of Mamun's most enduring legacies was the introduction of Turkish slaves as soldiers into the Muslim armies. These slave soldiers, the Mamluks, were eventually adopted throughout the Islamic world, and they gained power on their own in Egypt in the mid-thirteenth century. Upon Al-Mamun's death in 833, he was succeeded by another brother, Al-Mu'tasim (r. 833–842).

See also: ABBASID DYNASTY; CALIPHATES; HARUN AL-RASHID; ISLAM AND KINGSHIP.

MANCHU DYNASTY. *See* CH'ING (QING) DYNASTY

MANGBETU KINGDOM (ca. 1800s C.E.)

Short-lived African kingdom located in the northeastern territories of what is now the People's Republic of Congo.

In the early nineteenth century, a group of migrants from the north arrived in the savannah territories of northeastern Congo, led by a man named Nabiembali. These people were the Mangbetu, and the area they chose to settle was already occupied by Pygmies, primarily the Mbuti, and several Bantu peoples. The newcomers quickly settled in, establishing communities and intermarrying with their neighbors. Rather than becoming assimilated to the preexisting peoples, however, the Mangbetu established themselves as the locally dominant group, and in 1815 Nabiembali (r. 1815–1860) declared himself king.

The Mangbetu immigrants brought with them religious beliefs and rituals that centered upon a creator god, variously referred to as Kilima or Noro. As king, Nabiembali claimed divine, or at least semidivine, status and required that royal ancestors be venerated. His efforts to establish a ritual justification for rule is not uncommon in monarchical systems. By invoking divinity, a king strengthens his claim to authority, and by establishing a cult of ancestral worship he creates a sense of historical depth for the ruling lineage, for it implies that the right to rule extends back through many generations. The invocation of divinity assumes an even greater importance when the ruling elite is attempting to graft itself onto an existing population. It provides a way to more quickly institutionalize a regime that has no grounding in long-standing local tradition.

Nabiembali's reign was a long one, lasting forty-five years. While successful in consolidating his kingdom, he was less so in creating a stability that would outlast his reign. Nabiembali died in 1860, and the years following his death were a time of turmoil as his sons fought for the throne. One of these sons, Munza, finally succeeded in making good his claim to rule, ascending the throne in 1867.

Munza (r. 1867–1881?) became the first ruler to welcome European visitors into Mangbetu territory. In 1869, a German explorer named Georg Schweinfurth presented himself to the Mangbetu court and recounted his experiences in a volume entitled *Im Herzen von Afrika* (In the Heart of Africa) (1874). In his book, Schweinfurth described the court art of the Mangbetu, which included statuary as well as pottery, musical instruments, and other items, and which featured detailed carvings that were anthropomorphic in design.

Munza remained on the throne for about fifteen years, during which time he appears to have had difficulties with several of his neighbors to the north, particularly the Azande. It is not certain precisely when his rule came to an end, but it is known that his brother Azanga (r. ca. 1881–?) had taken the throne by 1881 and that Azanga received visitors at his court from both Italy and Russia.

In 1890, the twin problems of internal instability and external threat brought the Mangbetu kingdom to a premature end. Muslim slave raiders came into the territory from the north, seeking captives to supply the Sudanic slave markets. With them came Islam, and the Mangbetu royal lineages were soon replaced by Muslim rulers. The kingdom itself was broken up into smaller states, each of which became a Muslim sultanate. Within five years, even these were gone, abolished when the territory was taken by Belgian troops and made part of the colony known as the Belgian Congo.

See also: DIVINITY OF KINGS.

FURTHER READING

Hubbard, Maryinez. *A la recherche de la Mangbetu: Haute Zaire.* Brussels: Centre d'etude et de documentation africaines, 1975.

Schildkrout, Enid, and Curtis A. Keim. *African Reflections.* Seattle: University of Washington Press, 1990.

MANIPUR KINGDOM

(ca. 1300s B.C.E.–1949 C.E.)

A small but strategically situated kingdom in northeastern India, located among a series of valleys that connect India to Burma.

For centuries, the hills around the Manipur River in northeastern India were occupied by at least twenty tribes. Each had its own language and culture, but the Meithei tribe dominated. The name of the region and its people changed over the years, with dates uncertain. At various times, what became Manipur has been known as Tilli-Koktong, Poirei-Lam, Sanna-Leipak, Mitei-Leipak, and Meitrabak.

One of the earliest known kings of Manipur was Koikoi (r. ca. 1359–? B.C.E.), also known as Mariya Fambal-cha. When Koikoi took the throne in 1359 B.C.E. at age twenty-five, he introduced a new calendar known as Mari-Fam. Nearly three thousand years later, the calendar was changed again by King Kiyaamba of Manipur (r. 1467–1507 C.E.), who introduced the system of *Cheithaba* in which the year took on the name of a leading person. This change allowed even illiterate citizens to remember the year.

Written records from the earliest period of Manipur are called the *Puyas* or *Puwaris* ("Stories of Our Fathers"). According to the Puyas, the first of Manipur's 108 kings was Taangja Leelaa Paakhangba (r. 1445–1405 B.C.E.). These records are inconsistent, however, and there are a number of years, including 1129 B.C.E. to 44 C.E., without records.

Further complications in learning about the early history of Manipur have arisen because of the peculiar names of some of the rulers. For example, there was Yanglou Keiphaba (r. 968–983), whose name means "he who captured tigers at Yanglou," and Loitongba (r. 1073–1121), which means "he who ascended the throne together with his parents."

For centuries, Manipur remained isolated and little known. Although traders and military forces often passed along the Manipur River, they ignored the inhabitants of the region. This began to change, however, in the mid-eighteenth century C.E. In 1762, Burma invaded Manipur, and the kingdom's ruler, Raja Jai Singh (r. ca. 1760s), turned to the British for help. Burma invaded again in 1819 and destroyed much of the kingdom. In 1825, the Manipurs, led by Gambir Singh (r. 1826–1834), with British help, drove the Burmese beyond the Ningthi (Chindwin) River.

Manipur remained an independent kingdom until 1891, when a succession dispute developed over the claim to the throne by a five-year-old raja. Manipur was placed under British supervision as a result of the dispute. The British abolished slavery and built roads to link Manipur with other parts of India. When India gained its independence from Great Britain in 1947, the British handed over the Manipur kingdom to Maharaja Budhachandra Singh (r. 1947–1955), and India annexed the kingdom two years later, in 1949.

See also: INDIAN KINGDOMS.

MANSA MUSA (d. 1337 C.E.)

Ruler (r. ca. 1312–1337) of the Mali Empire, who built the city of Timbuktu into an enormously wealthy trading and cultural center, and whose *hajj* (pilgrimage) to Mecca brought the wealth of Mali to the attention of the world.

Although Mansa Musa's actual birth date is unknown, it is likely that he was born sometime in the late thirteenth century. A child of royalty, he is believed by some scholars to have been the grandson of Sundjata Keita (r. ca. 1230–1255), the founder of the great state of Mali.

A child of privilege, Mansa Musa received an education that befitted a member of the elite. This included training in the Arabic language and schooling in the central tenets of the Islamic faith. He came to the throne in the early fourteenth century, but the exact date is uncertain. Some scholars claim that he became king in 1307, whereas others claim 1312 as the first year of Mansa Musa's reign.

How Mansa Musa came to the throne is equally uncertain. It is known that the death of Sundjata Keita was followed by a time of political chaos in Mali, during which at least six different rulers struggled to hold power, only to be toppled by rival claimants to the throne. When Mansa Musa took the throne, however, he succeeded where his predecessors had failed. He moved quickly to stabilize the kingdom, and then he set about to expand his empire to include the great city-states of Timbuktu and Gao. These were among the most important trading centers of the Sahel, crucial nodes of the trans-Saharan trade network, and they generated immense wealth for whoever could claim them. By adding them to Mali's territorial possessions,

Mansa Musa became the ruler of the richest and most powerful empire in West Africa.

It was this wealth, and the use to which it was put, that earned Mansa Musa lasting fame. As a devout Muslim, the emperor felt a keen religious obligation to make the *hajj,* a pilgrimage to Mecca, which is the birthplace of the Muslim faith. All good Muslims, then as now, were required to make this journey at least once in their lifetime.

Mansa Musa's *hajj* was truly remarkable. He set forth in 1324 with a vast retinue of attendants and bearing a huge quantity of gold. At every stop along the route, he ordered the construction of a mosque, and upon his arrival in Cairo his outlays of gold were so great that he caused the devaluation of that precious metal. Mansa Musa spent so lavishly on the way to Mecca that he reportedly had to borrow money to finance his return trip to Mali.

During Mansa Musa's reign, the Malian Empire reached the pinnacle of its power and greatness. He invited the great scholars of his day to Niani, the imperial capital, and he sponsored the construction of numerous mosques and other important buildings throughout his realm. As a result of his efforts, Mali became one of the foremost seats of Islamic learning in the world.

Mansa Musa is credited with having ruled his empire in a spirit of tolerance. Although personally devout, he did not impose Islam upon his subjects, nor did he fight wars in the name of his religion. His rule was a time of great economic prosperity, peace, and security for Mali. After his death in 1337, subsequent emperors were unable to maintain the power and prestige that Mansa Musa had achieved. Their failure to do so paved the way for the eventual decline of the Malian Empire and its replacement as a regional power by the rising state of Songhai.

See also: MALI, ANCIENT KINGDOM OF; SONGHAI KINGDOM; SUNDJATA KEITA.

FURTHER READING
Levtzion, Nehemia. *Ancient Ghana and Mali.* New York: Africana Publishing, 1980.

MANSUR, AHMAD AL-

(1549–1603 C.E.)

One of the greatest of Morocco's rulers (r. 1578–1603), who extended the southern border of the kingdom to Timbuktu, along the southern reaches of the Sahara Desert.

Born into the ruling Sa'di dynasty, Ahmad al-Mansur was destined to rise to the position of emir (ruler) of all of Morocco. A canny administrator and able warrior, his reign was marked by successes in both domestic and foreign policy. Of singular importance was his skill in dealing with the many European powers—including France, Portugal, and Spain—who coveted the lands of North Africa. He successfully defeated an attempt at conquest by Portugal in 1578 and then played the various European competitors off against one another to keep his country free from colonizers.

Perhaps even more significantly, al-Mansur was successful in keeping his own putative masters, the Ottomans, from interfering in Morocco's rule. Morocco was, in fact, a part of the Ottoman Empire, but it profited from being so distant from the Ottoman centers of power in the Middle East that al-Mansur was able to rule with nearly complete autonomy. He took advantage of this freedom to create a strong, centralized government and a powerful army.

In 1590, al-Mansur found a use for his well-trained fighting forces when he decided to take control of the profitable trans-Saharan caravan trade that linked the gold, slave, and ivory-producing civilizations south of the desert with North Africa and the Mediterranean world. To this end, he sent his armies south through the desert to conquer the Songhai, whose West African empire then controlled much of the wealth of that trade.

Emerging victorious from the war with Songhai, al-Mansur gained possession of the fabled trading cities of Timbuktu and Gao. He soon discovered, however, that these prizes cost him far too much, because they were too difficult to defend, lying as they did so far from his own power base on the other side of the Sahara. In the end, Morocco gained little benefit from these acquisitions.

Al-Mansur died in 1603, leaving no one strong enough to carry on his work. The kingdom of Morocco soon slid into a period of decline. His sons fought among themselves for the right of succession, and the country that al-Mansur tried so hard to unify broke up into a collection of quasi-independent states within two years of his death.

See also: SONGHAI KINGDOM.

Maori Kingdoms

(ca. 900 C.E.–Present)

Kingdoms established by the Aboriginal people of New Zealand, the Maoris, who were descendants of Polynesian navigators who migrated to the islands of New Zealand perhaps as early as the ninth century. The Maori kingdoms offered stiff resistance to the British colonists who began coming to New Zealand in the 1800s.

According to Maori oral history, their different tribes are each descended from an individual who migrated to the islands from other parts of Polynesia. Although split into numerous tribes, the Maori maintain common traditions and trace their ancestry to these migrants, who came to New Zealand from the mythical land of "Hawaiki." Modern archaeology suggests that this mythical homeland of the Maori may have been the islands of Tahiti. Maori oral history claims that the ancestors of the various tribes arrived en masse around 1150, but archaeological evidence suggests that there were temporary Maori settlements in New Zealand as early as 850.

MAORI CULTURE

Socially, the Maori were separated into discrete but interconnected tribes, led by chiefs. Each tribe had its own village, organized around a common open area and a meetinghouse. Allegiance to Maori tribes was traced through both the maternal and paternal lines, and it seems that women enjoyed a very equitable position in Maori culture.

Near their villages, most tribes cultivated sweet potatoes, yams, and/or taro. The Maori were expert at exploiting the resources of the land, and within a few centuries of their arrival, they had deforested large areas of the islands and driven to extinction numerous native fauna, including the moa, a large flightless bird.

Conflict between Maori tribes was common, and most Maori believed that eating one's enemies transferred the power of a defeated individual to the victor. The first Europeans to visit New Zealand ran afoul of this practice when, in December 1642, several Maori warriors on the South Island of New Zealand attacked, killed, and cannibalized four crew members from the ship of Dutch explorer Abel Tasman. Tasman, perhaps understandably, directed his ship away from the islands but reported the existence of the islands upon his return to Europe.

In 1769, Captain James Cook attempted to make contact with the Maori, who were unimpressed. Later Europeans—whalers, sealers, and other profit-seekers—were intrigued by Cook's description of New Zealand as highly habitable and the Maori as highly intelligent. In general, the Maori welcomed these early visitors to the islands.

CONFLICT WITH EUROPEANS

As European immigration to New Zealand began to increase, so did competition for land between the newcomers and the native inhabitants, the Maori. When Great Britain claimed control of New Zealand in 1840, the situation deteriorated, and by 1845 many of the Maori tribes of the North Island had joined together to launch a series of violent raids on European settlements.

Fighting between Maori and Europeans continued periodically for the next few decades, primarily over the distribution of land. Concerned that the Maori efforts to protect tribal land were being weakened by continuing intertribal warfare, several of the tribes on the North Island united in 1857, electing one of their leaders, Pototau I (r. ca. 1857–?), as king. They also created a police force, judicial system, and a council of state to support the Maori cause of protecting land from European incursion.

Although not all Maori recognized the authority of King Pototau, most agreed that Maori land should be held in trust for future generations. In 1859, when Te Teira, a Maori of the Taranaki tribe, sold his land to a European, war erupted between the Maori and the British forces defending the colonist. At first, the fight seemed to go well for the Maori, who adopted guerrilla-type warfare against the better-armed British.

By 1864, however, the British had succeeded in defeating all of the important Maori fortified positions. The British government, having grown weary of dealing with the troublesome Maori, was willing to arrange a truce. The colonial government, however, was intent on gaining control of as much land as possible. By the end of the hostilities in 1872, the European settlers had confiscated huge tracts of Maori land.

The conflict with the Europeans splintered Maori culture and changed it irrevocably. Over the ensuing decades, however, the Maori managed to find a reasonable balance between assimilating into British New Zealand culture and maintaining Maori practices. Today, the traditional Maori culture is enjoying a revival among the many New Zealanders who consider themselves Maori, and there is a movement to reclaim land taken by white settlers.

See also: SOUTH SEA ISLAND KINGDOMS.

FURTHER READING

Higham, Charles. *The Maoris.* New York: Cambridge University Press, 1981.

MARATHA CONFEDERACY

(ca. 1713–1818 C.E.)

Alliance of Hindu kingdoms that freed most of India from Mughal domination in the eighteenth century.

In the late 1600s, the Marathas, a people of the western Deccan region of India, ended the control that the Mughal Empire had over much of southern and central India. In the absence of Mughal control, which had lasted more than a century, civil turbulence erupted across the region, as ancient disputes arose once again among the native inhabitants. The Mughal Empire had forcefully incorporated diverse states and ethnic groups, and many of them now craved autonomy. In response, the Peshwa, hereditary chief ministers of the Maratha Bhonsla clan, created the Maratha Confederacy in the early 1700s to keep the sprawling kingdom united.

THE KINGDOM

Initially, the first Maratha ruler, Sivaji I (r. 1674–1680), fought to consolidate the Maratha kingdom. He appointed a council of ministers that included the Peshwa, a military commander, a finance minister, and a chief justice. To suppress the constant threat of rebellion, Sivaji maintained a large army. He divided all citizens among three classes: the peasant class, the administrative class, and the military. The peasant class was understandably diverse; it included all citizens, no matter what their status, who were not in the government or the military. Sivaji placed these different groups in the peasant class because they paid all of the taxes in the confederacy.

The taxes were divided into two categories. The *sardeshmukhi* was a 10 percent income tax levied on all members of the peasant class. This tax was especially burdensome for poorer farmers and artisans.

The second tax, the *chauth,* was only levied on the Mughal population who remained in Maratha. In order to retain their land and possessions, the Mughals had to pay this excessive tax. Sivaji refused to tax government and military personnel because he needed their loyalty to ensure his power. But the crippling taxes unsettled the general population.

Sivaji recognized the growing unrest over taxes, but he lacked the skill to deal with it. Instead, he utilized warfare as a way to unite the country. Sivaji demonized neighboring kingdoms and convinced Maratha citizens that kingdoms such as Bengal and Rajput posed significant threats. Maratha therefore continually attacked its neighbors to prevent its own citizens from revolting. When Sivaji invaded Bengal and Rajput, he brutally ravaged the kingdoms, creating strong foreign hatred for his monarchy.

When Sivaji died in 1680, the monarchy began to crumble. In 1689, rebels assassinated Sivaji's son and successor, Sambhaji (r. 1680–1689). The Maratha kingdom then entered a period of upheaval, during which the Mughals regained some of their ascendancy by making Sivaji's grandson, Shahu (r. 1708–1749), a puppet king. During this time, the Maratha kingdom was divided between the north and the south. Shahu, with Mughal consent, ruled the north, while Rajaram (r. 1700–?), a powerful general, ruled the south.

ESTABLISHMENT OF THE CONFEDERACY

In 1713, a Maratha administrator named Balaji Bhat became Peshwa in Shahu's court. Bhat recognized that to regain Maratha's independence, he would have to empower the military leaders of the kingdom. He therefore constructed the Maratha Confederacy. The military commanders were given a great deal of control over their individual regions, but in return they pledged to support the Peshwa and follow his commands.

In 1720, the new Peshwa, Baji Rao I (r. 1720–1740), with the confederacy's support, once again freed Maratha from Mughal control. He also weakened Rajaram's control over the kingdom's southern region. Baji Rao I retained Shahu as titular monarch, but the Peshwa was now the kingdom's true ruler. Under his guidance, and with the military strength of the Confederacy, the Marathas rapidly expanded and gained increasing wealth. When Shahu died in 1750 with no immediate heir, the current Peshwa, Balaji Baji Rao (r.

1750–1761), dissolved the old position of monarch and became the Marathas's only official ruler.

Balaji Baji Rao's supremacy was brief, however. Both he and the leaders of the Confederacy had enjoyed widespread success. But as the confederacy's members gained greater wealth and military might, they refused to tolerate the Peshwa's command. Two generals, Ranoji Sindhia and Malhar Rao Holkar, began to openly defy Peshwa Balaji Baji Rao. In 1761, they joined with two other members of the Confederacy, Damaji Gaekwar and Raghuji Bhonsla, and attacked the Peshwa's forces at Panipat. Balaji Baji Rao's heir and cousin were killed, and Rao himself collapsed and died when he learned of his army's overwhelming defeat.

Consequently, the confederacy gained complete control over the Maratha kingdom. But rivalries among the four generals soon exploded, and the confederacy dissolved as they betrayed one another. Sindhia and Holkar eventually engaged in open warfare. The effort to overthrow the Peshwa had significantly weakened their forces, and internecine warfare now further reduced their strength. By 1771, civil war had made the Marathas highly vulnerable, and the confederacy and kingdom succumbed in 1818 to British forces as the British began their colonization of the Indian subcontinent.

See also: INDIAN KINGDOMS; MUGHAL EMPIRE.

FURTHER READING

Kadam, V.S. *Maratha Confederacy: A Study of Its Origin and Development*. New Delhi: Munshiram Manoharlal Publishers, 1993.

MARCUS AURELIUS (121–180 C.E.)

Emperor of Rome (r. 161–180) whose rule coincided with the end of the *Pax Romana* (Roman Peace) and the beginning of the decline of the Western Roman Empire.

Marcus Julius Aurelius was born in Rome on April 20, 121, to a family of high status and influence. His father died when Aurelius was still very young, and he was raised by his grandfather, who made certain that the boy was exposed to the best tutors available and persuaded Emperor Hadrian (r. 117–138) to serve as patron to the child. Hadrian complied, conferring honors on the boy long before he reached his adolescence.

In Rome at the time, it was common practice for the reigning emperor to adopt a young man of promise, and the adoptee frequently became the frontrunner for succession to the imperial throne. Hadrian had adopted Antoninus Pius, and he ordered Pius to adopt Marcus Aurelius in turn, thus placing the boy in line for eventual rule of the empire. In return, Aurelius dropped his family name (Julius) and became Marcus Aurelius Antoninus, in honor of his adoptive father.

When Hadrian died in 138, Antoninus Pius (r. 138–161) duly succeeded to the throne, and Aurelius, now seventeen years old, became his constant attendant and, later, adviser. With imperial patronage, Aurelius's life became a series of opportunities and promotions. He was named consul in 140 and then tribune in 147, becoming increasingly influential in Roman political circles. With Pius's death in 161, the Senate overwhelmingly affirmed Aurelius's right to succession.

Aurelius immediately recognized that the empire had become too vast to be ruled by a single emperor,

The rule of Marcus Aurelius is known as the Golden Age of Rome. His philosophical writings, the *Meditations,* are an intellectual, introspective examination of life, religion, and the universe. This marble bust of Marcus Aurelius dates from the second century C.E.

particularly at a time when the *Pax Romana* (the long-standing period of relative peace throughout the empire) was being challenged by new peoples massing on the borders and attacking far-flung settlements. Aurelius selected a man named Ceionius Commodus to share the imperial powers (Commodus took the imperial name Lucius Verus, r. 161–169). The co-emperors were immediately faced with several challenges. In the northern province of Britain, Picts and other indigenous peoples attacked and threatened to overrun Hadrian's Wall, which protected the Roman colony from its "barbarian" neighbors. In the east, local groups rose up to challenge Roman rule in Syria, Armenia, Mesopotamia, and other lands. Just when Rome's armies managed to quell these uprisings in 166, other peoples began to mass in the Danube region of Central and Eastern Europe. Among these were the Vandals, who would, in time, help bring down the empire.

In addition to these wars, Rome faced a number of natural disasters, from devastating earthquakes and floods to an outbreak of the plague. In addition, Aurelius's co-emperor, Verus, died in 169, leaving him to struggle on alone. The sudden shift in Roman fortunes, from a nation blessed with peace and great wealth to what seemed like disasters on all sides, led the people to panic. They turned to all sorts of superstitions to ward off the evil days that appeared to have arrived. This, and the knowledge that his son and chosen successor, Lucius Aelius Aurelius Commodus (r. 180–192), was ill-equipped to handle the challenges of empire, contributed to the sorrow of the final years of Marcus Aurelius's reign. He died near present-day Vienna, while attempting to quell an uprising among barbarians. A philosopher as well as an emperor, he left a legacy of philosophical musings called *Meditations*.

See also: HADRIAN; ROMAN EMPIRE.

MARGARET OF DENMARK

(1353–1412 C.E.)

Ruler of Denmark (r. 1387–1396), who united Denmark, Norway, and Sweden and set aside their traditional proscriptions against female rulers.

Margaret was the daughter of King Waldemar IV of Denmark (r. 1340–1375). Married at age ten to Haakon VI of Norway (r. 1350–1380), who was himself the son of Magnus II of Sweden (r. 1319–1364), Margaret seemed destined to unite the Scandinavian countries. Her only obstacle was her gender, as all three countries had long traditions and legal proscriptions against rule by women.

When Waldemar IV died in 1375, Margaret returned to the capital of Copenhagen from Norway with her five-year-old son, Olaf. She persuaded the barons and priests to accept her son as King Olaf II (r. 1376–1387) and to allow herself to rule as his regent until he was old enough to rule on his own.

During the next five years, Margaret skillfully adjudicated long-standing disputes between feuding Danish factions. She also provided relief for the poor, bolstered the Protestant church, improved the government bureaucracy, and generally astonished the royal council with her intelligence and courage. When her husband, King Haakon of Norway, died in 1380, Margaret returned to Norway, where the royal council of that kingdom quickly accepted the ten-year-old Olaf as king—on the condition that his mother act as Norway's regent as well. Margaret thus ruled as regent in both Norway and Denmark.

When Olaf came of age in 1385, he gained the Swedish Crown as well, based on his mother's record and reputation as regent. But Olaf died prematurely in 1387, and the fates of all three kingdoms—and all of Margaret's prodigious efforts to improve them—were suddenly at great risk.

Because the Danes had come to love and revere their "Margarete," the Danish council made her regent of the realm in 1386, overriding long-standing Scandinavian laws preventing female rulers. The Norwegians followed suit the same year, naming her regent of Norway for life. In 1389, the Swedes deposed their unsatisfactory king, Albert of Mecklenburg (r. 1364–1389), and joyously made Margaret their new queen.

For eight more years, Margaret continued ruling the Scandinavians during the first warless period of their history. Then, in 1396, she summoned the ruling bodies of all three of her realms to the city of Kalmar in Sweden, where the Kalmar Union was declared. This agreement stipulated that the three Scandinavian countries would be forever united under one ruler, while each country would keep its own laws and customs.

Margaret's prodigious political talents did not give her great foresight, however. She asked all three countries to accept her grandnephew, Eric of Pomerania, as their king and to allow her to continue as regent. All three countries accepted Margaret's request.

Margaret remained the de facto ruler until her death in 1412. Unfortunately—and predictably—her grandnephew Erik had greater imperial designs than his aunt; within a few years after Margaret's death, the Kalmar Union began to break apart because of his attempts to create a more imperial realm. Nevertheless, during her rule, Margaret had clearly demonstrated that there was no logical need for conflict between the Scandinavian states, and she affirmed that gender was irrelevant as a qualification for brilliant leadership and statesmanship.

See also: DANISH KINGDOM; HAAKON VI; KALMAR UNION; NORWEGIAN MONARCHY; SWEDISH MONARCHY; WALDEMAR I, THE GREAT.

MARIA THERESA (1717–1780 C.E.)

One of the most influential members of the Habsburg dynasty and the only woman in the history of that ruling family ever to attain the throne. Maria Teresa's full titles were archduchess of Austria, Holy Roman empress, and queen of Hungary and Bohemia (r. 1740–1780).

Maria Theresa was the second and last child born to the Holy Roman emperor, Charles VI (r. 1711–1740). The emperor had a son, Leopold, who was the legitimate heir to the throne, but the boy died in early childhood. The laws governing succession in the Holy Roman Empire prohibited a female from taking the throne. But with the death of his son, Charles VII decided to change the laws. In 1713, he issued a new law, the Pragmatic Sanction, which permitted a female heir to the Habsburg hereditary lands.

Born on May 13, 1717, after adoption of the Pragmatic Sanction, Maria Theresa was duly recognized by most European powers as the heir apparent. She was educated in statecraft, in keeping with her royal expectations. In February 1736, Maria Theresa married Francis Stephen of Lorraine, and the couple began a remarkably fertile family life, eventually producing sixteen children.

When Maria Theresa's father died in 1740, she was well prepared to assume the responsibilities of the empire. Unfortunately, among the European powers, Frederick II of Prussia (r. 1740–1786) re-fused to recognize the legitimacy of her accession, seeing an opportunity to expand his own territories by annexing the province of Silesia. To achieve his aims, Frederick launched the War of the Austrian Succession, which raged from 1740 to 1748. In the end, Maria Theresa lost Silesia, but gained recognition of her husband as Emperor Francis I (r. 1745–1765) of the Holy Roman Empire.

Although Francis I had the title, Maria Theresa held the power. By all accounts a pleasant man, Francis had no head for statecraft, so he deferred to Maria Theresa and her chief chancellor, Wenzel Anton von Kaunitz. Together, this pair launched much needed administrative and military reforms that greatly strengthened the empire and earned the empress great praise from subjects and courtiers alike.

Maria Theresa further strengthened her position by arranging marriages for her many children with powerful families throughout Europe. Such was the case for her daughter Marie Antoinette, who married the future King Louis XVI of France (r. 1774–1792) and became his queen. Another daughter,

Empress Maria Theresa of Austria was the only woman in the Habsburg Dynasty to rule on her own. An intelligent and enlightened ruler, her efforts to modernize the empire helped solidify Habsburg rule for decades to come.

Marie Caroline, married Ferdinand, the king of both Naples and Sicily (r. 1759–1816).

Unfortunately, Maria Theresa was less successful in her approach to foreign policy. Unable to forget the loss of Silesia, she insisted upon finding a way to punish Frederick II for having taken the territory from her empire. She therefore set out to create alliances with Russia and France in order to attack her old nemesis. In 1756, she felt she was ready, and she launched what became known as the Seven Years' War (1756–1763).

For all her diplomatic efforts, Maria Theresa's hoped-for alliance did not hold up. Neither France nor Russia remained loyal to her cause, both recognizing that Prussia was the more valuable ally. Without allies, Maria Theresa could not prevail in the war, and in 1763 she was forced to admit defeat. This was a bitter blow, made worse by the great personal loss she endured soon afterward: in 1765 her beloved husband died unexpectedly.

In accordance with the Habsburg laws of succession, Maria Theresa named her eldest son Joseph as co-regent, and he became emperor as Joseph II (r. 1765–1790). However, the empress was unwilling to relinquish her authority and continued to act as the effective ruler of the empire. Maria Theresa's reluctance to turn the empire over to her son was due, at least in part, to her profound distrust of Enlightenment ideas. A fervent Catholic, she greatly disapproved of her son's willingness to accommodate the non-Catholics (particularly the Protestants) among her subjects and his desire to reduce the influence of the Catholic Church over the empire. In fact, during her reign, Maria Theresa was distinctly unfriendly to Jews, and she forced Protestants to emigrate to Transylvania, the one area of her realm in which members of that denomination were permitted to practice their religion freely.

Maria Theresa never managed to realize her dream of restoring Silesia to the empire, but she did manage to acquire new territory in 1772. In that year she participated with Prussia and Russia in the partition of Poland, and for her efforts was rewarded with the territory of Galicia. Although she did not hand over the reins of the empire to her son Joseph II, Maria Theresa nonetheless did allow him some influence over policy during the latter years of her rule. For instance, she eventually permitted the free expression of religion other than Catholicism throughout the empire, and her edict abolishing the institution of serfdom on Crown lands was another policy that originated with her son.

Maria Theresa remained in power up to the time of her death, at age sixty-three, in 1780. Shortly before her death she had participated in a royal hunt, during which she contracted a bad cold. This appears to have turned into pneumonia, from which she never recovered. She died on November 29, 1780. Upon her death, Joseph II took the full reins of power and ruled until his death in 1790; he was succeeded by his younger brother, Leopold II (r. 1790–1792).

See also: AUSTRO-HUNGARIAN EMPIRE; FRANCIS I; HABSBURG DYNASTY; HOLY ROMAN EMPIRE; JOSEPH II; LEOPOLD II; MARIE ANTOINETTE.

FURTHER READING

Crankshaw, Edward. *Maria Theresa.* New York: Atheneum, 1986.

MARIE ANTOINETTE (1755–1793 C.E.)

Queen of France, the wife of Louis XVI (r. 1774–1792), who was a victim of the bloody Reign of Terror that followed the French Revolution.

A member of the Habsburg dynasty, Marie Antoinette was born on November 2, 1755, to Empress Maria Theresa of Austria and Holy Roman Emperor Francis I (r. 1745–1765). A much indulged, favored daughter of the imperial family, she grew up in the relaxed ambiance of the Habsburg court. Her fate as a princess, however, was to make an appropriate political marriage. Her mother determined that the most suitable match would be with the *dauphin* (crown prince) of France, the future Louis XVI. Thus, when Marie was fifteen, she was sent to the Paris court, where she was duly wed with all the splendor and opulence that befitted a royal pair.

The marriage of Marie and Louis was not a great success for many reasons. The dauphin was a homely, shy young man who was intimidated by his new bride. It appears that he also suffered a physical defect that made it impossible for him to consummate their marriage for the first seven years. Since providing an heir to the throne was a queen's primary duty, Marie Antoinette's failure in this regard made her a target for a great deal of gossip from an unsympathetic court.

In 1774, King Louis XV (r. 1715–1774) of France

died and Louis XVI, his grandson, became king. The young queen, resented for being a foreigner, immediately earned the disdain of the staid French nobility. It did not help matters that she attempted to ease her sense of isolation and loneliness due to a neglectful husband by surrounding herself with a group of young hedonists who encouraged her to hold lavish parties, spend excessively, and otherwise scandalize the French nobles. Rumors spread, accusing her of numerous affairs.

While this uproar swirled around her, Marie Antoinette was actually settling down from her early years of wild behavior. The king had had an operation that allowed him to consummate their marriage, and she finally produced the required heir, along with two daughters and another son. Marie's changed ways made no impression on the public or the royal court, however, and, in addition to widespread resentment and rumors, she was suspected of spying against France for the Austrian Empire.

By the late 1780s, the political climate in France was growing ominous. The nation was saddled with a huge debt, incurred largely because of France's support of the American Revolutionary War. Famine and poverty were widespread, and the memory of the dissolute young queen's behavior earned Marie Antoinette the hatred of the masses. Louis XVI attempted to institute reforms that would ease the suffering, but the nobility would not cooperate. In 1789 public unrest led to all-out revolution, and a Paris crowd stormed the Bastille—a prison, fort, and armory—to arm themselves.

As the French Revolution proceeded, some of the nobility fled France, realizing that the mob was out for blood. In 1789, Louis XVI was forced to leave his beloved palace at Versailles. When Marie finally persuaded him to flee the country in 1791, it was too late: the royal family was captured by an angry mob before they could reach safety outside France. The queen, king, and their children were imprisoned to await trial for treason against the republic.

In December 1792, King Louis XVI was hauled before a tribunal and found guilty; he was executed on the guillotine the following January. Marie remained in prison, but her children were taken from her and she was now alone. She did not have long to bemoan her fate, however. On October 14, 1793, it was Marie's turn to face the tribunal, where she was charged with treason and found guilty. On October 16, the queen was wheeled through the streets of Paris in an open cart to be vilified by a jeering mob, forced to mount the steps of the guillotine, and beheaded.

See also: Austro-Hungarian Empire; French Monarchies; Louis XVI; Maria Theresa; Regicide.

Marquesas Kingdoms

(200 b.c.e.–Present)

Polynesian kingdoms on the Marquesas Islands, an archipelago famed for the beauty of its landscape, that were almost completely depopulated by the introduction of European diseases. Of the ten Marquesas islands, only six are inhabited today.

Archaeological evidence shows that the beautiful Marquesas Islands were probably some of the earliest inhabited islands in the Pacifc Ocean region of Polynesia. First settled around 200 b.c.e., the islands were probably the dispersion point for Hawaiian settlers in 300 c.e.

Early tribes in the Marquesas dwelt in lush valleys separated from each other by mountains and seas. The inhabitants thus developed insular and warlike groups. Marquesans customarily tattooed their firstborn male or female child, and these children became the rulers. Each tribe had its own *haka-iki,* or chief, but power was decentralized, with no single king ruling the islands.

Early European visitors to the Marquesas described a light-skinned people decorated with elaborate blue tattoos, living in towns constructed of blocks of coral. Common apparel included loincloths and feathers. Dance was an important aspect of daily and religious life.

The Marquesas were among the first Polynesian Islands to be sighted by European explorers. In 1595, the Spanish explorer Álvaro de Mendaña de Neira landed and promptly named the islands after the Marquesa de Mendoza, a Spanish nobleman. In 1774, the English explorer, Captain James Cook, visited one of the Marquesas, and in 1791, an American captain, Joseph Ingraham, sighted the northwestern islands of Hatutut, Eiao, Motu Iti, Nuku Hiva, Ua Huku, Ua Pou, and Motu One. He named them the Washington Islands, a designation still used occasionally today.

In 1813 another American captain, David Porter, annexed Nuka Hiva, naming it Madison Island, but the annexation was never ratified by the U.S. Congress and the islanders. The French later established a colony on the same island when they took possession of the whole Marquesas archipelago in 1842. The French abandoned it seventeen years later but then took possession of the islands once more in 1870.

Although contact with the Europeans was intermittent, it proved disastrous for the Marquesan people. The introduction of European diseases and opium and periodic slave-raids wiped out 95 percent of the population, although some scholars have suggested that the Marquesans' continuation of tribal rivalries may have contributed to this decline. Today, fewer than 7,000 people live on the islands, a third of the population of the 1850s.

See also: SOUTH SEA ISLAND KINGDOMS.

MARRIAGE OF KINGS

Marriages of kings have often been arranged for political gain, for purposes of producing an heir, or for establishing a line of succession. It has generally also been considered important that kings marry someone of high social status. The nobility has sometimes frowned on the idea that one should marry for love. Politically strategic marriages could sometimes take years to negotiate and were intended to strengthen alliances, improve trade relations, or gain territory. In some cases, kings would marry several wives in order to maximize the potential political gains.

MARRIAGE FOR POLITICAL REASONS

Polygamy was common among the kings of ancient Egypt, who sometimes married their sisters. Typically, the king married one primary wife and had several secondary wives to help ensure an heir to the throne. It is believed that Egyptian pharaohs married hundreds of wives as a way of strengthening political ties with foreign countries.

Kings have also married off their daughters for political gain. For example, the Mongol Yuan dynasty of China (1260–1368) was known for using this strategy to control recently annexed territory. The Mongol emperor, Kublai Khan (r. 1260–1294), sought to prove military prowess by extending the borders of China. Instead of using force to control the territory of Koryo (present-day Korea), he was able to do so by arranging marriages between the two dynasties. Kublai Khan would send Yuan women to marry the kings of the

ROYAL RITUALS

MODERN ROYAL WEDDING CEREMONIES

Modern royal wedding ceremonies have typically been extravagant affairs, drawing on the practices of traditional wedding rituals while also suggesting a more forward-looking era. The marriage of Japan's crown prince Naruhito to Masako Owada in 1993 was just that. The ceremony took place in a small Shinto shrine. The bride wore a traditional wedding kimono and carried a small sword; the groom wore traditional eleventh-century court attire. As was the case with traditional Japanese royal marriage ceremonies, there was no music and no exchange of rings. The bride and groom recited their vows and prayed to the ancestors. The ceremony was followed by a modern, Western-style gala at the Imperial Palace in Tokyo.

Another wedding that combined traditional and modern practices took place in Morocco in the summer of 2002 with the union of King Mohamed VII to Princess Salma Bennani. The ceremony and celebration lasted for several days, complete with a procession of the Royal Guard on horseback, clad in white robes and turbans, through the city streets. Many Moroccans hoped that the marriage of King Mohamed VII, who still holds significant power, to the modern and educated Princess Salma would signify the beginning of a more progressive era for their country.

Koryo dynasty. The sons of these marriages would have succession rights to the Koryo throne but would also have loyalty to the Mongol family through their mothers. This tactic eventually allowed the Yuan dynasty to control Koryo as a vassal state.

Queen Mary I of England (r. 1553–1558) married the future King Philip II of Spain (r. 1556–1598) in 1553 with the hope of returning her country to Catholicism. For his part, King Philip II chose Mary to be his second wife in hopes of gaining England as an ally. Mary died in 1558, and England and Spain became enemies, in large part because of the Spanish Inquisition. It was also common practice for kings to marry the sisters of a deceased wife. When Mary I of England died in 1558, Philip tried to marry his widow's younger sister, Queen Elizabeth I (r. 1558–1603), but she turned down the proposal.

Royal marriages also served the purpose of spreading religious beliefs. For example, Islam spread in Indonesia during the thirteenth century as a result of the marriage of the first Muslim sultan of Pasai to a daughter of the ruler of Perlak, a region on the northern coast of Sumatra. Several marriages between Muslim and Hindu nobility took place at this time throughout Southeast Asia, encouraging the local populations to adopt the religious practices of their kings. In many cases, the monarchies forced new religions upon the general population.

MARRIAGE FOR LOVE

Although love was generally not considered a legitimate reason to marry, monarchs have sometimes wed for that reason. Two British kings, in particular did marry for love—King Edward IV (r. 1461–1483) and King Henry VIII (r. 1509–1547). Edward IV met Elizabeth Grey, a young widow whom he fell in love with and married secretly. He kept this a secret for five months, allowing the earl of Warwick to continue discussions about a possible royal marriage with a French bride. Henry VIII married his first wife, Catherine of Aragón, for diplomatic reasons—to maintain an alliance with Spain. When the marriage failed, Henry decided to marry Anne Boleyn, who was later executed on charges of witchcraft and adultery. Henry's marriage to Anne of Cleves was arranged for political reasons, but his wives Katherine Howard and Katherine Parr were chosen for love.

See also: BEHAVIOR, CONVENTIONS OF ROYAL; CONCUBINES, ROYAL; CONSORTS, ROYAL; INCEST, ROYAL; KINGS AND QUEENS; POLYGAMY, ROYAL; QUEENS AND QUEEN MOTHERS; ROYAL FAMILIES; SUCCESSION, ROYAL; WEDDINGS, ROYAL.

FURTHER READING

Weir, Alison. *The Six Wives of Henry VIII.* New York: Grove Press, 1992.

MARTEL, CHARLES (ca. 688–741 C.E.)

Frankish ruler (r. 714–741), called mayor of the palace, who is credited with reuniting northern France, stopping the Moorish advance into Gaul, and reuniting the Merovingian kingdom.

Charles was the illegitimate son of Pepin of Heristal (Pepin II), mayor of the palace, and the grandfather of Charlemagne (r. 768–814). When Pepin died in 714, Charles did not inherit the right to rule, but first had to defeat Chilperic II of Neustria and then claim neighboring Austrasia, the northeastern portion of the Merovingian kingdom of the Franks. Charles was not king, but he held the title of mayor of the palace, a traditional Merovingian title for the leading noble who held power behind the throne.

Repeated military victories won Charles allies and wealth, and some of the wealth obtained, often by plunder, was distributed to his supporters. There is a possibility that he also took Church lands to reward his friends. He earned his nickname Martel ("the Hammer") in 732 when he defeated the Moors at Poitiers, an action credited by some with ending the Islamic advance deeper into Europe. This victory and others also increased his power and that of the Franks, ultimately making Charles leader of the most powerful state in Western Europe.

When Charles Martel died in 741, his son, Pepin the Short (Pepin III), became the mayor of Neustria and the first king of the Franks (r. 751–768) of the Carolingian dynasty. Pepin's son was Charlemagne.

See also: CAROLINGIAN DYNASTY; CHARLEMAGNE; FRANKISH KINGDOM; MEROVINGIAN DYNASTY; PEPIN DYNASTY; PEPIN THE SHORT (PEPIN III).

MARY I, TUDOR (1516–1558 C.E.)

Queen of England (r. 1553–1558) who attempted to restore England to Roman Catholicism. Her reign was plagued by problems that she was ultimately unable to resolve.

Mary Tudor was born on February 16, 1516, to King Henry VIII (r. 1509–1547) and his first wife, Catherine of Aragon. As a child, Mary and her father were close. Kind, loving, and devoted to both her parents, she was also an only child—a fact that changed English history forever.

Although Catherine of Aragón became pregnant seven times during her twenty-year marriage to Henry, Mary was the only child of the union to survive past infancy. Catherine's failure to produce a male heir led Henry to break with the Catholic Church. In 1531 Henry, now head of his own Church of England, declared his marriage to Catherine void and sent her away from court without Mary. Fearful that Mary would side with her mother, Henry also sent her away and did not see her again until 1536. Mary continued to practice Roman Catholicism, despite her father's split from the Church.

Henry's marriage to Anne Boleyn produced another daughter, Elizabeth. Shortly after Elizabeth's birth in 1533, Henry had Mary declared illegitimate and sent her to live as a lady-in-waiting in her baby sister's household at Hatfield outside London. It is said that when Mary arrived there, the duke of Norfolk asked her if she wished to greet the princess. Mary—with a self-possession like her father's—answered that she was aware of no princesses in England other than herself.

Like Catherine of Aragón before her, Anne Boleyn also failed to give Henry a male heir. In 1536, she was executed on a charge of adultery, and Elizabeth was declared illegitimate. That same year, Henry married Jane Seymour, who became an advocate for Mary and persuaded Henry to bring his eldest daughter back to court. When Mary was presented again to Henry, he proclaimed to his courtiers that he was glad he had not heeded their advice and put her to death. Mary, who evidently had not realized how dangerous her position had been, fainted upon hearing this.

Henry's wish for a male heir was fulfilled in 1537, when Jane Seymour gave birth to a son, Edward. Mary, whose mother had died in 1535, accepted her brother as rightful heir to the throne. Sadly, just as she gained a brother, Mary lost the stepmother who had done so much for her; Jane Seymour died of complications from childbirth in 1537.

At Henry's death in 1547, Edward succeeded to the throne as Edward VI (1547–1553). Although Mary and Edward had been close, Mary left court soon after his coronation because she could not continue to practice her Catholic religion there.

Edward VI died in 1553 at age fifteen. As the young king lay on his deathbed, advisers persuaded him to bequeath the throne to his cousin, Lady Jane Grey. A few days later, Lady Jane was proclaimed queen of England and one of her supporters was sent to arrest Mary. Mary was alerted to the plot, however, and escaped to Norfolk. Meanwhile, the coalition supporting Lady Jane dissolved, and Mary was proclaimed queen on July 19, 1553. Jane Grey and several of her supporters were arrested for treason. Three were executed, but Mary forgave Jane because it was clear that the girl had been manipulated.

Late in 1553, Mary's announcement that she would marry Philip of Spain (the future Philip II, r. 1556–1598) sparked a rebellion in England by those who feared the consequences of foreign influence. When the rebellion was put down in 1554, the leaders were executed, and Mary was persuaded to execute Jane Grey as well, since the young girl might serve as a rallying point for other rebellious factions. Mary also imprisoned her sister Elizabeth, believing that she had participated in the rebellion.

From the beginning of her reign, Mary had been anxious to restore the Catholic Church in England. Mary ordered nearly 300 Protestants burned to death, earning her the infamous nickname Bloody Mary. Her primary motive, however, was not religious. Those who opposed her reinstatement of Catholicism in England also questioned her right to rule; thus, the executions were motivated by political considerations as well as religious ones.

The reign of Mary I was plagued by rebellions, epidemics, and crop failures. Even her marriage was a disaster. Mary was in love with her husband, but Philip did not return her affection and spent much of their marriage in Spain. The couple had no children.

In November 1558, it was clear that Mary was dying. On the advice of her counselors, she named her younger sister Elizabeth as her heir. Mary I died on November 17, 1558; she was forty-two years old. She was succeeded on the throne by her sister, who reigned as Elizabeth I (r. 1558–1603).

See also: EDWARD VI; ELIZABETH I; HENRY VIII; PHILIP II; SUCCESSION, ROYAL.

FURTHER READING

Erickson, Carolly. *Bloody Mary.* New York: St. Martin's Press, 1998.

Meyer, Carolyn. *Mary, Bloody Mary.* San Diego, CA: Harcourt Brace, 2001.

Ridley, Jasper. *Bloody Mary's Martyrs: The Story of England's Terror.* New York: Carroll & Graf, 2002.

MARY II. *See* WILLIAM AND MARY

MARY, QUEEN OF SCOTS

(1542–1587 C.E.)

Member of the House of Stuart (Stewart), who ruled as queen of Scotland (r. 1542–1567) and queen of France (r. 1559–1560), and whose son, James VI of Scotland (r. 1567–1625), succeeded to the throne of England as King James I (r. 1603–1625).

Mary Stuart was born on December 7 or 8, 1542, at the royal palace of Linlithgow in central Scotland. Mary was the daughter of King James V of Scotland (r. 1513–1542), who died just six days after her birth. Her mother was Mary of Guise, a member of the powerful Guise family of France, who became regent for Mary upon James's death and sent the young queen to be brought up at the French court. Mary's education included Latin and Greek.

MARRIAGE AND EARLY RULE

In April 1558, at Notre Dame Cathedral in Paris, Mary Stuart married the French dauphin (heir to the throne), the future Francis II (r. 1559–1560), the son of King Henry II (r. 1547–1559) and Catherine de Medici. The following year, Henry II died and Francis became king. Mary's tenure as queen of France was short-lived, however. Francis II died in December 1560, and Catherine de Medici took power as regent for her son, Charles IX (r. 1560–1574). Meanwhile, Mary of Guise had died, and Mary returned to Scotland in 1561 to assume the full mantle of rulership.

Mary's upbringing had taught her little about Scotland, which had become increasingly Protestant under the influence of the Scottish reformer John Knox. After Mary's return, there was a great deal of friction between her and Knox. Knox believed that Mary was unsuited to be queen; not only was she Catholic, but as a woman, she was inferior and had no right to be ruler. Although Mary made no effort to restore Catholicism in Scotland, the Catholic

Masses she attended in her chapel were often disrupted by zealous mobs, and Knox frequently denounced Mary from the pulpit of Protestant churches.

Mary relied heavily on her half-brother, the Protestant earl of Moray, for advice and counsel. Because of this, and because she sought to be acknowledged by Elizabeth I of England (r. 1558–1603) as heir to the English throne, Mary made no attempt to limit the growth of Scottish Protestantism. Some scholars cite Mary as an example of toleration; others argue that her acceptance of Protestantism accounts, in part, for her failure as queen. For by allowing Presbyterianism, the Scottish sect of Protestantism, to become Scotland's official religion, she lost the backing of her Catholic population and was unable to depend on them in a crisis.

COURT INTRIGUE AND SCANDAL

In April 1565, Mary became captivated with her cousin Henry, Lord Darnley, who was nominally Catholic. To prevent their marriage, the earl of Moray and his Protestant allies rebelled against the queen in what was later called the Chaseabout Raid. But when Mary insisted she would not reestablish Catholicism, Moray found few supporters and fled to England.

Soon after the marriage, Mary found Darnley to be a drunken and irresponsible husband who was disinterested in government matters. Finding no support from him, she turned to her secretary and trusted friend, David Riccio, for companionship and advice. Darnley became jealous, however, and in March 1566, Riccio was murdered in front of Mary, who was then six months pregnant. With help from the earl of Bothwell, Mary escaped from Holyrood Palace and returned to Edinburgh; ostensibly, she reconciled with Darnley. Her son James was born in June 1566.

Mary offered to pardon those involved in the Chaseabout Raid, but the offer was probably a bribe. On February 9, 1567, a house at which Darnley was staying was blown up, and his body was found strangled in the orchard outside. Public opinion against Mary ran high, with many accusing her of involvement in the murder.

Mary might have weathered the scandal had she behaved wisely and gone into seclusion to mourn. Instead, she attended a wedding the day after Darnley's death. Bothwell was publicly tried for the murder but acquitted for lack of witnesses. Worse, Mary

The last of the Stuart Dynasty to rule Scotland, Mary Queen of Scots had to give up the throne as a result of religious conflicts and court scandals. After fleeing Scotland, she was imprisoned by her cousin, Elizabeth I of England, and executed at age 44.

ratified grants to Bothwell and to others involved in the murder.

In April 1567, Bothwell, who had ambitions to be king, intercepted Mary on her way to Edinburgh. Within the next two weeks Bothwell received a divorce from his wife, and in May, he and Mary were married by Protestant rites, outraging many Scottish Protestants. A group of rebellious lords organized an army and met Mary and Bothwell, with their supporters, at Carberry Hill on June 15. Mary agreed to surrender to the lords, provided Bothwell was allowed to go. But the lords broke their promise and took Mary prisoner. She was forced to abdicate in favor of son James, who was crowned king at Stirling Castle on July 29, 1567. The earl of Moray was appointed James's regent.

ENGLAND AND THE FINAL YEARS

Mary escaped ten months later, disguised as a countrywoman. She gathered a sizable group of supporters and confronted Moray and his forces at Langside, near the city of Glasgow. Mary's forces were defeated and, against advice, she fled to England seeking help from Queen Elizabeth. Before agreeing to help, Elizabeth demanded that Mary first clear herself of Darnley's murder. At a legal conference at York, Moray supplied a series of letters, known as the Casket Letters, as evidence against Mary. These were letters from Mary to Bothwell (since disappeared) that supposedly incriminated her in Darnley's murder. Mary thus became a prisoner of the English government and was placed in a series of castles, each more heavily secured.

Mary's next years were spent planning escape. She wrote to the duke of Norfolk, twice offering to marry him in exchange for his help escaping. Elizabeth discovered both plots. After the second, Norfolk was imprisoned in the Tower of London.

In 1571, Elizabeth became aware of what came to be known as the Ridolfi Plot. Ridolfi, an Italian banker, helped plan an invasion of England by Spain. Supposedly, this invasion would inspire English Catholics to revolt against Elizabeth, free Mary, and place her on the throne. Mary neither knew nor approved of the plot, but Elizabeth moved her to a more secluded prison and denied her all correspondence and visitors.

In 1583, Sir Francis Walsingham, a spy for Elizabeth, attempted to entrap Mary in another plot that had been uncovered, the Throckmorton Plot. Once again, the plot involved a Spanish invasion of England, with hopes of inspiring Catholics to rise up and free Mary. The evidence implicated Mary, who was imprisoned at Fotheringay Castle. The following year, Parliament passed the Act of Association, which stated that should anyone conspire to make Mary queen, Mary would be guilty of treason, whether or not she knew of the plot.

By 1586, conditions in England had become difficult for Catholics. Legislation had been passed making it treason to be a priest, to help a priest, or to attend Mass. In addition, the fines for nonattendance at church services had skyrocketed to twenty pounds a month per adult. Mary's failings were increasingly overlooked, and she had come to be seen as a Catholic martyr. English Catholics held on to the hope that Mary would be England's next queen.

In early July 1586, Anthony Babington, a young Catholic nobleman, met with a group of Catholics planning to rescue Mary and crown her as queen.

Walsingham discovered the plot and seems to have encouraged it. Mary was allowed to receive and send correspondence again, and her letters to Babington were intercepted by one of Walsingham's agents. In one letter, Babington spoke of removing Elizabeth, and Mary replied with approval. Soon after, Babington was arrested and executed, and Mary was charged with treason.

At Mary's trial on October 15, 1586, the former Scottish queen remained calm, denying the court's jurisdiction and defending her innocence. Found guilty of conspiring against Elizabeth, she was executed on February 8, 1587.

See also: ELIZABETH I; JAMES I OF ENGLAND (JAMES VI OF SCOTLAND); SCOTTISH KINGDOMS; STEWART DYNASTY; STUART DYNASTY.

FURTHER READING

Fraser, Antonia. *Mary Queen of Scots.* New York: Delta Trade Paperbacks.

Lewis, Jayne Elizabeth, ed. *The Trial of Mary Queen of Scots: A Brief History with Documents.* New York: Bedford/St. Martin's Press, 1999.

Wormald, Jenny. *Mary Queen of Scots: A Study in Failure.* London: George Philip, 1988.

MATARAM EMPIRE

(ca. 860–late 1700s C.E.)

A kingdom of Central Java that had two flourishing periods. The first, which lasted until about 1000, was Hindu, and the second was Islamic.

FIRST MATARAM KINGDOM

The Matarams first established their leadership in central Java when they replaced the Buddhist Sailendra rulers, who shifted their seat of power to Srivijaya (Palembang). As a Hindu dynasty, these Matarams built a large complex of temples during the ninth and tenth centuries. The most famous was a set of temples called Lara Jonggrang, also known as Tjandi Prambanan (Prambanan Temple) because it was located near the village of Prambanan. It was probably built by the Hindu Mataram king Dhaksa, in the beginning of the tenth century, to worship the Hindu god, Siva (Shiva). It is Indonesia's biggest Shiva temple. Lara Jonggrang means "Slender Maiden," which is what the neighboring people called a large statue of Shiva's wife, the Hindu goddess Durga, that was in the temple. By about 900, the Mataram Empire extended over all of central and eastern Java. But around 1010, in response to requests by the Brahmans, the Eastern Java ruler Airlangga became king of this Hindu Empire.

SECOND MATARAM KINGDOM

The second flourishing period of the Mataram Empire in Java was from the late sixteenth to the late eighteenth century. Earlier in the sixteenth century, two Islamic kingdoms reigned in central Java, Demak and Pajang. Senapati Ingalaga incorporated those kingdoms into the powerful Mataram Empire and became its first king (r. 1584–1601).

Senapati tried to unify eastern and central Java, but it was Sultan Agung (r. 1613–1645) who succeeded in expanding the Mataram Empire to its greatest power, including most of Java. He took over Surabaya and Madura and other port cities in northern Java, and then tried unsuccessfully, in 1628 and 1629, to capture Batavia from the Dutch East India company. Agung also started a holy war against infidels in Bali and Balambangan in the far east of Java. To develop Mataram internally, he promoted interisland trade. He also mixed Islam with the existing Hindu-Javanese tradition and instituted a new calendar derived from Islamic and Javanese customs in 1633. The arts during his rule combined Islamic and Hindu-Javanese aspects.

After Agung died in 1645, the Mataram Empire began to weaken, losing both control and land to the Dutch East India Company. By 1749, it was a vassal state of the Company. Wars of succession in Mataram led to a division of the kingdom into three distinct sultantes by 1757, one at Yogyakarta and two at Solo. The politically shrewd Dutch participated in these wars and took control of the whole area, becoming the first rulers of a unified Java.

See also: JAVAN KINGDOMS.

FURTHER READING

Coedes, George. *The Indianized States of Southeast Asia.* Honolulu: University of Hawaii Press, 1971.

Hall, D.G.E. *A History of South-East Asia.* 3rd ed. New York: St. Martin's Press, 1981.

MATSUHITO. *See* MEIJI MONARCHY

MAURYA EMPIRE (321–185 B.C.E.)

Empire established in northern India in 322 B.C.E. when the Indian leader, Chandragupta Maurya (r. 321–297 B.C.E.), simultaneously overthrew the Magadha kingdom and captured the eastern portions of the Indo-Greek Empire established by Alexander III, the Great (r. 336–323 B.C.E.).

RISE OF CHANDRAGUPTA

Chandragupta Maurya was a member of the royalty of the Maghada kingdom, possibly an illegitimate son of the king. The Maghada ruler questioned Chandragupta's loyalty, however, and had him exiled. Assisted by Chanakya, a Brahman priest who served as his adviser, Chandragupta rallied a formidable group of Maghadan dissidents and foreigners under Maghadan control. In a bold move, Chandragupta assaulted the Greek territories in the Indus River basin while Chanakya staged a violent insurrection in Pataliputra, the Magadhan capital, and slaughtered the entire royal family. Chandragupta then took the throne, marking the beginning of the Maurya Empire.

Chandragupta Maurya envisioned an empire that would surpass any in Indian history. When the Greeks, led by the general Seleucus, mustered their forces in 305 B.C.E., Chandragupta again defeated them. Seleucus then ceded much of the land comprising present-day Afghanistan to the Mauryas. While Seleucus struggled with rebels in Babylon, Chandragupta gradually absorbed the remainder of Afghanistan. He also extended the eastern frontier of his empire, conquering the Indian states of Bengal, the Punjab, and Bidar. Eventually, the Maurya Empire dominated all of Afghanistan and the Indian subcontinent north of the Narbada River.

CHANDRAGUPTA'S REIGN

To secure these conquests, Chandragupta and his son and successor, Bindusara (r. 297–272 B.C.E.), maintained a massive military force with four components: a large cavalry, more than two hundred thousand infantry soldiers, thousands of chariots, and approximately six thousand elephants. All members of the military were paid directly by the monarchy, received generous provisions, and paid little or no taxes.

Chandragupta's generosity toward the military was highly calculated. Because of his bloody succession to power, Chandragupta continuously feared assassination attempts by Maghadan loyalists, and he used the military as a deterrent. Chandragupta also employed an extensive secret police force to unearth any plots against him. Chandragupta placed these spies in his court, the civil administration, and even in the general populace. These agents also spread propaganda about Chandragupta's munificence as a monarch.

The brutal penal system of the Maurya Empire also stemmed crime and insurrection. Chandragupta adopted a policy of *dandaniti* ("the science of punishment"), under which torture was commonly used to elicit confessions. Even minor thefts were punished by mutilation, while capital punishment was the penalty for homicide, larceny, or damaging royal property. Because all artisans were government employees, assaulting one of them also resulted in death.

Although the Mauryan judicial system was incredibly harsh, the overall government was highly effective. Despite his fears of conspiracy, Chandragupta realized that he could not manage his vast empire without capable ministers and efficient departments. First, he divided the empire into four provinces and appointed a viceroy to administer each one. Then, each city was divided into four wards with a prefect in charge of each. Subprefects, each responsible for ten to forty families, served under the prefects and oversaw fire prevention, sanitation, and the municipal courts. Most importantly, the subprefects maintained the census. Chandragupta demanded frequent, accurate counts of the populations in each city within the empire. The census data was used both for taxation and for security purposes—subprefects regularly reported arrivals and departures to Chandragupta's secret police.

Chandragupta also formed six commissions to regulate Mauryan society. The first commission oversaw all artisans, whom Chandragupta had denoted as government employees. This group set wages, inspected all products, and determined market prices. The second commission accommodated all foreign visitors, securing lodging for them, providing a safe escort, and monitoring their activities. Another group compiled the census information and meticulously recorded births and deaths to ensure accurate taxation. Finally, the last three commissions manipulated all trade within the empire. They levied and collected a sales tax on all products, enforced excise

ROYAL PLACES

PATALIPUTRA PALACE

Despite his constant fears of conspiracy, Chandragupta Maurya maintained an opulent palace at the Maurya capital of Pataliputra in northern India. The palace was filled with riches and diversions, and Greek ambassadors recounted that its massive timber pillars were decorated with golden vines and animal figures shaped from silver. The palace housed an elaborate park containing ponds, trees, and small temples. All of the palace's utensils were fashioned from gold, and all members of the court wore fine garments. A brigade of women warriors guarded Chandragupta, and he maintained a large harem. A large hunting preserve bordered the grounds, and the palace housed a small arena for both human and animal combat. Gambling was also a common distraction at the palace. When Asoka converted to Buddhism, however, he discontinued many of these practices. Court members dressed more plainly, and the palace's ostentatious ornaments were stored away. Although the palace no longer stands, descriptions of it reveal that it rivaled any in Asia or Africa.

taxes on products such as liquor, and oversaw the empire's agricultural industry. Chandragupta had declared that all land belonged to the monarchy, but farmers were given lifelong leases to their lands. A lease could be terminated, however, if a government inspector believed that the land was not being satisfactorily cultivated.

ASOKA'S ASCENDENCY

The reign of Chandragupta Maurya ended in 297 B.C.E. According to legend, he followed the Jain tradition of abdicating the throne and starving himself to death. He was succeeded on the throne by his son Bindusara, who maintained the empire during a twenty-five year reign.

When Bindusara died in 272 B.C.E., his son Asoka sought the Maurya throne. Although Asoka had served as a viceroy and was the appointed heir, his brothers disputed his succession and Asoka was forced to suppress them. Consequently, his actual coronation did not take place until 268 B.C.E., four years after Bindusara's death.

Asoka shared his grandfather's dream of a sprawling Maurya Empire. In 257 B.C.E., he invaded Kalinga, an Indian state located on the Bay of Bengal, in order to achieve his grand vision. The war with Kalinga was extremely ferocious, and both sides suf-

fered serious casualties. When the Maurya army finally triumphed after several months of combat, Asoka's forces plundered the Kalinga capital and viciously slaughtered countless civilians.

The carnage appalled Asoka. To atone for his perceived transgression, he converted to Buddhism and adopted a pacifist policy. Under the tutelage of the Buddhist monk Upagupta, Asoka toured the Buddhist holy sites, became a vegetarian, and served briefly as a monk in a Buddhist monastery. When Asoka returned to Pataliputra, he embraced the Buddhist "Law of Piety" as his governing principle. This law stipulated three obligations: honesty, reverence for all elders, and unwavering respect for animal life.

Using these principles, Asoka instituted monumental changes in the Maurya government. He set strict rules for the compassionate treatment of slaves and servants, promoted religious toleration, and generously supported charitable causes. He also sharply curbed the government's use of torture and reduced government corruption.

Asoka commissioned large numbers of Buddhist missionaries. At first, he sent them to adjoining kingdoms to ensure them of Maurya's peaceful intentions. Soon, however, he also began sending missionaries throughout Asia, to Africa, and even to Europe. These Buddhist missionaries successfully converted populations in Burma, Thailand, China, and Japan. Under Asoka's guidance, Buddhism thus became one of the world's major religions and deeply influenced the development of the Asian continent.

As he grew older, Asoka worried increasingly that Maurya's adherence to Buddhism would decrease after his death. To prevent this, he installed large rocks around the empire inscribed with Buddhist principles. These rocks, known as the rock edicts, first appeared around 258 B.C.E. Asoka periodically distributed other edicts across the kingdom. Finally, in 242 B.C.E., he issued the Seven Pillar Edicts, inscribed on more than thirty thousand pillars across the Maurya Empire. Above all, the Seven Pillar Edicts encouraged the Maurya public to observe the Law of Piety.

DECLINE OF THE EMPIRE

Despite his efforts, Asoka's fears proved accurate. When he died in 232 B.C.E., his two grandsons, Jalauka (r. 232–225 B.C.E.) and Dasaratha (r. 232–225 B.C.E.), divided the empire between them. Neither ruler embraced Buddhism, and the religion gradually lost its influence in the empire. The two brothers also lacked their grandfather's administrative skills. As a result, the empire became increasingly fragmented, as members of the royal family claimed portions of the provinces for themselves.

The last Maurya monarch, Brihadratha (r. 187–180 B.C.E.), was assassinated in 180 B.C.E. The head of the military, Pushyamitra Sunga (r. 180–151 B.C.E.), seized control of the highly weakened empire and founded the Sunga dynasty. During their ascendancy, the Maurya rulers had introduced a highly organized government that provided a model for later Indian governments and that had helped establish Buddhism as one of the world's major religions.

See also: ASOKA; CHANDRAGUPTA MAURYA; INDIAN KINGDOMS; INDO-GREEK KINGDOMS; KALINGA KINGDOM; MAGADHA KINGDOM; SUNGA DYNASTY.

FURTHER READING

Mukherjee, Bratindra. *The Character of the Maurya Empire.* Calcutta: Progressive Publishers, 2000.

MAUSOLEA, ROYAL. *See* FUNERALS
AND MORTUARY RITES

MAXIMILIAN (1832–1867 C.E.)

Emperor of Mexico (r. 1864–1867) who was a member of the Habsburg dynasty and brother of Austrian emperor Francis Joseph (r. 1848–1916). Maximilian was installed as ruler of Mexico by French emperor Napoleon III (r. 1852–1870) during the brief period of French interference in Mexican affairs known as the French Intervention (1861–1867).

Ferdinand Maximilian was born on June 6, 1832, in Vienna, Austria, to Archduke Francis Karl and Archduchess Sophie. As befitted a youth of imperial birth, Maximilian served in the Austrian navy and then went into politics, acting as governor-general of Lombardy until 1859. Consistent with his social and political status, he married Charlotte, the daughter of King Leopold I of Belgium (r. 1831–1865).

While Maximilian served in Lombardy, a civil war broke out on the other side of the globe in Mexico between conservative and liberal factions. The war, known as the War of the Reform (1858–1861), was won by the liberals, who installed Benito Juarez as Mexican president. The Mexican conservatives turned to Europe for help.

Initially, Britain, France, and Spain all offered to help restore Mexican conservatives to power, but the British and Spanish decided to withdraw. However, Napoleon III of France saw an opportunity to increase France's imperial holding in the Americas. In 1863, French forces invaded and captured the Mexican capital, overthrew the liberal government, and prepared to establish a monarchy.

Needing an emperor, Napoleon offered the job to Maximilian, who agreed to take the position if the Mexican people truly wanted him to rule. A sham vote was held (voting rights were restricted to areas under firm control of the French forces), and results seemed to show that the Mexicans approved of Maximilian. Meanwhile, the French promised to leave some 25,000 troops in Mexico City until Maximilian could create a loyal army of his own.

Maximilian and his wife Charlotte (whom the Mexicans called Carlotta) arrived in Mexico City on May 28, 1864. Much to Maximilian's surprise, the popular support he anticipated was all but nonexistent, and the royal couple was shunned by all but the conservative elite. Moreover, the United States, which opposed any European political presence in the Americas, did not recognize Maximilian's authority to rule.

Lacking local or regional support, Maximilian made some effort to improve his popularity. He began with small gestures, such as delivering all public addresses in Spanish. Soon, however, he began supporting causes dear to the hearts of the Mexican people—causes that were bound to alienate and anger his core of conservative supporters. Maximilian advocated the separation of church and state, particularly through the confiscation and redistribution of church-owned properties. Doing so incurred the wrath of Mexico's Catholic clergy and caused the conservative elite to turn against him as well.

Although the civil war in Mexico was ostensibly over, sporadic fighting still occurred in the countryside, and Maximilian depended on French troops to maintain order. Convinced that these uprisings were the work of common outlaws and criminals, he ordered that all captured rebels be executed. In reality, the uprisings were the work of liberal supporters of Benito Juarez, who were mounting resistance to French and European control.

Meanwhile, France was negotiating a new relationship with the United States, which wanted Napoleon to withdraw all French troops from Mexico. Napoleon complied in 1866, leaving Maximilian without military support. The empress Carlotta sailed to France to beg for continued French support, but Napoleon refused.

Without protection, Maximilian found himself at the mercy of Juarez's guerrilla army. More courageous than smart, and perhaps out of desperation as well, Maximilian decided to defend his throne and assume personal command of the few forces he had mustered. Juarez's forces arrived in Mexico City in February 1867 and laid siege to the nearby city of Querétaro, where Maximilian had chosen to make a stand. Querétaro fell to the guerrillas on May 5, 1867, and Maximilian was captured. A little more than a month later, on June 19, 1867, he was executed by a firing squad.

See also: AMERICAN KINGDOMS, CENTRAL AND NORTH.

MAXIMILIAN I (1459–1519 C.E.)

Holy Roman emperor (r. 1493–1519) and German king (r. 1493–1519), who inherited an empire in decline, fought in vain to regain its former glories, but extended its influence through clever matrimonial alliances.

Maximilian was the son of Holy Roman Emperor Frederick III (r. 1440–1493). As a young man, Maximilian impressed everyone with his physical presence, intelligence, courage, and goodwill. His contemporary, the Italian statesman Niccolo Machiavelli, called him "a pattern of many princely virtues." Chosen emperor-elect in 1486, Maximilian took an ever-increasing share of imperial duties until his father's death in 1493, at which time Maximilian took the throne of both the Holy Roman Empire and the German kingdom.

As emperor, Maximilian dreamed of returning the Holy Roman Empire to its former grandeur. Accomplishing this feat, however, would have required the energy of a Charlemagne (r. 768–814) and the skill of a Julius Caesar (r. 49–44 B.C.E.). The apathy of his father, Frederick III, had already allowed Hungary, Bohemia, and several smaller states to secede or drift away from the imperial fold. Maximilian's own campaigns into Italy against the veteran Pope Julius II were a woeful failure. Although Maximilian fought on many fronts, he won few battles.

Maximilian knew that the imperial bureaucracy was corrupt and inefficient, and he attempted reasonable, intelligent reforms. But whenever confronted with the slightest personal inconvenience, he bypassed his own reforms in the name of expedience, and this undermined his own authority for change. Maximilian even ignored or overturned laws such as those he had enacted at the historic Diet at Worms in 1495, where he had prevailed upon the Reichstag (the imperial assembly) to outlaw wars of personal profit. When thwarted by reluctant German princes, who feared a more powerful central government, Maximilian set up his own courts and financial institutions, which operated outside of the Reichstag's control.

Toward the end of his reign, after many military, financial, and political disappointments, Maximilian embarked upon a far more successful diplomatic path—the arrangement of clever marriages. For his son, Philip, he accepted an offer by King Ferdinand II of Aragón (r. 1479–1516) for the hand of Ferdinand's mentally disturbed daughter, Juana, the sole heir of the kingdoms of Aragón and Castile. Maximilian brought Bohemia and Hungary back into the sphere of influence of his Habsburg dynasty by arranging a dual marriage of his grandchildren to the son and daughter of King Ladislas II (r. 1471–1516), who wore the crowns of both countries.

Maximilian's greatest legacy, however, was his patronage of education and the arts. Reputed to speak eight languages himself, Maximilian is sometimes credited as the primary cause for blending South and North German dialects into a common language. He opened or expanded universities and academies throughout his realm, inviting humanists from Italy to attend his court in Vienna. He also supported German thinkers and artists—including the artist Albrecht Dürer—to the full extent of his finances.

Before Maximilian died, he considered himself a failure. But despite the unsuccessful skirmishes of his early years, he had brought art and prosperity to Germany, and he had sown the seeds that would widen the Habsburg influence to its greatest extent within two generations. Upon his death in 1519, Maximilian was succeeded on the imperial throne by his grandson, Charles V (r. 1519–1558), who also ruled as King Charles I of Spain (r. 1516–1556).

See also: CHARLES V; FERDINAND II; HABSBURG DYNASTY; HOLY ROMAN EMPIRE.

MAYA EMPIRE (1800 B.C.E.–1524 C.E.)

Pre-Columbian civilization that inhabited a large territory extending across the Yucatán Peninsula in Mexico and including parts of Guatemala, Belize, and the western areas of Honduras and El Salvador.

During their long historical development, the Mayas never formed a unified state. Nevertheless, they shared a number of Maya dialects and other cultural patterns, including an elaborate calendar, writing, massive architecture, and polychrome pottery.

Scholars have divided the area inhabited by the Maya-speaking people into three subregions: the Southern Subregion, including the Guatemalan highlands and Pacific Coast; the Central Subregion, comprising northern Guatemala and contiguous lowlands to the east and west; and the Northern Subregion, consisting of the Yucatán Peninsula.

PRE-CLASSIC PERIOD
(1800 B.C.E.–250 C.E.)
The origins of the Maya-speaking people are still unclear. Some scholars believe that they could have been immigrants proceeding from the Mexican Gulf

Coast, while others argue that they originated in the Guatemalan highlands.

Whatever the case, around 1800 B.C.E., there were a number of Maya villages in the Southern Subregion. Each settlement had a maximum of about 1,000 inhabitants. The main economic activity was agriculture, and the people supplemented their diet by hunting, fishing, and gathering. These early Mayas practiced a method of cultivation known as "slash and burn," in which they cut the vegetation of the area where they planned to sow and then set it on fire, increasing its immediate fertility. Over time, however, this practice caused the soil to lose its fecundity, forcing the Maya to cultivate another area.

The early Maya settlements had commercial links with each other and gradually extended their trade routes to other regions. Some Maya settlements exchanged goods with the Olmec civilization of the Mexican Gulf Coast, west of the Yucatán Peninsula.

The Maya were renowned for their architecture, today comprising some of the most magnificent ruins in the Americas. The ancient city of Chichén Itzá on Mexico's Yucatan Peninsula is dominated by the Pyramid of Kukulkán, which towers over the other buildings at the site.

THE AZTEC AND MAYA EMPIRES

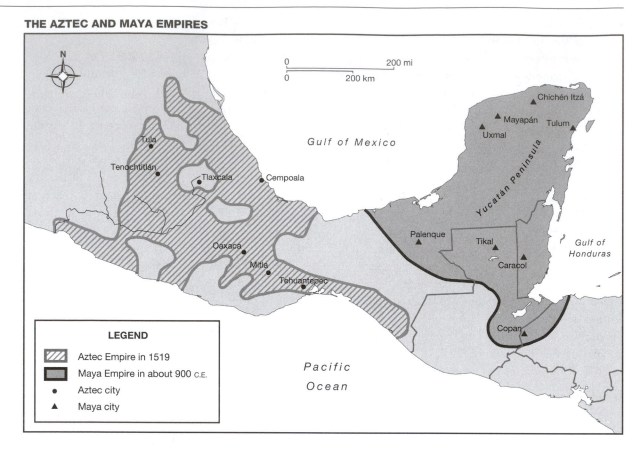

LEGEND

▨ Aztec Empire in 1519

▦ Maya Empire in about 900 C.E.

• Aztec city

▲ Maya city

The Olmecs, in turn, influenced the Maya religion and astronomy, contributing to the development of both a calendar and writing.

According to scholars, by the late Pre-Classic period some Maya settlements already exhibited a certain degree of political centralization. Urban centers like Kaminaljuyú, Tik'al, and Nakbe dominated other minor settlements, demanding tribute from them. There was also an internal social division, and emerging elites organized construction projects, supervised trade, and led public ceremonies.

CLASSIC PERIOD (250–900 C.E.)

In the early Classic period (250–600), the city and empire of Teotihuacan—located on the northeast side of the Valley of Mexico—exerted a powerful influence over Maya civilization. In some cases, it seems that invaders from Teotihuacan took over Maya settlements, while in other instances, it appears that the links were mainly commercial. Around 400, a Teotihuacan force occupied the Maya city of Kaminaljuyu and developed a hybrid culture combining Teotihuacan traditions with Maya ones. In the Maya center of Tik'al, a mythical king called "Fire Is Born" (who pos-

sibly came from Teotihuacan) removed the native rulers and started a new ruling dynasty.

Around 600, Teotihuacan's influence in Mesoamerica waned, possibly due to climatic changes that contributed to the decline of that civilization. As Teotihuacan's influence decreased, a number of independent Mayan kingdoms emerged. The largest of these kingdoms were Tikal and Copan (in Guatemala), Kalak'mul (in the Campeche region of Mexico), Caracol (in Belize), and Palenque (in western Honduras). These kingdoms established temporary alliances with each other. The capital city of each kingdom controlled political, religious, and economic activities. Agriculture remained the main economic activity, complemented by hunting and gathering.

Tik'al was the most populous Maya center in the late Classic period. Estimates on its maximum total population vary between 10,000 and 90,000 inhabitants. It had a total of about 3,000 structures, including six large temple pyramids that consisted of a series of superimposed platforms made of rocks and cement, covered with blocks of limestone.

Tik'al and other sites of the Classic period also contained smaller pyramid-like buildings that could have served as palaces with administrative functions. The royal elites exacted tribute and labor from commoners, who had to work in the official construction projects. The importance of both crafts and trade increased during the Classic period, and war remained an important activity.

Each Maya kingdom in the Classic period was ruled by a monarch belonging to a royal lineage that traced its descent from a common ancestor. Customarily, the eldest son or younger brother succeeded to the throne upon the death of a king. However, there could be some variations; in fact, Palenque had at least two female rulers. An advisory council, composed of the leaders of noble families, helped the king to govern. The members of these families were also in charge of the main civil and ecclesiastical positions.

Maya priests prepared the religious and agricultural calendar, took care of rituals, and wrote historical chronicles. They also carried out human sacrifices to appease the gods and avert disasters. The king played a crucial role in Maya public ceremonies. He also led his kingdom into wars to gain power, resources, and prestige. According to scholars, although the Mayas of the Classic and Postclassic period practiced human sacrifices, this never reached the scale of the Aztecs. Most probably, prisoners captured during battles were used as sacrificial victims.

By the end of the Classic period, around 800, the southern lowlands of the Maya region experienced a gradual decline and collapse. According to experts, the region had an excess of population, totaling around 10 million, while cities like Tik'al, Kalak'mul, and Caracol each had about 100,000 inhabitants. As a result of these large populations, internal and external conflicts over resources became more frequent and violent. Severe climatic changes worsened the situation. As a result, the Maya settlements in the central and southern region gradually lost population and declined both economically and politically.

POSTCLASSIC PERIOD (900–1524 C.E.)

In the Postclassic period of Maya history, northern Yucatán was the most populated area of the Maya region. A number of kingdoms emerged at that time, each organized around trade and war. Maya cities in this period were located close to commercial routes, and defensive walls surrounded the majority of major settlements.

Early in the Postclassic period, the most promi-

nent settlement was Chichén Itzá, a city strongly influenced by the Toltec civilization, which had originated in northern Mexico and extended its dominion over much of central Mexico. Around 1200, Chichén Itzá began to decline, but another city, Mayapán, rose to power and unified most of the Yucatán. The rulers of Mayapán, who belonged to the "Cocom" lineage, governed the Yucatán Peninsula for 250 years. During their rule, most major settlements invested large amounts of labor in building defensive walls, indicating the regularity of warfare. Around 1450, the rebellious Maya lineage of the "Xiu" defeated Mayapán and sacked the city. Northern Yucatán was divided into sixteen autonomous kingdoms, which lasted until the arrival of the Spanish conquistadors in the early sixteenth century.

See also: AMERICAN KINGDOM, CENTRAL AND NORTH.

FURTHER READING

Coe, Michael D. *The Maya*. 6th ed. New York: Thames & Hudson, 1999.

Sharer, Robert J., Silvanus G. Morley, and George W. Brainerd. *The Ancient Maya*. 5th ed. Stanford, CA: Stanford University Press, 1994.

MAYORS OF THE PALACE. *See*

CAROLINGIAN DYNASTY

MBEMBE NZINGA. *See* AFONSO I

MBUNDU KINGDOMS

(1500s–early 1900s C.E.)

Kingdoms formed by the Mbundu people, one of several ethnic groups in what is now the Republic of Angola in southwest Africa. There were two Mbundu kingdoms, one centered at Matamba and the other called Ngola (also the Mbundu term for "ruler"). It is from the latter of these two kingdoms that the modern nation of Angola takes its name.

The Mbundu states arose in the sixteenth century, as groups of Mbundu people settled along the shores of the Kwanza River where it flows through west-central Angola. These migrants came to the region at that time to escape the pressures of expansion by the kingdom of Kongo, and to avoid being captured in the slave raiding then prevalent in that kingdom. The Mbundu kingdoms did not remain independent for long, however. The Portuguese laid claim to the territory in 1620, and the Mbundu states remained under Portuguese colonial rule until Angola gained its independence from Portugal in 1975.

Perhaps the most celebrated of the Mbundu rulers was Queen Njinga (r. 1624–1629), who ruled the kingdom of Ngola. In 1629, the Portuguese forced Njinga out of power for being less than fully cooperative in realizing their interests in the slave trade. Njinga was not without resources, however, and she made an alliance with a warlike group called the Mbangala (also known as Jaga). With their assistance, Njinga set out to establish a new kingdom, which she succeeded in doing by conquering the other Mbundu kingdom of Matamba and subjugating the people there to her rule in 1630.

Although Njinga enjoyed sovereignty in her new territory, she never renounced her right to rule Ngola. In 1641, she attempted to make good her claim by allying herself with the Dutch, who vied with Portugal for control over the region. The Portuguese prevailed, however, and Njinga was forced to recognize that she would never again regain the throne of Ngola.

Ever the pragmatist, Njinga decided that if she could not beat the Portuguese it might be best to join them. In 1656, she professed herself a Catholic, thus hoping to ingratiate herself with the Portuguese. This seems to have gained her some measure of acceptance, for in 1657, the Portuguese offered her a treaty of peace, ending three decades of conflict between them. Njinga, now known by her Christian name of Ana de Sousa, ruled at Matamba in relative peace for six more years, until her death in 1663.

By the late 1800s, Portuguese colonial authorities had expanding their rule throughout much of the area of present-day Angola. Their expansionism put great pressure on the various indigenous states, including the kingdom of the Mbundu. After about 1850, these states tried to compete economically with the Portuguese. But they failed, and between 1890 and 1922 all the states, including the Mbundu kingdom, had lost their autonomy as a result of military campaigns launched against them by the Portuguese.

In 1951, Angola officially became an overseas province of Portugal, and the indigenous peoples became subject to harsh repression. Then, after Angola gained its independence from Portugal in 1975, the new nation was wracked by periods of civil war until the early 1990s. Today, the Mbundu are the second largest group in Angola. They dominate the capital city of Luanda, a number of coastal towns, and the Malanje highlands in the east.

See also: AFRICAN KINGDOMS.

MEATH KINGDOM

Ancient and medieval kingdom in central Ireland that was one of five early Irish provinces. The western part, or Mide ("middle kingdom" in the Gaelic language), consisted of the areas of Offaly, Longford, and Westmeath; in the eastern part of the kingdom, the regions of Meath, Louth, and north Dublin formed Brega ("the heights" in Gaelic).

According to legend, sometime in the first century C.E., the Irish high king, Tuathal Techtmar (r. dates unknown), the ancestor of the Uí Néill (O'Neill) dynasty, carved the kingdom of Meath out of the other four Irish provinces and made it the seat of his kingship. He did this so that he would not be biased in favor of his own province during his rule.

The Uí Néill drove the Uí Failge and other tribes from Meath into the kingdom of Leinster and took over Tara, the seat of the high kings, in the fifth century. One branch of the Southern Uí Néill, the Clann Cholmain, became the kings of Meath. Their seat of kingship was located at the cult center of Uisnech, the meeting point of the five provinces. Another branch of the Uí Néill, the Síl nÁedo Slaine, ruled Brega, where Tara was located. Both branches of the dynasty claimed descent from Diarmait MacCerrbel (r. ca. 544–565), the great-grandson of the founder of the Uí Néill dynasty, Niall of the Nine Hostages (r. ca. ?–450), and king of Meath and high king of Ireland.

The high kings of Ireland frequently interfered in the running of Meath. One such Irish high king, Aodh Mac Neill (r. 797–819), divided Meath between Conchobar (r. 803–833) and Ailill (r. 799–803), the sons of the high king Donnchad mac Domnall (r. 770–797), but Conchobar soon killed his brother and reunited the kingdom.

In the late tenth and early centuries, Maelsechnaill mac Donnail (r. 980–1022) of Clann Cholmain, the king of Meath and high king, extended his rule into Brega, raided Dublin, and exacted tribute from the Vikings. His successors were not as strong, however. In the eleventh century, as the power of the Uí Néill waned, Meath dwindled into a number of minor kingdoms, and the dominant powers in the area fought for its territory. In time, puppet kings of Meath were appointed by the O'Connor kings of Connaught and the MacMorrough kings of Leinster.

When Henry II of England (r. 1154–1189) invaded Ireland in 1171, he granted Meath to a Norman noble, Hugh de Lacey, in gratitude for his service. The only powerful king in the area, Tiernan O'Rourke of Breifne (r. dates unknown), who had expanded his rule into Meath, opposed the Normans but was killed by de Lacey. High king Rory O'Connor (r. 1166–1186) also fought de Lacey, but eventually came to an agreement with him. The area around Dublin, called the Pale, which included parts of Meath, continued to be occupied by the English throughout the Middle Ages.

See also: CONNAUGHT KINGDOM; IRISH KINGS; LEINSTER KINGDOM.

MEDES KINGDOM (ca. 700–550 B.C.E.)

Short-lived kingdom in the ancient Near East that was important for its alliance with the Babylonians in toppling the powerful Assyrian Empire.

Relatively little is known about the Medes kingdom, other than what has been determined from studying the artifacts of other cultures of the time. It is believed that there were originally at least six separate Median tribes living near each other in what is now present-day Iran. Around 700 B.C.E., a legendary Median leader named Deioces (Dioces) (r. ca. 699–647 B.C.E.) united the tribes into one kingdom under his rule. During his reign, however, armies of the powerful Assyrian Empire invaded Median territory, and the Medes were made subjects of the Assyrians. Around 647 B.C.E., the Assyrians sent Deioces into exile.

The Median king, Phraortes (Kshathrita) (r. ca. 647–625 B.C.E.), eventually managed to drive out the Assyrians and reassert Median independence. He also subjugated the Persians and established the capital of his kingdom at Ecbatana. When the Median kingdom was overrun by the Scythians around 625 B.C.E., Phraortes was killed in battle.

Phraortes's son and successor, Cyaxares (r. 625–585 B.C.E.), ruled the Medes kingdom during its peak of power. First, he had to endure the rule of the Scythians for twenty-eight years. But, after reinforcing his army, Cyaxares drove out the Scythians and then proceeded to defeat the Persians. Around 615 B.C.E., he also invaded Assyria. In 614 B.C.E., after joining forces with the Babylonians and his former enemies, the Scythians, he captured and leveled the Assyrian city of Ashur.

The Median alliance with the Babylonian king, Nabopolassar (r. 625–605 B.C.E.), was reinforced when Cyaxares's daughter, Amytis, married Nabopolassar's son, the future king Nebuchadrezzar II (r. 604–562 B.C.E.), in 613 B.C.E. The friendship between Cyaxares and Nabopolassar greatly benefitted both sides over the years as they helped fight each other's battles.

In 612 B.C.E., the Medes joined the Babylonians in their fiercest fight yet when they again challenged the Assyrians. Together, they managed to capture the strongly defended Assyrian capital city of Nineveh. Over the next few years, the Medes and Babylonians crushed the Assyrians and captured their remaining strongholds, bringing to an end the mighty Assyrian Empire.

The Babylonians took most of the conquered Assyrian territory, but the Medes annexed the northern and eastern parts. Cyaxares expanded his territory farther to the north and to the west, venturing into Armenia and then capturing Cappadocia (in present-day Turkey), which was part of the kingdom of Urartu. When a boundary dispute with king Alyattes (r. 610–560 B.C.E.) of the kingdom of Lydia in Anatolia (present-day Turkey) could not be resolved, Nebuchadrezzar II of Babylonia, Cyaxares's son-in-law, settled the dispute by creating the dividing line at the Halys River.

Cyaxares was succeeded by his son, Astyages (r. ca. 585–550 B.C.E.), and the kingdom remained peaceful for about three decades. However, the Persian leader, Cyrus of Anshan, became increasingly discontented with his status as a vassal of the Medes. Around 553 B.C.E., Cyrus revolted to gain his independence. Astyages's general, Harpagus, betrayed him and brought part of Astyages's own army to fight against him. Cyrus, who became known as Cyrus the Great (r. 559–530 B.C.E.), conquered the Median territory and incorporated it into the Persian Empire, putting an end to the Medes kingdom around 550 B.C.E.

See also: ASSYRIAN EMPIRE; CYAXARES; CYRUS THE GREAT; NABOPOLASSAR; NEBUCHADREZZAR II; PERSIAN EMPIRE; SCYTHIAN EMPIRE.

MEDICI FAMILY (ca. 1400s–1737 C.E.)

One of the most wealthy and powerful families in Italian history, particularly in the city of Florence. Though only rarely did any member of the Medici family hold political office, their influence was immense. From the time of the Medicis' rise in the fifteenth century until their demise in the mid-eighteenth century, rivals challenged Medici power. However, various shrewd figures in the family helped ensure their control and power, and did much for the cultural and political development of Italy.

ORIGINS AND EARLY YEARS

The Medici family name appears as early as the twelfth century, connected with the emerging industries of banking and finance. They enjoyed only moderate prominence, however, until the fifteenth century, when Giovanni di Bicci de' Medici consolidated the family's wealth and left it one of the richest in Europe at his death in 1429. This wealth became the basis of the future political power of the Medici family.

Giovanni's death left the Medici family vulnerable to business rivals, and they were driven out of Florence for a brief time in 1433 by the Albizzi family. They soon returned, however, led by Giovanni's son, Cosimo de' Medici (Cosimo the Elder), who was the first Medici of true political importance.

CONSOLIDATION OF FAMILY POWER

Cosimo de' Medici had a special aptitude for economic affairs, and under his control, the family's fortunes increased exponentially. Cosimo's vast wealth enabled him to fund a variety of public projects, and his contributions to the Florentine government gave him a powerful voice in local affairs. One of the greatest patrons of art and education in European history, Cosimo almost singlehandedly pushed Florence to the forefront of cultural development and placed his native city at the center of the Italian Renaissance. Cosimo's death in 1464, which brought his son Piero de' Medici to the head of the family, was greatly mourned throughout Europe.

Piero de' Medici was plagued with poor health and consequently ran the family for only a few years. He enjoyed much of the same popularity as his father, though a rival family, the Pitti, did make an attempt on his life following Cosimo's death. Piero died in 1469, passing leadership of the family to his two sons, Lorenzo and Giuliano de' Medici. A plot, led by Pope Sixtus IV and members of the rival Pazzi family, succeeded in murdering Giuliano in 1478, but left Lorenzo in charge of the family and generated much sympathy and support for the Medicis in Florence.

Lorenzo de' Medici gained an unprecedented popularity and is frequently known as Lorenzo the Magnificent. Though it cost his family a great deal of money to do so, Lorenzo patronized and promoted the work of artists such as Botticelli and Michelangelo; his patronage further cemented Florence's position as the leading cultural and scholastic city of its time. Lorenzo was also a major figure in international politics and tried hard to maintain the precarious balance of power among the numerous small kingdoms of the Italian Peninsula. Lorenzo's power and some illicit political activities (he took control of Florence's treasury, largely to his personal gain) did garner him some enemies, chief of whom was the Dominican priest Girolamo Savonarola, who attacked the Medici family as corrupt and irreligious.

CHALLENGES OF MAINTAINING POWER

Lorenzo's death in 1492 created a crisis for the Medici family, as his son Piero de' Medici was quickly driven from power by the twin forces of Savonarola and an invading French army. Savonarola became the de facto ruler of Florence, though the populace soon turned against him, and the city went through an extended period of civil unrest. The Medicis were restored in 1512 at the behest of Spain and the Holy League, a group led by Pope Julius II that was aimed at removing French influence from the Italian Peninsula.

The Medicis returned to prominence with Giuliano de' Medici, Piero's younger brother, at their helm. Giuliano presided over the family for just four years, from 1512 to 1516, but managed to secure international support for the Medicis by marrying into the powerful Savoy dynasty of Sicily.

Upon Giuliano's death in 1516, another Lorenzo de' Medici, the son of Piero and grandson of Lorenzo

The powerful Medici family of Florence included highly influential figures, such as the political leader Cosimo de Medici. Shown in this portrait by Jacopo Pontormo, Cosimo was a capable ruler, as well as a patron of the arts, who helped position Florence at the center of the Italian Renaissance.

the Magnificent, became head of the Medici family. Lorenzo advanced the political aims of the Medici family by being installed as duke of Urbino by Pope Leo X, who was his uncle and a younger son of Lorenzo the Magnificent. Lorenzo continued the Medici family's traditional patronage of the arts; his tomb at the Church of San Lorenzo, built by Michelangelo, is still a popular attraction in Florence.

Lorenzo's death in 1519 pushed the family toward more turmoil. Lorenzo's successor Giulio, the illegitimate son of the murdered Giuliano, held control of the family for four years before being named Pope Clement VII in 1523. When Giulio became pope, he turned over the family to Alessandro de' Medici, a very unpopular figure who may have been Giulio's illegitimate son (some historians believe that Alessandro's father was Lorenzo of Urbino). Giulio used his papal power to have Alessandro named duke of Florence, but he could not prevent the ultimate undoing of his successor. Hated by the Florentine people,

Alessandro survived diplomatic challenges to his power only to be murdered in 1537 by Lorenzino de' Medici, a close relative and companion.

The death of Alessandro brought Cosimo I de' Medici to power. Cosimo I, duke of Florence (r. 1537–1574), was a descendant of the brother of Cosimo the Elder, and thus the first member of the family's lesser branch to assume power. Cosimo was a powerful ruler, and under his command Florence enjoyed its most prominent international position as it came to control several nearby territories, including Siena. Shortly before his death in 1574, Cosimo was named grand duke of Tuscany by Pope Pius V. While he was a beneficent patron of the arts, Cosimo is most often remembered for his authoritarian rule. His death brought his son Francesco (r. 1574–1587) to the duchy and foreshadowed the decline of the Medici family in Florence.

THE LONG ROAD TO RUIN

While Cosimo was consolidating his power in Florence, Catherine de' Medici, the daughter of Lorenzo of Urbino, was strengthening hers in France. Catherine had married Henry II (r. 1547–1559), who became king of France in 1547. Henry's death in 1559, followed by that of his son Francis II (r. 1559–1560) in 1560, left Catherine as one of the most powerful figures in Europe. Catherine de' Medici was perhaps most notable for her role in the Saint Bartholomew's Day Massacre, in which nearly 75,000 French Protestants were murdered, largely at her behest.

Back in Florence, Francesco de' Medici set the family on the path to decline, as he allowed the increasingly strong Austrian Habsburg dynasty to assume a position of great influence throughout Tuscany. Francesco's daughter, Marie de' Medici, became queen of France through her marriage to King Henry IV (r. 1589–1610). Marie is best known for precipitating the rise of French Cardinal Richelieu, who, as chief adviser to King Louis XIII (r. 1610–1643), worked to increase the power of the French Crown and destroy the Huguenots (French Protestants).

Francesco was succeeded as grand duke of Tuscany in 1587 by his younger brother, Ferdinand I (r. 1587–1609), who tried to make up for some of Francesco's mistakes. A patron of the sciences, Ferdinand secured an academic position in the University of Pisa for Galileo Galilei. After Ferdinand died in 1609, his son and successor, Cosimo II (r. 1609–

1621) carried on his father's patronage of the sciences in general and Galileo in particular. Cosimo suffered from poor health and died in 1621, passing the duchy to his son, Ferdinand II de' Medici (r. 1621–1670)

Although Ferdinand II was also interested in advancing scientific knowledge, he was unable to prevent Galileo from being tried by the Church during the Inquisition. Ferdinand was not a skilled leader, and the economic importance of Florence steadily declined during his reign. His death in 1670 made his son, Cosimo III (r. 1670–1723), grand duke of Tuscany.

Cosimo III was an irresponsible ruler whose religious intolerance and financial malfeasance drove the city of Florence, the region of Tuscany, and the Medici family itself virtually to ruin. His death in 1723 brought his son, Giovanni Gastone (r. 1723–1737), to power, but there was little that Giovanni Gastone could do to repair the damage of his predecessors' reigns. Giovanni Gastone de' Medici is best remembered for the monument to Galileo he had built at the Santa Croce Church in Florence. He left no male heir upon his death in 1737, and consequently the duchy of Tuscany went to the House of Lorraine, and the Medici family line came to an end.

See also: HENRY IV (FRANCE); ROYAL FAMILIES; SAVOY DYNASTY.

FURTHER READING

Hibbert, Christopher. *The House of the Medici: Its Rise and Fall.* New York: Perennial, 1999.

MEHMED II, THE CONQUEROR

(1432–1481 C.E.)

Ottoman sultan (r. 1444–1446, 1451–1481) whose conquest of the ancient Byzantine city of Constantinople and other lands gained him the title Fatih Mehmed, or Mehmed the Conqueror. Although the career of Mehmed II began with failure after failure, his eventual military triumphs made him one of the best-known Ottoman sultans.

The third son of Sultan Murad II (r. 1421–1451), Mehmed was born in Edirne, then the Ottoman capital. He was never expected to rule the empire, but after the early deaths of his older brothers he became his father's heir. In 1444, when Mehmed was only twelve years old, Murad II abdicated and Mehmed began his first reign.

The enemies of the Ottomans perceived Mehmed's youth as a sign of weakness, and the empire was besieged by a European crusade and internal division. The young Mehmed was unable to cope with the challenges, so Murad II reclaimed the throne in 1446 at the behest of various powerful Ottoman interests. Mehmed spent the next five years at the provincial capital of Manisa, but when Murad II died in 1451, he once again became the Ottoman sultan.

Mehmed's second reign was far more successful. After working to secure the support of those who had helped depose him previously, he turned his attention to the prize that had attracted the Ottomans since their rise to power: the city of Constantinople, the capital of the Byzantine Empire, called by many the finest city in the world. Previous sultans had taken much of the territory around the city, also known as Byzantium, but failed to defeat the remaining stronghold. Mehmed's siege of the city began in 1453, and a combination of force and clever tactics won him the prize. On May 29, 1453, Constantinople fell to the Ottomans and became their new capital.

Mehmed spent much of his reign reconstructing the sacked city and raising it to new heights of power and beauty. He encouraged members of various ethnic and religious groups to settle in the city, repopulating his new capital with traders and talented subjects regardless of their origins. Mehmed's policy of religious toleration led him to establish a system of leadership for each religious group in the city, with patriarchs for the Greek and Armenian Christians and a grand rabbi to head the Jewish community.

Mehmed continued to expand his territory throughout his reign. Twenty years after the fall of Constantinople, he defeated a major Turkmen rival at Bashkent, extending Ottoman control throughout Anatolia (present-day Turkey). He conquered Trebizond, the capital of another Greek Christian state, in 1461, and established control over much of the Balkans, including Serbia in 1459 and Bosnia in 1463.

Mehmed was known as an enlightened leader who wrote poetry, encouraged education and theological discussion, and had his portrait painted by the great Venetian painter Gentile Bellini. However, he left a more troubling legacy by providing legal sanction for the practice of fratricide among Ottoman princes, supposedly ensuring the accession of the most capable candidate. Fatih Mehmed died on a military campaign in 1481 and was succeeded by his son, Beyezid II (r. 1481–1512).

See also: BEYEZID II; OTTOMAN EMPIRE; SULTANATES.

MEIJI MONARCHY (1868–1945 C.E.)

The imperial system of Japan between the Meiji Restoration of 1868 and the Japanese defeat in World War II.

The Meiji monarchy is named after Emperor Mutsuhito (r. 1867–1912) of the Yamato dynasty, who was given the reign-name of Meiji ("enlightened rule"). The Meiji monarchy was marked by a blend of traditional Japanese and Western elements.

The Meiji Restoration was, in fact, a revolution against the Tokugawa shogunate. It was called a restoration because the Japanese imperial house had been restored to power after a long period of control by the shoguns. In practice, however, the emperor Mutsuhito, who took the throne in 1867 at age fifteen, was essentially only a figurehead. Real power was held by a group of politicians from samurai houses, many of whom became leaders in the Meiji Restoration. These leaders are referred to by historians as the "Meiji oligarchy."

Although the emperor played only a limited political role in the Meiji Restoration, his symbolic role was immense. The connection of the emperor with government authority was emphasized by the abandonment of the old capital, Kyoto, by the imperial family, and the move to the shogunal capital and administrative center, Edo, which was renamed Tokyo ("Eastern capital").

Under the restoration, the emperor and the imperial house were promoted as the focus of Japanese

Mutsuhito, the 122nd emperor of Japan, transformed his country from an isolated feudal state into a world power. His reign took the name Meiji ("enlightened rule"), and his resumption of imperial rule after the military domination of the shoguns is known as the Meiji Restoration. This nineteenth-century woodblock print shows the emperor holding council, as the nation prepares to wage war against China.

ROYAL PLACES

THE IMPERIAL PALACE IN TOKYO

The Japanese Imperial Palace in Tokyo was built in the late 1800s on the site of Edo Castle, the old headquarters of the Tokugawa shoguns, which had burned in 1873. By occupying this site, the emperor made concrete the transfer of authority from shoguns to emperors that occurred during the Meiji Restoration. Located on a hill, the palace combined a mixture of European and Japanese styles. During World War II, many of the palace buildings from the Meiji era were destroyed in bombings, and most of the current structures date from the postwar period. The Imperial Palace grounds, one of the few open spaces in crowded Tokyo, are screened from the city by moats and forests, and the palace itself remains secluded from public view.

religious loyalty, with a strong emphasis on the divinity of the emperor and the descent of the imperial house from the sun-goddess Amaterasu Omikami. The religious assertions of Meiji ideology were drawn from Japan's indigenous religion, Shinto. The system of emperor-worship is called State Shinto. A government decree in 1872 established the emperor's birthday as a religious holiday.

Meiji ideology also drew on Confucianism, proclaiming the emperor as father of the nation. The patriarchal nature of the Meiji monarchy was reinforced by restricting succession to males by a law issued in 1889. This had not been required previously; pre-Meiji Japan had seen many reigning empresses. Like the institution of primogeniture (inheritance by the oldest male) in Western culture, this change in the Japanese system of succession was influenced by contemporary Western models of monarchy.

By contrast with Shinto and Confucianism, Buddhism and Christianity were frowned upon as religions of foreign origin that were harder to reconcile with the divine claims of the emperor. Although Buddhism had long had a place at the Japanese imperial court, Buddhist ceremonies were now banished from the imperial palace, and the great rites of passage accompanying births, deaths, and marriages in the imperial family were purged of Buddhist elements. The edict, *Imperial Rescript on Education*, enacted in 1890, combined emphasis on the Confucian virtues of filial piety and devotion to the public good with a claim for

the eternal nature of the Japanese monarchy and its relation to its subjects. Japanese children were required to memorize it in school. This emperor-centered view of Japanese existence, which had little precedent in pre-Meiji Japanese history, was reasserted in an even stronger form in 1937, with the edict *Kokutai no Hongi* (Basic National Principles), issued by the Ministry of Education.

Unlike previous Japanese regimes, the Meiji state was a constitutional monarchy, the first nation outside Europe or European colonies to possess a written constitution. However, both Meiji constitutions, in 1868 and 1889, were presented as imperial decrees under the emperor's authority. In practice, the 1889 constitution limited the emperor's power by requiring his decrees to be signed by a government minister. However, unlike the British system in which the monarch was subordinate to whichever group held a majority in Parliament, the Meiji oligarchy looked to the combination of a constitution and an authoritarian monarchy for inspiration. The imperial cabinet was considered responsible to the emperor rather than the parliamentary body, the Diet, and the armed forces also expressed personal loyalty to the throne. This made it difficult for any civilian prime minister to fully control the military, whose leaders had an independent connection to the emperor. The emperor also was charged with responsibility for mediating disagreements between the two houses of the Diet.

The central role of the emperor in Meiji politics and culture was reinforced by allowing the emperor to be seen more regularly by the Japanese people. Pre-Meiji emperors had lived in seclusion, seldom leaving the imperial palace in Kyoto. But the Meiji rulers traveled over many areas of the country, even using Japan's new railroad system.

Although aspects of the Meiji system persist in Japanese culture and politics to the present day, the Meiji monarchy ended with the defeat of Japan by the United States and its allies in World War II. The victors forced Emperor Hirohito (r. 1926–1989), the grandson of Emperor Mutsuhito, to renounce his claim to divine status. They also imposed a new constitution, which separated the emperor from politics. These changes destroyed the basis of the Meiji monarchy.

See also: DIVINITY OF KINGS; HIROHITO; NATIONALISM; SACRED KINGSHIPS; YAMATO DYNASTY.

FURTHER READING

Fujitani, Takashi. *Splendid Monarchy: Power and Pageantry in Modern Japan.* Berkeley: University of California Press, 1996.

Keene, Donald. *Emperor of Japan: Meiji and His World, 1852–1912.* New York: Columbia University Press, 2002.

MENANDER (115–90 B.C.E.)

The best-known ruler of the Indo-Greek kingdoms that arose in Central Asia and northern India in the late second and first centuries B.C.E. Menander was an intellectual whose public conversion to Buddhism extended his influence throughout much of India.

Lacking archaeological or documentary evidence, scholars have found it difficult to determine the dynasties and precise dates of most of the Indo-Greek rulers of Bactria and other Indo-Greek kingdoms. This includes knowledge of Menander. The region of Bactria was located in Central Asia between the Hindu Kush Mountains and the Amu Darya or Oxus River. While there is casual reference to these Indo-Greek rulers in classical Greek and Indian texts, their very existence can be proved only by the quantity and distribution of the coins minted during their reigns.

Menander was a successor of the great Bactrian ruler, Demetrius II (r. ca. 180–165 B.C.E.) and the dynasty of King Euthydemus I (r. ca. 235–200 B.C.E.). Menander's kingdom consisted of an area that extended from the Kabul Valley in the west to the Ravi River in the east, and from the Swat Valley in the north, to Arachosia in Afghanistan in the south. However, the extremely wide distribution of Menander's gold and silver coins suggests that his influence was far greater than his kingdom and that he sought control over the Ganges Valley and captured what remained of the kingdom of Magadha.

Ancient Indian tales tell of Menander's alliance with the kings of the northern Indian cities of Panchala and Mathura in an expedition against the Sunga ruler of Pataliputra after the fall of the Mauryan Empire around 185 B.C.E. However, Pataliputra, the ancient capital of Magadha (south Bihar), remained under Sunga control until 73 B.C.E.

Menander's coins also attest to the duration of his reign, the wealth of his realm, and the nature of his personal philosophy. Menander is not depicted as a conqueror on the coins. Instead, his image is gentle and almost effeminate, with delicate features and curls. Furthermore, the inscriptions on Menander's coins describe him as *Basileos* (king) and *Soter* (savior) rather than conqueror or patriot. The appearance of the Buddhist prayer wheel on his coins complete his image as a king devoted to Buddha.

Buddhists claim that Menander, who protected them from persecution by the Sungas, converted to Buddhism after a public debate with the Buddhist philosopher monk, Nagasena. The *Milinda-pañha* (The Questions of Milinda) is a lively discussion of Buddhist theologic and philosophic doctrine. In this work, Nagasena answered questions and dilemmas posed by King Milinda, who is clearly Menander. Written in Sanskrit by an unknown author, the *Milinda-pañha* is the one nonsacred work whose authority Buddhist commentators, such as Buddhaghosa, readily accept.

According to Buddhist tradition, Menander quietly handed over his kingdom to his son, Strato (r. ca. 130–95 B.C.E.) However, the later Greek historian, Plutarch, claimed that Menander died in battle. Many Central Asian and Indian cities built monuments to enshrine Menander's ashes after death.

See also: BUDDHISM AND KINGSHIP; COINAGE, ROYAL; INDO-GREEK KINGDOMS; SUNGA DYNASTY.

MENELIK II (1844–1913 C.E.)

Emperor of Ethiopia (r. 1889–1913), notable for his efforts at modernization and for expelling Italian colonial interests from the nation.

Menelik was born in 1844 in Shewa, a kingdom under the authority of the Ethiopian Empire. His father was Malakot, king of Shewa (r. 1847–1865). Because he was expected to assume the Shewa throne one day, Menelik was educated in the Ethiopian Orthodox Church and was trained in both the military and political sciences. Perhaps most important to his development as a future ruler was that, during his early life, he had good role models. Both his father and grandfather, Sahle Selassie (r. 1813–1847), had been Shewa kings, and Menelik also had the opportunity to observe the court of the Ethiopian emperor, Tewodros II (r. 1855–1868).

KING OF SHEWA

Upon the death of Malakot in 1865, Menelik inherited the throne of the Shewa state. He had great ambitions, however, and soon set his sights on the Ethiopian throne. His ambition did not escape Tewodros's notice, much to the young Menelik's detriment. Tewodros, concerned that Menelik and some others might attempt to challenge his rule, ordered these potential rivals to be imprisoned.

Menelik eventually escaped Tewodros's custody and made his way back home to Shewa. When Tewodros died in 1868, Menelik made an unsuccessful attempt to claim the Ethiopian throne, ultimately losing to Yohannes IV (r. 1872–1889). Chastened by his failure, Menelik returned to Shewa, where he busied himself by increasing his regional power. Over time, he succeeded in shifting Ethiopia's center of economic and political power from the capital of Addis Ababa to his own seat of power in Shewa. Upon the death of Yohannes IV in 1889, Menelik mustered an army and successfully seized the Ethiopian throne.

RULE AS EMPEROR

Menelik's rule began with a disaster. He signed a treaty that opened the door to invasion and annexation by Italy. This led to a bloody war that lasted until 1896. At a great battle fought in the vicinity of Adowa, in northern Ethiopia, in 1896, Menelik's forces finally succeeded in forcing the Italians to forsake all claims to Ethiopian territories. He then em-

Heir to the throne of the Shewa Kingdom in eastern Africa, Menelik II seized power in Ethiopia in 1889. As emperor, Menelik II secured his nation's independence from Italy, expanded the country through conquest, and modernized it by improving trade and communications.

barked on a policy of expansion, and by 1906 he had doubled the territory under his control.

With his kingdom secure, Menelik turned his attention to bringing Ethiopia into the modern world. He imposed taxes and used the revenues from them to transform Addis Ababa into a center for politics and economics. He created the Addis Ababa-Djibouti Railway, which greatly improved trade and communications throughout the region. Through such efforts, Menelik brought Ethiopia a degree of international respect and authority greater than it had ever known.

In 1909 Menelik II suffered a stroke that rendered him incapable of continuing to rule. He eventually lapsed into a coma, and lingered near death for several years. During this time, effective rule over the kingdom passed to his grandson, Lij Iyasu (r. 1913–1916). Menelik died in December 1913, at which time Lij Iyasu was crowned Ethiopia's king. He was overthrown three years later.

See also: GALAWDEWOS; HAILE SELASSIE I; TEWODROS II.

FURTHER READING

Marcus, Harold G. *The Life and Times of Menelik II: Ethiopia 1844–1913.* Lawrenceville, NJ: Red Sea Press, 1995.

MENES (flourished ca. 3100 or 3000 B.C.E.)

Traditionally considered the first king of a unified Egypt and founder of Egypt's first ruling dynasty. According to legend and some historical records, Menes (which is a Greek name) was a ruler from Upper (or Southern) Egypt who defeated Lower (or Northern) Egypt and unified the two kingdoms into one empire. He then became the first king, or pharaoh, of the First Dynasty of a united Egypt.

Some archaeological evidence suggests that Menes may be the same person as King Narmer, who also was credited with unifying Egypt because of scenes carved on the famous Narmer Palette (an artifact discovered at the pre-dynastic capital of Hierakonpolis and believed to date from about 3200 B.C.E.). One side of the slate palette depicts Narmer wearing the crown of Upper Egypt and clubbing an enemy; the other side shows him wearing the crown of Lower Egypt and looking over his defeated enemies.

Menes also is sometimes identified as a king named Scorpion (who signed his name with a hieroglyph of a scorpion) because other artifacts portray that king in a similar victory scene. Many experts now believe that Menes is the same person as King Aha (who may have been Narmer's son), because "Men" is written next to Aha's name in some places and he was the first king with significant monuments all around Egypt.

Whatever his real identity, after becoming king, Menes founded the capital city of Memphis (not far from Cairo, the current Egyptian capital). It was an excellent location—easy to defend because it was on an island in the Nile and strategically located at the border between the old and new kingdoms. Menes oversaw the construction of many irrigation channels from the Nile, which improved the productivity of neighboring fields. By the end of Menes's rule, Memphis was a flourishing commercial city and the core of Egypt.

Legend has it that Menes reigned for sixty-two years and was then killed by a hippopotamus. This account may have arisen because in ancient Egypt the hippopotamus was a symbol for a foreign enemy; so perhaps Menes just died defending his empire. If Menes was truly King Aha, then his heir was his son Djer, whose mother Neithotep served as queen until Djer was old enough to serve as king.

See also: EGYPTIAN DYNASTIES, ANCIENT (BEFORE EIGHTEENTH DYNASTY).

MERCIA, KINGDOM OF

(flourished ca. 600–918 C.E.)

One of the seven kingdoms of Anglo-Saxon England, occupying roughly the same area as the modern-day Midlands. The kingdom of Mercia was an independent state from about 600 to 886 and then a semi-independent territory until the death of its last significant ruler, Ethelfled, in 918.

Mercia gained primacy over the other states of the Anglo-Saxon heptarchy (Wessex, Essex, Sussex, East Anglia, Kent, and Northumbria) during the reign of Penda (c. 632–654), who extended the boundaries of the kingdom and established dominance over Wessex and East Anglia. Penda himself steadfastly refused to convert to Christianity, which was spreading rapidly across England, but he made no objection when his son, Paeda, converted in order to marry the daughter of Oswy of Northumbria—nor did he object to a mission from Northumbria sent to convert his people.

When Penda died in battle against Oswy of Northumbria in 656, Mercia fell briefly under Northumbrian control for three years, although Penda's son Paeda was granted limited rule. Mercian supremacy was reestablished, however, when another of Penda's sons, Wulfhere (r. 658–675), took the throne and once again expanded the kingdom's boundaries.

Mercian hegemony held throughout the eighth century, strengthened by the reigns of Ethelbald (r. 716–757) and his cousin Offa (r. 757–796). Offa, the last strong king of Mercia, in addition to declaring himself overlord in Kent and Sussex, had Ethelbert, king of East Anglia, beheaded so that he could rule that country as well. Offa also secured his interests in Wessex and Northumbria by marrying his daughters to the rulers of those kingdoms. The land work on the eastern border of modern Wales, known as Offa's Dyke, was built in his reign as a defense against the Welsh.

After Offa's death in 796, Mercia declined as a power. Attacks from neighboring kingdoms and the incursions of the Danes drained Mercia of resources until 886, when the eastern portion of the kingdom became part of the Danelaw and the western part came to be controlled by Wessex. The last noteworthy ruler of the kingdom, Ethelfled (r. 911–918), the daughter of Alfred the Great of Wessex (r. 871–899), ruled over a semi-independent Mercia, first as consort of Ethelred, earl of Mercia, and later alone. Ethelfled built cities and oversaw military campaigns. With her brother, Edward the Elder of Wessex (r. 899–924), she recaptured Derby, Leicester, and York from the Danes.

See also: ALFRED, THE GREAT; ANGLO-SAXON RULERS; DANISH KINGDOM; NORTHUMBRIA, KINGDOM OF; WESSEX, KINGDOM OF.

MERINA KINGDOM (1783–1896 C.E.)

Kingdom located in the central region of Madagascar, a large island off the southeastern coast of Africa, that ruled as the dominant kingdom on the island in the 1800s.

Prior to 1787 Madagascar was home to a number of small centralized kingdoms; historians identify eighteen different states. In the interior of the island, the land controlled by the Merina people, a ruler named Andrianampoinimerina (r. 1783–1809), took the throne in 1783 and soon united many of the Merina people under his rule. Andrianampoinimerina spent his twenty-three-year reign absorbing all the remaining neighboring states under his authority and can thus be said to be the first true Merina king. Like all the Madagascar states, the wealth of the Merina kingdom was heavily based on the slave trade that serviced markets in the Persian Gulf and beyond.

Andrianampoinimerina was succeeded on the throne of Merina by his son Radama I (r. 1810–1828), who built upon the work of his father by expanding his territory until it extended from one side of the island to the other. Radama I was helped in this enterprise by

an alliance with the British, who modernized and equipped his army. In return, however, Radama had to agree to outlaw the slave trade, which had previously formed the bulk of the kingdom's revenues. Radama's reign was marked by increased European missionary activity in Merina and by a great loss of life as a result of his wars of expansion.

Upon the death of Radama I in 1828, he was succeeded on the throne by his wife, Ranavalona I (r. 1828–1861). Suspicious of foreigners, Ranavalona rejected her husband's pro-Western policies. She declared Christianity illegal and followed a policy that isolated Merina and withdrew it from participation in the world beyond Madagascar's borders. During her rule, the Merina kingdom was also wracked by intermittent civil war as factions fought for control.

Ranavalona I was succeeded by her son, who took the royal name of Radama II (r. 1861–1863) but may not have been an actual son of the former king. Radama attempted to return Madagascar to a pro-Western stance, but his court officials were so outraged by this effort that they had him assassinated just two years after he took the throne.

Radama II was succeeded by his widow, Queen Rasoherina (r. 1863–1868), who attempted to continue her husband's policies of welcoming contact with the West, particularly the French. This effort would prove to be the undoing of the Merina kingdom, however. The French were more interested in territorial acquisition than in political alliance, and France's desire for territory eventually led to the end of the Merina kingdom.

The next rulers of the Merina kingdom—queens Ranavalona II (r. 1868–1883) and Ranavalona III (r 1883–1896)—ruled in name only. During their reigns, the prime minister, Rainilaiarivony, exercised actual control over Merina. By this time, the Merina kingdom had expanded to include all of Madagascar except the far south and part of the western portion of the island.

In 1883, French forces bombarded and occupied the Merina settlement of Tamatave, and within two years they had declared the whole of Madagascar a French protectorate. This protectorate status was recognized by the British, who had been vying with the French for control in Madagascar for a number of years. For the next few years, the Merina kingdom attempted to resist French rule, and heavy fighting took place periodically. In 1896, however, French forces defeated Merina and declared Madagascar a

French colony. The French formally abolished the Merina monarchy, and the kingdom came to an end.

See also: AFRICAN KINGDOMS; MADAGASCAR KINGDOMS; RADAMA I; RADAMA II; RANAVALONA I, MADA.

FURTHER READING

Brown, Mervyn. *A History of Madagascar.* Princeton, NJ: Marcus Weiner Publishers, 2002.

Kottak, Conrad P. *Madagascar: Society and History.* Durham, NC: Carolina Academic Press, 1986.

MEROVINGIAN DYNASTY

(457–751 C.E.)

Frankish dynasty of kings that ruled in Western Europe immediately following the fall of the Roman Empire.

The Franks were a Germanic tribe that entered the Roman province of Gaul, now France, in the early fourth century. They generally had a good relationship with the Romans, often serving in their armies and defending the northern frontier of the western empire until its fall in 476.

The Merovingians owe their family name to Merovech (r. 447–457), the chief of a group of Franks known as the Salian Franks. Little is known about this legendary hero. He and other Frankish leaders, such as Childeric I (r. ca. 457–481), are best known for their military victories against other Germanic peoples, most notably the Visigoths, Saxons, and Alamanni in the last decades of the Roman Empire.

The era immediately following the fall of Rome witnessed a pivotal transformation in the history of Europe, during which new economic, political, social, and cultural institutions replaced those of ancient Rome. This change resulted in the development of various regional European societies. The Merovingians were rulers of the largest and most powerful of these new European regions—the Frankish kingdom that eventually became the nation of France.

KING OF ALL FRANKS

The son of Merovech, Childeric I, inherited the mantle of leadership from his father. But the first Merovingian leader to unify the Frankish peoples under one rule was Childeric's son, Clovis I (r. 481–511), who was the founder of the Frankish monarchy. Clovis was the first Frankish king to have laws written down. Although Roman law served as the basis of Frankish law, some elements of Germanic legal traditions survived, such as the punishments for various crimes.

One element of Frankish law proved very important in the history of the Merovingian dynasty. According to Frankish legal custom, property was equally divided among male offspring. This applied

ROYAL RELATIVES

CLOTILDA

One of the most ignored aspects of Frankish history is the role played by women. Yet one of the more important aspects of early Frankish history hinged upon the actions and persuasive ability of a woman. Clotilda, a Christian, was the wife of Clovis I. After the Franks scored a decisive victory over the Germanic Alemanni tribe, Clotilda convinced her husband that God had aided him in his victory. As a result, Clovis converted to Christianity. This decision was important because the relationship between the Franks and the Roman Church would be decisive in shaping Western European society. Ironically, the Carolingians were able to depose the Merovingians partly because of their alliance with the papacy. Later, the greatest Frankish king, Charlemagne (r. 768–814) became emperor with the support of Pope Leo III.

even to a king. Thus, after the death of Clovis in 511, the kingdom of the Franks was divided among his sons. These separate kingdoms later took the names of Austrasia, Neustria, and Burgundy. For the next several centuries, the descendants of Clovis ruled over portions of the Frankish lands, only occasionally unifying them.

Unification of the Frankish kingdoms usually occurred only after decades of conflict between rival brothers. In 558, for example, Clovis's son, Lothair (r. 511–561), temporarily reunified the Franks by defeating his three brothers—Theodoric I (r. 511–533), Chlodomer (r. 511–524), and Childebert (r. 511–558)—over the course of many years of rivalry and conflict.

But upon Lothair's death in 561, his four sons—Sigibert I (r. 561–575), Charibert (r. 561–567), Guntram (r. 561–593), and Chilperic I (r. 561–584)—split the Frankish lands once again. This tradition continued throughout the rule of the Merovingians and their successors, the Carolongian dynasty. It did not end until 987 with the advent of the first true French king, Hugh Capet, the founder of the Capetian dynasty.

THE MAYORS OF THE PALACE

After the reign of Dagobert I (r. 629–639), the Merovongian kings fell under the control of the mayors of the palace. Originally created as a royal office in charge of the daily business of the royal household, the mayors came under the control of a single family, the Carolingians, and gradually gained control of the important elements of royal power.

The office of mayor of the palace gave the Carolingians almost complete control over the royal treasury. As a result, they enriched themselves and gave favors to important allies. They also led the royal armies in battle, proving themselves to be able warriors. The Carolingians also closely allied themselves with the Roman Church, the support of which lent legitimacy to any European ruler.

The Merovingian kings after Dagobert I were known as the *rois fainéants,* or idle kings, because they were entirely subject to the Carolingian mayors of the palace and did little to actually rule the kingdom. In 751, Pepin the Short (Pepin III) (r. 751–768), the Carolingian mayor of the palace, deposed the last Merovingian king, Childeric III (r. 743–751), and the Carolingians officially took the title of king of all the Franks.

See also: Capet, Hugh; Carolingian Dynasty; Charlemagne; Clovis I; Frankish Kingdom; French Monarchies; Lothair I; Salian Dynasty.

FURTHER READING

Gregory of Tours. *The History of the Franks.* New York: Penguin Books, 1974.

James, E. *The Franks.* New York: Blackwell Publishers, 1991.

Pirenne, Henri. *The Economic and Social History of Medieval Europe.* San Diego, CA: Harcourt Brace, 1989.

Merovingian–Frankish Kingdom (486–751 c.e.)

Kingdom in Western Europe founded by a Germanic tribe, the Salian Franks, which laid the foundation for the development of the kingdom of France.

The Merovingian-Frankish kingdom was founded by the Frankish ruler Clovis I (r. 481–511), who united various Frankish peoples under one rule in 486 c.e. Clovis, who became leader of the Salian Franks in 481, launched an expansion of Frankish territory into the Roman province of Gaul. In 486, he overthrew a Roman army and established the Merovingian dynasty, which took its name from Clovis's grandfather, a Frankish chief named Merovech (Merovaeus).

Clovis moved the Frankish capital to Paris, thus establishing the importance of the city to the Merovingian kingdom and, later, to France. On Clovis's death in 511, his kingdom was divided, according to Frankish custom, among his four sons: Theodoric, Chlodomer, Childebert, and Clotaire.

DIVISION AND RIVALRY

Theodoric I (also known as Thierry) ruled as king of Metz from 511 to 533. His brother Chlodomer, king of Orléans, reigned from 511 to 524. Childebert, king of Paris, ruled that part of the kingdom from 511 to 558, while Clotaire (Lothair) was king of Soissons beginning in 511. Clotaire became king of all Franks in 558 following the deaths of his brothers and Theodoric's heirs. Thus, the Frankish kingdoms were temporarily reunited under Clotaire after years of rivalry.

The four kingdoms were split and rejoined sev-

ROYAL PLACES

ST. DENIS

The first abbey of Saint-Denis was founded during the rule of the Merovingian king, Dagobert I. The first bishop of Paris had been St. Denis (Dionysisus), who was martyred with several companions in 270 C.E. They were buried a few miles north of Paris and a small chapel was built on the location. By the fifth and sixth centuries, the site was a noted destination for pilgrims.

In 630, Dagobert I established an abbey for a Benedictine monastery on the site and replaced the chapel with a basilica. Successive kings continued to support the abbey of St. Denis, which soon became one of the richest and most prestigious abbeys in Europe.

Dagobert was buried at the abbey of St. Denis, which subsequently became the burial site of most French kings and queens, including Louis XVI and Marie Antoinette. Although many of the tombs at the abbey were desecrated during the French Revolution, restoration took place under the Bourbon kings of France.

eral times over the ensuing years, with some changes in name along the way. The Frankish kingdom of Austrasia included eastern France, western Germany, and the Netherlands; Burgundy included southeast France and eventually extended to Arles and Switzerland; and Neustria covered the territory around the Seine and Loire rivers, including Soissons and Paris.

Much of the history of the Merovingian-Frankish kingdom was marked by dynastic war and violent rivalry. One of the most bitter was between two queens, Fredegunde of Neustria and Brunhilda (Brunehaut) of Austrasia. Brunhilda, daughter of a Visigoth king of Spain, was married to Sigebert I (r. 561–575). Her sister, Galswintha, was married to Sigebert's brother, Chilperic I (r. 561–584), who ruled Neustria.

In 567, Fredegunde, who had been Chilperic's mistress since before his marriage to Galswintha, persuaded him to murder Galswintha. Seeking revenge for the murder of her sister, Brunhilda urged war against Neustria. Even after Sigebert and Chilperic were killed (in 575 and 584, respectively), the war continued between the two queens, who served as regents for their sons.

Fredegunde died in 597. Meanwhile, Brunhilda's ruthlessness eventually led to her downfall. The

mayor of the palace, the official in charge of the business of the royal household, was Pepin of Landen (Pepin I), a member of the Carolingian family. Aided by Arnulf, the bishop of Metz, Pepin betrayed Brunhilda to Fredegunde's son, Clotaire II (r. 584–629), king of Neustria.

DECLINING POWER OF THE MEROVINGIAN KINGS

Clotaire II became king of Neustria in 584. By 613, he had become king of all Franks, although most of the power in the kingdom was wielded by the mayor of the palace, Pepin of Landen, and Bishop Arnulf.

To administer their vast holdings, the Merovingian kings depended on an entourage of officials. Over several generations, the cash-poor Merovingians awarded these officials with favors and property. Initially, the land was held only for the lifetime of the owner. But by the end of the sixth century, ownership had become hereditary. The result was the creation of a powerful class of land-based aristocrats. The most powerful of all was the *major-domus,* the mayor of the palace.

In 623, Pepin and Arnulf forced Clotaire II to designate his son, Dagobert I (r. 629–639), as king, although they ruled for him until 623. Eventually, however, Dabogert I became sufficiently strong to break free of the influence of Pepin and other powerful Frankish nobles. Pepin retired to Aquitaine, where he worked to extend his power to include Basques and Bretons. Dagobert's successors, meanwhile, became known as *rois fainéants* ("idle kings") because they let their power trickle away into the hands of the hereditary mayors of the palace.

DECLINE OF THE MEROVINGIANS

The marriage of Pepin I's daughter and Bishop Arnulf's son produced Pepin of Heristal, who served as mayor of the palace of Austrasia from 680 to 714. In 687, after defeating the Neustrians at the battle of Tetry, Pepen of Heristal had himself proclaimed mayor of all Frankish territory except Aquitaine. Although the Merovingians retained power in name, Pepin of Heristal's victory guaranteed the rise to power of the Carolingian dynasty. His illegitimate son, Charles Martel (r. 714–741), succeeded him as mayor of the palace and achieved a significant victory when he repelled Moorish invaders between Tours and Poitiers in 732.

Martel's son, Pepin the Short, also served as mayor of the palace under the Merovingian king, Childeric III (r. 743–751). Pepin sought and received permission from Pope Zacharias to depose Childeric, the last of the Merovingian kings. He then assembled nobles and powerful clergy at Soissons in 751 and was declared King of the Franks, while Childeric was sent to a monastery.

In 754, Pope Stephen II traveled to France, where he personally anointed Pepin (r. 751–768) as king. This marked the end of Merovingian rule and the beginning of the Carolingian dynasty. In return for the recognition of legitimacy to rule, Pepin led his armies into Italy in 755 against the Lombards, who had been threatening papal power. His successful campaign led to the establishment of the northern part of the Papal States, after Pepin gave the pope a gift of land that became known as the Donation of Pepin.

The period of the Merovingian-Frankish kingdom was a time when the political, cultural, and economic institutions of the Roman period broke down almost completely after the fall of the Roman Empire, to be replaced by new regional divisions and societies. It was also a period in which towns and cities throughout Western Europe went into decline and were replaced by the rural holdings of the landed aristocracy, laying the foundations for the development of medieval feudalism.

See also: CAROLINGIAN DYNASTY; CLOVIS I; FRANKISH KINGDOM; LOTHAIR I; MARTEL, CHARLES; MEROVINGIAN DYNASTY; PEPIN THE SHORT (PEPIN III).

FURTHER READING

Koenigsberger, H.G. *Medieval Europe, 400–1500.* New York: Longman, 1987.

Sauvigny, G. de Bertier de, and David H. Pinkney. *History of France.* Arlington Heights, IL: Forum Press, 1983.

Tierney, Brian, and Sidney Painter. *Western Europe in the Middle Ages, 300–1475.* 6th ed. Boston: McGraw-Hill, 1999.

MEWAR KINGDOM. *See* UDAIPUR KINGDOM

MEXICAN MONARCHY

(1822–1823 C.E., 1864–1867 C.E.)

Failed monarchies that ruled Mexico after its independence from Spain in 1821, before the country became firmly established as a republic. The first monarchy was led by Mexican revolutionary Agustín de Iturbide, who ruled from 1822 to 1823. The second was headed by Austrian archduke Maximilian, who ruled as emperor of Mexico from 1864 to 1867.

ITURBIDE'S RULE

In 1820, Mexican-born General Agustín de Iturbide overthrew the existing Spanish government in Mexico. On February 24, 1821, he proclaimed the Plan of Iguala, which called for independence from Spain, declared Catholicism the official state religion, and annulled distinctions between Spanish immigrants and Mexican-born individuals. According to the Plan, Mexico would become a constitutional monarchy, and a congress would invite the Habsburg monarch of Spain, King Ferdinand VII (r. 1813–1833), to rule.

The Plan of Iguala did not state clearly if Ferdinand could govern both Spain and Mexico at the same time. If the Spanish king rejected the invitation, the throne would be offered to a member of another European reigning family. On August 24, 1821, the new Spanish viceroy of Mexico, Juan O'Donojú, capitulated to

Iturbide's demands and signed the Treaty of Córdoba, accepting the Plan of Iguala. The text of the treaty was then sent to King Ferdinand for his approval.

In September 1821, Iturbide entered Mexico City and assumed the leadership of the country. He appointed a governing junta, or council, to fulfill legislative functions until parliamentary representatives were elected. The Constituent Congress began its meetings on February 24, 1822. Shortly after, it became known that the Spanish king had refused to approve the Treaty of Córdoba. Subsequently, the Congress elected Iturbide emperor on May 19, 1822.

From the beginning of Iturbide's rule, the emperor and the Congress competed for political superiority. Iturbide also struggled with financial difficulties, regional tensions, and discontented military officers. On

October 31, Iturbide dissolved the Congress and created a legislative junta that was subject to the emperor.

Following a series of rebellions led by disgruntled military officials, a coalition commanded by General Antonio López de Santa Anna declared the republic, in the Plan of Casa Mata (February 1, 1823). In order to avoid a civil war, Iturbide abdicated on March 19 and fled Mexico with his family. After brief stays in Italy and England, Iturbide decided to try to regain power in Mexico. On July 17, 1824, he disembarked on the eastern coast of Mexico and was arrested by local authorities. He was executed two days later.

MAXIMILIAN'S RULE
After Iturbide's failed rule, Mexico adopted a republican system of government. From 1823 to the early

The short-lived Mexican monarchy lasted from 1864 until the execution of Emperor Maximilian by a republican firing squad on June 19, 1867. The French impressionist Edouard Manet painted this famous scene of Maximilian's execution not long after his death.

1850s, the country experienced a period of great political instability, characterized by brief governments, military coups, and constant struggle between Liberal and Conservative politicians. Beginning in 1855, the Liberals in power introduced a series of reforms, including the abolition of military and ecclesiastical courts, and the confiscation of ecclesiastical property.

In 1857, those reform measures led to the War of the *Reforma* between Liberals and Conservatives. By late 1861, Liberal leader Benito Juárez succeeded in taking Mexico City from the Conservatives. Afterward, Juárez declared that the payment of all of Mexico's foreign debts would be postponed. In response, England, Spain, and France captured the port of Veracruz. Juárez negotiated with the Europeans and obtained the withdrawal of British and Spanish forces. However, French emperor Napoleon III (r. 1852–1870) kept his troops in Mexico to promote the establishment of a monarchy. Napoleon expected to give the Mexican Crown to Austria in exchange for territorial concessions in Europe. He thus offered the Mexican throne to Archduke Maximilian, the younger brother of Austrian emperor Francis Joseph (r. 1848–1916).

Mexican Conservatives, who favored the monarchical regime and wanted to overturn Liberal reforms, supported Napoleon. After long negotiations, the French emperor and Maximilian reached an agreement. In exchange for military and material support to consolidate his rule in Mexico, Maximilian would later provide financial compensation to France. On April 10, 1864, the Austrian archduke accepted the newly created throne from a group of Mexican monarchists. Maximilian and his wife Carlotta, the daughter of King Leopold I (r. 1831–1865) of Belgium, arrived in Mexico City on June 12, 1864.

As emperor of Mexico, Maximilian alienated himself from the Conservatives by ratifying the Liberal reforms. He also failed to improve the economy or build up a military basis of support. Meanwhile, the Liberals fought fiercely against the French intervention. In late 1866, Napoleon decided to withdraw his troops from Mexico, due to increasing national and international opposition and the possibility of a war with Prussia, leaving Maximilian with no support. Napoleon encouraged Maximilian to abdicate the throne, but Maximilian refused. Assuming command of the imperial troops himself, he was cap-tured by Liberal forces on May 15, 1867. In accordance with a decree previously issued by Benito Juárez, Maximilian and his closest collaborators were executed on June 19. The Liberals regained control of the country, and reestablished a republican form of government.

See also: Aᴍᴇʀɪᴄᴀɴ Kɪɴɢᴅᴏᴍs, Cᴇɴᴛʀᴀʟ ᴀɴᴅ Nᴏʀᴛʜ; Mᴀxɪᴍɪʟɪᴀɴ I; Nᴀᴘᴏʟᴇᴏɴ III.

FURTHER READING

Anna, Timothy E. *The Mexican Empire of Iturbide*. Lincoln: University of Nebraska Press, 1990.
Cunningham, Michelle. *Mexico and the Foreign Policy of Napoleon III*. New York: Palgrave, 2001.

Mɪᴅᴀs (700s–600s ʙ.ᴄ.ᴇ.)

Mythological and historical ruler of the kingdom of Phrygia in Anatolia (present-day Turkey), best known for his legendary "golden touch," which allowed him to turn objects into gold by touching them.

The historical king Midas is first mentioned around 700 ʙ.ᴄ.ᴇ. in an inscription recording his dedication of a throne to the Oracle of Apollo at Delphi in Greece, thereby strengthening ties between Phrygia and Greece. The ancient Greek historian Herodotus mentions Midas in an account of this dedication, and he points out that the Phrygian ruler was one of the first non-Greeks to make an offering to the Greek god Apollo.

According to Greek legend, however, Midas's relationship with Apollo was not restricted to religious offerings. According to ancient Greek and Roman myths, Midas was chosen to be a judge in a musical contest between Apollo and the satyr Marsyas (or Pan, in some versions of the myth). Midas ruled against Apollo, who promptly turned the king's ears into those of an ass.

The most famous of Midas's legendary exploits, however, may have reflected a Greek conception of Midas and the Phrygians as fabulously wealthy—a notion borne out by modern-day excavations at the ancient Phrygian capital of Gordium (in present-day Turkey). According to legend, Midas was given a single wish by the god Dionysus after capturing the satyr Silenus, a companion of the god. Midas requested that all he touched be turned to gold. Once the wish was granted, however, he was horrified to realize that he had condemned himself to death by starvation, since even the food he touched turned to gold. Upon appeal, Dionysus agreed to reverse the wish if Midas bathed in the river Pactolus. This was the mythical explanation for that river's golden sands.

The historical king Midas likely did not have as happy an ending as occurred in his most famous legend. Threatened by an army of Assyrians in 709 B.C.E., Midas sent the Assyrian king Sargon II (r. 722–705 B.C.E.) a letter of submission, which Sargon accepted. However, during the reign of Sargon's successor, Sennacherib (r. 704–681 B.C.E.), hordes of Cimmeran invaders from beyond the Black Sea descended upon Anatolia and the Near East, and both Phrygia and the Assyrian Empire crumbled. Tradition has it that Midas committed suicide when he realized that Phrygia would never again be a political power.

See also: ASSYRIAN EMPIRE; MYTH AND FOLKLORE; PHRYGIA, KINGDOM OF; SARGON II; SENNACHERIB.

MIDDLE EASTERN DYNASTIES

The dynasties and rulers that shaped the history of the Middle East, ranging from the earliest days of Mesopotamian civilization to the present-day dynasties that continue to rule much of the Arabian Peninsula. The many dynasties and rulers of the Middle East, from ancient to modern times, are a varied group. While there is little but geography to bind them together across time, in the various periods of history there have been many factors in common, as well as stark differences, among Middle Eastern dynasties and the civilizations they ruled.

DYNASTIES OF THE ANCIENT MIDDLE EAST

The dynasties of the ancient Middle East ruled a collection of small city-states and vast empires, formed by means of conquest and generally governed by autocratic rulers. In the majority of these civilizations there was a strong correlation between dynasties and deities.

The ancient Egyptian dynasties believed in divine kingship, but in other civilizations the relationship between god and ruler was more complex. In ancient Sumer, for example, kings were believed to rule with the aid and blessing of the gods, but they also sometimes came into conflict with a powerful priesthood. The Hittites worshiped their deceased kings as deities, yet viewed the living monarchs as human and subject to law. Similarly, the Amorite king Hammurabi of Babylon (r. 1792–1750 B.C.E.) claimed that his famous code of law was divinely inspired. Sargon of Akkad (r. ca. 2334–2279 B.C.E.) was said to be the son of a high priestess.

Many Israelite rulers, such as King Solomon (r. ca. 970–930 B.C.E.), were priest-kings with strong religious and judicial roles in addition to monarchical or military ones. The Hasmonean dynasty, founded by Judas Maccabeus (r. ca. 166–161 B.C.E.), was headed by Jewish priest-kings who at one point ruled much of Palestine. Cyrus the Great of Persia (r. 559–530 B.C.E.) believed that he had been divinely destined to rule the world, and, indeed, he conquered much of the Middle Eastern region.

Hereditary rule was common among early Middle Eastern dynasties, but its course was rarely smooth. Since no system of primogeniture (inheritance by the oldest son) existed in many of the early Indo-European and Semitic dynasties, infighting among potential heirs was a common occurrence and contributed to the weakening of many early empires. Succession conflicts posed a problem for the Hittites, as well as for some Assyrian kings, such as Ashurbanipal (r. 669–627 B.C.E.), whose civil war with his brother in 652 B.C.E. was highly destabilizing for the Assyrian Empire.

Intermarriage among the early dynasties was a common way of resolving disputes among dynasties. For example, one Assyrian king married his daughter to a Babylonian, and Ramses II of Egypt (r. 1279–1212 B.C.E.) took a Hittite princess as a bride. Similarly, King David of Israel (r. ca. 1010–970 B.C.E.) took wives from a number of conquered territories, using marriage to cement his rule.

GRECO-ROMAN AND PERSIAN DYNASTIES

The Middle East was dominated by Greco-Roman and Persian dynasties from around the fourth century B.C.E. until the rise of Islam in the sixth century C.E. When the Eastern Mediterranean was not directly ruled by Greece or Rome, local dynasties of Hellenistic dynasties, such as the Seleucid dynasty of Syria and the Ptolemaic dynasty of Egypt, took their place.

Other small dynasties flourished around the edges

of the great imperial territories during the Pax Romana ("Roman Peace), building kingdoms whose wealth and power were based on control of trade routes that connected the Arabian and Mediterranean seas. Two such dynasties, similar in nature, were the Nabataeans of Petra (in present-day Jordan) and the Palmyrans of Syria, although both were eventually repressed by Rome.

The fracturing of the empire of Alexander the Great (r. 336–323 B.C.E.) after Alexander's death in 323 B.C.E. gave rise first to the Parthian dynasty and then to the Sassanid dynasty in Persia. The Sassanids explicitly linked their dynasty to the Persian Empire of Cyrus the Great and Darius I (r. 521–486 B.C.E.). The Sassanid ruler Shapur I (r. ca. 222 C.E.) titled himself King of Kings of Iran and non-Iran. The Sassanid dynasty also bore a strong link to the Zoroastrian religion.

Further west, the Byzantine Empire arose from the division of the Roman Empire after 330 C.E., and the Byzantine emperors eventually conquered much of the Middle East. Like the Sassanid rulers of Persia, the Byzantine emperors derived legitimacy from a strong religious base, in their case of Greek Christianity, as well as political and military might. Some of Byzantium's Arab subjects, including the vassal dynasty of the Ghassanids (in modern-day Syria, Jordan, and Israel), were also strongly Christian and remained loyal to Byzantium partially for religious reasons. Meanwhile, in pagan Arabia, strong tribal families and clans became prominent in the fifth and sixth centuries, including the Banu Ummayya and the Beni Hashem, the forerunners of some of the major Arab dynasties of the Islamic age, including the Umayyads and Hashemites.

THE ISLAMIC AGE

After the death of the Prophet Muhammad in 632, his Islamic followers conquered territories throughout the Middle East, converting many of their new subjects to the new religion. Islamic dynasties, like their pagan and Christian forerunners, had an important element of faith. In contrast to many earlier dynasties, however, the Islamic Middle Eastern dynasties rejected ideas of divine kingship. Despite early Islam's distaste for the concept of worldly kingship, a split developed between the political and religious leaders in most Islamic dynasties. Nonetheless, the leaders of these dynasties, including the Umayyads, Abbasids,

and some of the Ottomans, continued to use the title "caliph," with its connotation of religious stewardship over the community of Muslims.

Islamic dynasties throughout the Middle East bore close ties because of their religious commonalities, but sharp differences existed as well. In contrast to the many Islamic dynasties that embraced the dominant Sunni form of Islam, the Safavid dynasty in Persia (1501–1736) based its right to rule on its heritage of the Shi'a (Shi'ite) branch of Islam and declared Shi'a the state religion.

Many Islamic dynasties had strong martial roots—from the Umayyads, who forged their rule in war, spreading Islam across the Middle East, but were transformed into an urban hereditary dynasty, to the Mamluks, a military caste that rejected the idea of hereditary rule. The Seljuqs (1038–1303) and Ottomans (1280–1923), with their Turkic languages and Central Asian heritage, started out as mobile, seminomadic warrior dynasties. Later Ottoman sultans, however, withdrew from active campaigning as their empire became one of the large "gunpowder empires" (which included the Safavids of Persia and the Mughals of India), so named for their military prowess and rapid conquests.

Ottoman inheritance patterns also shifted over time: in the beginning, a law of fratricide led sultans to eliminate other male heirs, for like many other Middle Eastern dynasties, selection of the fittest male relative, rather than primogeniture (inheritance by the oldest son), was used as a method of transferring rule. Many Arab dynasties still in power today follow a similar system, in which the ruler can decide which of his close male relatives will inherit the throne.

MODERN MIDDLE EAST

Many countries in the Middle East today are still ruled by monarchs (both constitutional and autocratic). The Saudi dynasty still holds sway in Saudi Arabia, while the Hashemite kingdom of Jordan is the latest manifestation of the Hashemite dynasty's rule. Emirs from various Arab dynasties still rule Kuwait, the United Arab Emirates, Bahrain, and Qatar, while Oman is one of the few remaining sultanates in the world. Although these dynasties, ruling small nation-states, are a far cry from the imperial dynasties of the past, their presence proves that Middle Eastern dynasties continue to remain influential in the politics of the region.

See also: ABBASID DYNASTY; ACHAEMENID DYNASTY; AYYUBID DYNASTY; BUYID (BUWAYHID) DYNASTY; FATIMID DYNASTY; HASHEMITE DYNASTY; ISLAM AND KINGSHIP; KASSITES; MAMLUK DYNASTY; OTTOMAN EMPIRE; PAHLAVI DYNASTY; PTOLEMAIC DYNASTY; SAFAVID DYNASTY, SAFFARID DYNASTY; SASANID DYNASTY; SELJUQ DYNASTY; UMAYYAD DYNASTY.

FURTHER READING

Goodwin, Jason. *Lords of the Horizons: A History of the Ottoman Empire.* New York: Picador, 2003.

Hourani, Albert. *A History of the Arab Peoples.* Cambridge, MA: Belknap Press of Harvard University Press, 2002.

Kostiner, Joseph, ed. *Middle East Monarchies: The Challenge of Modernity.* Boulder, CO: Lynne Reinner, 2000.

Mansfield, Peter. *A History of the Middle East.* New York: Penguin, 1992.

Sicker, Martin. *The Pre-Islamic Middle East.* Westport, CT: Praeger, 2000.

MILAN, DUCHY OF

A duchy in northern Italy, ruled for generations by the Visconti and Sforza families.

One of the wealthiest duchies in Renaissance Italy, the duchy of Milan emerged in the late Middle Ages from the independent city-state of Milan, which, like other Italian city-states of the period, was loosely subordinated to the Holy Roman Empire. Because of the duchy's great wealth and power, it often became a battleground as countries such as France, Germany, and Spain sought to control it and shape not only its destiny, but that of all Italy.

THE VISCONTI

In 1287, the Visconti family emerged as the leading family of the city-state of Milan, ruling as lords of Milan until 1395, when the title of duke was bestowed on Giovanni Galeazzo Visconti (r. 1378–1402) by the Holy Roman emperor, Wenceslas (r. 1378–1400). The elevation of Giovanni to duke marked the beginning of the duchy of Milan.

Giovanni Galeazzo was an important patron of Renaissance art and architecture, and during his rule the Milan duchy reached its height of power and became one of the most important states in Italy. He also reformed and centralized the government of the duchy, promoted economic development, and conquered various city-states and territories as far south as Siena and Pisa. He died while preparing to attack Milan's main enemy, the city-state of Florence.

Upon Giovanni Galeazzo's death in 1402, the title of duke passed first to his son, Giovanni Maria Visconti (r. 1402–1412), who was assassinated by rivals in 1412, and then to his other son, Filippo Maria Visconti (r. 1412–1447). Both were weak rulers, and during their reign, Milan lost a number of territories that had been conquered by their father and his predecessors.

Under the Visconti, the duchy of Milan had a combination of feudal, civic, and bureaucratic elements. Much of the rural land in the duchy was held by vassals of the duke. In the cities, local civic government coexisted with ducal officials, such as the *comissario*, who represented the duke's political interests, and a *referendario*, who represented his financial interests. The central institutions of the duchy were organized into a series of councils and departments, all of which followed a chain of command that went back to the duke. The duchy of Milan was one of the most advanced bureaucratic states of its time, and it was one of the first to appoint a resident ambassador to a court outside Italy, that of the French king. The ruling family of the duchy was also deeply intertwined with the Catholic Church, controlling much ecclesiastical patronage.

Duke Filippo Maria Visconti died in 1447, killed during a bloody war against the Venetians. His death was followed by the formation of a short-lived republic called the Ambrosian Republic, named after the fourth-century bishop of Milan, Saint Ambrose. Filippo Maria had left no clear heir, but his illegitimate daughter Bianca was married to Francesco Sforza, one of Italy's leading *condottiere*, or military leaders. Francesco used his marriage to claim the dukedom in 1450, founding a new line of rulers.

THE SFORZA

Because of the irregularity of the Sforza succession, it took some time for the Holy Roman Empire and other leading European powers to recognize Francesco as duke. Moreover, the king of France, Charles VII (r. 1422–1461), had a claim on Milan through Visconti ancestry. Nevertheless, Francesco (r. 1450–1466) retained control of the duchy and became a leading Italian statesman during his reign.

Under Francesco's guidance, Milan enjoyed a period of peace and prosperity that lasted until his death in 1466. He was succeeded by his much less competent son, Galeazzo Maria Sforza (r. 1466–1476), who was self-indulgent, cruel, and extravagant. Galeazzo ruled Milan until assassinated by a disgruntled courtier in 1476. He was succeeded by his eight-year-old son, Giovanni Galeazzo (r. 1476–1494).

During the rule of Giovanni, the real power was held by his uncle, Ludovico Sforza. Ludovico (r. 1494–1500) succeeded to the dukedom himself on the death of Giovanni in 1494. Ludovico's rule was a time of great cultural splendor in Milan, and he was a patron of the great Renaissance artist, Leonardo da Vinci. However, Ludovico is best known for a disastrous alliance he made with France, which led to a French invasion of Italy in 1499. The French deposed Ludovico, and he was imprisoned. King Louis XII of France claimed Milan, and French rule of the duchy lasted until 1512. Like other Italian states of the period, Milan lost its independence and became a political prize of a non-Italian state.

In 1512, Swiss forces, allied with other European powers against France, invaded Milan and ended French rule of the duchy. They restored to the throne Ludovico's eldest son, Massimiliano (r. 1512–1515). Massimiliano ruled as a puppet of the Swiss, to whom he ceded some northern Milanese territories. He later handed over power to Francis I (r. 1515–1547) of France in 1515, after the French victory over the Swiss at the battle of Marignano. Massimiliano renounced his claim on Milan and spent the rest of his life in France, receiving a pension from Francis I.

Massimiliano's younger brother, Francesco II (r. 1521–1535), recovered the dukedom after the French were defeated by the army of the Holy Roman emperor, Charles V (r. 1519–1558), at the battle of Bicocca. However, Francesco II spent most of his reign under the domination of the Holy Roman Empire. Francesco died without an heir in 1535. His death marked the end of Milanese independence, and the title duke of Milan went into the possession of the Spanish Crown.

See also: CHARLES V; HOLY ROMAN EMPIRE.

FURTHER READING

Holmes, George, ed. *Oxford Illustrated History of Medieval Europe.* New York: Oxford University Press, 1988.

MILITARY ROLES, ROYAL

The various functions of the monarchy as relating to the exercise of military power. Although the centuries following the eighteenth-century Enlightenment have seen a marked decrease in military-based monarchs—and monarchies in general—several kings and queens had a close relationship with the military all the way into the twentieth century.

From the very beginnings of monarchy, military power was a necessary condition for rule. According to Chinese tradition, for example, the early Shang (Yin) dynasty (ca. 1523–1027 B.C.E.) began with a military uprising led by a local warrior and tribal chief named Tang, who overthrew the Xia (Hsia) dynasty and its tyrannical ruler, Chieh.

Similarly, the First dynasty of Egypt (ca. 3100–2905 B.C.E.) was founded by Menes, a military leader said to have united the two major regions of Egypt. Numerous other Egyptian pharaohs were great military leaders as well, including several of the best-known pharaohs—such as Djoser, Thutmose III, Rameses I, Seti I, and Rameses II, who is often noted as one of the great warriors of the ancient world.

The close connection between royal power and military might did not end with the Egyptians, who were in fact ultimately conquered by a foreign king, Alexander the Great of Macedon (r. 336–323 B.C.E.). Virtually all of Alexander's thirteen-year reign was spent abroad in military conquest, and in that short amount of time he spread Greek culture and ideals to much of the known world. In fact, Alexander is much better remembered as a military leader than as a political administrator, and the lands he conquered were so poorly governed that his empire collapsed almost immediately upon his death. His lands were later taken over by another society frequently led by generals, the Roman Empire, which had several skilled military leaders as ruler, including Julius Caesar (r. 49–44 B.C.E.); Augustus (r. 27 B.C.E.–14 C.E.); Tiberius (r. 14–37); Trajan (r. 98–117), and Marcus Aurelius (r. 161–180).

The early medieval period saw the rise of Charlemagne (r. 768–814), whose empire was stretched to great lengths thanks to his almost ceaseless military conquests. Despite the success of Charlemagne and a few other great leaders—including Richard I of England (r. 1189–1199) and Genghis Khan of Mongolia (r. 1206–1227)—the Middle Ages were marked by the rise of professional warriors under feudal lords, thus somewhat lessening the military role of monarchs.

Numerous kings continued to serve in battle in the Middle Ages, but the combination of military and political talent was rapidly becoming less necessary as the years wore on. The increasing use of professional armed forces hastened this trend, although the seventeenth and eighteenth centuries witnessed the rise of two of the greatest military leaders of all time also serving as monarchs—Gustavus Adolphus of Sweden (r. 1611–1632) and Peter the Great of Russia (r. 1682–1725).

By the eighteenth century, the armies of many kingdoms were almost fully professional, a trend indicated by the fact that King George II of England (r. 1727–1760) became the last British monarch to lead troops in battle, during the War of the Austrian Succession in 1743.

The post-Enlightenment era began with an exception to this trend of nonmilitary rulers—Napoleon I of France (r. 1804–1815), perhaps the greatest military leader of all time. Unlike military kings such as Gustavus Adolphus and Peter the Great, Napoleon was a general who rode his military conquests to the throne, rather than a monarch who was also a military leader. Perhaps partly as a result, his domestic policies achieved only limited success.

The other great military monarch of the nineteenth century, southern Africa's Shaka Zulu (r. 1818–1828), was a warrior who had no real skills as a politician and consequently incurred the disfavor of his people.

The line of monarchs who were successful both militarily and politically effectively ended with Napoleon, and the nineteenth and twentieth centuries saw monarchs become military leaders in symbol and diplomacy only, rarely on the battlefield. The rise of democratic governments around the world in these centuries has further limited the military role of monarchs in modern history.

Monarchs today serve more as representations of national unity than as actual leaders, and this extends from the legislative branches of government to the front lines of combat. Recent monarchs who have been especially successful as inspirational figures for their military forces include George V (r. 1910–1936) and George VI (r. 1936–1952) of Great Britain, and Emperor Hirohito of Japan (r. 1926–1989). Although some members of various royal families have served

or continue to serve in their nations' militaries, the age of monarchs as battlefield leaders has passed.

See also: ALEXANDER III, THE GREAT; CHARLEMAGNE; CONQUEST AND KINGSHIPS; GENGHIS KHAN; NAPOLEON I (BONAPARTE); POWER, FORMS OF ROYAL; SHAKA ZULU.

FURTHER READING
Spellman, W. M. *Monarchies, 1000–2000.* London: Reaktion, 2001.

MINAMOTO RULERS

(ca. early 1100s–1330s C.E.)

Warrior family from the northern Kanto region of Japan who played a determinant role in the ceaseless interclan struggles for power and for influence at the imperial capital during the latter Heian period (794–1185).

Known as *Seiwa Genji*, the Minamoto clan was descended from the Emperor Seiwa (r. 858–876). Minamoto samurai first established themselves at the imperial court in the late 1000s through their service to regents from the Fujiwara clan, who hired the Minamoto both as bodyguards and to put down provincial unrest.

RISE OF THE MINAMOTO
In 1028, Minamoto Yorinobu (968–1048) assisted the Fujiwara imperial regent in defeating a local rebellion in the east. His victory solidified both Minamoto influence at court and their power locally in eastern Japan.

During the Earlier Nine Years' War (1051–1062), the victories of Minamoto Yoshiie (1039–1106) and his father Yoriyoshi (988–1075) preserved imperial interests and secured the ascendancy of the Genji clan over other clans in northern Japan. Yoshiie's subsequent victories during the Later Three Years' War (1083–1087) reaffirmed the Minamoto power as an independent force since these battles were waged independently and not in the service of the emperor.

A man of legendary military genius and one of the clan's revered ancestors, Yoshiie forged the Minamoto samurai into a formidable army, respected and feared across Japan. Many local leaders put their lands under Yoshiie's control in return for armed protection.

TIMES OF DISTURBANCE

The Minamoto fortunes declined temporarily after the defeat of Tameyoshi (1096–1156) during the Hogen Disturbance (1156), which was kindled by the struggle between the followers of retired Emperor Sutoku (r. 1123–1142) and Emperor Go-Shirakawa (r. 1155–1158). The two court factions enlisted forces from opposing warrior factions, each of which was in turn made up of allied Minamoto and Taira fighters. Tameyoshi's son Yoshitomo (1123–1160) fought with the victorious Taira group against his father.

Though short, the bloody Hogen conflict marked a major decline in Fujiwara influence, a rise in the imperial court influence of Taira Kiyomori (1118–1181), and a personal attempt, eventually unsuccessful, by Go-Shirakawa to restore rule to the person of the emperor. Yoshitomo refused to execute his defeated father, Minamoto Tameyoshi, but a kinsman obliged, maintaining it would be disgraceful for Tameyoshi to be killed by a victorious Taira.

Disappointed in his gains, Yoshitomo soon became restless and in 1159 turned on his former Taira ally. Kiyomori successfully rallied his followers and defeated Yoshitomo. For unknown reasons, Kiyomori spared the lives of Yoshitomo's children—perhaps due to his attraction to Yoshitomo's concubine. However, Kiyomori's clemency led to his own downfall two decades later at the hands of the Minamoto sons he had spared, Yoritomo and Yoshitsune.

The final clash between the Minamoto and Taira clans, the Genpei War (1180–1185), began in 1180 when a disaffected imperial prince called for Minamoto support against the imperial ascension of the infant prince Antoku (r. 1180–1185), a grandson of Taira Kiyomori.

Minamoto Yoritomo, now the head of his clan, successfully enlisted a large number of warrior vassals, including disaffected members of the Taira family. The five-year war engulfed Japan in clan struggles that raged across the country, simultaneously pitting local forces against the central imperial powers.

A great strategist and organizer, Yoritomo relied heavily on his younger half-brother, Yoshitsune, for military success. In 1185 Yoshitsune's army annihilated the Taira forces at the decisive sea battle of Dannoura.

MINAMOTO SHOGUNS

The rise of the Minamoto samurai culminated in the military triumphs of Yoritomo (r. 1192–1195) and his brother Yoshitsune over their Taira family (also known as the Heike), their rivals during the Genpei War. The Minamoto victory in 1185 signaled the end of the primacy of civil and religious government at the imperial court in Kyoto and the beginning of rule by an independent warrior class over a regime called the Kamakura shogunate.

In 1192, Yoritomo legitimized his rule by forcing the thirteen-year-old emperor to name him the first *seii tai-shogun* ("barbarian-subduing generalissimo"). The appointment honored and continued the centuries-old Japanese tradition of duality in government, whereby those who wielded real power sought sanction by an appointment or title bestowed in the name of the highest power embodied in an emperor of divine descent.

Yoritomo's government was known as the *bakufu* ("field tent headquarters" of a military campaign), which came to stand for the shogunate itself. Yoritomo located the *bakufu* in Kamakura, his family base about 30 miles from modern-day Tokyo, hence the Kamakura shogunate (1192–1333).

By institutionalizing the role of shogun as military leader defending the imperial court, the Minamoto rulers established the feudal military rule that governed Japan until the Meiji Restoration in 1868.

See also: KAMAKURA SHOGUNATE; YORITOMO.

MINANGKABAU KINGDOM

(flourished 1300s C.E.)

Buddhist kingdom located in western part of Sumatra that flourished briefly in the fourteenth century.

The Minangkabau region in highland West Sumatra enters history in the early fourteenth century. Around 1343, a ruler known as Adityavarman (r. 1343–1374) established a center of power in Jambi (which he called Dharmasraya) and then moved his capital to the Tanahdatar area (near present-day Pagarruyung).

Adityavarman seems to have come from the court of the Majapahit Empire of eastern Java, which claimed suzerainty over the main populated areas of Sumatra's eastern coast. His father may have been a Javanese prince who married a Sumatran princess captured during an expedition in 1275 sent by the kingdom of Singasari, the predecessor state to Majapahit. Thus, Adityavarman may have been sent as a viceroy, with the idea that his maternal connections with Sumatra would stand him in good stead.

Before long, however, Adityavarman decided to declare himself independent from Majapahit control. He moved his capital from the lowlands of Sumatra's east coast to the Minangkabau highlands. This move may have had two motives: to distance himself from the reach of Majapahit's revenge for his betrayal; and to oversee the sources of gold that were plentiful in the Tanahdatar region. In one of his inscriptions, Adityavarman explicitly calls himself *Kanakamedinindr* ("Gold-land Lord").

How Adityavarman succeeded in transplanting a Javanese-style court into the Sumatran highlands is unknown. Yet, he left a large number of inscriptions dating over a period of thirty years, evidence that he had a long reign. He also was a faithful adherent of a form of esoteric Buddhism, probably initiated into a cult of Bhairawa, a deity with demonic features. An enormous statue unearthed near Padang Roco in western Sumatra depicts Bhairawa with eyes bulging in a threatening manner, with snakes for armbands, skull bowl, and sacrificial knife, standing on a pile of corpses and skulls.

One of the inscriptions attributed to Adityavarman mentions a crown prince, Ananggavarman. Adityavarman's dream of an esoteric Buddhist kingdom in the mountains of Sumatra, enriched by the gold of many mines, does not seem to have survived him, however. Ananggavarman himself never produced any known inscriptions. After Adityavarman's last inscription, West Sumatra and Minangkabau disappear from history, reappearing only when the Portuguese enter the region in the early sixteenth century.

Tanahdatar (Pagarruyung) played the role of a powerful moral force in later Sumatran politics. The endorsement of its rulers was sought after by claimants to thrones elsewhere in Sumatra. But the region around the city was already Muslim by the late 1600s, when the first outside visitor to the area, a Portuguese named Tomas Diaz from Melaka, viewed the capital. Memories of Adityavarman's kingdom perhaps survive most vividly in the legend of the wars between Datuk Katumenggungan and Datuk Pepatih nan Sebatang. One was an autocrat, and the other an advocate of a more democratic system of government. The two forms of *adat*, or customary law, still exist in different villages of Sumatra today.

See also: SAMUDERA-PASAI; SOUTHEAST ASIAN KINGDOMS; SRIVIJAYA-PALEMBANG EMPIRE.

FURTHER READING

Miksic, John, ed. *Indonesian Heritage: Ancient History*. Vol. 1. Singapore: Archipelago Press, 1996.

Reid, Tony, ed. *Indonesian Heritage: Early Modern History*. Vol. 3. Singapore: Archipelago Press, 1996.

Ricklefs, M. C. *A History of Indonesia Since c. 1200*. Stanford, CA: Stanford University Press, 2001.

MING DYNASTY (1368–1644 C.E.)

Chinese dynasty that restored native rule to China and instituted an extended period of internal peace and prosperity. The Ming dynasty returned native rule to China after a century of foreign domination by the Mongols. Lasting nearly 300 years, the Ming era was a time of prosperity. The population grew, literature and the arts flourished, and Chinese ships explored distant lands for the first time. Ming rule was also marked by a highly centralized government and increasing isolation from the rest of the world. Although it was an era of domestic peace, the constant threat of foreign invasion drained the empire's resources.

RETURN TO CHINESE RULE

The Ming ("brilliant") dynasty was founded in 1368 by Zhu Yuanzhang, later known as Hungwu (r. 1368–1398), a peasant who had experienced the desperate poverty and suffering of the final years of Mongol rule. A talented leader, Hungwu led his rebel troops to victory over the Yuan dynasty, establishing his capital in the city of Nanjing. The Yuan rulers fled to Mongolia, where they would remain a constant menace to the new dynasty.

Hungwu restored traditional Chinese customs, reinstituting the rituals of Confucianism that had been neglected by the Yuan. He revived agriculture, which had deteriorated under the Mongols. Hungwu kept taxes low by carefully restricting government spending. He barred from politics all eunuchs—the castrated men who served the imperial family within the Forbidden City, and whose involvement in politics had plagued previous dynasties with debilitating power struggles. Paranoid and ruthless, Hungwu executed all rivals. He eliminated the post of prime minister, creating a highly centralized administration in which all parts of the government were under his control. This system laid a great burden on his successors, handing them a workload that would challenge the abilities of even the most conscientious Ming emperors.

STRENGTH AND PROSPERITY

Hungwu's son, Yung Lo (Yongle) (r. 1402–1424), ruled China at the height of Ming power. Moving the capital to Beijing, he fortified the city with walls and built the famous Forbidden City, a sprawling complex of 9,000 rooms that housed the imperial palaces. He led several great campaigns against the empire's Mongolian rivals to the north.

Reversing Hongwu's prohibition on eunuch in-

volvement in politics, Yongle restored eunuchs to a position of power. In 1405, Yongle sent his grand eunuch, Zheng He, on the first of seven naval missions that would reach as far as the shores of India and Africa. Chinese ships and charts had been the most advanced in the world since the eleventh century, but this was the first official expedition to the West. The goal of these expeditions was diplomatic, not commercial. Mistrustful of trade, the Ming sought to enroll new tributaries—nations that would acknowledge Chinese superiority. The expeditions returned with foreign emissaries and oddities. One trip brought back a giraffe. The expeditions ended in 1433, a victim of dwindling state resources and the disapproval of Confucian scholars who viewed trade and foreign contact as dangerous. This marked the end of Chinese power on the sea.

While China's boundaries did not expand under the Ming, the dynasty brought prosperity and an extended period of peace within its borders. Trade with the West introduced into China plants from the New World, including sweet potatoes, maize, and peanuts. These new plants created an agricultural boom that contributed to a doubling of the Chinese population. Regional specialization in agriculture and manufacturing increased as provinces refined the production of cotton, silk, tobacco, sugar cane, and porcelain. Despite the government's suspicion of profit and commerce, foreign demand for Chinese products like silk and porcelain grew, leading to an inflow of silver.

ARTS AND CULTURE

The Ming saw a rapid expansion of publishing and a flowering of popular literature. In the sixteenth and seventeenth centuries, the number of books published in the vernacular grew dramatically. Before this time, most books were written in the scholarly style accessible only to the highly educated. Now those with only a basic education could enjoy the period's explosion of popular plays, novels, and how-to books. Some of China's greatest novels were written during the Ming period, including the famous *Journey to the West* by Wu Chengen (1500?–1580) and *The Romance of the Three Kingdoms*, attributed to Lo Guanzhong, who wrote in the late fourteenth century.

Imperial patronage of ceramics created some of the world's finest porcelain under the Ming. The imperial kilns at Jingdezhen in Jiangxi province, estab-

Ming Dynasty

HUNG WU* (HUNGWU)	1368–1398
CHIEN WEN	1398–1402
YUNG LO	1402–1424
HUNG HSI	1424–2425
HSUAN TE	1425–1435
CHENG T'UNG	1435–1449
CHING T'AI	1449–1457
T'IEN SHUN	1457–1464
CH'ENG HUA	1464–1487
HUNG CHIH	1487–1505
CHENG TE	1505–1521
CHIA CHING	1521–1567
LUNG CH'ING	1567–1572
WAN LI	1572–1620
T'AI CH'ANG	1620
T'IEN CH'I	1620–1627
CH'UNG CHEN	1627–1644

*Indicates a separate alphabetical entry.

ROYAL PLACES

MING TOMBS

Thirty miles northwest of Beijing, thirteen Ming emperors lie buried in a magnificent complex of tombs in a valley south of the Tianshou Mountains. Laid out according to the principles of *feng shui*, the Ming Tombs are the most complete set of tombs to survive from any Chinese dynasty. Emperor Yongle (r. 1402–1424), the third Ming emperor and builder of the Forbidden City, chose the site and built the first and largest of the tombs. Known as *Changling*, the structure is a replica of the Hall of Supreme Harmony, the largest hall in the Forbidden City. Similar tombs were erected for all subsequent Ming emperors (except for Jingtai), who were buried with their empresses and concubines beneath mounds of earth adjacent to buildings that resemble Ming imperial palaces. The most extravagant tomb was constructed for Emperor Wanli (r. 1572–1620), who was buried in an underground palace filled with treasures.

A "Spirit Road" runs through the complex, lined by large sculptures of animals and imperial advisers. The Ming rulers revived the practice of ancestor worship, performing ritual sacrifices at the tombs of their predecessors. These ceremonies were designed to both honor their ancestors and enlist their aid.

lished in the late fourteenth century, supplied porcelain to the Ming emperors and to traders eager to meet the growing foreign demand for the exquisite porcelain with its distinctive blue-and-white designs.

Despite Ming resistance to foreign influence, a few foreigners managed to infiltrate the Middle Kingdom, as China was known to itself. Notable among these was Matteo Ricci (1552–1610), the famous Italian Jesuit who in 1601 received permission to reside in Beijing. Ricci attempted to win followers for Christianity by sharing his knowledge of Western science. He remained in China until his death in 1610, having managed to convert some Chinese officials to his faith.

In philosophy, Wang Yangming (1472–1529) challenged orthodox Confucianism, with its emphasis on obedience to authority, and instead espoused intuitive moral knowledge over painstaking rational investigation. He introduced the subversive idea that all people—even the uneducated—possessed access to this form of knowledge.

The Ming maintained the Chinese system of selecting civil servants with a national examination that tested knowledge of classical Chinese texts. Regional quotas were instituted to avoid the domination of this system by scholars from the more educated, prosperous areas.

ISOLATION AND COLLAPSE

In contrast to Mongol rule, when China was part of a vast, thriving trade network, the Ming era was marked by its emperors' efforts to withdraw from the world. Typical of Chinese rulers, the Ming held the Confucian view that land was the source of national wealth, viewing trade and industry with distrust. Foreign contact was also viewed with suspicion. To control and limit trade, the Ming required that it be conducted within the confines of the tribute system. However, the isolationist policies of the Ming merely encouraged the growth of smuggling and piracy. Pirates terrorized coastal towns, raiding and looting. In 1577, Portugal was allowed to establish Macao as a trading center in exchange for Portuguese help in fighting the local pirates.

After the middle of the fifteenth century, outside pressure increased from the hostile Mongol and

Manchu lands to the north. In 1449, the Mongols captured Ming emperor Zhengtong (r. 1435–1449; 1457–1464). (Rather than pay the requested ransom, the Ming court opted for installing a new emperor.) In 1542, the Mongols killed or captured 200,000 Chinese in a single month. The Ming responded defensively, increasing their isolation by withdrawing behind the Great Wall and expending massive sums of money to reinforce and extend it.

The highly centralized system established by Hongwu had left later Ming emperors without the support of a prime minister and his staff to help in the administration of the empire. This led to an increasing reliance, after Yongle's time, on the imperial eunuchs to aid in the daunting task of governing the vast Chinese empire. By the middle of the fifteenth century, eunuchs had established their own bureaucracy, which possessed control over much of the government's administration. Power struggles between the official bureaucracy and the eunuchs paralyzed government.

Emperor Wanli (r. 1572–1620) became so disillusioned with the infighting at court that he withdrew completely from his imperial duties and refused to leave the Forbidden City. As the only servants allowed inside the Forbidden City, the eunuchs became the sole source of contact between the emperor and the world outside. This opened the way for complete government control by the eunuchs.

By the early seventeenth century, the Ming government was nearly bankrupt, a consequence of Wanli's extravagant spending and constant military campaigns against the Mongols. At the same time, a series of natural disasters left millions dead from disease and starvation. Without money, the imperial government could not respond effectively to the situation. Unrest and revolt spread, and rebel leader Li Zicheng seized Beijing in 1644. Recognizing the end, Chongzhen (r. 1627–1644), the last Ming emperor, hung himself from a tree in the imperial garden. Invaders from Manchuria arrived later that year to defeat Li Zicheng and proclaim the Ch'ing dynasty.

See also: CH'ING (QING) DYNASTY; HUNG WU (HUNGWU); WANLI; YUAN DYNASTY.

FURTHER READING

Twitchett, Denis. *The Cambridge History of China: The Ming Dynasty.* Vol. 8. New York: Cambridge University Press, 1998.

MINOAN KINGDOMS

(2000–1375 B.C.E.)

An ancient Bronze-Age Mediterranean civilization, centered on the island of Crete, that was mysteriously destroyed sometime after 1375 B.C.E.

Most of what is known today about Minoan culture is based on archaeological evidence rather than historical documents. Although the Minoans did leave written records, only the latest of their three forms of writing is decipherable to scholars. Existing examples of this script show that it was used solely as a recordkeeping aid; the content is therefore somewhat disappointing as a historical record.

Fortunately, the Minoans were great artists and builders, and the remains of many of their works have survived through the ravages of the millennia, as well as through Crete's frequent earthquakes, allowing scholars to reconstruct part of the story of the Minoan civilization. The most conspicuous remains of Minoan civilization are their immense palaces. First built around 2000 B.C.E., the main palaces of Knossos, Phaestus, and Malia were all destroyed around 1700 B.C.E., probably by an earthquake. They were then rebuilt in an even more elaborate fashion.

One of the most striking of Minoan achievements is the monumental palace at Knossos. A center for ritual, trade, storage, and political and economic activity, the palace at Knossos had hundreds of rooms and a floor area of more than three acres. One of the remarkable features was its indoor plumbing, with water provided by hundreds of miles of aqueducts. By the late fifteenth century B.C.E., the population in and around the palace of Knossos likely numbered in the tens of thousands.

No names of Minoan kings have survived in Minoan records. However, Greek legend claims that there was a Minoan King named Minos (for whom the civilization was later named), who ruled the island of Crete with his brothers, Rhadamanthys (who supposedly ruled Phaestus), and Sarpedon (who controlled Malia).

The power of Minoan monarchs was probably limited and may have been more on the scale of a chief rather than a king. Until 1470 B.C.E., when evidence suggests that the various Minoan territories were unified under the control of the palace at Knossos (and probably the mainland Greek Mycenaeans), the palaces at Knossos, Malia, and Phaestus probably acted as largely independent city-states.

One of the sites of the ancient Minoan civilization of Crete is the palace of Knossos, an enormous complex that included shrines and temples, residences, workshops, storerooms, and courtyards.

The Minoan economy was also centered on the three great palaces. Agricultural surplus, which may have been produced by slave labor, and raw materials were routinely gathered together, organized, and redistributed by an extensive palace bureaucracy. Craft production was highly skilled and probably overseen by a noble class. Jewelry, textiles, and pottery were then funneled into an extensive trading network, which was also controlled primarily by the nobles of the Minoan state.

This trading system formed the basis both for the relative wealth of Minoan civilization and its widespread cultural influence. The Minoans were unrivaled in their naval supremacy, largely because of their superior ships, and they had trade routes as distant as Egypt, Sumer, and Syria, as well as close trading ties to the Greek mainland and the remainder of the Aegean Sea.

Women played a central role in many Minoan rituals, particularly those involving the chief Minoan deity, a fertility/mother goddess. Religion seems to have had a central part in Minoan life. Shrines were scattered thickly throughout Crete, in palaces, caves, next to running water, and on desolate hilltop sites, and women may have had considerable power through their religious positions.

Some historians suggest that both women and men participated in the dangerous Minoan ritual of bull-leaping. A participant, sometimes alone, sometimes a member of a team, would stand still as a charging bull rushed forward until it was close enough for the individual to grab onto the bull's horns and vault over its back. The Minoans also ritually sacrificed bulls and often made agricultural offerings as well.

Sometime after around 1470 B.C.E., a volcano on the nearby Aegean island of Thera erupted with an enormous explosion, and the palaces of Phaestus and Malia, as well as all of the smaller Minoan cities, were destroyed. Evidence suggests that during that time or just afterward, the Mycenaeans of mainland Greek took control of Knossos and the remains of

Minoan power. During this chaotic period, Minoan civilization began a steep and rapid decline. By 1200 B.C.E., the Minoan civilization was dead, the last of its palaces in ruins.

See also: MYCENAEAN MONARCHIES.

FURTHER READING

Cadogan, Gerald. *Palaces of Minoan Crete.* London, New York: Routledge, 1991.

Castledon, Rodney. *Minoans: Life in Bronze Age Crete.* New York: Routledge, 1993.

Higgins, Reynold. *Minoan and Mycenaean Art.* Rev. ed. New York: Thames & Hudson, 1997.

MISSISSIPPIAN CULTURE

(ca. 800–1700 C.E.)

The last indigenous Native American culture to develop in North America before the European colonial period, located in the central and lower Mississippi Valley.

The Mississippian culture extended over a large part of the present-day Southeastern and Midwestern United States, including the river valleys of the Mississippi, Alabama, Georgia, Arkansas, Missouri, Kentucky, Illinois, Indiana, and Ohio. Mississippian culture also extended as far north as Wisconsin and Minnesota and as far west as the Great Plains.

EARLY LIFE

An agriculture-based society, with crops such as corn, beans, and squash, the Mississippian culture developed on the low-lying fertile land bordering the Mississippi River and its tributaries. The people lived in complexes of villages dominated by a larger town and governed by priest-rulers or chiefs.

The heart of Mississippian towns was a ceremonial plaza, with a temple or chief's dwelling atop one or more oval or pyramid-shaped earth mounds built around the plaza. Sometimes less important leaders also lived on mounds, but the highest mound was always designated for the temple of the chief priest.

When the chief priest died, his temple was torn down and another layer of earth was added on the mound for his successor. Social status was measured by the proximity of one's home to the plaza. This was a characteristic type of settlement in parts of Mexico

and Guatemala from about 850 B.C.E., but it only entered North America with the Mississippian culture.

ECONOMIC GROWTH

During the earliest phase of the Mississippian culture (ca. 800–1000), known as the Emergent Mississippian period, there seems to have been widespread trade in exotic goods. Village sites found near saline springs indicate that salt became a main product for trade. There is also evidence that agriculture was gaining importance, with corn in more abundant supply and tools made for rigorous farming.

After 1000, agriculture continued, and wild seeds, fruits, and nuts were harvested as well. Streams and rivers provided abundant fish and shellfish, and the bow and arrow added hunting to the culture's means of obtaining food.

Clearly, the economy and communications networks were improving as well, since it is apparent that exotic goods made their way to even the smallest and most remote farmsteads. There is also evidence that home crafts, sold to supplement the agricultural economy, were produced by skilled artisans at even the most remote locations. Excavations have revealed the existence of materials such as mica and shell that local artists probably made into objects for trade or decorative or ceremonial items.

To facilitate the growing trade, market centers emerged at strategic spots close to the source of valuable goods and along principal travel routes. Current-day St. Louis was one of those centers; and the site of Cahokia, across the Mississippi River in Illinois, was once the main economic, political, and religious center of Mississippian culture.

Prehistoric urban centers such as Cahokia were most important from about 1050 to 1150. Around that time, however, social stability began to weaken, with competition apparently arising between centers for control of the trade networks, and between growing numbers of high-ranking civic and religious leaders for power. The economy may have been further destabilized by deterioration of the environment due to overpopulation.

As a result of these and possibly other causes, the population and influence of the large Mississippian centers decreased between 1300 and 1400. Trade networks also became significantly smaller or were totally abandoned. Cities were decentralized into small villages, which remained largely dependent on agriculture or returned to the less complex and more mobile existence of hunting and gathering. As a result, when the Europeans arrived, they found abandoned centers that still contained earthen mounds.

The people of the Mississippian culture did not have immunities to the illnesses brought by Europeans to the Americas. Even the common cold proved virulent. Thus the diseases the Europeans brought with them, as well as their attacks against native peoples, accelerated the decline of the Mississippian culture.

See also: AMERICAN KINGDOMS, CENTRAL AND NORTH.

FURTHER READING

Smith, Bruce D., ed. *Mississippian Emergence.* Washington: Smithsonian Institution Press, 1990.

MITANNI KINGDOM

(ca. 1500–1260 B.C.E.)

Kingdom of the ancient Near East whose rulers rose from obscurity in the decades before 1500 B.C.E. to rule over a large empire that stretched from the Zagros Mountains (on the eastern border of present-day Iraq) all the way to the Mediterranean Sea. Although Mitanni successfully fended off repeated invasions by the Egyptians, the kingdom succumbed after only about 250 years to attacks from its own neighbors, the Hittites and the Assyrians.

Sometime between 2300 and 2000 B.C.E., nomadic peoples speaking Indo-European languages began migrating into the ancient Near East from their ancestral lands north of the Black Sea. The largest group of migrants continued into Iran and India, and another group moved into present-day Turkey to become the Hittites. Still another group of these Indo-European migrants apparently settled in northern Iraq. They became an aristocratic ruling class who ruled over of a large portion of a local people known as the Hurrians.

Hurrian tribes, whose language was neither Semitic nor Indo-European, had established their own dominance in the region not long before the arrival of these new migrants. Based on archaeological evidence, historians believe that it was the Mitanni who brought skilled horsemanship and the use of spoke-wheel chariots to the Hurrians, as well as elements of the old Indo-European religion. The Mitanni established their capital at a city named Wassukkani, probably located in the Khabur River area.

The first Mitanni kings whose names are known were Shuttarna I (r. ca. 1560 B.C.E.) and Parattarna (r. ca. 1530 B.C.E). Parattarna's successor, Saustatar (r. ca. 1500–1450 B.C.E.), earned his fame by sacking and looting the great Assyrian palace at Ashur. Under Saustatar, Mitanni also gained new territory on the borders of the neighboring Hittite Empire. Mitanni reached the height of its power in the 1400s B.C.E., and by around 1420 B.C.E. its empire stretched from the Mediterranean to northern Iran.

For much of its existence, the Mitanni kingdom vied with Egypt for control of Syria and Palestine. The two kingdoms eventually agreed to a peaceful division of the region, sealed with several marriages between the two royal families. The last independent Mitanni king, Tushratta (r. ca. 1385–1350 B.C.E.), not only sent his daughter to marry Pharaoh Amenhotep III of Egypt (r. 1386–1349 B.C.E.), but when the pharaoh took ill, he dispatched a physician with the image of the goddess Ishtar of Nineveh, famed for her curative powers. This helped neither Amenhotep, who died soon after, nor Tushratta himself, who gained nothing from the gesture.

During the reign of Tushratta, the Hittites sacked the Mitanni capital city of Wassukkani. Not long afterward, Tushratta was murdered by one of his own sons in a palace intrigue. Soon after, Mitanni was absorbed into the Hittite Empire. Hittite control did not last long, but a new and more dangerous threat later emerged—Assyria.

By about the thirteenth century B.C.E., the resurgent Assyrian Empire had become a powerful and aggressive force that posed a serious threat to Mitanni. Around 1260 B.C.E., the Assyrians overwhelmed the remnants of Mitanni and absorbed the kingdom into their own growing empire. Although the Mitanni kingdom disappeared, the Hurrian culture survived and eventually exerted a powerful influence on the Hittites.

See also: ASSYRIAN EMPIRE; EGYPTIAN DYNASTIES, ANCIENT (EIGHTEENTH TO TWENTY-SIXTH); HITTITE EMPIRE; MIDDLE EASTERN DYNASTIES.

MIXTEC EMPIRE (1500 B.C.E.–1520 C.E.)

Pre-Columbian empire that developed in the south-central area of Mexico. Scholars have divided the

Mixtec prehistory into four phases: Cruz (1500–200 B.C.E.), Ramos (200 B.C.E.–300 C.E.), Las Flores (300–1000), and Natividad (1000–1520). In each of these phases, the economic development of the Mixtec Empire was strongly influenced by the three climatic zones found within the empire: the Mixteca Alta (High Mixtec), Mixteca Baja (Low Mixtec), and Mixteca Costa (Coastal Mixtec).

During the Cruz phase of the empire, the Mixtec communities comprised a central village and a number of subject hamlets, a structure that indicated a basic hierarchical organization of society. The majority of the settlements had a limited number of inhabitants. The main economic activity was agriculture, supported by irrigation techniques and terracing of fields.

In the Ramos phase, some Mixtec villages experienced a significant population growth. One of these was Yucuita, located in the Mixteca Alta. There is evidence of conflict among chiefdoms during this period, as many of the emerging towns were located on elevated hilltops, suggesting a fortified status. There is also evidence of tribute and trade, as well as craft specialization.

In the Las Flores phase of the empire, the Mixtec settlements experienced rapid population growth, becoming true city-states. Disputes among the different city-states were frequent, as indicated by archaeological and historical evidence. Around 900, the Mixtec Empire began spreading southward into the Valley of Oaxaca, and by the fourteenth century, the Mixtec had overshadowed their greatest rivals, the Zapotecs, whose civilization was centered in southern Oaxaca. The Mixtec had a strong influence on the Zapotecs, especially at the Zapotec city of Monte Albán. According to some scholars, Monte Albán controlled the Valley of Oaxaca directly, but the issue is still debated. The largest site in this region of the empire was Yucuñudahui, which comprised a number of ceremonial spaces, residential areas for the elite and commoners, and a ball court.

During the Natividad phase, the centralized city-states of the Mixtec Empire were divided into a number of smaller chiefdoms, or *cacicazgos*. Each of these chiefdoms was comprised of a head town surrounded by subjected villages. The head towns contained administrative and ceremonial buildings, religious monuments, and elite and nonelite residential areas. Their populations ranged from 2,500 to 25,000 inhabitants. *Cacicazgos* established short-term alliances with each other for political and military

purposes. In the late fifteenth century C.E., the Aztecs attempted to conquer Oaxaca. Some Mixtec and Zapotec chiefdoms allied with each other and succeeded in resisting the Aztec invasion. When the Spaniards arrived in the area, in the 1520s, the most important Mixtec chiefdom was the *cacicazgo* of Tilantongo, located in the Mixteca Alta.

See also: AZTEC EMPIRE; SOUTH AMERICAN MONARCHIES; ZAPOTEC EMPIRE.

MOCHE KINGDOM (ca. 100–600 C.E.)

A pre-Columbian civilization of Peru that flourished prior to the rise of the Incas and, with the Nazca civilization, constituted the Huari (Wari) culture.

The Moche were a people who arose to dominate the portion of Peru surrounding the modern city of Trujillo between 100 and 600. As the Moche never developed a writing system and had been dispersed and had declined long before the arrival of the Spanish, there is little documented information available. All that can be known about their society and culture must be deduced from the archaeological record they left behind.

Among the most informative sources available to scholars about the Moche are their massive pyramids, which appear to have served as both tombs and ritual centers. The most significant pyramid found to date is located in Sipan, where the mummified remains of a man, dubbed "Lord of Sipan" by archaeologists, were recovered in 1987. The identity of the mummy, and verification as to whether or not he was a ruler, have yet to be determined.

What can be postulated is that the Moche had a highly stratified society, with ranks that included warriors, priests, merchants and artisans, and farmers. They were technologically well-developed, as can be inferred from the impressive system of dams and aqueducts that they left behind. The distribution of Moche ceramics and textiles throughout the region suggests that they were the dominant culture, and it is presumed that they backed up their economic and cultural ascendancy with military strength.

The latter years of the Moche kingdom seem to have been marked by no major disasters. Nonetheless, the Moche ceremonial centers seem to have been abruptly abandoned sometime in the late 500s. The timing of this event coincides with the rise of the

The pre-Columbian Moche civilization flourished in Peru from the first to seventh centuries C.E. The Moche built massive pyramids, such as the Pyramid of the Moon, which served as both tombs and ritual centers where priests sometimes performed human sacrifices.

militaristic Tiahuanacans around Lake Titicaca, but there is no evidence that Moche settlements were attacked or damaged by war. This pattern of sudden cultural flourishing and equally abrupt dissolution is a familiar one in many parts of Mesoamerica and South America.

In cultures for which more plentiful historical data exist, this pattern has been attributed to the style of administration practiced by many of the kingdoms and empires of the region. It appears that although the dominant cultures expended much of their resources on wars of conquest, they devoted little or none to creating any integrating structure to bind their conquered territories to themselves. Thus, when their armies moved on to other conquests, there was little to hold the subject peoples to the empire except fear of retribution should they revolt.

Should the ruling power show signs of weakness, the subordinate peoples could, and presumably did, "vote with their feet" by migrating out of the area. Then, lacking a sufficient tribute-paying base of agricultural communities to support the ceremonial and urban centers, the dominant culture itself was vulnerable to conquest by an upstart power.

Although it is unknown whether this is what occurred with the Moche, it is known that their disappearance as a regional power occurred with great rapidity. Within a very short time their ceremonial centers were appropriated by peoples associated with Tiahuanaco, and eventually their lands became a part of the great Incan Empire.

See also: HUARI EMPIRE; INCAN EMPIRE; NAZCA KINGDOM; SOUTH AMERICAN MONARCHIES.

MOCTEZUMA II (ca. 1480–1520 C.E.)

Last emperor (r. 1502–1520) of the Aztecs, who was overthrown by the Spanish conquistadors led by Hernando Cortés.

Moctezuma II (also called Montezuma) was born Moctezuma Xocoyotl ("the youngest") around 1480. He was the youngest son of the reigning Aztec emperor, Axacayatl (r. 1460–1481). Because leadership among the Aztecs was not hereditary, there was no absolute certainty that the boy would one day become emperor, particularly as he was not the ruler's eldest son. He was of noble birth, however, and was educated according to his class. He received instruction in the arts, sciences, and humanities of his time. He was also trained in the skills of the warrior, for the Aztecs were a very militaristic people.

Only a year or so after Moctezuma's birth, his imperial father died and was succeeded by two uncles, Tizoc (r. 1481–1486) and Ahuitzotl (r. 1486–1502). During his rule, Ahuitzotl made a name for himself by leading incessant campaigns against neighboring peoples, effectively doubling the territory held by the Aztecs by the time his reign ended. The principal reason for these wars appears to have been to take captives, for Ahuitzotl was deeply committed to offering sacrifices to the Aztec gods, and the preferred sacrificial victims were captured war slaves. Ahuitzotl sacrificed huge numbers of people: as many as 20,000 victims were killed in a single ritual event celebrating the end of a war.

When Ahuitzotl died in 1502, Moctezuma was twenty-two years old and living the quiet life of a religious scholar. His erudition, as well as his skill in battle, brought him to the attention of the council of nobles who convened to choose a new ruler, and they named him to the throne. His profound interest in theology, however, would soon prove to be the undoing of his rule and of his entire people.

At first, Moctezuma appeared to fulfill all the expectations of his councillors. At war, he was as fierce as any of his predecessors, and he personally led his armies to victory in more than forty campaigns. His commitment to ritual earned him the approval of the priesthood, and his administrative skills led to the building of new temples, the refurbishment of old ones, and the creation of an extraordinary aqueduct system that opened up new expanses of cropland to supply the capital city of Tenochtitlan. At the same time, however, he displayed a cruel streak, quick to impose brutal punishment upon those who displeased him, and subject peoples within his empire soon began to rise in minor rebellions against his rule.

These rebellions need not have proved fatal to Moctezuma's rule, however. After all, he controlled a supremely powerful army and was but one of a long line of fierce emperors. What brought him down in the end were his religious beliefs, as well as his inability to understand the motives and tactics of a newcomer to his lands: the Spanish conquistador, Hernando Cortés.

When Cortés sailed his fleet into the port of Veracruz on the Caribbean coast in 1519, he sent emissaries to the Aztec ruler at Tenochtitlan. Moctezuma, steeped in the mythology of Aztec religion, knew the legend of the great god Quetzalcoatl, who had promised to return to the Aztecs in the guise of a pale-skinned, bearded man. Now there was a visitor who fitted the description, and he sought a royal audience. Not all of Moctezuma's advisers were convinced that this newcomer was indeed the incarnation of a god, however. In the end, caution prevailed, and rather than welcome the Spaniards into Tenoctitlan, Moctezuma sent a huge offering of goods and gold to Cortés, hoping to induce him to leave the region.

Cortés appreciated the gift but had no intention of leaving. He ordered his fleet to be burned in the harbor to ensure that his forces could not leave, and he prepared to wait until Moctezuma agreed to see him. The Aztec emperor finally relented, permitting Cortés and a party of soldiers to enter Tenochtitlan. The Spaniards were awed to see a city greater in size and population than any in Europe at that time. Realizing that a direct attack against so many would be doomed to failure, Cortés instead persuaded Moctezuma to allow a small party of Spaniards into the palace, where he and his men quickly took the emperor hostage.

Moctezuma quickly crumbled, converted to Christianity, and swore allegiance to Spain—all in an effort to preserve his life. The strategy seemed to work at first, and he was allowed to serve as a puppet ruler for awhile. However, during a time when Cortés was absent from Tenochtitlan, a conflict arose between the Aztecs and the Spanish, leading to the slaughter of thousands of Aztecs. The people stormed the palace demanding that the Spanish surrender, but the soldiers sent Moctezuma out to try to calm the mob. Instead of respect, he was met with catcalls, jeers, and thrown rocks, one of which struck him and knocked him down. He died two weeks later. The specific cause of his death is unknown. Moctezuma may have died as a result of this injury, or he might have been killed by the Spanish, who may have decided that he was no longer useful to them.

See also: AZTEC EMPIRE; SOUTH AMERICAN MONARCHIES.

FURTHER READING

Thomas, Hugh. *Conquest: Moctezuma, Cortes, and the Fall of Old Mexico.* New York: Simon & Schuster, 1993.

MON KINGDOM

Powerful kingdom in Myanmar (Burma) also known as *Hanthawaddy Kingdom* (Kingdom of the Mon People).

The Mon moved south from western China to southern Thailand's Chao Phraya River basin around the sixth century C.E. Their first kingdoms were connected to China and to the ancient Cambodian kingdom of Funan. The Khmer civilization also had a powerful influence on them.

During the following centuries, the Mon migrated west to southern Myanmar's Irrawaddy River Delta and took for their state religion the Theravada Buddhism practiced in Ceylon (Sri Lanka) and southern India. They also acquired India's Pali script. They put down roots in southern and southeastern Myanmar by 825, introducing the country to both Buddhism and writing. The Mon were experts in agriculture as well. They were skilled in irrigation and used the river basins to create fruitful paddy fields.

The Mon kingdom was conquered by the Pagan kingdom in 1057. It regained its independence and its territory in Martaban and Pegu under King Wareru, a son-in-law of Rama Kamheng, after the Pagan decline in 1287. During the following 200 years, there was constant fighting between the Mon and the Burmans; but the Mon remained independent until they were finally dominated by Toungoo Myanmar in 1539. The height of the Mon kingdom during those years was under King Thammachedi (Dammazedi) (r. 1472–1492).

In the mid-eighteenth century, the Mon rose up again and set up their kingdom at Pegu, but it lasted only about ten years. The Burmans defeated the Mon in 1757, when their ruler, Alaungpaya, demolished Pegu and killed tens of thousands of Mon, including a large number of children, pregnant women, and scholarly priests. The Burmans murdered more than three thousand priests at Pegu and thousands of others in the countryside, and Burman priests occupied their monasteries. The Burmans also destroyed much of the Mon literature, which had been written on palm leaves, and they prohibited use of the Mon language. The Mon were totally oppressed, and their property and belongings were ruined.

The Mon never became independent again. Some of them escaped and took refuge in Siam (Thailand), and there are still some Mon in southeastern Myanmar. They continue to be skilled in agriculture, mainly cultivating rice and fish. They build and live in wood-framed, thatch-roofed houses on piles. The women craft pottery and bamboo-woven mats and cloth. Mon villages have granaries, cattle, pagodas, and monasteries that also serve as schools. Although the Mon believe in spirits, especially the house spirit, they remain devoted Buddhists.

See also: ALAUNGPAYA DYNASTY; PAGAN KINGDOM; RAMA KHAMHENG.

FURTHER READING

Tarling, Nicholas, ed. *The Cambridge History of Southeast Asia: Volume 2, Part 1, From c. 1800 to the 1930s.* New York: Cambridge University Press, 2000.

MONARCHS, AGES OF

Many monarchs have come to their positions as children. A child king or queen could have been the next in the line of succession, and thus the rightful heir. In some cases, a ruler has been a person of royal blood chosen by the powers around the throne specifically because their youth made them able to be controlled by the regents who would rule on their behalf until maturity. Often regents have been relatives. Although some were power-hungry and promoted their own agendas, many were benevolent advisers to the young rulers.

DANGERS TO YOUNG MONARCHS

Being in line for the throne at a very young age has often been a dangerous position. Edward V of England (r. 1483), who should have inherited the Crown from his father, Edward IV (r. 1461–1483), vanished in the Tower of London in 1483 at the age of twelve, along with his ten-year-old brother—perhaps murdered at the behest of his uncle, who became King Richard III (r. 1483–1485). King Rattha (Ratsada) of Thailand (r. 1534) was only five when he inherited the throne from his father, King Bòromoraja IV (r. 1529–1534), but he only lasted on the throne for five months before he was executed by his cousin, who became King Chairacha (P'rajai) (r. 1534–1547).

Ivan VI (r. 1740–1741) became tsar of Russia when he was just two months old, and he ruled for one month with his mother as regent. He was overthrown by a cousin, Elizaveta Petrovna, the daughter of Peter the Great (r. 1682–1725), whose claim to the throne was probably better than that of Ivan. Ivan and his mother were exiled and imprisoned. Ivan died at age twenty-four in a botched rescue attempt, having spent almost his whole life a prisoner.

YOUNG MONARCHS WHO NEVER OUTGREW THEIR REGENTS

Charles IX of France (r. 1560–1574) was ten years old when he inherited the throne in 1560. His formidable mother, Queen Catherine de Medici, was regent until he was declared an adult at age thirteen, and she continued to exert real power throughout Charles's reign. Catherine is thought to have been the instigator behind the major event of Charles's reign, the tragic St. Bartholomew's Day Massacre of Protestants by Catholics in August 1572.

King Edward VI of England (r. 1546–1553) inherited his kingdom from his father, Henry VIII (r. 1509–1547), when he was nine years old. His uncle, Edward Seymour, served as regent, and although Seymour truly loved Edward, he could not resist using his power to further his own favorite cause: Protestantism. Edward was a gentle, studious, and deeply religious boy, who died of tuberculosis at age sixteen. Upon his death he was succeeded on the throne by his Catholic half-sister, Mary I (r. 1553–1558), which led to a period of extreme religious strife in England.

YOUNG MONARCHS WHO WENT ON TO RULE SUCCESSFULLY

The Holy Roman emperor Otto III (r. 983–1002) was only three years old when his father, Otto II (r. 973–983), died in 983. His mother, Theophano, became regent, and after Theophano died in 991, his grandmother, Adelheid, the widow of Otto I (r. 936–973), took over as regent until 994. On his fourteenth birthday, Otto told his grandmother that he was an adult and no longer wished to be ruled by a woman. Adelheid retired to a convent, where she lived so virtuously that 100 years after her death she was named a saint.

Louis XIV (r. 1643–1715) was not quite five years old when his father died and he came to the throne of France. His mother, Anne of Austria, served as regent until 1651, when Louis, at the age of fourteen, was considered to be an adult. However, the real power all along was in the hands of Cardinal Mazarin, the prime minister. Hatred of Cardinal Mazarin among the people of Paris and some of the nobility led to an uprising against the Crown in 1648. During the unsettled years of civil war that followed, Louis suffered danger and privation. Mazarin succeeded in putting down the rebellion in 1653, and Louis determined never to let anything like that happen again. When Mazarin died in 1661, the twenty-three-year-old Louis announced to his astonished ministers that he intended to take full responsibility for governing the country. He became the "Sun-King," one of the most absolute monarchs in history, famous for his statement "L'état, c'est moi"—"I am the state."

Pedro II (r. 1831–1889) became emperor of Brazil at age five after the abdication and flight to Portugal of his father, Pedro I (r. 1822–1831). His mother, Dona Leopoldina, had already died. A committee of three regents was chosen to govern until Pedro's eighteenth birthday. Pedro passed a lonely childhood, choosing as a father figure and friend a former stable groom, an Englishman named Richard Shelley. Pedro loved to study and developed a liberal outlook. As emperor, he sought to modernize his country, promote education, and abolish slavery (this last was done in stages and was achieved by 1888). His reforms alienated the conservative elements of his country but did not seem radical enough for the liberals. Eventually, he was forced to abdicate in favor of a republican form of government, and his whole family was forced into exile. But Pedro is considered to have made great strides in preparing Brazil to be a democratic country.

See also: ABDICATION, ROYAL; ACCESSION AND CROWNING OF KINGS; DEACCESSION; DETHRONEMENT; IN-

MONARCHY

A political system or form of government that is headed by a ruler who has a hereditary tenure of authority. The ruler, or monarch, of a monarchy may be chosen or elected, or may have achieved rule through conquest or heredity. Monarchies are generally one of two types: absolute monarchy and limited monarchy.

In an absolute monarchy, the temporal rights of a monarch may be unlimited. In addition, absolute monarchs frequently derive the legitimacy of their powers directly from a god—either explicitly or implicitly. This idea gave rise to the notion of "the divine right of kings."

No monarchy is totally absolute; that is, there is almost always some means of appealing or limiting any ruler's decisions. Nevertheless, it is reasonable to call rulers absolute when they summarily execute their own citizens without recourse to appeal or when they engage their domains in unpopular wars.

Many of the satraps (governors) and monarchs who ruled the various countries of the ancient Near East during the first and second millennia B.C.E. were absolute monarchs. One such ruler was King Mithradates the Great (r. 120–64 B.C.E.) of Pontus in Asia Minor (present-day Turkey).

Limited or constitutional monarchies constrain the rights and powers of their rulers by subjecting their decisions to the rulings of a council or legislature. Early examples of limited monarchies may be found throughout Europe within the last millennia. A classic example is the British monarchy of King John of England (r. 1199–1216), whose royal powers were limited by the Magna Carta (1215)—an agreement imposed upon him by the powerful barons of England.

Modern constitutional monarchies, such as in Great Britain and Sweden, retain their monarchs in a purely symbolic capacity. Queen Elizabeth II (r. 1952–present), for example, has virtually no power other than as the symbolic head of state.

See also: BODIES, POLITIC AND NATURAL; DIVINE RIGHT; DUAL MONARCHIES; REALMS, TYPES OF; RELIGIOUS DUTIES AND POWER.

MONARCHY FORMATION, MYTHS OF

Legendary stories concerning the origin of a kingdom or its ruler that generally play a role in establishing lineage and legitimacy.

Myths concerning the foundation of many kingdoms have supported the legitimacy of those realms by purporting that the rulers were descendants and representatives of a god or gods. Disloyalty to the ruler was thus seen as a sign of disrespect for the gods. Attributing divinity to a monarch sanctioned the rule and increased the loyalty of the people. Belief in the ruler's divinity also entailed the notion that the well-being of the monarch ensured the prosperity of the kingdom.

Great cities are generally the centers of great power. As a result, myths of the foundation of cities and of the formation of monarchies are often tied together. In one myth about the founding of ancient Rome, for example, Romulus and Remus, sons of the god Mars and a vestal virgin, were suckled by a she-wolf and later taken in by a shepherd and his wife. When they were young men, Romulus killed his brother in an argument and became the first of seven kings of the city of Rome. When Romulus died, he was said to have become a god. In Virgil's account of Rome's founding, the Trojan warrior Aeneas fled the city of Troy when it was destroyed by the Greeks, and he eventually founded and became king of Rome.

The Incas had various versions of the myth of their creation. Each, however, seems to claim that Manco Capac, the first human, was the son of the sun. Each subsequent human was then also a descendant of the sun, and the work of uniting the various Andean tribes was thus seen as a divine mission.

On the other side of the world, the Japanese foundation myth shares the belief that direct descendants of the sun goddess Amaterasu established the royal house of Japan. The present Japanese emperor, Akihito (r. 1989–present), is the one hundred twenty-fifth ruler in a direct line from the first emperor Jimmu (r. ca. 660?–581? B.C.E.).

The Korean foundation myth, asserting that the part-human, part-divine being Tangun founded the monarchy, dates back more than four thousand years. According to one version, Tangun lived more than nineteen hundred years and then became the mountain god. However, North Korea boasts that the burial chamber at Mount Daebaik is that of Tangun.

Belief in the divine right of kings in Christian and Hebrew monarchies was based on the description of kings as God's anointed in the Hebrew Bible. Anointing the king has been an important part of Western coronation ceremonies for centuries. In France, for example, the coronation ritual is rooted in a myth surrounding Clovis (r. 481–511), an early Frankish king and the founder of the Merovingian dynasty. According to tradition, the appearance of a dove from heaven, bearing oil for Clovis's anointing, was a sign of divine will.

The Irish foundation myth combines classical, pagan, and Christian beliefs. The Firbolgs, who, according to legend had escaped slavery in Greece by taking over their masters' ships, first inhabited the island. Then the people of the goddess Danu (known as the Tuatha De Danaan), a northern race of builders and craftsmen, conquered them. Later, the sons of Mil, who were descendants of Noah, unseated the Tuatha De Danaan and established the Milesian race on the island.

Throughout history, monarchs have found it expedient to disseminate the idea that, if they did not represent a god or goddess in human form, at least their royal authority was god-given. In addition to divine sanction, possession of historic emblems of kingship could confer the sense of legitimacy to a ruler. Edward I of England (r. 1272–1307), for example, removed the ancient Stone of Scone from Scotland as a symbol of his authority over that kingdom. According to legend, the Hebrew patriarch Jacob used the stone at ancient Bethel in Palestine, and later, Irish kings used it before it was brought to Scotland.

See also: Accession and Crowning of Kings; Descent, Royal; Divine Right; Divinity of Kings; Earth and Sky, Separation of; Enthronement, Rites of; Heavens and Kingship; Kingly Body; Myth and Folklore; Sacred Kingships.

Mongkut (Rama IV)

(1804–1868 c.e.)

King of Siam (r. 1851–1868), known for welcoming Western-style reforms and progress into his country. Called King Phrachomklao in Siam (modern-day Thailand), Mongkut (also known as Rama IV) was the model for the king in the play *The King and I,* which was based on memoirs published by a court governess and English teacher, Anna Leonowens.

The forty-third child of King Rama II (r. 1809–1824), Mongkut was born to a queen and was thus in line for the throne. He was only twenty when his father died in 1824, however, and he was passed over in favor of his older and more experienced half-brother Chetsadabodin, who reigned as King Phranangklao (Rama III) (r. 1824–1851).

Not needed to rule, Mongkut decided to live as a Buddhist monk. He remained in a religious order for twenty-six years, during which he totally embraced the early Buddhist traditions and gained a thorough personal knowledge of his country and its people. In his travels as a monk, Mongkut also met many foreigners and learned much about the outside world, especially in the fields of science and technology.

Mongkut became a scholar and also abbot of a monastery in Bangkok, which he turned into a center for intellectual debate. The center eventually attracted American and French Christian missionaries and people who had an interest in learning Western languages and science. Mongkut also developed a reformed Buddhism that eventually became the Thammayut order, which to this day is the intellectual core of Thai Buddhism.

Mongkut's enthusiasm for the West was shared by influential friends, including many important princes and nobles. These friends helped influence the choice of Mongkut as successor to the throne upon the death of his brother, Rama III, in 1851.

As king, Mongkut retained his human warmth and deep religious beliefs, while remaining aware of progress in the world outside his country. He introduced and promoted various Western innovations and guided his kingdom capably while warding off French and English territorial aspirations. Indeed, he was able to maintain his country's independence, making it the only nation in Southeast Asia that never fell under Western domination.

Mongkut died of malaria on his sixty-fourth birthday in 1868. He contracted the disease while watching a solar eclipse (which he had predicted himself) from a mosquito-infested viewing area. Upon Mongkut's death, the throne passed to his son Chulalongkorn, who became King Rama V (r. 1868–1910).

See also: Chulalongkorn; Siam, Kingdoms of; Southeast Asian Kingdoms.

MONGOL DYNASTY. *See* YUAN

DYNASTY

MONGOL EMPIRE (1206–1481 C.E.)

Great empire of Asia that, at its peak, was the largest land empire in history. At one time or another, the territory controlled by the Mongols included Armenia, Turkestan, Persia (present-day Iran), China, Mongolia, Korea, parts of Russia, and Southeast Asia. Although the Mongols are remembered chiefly for the savagery of their conquests, they fostered important cross-cultural exchanges between East and West.

The traditional Mongol lifestyle was (and remains) nomadic. Skilled horsemen, the Mongols spent their lives constantly on the move, searching the vast Central Asian steppes for new grazing pasture for their herds of horses, sheep, goats, and cattle. Mongol society was organized into families, clans, and tribes. Tribes became known by the names of their most important clans. Intertribal skirmishes were common, and much of the Mongol conception of manhood was based on soldiering skills, so when ambitious men took the initiative to unite tribes, they gained control of considerable military force.

EARLY DEVELOPMENT

The first Mongol tribal confederations took place under the Xiaong-Nu tribe, which dominated much of Central Asia from about 300 B.C.E. to 48 C.E. The Xiaong-Nu launched numerous attacks against China in the first and second centuries B.C.E. and first century C.E., posing a serious threat to that relatively young state. Mongol incursions into Chinese territory provided the impetus for the construction of the Great Wall of China.

After the Chinese Han emperor, Kuang Wu Ti (Guang Wudi) (r. 25–57), instituted a particularly aggressive diplomatic and military policy against the Xiaong-Nu, the confederation gradually splintered, and by the fifth century, the Mongol confederation had completely disintegrated. Evidence suggests, however, that a branch of the Xiaong-Nu tribe may have migrated westward and become the ancestors of the European Turks.

After the disintegration of the confederation, the Mongols remained largely unfederated for more than six centuries, until the rise of a Mongol tribe, the Khitan, who established control over much of Manchuria and parts of northern China. There, the Khitans established the Liao dynasty (907–1125) and allied themselves with another tribal confederacy known as "All the Mongols." The Liao dynasty fell in 1125 to the Juchen, who were aristocratic successors to the Khitans.

GENGHIS KHAN AND HIS SONS

In the late twelfth and early thirteenth centuries, a Mongol leader named Temuchin (Temujin), later known as Genghis Khan (r. 1206–1227), managed, despite overwhelming odds and primarily on the strength of personal charisma, to gain control of the "All the Mongols" League. In 1206 Temuchin had himself named *khan* ("lord" or "prince") of all the Mongol tribes of the Asian steppes, decimating the power of the Tatars and the Juchens in the process. Genghis left no aristocratic strongholds to provide him with competition. Once named *khan,* he placed members of his family in control of thousands of families and huge swaths of land, replacing the old clan and tribal structure of the Mongols with a system of feudalism.

Having created a stable political structure at home, Genghis was free to lead his Mongol armies, for the first time, out of the confines of the steppe. Between 1207 and 1227, Genghis extended the boundaries of his growing empire from Beijing in the east to the Caspian Sea in the west, adapting his tactics to fit the situation and adopting foreign ideas whenever they suited his plans. His early conquests seem to have been undertaken primarily for plunder. After a bloody war with the Muslim state of Khwarezm in Central Asia in 1219, the Mongols acquired their reputation for needless savagery.

When Genghis Khan died in a battle against the northwestern Chinese border state of Hsi Hsia in 1227, the empire was split, as he had directed, among his four sons, although the third son, Ogodei, was considered chief among them and received the title "Great Khan." Genghis's son Jochi had died before his father, so the western part of the empire went to Jochi's son, Batu (r. 1227–1255). Tolui (r. 1227–1233) received the Mongol homeland in the eastern part of the empire, while Chagatai (r. 1227–1242) was given control of the south.

During the reign of Ogodei (r. 1227–1241), the

Mongol empire held together and even expanded its territory. In Tolui's region, Mongol armies made advances deep into China. In the west, Jochi's son and successor, Batu (r. 1227–1255), established the Golden Horde khanate, a Mongol state that comprised most of Russia.

After Ogodei's death in 1241, however, the empire descended into a period of interregional warfare. Tolui's son, Mongke (r. 1251–1259), seized power in 1251 and ruled China and the eastern part of the empire until his death in 1259, at which point the khanate was taken over by his brother, Kublai Khan, the empire's next great ruler.

KUBLAI KHAN AND TAMERLANE

Unlike his predecessors, Kublai (r. 1260–1294) was a great administrator as well as a soldier. After defeating the Sung (Song) dynasty of China, he established the Yuan (Mongol) dynasty, which ruled China until 1368. Under Kublai's rule, the Mongols encouraged foreign trade and scholarship. It was to his royal court that the Venetian explorer and tradesman, Marco Polo, traveled in the thirteenth century,

opening a trade route from east to west that likely contributed to the European discovery of the Chinese inventions of gunpowder and the compass.

Kublai ruled the Mongol Empire primarily from China, and even during his reign, control of the further reaches of the empire was largely nominal. The Mongols, unaccustomed to dealing with government bureaucracy, let the Yuan dynasty be administered primarily by Chinese civil servants. This policy led eventually to the loss of China to the Ming dynasty in 1368.

After the fall of the Yuan dynasty, the Mongol Empire underwent a brief revival under Timur Leng, or Tamerlane (r. 1370–1405), a member of an Islamic Mongol tribe in the Central Asian region of the empire that had once been ruled by Genghis's son, Chagatai. Tamerlane was responsible for both the destruction of Islamic centers, including Baghdad and Damascus, and the construction of the magnificent Mongol capital of Samarkand, to which he deported foreign artists before reducing their home cities to bloody rubble. Under his rule, the Mongol Empire reached its largest extent, stretching from

THE MONGOL EMPIRE, LATE 13TH CENTURY C.E.

Mongolia in the east to the Mediterranean Sea in the west.

Tamerlane established the Timurid dynasty, which survived for a century after his death. However, after Tamerlane died in 1405, the Mongolian Empire began disintegrating once more without a single powerful leader to unite it. In the sixteenth century, as the Timurid dynasty was ending, one of Tamerlane's descendants, Babur (r. 1526–1530), moved south and established the Muslim Mughal dynasty and empire in India. By this time, however, the traditional nomadic Mongol people had, by and large, retreated from the world stage, returning to the arid steppes of their homeland.

See also: GENGHIS KHAN; GOLDEN HORDE KHANATE; KUBLAI KHAN; LIAO DYNASTY; MING DYNASTY; SUNG (SONG) DYNASTY; TAMERLANE (TIMUR LENG); YUAN DYNASTY.

FURTHER READING
Morgan, David. *The Mongols.* Oxford: Basil Blackwell, 1986.

MONIVONG, KING (d. 1941 C.E.)

Cambodian king (r. 1927–1941) who ruled during the French colonial period. During his reign, the French encouraged a large influx of Vietnamese immigration into Cambodia.

The son of King Sisowath (r. 1904–1927) of Cambodia, Monivong took the throne after his father's death in 1927. French colonial authorities in Indochina played a significant role in choosing Monivong to succeed as king, and he remained largely subservient to the French throughout his rule.

During Monivong's reign, Cambodian nationalism began to emerge, as the population of the country became increasingly educated. Nationalists favored greater autonomy from France and less Vietnamese influence as well. In the 1930s, Cambodian students petitioned the king, complaining of favoritism shown to Vietnamese students in the elite school, the Lycée Sisowath, in Phnom Penh, the capital. In 1936, nationalists began publishing *Nagara Vatta* ("Angkor Wat"), Cambodia's first Khmer-language newspaper. Its editorials frequently criticized French colonial policies, but its greatest wrath was directed against the Vietnamese because of the past exploitation of

Cambodia and current control of most of the nation's civil service and professional positions.

King Monivong died in 1941 and was succeeded on the throne by his nineteen-year-old grandson, Prince Norodom Sihanouk (r. 1941–1955; 1993–2004). It is believed that the French chose Prince Norodom rather than Monivong's son, Prince Monireth, because the nineteen-year-old Norodom was younger and more supportive of French interests.

See also: CAMBODIAN KINGDOMS; NORODOM SIHANOUK.

MONOPOLIES, ROYAL

Type of economic organization that gives one person or group sole control of an industry, a product, an institution, or even an idea.

Throughout history, most of the world's monarchs enjoyed the legal prerogative to create monopolies of all sorts. These were usually instituted to promote a royal program or to help the monarch control the populace and maintain power. Some monopolistic arrangements gave the ruler control over certain institutions or functions of government. Others established systems of censorship, giving the Crown control over intellectual culture. More often, however, monarchs created economic monopolies to establish or protect industries and to increase revenues for the state.

MONOPOLY AS A FUNCTION OF GOVERNMENT

Most monarchies had monopolies as one of the basic functions of government. For example, only the Crown could issue currency in most cases, and frequently the monarch alone was the ultimate source of justice. Monarchs controlled the royal court system, appointed royal judges and officials, and were usually the court of last resort in appeals cases. This not only served as a source of royal power, but also allowed monarchs to be the final arbiters of what was deemed legal or illegal in their kingdoms.

Some monarchs used intellectual monopolies to control the ideas that would influence their subjects. In the pre-industrial era, European rulers often employed royal censors, who read every new book published and banned those critical of the monarch, royal programs or policies, or the official state religion. The Manchu emperors of China actually dictated what events, information, and ideas could appear in the histories of the empire. Only those works that the emperor himself had edited were considered authentic.

Most rulers had one official religion. Those who adhered to other beliefs were persecuted. Only those who followed the official state religion could attain status or rank in society. For example, in the sixteenth and seventeenth centuries C.E., the rulers of the Ottoman Empire filled their bureaucracies with men who shared their Muslim belief. Intellectual monopolies such as this, or over ideas, increased the emperor's power and prestige.

ECONOMIC MONOPOLIES

More often, monarchs created economic monopolies, and it is these institutions that are most often associated with the word "monopoly." Industrial monopolies were frequently used to establish a new industry where none had existed before or to establish trade in a new market. In a similar way, European monarchs frequently gave exclusive rights for the establishment of new manufactures in their territories to a single artisan or firm. Rulers hoped that these manufactures would create new domestic industries to stimulate economic growth or more often to supplant imported foreign products.

In the seventeenth century, for example, French minister and statesman Jean Baptiste Colbert instituted a scheme to replace most of the fashionable Italian laces that were currently popular in French clothing with similar products created in France. He imported Italian artisans, granted them the exclusive right to manufacture and sell laces for a fixed period, and gave them exemptions from certain taxes. Moreover, the king, Louis XIV (r. 1643–1715), gave these artisans the prestige of being a "royal manufacture"—that is, the sole supplier of lace to the royal family and court. A similar prestigious award still exists in Great Britain, where suppliers of products to the royal family receive a "royal warrant" to display on their products.

FOSTERING TRADE AND COLONIZATION

Royal monopolies were also used to open new markets for trade and to colonize new territories. In the seventeenth century, the Crown granted the French West India Company, a private trading company, the exclusive right to conduct trade with the French West Indies. Other traders were not permitted to do business with the French-controlled islands, and the company was exempted from import duties on goods brought back to France.

Similarly, the English East India Company, which operated from the early 1600s to late 1800s, had a royal monopoly on British trade with the East Indies, including the right to import tea to the American colonies. This monopoly, and the import tax associated with it, contributed to the disaffection of the American colonists, leading to the "Boston Tea Party" and, ultimately, to the American Revolution.

The English and French Crowns also issued land-grant monopolies to certain trading and joint-stock companies for the purpose of colonizing North America. William Penn held one such grant for the colony of Pennsylvania, giving him the exclusive right to distribute and sell land there.

GENERATING REVENUE

Monopolies on industry and trade were issued primarily to generate revenue for the Crown. In such cases, the monarch received a share of the profits in return for the exclusive right to harvest or manufacture the product and sell it. For example, Chinese emperors issued licenses to suppliers of ginseng, while the rulers of the Ottoman Empire established an opium monopoly to help fund their military efforts against the Greeks in the nineteenth century.

In the sixteenth century, the Spanish Crown gave a tobacco monopoly in their South American colonies to only a few companies in return for the tax revenues.

Although historians have debated whether or not economic monopolies were truly successful in establishing new industries, it is clear that they generated revenue for the state. Monopolies were an important tool for the world's royal families to increase their own wealth as well as to forward economic, political, and intellectual programs.

See also: COMMERCE AND KINGSHIP; PATENT LETTERS, ROYAL; TAXATION.

MONTENEGRO KINGDOM

(1878–1918 C.E.)

Small kingdom in the Balkan region of Europe that began as a principality and did not establish a kingship until the early twentieth century. The history of Montenegro is intricately entwined with that of the kingdom of Serbia.

In the 1300s, the region of Montenegro was the independent principality of Zeta and was part of the Serbian Empire. When the Ottoman Turks defeated Serbia at the battle of Kosovo in 1389, Montenegro became a haven for Serbian nobles fleeing Turkish rule. Although the Ottomans did not recognize Montenegro's independence, the principality managed to maintain its autonomy and, unlike other Balkan states, did not become a Turkish tributary. However, the Montenegran princes ruled only a small area, and in 1459, it finally fell under Ottoman control.

Between 1515 and 1851, Montenegro was ruled by a series of *vladikas*, or priest-bishops, who were assisted by civil governors. The episcopal succession was made hereditary under Danilo I (r. 1696–1735), who founded the Petrovich-Niegosh dynasty. Because the bishops could not marry, the office passed from uncle to nephew rather than from father to son. During Danilo's rule, Montenegro established political ties with Russia, securing an alliance against the Ottomans, who still threatened the principality. From that time forward, the Russian tsars were considered the spiritual overlords of the vladikas.

Prince Peter I (r. 1781–1830), the grandnephew of Danilo I, instituted a number of reforms in Montenegro in an attempt to end the traditional blood feuds and lawlessness that had plagued the country. Also during Peter's reign, in 1799, the Ottoman sultan, Selim III (r. 1789–1907), recognized Montenegran independence.

In 1852, under the rule of Prince Danilo II (r. 1851–1860), Montenegro was secularized, as Danilo transferred the traditional ecclesiastical duties of the prince to an archbishop. Danilo also defeated the Ottomans at the battles of Ostrong (1853) and Grahovo (1858), confirming the principality's independence. Assassinated in 1860, Danilo II was succeeded by his nephew, Nicholas I (r. 1860–1921).

During the reign of Prince Nicolas I, the major powers of Europe met in 1878 to reconsider the terms of an agreement made with the Ottoman Empire. The Congress of Berlin recognized Montenegro as an independent state under Nicolas I, who proclaimed himself king in 1910, thus officially changing the country to a kingdom. The Congress of Berlin also granted Montenegro additional territory in the region, including a narrow outlet to the Adriatic Sea.

During World War I, Montenegro's armies joined forces with Britain, France, and the other Allied powers. In 1915, however, Montenegro was defeated by Austria and occupied, forcing Nicolas I and his family to flee to Italy. In the ensuing chaos at the end of the war, King Peter I of Serbia (r. 1903–1921) took advantage of Montenegro's lack of a central political organization to advance his own ambitions, and he annexed the kingdom in 1918.

The Montenegran people, for the most part, opposed the annexation by Serbia and staged the Christmas Uprising on January 7, 1919. This revolt soon turned into a full-scale war between the Serbians and Montenegrans that lasted until 1926. During the revolt, in 1921, Nicolas I was deposed. He was succeeded first by his son, Danilo I (r. 1921), who abdicated soon after taking the throne. He, in turn, was succeeded by his nephew, Michael II (r. 1921–1922). Michael ruled for only a year, after which he resigned his rights as king, ending the Montenegran kingdom.

In the next few decades, Montenegro was unable to regain its independence. However, in 1946, the former kingdom became part of the Republic of Yugoslavia, along with Serbia, Bosnia, Herzegovina, Croatia, and Slovenia. Montenegro remained part of Yugoslavia until that state began to disintegrate in the early 1990s. In 1992, Montenegro and Serbia declared themselves a new Federal Republic of Yugoslavia under President Slobodan Milosevic. But after a period of civil strife in the Balkan region, Montenegro and Serbia formed a loose federation of two republics in 2003.

See also: OTTOMAN EMPIRE; SERBIAN KINGDOM.

FURTHER READING

Stavrianos, Leften Stavros. *The Balkans Since 1453.* New York: New York University Press, 2000.

Temperly, H. W. *History of Serbia.* New York: AMS Press, 1970.

MOREA, DESPOTATE OF

(1349–1460 C.E.)

Autonomous Byzantine principality, or despotate, on the Peloponnesian Peninsula of Greece that was the last bastion of the Byzantine Empire.

The principate of Morea was created in 1349 by John VI Cantacuzenus (r. 1347–1354), the ruler of the Byzantine Empire. He named his younger son Manuel as despot ("lord") of Morea, hoping to prevent further unrest in an empire already weakened by civil war.

In 1354, John VI was forced to abdicate the throne of the Byzantine Empire by John V Palaeologus (r. 1354–1376) of the Palaeologan dynasty, for whom Cantacuzenus had been acting as reigning regent and co-emperor. Despite his father's loss of the throne, Manuel managed to retain control of Morea.

Maintaining control of Morea was no easy matter, however. A significant barrier—the Hexamilion wall—blocked the narrow isthmus that connected the Peloponnesus to the rest of Greece. Yet, Manuel had assumed control over a territory coveted not only by the Byzantine Palaeologi dynasty, but also by the Latins to the west and the Ottoman Turks to the east. Manuel succeeded not only in defending against these threats, but also in laying the foundation for a state that would become the center of late Byzantine culture. He failed only in securing the succession of his heirs; after his death in 1380, the Palaeologi seized the principate of Morea.

By 1393, the Morea was under the control of Theodore I Palaeologus (r. 1393–1407), son of the emperor John V. For strategic reasons, Theodore I chose to accept Turkish sovereignty but continued to rule Morea as an independent state. He arranged a large emigration of settlers from Albania in order to bolster Morea's population and workforce, and perhaps also to weaken and divide the ever restive factions of local Greek nobility.

Theodore I ruled from Mistra, a relatively young city established in 1249 near the site of ancient Sparta. He began a series of building projects in the city, a policy continued by his son and successor, Theodore II Palaeologus. By 1425, Mistra was filled with churches, palaces, and monasteries, and it attracted a vibrant community of artists and scholars. The cultural center of the Byzantine Empire shifted to the city from Constantinople.

The mid-1400s was a period of ascendancy for Morea. By 1430, the principate controlled all of the Peloponnesian Peninsula, except for the harbors of Corone, Nauplia, and Medone, which were ruled by the Republic of Venice. At the same time, however, the Byzantine Empire was crumbling against the advances of the Ottoman Turks. In 1446, the Ottomans destroyed the Hexamilion wall, and the two co-despots, Constantine XI and Thomas, barely escaped back to Mistra. The capital city was spared by a particularly harsh winter that prevented the Ottoman armies from reaching it, but the Morean countryside was ravaged. The Ottomans then turned their attention temporarily to other fronts.

Constantine XI (r. 1448–1453) became the last Byzantine emperor in 1448, when he took the throne upon the death of his brother, John VIII (r. 1425–1448). This left Thomas and another brother, Demetrius, to rule in Morea. Constantine ruled from Constantinople, where he died during the final defense of the city in 1453, when it fell to the Ottoman Turks. In 1460, Thomas and Demetrius, the two remaining despots of Morea, surrendered to the Ottoman sultan, ending this last minor outpost of Byzantine power.

See also: Byzantine Empire; Ottoman Empire; Palaeologan Dynasty.

FURTHER READING

Norwich, John Julius. *Byzantium: The Decline and Fall.* New York: Alfred A. Knopf, 1996.

MORTUARY RITES. *See* Funerals and Mortuary Rites

MOSHOESHOE I (1786–1870 C.E.)

Founder and king (r. 1830–1870) of the Sotho, also called Suto, kingdom of southern Africa.

Moshoeshoe was born in 1786 in the village of Menkhoaneng (in present-day Lesotho) to parents who were descended from chiefly lineages. His father was Mokhachane, a minor chief among the Koena people. His mother was Kholu, daughter of the chief of a neighboring group. He was given the birth name of Lepoqo.

A boy of such a background could aspire to leadership, but Moshoeshoe determined early in life that he wanted more than to follow in his father's footsteps as a minor chief. His ambition was matched by an imperiousness that threatened to derail his dreams. Moshoeshoe was quick to retaliate, often violently, against anyone who offended him. It was only after he overcame his tendency to excessive violence, bowing to the wisdom of trusted advisers, that Moshoeshoe began to amass a significant following.

Having learned to control his temper, Moshoeshoe next learned the importance of forming alliances with neighboring villages and lineages. This, he realized, was best done by marrying the daughters of powerful families, creating ties of kinship that he could call upon when he needed support or assistance. In this way, Moshoeshoe expanded his influence throughout the region. By 1830 he had forged these alliances into a nation, which was called Basotho, and he enthroned himself as king. (The prefix "Ba-" is commonly used in Bantu languages to denote a personal plural. Thus "Basotho" translates to "Sotho people.")

Moshoeshoe's rule coincided with a period of intense colonial activity in southern Africa. The dominant colonial power was Great Britain, but there was pressure from the land-hungry Afrikaaner settlers (of Dutch ancestry) of South Africa as well. This ultimately led to war, as Moshoeshoe attempted to expel European interlopers from his territory.

In 1852, Moshoeshoe managed to defeat a well-equipped invasionary force led by the British, but warfare continued for another fifteen years, as more British settlers arrived and as Afrikaaners continued to move up into the region from the south. Finally, Moshoeshoe petitioned the British for protectorate status for the Basotho kingdom. This was granted in 1868, permitting him to maintain a degree of autonomy for his kingdom and bringing an end to the chronic warfare that plagued his realm.

See also: AFRICAN KINGDOMS.

FURTHER READING

Thompson, Leonard. *Survival in Two Worlds: Moshoeshoe of Lesotho, 1786–1870.* Oxford: Clarendon Press, 1975.

MOSSI KINGDOMS

(1500s C.E.–Present)

A collection of small kingdoms founded in the fifteenth century in what is now Burkina Faso. The Mossi kingdoms survive to this day, although the power of the kings is subordinated to the national government.

The Mossi kingdoms of Burkina Faso (formerly called Upper Volta) originated outside their current territory, which centers on the White Volta River basin. The founders of the kingdom are believed to have been migrants from the Dagomba and Mamprusi kingdoms of northern Ghana. These people, who came to be called the Mossi or Moose, therefore, already possessed a tradition of monarchical government. According to oral tradition, the first Mossi king was Ouedraogo (r. dates unknown), who was said to be the grandson of a Mamprusi king named Nedega (r. dates unknown).

Ouedraogo established his kingdom, named Tenkodogo, in the southern portion of the White Volta River basin, sometime in the 1500s. Sons of the king were sent out to expand the kingdom's territory and ultimately were granted kingdoms of their own among the newly conquered peoples, who were assimilated into the Mossi. In the end, more than twenty such kingdoms were formed, including Tenkodogo, Ouagadougou, Yatenga, and Boussouma.

By the 1600s, the more powerful of the Mossi kingdoms had become highly developed, with great social and political stratification and a growing ministerial class, as well as an elaborate political network. Integration of the outlying villages with the capital in Ouagadougou, for instance, was accomplished by recruitment of rural youths into service or marriage in the king's court.

Such relationships created ties of loyalty that connected the populace with the king. Conversely, the king used his outlying villages as repositories for his political rivals, sending potential troublemakers to govern distant areas and thus diminishing their potential for causing trouble in the capital.

This policy of sending potentially dangerous rivals away from the capital was the general impetus behind the proliferation of Mossi kingdoms. A king with many sons faced threats on two fronts. As his sons matured, one or more might grow weary of waiting for their father to vacate the throne. This, in turn, might inspire in the royal offspring the idea of hastening the king to his death. Even were the king to escape this danger and live out his life in peace, succession to the throne at the time of his death could still be highly contested, if all his sons vied for succession.

To avoid these potentially disastrous outcomes, Mossi kings maintained the practice of carving out portions of territory and granting these lands to political rivals. Better still, the king often charged his sons or rivals with the task of conquering new lands. By promising them the right to rule over newly conquered territory, the king could satisfy all their kingly ambitions, while eliminating the danger of a palace coup or a bloody war of succession.

See also: AFRICAN KINGDOMS; DAGOMBA KINGDOM; MAMPRUSI KINGDOM.

MUGHAL EMPIRE (1526–1857 C.E.)

Empire that began in Kabul (in present-day Afghanistan) during the sixteenth century and eventually controlled most of India.

The Mughal Empire emerged when Babur (r. 1526–1530), the ruler of Kabul, defeated the Lodi sultan in 1526 at the first battle of Panipat and gained control of Delhi. Utilizing his heavily armed, expertly trained army, Babur rapidly conquered the Rajputs at the battle of Ghagra in northwest India, then swept across northern India and seized the states of Bihar and Bengal. These victories established the Mughal Empire as the predominant force in northern India.

INITIAL CHALLENGES

Because Babur's conquests occurred rapidly during a four-year period, the Mughal army was deeply strained. Babur and his son and successor, Humayun (r. 1530–1540), continually faced rebellions during their reigns. The Suri dynasty even deposed Humayun for a fifteen-year period from 1540 to 1555, but he was then restored to the throne and reigned for another year.

When Humayun's son, Akbar (r. 1556–1605), became the Mughal sovereign in 1556, he quashed all internal rebellions and expanded the empire. He initially conquered the remaining portions of northern India; then he captured parts of the Deccan, in central India, including the state of Berar.

After these successes, Akbar developed Mughal government and society. First, he proclaimed the unchecked power of the emperor. The emperor was the military commander, wrote all the laws, and served as the empire's chief justice. Four ministers were appointed to oversee the military, finances, industry, and the judiciary, but these roles were only advisory and the ministers had no actual authority.

MUGHAL EMPIRE

Mughal Dynasty

BABUR*	1526–1530
HUMAYUN	1530–1540

Suri Dynasty

SHIR SHAH SUR	1540–1545
ISLAM SHAH	1545–1553
MUHAMMAD 'ADIL	1553–1555
IBRAHIM III	1555
SIKANDAR III	1555

Mughal Dynasty

HUMAYUN (RESTORED)	1555–1556
AKBAR, THE GREAT*	1556–1605
JAHANGIR*	1605–1627
SHAH JAHAN I*	1627–1658
AURANGZEB*	1658–1707
BAHADUR SHAH I	1707–1712
JAHANDAR SHAH	1712–1713
FARRUKSIYAR	1713–1719
RAFID-UD-DARAJAT	1719
SHAH JAHAN II	1719
MUHAMMAD SHAH	1719–1748
AHMAD SHAH	1748–1754
'ALAMGIR II	1754–1759
SHAH 'ALAM II	1759–1806
AKBAR II	1806–1837
BAHADUR SHAH II	1837–1858

*Indicates a separate alphabetical entry.

MUGHAL GOVERNMENT AND SOCIETY

Akbar recognized the need for an efficient government to manage the sprawling domain. Therefore, he divided the empire into fifteen provinces called *Subas.* Each province was subdivided into districts called *Sarkars,* while these districts were separated into groups of villages called *Parganas.* Each province had two governors. The *Nazim* were officials who controlled local military and administration; the *Dewan* handled tax collections. Within each district, the emperor appointed an individual to serve as justice of the peace. Furthermore, an official called a *Kotwal* was appointed to each major city to supervise local affairs.

All officials answered directly to the emperor. Akbar created the *mansabdars,* a civil service structure with thirty-three levels. Advancement from level to level depended solely upon the emperor's patronage, and Akbar limited his appointments to individuals from his native region. As a salary, the appointees were either given land grants or received a specified portion of the revenue from their province, district, or city. Aware of the threats his predecessors had faced, Akbar also placed spies in each province to monitor the actions of his officials.

Economically, land was the most precious commodity in the Mughal Empire, and it generated the most revenue. Akbar developed an elaborate system that classified land according to its fertility. He then set an average annual production figure for each classification. The government collected one-third of the production figure for each farm even if the farm produced less than the set figure in a given year. Akbar made allowances for conditions such as drought and at times collected one-third of the actual crop.

The monarchy also levied a heavy tax on all exports and imports, exacted heavy tributes from conquered kingdoms, created a poll-tax, and monopolized all of the empire's major industries. The Mughal emperor controlled the production of cotton, silk, spices, and indigo. The military manufactured its own weapons so that it was not dependent on any foreign

A masterpiece of Mughal architecture, the Taj Mahal in Agra, India, was built in the early seventeenth century by the Emperor Shah Jahan as a mausoleum for his wife. The white marble structure represents the throne of god in paradise and is a monument to eternal love.

THE PEACOCK THRONE

The peacock throne epitomized the extravagances of the Mughal Empire. During his reign, Shah Jahan commissioned the construction of seven magnificent thrones to represent the wealth and power of the empire. The most ornate of these was the peacock throne. More than six feet tall and made of marble and gold, the throne was covered with diamonds, rubies, and emeralds. The diamonds were each ten carats, and there were 108 rubies and 116 emeralds. Atop the throne sat a jeweled peacock made of sapphires, gold, a massive diamond, ruby, and pearl. As bloody feuds weakened the Mughal monarchy, the peacock throne came to symbolize the monarchy's infatuation with opulence and its lack of concern for civil affairs. When Nadir Shah, a Persian invader, looted Delhi in 1739, he stole the throne and took it to Persia, a final sign that the Mughal empire had crumbled.

suppliers. In addition, the military was given generous provisions to ensure its loyalty and strength.

Although Akbar heavily taxed the empire's citizenry, he did not physically oppress them. He enacted a policy of religious toleration. Hindus were not allowed to hold government positions, but they did not suffer persecution and were even encouraged to practice their religion. Furthermore, Akbar amply rewarded all who proved their allegiance to him. Consequently, the northwestern Rajput states, which had previously chafed under Mughal domination, became staunch Mughal allies during Akbar's reign.

Magnificent public projects became an important part of Mughal rule. Mughal emperors constructed ornate palaces, fortresses, and mausoleums—such as the Taj Mahal in Agra, constructed in the 1600s by Shah Jahan I (r. 1627–1658). They surrounded them with cities featuring improved transportation, sanitation, and education systems. During Akbar's rule, he assembled the empire's finest painters, writers, and scientists and lavishly funded their endeavors. Mughal poets combined Persian and Hindi to create a new language, named Urdu.

DECLINE OF THE MUGHALS

The achievements of Akbar's reign became the excesses of future Mughal emperors, however. When Akbar died in 1605, his son and successor, Jahangir (r. 1605–1627), expanded the empire south into the Indian subcontinent. This expansion, however, exerted an increasing strain on the empire's resources. During his reign, Jahangir failed to maintain the military as Akbar had done. Mughal forces were no longer well trained, and their equipment lacked the superiority it had once held. Moreover, Jahangir lacked Akbar's administrative capabilities. During his reign, the provincial governments steadily lost their efficiency as many positions became hereditary rather than appointed.

Most importantly, a dynastic disturbance unsettled the emperor's strength. Jahangir's oldest son, Shah Jahan, was the nominal heir. But when Shah Jahan feared that he would be supplanted, he rebelled against his father. Although the two were reconciled, the dispute damaged the image of the infallible emperor that Akbar had meticulously created.

This image was shattered in 1658, when Shah Jahan died and his four sons battled for control of the throne. After a protracted power struggle, Aurangzeb (r. 1658–1707) emerged as the new Mughal emperor. However, the feud had shaken the stability of the empire, and Aurangzeb decided that only a brutal display of power could restore the monarchy's preeminence. Therefore, he assembled a massive army and pushed farther south into the subcontinent. During Aurangzeb's reign, the Mughal Empire extended from the Himalayas in the north to Cape Comorin in the south.

THE MUGHAL EMPIRE

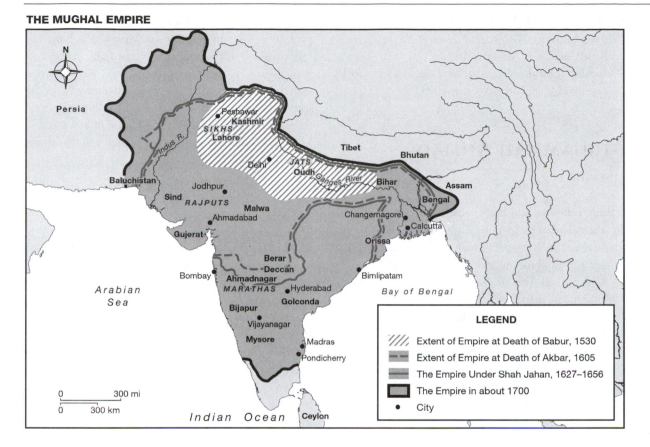

But Aurangzeb also repealed many of Akbar's social policies. Most tellingly, he abandoned the empire's tradition of religious toleration. Aurangzeb declared Islam to be the empire's official religion, and he stripped Hindus of many of their social privileges. Hindus could not openly practice their religion, they were more heavily taxed, and their lands were frequently confiscated and granted to Islamic citizens.

The consequences of Aurangzeb's actions were immediate, as Hindu rebellions erupted across the expanded empire. In southern India, Shivaji united the Marathas and steadily drove the Mughals back north. The Hindus in Rajputana, who had faithfully served the previous Mughal emperors, also withdrew their support, forcing Aurangzeb to divert his forces to regions that had long been part of the empire. Aurangzeb had pushed the Mughal Empire to its greatest limits, and the strain of this expansion ultimately undermined its very foundation.

After Aurangzeb's death in 1707, the empire quickly lost its dominance. Struggles over succession repeatedly weakened the monarchy. The Mughal army suffered numerous defeats and systematically relinquished the vast regions it had previously conquered. Finally, in 1761, Ahmad Shah Abdali led a massive force that crushed the remnants of the Mughal army at Panipat. Furthermore, European agents manipulated the empire for their own advantages. The Mughal emperors had allowed Portuguese, Dutch, French, and British traders to operate freely in the empire. But the Europeans always sought to control India, and they constantly influenced affairs at the court.

Despite the Mughal defeat and the battle of Panipat in 1761, the empire lasted another century, primarily because the rivalries among the Hindu kingdoms in India prevented them from uniting as a central authority. The British also became an increasingly controlling force. Finally, in 1858, the British deposed Bahadur Shah II (r. 1837–1858), the last Mughal emperor, after he allegedly abetted the Sepoy Mutiny. The Mughal Empire, once the most opulent in Asia, became a British colony.

See also: AKBAR THE GREAT; AURANGZEB; BABUR; INDIAN KINGDOMS; JAHAN, SHAH; JAHANGIR; MARATHA CONFEDERACY.

FURTHER READING

Hintze, Andrea. *The Mughal Empire and Its Decline.* Brookfield, VT: Ashgate, 1997.

Richards, John F. *The Mughal Empire.* New York: Cambridge University Press, 1993.

MUHAMMAD AHMAD

(1844–1885 C.E.)

Islamic religious and nationalist leader in the Anglo-Egyptian Sudan region of Central Africa, who struggled successfully to overthrow British and Egyptian power and establish an independent Islamic state.

Muhammad Ahmad was the son of a shipbuilder from Dongala district of Nubia (Sudan), and his family claimed to be descended from the Prophet Muhammad. He grew passionate about the Islamic religion at an early age. Rather than teach, he became a mystic certain that his mission was to purify Islam. Before long, he had gathered a group of disciples.

In 1881, Muhammad Ahmad claimed that he was the "Mahdi"—considered, in Sunni Islam, to be a divinely led restorer of the faith who will eventually return justice to earth and make Islam universal. Muhammad Ahmad was not the only one to claim to be the Mahdi, but he was the most famous. Like most who did, he sought to reform established authority.

At the time, Egypt (then part of the declining Ottoman Empire) ruled the Sudan, while Great Britain had economic and political interests there as well. The majority of people in the region were heavily oppressed by taxes and by the Egyptian military occupation. As Mahdi, Muhammad Ahmad took it upon himself to overthrow Egyptian and British power over the Sudan and to make his country an Islamic state.

Muhammad Ahmad accomplished this goal in January 1885, creating an independent Islamic state with its capital at Omdurman. His reign was cut short by his death just five months later, however, shortly after he captured the vitally important city of Khartoum.

Despite Muhammad Ahmad's short rule, his influence was significant. The government he established was considered the first real Sudanese nationalist government, and he enforced a universal religious regime whose requirements he claimed God transmitted to him in visions.

Muhammad Ahmad's reforms of Islam included prohibiting the pilgrimage to Mecca (the *hajj*) and replacing it with a requirement to fight in the holy war against nonbelievers (the *jihad*). His disciples, called Mahdists, made regular pilgrimages to his tomb at Omdurman after his death, but they were defeated in 1898 by an Anglo-Egyptian army led by Lord Kitchener, a victory that brought Sudan under British control.

See also: EGYPTIAN KINGDOMS, MODERN.

MUHAMMAD ALI (ca. 1769–1849 C.E.)

Pasha of Egypt who worked to reform and modernize his country, while serving as its de facto ruler.

Muhammad Ali was born in humble circumstances in Ottoman-ruled Albania. Because of the Ottoman system of recruiting soldiers and bureaucrats from throughout the empire, he was able to rise rapidly through the ranks of the army on the basis of his skill as a soldier, his political intelligence, and his unbounded ambition.

When France invaded Egypt in 1798, Muhammad Ali commanded the Ottoman force that tried to expel the forces of Napoleon Bonaparte from the Ottoman territory. In the early 1800s, Ali managed to beat back French and British colonization attempts in Egypt, although both powers remained influential in the region. In 1805, the Ottoman sultan appointed him pasha, or governor, of Egypt.

Despite his technical status as a vassal of the Ottoman sultan, Muhammad Ali ruled Egypt with near independence. In 1811, he purged Egypt of the leaders of the Mamluk military caste that had governed the country since 1250 by inviting several hundred Mamluks to a banquet, where they were ambushed and killed.

As pasha, Ali pursued a relentless program of modernization, especially in military reform and the creation of a national army. He also reorganized the administrative and educational systems of Egypt and pursued various public works projects with the use of peasant conscript labor.

Ali's military victories were extensive. He subdued the Wahhabis, a rebellious Islamic movement in Arabia, and in 1820 attempted to conquer the Sudan. Throughout the 1820s, he fought successfully with Ottoman forces attempting to quell the rebellion in Greece. In 1827, however, combined British, French, and Russian forces defeated Ai's fleet at Navarino, a seaport in the Peloponnesus region of Greece.

To gain Ali's support in fighting the Greek revolt, Sultan Mahmud II (r. 1808–1839) had pledged to make Ali pasha of Syria as well as Egypt. The sultan failed to do so, however, and in 1839 Ali and his son Ibrahim Pasha began a revolt of their own, invading Syria and attacking Asia Minor (present-day Turkey).

Pressure from European nations that wanted to maintain the Ottoman Empire's position eventually forced Ali to end the revolt, however. As a compromise, the sultan recognized a hereditary governorship of Egypt for Ali's family. Muhammad Ali died in 1849, having made his family overlords of a modernized and increasingly independent Egypt.

See also: EGYPTIAN KINGDOM, MODERN; MAMLUK DYNASTY; OTTOMAN EMPIRE.

MUHAMMAD V (1909–1961 C.E.)

Sultan (r. 1927–1957) and king (r. 1957–1961) of Morocco, who was responsible for negotiating Morocco's full independence from France. Born in Fez, Morocco, on August 30, 1909, Muhammad was the third son of Sultan Moulay Yusuf (r. 1912–1927) of the Alawite (or Alaouite) dynasty, which had ruled Morocco since 1660 and traced its roots to the Prophet Muhammad.

Upon the death of his father in 1927, Muhammad V became sultan of Morocco at age eighteen. Although the Alawite dynasty remained in power, Morocco had been a French protectorate since 1912. An ardent nationalist, Muhammad had an excellent relationship with the French and hoped to gain independence gradually for Morocco. His hopes of French cooperation were dashed, however.

While Muhammad was in Tangier in April 1947, riots broke out in the city of Casablanca, and many thought that French police had fired unnecessarily on Moroccans. Muhammad responded by giving a speech at Tangier in which he demanded Morocco's complete independence, reviving a nationalist movement that had been simmering for years.

In 1953, the French ousted Muhammad V and exiled him and his family to Corsica and then Madagascar, angering Moroccan nationalists and all who considered him the country's spiritual leader. His popularity grew during his two-year exile, while fighting between the French and various Moroccan factions escalated.

Eventually, the French relented and restored Muhammad V to power in 1955. Ensuing negotiations led to Morocco's limited home rule in February 1956 and to full independence on March 2, 1956. More popular than ever, Muhammad V meted out responsibilities to various factions so none could become too powerful. He also strove to create a constitutional monarchy with a modern government that gave him an important role.

Muhammad worked to keep radical factions from proceeding too quickly and sought to train people to fill new posts, including police and military forces to control unruly elements. Indeed, there was opposition to the new independent government—from parts of the Army of National Liberation (which wanted total expulsion of the French army despite negotiated compromises), and from some Berber tribes reviving ancient internal disputes. New political parties also caused divisions and instability in the government.

Muhammad V assumed the title of king in 1957, and took direct control of Morocco in 1960. To show he was not establishing a dictatorship, he pledged to create a written constitution by the end of 1962 that would give Moroccans a representative government. Muhammad V died unexpectedly after minor surgery in February 1961, before completion of the constitution. The Crown passed to his thirty-two-year-old son, Hassan II (r. 1961–1999).

See also: HASSAN II.

MUHAMMAD XII (BOABDIL)

(d. 1534 C.E.)

Last Muslim ruler (r. 1482–1492) of the Moorish kingdom of Granada on the Iberian Peninsula, known to the Spanish as Boabdil, a corruption of the first part of his full name, Abu abd-Allah.

Abu abd-Allah Muhammad XII, also known as Boabdil, was the son of Sultan Muley Hacen (Abu-al-Hasan Ali) (r. 1464–1482) of Granada and a member of the Nasrid dynasty. When Muley Hacén refused to pay his annual tribute to the Christian kingdom of

Castile in 1481 and took the town of Zahara, he triggered a final struggle between Christians and the Moors in Iberia.

As war raged between the two groups, Boabdil, supported by the powerful Abencerrajes family of Granada, seized the throne from Muley Hacén and plunged the kingdom into civil war as well. Muley Hacén, with the help of another powerful family, the Zegries, was successful in retaking Granada from his son, whom he deposed in 1483. But Muley Hacén's triumph was short-lived. His brother, Muhammad az-Zaghal, backed by a third important family, the Venegas, deposed him and retook Granada in 1485.

Meanwhile, Boabdil had been taken prisoner at Lucena in 1483 by Ferdinand II of Aragón and Isabella I of Castile, the so-called Catholic kings. Boabdil bargained for his freedom by agreeing to hold Granada as a fiefdom under the Catholic monarchs. The agreement specified that, in exchange for help in retaking Granada, Boabdil would cede the lands currently controlled by az-Zagal to the Catholic kings. Meanwhile, part of Granada, including the great Moorish palace, the Alhambra, lay in the hands of Muley Hacén.

Muley Hacén and az-Zaghal formed an alliance to defend the Alhambra and forced Boabdil to retreat and take refuge at the court of Ferdinand and Isabella. But Boabdil mounted a renewed, and successful, campaign to take the Alhambra in 1485 upon the death of Muley Hacén.

Having regained Granada, Boabdil reneged on his agreement with Ferdinand and Isabella, refusing to surrender the lands he had promised them. In response, Christian forces laid siege to Granada in 1491. Despite a gallant defense of the city by its Moorish inhabitants, by the end of the year the situation was dire. Boabdil was finally forced to surrender the city to Ferdinand and Isabella on January 2, 1492. With the conquest of Granada, the Christian *reconquista* (reconquest) of the Iberian Peninsula was complete, and Moorish rule in Iberia was ended after more than seven hundred years.

According to tradition, as Boabdil left Granada, he looked back on the beautiful Moorish city one last time and wept. The spot from which he supposedly looked back upon his beloved city is still known as "the last sigh of the Moor." Allowed to retire to lands in the Alpujarras region of Andalucia (the southernmost province of Iberia), Boabdil left there in 1493 to journey to Morocco, where he took refuge in the

court of his kinsman, the ruler of Fes. It is reputed that Boabdil died in battle in Morocco in 1534 while fighting for his kinsman.

See also: FERDINAND II; GRANADA, KINGDOM OF; IBERIAN KINGDOMS.

MU'IZZI (SLAVE) DYNASTY
(1206–1290 C.E.)

Dynasty of rulers in India, founders of the Delhi sultanate, that was started by military slaves of the Muslim Giurid dynasty of Afghanistan.

In 1193, the Giurid sultan, Muhammad of Ghur (r. 1163–1203), conquered the Indian city of Delhi and left a slave lieutenant, Qutab-ud-din Aybak, in charge when he returned to Afghanistan. After Ghur was assassinated by opponents, Aybak (r. 1206–1210) declared independence and laid the foundation for the Mu'izzi, or Slave dynasty. Aybak proclaimed himself sultan of Delhi and established a new state centered there, the Delhi sultanate.

Known for his generosity, Aybak began construction in Delhi of the Qutb Minar, a structure that celebrated the rise of Muslim rule in India. When Aybak died in an accident in 1210, power passed to his son, Aram Shah (r. 1210–1211), who lacked the experience and the credibility of his father. As a result, his advisers, the Turkish nobles, stepped in and helped another military slave, Iltumish, defeat Aram Shah and take the throne.

Iltutmish (r. 1211–1236), also known as Shams-ud-din, had been the foremost military slave of Sultan Aybak and had become his master's son-in-law when he married Aybak's daughter.

The greatest of the Slave kings of Delhi, Iltutmish maintained a strong central army. With it, he consolidated Turkish conquests in northern India and added new territory to the growing empire, while defending it against the Mongols, who loomed as a serious threat. He also completed the construction of the Qutule Minar and created a new form of currency. Iltumish established a monarchical form of government in Delhi and created a new governing class. A patron of the arts and learning, he was also considered a religious and wise leader.

Iltutmish wanted his daughter, Radiyya, to succeed him to the throne. But the nobles of Delhi chose his son, Rukn-ud-din Firuz, instead. As sultan, Firuz I (r. 1236) left the administration of the sultanate to his mother, Shah Turkan. But this led to revolts in the provinces and to the deaths of both Firuz and his mother. The nobles then turned back to his sister, Radiyya.

Radiyya Begum (r. 1236–1240) was the first and only woman to rule the Delhi sultanate. Radiyya was a strong and capable ruler, but when she appointed an African to an important position at her court, the Turkish nobles rebelled and murdered her in 1240.

For the next twenty-six years, the Mu'izzi dynasty suffered from poor leadership under a series of weak rulers. This ended in 1266, when Ghiyasuddin Balban (r. 1266–1287) seized the throne. A practical man with an iron hand, Balban paid great attention to the production of arms and weapons. He built forts, maintained a strong army, and developed a network of spies. Balban suppressed all revolts in the sultanate and maintained order throughout the state. During his strong rule, the Mongols continued to pose a serious threat, but they were unable to penetrate into India.

After Balban died in 1287, the Slave dynasty rapidly declined under the rule of his grandson, Kayqubadh (r. 1287–1290), and great-grandson, Kayumarth (r. 1290). When Kayumarth was deposed in 1290 by the Khaljis, another Afghan dynasty, the Mu'izzi dynasty came to an end.

See also: DELHI KINGDOM; KHALJI DYNASTY; SOUTH ASIAN KINGDOMS.

MUNSTER KINGDOM

(ca. 450–1596 C.E.)

Ancient and medieval kingdom in southwest Ireland that, before it was divided in two in 1118, was the largest of the early Irish kingdoms. Munster (*Mumu* in Gaelic) has long been considered the place of the mythical beginnings of Ireland. The kingdom has a rich legendary tradition but few reliable sources for its early history.

EARLY HISTORY

According to ancient legend, the Eóganachta, the ruling dynastic group of Munster, were descended from Eibhear Fionn (Eber Finn), one of the sons of Míl Espáne, the first Celtic ruler of Ireland. The Eóganachta took their name from the legendary Eógan Mór, who was said to be a distant descendant of Eber Finn. Early in its history, Munster consisted of five "fifths," or subkingdoms: Thomond in the north, Desmond in the south, Ormond in the east, Medón Muman or mid-Munster, and Iarmumu, or west Munster.

Many historians consider Conall Corc (flourished ca. 450) the first historical king of Munster, and the Eóganachta are said to be descended from him. Conall worked with Patrick, the Christian missionary and patron saint of Ireland, to codify native Irish law. He established the seat of kingship on the Rock of Cashel in County Tipperary in southern Ireland. An eighth-century legend has an angel appearing at Cashel to make the land fertile for Conall and his descendants. The kings of Munster at Cashel considered their kingship equal to that of Tara, the seat of the High Kings of Ireland in the north.

PARTITION OF THE KINGDOM

In the tenth century, the Eóganachta were divided into two hostile groups. The struggle between them coincided with a contest for the throne of Munster between the Eóganacht Chaisil (a branch of the eastern Eóganachta who lived around Cashel) and the Dál Cais (O'Briens) of Thomond, who claimed to be the descendants of Cormac Cas, the brother of Eógan Mór. The Dál Cais had built up their power by forming alliances against the kings of Cashel. On the death of King Donnchadh II mac Ceallachian (r. ca. 961–963) in 963, the Dál Cais seized the throne of Cashel. The Eóganachta fought against their rule but were pushed back to the south into Desmond.

In the eleventh century, the leading branch of the Eóganachta took the name MacCarthy from Carrthach, king of the Eóganacht Chaisil (d. 1045). The first king to use this name was his son, Muiredach (d. 1092).

A number of O'Brien kings also were high kings of Ireland. The most famous of these was Brían mac Cennétigh, known as Brian Boru (r. 978–1014), who extended his power to the high kingship. Brian died while fighting a coalition of the Vikings and forces of the kingdom of Leinster at the battle of Clontarf in 1014.

The feud between the two branches of the Eóganachta continued for fifty years, until 1092, when the two parties realized that they needed to unite against the O'Briens and gave their support to Tadgh MacCarthy in a struggle to defeat King Muirchertach O'Brien (r. ca. 1086–1119). Muirchertach was confident of victory until his allies deserted him and rallied around Tadgh. In 1119, Muirchertach was forced to accept the Treaty of Glanmire, which partitioned Munster into two kingdoms, Thomond in the north and Desmond in the south. King Tadhg I MacCarthy Mór (r. 1118–1123) returned his dynasty to the capital of Cashel.

In 1171, King Dermod I of Desmond (r. 1144–1185) submitted to King Henry II of England (r. 1154–1189) as his feudal lord, hoping to gain an ally in his struggle against the king of Thomond, Domhnall Mór O'Brien (r. 1168–1194). Domhnall submitted as well, but Dermod was regarded as the greatest traitor in Irish history for this act, which paved the way for English rule in Ireland.

LATER HISTORY

In the thirteenth century, the Desmond kings defended themselves against the Norman knights who had begun moving into the kingdom and seizing estates for themselves. King Finghin V (r. 1252–1261) defeated a Norman army led by John FitzThomas. By the fourteenth century, however, the Norman barons had returned and settled in Munster.

In 1541, Henry VIII of England (r. 1509–1547) declared himself king of Ireland. King Murrough O'Brien of Thomond (r. 1539–1541) surrendered his half of the kingdom, but Henry met with resistance from the last MacCarthy king of Desmond, Donal IX (r. 1558–1565). In 1565, when Donal refused to surrender his title and kingdom to Elizabeth I (r. 1558–1603), he was kidnapped and taken to the English court, where he was forced to submit. With his act of submission to Elizabeth, the kingship in Munster came to an end.

See also: BORU, BRIAN; IRISH KINGS.

FURTHER READING

Byrne, Francis John. *Irish Kings and High-Kings.* 2nd ed. Portland, OR: Four Courts Press, 2001.

Ellis, Peter Beresford. *Erin's Blood Royal: The Gaelic Novel Dynasties of Ireland.* New York: Palgrave Macmillan, 2002.

O Corrain, Donnchadh. *Ireland Before the Normans.* Portland, OR: Four Courts Press, 2004.

MUSIC AND SONG

The development of music has often depended on the patronage of monarchs, and kings have felt free to treat musicians as servants. Yet music has at different times in history been regarded as the source of special power, and kings have needed musicians to consolidate their prestige and their hold on people's minds. As an example of the perceived power of music, when dictator Milton Obote of Uganda wished to destroy the power of the Kabaka, the hereditary ruler of the Kiganda tribe, in 1966, one of the steps he took was to kill the court musicians and destroy their instruments.

MUSIC IN THE AFTERLIFE

The excavation of the 4,500-year-old cemetery at Ur, in Iraq, revealed a tomb containing the remains of a queen, Pu-Abi, who was buried not only with magnificent jewelry and artworks and the remains of nearly twenty attendants, but with musical instruments and the skeleton of a harpist who was buried in a sitting position as though ready to play. The instruments are a harp and two lyres, all made of rich materials including silver, gold, and lapis lazuli, and intricately decorated with motifs such as bulls' heads. These and similar instruments and musicians found in neighboring royal graves show that for the ancient Mesopotamian rulers music was an essential element of life to take with them into eternity.

MONARCHS AS MUSIC LOVERS

The biblical Book of Samuel tells how King Saul (r. 1020–1010 B.C.E.) was troubled by an evil spirit and found relief only when the young shepherd David played the harp for him. Eventually, Saul's jealousy of David's growing popularity caused him to throw his spear at David as he played, but at first when David played, "Saul was refreshed, and was well, and the evil spirit departed from him."

Music formed a vital part of the splendor of the royal court of French king Louis XIV (r. 1643–1715) at Versailles, especially the music of the Italian-born composer Jean-Baptiste Lully. Lully composed and directed instrumental music, ballets, and operas during his thirty-four-year tenure at Louis's court. He knew well the art of flattering the king and managing the complex play of personalities at the court. He died as a result of an infection in his foot, which he had injured with his staff while beating time with it as he accompanied a rehearsal of a Mass to celebrate the king's recovery from an illness.

Ludwig II of Bavaria (r. 1864–1886) may have taken love of music further than any other king. From early childhood he had identified with a figure from German mythology, the swan-knight Lohengrin. At age fifteen he saw a performance of the opera *Lohengrin* by Richard Wagner, which moved him so much that he made a promise: If he became king, he would seek out Wagner and give him any help he might need.

When Ludwig did succeed to the throne, at age eighteeen, his envoys had trouble finding Wagner, who was hiding from his creditors; but they eventually succeeded in letting the composer know that Ludwig would give him everything he needed to produce his operas on the scale they deserved. The young monarch and the fifty-year-old composer met in December 1864 and were friends until Wagner's death.

Ludwig wrote to Wagner after watching a performance of one of his operas: "You are a god-man, the true artist by God's grace who brought the sacred fire down from heaven to earth, to purify, to sanctify and to redeem!" Wagner respected Ludwig's mystical preoccupations but urged the king to pay more attention to managing his kingdom. The fact is that Ludwig's hold on reality was precarious. He managed to find money to give Wagner an allowance and a series of houses, and to build the opera house at Bayreuth, which is still home to an opera festival, but his kingdom was falling apart. Not long after Wagner's death in 1883, Ludwig was certified insane and deposed; he drowned in 1886. Wagner's work is his most lasting achievement.

MONARCHS AS MUSICIANS

Many monarchs have not only employed musicians and been patrons to musicians and composers but have played music themselves. Maya rulers of the Late Classic period (600–800) maintained large staffs of musicians; their painted vases show the use at court of conch-shell trumpets, long wooden trumpets, standing drums, and flutes. But one Mayan vase also shows a ruler (identified by his elaborate feathered headdress) shaking a rattle himself, while his wife dances to the rhythm.

The Roman emperor Nero (r. 37–68) was trained as a musician. The Roman historian Suetonius re-

ports that when a great fire swept Rome in 64, Nero sang a song about the destruction of Troy as he watched from a tower as Rome burned. Suetonius also describes Nero's many public performances as a singer, and how no one was allowed to leave during the performance—"insomuch, that it is said some women with child were delivered there."

King Henry VIII of England (r. 1503–1547) is most famous for the high-handed way he treated marriage. But he was a highly educated and cultured man who loved music. He employed seventy-nine musicians in his Chapel Royal, whose job was to provide music at the religious services the king attended daily. Whenever he traveled he was accompanied by at least some of his court musicians. Henry also was an accomplished instrumentalist, playing bagpipes, recorders, and virginals (an early keyboard instrument). He even composed several pieces of music. He is thought to have composed the song "Greensleeves."

The most accomplished royal musician was probably Frederick II, the Great, of Prussia (r. 1740–1786). In the lulls in the fighting of the War of the Austrian Succession (1740–1748) and the Seven Years' War (1756–1763), Frederick found time to learn to play the flute at an almost professional standard, to listen to and support the work of great composers such as C.P.E. Bach and Johann Joachim Quantz (who was Frederick's flute teacher), and to compose over one hundred pieces of music himself.

See also: BEHAVIOR, CONVENTIONS OF ROYAL; EDUCATION OF KINGS; LITERATURE AND KINGSHIP.

MUTESA I (ca. 1830s–1884 C.E.)

Ruler (r. 1856–1884) of the Ganda kingdom (Buganda), noted for his success in maintaining Buganda's relative autonomy during the height of European colonial competition.

Mukabya Mutesa was born in the late 1830s, the son of Kabaka Suna II (r. ca. 1825–1856), who then ruled the kingdom of Buganda. As but one of some sixty-one claimants to the throne, Mutesa rose to power with the help of his mother, Muganzirwazza, who was a member of a powerful kinship-based faction called the Elephant Clan. Muganzirwazza succeeded in placing her son on the throne after Kabaka Suna's death by forming an alliance with the king's prime minister, Katikiro Kayira. When Mutesa took the throne in 1856, he was a young man in his mid-twenties.

As ruler, Mutesa looked outward, beyond the borders of his kingdom, welcoming new influences. For instance, he increased Buganda's wealth by encouraging trade with the wealthy Swahili who came into Buganda from their city-states on the East African coast. He even went so far as to learn to speak the traders' language fluently. Mutesa also opened his kingdom to Islam, although he favored the incorporation of Islamic tenets and practices into the indigenous religious tradition called Lubaale.

Mutesa's belief that Islam could complement Lubaale was less widely accepted by his subjects, however. Young Islamic converts, offended by Mutesa's refusal to reject outright the beliefs of his forebears, denied the legitimacy of Mutesa's rule. Throughout his reign, this frequently led to outright rebellion. Mutesa responded to these revolts with force, executing many of his rebellious Muslim subjects. The conflict between Islamic converts and traditional religionists remained a continuing source of trouble within the Ganda kingdom.

Adding to Mutesa's difficulties was Egypt, which embarked upon a campaign of expansion and threatened to overrun Buganda's northern border. To strengthen his defenses, Mutesa sought to create friendly relations with the British. He invited missionaries from the British-based Church Mission Society to Buganda, expecting in return that Great Britain would provide some protection against the Egyptians. This was a time when various European powers looked hungrily upon the African continent, each hoping to establish or expand its colonial presence. The British were thus pleased to find a local king who was so welcoming to their representatives.

With the arrival of the British Christians, the French were spurred to send their own missionary representatives, whom Mutesa welcomed with equal warmth. Both the British and the French hoped to use their missionary presence in the region to lay the groundwork for an eventual claim to territory. But Mutesa hoped to use the competing religious agendas, as well as the underlying political ones, to secure his own position by playing them off against one another.

For his plan to work, Mutesa had to maintain a difficult political balance in his dealings with the French and the British. Among his own people, he faced a daunting task as well. As the various mission-ary groups gained converts, rival factions were formed within the kingdom, ostensibly on religious grounds but with political ramifications as well. The (primarily Protestant) British-led converts were opposed to the (primarily Catholic) converts won by the French missions, and both these groups were opposed to the converts to Islam. These rivalries frequently threatened to break out into open violence.

It is a mark of Mutesa's charisma and strength of will that he succeeded in maintaining the necessary balance among all these constituencies. In fact, he succeeded so well that he brought his nation to the peak of its power and prosperity. When Mutesa died in October 1884, his son Henrique I (r. 1884–1888) succeeded him on the throne. But Henrique lacked his father's skill at keeping the rival factions in check, and a bloody civil war ensued soon after he took the throne.

See also: GANDA KINGDOM.

MYCENAEAN MONARCHIES

(2000–1200 B.C.E.)

Ancient kingdoms in Greece established by the Achaeans, or Mycenaeans, between 2000 and 1200 B.C.E.

Around 2000 B.C.E., a group of Indo-European peoples known as the Achaeans invaded the Greek Peninsula, where they conquered and intermarried with the indigenous population. Within a few centuries, the Achaeans, also known as the Mycenaeans, dominated much of Greece and the Aegean Sea. About five hundred years after their original invasion of Greece, the Achaeans conquered the Minoans, a major Mediterranean power centered on the island of Crete, and adopted many aspects of Minoan culture. As Minoan civilization declined, the Mycenaeans inherited rich Minoan trade networks with Egypt and Mesopotamia. Unlike the Minoans, the Mycenaeans pursued their aims through violence and war. As a result, they became the most powerful people in the ancient Aegean world.

The warrior ethos of the Mycenaeans is best represented in the *Iliad* and the *Odyssey,* the ancient epics of the Greek poet Homer. Homer's works describe a world of warrior-kings in pursuit of honor and glory. Success in battle, not birth or wealth, determined one's value in Mycenaean society. Great warriors, such as Achilles and Ajax, fought against Paris, Hector, and other heroes of Troy, the Mycenaeans' great rival, in the Trojan War, which Homer described in the *Iliad*. The *Odyssey* follows the Greek warrior Odysseus on his turbulent and much interrupted trip home after the Greeks defeated the Trojans. The cultural values revealed in the *Odyssey* differ from modern ideas of honor and glory. Odysseus used cunning to overcome obstacles, often lying and cheating his way out of difficult situations. Mycenaean leaders, though powerful fighters, were also wily and deceitful when necessary.

Homer's epics along with archaeological discoveries reveal that the Mycenaeans practiced a simple form of monarchy. Most of the kingdoms founded by these warriors were no larger than city-states. In addition, Mycenaean kings were typically aided by a ruling council, which consisted of the noblemen of the kingdom. This practice differentiated the Mycenaeans from the other ancient civilizations around them, such as Egypt and Mesopotamia, which had powerful absolute monarchs who ruled over vast territories. The practice of the Mycenaean monarch conferring with a council laid the foundations of later Greek democracy.

Mycenaeans copied aspects of Minoan culture other than their trade practices. The Minoans had built large, complex palaces that served as political, economic, and social centers. The best example of this is the palace at Knossos on the island of Crete. The Mycenaeans also built large palaces, but unlike the Minoans, they erected huge defensive walls around them. The need for such walls reflects the violent nature of Mycenaean society.

The Mycenaeans were a warlike people who forged a powerful kingdom in the ancient Mediterranean world. Among the remains of Mycenae is the Lion's Gate at the entrance to the royal palace.

Mycenaean kings had disappeared by the end of the thirteenth century B.C.E. Invasions, including those from a group of Indo-Europeans called Dorians from the north and from a maritime people simply known as the Sea Peoples from the south, ushered in a period of decline for Mycenaean civilization. After invaders destroyed the two major cities of Mycenae, Pylos and Tiryns, the surviving Mycenaeans dispersed throughout the lands surrounding the Aegean Sea.

See also: ATHENS, KINGDOM OF; EGYPTIAN DYNASTIES, ANCIENT (BEFORE EIGHTEENTH DYNASTY); MINOAN KINGDOMS; PERGAMUM KINGDOM; SPARTA, KINGDOM OF; TROJAN KINGDOM.

MYSORE KINGDOM

(ca. 200s–1947 C.E.)

Kingdom in the interior of the southern Indian Peninsula whose early history is lost but whose power held back the encroachment of British colonialism in that region in the eighteenth century.

From the early fourth century B.C.E. until about 180 B.C.E., the kingdom of Mysore was part of the Maurya Empire, India's first imperial realm. After the collapse of the Maurya Empire in the late second century B.C.E., Mysore (the Hindu word for "buffalo town") was divided into three parts. The northern part came under the control of a minor local dynasty, the Kadamba dynasty. Southern Mysore was controlled by the Chera dynasty, which ruled the southwestern coast of India until they were replaced by the Chola dynasty in the eighth century C.E. The Pallava dynasty governed the east side of Mysore until the eleventh century, when all of Mysore and most of the Deccan region of India came under the rule of the Calukya dynasty.

The Hoysala dynasty, whose rule originated in the Deccan region in the eleventh century, gradually took over Mysore in the twelfth century as the power of the Chalukyas declined. The strength of the Hoysala dynasty was broken, in turn, in the mid-fourteenth century by the Muslims of the Delhi sultanate under Mohammed Tughluq (r. 1320–1324) and his successors.

With the dissolution of the Tughluq dynasty—due mainly to poor administration—in the early fifteenth century, Mysore and most of southern India came under the influence of the Vijayanagar dynasty. The Vijayanagars revived Hindu beliefs throughout their realm and, while tolerant and respectful of the Muslims, they managed to confine Muslim power to the northern parts of India until the late sixteenth century.

In 1565, Vijayanagar lost the battle of Rakasa-Tangadi to the combined Muslim armies of the states of Bijapur, Ahmadnagar, and Golconda. In the aftermath, Mysore came to be ruled by a number of local princes, the Rajas (or Wodeyars) of Mysore.

By the mid-1700s, a Muslim of peasant stock named Haider Ali had risen to prominence in Mysore. An army commander who had studied European military tactics, he became the virtual ruler of Mysore by 1761. Haidar Ali (r. ca. 1761–1782) wanted to work with the British, who were a growing power in India. But the British, with the help of the Maratha dynasty of the western Deccan region and Nizam Ali Khan, the ruler of Hyderabad, attacked Haider Ali and Mysore.

Haidar Ali defeated the British army of Bombay in 1766. Three years later, in 1769, the British promised to help Haidar Ali if he was attacked by other Indian states, but when the Marathas invaded Mysore in 1771 the British would not help. Haidar Ali then turned against the British and, supported by European soldiers of fortune, he annihilated a British force of four thousand soldiers in 1789.

When Haidar Ali died in 1782, his son, Tipu (r. 1782–1799), took command of Mysore. The well educated Tipu set out to modernize the economy by reforming agriculture and manufacturing, including an arms industry. Tipu made peace with the British in 1784, but his invasion of a state under British protection a few years later provoked renewed fighting. Heavily outnumbered and outgunned, Tipu lost the third Mysore war (1790–1792) to the British.

After a short period of peace, Tipu began seeking help from France, a move that antagonized the British and led to the fourth and final Mysore War (1799). British forces stormed Tipu's fortress at Srirangapatnam, where they killed Tipu and sacked the city. After Tipu's defeat, the British reinstalled the Wodeyars to power in Mysore, with sufficient safeguards to ensure continued British dominance of the region until India gained independence in 1947.

See also: COLONIALISM AND KINGSHIP; INDIAN KINGDOMS; MAURYA EMPIRE; TUGHLUQ DYNASTY; VIJAYANAGAR EMPIRE.

MYTH AND FOLKLORE

Legendary stories and popular tales, often featuring rulers or their ancestors that play a significant role in the historical and cultural heritage of nations and peoples.

Kings and queens, both real and imaginary, are prominent characters in the myth and folklore of many cultures. Furthermore, many of the rituals of kingship have their origin in myth, as do the legendary kings and queens who appear in folkloric rituals, customs, and performances.

LEGENDARY KINGS AND GOD-KINGS

Legends and myths may sometimes feature real kings and queens. In one popular Scottish legend, for example, Robert I (Robert the Bruce) (r. 1306–1329) found renewed strength for his fight against the English by watching a spider's continued attempts to spin its web.

Other mythical kings are the invention of popular imagination. Prester John was a mythical priest-king of the Middle Ages who was said to rule a wealthy and virtuous Christian kingdom in Africa or Asia. Many Christian adventurers and pilgrims searched for his kingdom, a sign of hope for areas that at that time were occupied by the Muslims. Other rulers might be either real or mythical, such as King Arthur and the Indian queen Minatci, about whom there is no reliable historical evidence.

Kings, especially those who originated a dynasty, are often identified with a god, and subsequent kings are thought to be incarnations of him. The king is often considered the son of the sky god, but he may also represent the thunder god when he is at war. Often, kings were thought to be married to the goddess of their people. In Ireland, for example, a story is told about a prince meeting an ugly old woman whom he had to agree to marry. When he did so, she turned into the beautiful young goddess of sovereignty.

KINGS AND HERO MYTHS

Over time, philosophers developed rational explanations for the idea of a god/king. For example, the Greek writer Euhemerus, who lived in the third century B.C.E., believed that mythological figures such as King Theseus of Athens were real historical people who were ignorantly worshiped as gods after their deaths.

In modern times, scientists and literary scholars have developed their own theories. In his book, *The Hero* (1936), British scholar Lord Raglan developed the ideas of the myth-ritual school, begun by British folklorist Sir James George Frazer, to explain many of the details in myths. According to Raglan, the mysterious circumstances of the hero's birth include being the reputed son of a god. After his expulsion by his father and being brought up by foster parents, he goes to his future kingdom and kills the king. Eventually, he, too, is driven from the throne and meets a mysterious death.

Raglan believed that the original real murder of the weakened king eventually became a symbolic ritual and then a myth. The death and disappearance of the king are associated with the death and resurrection of the sky god, which restores fertility to the land. In his book, *The Myth of the Birth of the Hero* (1909), Freudian psychoanalyst Otto Rank studied the legendary Greek king Oedipus and other early king-heroes and concluded that the hero's killing of his royal father is a fulfillment of unconscious Oedipal desires to usurp the father and his power.

One of the most discussed myths in the Western world is that of the Arthurian Grail and its wounded Fisher-King. For English anthropologist Jessie Weston, a follower of myth-ritual theory, the king is wounded in his sexual organs and infertile, and thus the land is infertile also. To French anthropologist Claude Levi-Strauss, for whom myths are about the dialectical relationship between opposites, the myth embodies the tension between two worlds: the terrestrial king, Arthur, which is full of questions, and the heavenly realm, with its immobile Fisher-King, where there are answers no one asks for.

MYTHICAL MOTIFS

One widespread myth is that of a king who is not really dead but will return, like King Arthur, Frederick Barbarossa, or Constantine. Another motif is the recognition of the true king through his ability to control symbols of kingship.

In one Scythian myth, a burning gold cart, sword, and cup fall from the sky. The youngest son of King Targitaus is able to grasp them after his older brother fails, and he becomes king. The cart symbolizes the king's control of agriculture, the sword control of war, and the cup the sacred priesthood. A similar story about the sword in the stone, Excalibur, pulled out by the young future king Arthur, is a part of Arthurian legend.

ROYAL RITUALS

INDONESIAN PUPPET RITUALS

The *wayang* puppet performances of Java began as rites to worship gods who were royal ancestors. *Wayang* comes from a word that may have meant "shadow" or "spirit." The *wayang* began as performances by masked dancers and shadow puppets, but there are also *wayang golek* or colorfully painted wooden rod puppets. The *wayang* was an outgrowth of shamanism, with a master who was in contact with the spirit world. The *dalang* (puppeteer) is an intermediary between heaven and earth.

The first mention of *wayang* performances dates to the ninth and tenth centuries C.E. According to a traditional manual for puppeteers, the *Serat Pakem Sastramiruda*, the legendary eleventh-century king and seer Jayabaya had images of his ancestors drawn on palm leaves. This was the beginning of the shadow puppets.

The Mataram kings traced their descent from the Hindu god Shiva, and court artists used puppets to illustrate stories from the great Indian epics, the *Ramayana* and the *Mahabharata*. The *Ramayana* recounts the adventures of Prince Rama, an incarnation or avatar of Vishnu. In the *Arjuna Wiwaha*, which is based on the *Mahabharata*, the sacred warrior Prince Arjuna fights evil in the world with the help of the gods. In addition to kings, princes, princesses, demons, and ogres, there is a clown figure who provides comedy and is also a spokesman for the *dalang*.

With the coming of Islam to Java in the fourteenth and fifteenth centuries C.E., a puppet tradition developed that combined Islamic moral teachings and Sufi mysticism with Hindu elements. The puppets still play an important cultural role in Indonesia. Modern puppeteers still go through spiritual training before beginning their work, though some old-timers claim that modern *dalang* are concerned only with showmanship and popularity.

KINGS AND QUEENS IN FOLKLORE AND FAIRY TALES

A large number of fairy tales feature kings and queens as major characters. The American psychologist Bruno Bettelheim finds that kings and queens in these stories represent parents, who seem immensely powerful to the child, and individuals play out their conflict with their parents through the tales. The narcissistic queen in the Snow White story exhibits jealousy of her daughter, who must resolve her inner conflicts with her. For the Jungian psychoanalyst Marie-Louis von Franz, the king represents the self, or psychic whole of the individual. Often there is a king with three sons, but no queen, who is dead; this is usually interpreted to mean that the masculine is crippled without the feminine and must be restored through the hero son's marriage with the princess (anima).

Literary fairy tales written by modern authors often contain characters that have attained a mythical status of their own. These include Hans Christian Andersen's "The Emperor's New Clothes," whose main character stands for the empty self-importance of royalty and its willingness to believe flattery. The Snow Queen in Andersen's story of the same name is a memorable archetype of coldness.

There are many rituals and customs in folk culture having to do with the election of mock kings or so-called Lords of Misrule. In medieval Europe, for example, the King of Fools was elected at the

New Year to preside over a symbolic overturning of authority, in memory of how God humbles the proud and exalts the humble. In England, kings and queens of the May were elected and engaged in a Maypole dance, perhaps the survival of a fertility ritual.

The mythical meaning of kings and queens has changed greatly throughout history. Some people have interpreted them as gods, or symbols of heaven; for others, royal figures are aspects of ourselves. But the meaning that people give to real kings and queens, as well as to mythical or legendary ones, is always greater than the actual power and meaning that they possess.

See also: ARTHUR, KING; DIVINITY OF KINGS; EARTH AND SKY, SEPARATION OF; HEALING POWERS OF KINGS; HEAVENS AND KINGSHIP; LITERATURE AND KINGSHIP; MONARCHY FORMATION, MYTHS OF; SACRAL BIRTH AND DEATH; SACRED KINGSHIPS.

FURTHER READING

Herbert, Mimi, with Nur S. Rahardjo. *Voices of the Puppet Masters: The Wayang Golek Theatre of Indonesia.* Honolulu: University of Hawaii Press, 2002.

Lindhal, Carl, John McNamara, and John Lindow. *Medieval Folklore: An Encyclopedia of Myths, Legends, Tales, Beliefs and Customs.* Santa Barbara, CA: ABC-CLIO, 2000.

Perry, John Weir. *Lord of the Four Quarters: The Mythology of Kingship.* New York: Paulist Press, 1991.

MZILIKAZI (ca. 1790–1868 C.E.)

Founder and first ruler (r. 1837–1868) of the Ndebele kingdom, which arose as a result of the great demographic upheavals that also produced the Zulu kingdom.

Mzilikazi began as a warrior in the formidable army of Shaka Zulu (r. 1816–1828), where he earned the respect of his leader and fellow soldiers for his courage in battle and quick intelligence. Unfortunately, Mzilakazi was also proud, ambitious, and perhaps a little greedy. Shaka had entrusted him with the command of a band of fighters, sending them out to raid for cattle. Mzilikazi decided to keep the beasts rather than send them to his general. To make matters worse, he then insulted Shaka's repre-

sentatives when they came to demand an explanation for his actions.

Mzilikazi must have known that this behavior would soon call down upon him the wrath of Shaka. Rather than face the consequences of his actions, he gathered a number of fellow warriors and headed north, planning to establish himself as a king in his own right. He succeeded, creating the Ndebele kingdom by means of military conquest.

Mzilikazi followed a straightforward plan of action, conquering local peoples who were no match for his formidable army. In this way, he employed the same tactics that had worked so well for his former leader, Shaka. After overrunning a village, Mzilakazi would destroy the crops, herds, and houses. After killing villagers who were too old or too young to be of use to him, he forced the surviving men to join his army and gave all captured women to his soldiers as wives. In a very short time, Mzilakazi succeeded in terrifying the local peoples into submission to his rule.

No matter how thoroughly he managed to subdue the local people, however, Mzilikazi could never relax his guard. He knew that Shaka would never forget the insult done to him on that long-ago cattle raid. Mzilikazi knew that Shaka had sent troops in pursuit and, because of this, Mzilikazi was forced to remain on the run for years.

It took Mzilikazi until the 1830s to defeat enough Zulu forces to earn a respite from Shaka's vengeance. Exhausted from years of constant warfare, he created a capital city in Bulawayo (present-day Zimbabwe). Still more a general than a king, however, Mzilikazi continued to lead military campaigns, including attacks on Afrikaaner settlements.

The Afrikaaners (white settlers of Dutch ancestry) were forced to sue for peace in 1852, finally permitting Mzilikazi to concentrate on administering his kingdom.

Mzilikazi's rule was absolute for a time, but in 1860 migrants fleeing European gold hunters poured into the region. The newcomers challenged his authority, but through force of will and his powerful army, Mzilikazi managed to remain on the throne until his death in 1868. He was succeeded by his son, Lobengula (r. 1868–1893).

See also: LOBENGULA; NDEBELE KINGDOM; SHAKA ZULU; ZULU KINGDOM.

General Index

O

Biographical Index

Photo Credits Volume Two

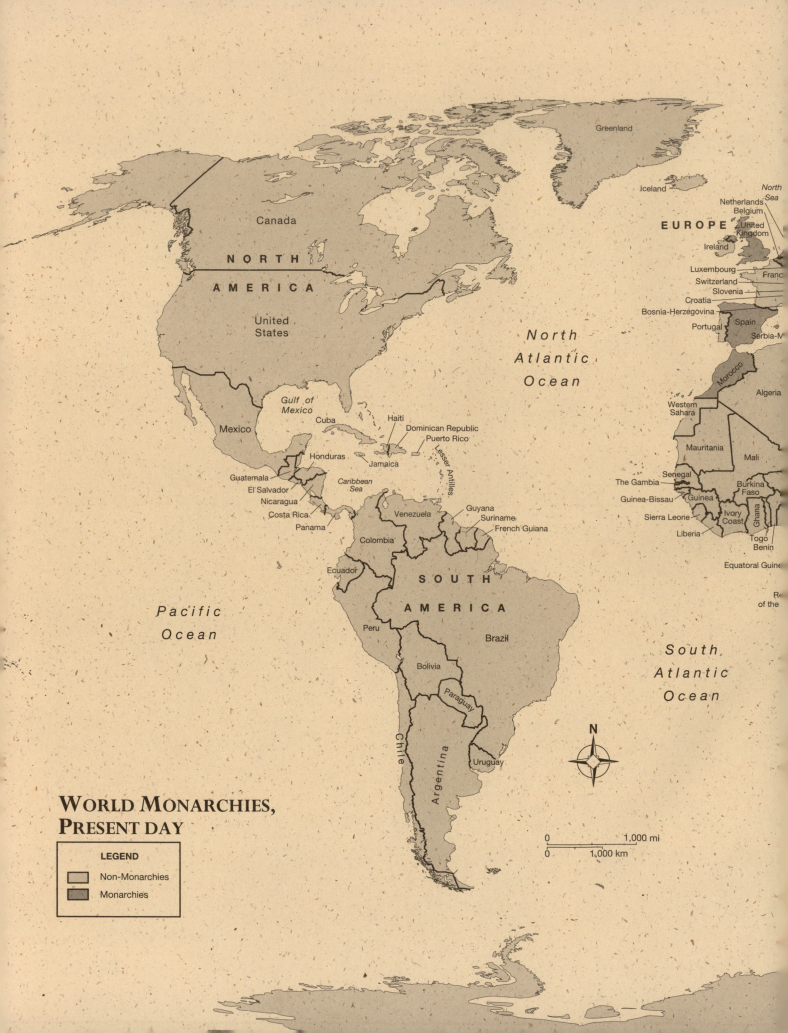

World Monarchies, Present Day

LEGEND
Non-Monarchies
Monarchies